# A HISTORY OF
# THE WORLD CUP

# A HISTORY OF THE WORLD CUP

## 1930–2018

*Clemente Angelo Lisi*

ROWMAN & LITTLEFIELD
*Lanham • Boulder • New York • London*

Published by Rowman & Littlefield
An imprint of The Rowman & Littlefield Publishing Group, Inc.
4501 Forbes Boulevard, Suite 200, Lanham, Maryland 20706
www.rowman.com

6 Tinworth Street, London SE11 5AL, United Kingdom

British Library Cataloguing in Publication Information Available

**Library of Congress Cataloging-in-Publication Data**

Names: Lisi, Clemente Angelo, 1975- author.
Title: A history of the World Cup : 1930-2018 / Clemente A. Lisi.
Description: New Edition. | Lanham : Rowman & Littlefield, [2019] |
    Includes bibliographical references and index.
Identifiers: LCCN 2018055638 (print) | LCCN 2018055763 (ebook) | ISBN
    9781538108338 (electronic) | ISBN 9781538108321 (paper : alk. paper)
Subjects: LCSH: World Cup (Soccer)—History—20th century. | Soccer—
    History.
Classification: LCC GV943.49 (ebook) | LCC GV943.49 .L573 2019 (print) |
    DDC 796.334/66809—dc23
LC record available at https://lccn.loc.gov/2018055638

♾™ The paper used in this publication meets the minimum requirements of
American National Standard for Information Sciences—Permanence of Paper
for Printed Library Materials, ANSI/NISO Z39.48-1992.

Printed in the United States of America

For my family

# CONTENTS

# CONTENTS

# FOREWORD
## Bruce Murray

I have achieved a lot during my playing career. I won two NCAA titles with Clemson, played with Millwall in England, and was inducted into the National Soccer Hall of Fame. Only 18 when I made my U.S. senior national team debut, I was still in college when I was called up to start against England in a friendly game at the Los Angeles Coliseum. We lost 5–0, but for me it was the beginning of a stellar career. Playing for the United States always filled me with great pride—whether it was the Olympics, Copa America, or Gold Cup. It is something I will carry with me for the rest of my life.

One of the biggest highlights, of course, was playing at the World Cup. Just qualifying for the 1990 World Cup—the only one I ever played in—would have been enough. I was part of the first U.S. team to do so in 40 years. It was a truly monumental feat. The national team was just starting to come into its own during the late 1980s. I was very lucky to have been a part of that historic run. I played with some of the greatest players in American soccer history—Tony Meola, John Harkes, Tab Ramos, and Peter Vermes, just to name a few. All are considered pioneers of the sport, helping the game grow throughout the 1990s.

I also had the unique experience of playing with the previous generation, players like Ricky Davis, Kevin Crow, and Arnie Mausser as well as players who gained popularity afterward at the 1994 World Cup such as Cobi Jones, Alexi Lalas, Thomas Dooley, and Earnie Stewart. I served as a bridge between two generations of American players—all very important to the development and growth of soccer in the United States.

With the 1990 World Cup approaching and the 1994 tournament (played on American soil) on the horizon, we were under a lot of pressure to qualify for Italia '90. Bob Gansler, our coach at the time, went with college players over the old pros of the time. He gambled—and it paid off. We faltered at the start but were able to pull it out in the final game against Trinidad & Tobago. I will never forget Paul Caligiuri's now-epic goal and how it silenced the crowd in Port-of-Spain that November afternoon in 1989. We finally showed everyone that we were legitimate and proved it on the field. As far as I am concerned, the region—indeed, the world—was put on alert. Nowadays, the United States qualifies for the World Cup with ease and regularly gets into the knockout phase.

At the time, however, things were very different. Seven months after we had qualified, no one expected much from us once we got to Italy. These were the days before Major League Soccer, social media, and wall-to-wall television coverage. Soccer was still on the sidelines of the American sports landscape, relegated mostly to Spanish-language television and ethnic neighborhoods across the country. The game had not entered the living rooms of most Americans. Despite that, there were Americans in the stands when we took on Czechoslovakia in Florence in our first game. The result, a 5–1 loss, was highlighted by a Caligiuri goal. In our second game against Italy, at Rome's Olympic Stadium, we were greeted by thousands of flag-waving Italians. We lost only 1–0, but Vermes's shot that failed to go in could have changed the outcome. The World Cup is made up of many great moments and, as I learned, even more what-ifs. I even scored a goal at that tournament (one of 21 career goals for the United States in full international matches) during our final group game against Austria in Florence. Of course, I am proud of the other 20 goals I scored in a U.S. jersey in exhibition matches against club teams. At the time, the U.S. played against many foreign clubs, and I was fortunate enough to have scored against Italian teams such as Roma and Fiorentina, as well as Sheffield Wednesday of England. Despite that goal against Austria, we still lost 2–1 and finished the tournament 0–3. Nonetheless, we went home with our heads held high.

The World Cup is filled with great moments and story lines. Soccer in general—and the World Cup in particular—is about bringing together people of different races and cultures. I experienced this competition both firsthand as a participant and years later as a fan. This book does a wonderful job of highlighting those many moments—putting them into context and creating a detailed timeline for future generations to enjoy.

Soccer in the United States has grown immensely over the past three decades. This book is a fantastic way for fans, both old and new, to immerse themselves in the World Cup. It is a reference book every fan should have.

*Bruce Murray was a professional soccer player from 1988 to 1995. He was an attacking midfielder/striker who played for the United States 86 times and scored 21 goals. He played in both Europe and domestically in the American Soccer League, American Professional Soccer League, and A-League. He was also a member of the U.S. team that placed third at the 1989 FIFA Futsal World Championship. Murray was inducted into the National Soccer Hall of Fame in 2011. He currently coaches the Bethesda Soccer Club in Maryland.*

# ACKNOWLEDGMENTS

A project of this magnitude requires a lot of help along the way. I would like to thank the many journalists whose articles and books provided me with information on past World Cups. I also want to thank those who helped make this book possible, including my wife, Kate, for all her patience and for dealing with my absence in the summer of 2014 so I could travel to Brazil for the World Cup. I would also like to thank my parents, Franco and Rachele, and my sister, Paola, for their words of encouragement. A special thanks goes to J Hutcherson at USSoccerPlayers.com for giving me a place to write about the world's greatest game. I would also like to thank my editors over this book's many editions, from Stephen Ryan to Kellie Hagan to Christen Karniski, along with everyone at Rowman & Littlefield, for believing in this book's updated edition and helping to make it a reality. I would also like to extend my gratitude to all the players and coaches who gave their time so I could compile this extraordinary story. My gratitude also goes to FIFA for providing me with official game reports and access to video and photographs. Finally, I want to offer my special thanks to former U.S. star Bruce Murray for writing the foreword. His experiences and knowledge of the game added credibility to this book.

# INTRODUCTION

*Some people believe football is a matter of life and death.
I'm very disappointed with that attitude. I can assure you
it is much, much more important than that.*

—Former Liverpool coach Bill Shankly[1]

I am a soccer junkie. The sport has been in my blood since I was a
child. Actually, given that my parents were born in Italy, I'd argue
that somewhere in my DNA is a "soccer gene." Though scientists have
never found it, I'm sure it exists. I first learned of soccer's existence, and
the passion it can evoke, in the summer of 1982. I was just six years old
and on vacation in Italy with my parents and younger sister. Not too
far away, the World Cup was being contested in Spain. Unknown to me
at the time, I was falling in love with the sport.

Italy had started the tournament off on the wrong foot but had
steadily picked up steam during the knockout rounds. That summer
was truly a magical time. I remember watching the World Cup final
between Italy and West Germany on my grandmother's TV in Naples,
fascinated with what these athletes were able to do with a ball. Italy's
star striker Paolo Rossi, affectionately nicknamed *Pablito* by the Argentine press four years earlier for his small stature, was the first player I
enjoyed watching. He scored goals—lots of them—and the crowds, both
in the stadiums and huddled around the television, loved him. Naples
is a city overflowing with passion and zest for life—and has always had

a great love for soccer. During the game, the streets around my grand-mother's apartment building were empty. The nation held its breath. I knew something monumental was about to happen but exactly *what* was hard for me to understand.

Then it happened.

Italy beat West Germany, 3–1. My memories of that game include Rossi's first goal, Marco Tardelli's long-range shot that wound up in the back of the West German net, and his subsequent goal celebration. The final whistle brought with it an explosion of joy in the stands and across Italy, including the narrow, cobble-stoned streets near my grandmother's four-story building. The emotional phrase, "*Campioni del Mondo! Campioni del Mondo! Campioni del Mondo!*" shrieked from Italian TV commentator Nando Martinelli's raspy voice as I jumped up and down with joy. I still remember my father crying—the first time I'd ever seen him do that—and people in the neighborhood waving Italian flags from their windows and on the streets. I was fascinated. All of this emotion for a game! My father grabbed me by the hand to join the throng of fans who had started cheering in the streets. Chants of "E-TAL-YA! E-TAL-YA! E-TAL-YA!" filled the night sky as I stood in the street and proudly waved an oversized green, white, and red flag affixed to a wooden stick.

I was hooked. Since that night, my love for the sport has blossomed over the years. My love affair with soccer, particularly when I was a child, has always put me in the minority among American sports fans. While soccer is the world's biggest religion—cutting across ethnicity, ideology, and gender like nothing else—it has always had to compete in this country with baseball, football, basketball, and hockey for attention. Growing up in New York, near the United Nations, afforded me the chance to make friends with children from around the world. Some didn't always speak English, but we all bonded because I always showed up to school with a soccer ball. One of the most upsetting experiences I had as a child was watching my soccer ball get run over by a bus. Thankfully, my parents bought me a new ball the next day.

Despite having a group of friends who hailed from far-off places like Albania, Turkey, and Uruguay—all of whom had an appreciation for what the Brazilians call the "Beautiful Game"—it wasn't easy to play in an organized league when I was growing up. I grew up during the 1980s, a time when this country had become a soccer backwater following the collapse of the North American Soccer League. All the hoopla that had come with the New York Cosmos had suddenly packed up and left town like a traveling circus. The only games I could watch on TV were a few weeks old and in Spanish. While other kids watched baseball and football, I grew up watching Spanish-language soccer announcers like Tony Tirado, Norberto Longo, and Andreas Cantor—whose trademark "GOOOOOOOAAAALL!" outburst resonated in my living room years before most Americans had ever heard it.

When I was twelve, my parents signed me up for a soccer league at a local YMCA. I was very excited. This was my chance to play like the stars I had seen on TV. Maybe I could score goals like Diego Maradona or dribble like Michel Platini. To my dismay, I was the only kid who had signed up. My dad and I had a brief chat with the coach, a short, dark-skinned man from Trinidad. I recall that we traded stories on that day about how great soccer was and how Americans just had no appreciation for it: a conversation that I know takes place somewhere in this country on a daily basis. In 1988, I cheered FIFA's decision to award the 1994 World Cup to the United States, although it ultimately failed in its goal of establishing soccer as a major sport. There are, however, signs that soccer is raising its profile in this country's saturated sports market. The signing in January 2007 of English superstar David Beckham by the Los Angeles Galaxy and interest by the U.S. Soccer Federation to host the 2022 World Cup show that soccer is a game that is here to stay.

Every four years, sports fans across this country jump on the World Cup bandwagon just like they do with curling during the Winter Olympics and gymnastics at the Summer Games. Once the World Cup comes to an end, so does everyone's interest. Not me. I live and breathe the game seven days a week, particularly on Sunday mornings when I get up early just to watch Italian League games. I have watched Serie A games on Sunday mornings since I was eleven, getting up before everyone else in my family so I could fix the rabbit ears on my 13-inch TV and clear up the fuzzy UHF signal that came into my living room courtesy of the now-defunct WNYC/Channel 31 in New York. If that sounds like a passionate fan, try sitting with your ear affixed to a radio for two hours listening to a game. Yep, I did that too—just to listen to teams like Napoli, Juventus, and AC Milan play—before the proliferation of satellite television during the late 1990s.

While many Americans love to watch a baseball game on a summer afternoon, my primary love has always been soccer. Most Americans have always had a problem with soccer because the rule against touching the ball with one's hands usually makes for a low-scoring game. The game is appealing just for that reason. People around the world can relate to that struggle to score, putting their emotions into a sport where even one goal can mean everything—just like in life. Some scoreless games are full of drama and excitement. Sophisticated fans can appreciate a final score of 0–0, while casual viewers just see a bunch of zeroes. If they realized that a typical soccer game is no different from a pitcher tossing a no-hitter, more people in this country would embrace the sport.

Above all, I love the World Cup—not only because it showcases so many of the sport's greatest players at one tournament—but because it allows my very private joy to become a public celebration. Every four years, soccer fans are allowed to come out of the closet. They crowd bars across the country and cheer on their national teams in full view of others, a practice that often includes wearing your favorite team's jersey and donning face paint. Perceptions are slowly changing. The 2014 World Cup enjoyed a ratings success in this country and today more children play the sport, both in city parks and on lush, suburban fields. I have reason to believe—based on conversations with people in soccer circles and everyday sports fans—that many people became converts after witnessing on TV the atmosphere of the fans inside German and South African stadiums. The constant chanting, displays of national pride, and unabated joy following the scoring of goals gave sports fans in this country something different than the canned enthusiasm generated by the public announcing systems at most American stadiums.

If you're hearing snickers right about now, it's probably soccer's detractors (and there are many of you out there), who have been trying to dismiss the game as a "foreign" sport for years, arguing that it has no place in the American sports landscape. True, soccer is unlike American sports. The game features two halves with a clock that never stops. Each half is one continuous 45-minute play or opera with players running up and down the field, maintaining possession of the ball before stringing together a series of passes all in an effort to score a goal. On its surface, soccer seems very easy to play: just kick the ball into the goal. Yet goals are rare. Perhaps soccer's greatest appeal lies in that contradiction—a simple game that is difficult to play well. Goals are treasured because they are so tantalizingly difficult to score. Even the craftiest striker can be stripped of the ball by a slower, but wiser, defender who has perfectly anticipated his opponent's next move. On the other hand, even the smartest defender could be fooled by a striker who has learned to glide one way, then dart the other. The game's beauty lies in the artistry and power of its players.

The aim of this book is to recount the history of the World Cup to an American audience largely unfamiliar with the tournament's past. There are some readers who may be new to the game and want to know more about its past. Maybe you were bitten by the soccer bug for the first time while watching the 2014 World Cup and are hungry for more details. Some of you may already enjoy reading about the game and want to add another World Cup book to your collection. No matter what the reason is, this book pulls together the tournament's greatest games and players into one comprehensive history. For me, the greatest moment in sports is when two national teams step onto the field and prepare to play each other. The next best moment is when they line up before the cameras and listen to the national anthems. Then the referee places the ball on the midfield line and the game begins. The world watches. And the fun is just about to begin.

This book has been a labor of love and the dream of a lifetime. I watched more than 400 World Cup games and hundreds of hours of archived footage culled from a variety of places in order to make this book a reality. I delved into this project with the exactness and accuracy of a journalist and all the love and ardor of a fan. For the lifetime fan, I hope this book is a pleasurable trip down memory lane. For the novice, I hope it triggers enough interest in the game to become a true fan. If I've learned one thing, it's that the beautiful game is in the eye of the beholder. I hope you will feel the same way about the game as I do after reading this book.

## NOTE

1. Coach Shankly's quote was named as the greatest football saying in 2006. news.sky.com/skynews/article/0,,91167-13531842,00.html, retrieved March 2007.

# 1

# THE WORLD CUP
# IS BORN

There is no sporting event more popular than the World Cup. For one month every four years, hundreds of millions of people turn their attention to the tournament, which features the most talented players on the planet proudly representing their countries. Wars stop. People call in sick to work. Nothing else seems to matter. Fans pack into bars to watch games or choose to stay home for days at a time glued to their TV sets. The first World Cup, won by Uruguay in 1930, featured just thirteen teams and today, the tournament includes thirty-two nations. The final match itself is watched by an estimated audience that surpasses one billion global viewers. Soccer is without a doubt the planet's pastime with the World Cup representing the sport's biggest event. The game, however, wasn't always so popular. A little over a century ago, soccer was primarily played by English private school students but with the help of colonialism, it rapidly spread to become the world's number one spectator sport.

Trying to figure out who was the very first to play soccer is a little like answering the question who invented spaghetti. Though the Chinese can lay claim to both, the general belief is that it was the British who set the rules for the modern game in 1863. The game of soccer, known as football throughout most of the world, got its start during ancient times. An early form of the game called *tsu-chu* was played by the Chinese around 1700 B.C.E. during the Han Dynasty.[1] The game consisted of players kicking a leather ball filled with feathers into a small net kept in place by long bamboo sticks.[2] In Europe, a similar game was played by the Greeks called *episkyros*.[3] The game was played on a field where players used their hands and feet to move the ball past a goal line. The Romans also played a version of the same game called *harpastum*, played with a small ball on a rectangular field marked by boundary lines.[4] The object of the game was for players to pass the ball, using their hands, to get it over the opponents' boundary line. Roman armies eventually imported the game to Great Britain in 43 A.D., where it grew into a popular pastime of the masses during the eighth century under the name mob football.[5] Games were more like a bloody battle than a sporting spectacle and featured punching and biting. The game, which involved moving the ball to a predetermined spot using one's hands and feet, featured hundreds of players. It posed such a public nuisance that several attempts were made to have it banned.[6] In Italy, another soccer precursor called *calcio*—which to this day remains the Italian name for soccer—developed in Florence in the 1500s during the Renaissance. The games were rugged, much like mob football, and took place in Santa Croce square, which is roughly 100 yards long and 50 wide—about the size of a modern soccer field.[7] Like the British version, players used their hands.

Soccer took its first modern steps on October 26, 1863, when thirteen men representing ten English and Scottish teams met at Freemasons' Tavern in London to come up with a set of rules that would govern the sport. A group of dissidents favored rules associated with the Rugby School, where players were allowed to use their hands and engage in rough tackles. Another group backed a version called the Cambridge Rules, which had been adopted by most British universities in 1848. Instead of coming up with a compromise, there was a rift and the sport was divided into two games—rugby and soccer.[8] On December 8, 1863, eleven London teams created the Football Association with a single set of rules that did away with violent tackles. Another rule was added six years later that banned any handling of the ball—a change that would usher the start of modern soccer and forever separate it from rugby. Here were the original rules[9]:

1. The maximum length of the ground shall be 200 yards, the maximum breadth shall be 100 yards, the length and breadth shall be marked off with flags; and the goal shall be defined by two upright posts, 8 yards apart, without any tape or bar across them.

2. A toss for goals shall take place and the game shall be commenced by a place kick from the center of the ground by the side losing the toss for goals; the other side shall not approach within 10 yards of the ball until it is kicked off.

3. After a goal is won, the losing side shall be entitled to kick off and the two sides shall change goals after each goal is won.

4. A goal shall be won when the ball passes between the goalposts or over the space between the goalposts (at whatever height), not being thrown, knocked on, or carried.

5. When the ball is in touch, the first player who touches it shall throw it from the point on the boundary line where it left the ground in a direction at right angles with the boundary line, and the ball shall not be in play until it has touched the ground.

6. When a player has kicked the ball, any one of the same side who is nearer to the opponent's goal line is out of play and may not touch the ball himself, nor in any way whatever prevent any other player from doing so, until he is in play; but no player is out of play when the ball is kicked off from behind the goal line.

7. In case the ball goes behind the goal line, if a player on the side to whom the goal belongs first touches the ball, one of his side shall he entitled to a free kick from the goal line at the point opposite the place where the ball shall be touched. If a player of the opposite side first touches the ball, one of his side shall be entitled to a free kick at the goal only from a point 15 yards outside the goal line, opposite the place where the ball is touched, the opposing side standing within their goal line until he has had his kick.

8. If a player makes a fair catch, he shall be entitled to a free kick, providing he claims it by making a mark with his heel at once; and in order to take such a kick he may go back as far as he pleases, and no player on the opposite side shall advance beyond his mark until he has kicked.

9. No player shall run with the ball.

10. Neither tripping nor hacking shall be allowed and no player shall use his hands to hold or push his adversary.

11. A player shall not be allowed to throw the ball or pass it to another with his hands.

12. No player shall be allowed to take the ball from the ground with his hands under any pretext whatever while it is in play.

13. A player shall be allowed to throw the ball or pass it to another if he made a fair catch or catches the ball at the first bounce.
14. No player shall be allowed to wear projecting nails, iron plates, or gutta percha (a sticky latex sap) on the soles or heels of his boots.

These new rules spread throughout Britain. What really solidified the Football Association's authority over the sport was the creation of a tournament. The first organized modern soccer competition, known as the Football Association Cup, was a single elimination tournament created in 1871—still played today. The first trophy was won a year later when Wanderers of London defeated the Royal Engineers of London, 1–0. In 1873, the same competition featured fifteen teams and games attracted thousands of fans. Nine years later, the number of teams swelled to seventy-three. The competition is still open to all professional and amateur teams in England with the championship game staged at London's Wembley Stadium. The creation of club tournaments eventually gave rise to the conception of national teams. The first game between two countries took place in 1872 when England played Scotland with the then-novel idea that each team would be represented by eleven of its best native-born players. The game in Glasgow ended 0–0. In England, being chosen to play for the national team was so prestigious that, starting in 1886, players were presented with a velvet cap for each appearance. The term *caps* is still used to describe the number of times a player has played for his national team. The scope of international competition near the end of the nineteenth century was limited to teams hailing from Great Britain. At the inaugural modern Olympic Games in 1896, soccer was not one of the events. Not before long, though, the passion the British had for the game would spread across the world. In time, soccer would become the world's game.

In this country, English settlers brought an early version of soccer here with them in the seventeenth century. The game went on to gain prominence during the nineteenth century at a number of colleges, including Harvard and Yale. The turning point for the sport came when Harvard adopted rugby football rules, a decision that would stifle the development of soccer and open the doors for the popularity of American football. Other colleges soon followed suit and soccer all but disappeared from the American sports landscape. Soccer made a brief comeback during the 1920s following mass immigrations from Europe, but its first national sanction did not take place until 1959 when the National Collegiate Athletic Association recognized the game as an official collegiate sport worthy of a national tournament.

Initially, students attending prestigious British schools played soccer and competed as amateurs. After graduation, these players—unknown to them—became soccer ambassadors, exporting the game to foreign lands. These men created a "soccer diaspora" since Great Britain was a colonial power with far-reaching international interests. In Latin America, the game became known simply as fútbol. The spread of the British Empire also gave rise to the creation of domestic leagues. The manner in which soccer spread to Italy is typical of how countries outside of Britain took a liking to the sport. A group of Brits living in northern Italy founded a sports team in 1892 called the Genoa Cricket and Football Club. Genoa was a bustling business center at the time and the British were active in the port trade, working on cargo ships and bringing goods to and from England. The cricket part of the club never took hold, while soccer gained broader acceptance. The team, made up solely of British players, only played a few games since opponents were hard to find. Whenever they did play, however, thousands gathered to watch. What transpired a few years later would forever change the way the country shaped like a boot played sports: In 1896, the team allowed Italians to play just as other clubs were beginning to sprout up across the peninsula. A year later, Juventus was founded and over the next century would go on to become the country's most successful club team. In 1898, the Italian championship was established and won by Genoa, which featured seven Italians on its roster. The club retains its English name to this day.

Similarly, British workers in South America spearheaded the spread of the sport there. Soccer made its way to Argentina after two British teachers, Watson Hutton and Isaac Newell, traveled to the country in 1880 to run several schools. Hutton and Newell became soccer pioneers, founding two teams, Rosario Central in 1889 and Newell's Old Boys in 1905. Both clubs exist to this day and continue to have a large following both at home and abroad. Brazilians, known the world over for their soccer skills, fell in love with the sport after Charles Miller, a Brazilian by birth who had been educated in England, introduced the sport to the Brazilian people in 1895 by organizing several teams at British-owned companies so that workers could play on a recreational level. Miller's passion for the game helped spur the creation a year later of CR Flamengo, the country's first club team, with the hopes of someday playing against other amateur sides.

In 1900, Olympic organizers included soccer at the Summer Games by allowing just three teams to participate—Belgium, Great Britain, and the host country, France. The British, represented by the London-based club Upton Park, won the gold medal. Although soccer may have originated and developed in Britain, the sport's governing body, the Fédération Internationale de Football Association (FIFA), was founded in May 1904 with seven members: France, Belgium, Denmark, Spain, Sweden, Switzerland, and Holland. FIFA included solely European nations until South Africa joined in 1909, followed by Argentina and Chile in 1912 and the United States in 1913. FIFA's role was to oversee all national federations. Britain's four associations (England, Scotland, Northern Ireland, and Wales) joined FIFA in 1915, only to leave five years later due to political tensions connected to World War I. The British wanted Germany and its allies, Austria and Hungary, thrown out of FIFA. Unable to gain support from other members, Britain's four federations pulled out. Other tensions arose. In 1921, the Belgian Football Association announced it would allow teams to pay players—who were considered amateurs because they were not financially compensated—for the time they had to take off from their jobs to play games. Italy, France, Norway, and Switzerland all implemented the same rule. FIFA did not have any guidelines addressing clubs paying players and said individual federations were allowed to come up with their own regulations. The British resisted compensating or rewarding players with money—a practice commonly referred to as "broken-time payments"—for any work missed because of playing commitments.

Britain's four federations rejoined FIFA in 1924, only to leave for a second time four years later after getting into another disagreement over the definition of an amateur player and whether they should be paid. The British would not become a FIFA member again until after World War II, missing out on the first three World Cup tournaments. Ultimately, the creation of FIFA made organizing a competition like the World Cup a reality. The Olympic soccer tournament at the time only featured amateurs, a decision that FIFA did not accept. FIFA president Jules Rimet and French Football Association secretary Henri Delaunay realized that amateurs were not the only ones playing the sport. But

FIFA and the IOC were at odds over who should control the Olympic soccer tournament and the fight over what constituted an *amateur player* helped further fuel the debate. "We must implement a tournament which represents us," said Delaunay.[10]

In 1926, Rimet and Delaunay proposed the creation of a competition open to all national federations that would include both amateurs and professionals. FIFA, realizing that the Olympics limited soccer because it did not allow the best players to participate, agreed on May 26, 1928, at a meeting in Amsterdam that the World Cup would be played every four years beginning in 1930. Determining the format of the tournament was just the first hurdle FIFA had to overcome. Another determination to make was location. Holland, Italy, Spain, Sweden, and Uruguay all submitted bids. Sweden and Holland eventually withdrew and backed Italy's candidacy. Rimet had other plans. His goal was to make the sport truly global and he favored Uruguay's bid. He argued that the country should host the tournament because it was the strongest team in the world after winning two consecutive Olympic soccer tournaments in 1924 and 1928. FIFA named Uruguay as the host nation in 1929 and it gave French sculptor Abel Lafleur the task of designing the trophy.

After years of wrangling, the stage had been set. National federations could finally field their best players for a chance to become world champion. The original World Cup trophy bore Rimet's name and was contested three times during the 1930s, before World War II put a twelve-year stop to the competition. When the tournament resumed, the World Cup quickly emerged as one of the greatest sporting events on the planet. Held every four years since 1950, the World Cup entered a new era with two key decisions: FIFA decided in July 1988 to award the tournament to the United States—the first time it would ever be played outside Europe or South America—and again in May 1996 when it granted South Korea and Japan the rights to co-host the competition in 2002.

Interestingly, the World Cup has produced only eight different winners during the past eighty years. It has also been highlighted by a series of dramatic upsets like the United States' defeat of England in 1950, North Korea's victory over Italy in 1966, and Cameroon's upset of Argentina in 1990, to name just a few. Today, FIFA boasts 205 federations and rivals only the United Nations when it comes to membership.

The World Cup is the Super Bowl, Wimbledon, and Olympics all rolled into one. A global TV audience of 700 million watched the 2010 World Cup final in Johannesburg between Spain and the Netherlands. After nearly a century, the World Cup remains the embodiment of every soccer player's ambition and the dream of billions of fans.

## NOTES

1. Elio Trifari and Charles Miers, *Soccer! The Game and the World Cup* (New York: Rizzoli International Publications, 1994), 26.

2. Trifari and Miers, *Soccer! The Game and the World Cup*, 26.

3. Trifari and Miers, *Soccer! The Game and the World Cup*, 26.

4. Trifari and Miers, *Soccer! The Game and the World Cup*, 26.

5. Trifari and Miers, *Soccer! The Game and the World Cup*, 26.

6. Trifari and Miers, *Soccer! The Game and the World Cup*, 27.

7. Trifari and Miers, *Soccer! The Game and the World Cup*, 27.

8. Trifari and Miers, *Soccer! The Game and the World Cup*, 30.

9. The list of rules is quoted from the site, "About: World Soccer," worldsoccer.about.com/cs/theposts/a/origrules_2.htm.

10. Andres Cantor, *Goooal: A Celebration of Soccer* (New York: Simon & Schuster, 1996), 18.

# ( 2 )

# THE FIRST STEPS

## 1930

The battle to host the first World Cup led to widespread bitterness, eventually turning into a tournament boycott on the part of many European nations. Holland, Sweden, Italy, Spain, and Hungary decided not to send teams following a failed bid by the Italians. In less than three decades, FIFA's membership had ballooned to forty-one countries, but with two months to go before the start of the tournament in Uruguay not a single European country had accepted an invitation to play. Another set of European countries—Germany, Austria, Czechoslovakia, and Switzerland—also declined, arguing that the two-week boat journey to South America was not worth the trouble. The organizers had even offered to pay for the transatlantic journey, but that wasn't enough to convince the boycotters. At the same time, the British (England, Scotland, Wales, and Northern Ireland) were ineligible because they were not FIFA members. The only countries who agreed to embark on the long trip were France, Belgium, Romania, and Yugoslavia. The French went because it was the home of Rimet. Belgium—also under FIFA pressure to attend—eventually agreed to send a team. Romania decided to participate after King Carol, a rabid sports fan, had promised in 1928 to send a team. Yugoslavia was persuaded by the goodies organizers had offered them, which not only included an all-paid voyage on the cruise ship *Florida*, but hotel accommodations once they made landfall in the capital, Montevideo.[1] The other three European teams boarded the *Conte Verde*, where players spent much of the time on the ship's deck training for the tournament.[2] The Americas had a healthy representation that included Uruguay's neighbor and soccer rival, Argentina, along with Brazil, Paraguay, Peru, Bolivia, and Chile. Mexico and the United States rounded out the field of thirteen nations. The first World Cup took place from July 13 to July 30, 1930. The teams were placed into four groups—three pools of three countries and a fourth consisting of four—with all the games taking place at three venues scattered around Montevideo. The four group winners would advance to the semifinals. The teams were divided in the following way:

Pool 1: Argentina, Chile, France, and Mexico
Pool 2: Yugoslavia, Brazil, and Bolivia
Pool 3: Uruguay, Romania, and Peru
Pool 4: The United States, Paraguay, and Belgium

In the planning stages, organizers decided to build a stadium worthy of hosting the big event. The stadiums where two of the country's biggest club teams, Nacional and Peñarol, played were not large or modern enough to stage the championship game. The government decided to build a new stadium in Montevideo and hired architect Juan Scasso to design it. The venue would be named the Centenario in commemoration of the country's one hundred years of independence. Construction began in February 1930 but the stadium would not be completed until five days after the tournament had already begun. The Centenario's completion was better late than never and the country could boast being the home to a 100,000-seat facility that at the time was the envy of the soccer world. Uruguay was a hotbed for soccer at the start of the twentieth century. The team, which featured gifted midfielder José Leandro Andrade, had entertained crowds around the world in the decade leading up to the World Cup. At the 1924 Olympic Games, Uruguay traveled to Paris and for the first time a South American team had taken the long trip to Europe for an official competition. The Olympic soccer tournament was a huge success and the final between Uruguay and Switzerland attracted more than 50,000 fans. At the inaugural World Cup, the Uruguayans were clearly the favorites after Europe's most powerful teams failed to show up. The team prepared for the competition by going into complete isolation two months before the start of the World Cup at the opulent

Prado Park Hotel in Montevideo. The players were forced to live a monastic life, even having to adhere to a strict curfew. When goalkeeper Antonio Mazzali, a two-time Olympic gold medalist, failed to return to the hotel on time one night, he was booted from the team.

## Group Play

The tournament opened on July 13 at Pocitos Stadium, which was home to club team Penarol. A crowd of just 1,000 gathered to watch France defeat Mexico, 4–1, in the very first World Cup game. The French won despite being down a player (FIFA would not allow substitutions at the World Cup until 1970) after goalkeeper Alex Thépot was kicked in the jaw while trying to make a save. Rimet's dream of a global tournament had finally come to fruition and it was fitting that the first goal was scored by a Frenchman, Lucien Laurent, after just nineteen minutes.

Two days later, France and Argentina met at Parque Central Stadium, which housed club team Nacional. Argentina, one of the favorites to win the tournament, yearned to be crowned world champions. Two years earlier, Argentina had lost the Olympic final to Uruguay, only to retain the South American Championship (known as the Copa America) one year later. Thépot was back between the posts and it was his heroics that kept France in the game. Despite Thépot's brilliant goalkeeping performance, Argentina's potent attack was finally able to crack the French defense when Brazilian referee Almeida Rego awarded a free kick just outside the penalty box in the 81st minute. Luis Monti quickly took the kick just as the French were lining up their wall and Marcel Pinel fired off a powerful shot past Thépot. The French countered, hoping to tie the game, but Rego whistled three times to signal the end of the contest at the very moment Marcel Langiller was slicing through the Argentine defense. Right after he blew the whistle, Rego consulted his watch and realized there were still six minutes left to play. The French players vehemently protested as dozens of Uruguayan fans, who had cheered against the Argentines, stormed the field. Rego tried to restore order, but the chaos that ensued made it nearly impossible for the game to restart. The game resumed a few minutes later and the final minutes played out with some help from the police—who escorted the enraged fans off of the field at gunpoint—but the score remained the same: Argentina 1, France 0.

Chile, who breezed to the top of the group standings with 4 points after defeating Mexico 3–0 and France 1–0, had to get past Argentina in its last game for a shot at the semifinals. Chile's 1–0 win over France had come on July 19 at the newly completed Centenario Stadium, a match that was followed up with a showdown between Argentina and Mexico. The Argentines, even without their captain Manuel Ferreira, who had returned home to take a law exam, were too much for Mexico to handle. Argentina jumped out to a 3–0 lead after just seventeen minutes thanks to two goals from striker Guillermo Stabile and one from Adolfo Zumelzú, who had replaced Ferreira in the starting lineup. The Mexicans scored seven minutes before halftime when Manuel Rosas converted the World Cup's first penalty kick. Up 3–1, Argentina padded its lead, scoring two more goals in the first ten minutes of the second half. Incredibly, the Argentine team almost lost its commanding 5–1 lead. Felipe Rosas took a cue from his brother Manuel and scored Mexico's second goal in the 65th minute before Stabile netted his third goal—and the World Cup's first-ever hat trick—in the 80th minute, lifting Argentina to a 6–3 win. Despite the victory, Argentina was left to ponder how they could have given up three goals to Mexico. Argentina knew it needed to field a tighter defense if it hoped to defeat Chile and reach the semifinals.

On the eve of the tournament, no one had doubted Argentina's place in the semifinals. But after witnessing Argentina give up three goals to Mexico, the Chileans believed they had a chance to pull off the upset. Ferreira was back and Juan Evaristo was brought in to reinforce the Argentinean midfield. Chile made its own changes and replaced wingers Tomas Ojeda and captain Carlos Schneeberger with Guillermo Arellano and Juan Aguilera. Argentina and Chile met on July 22 at the Centenario. The winner would go through to the semifinals. Stabile, who was now the tournament's top scorer with three goals, netted his fourth in the 12th minute, then added a second two minutes later to give Argentina a 2–0 lead. The Chileans pulled one back with Guillermo Subiabre in the 16th minute. Once again, Argentina's defense had not been able to stop an opponent from scoring. The game also featured some violence to go along with the scoring. A free-for-all broke out on the field right before halftime following a vicious foul by Monti and police officers had to intervene to restore order. Once the dust cleared, both teams went to their respective locker rooms with Argentina holding on to a slim 2–1 lead. Fortunately, the second half was violence free. Chile continued to put the pressure on Argentina's vulnerable defense, but goalkeeper Angel Bossier made a series of saves to preserve the lead. Evaristo would score a third for Argentina in the 51st minute to cap off a 3–1 win. Argentina was through to the semifinals.

## GUILLERMO STABILE

A natural goalscorer, Guillermo Stabile was the World Cup's first top scorer with eight goals in just four games at the 1930 tournament. Born in Buenos Aires in 1905, Stabile played for Huracan at the time of the inaugural World Cup but soon thereafter, like so many other top South Americans in the 1930s, he found the lure of money too great and joined Italian club, Genoa. He was proclaimed a hero after netting a hat trick in his debut against rival Bologna. Stabile moved to Napoli in 1935, before finishing his career in the French league with Red Star Paris a year later.

Surprisingly, Stabile started the 1930 World Cup on the bench. He watched as his teammates beat France 1–0. He played the next game against Mexico, hitting a hat trick to lead Argentina to a 6–3 win. He scored two goals in the next match against Chile in a 3–1 victory, two more in the semifinals against the United States in a 6–1 drubbing, and one more in the final, where Argentina defeated rival Uruguay, 4–2. In 1936, after completing his move to Red Star Paris, Stabile became a French citizen. Though he never played in another World Cup, Stabile played for France and once scored four goals against Austria.

After retiring, Stabile coached Argentina from 1939 to 1960, in a total of 127 matches, making him one of the few coaches with more than one hundred international games under his belt. Stabile coached Argentina to six Copa America titles in 1941, 1945, 1946, 1947, 1955, and 1957. The team he coached in 1957 is considered by many to be the greatest Argentine squad of all-time.

Stabile died in 1966 at age 60.

### World Cup Career Statistics

Tournaments played: 1
Games: 4
Goals: 8

Group 2 opened on July 14 with a game between Yugoslavia and Brazil at Parque Central Stadium. The hype surrounding the Brazilians, one of the pre-tournament favorites, appeared to do them little good. Alexsandar Tirnanić and Ivan Beck gave Yugoslavia a 2–0 lead in the first half. The Brazilians got a goal from its captain, Preguinho, in the 62nd minute, but it would be the Yugoslavs who would hang on for the 2–1 win. The loss dealt a severe blow to Brazil's chances of moving on to the semifinals. Yugoslavia would clinch a semifinal spot three days later after defeating Bolivia 4–0 at Parque Central Stadium. The Yugoslavs made just one change to its starting lineup, taking out Branislav Seculic on the left wing and replacing him with Dragutin Najdanović. After a scoreless first half, Yugoslavia put on a spectacular offensive display, hitting the target four times in a span of twenty-five minutes. The triumph officially eliminated Brazil. The Brazilians may have been eliminated, but they left an indelible mark on the competition: players using a single name or nicknames. Brazilian society has had an affinity for nicknames for centuries and players—just like doctors, lawyers, and even politicians—use single names or nicknames, a tradition that has its roots in slavery. When the English introduced soccer to Brazil, the fans referred to the players solely by their surnames. As the game grew in popularity, nicknaming took over. When the Brazilian national team played its first game in 1914, the team featured a striker called Formiga, which is Portuguese for "ant." The use of single names by Brazilian players are used to this day.

Group 3 opened on July 14 with Romania and Peru at Pocitos Stadium in front of a crowd of just 300. The Romanians, an odd assortment of workers who had been given the month off from their day jobs by King Carol to play in the tournament, defeated Peru 3–1. The crowd also watched one of the tournament's most violent games. Romanian defender Adalbert Steiner broke his right leg following a rough tackle. Peru captain Mario De Las Casas was the first player to receive a red card at the World Cup when Chilean referee Alberto Warken booted him from the game following his violent tackle on Steiner.

Hosts Uruguay, called the *Celeste*—Spanish for sky blue because of the color of the team's shirts—made its much-anticipated debut on July 18 at the Centenario so it would coincide with the 100th anniversary of the country's independence. Despite delaying Uruguay's game against Peru by five days, the stadium was still not completed and scaffolding was visible along most of it. The stadium could seat 100,000 spectators, but its capacity was reduced to 70,000 because there was still work being done. Peru had put on a disappointing performance against Romania and the hosts were banking on exploiting their opponent's weak defense. As a result, Uruguay, along with its enthusiastic fans, was expecting to coast to victory. How wrong it would be. The first half ended scoreless. The crowd would get what it wanted fifteen minutes into the second half when Héctor "Manco" Castro, who was missing part of his right arm, took a pass from Pedro Petrone to score the game winner. Uruguay had won the game 1–0, but changes needed to be made if it hoped to earn a victory against Romania.

On July 22, Uruguay and Romania met at the Centenario Stadium. This time, Uruguay was supported by 80,000 fans, all of whom were expecting a win. Uruguay coach Alberto Suppici tinkered with the lineup and replaced defender Domingo Tejera with the faster and more experienced Ernesto Mascheroni. Suppici also changed things upfront and Pablo Dorado, Peregrino Anselmo, and Héctor Scarone all came off the bench. The changes worked. Dorado grabbed the game's first goal after just seven minutes and Scarone added a second goal seventeen minutes later. Anselmo scored a third in the 30th minute and José Pedro Cea added a fourth just five minutes later to complete Uruguay's 4–0 rout. The two-time Olympic champions had booked a trip to semifinals and their four-goal performance clearly made them favorites to become world champs.

The U.S. team competed in Group 4 with Belgium and Paraguay. The Americans had lost 11–2 to Argentina just two years earlier at the Olympics, but this time they fielded pros, not amateurs, and FIFA made them a top seed. The United States was coached by Irish-born Jack "Jock" Coll, who had moved to this country from Scotland in 1922. Coll coached several teams in the American Soccer League, including the Brooklyn Wanderers, and quickly rose to prominence as one of America's most talented coaches. The American team, which arrived in Uruguay from Hoboken, New Jersey, aboard the SS *Munargo*, also featured six British-born players: Alec Wood, James Gallacher, James Brown, Andrew Auld, Bart McGhee, and George Moorehouse—all of whom had moved to this country as young men. These players were by no means "ringers"—as some have defined them—and had developed most of their skills playing in the then-burgeoning ASL. Moorehouse was the only player on the team who had spent time in Britain's professional ranks, although that experience was limited to playing in just two games with Tranmere in England's Third Division.

The U.S. team made its tournament debut on July 13 against Belgium. The game drew 10,000 spectators at Parque Central Stadium. The Americans proved too talented for the Belgians, with McGhee scoring two goals and Bert Patenaude adding another for the 3–0 win. The victory was the first for the U.S. side at a major soccer tournament. Four days later, the United States squared off against Paraguay at Parque Central Stadium and this time a crowd of just 800 would witness another American triumph. Paraguay was a team beaming with confidence on the eve of the tournament. Paraguay had defeated Uruguay, 3–0, in the previous year's Copa America and was hoping to win the group this time around. Despite Paraguay's confidence, the Americans were the ones to take the lead with Patenaude's goal after ten minutes. Tom Florie scored five minutes later and Patenaude added a third in the 50th minute to seal the 3–0 win and a spot in the semifinals. Debate rages to this day over who scored the United States' second goal. While FIFA records credit Florie with the goal, the U.S. Soccer Federation claims it was Patenaude. That would make American Patenaude—and not Stabile of Argentina—the first player to record a hat trick in the World Cup. The box score published in newspapers at the time, including Argentina's *La Prensa* and Brazil's *O Estádio do Sao Paulo*, credit Patenaude with all three tallies. The discrepancy is believed to have resulted from the fact that players at the time wore no numbers on the back of their jerseys and that Patenaude had been mistaken for Florie by the official scorekeeper. In 2006, FIFA officially revised its record books and attributed Patenaude with the triple strike and, therefore, he is now the first player to have recorded a hat trick at the World Cup.

## Semifinals

Controversies aside, the United States had posted two impressive wins in group play, but had to overcome Argentina if it wanted to book a trip to the final. Argentina had earned widespread praise for its defeat of Chile and was certainly the toughest opponent the United States had faced to date at the tournament. On July 26, an estimated crowd of 80,000 filled the Centenario to watch the clash between the United States and

Argentina. Complicating matters for both teams was the drenched field that had flooded during a storm the night before. Ultimately, the field conditions were the last thing to emerge as a problem. The game turned violent very quickly. Any chance the U.S. team thought it had of reaching the final match lay in ruins after midfielder Raphael Tracy had his right leg broken after ten minutes. That wasn't all. Auld continued to play with a serious mouth injury after being kicked in the face. Despite that, the American team, which started its six British-born players for the third straight game, were able to hold off Argentina to just one goal in the first half, scored by Monti in the 20th minute. However, the second half was characterized by a barrage of Argentine attacks that would guarantee Argentina a spot in the final. Alejandro Scopelli created repeated opportunities for Stabile and Carlos Peucelle, who each scored a pair of goals. Three of those goals came in the span of seven minutes late in the second half and Scopelli added a goal of his own to give Argentina a 6–0 lead. The Americans' lone goal came from Brown with two minutes left at the end. Though Argentina had won 6–1, the Americans were not impressed with the South Americans' brutal playing style or the officiating of Belgian referee Jean Langenus. Tensions ran so high that when Langenus whistled a foul in favor of Argentina, Coll ran out onto the field and threw the team's medical equipment at him.[3] The Americans had put on a good showing, garnering them the attention of the soccer world, even though the feat was hardly noticed back home. Argentina, on the other hand, was already one of the strongest teams in South America and now wanted to prove it was the best in the world.

The other semifinal pitted Uruguay against Yugoslavia and was played the following day at the Centenario Stadium. A boisterous crowd of 93,000 greeted the hosts and the prospect of reaching the final was on everyone's mind. Those hopes were temporarily dashed when Seculic put Yugoslavia ahead after just four minutes. Dread turned to celebration when a goal by Cea and another by Anselmo in a span of two minutes put the *Celeste* ahead, 2–1. Amid the cheering of the home fans, Anselmo added a third goal fourteen minutes before the end of the first half—even though the ball had appeared to be out of bounds before the goal was scored—to take a 3–1 lead. Uruguay completed the rout in the second half, scoring three more goals in the final thirty minutes. Santos Iriarte scored in the 60th minute and Cea completed his hat trick when he added a goal in the 67th and 72nd minutes for the

6-1 win. Coincidentally, this semifinal game ended with the identical score as the Argentina–United States match. The result also confirmed that Uruguay was the team to beat at the competition. The win also pitted the hosts against its rivals Argentina in an all-South American final.

## The Final

The championship game was played on July 30 at the Centenario. A seemingly innocuous controversy overshadowed the buildup to the game as the teams incessantly bickered for days, reaching an absurd level of squabbling when the disagreement focused on which team should provide the game ball. In the end, the fight forced FIFA to mandate that Argentina provide the ball in the first half and the Uruguayans provide their own in the second. World Cup history was finally made at 2:10 p.m. when Uruguay and Argentina walked onto the field for a chance to become the first country to be crowned world champion. Thousands of Argentine fans had made the trip across the Río de la Plata on ferryboats for the chance to cheer on their team. Many never made it into the stadium after organizers refused to increase the capacity past 93,000 for safety reasons. The referee was not chosen until three hours before the start of the game for fear that he would be targeted by fans. The responsibility eventually fell to Langenus, who demanded a police escort and a boat ready for him after the game so he could quickly depart the country.[4]

The tense match broke open after just twelve minutes when Dorado put Uruguay ahead with a blistering shot that went through Botasso's legs. Argentina responded, tying the game eight minutes later when Peucelle picked up a pass from Francisco Varallo and beat goalkeeper Enrique Ballesteros with a high shot. Argentina took a 2–1 lead in the 37th minute on a Stabile goal from close range that turned out to be the game's most controversial occurrence. The Uruguayan players argued that Stabile was offside, but Langenus allowed the goal to stand and Argentina was in the lead. The second half was a different story. Just twelve minutes into the half, Cea was able to tie the game and, with the loud cheering of the home team behind them, the *Celeste* orchestrated an astounding comeback. Argentina was unable to use the counterattack to its advantage, cutting through the Uruguayan defense on several occasions. Argentina was a team that possessed great passing skills—a feature that allowed them to find open spaces and create scoring opportunities—but the Uruguayan defense was able to break up those plays. The Uruguayans put any doubt that victory was theirs to rest when Iriarte's ferocious 25-yard blast landed in the back of the net to put his team ahead, 3–2. Despite taking the lead, Uruguay feared that Stabile, who would finish the tournament's top scorer with eight goals, could tie the game at any moment. That moment, however, never came and Uruguay put the game away when Castro headed in a pass from Dorado in stoppage time—the additional minutes a referee is allowed to tack on to the end of each half because of time wasted for injuries and penalties—to seal the 4–2 victory. Rimet presented Uruguayan captain José Nazassi with the trophy at the end of the game, unleashing several days of celebrations across Uruguay. The government proclaimed the day after the final a national holiday. The Uruguayan team, which had gone undefeated at the tournament, could not have given its fans a better present in the year of its centenary.

*World Cup founder and FIFA president Jules Rimet (left) presents the trophy that bears his name for the first time in 1930 to Uruguay's Raul Jude, president of that country's soccer association (Credit: EMPICS).*

## 1934

The success of the first World Cup quickly turned the tournament into soccer's premier competition. Unlike the first World Cup where most European teams turned down invitations to participate, this time thirty-two of FIFA's fifty members wanted a shot at the trophy. In 1932, FIFA gave Italy the nod to host the tournament and fascist dictator Benito Mussolini—who had taken power in 1922 after marching on Rome and appointed prime minister by King Victor Emmanuel III—spared no expense. Not only did Mussolini want to show the world the supremacy of the fascist regime, but also how great his national team could be when pitted against other countries.

### Pre-Tournament Qualifiers and the Italian Advantage

The large number of entrants forced FIFA to implement its first World Cup qualification rounds. Teams were placed in groups of two to three in order to whittle down the field. Oddly, host country Italy also had to qualify for the competition. What a disaster it would have been had Italy lost in the qualifier and failed to reach the finals. But FIFA gave Italy an easy opponent and placed them in a bracket with Greece, who had formed its national team just four years earlier. The Italians won 4-0 and the Greeks forfeited the second game after the lopsided loss. Uruguay, meanwhile, had not forgotten how bad European turnout had been at the last tournament and decided not to send a team, repaying the Italians' snub four years earlier. This would be the first—and only—time a reigning world champion would not defend its title. Argentina, who had lost in the final four years earlier, was also at a disadvantage because its national team was composed solely of amateurs after club teams refused to release their players. The team arrived in Italy with second- and third-division players with little chance to lift the trophy. Argentine clubs feared that once its players arrived in Italy, that local teams there would induce the players to leave their native land and play for them. Indeed, the best soccer in the world was being played in Uruguay and Argentina, but that talent would be absent from the World Cup. Furthermore, the British—the modern missionaries of the sport—were again missing from the tournament because of its ongoing feud with FIFA. The tournament was played from May 27 to June 10 in eight cities: Naples, Rome, Florence, Genoa, Bologna, Milan, Turin, and Trieste. In an effort to keep the tournament competitive and ensure its financial viability, eight teams—Italy, Czechoslovakia, Brazil, Hungary, Austria, Argentina, Germany, and Holland—were seeded and would not meet each other in the first round. When the sixteen teams were finalized, twelve hailed from Europe. The only exceptions were the United States, Egypt, Brazil, and Argentina. Half of the teams that went to Italy, including the United States, Brazil, and Argentina, would go home after just ninety minutes of play because of the new knockout format.

Italy's biggest problem was the possibility of encountering Austria. Hugo Meisl coached the mighty Austrian team, nicknamed the *Wunderteam* for its supremacy and ease in which it defeated opponents. Born to a wealthy family, Meisl, who had governed the Austrian Football Association during the 1920s, eventually rose to prominence as his country's national team coach. Meisl was the driving force behind making soccer a professional sport in Austria and in 1927 invented the Mitropa Cup—a precursor to the European Champions Cup—even though his biggest achievements would come closer to the playing field. In 1912, Meisl made his debut on the Austrian bench in a 3–1 defeat over Italy in Genoa. He was in charge of the national team for just two years before going off to fight in World War I, but promptly returned to the Austrian bench following the armed conflict in 1919. The *Wunderteam*—regarded as the most powerful pre–World War II national team in Europe—was Meisl's brainchild. A 2–1 win over Czechoslovakia in April 1931 was the first in a fourteen-game unbeaten streak, a run that included eleven wins and three ties. The streak also included two impressive wins over Germany (6–0 in Berlin and 5–0 in Vienna) and a 5–0 thrashing of Scotland in May 1931. Austria would go on to earn its *Wunderteam* moniker after losing just three times in a span of thirty-one games between April 1931 and June 1934. One of those wins was a 4–2 victory over Italy in Turin on the eve of the World Cup finals—another sign the *Wunderteam* was destined to conquer the game's biggest prize.

The World Cup gave Italian organizers the chance to help the government create a positive image of their country and—why not?—win the trophy at the same time. Italy's road to World Cup glory was strewn with obstacles, despite the optimism exuded by Mussolini and tournament organizers. Czechoslovakia, Hungary, and Spain were also favored to win the title, though "Il Duce" had no doubt his beloved Italy would capture the trophy. Mussolini was not a big soccer fan—but to him the World Cup was more than a soccer tournament. It was an opportunity to show the world that his totalitarian regime had transformed Italy into a world power. As a result, Mussolini was very hands-on, even going as far as giving the players a pep talk in a Rome hotel on the night before their opener against the United States. The Italians, coached by Vittorio Pozzo, had set up camp nearly two months before the start of the competition in a small mountainside retreat near picturesque Lake Maggiore in northern Italy.

Pozzo, who had played for Torino for five seasons starting in 1905, was a master tactician in the tradition of Meisl. Paternalistic toward his players, Pozzo discovered his love for the game as a young man studying in England. Pozzo was named Italy's coach in 1929 and for the first time in the team's history a sole coach, rather than a committee, was allowed to select players. Pozzo was also a superstitious man, relying on two good luck charms to guide him through tough times. The first was a small shard of glass from a broken trophy that Italy had won against Hungary, 5–0, in 1930 in the final of the Gero Cup, a precursor to the European Championship.[5] He always carried it in his pocket and was often seen fiddling with it. The other was a one-way ticket to England that his family had purchased for him a few years earlier.[6] Lucky charms aside, the Italians were stacked with talent, including players the country had naturalized because of their Italian heritage. Worried that Italian superiority may not be enough to win the trophy, Mussolini ordered a decree that anyone with Italian ancestry was eligible to join the country's military. The *oriundi* (South Americans who had become Italian citizens and imported to play on the national team) included Monti, who had played in the final four years earlier with Argentina; Raimundo Orsi, who won a silver medal at the 1928 Olympics but who sat out the first World Cup; and Attilio Demaria and Enrique Guaita. Pozzo justified their presence by arguing that they had Italian-born fathers—if it stood that they could be called to serve in the Italian army, then they could certainly play soccer for their newly adopted country. "If they can die for Italy, they can play football for Italy," Pozzo said.[7] The Italian coach also devised what he called *Il Metodo* (The Method), utilizing a 2-3-5 formation with two defenders, three midfielders, and five strikers. This tactical system—first used by the Austrians, Czechoslovakians, and Hungarians and often referred to as the Danubian

School—was widely used during the 1920s. The combination of players relied heavily on a series of short passes and individual skill, which emphasized playing the ball on the ground. Pozzo's method, however, added more players to the midfield, creating a 2-3-2-3 formation. This made for a stronger defense and allowed for the effective use of the counterattack as an offensive weapon.

## Group Play

Italy opened the tournament on May 27 at Rome's National Stadium against the United States in front of 30,000 fans. The Americans, who had entered the competition late, had defeated Mexico, winners of the North American bracket, in an impromptu playoff game held in Milan just three days earlier. The Americans won 4–2 and the Mexicans made the long journey for nothing. Aldo "Buff" Donelli left his mark in the record books, becoming the first player in U.S. national team history to score four goals in one game. The Americans were not the same team that had reached the semifinals four years earlier. Only three players returned—Bill Gonsalvez, Moorhouse, and Florie, who at thirty-seven was the oldest player at the tournament—and the U.S. players were thrown together following a series of tryout games. The Americans hung on against the powerful Italians, at least for the first eighteen minutes. That's when the Italians opened the scoring with Angelo Schiavio. Italy went up 2–0 when Orsi scored two minutes later. Schiavio put the game out of reach in the 29th minute to make it 3–0. The outmatched Americans scored their lone goal in the second half with Donelli.

Nicknamed "Buff" because of his fascination with "Buffalo" Bill Cody, Donelli was born in 1907 in Morgan, Pennsylvania, and grew up playing football and soccer. At age fifteen, he joined the Morgan Strasser Football Club of Pittsburgh in 1922 and spent eight seasons with the team. At the same time, Donelli also played football for Duquesne University and was a center and running back from 1926 to 1929. In his final season, Donelli captained the first undefeated team in school history. To date, Donelli's name is one of the most hallowed in Duquesne football history. A year later, Donelli opted to play soccer and signed with the Curry Silver Tops FC and was eventually selected to play on the U.S. team.

Despite Donelli's goal, the Italians—nicknamed the *Azzurri* (The Blues) because of the color of their jerseys—were still determined. Much to the delight of Mussolini and the crowd, Giovanni Ferrari made it 4–1 in the 63rd minute and Schiavio completed his hat trick a minute later. Orsi got on the scoreboard once again, notching his second of the game, and Giuseppe Meazza, one of the world's best players at the time, netted one to make the final tally 7–1. The win set a new World Cup record score and Meazza had developed into Italy's first soccer superstar.

Born in Milan in 1910, Meazza signed with Inter Milan in 1927, quickly forging a reputation as a ruthless finisher and possessing a potent shot that often left goalkeepers dumbfounded. In his third year at Inter, Meazza scored thirty-one goals in thirty-three league games during the 1929–30 season. In 1930, he was also given his first start for Italy, scoring twice in a 4–2 win over Switzerland. Meazza's exploits off the field often matched those on it. Meazza was the only player on the national team who was allowed to smoke and had a habit of drinking heavily before games. Though garnering great success as a striker, it was as a midfielder where Meazza would enjoy his greatest achievements. Pozzo's decision to move him further back during the World Cup proved to be a stroke of tactical genius.

The other six first-round games also took place on the same day. In Trieste, the seeded Czechoslovakians, who featured only players from club teams Sparta and Slavia Praha, had a tough time disposing of Romania. The Czechoslovakians were finally able to put the game away in the 69th minute when Jiří Sobotka won the ball and dished off a pass to Oldřich Nejedlý, who scored the winning goal in a 2–1 victory. At Florence's Berta Stadium, Germany outlasted Belgium, 5–2. The Germans got on the board in the 26th minute with Stanislaus Kobierski, but two goals by Belgium's Bernard Voorhoof in the 31st and 43rd minutes gave his team a stunning 2–1 halftime lead. A hat trick by striker Edmund Conen in the second half gave Germany the win.

At Mussolini Stadium in Turin, Austria defeated France 3–2 in overtime—despite Meisl's complaints on the eve of the game that his team was not fit. The *Wunderteam* appeared to get lucky early on after French striker Jean Nicholas suffered a head injury—although that didn't stop Nicholas from putting his team ahead, 1–0, after nineteen minutes. Austria tied the game with striker Matthias Sindelar in the final minute of the half. A scoreless second half gave way to a riveting overtime session. The game went Austria's way after just four minutes when Anton Schall put his team ahead, 2–1, with a goal that was blatantly offside. Two minutes later, with the French players still fuming, Austria scored again thanks to Josef Bican to make it 3–1. The French scored with six minutes left to play when Georges Verriest converted a penalty kick, but it was too little too late. The Austrians won, 3–2, and moved on to the next round.

In Genoa, Spain and Brazil squared off in what would be the most entertaining game of the first round. The Brazilians knew they didn't have a team that could compete for the title after internal disputes had prevented coach Carlo Rocha from fielding players from the Rio and São Paolo leagues. Spain, on the other hand, was an emerging soccer power thanks to its talented goalkeeper Ricardo Zamora. Spain took a 1–0 lead

## LEÔNIDAS DA SILVA

Recognized as the player who perfected the bicycle kick, Leônidas da Silva was born in 1913 in Rio de Janeiro, Brazil. He started his career with Brazilian club Sao Cristovao, but moved to Peñarol in Uruguay in 1933. After a season, he came back to Brazil to play for Vasco de Gama. Leônidas helped the club win the Rio State Championship. In 1934, Leônidas joined Botafogo and won another league title a year later. In 1936, he joined Flamengo, where he played until 1941, and was one of the first black players to play with the Brazilian club. Leônidas joined Sao Paulo in 1942 and stayed at the club until his retirement eight years later.

An outstanding striker, Leônidas played for Brazil at the 1934 World Cup—four years later, he left his mark on the tournament: He finished top scorer in 1938 with eight goals, scoring four times in the 6–5 overtime victory over Poland. Brazil coach Ademar Pimenta benched Leônidas in the semifinal against Italy. The Italians won the game, 2–1. Leônidas made 23 appearances for Brazil.

In 1953, Leônidas was named Sao Paulo's coach, before retiring for a career in broadcasting as a radio reporter. Leônidas died in 2004 from complications due to Alzheimer's disease.

### World Cup Career Statistics

Tournaments played: 2
Games: 5
Goals: 8

in the 18th minute following a perfectly executed José Iraragorri penalty kick. The Spaniards added a second goal nine minutes later with Isidro Lángara. The Brazilians were down, but not out. The team regrouped and pulled one back with Leônidas da Silva in the 56th minute. Spain guaranteed its passage to the quarterfinals when Lángara scored his second of the game to clinch the 3–1 win. Brazil's Valdemar de Brito made history when he became the first player at a World Cup to miss a penalty kick after Zamora deflected the shot with both fists. Once again, Brazil exited the World Cup after the first round. Valdemar went on to become a scout and would be forgiven decades later for discovering a young player named Pelé. As for Leônidas, who is widely credited with perfecting the bicycle kick, it would be another four years before he would burst onto the world stage as an impressive goalscorer.

Another South American team, Argentina, would also pack its bags early after losing to Sweden, 3–2, at Bologna's Littoriale Stadium. Argentina's loss was another sign the tournament was on its way to becoming an all-European affair. Despite featuring mostly young players, an inexperienced Argentina was able to delight the crowd—even taking the lead twice—but the Scandinavians would win the game with a goal from Knut Kroon with eleven minutes left to play. At Milan's San Siro Stadium, Switzerland defeated Holland, 3–2, in a dull game; the Swiss were able to win thanks to two goals by Leopold Kielholz.

At Ascarelli Stadium in Naples, Egypt made history by becoming the first African country to play in a World Cup match. Hungary wanted revenge for a shocking 3–0 loss inflicted on them by the Egyptians at the 1924 Olympics in Paris, and this time did not underestimate their opponents. Hungary made sure to put on the pressure early, resulting in a goal by Pál Teleki in the 12th minute. Gejze Toldi put the Hungarians comfortably ahead, 2–0, in the 30th minute. Egypt responded with a goal eight minutes later from Abdel Rahman Fawzi. The first half ended with Hungary on top, 2–1. The Hungarians dominated the second half and goals from Miklós Toldi in the 52nd minute and Ene Vincze seven minutes later led them to prevail, 4–2.

**Eight Teams Remain**

The quarterfinals were all played on May 31 and featured some of the World Cup's most competitive and, at the same time, vicious games. Germany, who had not appeared as strong as some had expected before the start of the tournament, played a disappointing game against Sweden in Milan. The game remained scoreless for an hour as both sides attempted in vain to get ahead under a driving rain. Germany was able to score two goals—both from Karl Hohmann—in a span of three minutes. Sweden was reduced to ten players after Ernest Anderrson suffered an injury. Despite being down a man, the Swedes scored in the 83rd minute thanks to striker Gösta Dunker. The German team had again strung together a lousy performance, but it was good enough to hold off Sweden, 2–1, and guarantee them passage to the semifinals.

The game between Austria and Hungary in Bologna lived up to expectations. Meisl changed his lineup and started the dwarflike Johann Horvath, a move that would pay off for the Wunderteam. Horvath wasted no time and scored after just five minutes. The game turned fierce following the goal. Italian referee Francesco Mattea lost control of the match and players on both sides were given free reign to run wild. In between all of the fouling, the Austrians added a second goal in the 53rd minute when striker Karl Zischek unleashed a potent shot past goalkeeper Antal Szabo. The Hungarians didn't let their defensive lapses get the best of them and pulled one back fourteen minutes later when Bela Sarosi, one of the few on the field able to keep his composure amid the mayhem, scored on a penalty kick. The Hungarians tried to tie the score, but saw their hopes dashed when striker Imre Markos was red carded. Austria won 2–1.

The clash between Czechoslovakia and Switzerland in Turin turned out to be the best game of the quarterfinals. The Swiss took the lead in the 18th minute after Kielholz scored on a breakaway. The Czechoslovakian team got its defense in order and managed to tie the score with Frantis˘ek Svoboda six minutes later. It added another goal three minutes into the second half with Sobotka. The Swiss managed to knot the game at two when Andre Abegglen was able to put the ball past goalkeeper František Plánička. The Czechs finally won the game, 3–2, when Nejedlý was able to score the game-winner seven minutes from the end. The victory meant a spot in the semifinals and a date with Germany.

The Italian team traveled to Florence to take on Spain in what would be one of the ugliest and roughest games of any World Cup. Italian captain Virginio Rosetta suffered an injury in the opening round against the U.S. team and ended up sidelined. The captain's armband went to veteran goalkeeper Giampiero Combi, but much to the dismay of the 35,000 fans in the stands at Berta Stadium—and the millions listening on the radio—it would be Zamora standing in front of the other goal who would garner all the attention. The Italians knew that Zamora, who played with Real Madrid, was a force to be reckoned with and they wasted no time trying to rough him up. Referee Louis Baert of Belgium let many fouls go unpunished; despite that, Spain was on the board first when a Luis Regueiro shot in the 31st minute was misplayed by Combi and went past him. The *Azzurri* tied the game a minute into the second half with Ferrari. The Spanish players protested, claiming Schiavio had impeded Zamora from getting to the ball. The protests were ignored and the goal stood. The game was headed into overtime, but 120 minutes was not enough to decide a winner. A replay would be played the following day—but this time with some changes.

The replay at Berta Stadium featured some of the same enthusiastic fans, but almost none of the same players. Both coaches called on fresh legs (five changes for the Italians and seven for Spain), but player after player collapsed from exhaustion during an unbearably humid afternoon. Baert was replaced by Swiss referee René Mercet, but his handling of the game would prove to be no better. Spain was forced to go without Zamora, who had been beaten up from the day before, and his backup, Juan José Nogués, did a decent job against the *Azzurri*'s front line. Meazza scored the game's only goal on a header in the 12th minute to catapult the Italians to the semifinals. Spain had two goals disallowed for having players offside. Both were disputed by the Spanish. The officiating was immediately called into question and Mercet was suspended by the Swiss Football Association for his lousy performance. The Italians, who with talent and some luck, would face the dreaded Austrians in the semifinals. Mussolini, who was sitting in the VIP section, had gotten his wish and now the host country was one step away from the final. Mussolini's Italy appeared to be on a collision course to meet Adolf Hitler's Germany in the final. But first, the weary Italians had to overcome Austria in Milan, while the Germans faced Czechoslovakia in Rome.

## Semifinal Action

On June 3, Italy and Austria met in a game that had all the talent and intensity of a final. Both teams played under a heavy rain as 60,000 fans rooted on the *Azzurri*. The Austrians, who relied heavily on passing to open up scoring chances, were at a disadvantage on the muddy Milan field and the Italians were able to shut down Sindelar in the midfield. Austria's star forward was unable to create any scoring chances. The Italians, led by the efforts of Orsi and Monti, took the lead in the 19th minute with Guaita, who tapped in a rebound after goalkeeper Peter Platzer was unable to hold on to a powerful Schiavio shot. Austria tried to push the ball forward, but Horvath's absence because of injury further handicapped the *Wunderteam*. The Austrians could only muster one shot on goal in the first half and both sides headed to the locker rooms with Italy holding on to a 1–0 lead. Austria came out strong in the second half, but Combi was the star in goal, smothering shot after shot. The Austrian barrage made a desperate last-ditch attempt to tie the game when Karl Zischek broke through the defense, but his shot was wide. The Italians won 1–0 and were in the final. The dictator's propaganda machine—complete with rallies across Italy following each win—was in full swing. In the meantime, Austria's loss marked the end of an era. The *Wunderteam*'s string of victories would not result in a World Cup title. Gone was the era of Austria's domination of European soccer and any chance at World Cup glory.

The other semifinal, also played on July 3 after organizers had determined to play both of them on the same day, featured Germany against Czechoslovakia. The Germans, who were one of the pre-tournament favorites, had put on a dreary showing in the two previous rounds, while the Czechoslovakians had clearly been the most entertaining team at the competition. The Germans were caught off guard early on and Czechoslovakia took the lead in the 21st minute with Nejedlý, who tallied his third goal of the tournament. The Germans regrouped and tied the game in the 50th minute when Rudolf Noack's shot beat Plánička. The Germans almost took the lead a few minutes later, but Lehner's shot was smothered by Plánička. Czechoslovakia scored again in the 60th minute when Nejedlý slammed the ball into the German goal after an Antonín Puč free kick hit the crossbar. Germany was unable to mount a comeback and Nejedlý completed his hat trick in the 81st minute to lift Czechoslovakia to a 3–1 win.

### The Debut Consolation Game

Germany and Austria met on June 7 in Naples in the first-ever third place game at a World Cup. The Germans built a 3–1 halftime lead as the weary Austrians sluggishly tried to keep up. The *Wunderteam* showed signs of fatigue following its loss against Italy four days earlier in the Milan mud and offered little resistance, falling behind 1–0 on a goal by Lehner after just thirty seconds—the quickest goal of the tournament. The Germans went on to win 3–2. Upon the Austrians return to their country, many in the country blamed the team's poor showing on Meisl, who promptly resigned. The Austrian FA declined his resignation and Meisl remained at the helm—at least for now.

## The Final

Austria's downfall was the last thing on Mussolini's mind. The dictator was focused on winning the trophy and made his presence felt the night before the final, giving the Italian players one of his impassioned pep talks. "If the Czechs play fair, we'll play fair. That's the most important thing," Mussolini told them. "But if they want to play dirty, then we Italians have to play dirtier."[8] Pozzo and his players had the entire pressure of a country on them. If that wasn't enough, they faced a tough opponent in the Czechoslovakians. On June 10, Italy collectively held its breath. The political use of the World Cup was working wonders for Mussolini and with one game left to win it all, an Italian victory would be the perfect ending to a memorable tournament for the dictator. Czechoslovakia had played a stylish brand of soccer in the previous three games and looked capable of pulling off a win. Both teams were captained by their goalkeepers: Combi, who was playing his 47th and last international game, while the equally capable Plánička defended the Czechoslovakian goal with his trademark catlike reflexes. The game would also be a contrast of styles. The Italians had power and stamina. The Czechoslovakians featured artistry and skill. Despite both teams' offensive approaches, it took seventy minutes before a goal was scored. Puč kicked a corner and when the ball came back to him, he successfully fired off a powerful shot from a nearly impossible angle to put Czechoslovakia ahead, 1–0. The Czechoslovakians were unable to finish off the Italians when Svoboda's shot slammed against the post. Italy never gave up. With ten minutes remaining, the *Azzurri* scored a remarkable equalizer when Orsi, off a pass from Guaita, ran through the Czechoslovakian defense and faked a shot with his left foot. Instead, he shot the ball with the outside of his right to send a curling, dipping ball over the hands of a helpless Plánička.

The teams had been evenly matched for much of the game. Overtime would prove to be a contest of endurance. The Italians were the fitter team, but were handicapped by an injury to Meazza. Nevertheless, his injury turned into a mixed blessing in the 95th minute. The Czechoslovakians didn't bother to mark the limping Meazza. When he got the ball on the wing, Meazza decided immediately to cross it to Guaita. The Argentine-born midfielder then passed the ball to Schiavio, who was able to blow past a defender and beat Plánička with a shot that crept in just under the crossbar. The trophy belonged to Italy and the celebrations spilled into the streets of Rome. Pozzo, who was carried off the field atop his players' shoulders, was hailed a national hero. Mussolini was also present, like he had been for all of Italy's games, and he applauded the effort as the players celebrated on the field. Standing upright, proud, and sporting a yachting cap, the dictator gave off a neutral appearance, even though he must have been delighted inside to see the Italians win. Mussolini immediately ordered that Meazza and his teammates receive a cash prize of $17,000 each for their success. Monti added a championship to the runners-up medal he had been awarded with Argentina four years earlier, earning him the distinction of becoming the first, and only, player to receive successive World Cup honors with different nations. Italy's triumph also capped off a controversial tournament, one marred by violent games and poor refereeing. The victory may have been sweet for Mussolini, but outside the country, the tournament's outcome had left many with a bitter taste in their mouths.

## 1938

Victories by Uruguay and Italy showed how important home-field advantage could be at the World Cup. Mussolini had used the World Cup to his advantage as a propaganda tool, in the same way Hitler had done with the 1936 Berlin Olympics. Now, with Europe teetering on the brink of war, FIFA was diplomatic over its choice of who would host the 1938 tournament. The third edition of the World Cup was awarded to France in 1936 with 40 of FIFA's 54 members voting in favor of the bid. The French were hopeful they could win the trophy named after a

Frenchman. Argentina, which won the 1937 Copa America, also applied to stage the finals, believing the venue would alternate between South America and Europe. However, FIFA was mindful of the traveling difficulties encountered the first time to Uruguay. FIFA's membership had blossomed to 57 nations by 1938, and most of those countries hailed from Europe. To FIFA, it made sense to give the World Cup to a European country. FIFA's choice was also out of loyalty to Rimet, the man who had played such a large part in getting the tournament started a decade earlier. The choice angered Argentina, which—along with Uruguay—boycotted the tournament.

The Italians, who automatically qualified as champions, had won the gold medal at the 1936 Olympics and returned to the World Cup with a revamped roster. Pozzo's team was stronger and more refined than the one he had fielded in 1934 and it revolved around veterans Meazza and Ferrari. This time, the team featured defenders Alfredo Foni and Pietro Rava, along with brilliant goalscorers Silvio Piola and Gino Colaussi. Piola, who had replaced Meazza as the country's most talented striker, was born in 1913. He had begun his pro career at the age of sixteen with Pro Vercelli, one of Italy's strongest clubs at the time. At age twenty-one, Piola made his national team debut in March 1935, scoring both goals in a 2–0 victory over Austria. The previous year, Piola had signed with Lazio and would go on to spend eight seasons with the Rome-based club before playing for Torino, Juventus, and Novara.

Meanwhile, the Nazi invasion and occupation of Austria ended that country's hopes of participating in the World Cup. Hitler admired Mussolini's move to naturalize players in 1934—which was the impetus for Germany's annexation of his native Austria. The Germans decided to bolster their chances of winning the trophy and plucked several Austrian players for its national team after having Hitler's theory of Aryan superiority destroyed by Jesse Owens at the 1936 Berlin Olympics. German tanks rolled into Austria. The *Wunderteam* was no more and Sindelar, who had played for Austria at the World Cup four years earlier, refused to don a German jersey.

Sindelar was born in 1903 in the village of Kozlov, located in present-day Czech Republic. Sindelar's father, who worked as a mason, moved his family to Vienna in search of a better life. The Sindelars, which included little Matthias and his three sisters, moved to the Viennese suburb of Favoriten, an industrial town dotted with factories and vacant lots. It was on those bare swaths of dirt where Sindelar first played soccer. Sindelar, who made his pro debut with Hertha Vienna in 1918 at age fifteen, is widely considered Austria's greatest player ever. He exuded an elegant style and was able to move across the field quickly because of his lean, muscular physique. His ability to slip through opposing defenses like a sheet of paper earned him the nickname *Der Papierene* (The Paper Man). Sindelar, who stood 6'1" and weighed just 165 pounds, was no fragile athlete, often battling players one on one for balls before going on one of his legendary runs that often resulted in a goal. Austria's fourth-place finish at the 1934 World Cup had marked the beginning of the end for the *Wunderteam*. On January 24, 1937, Meisl took his place on the Austrian bench for the last time. The team gave Meisl a farewell victory, defeating France 2–1 in Paris. Meisl died a few weeks later at age fifty-five. On top of that, the Nazi occupation of Austria ended any hope of the *Wunderteam* ever competing at the 1938 World Cup. But before the Germans could purge Austria's roster—and claim Sindelar as one of their own—a game was organized between both teams. On April 3, 1938, Austria defeated Germany 2–0 with Sindelar scoring one of the goals.

When he was drafted into the "Greater Germany" team for the World Cup that summer, Sindelar tried everything to get out of it, even claiming his age and nagging knee injuries would make it difficult for him to play. But the political upheaval of the time was starting to affect Sindelar, who began to go through a psychological crisis. Not only was Austria falling apart, but so was his personal life. A few days before his 36th birthday on January 23, 1939, Sindelar died of asphyxiation as a result of carbon monoxide poisoning. Lying next to him on the bed was an unconscious Italian prostitute named Camilia Castagnola, who he had met only a few days earlier. She never came out of her coma. Sindelar's death has been shrouded in mystery and an official investigation conducted by the Nazi's over a two-day period deemed it an accident. Historians speculate it was a murder-suicide or even a double homicide, but there's little evidence left to work with after so many decades. Some 15,000 mourners lined the streets of Vienna the day of Sindelar's funeral, bidding farewell to an athlete who had embodied the nation.

Austria's loss almost turned into England's gain. The British associations, still not members of FIFA, were invited to play at the World Cup.

All four declined. The vacancy left by Austria led FIFA to invite the English players again, but they refused, saying they didn't have enough time to prepare for the competition. FIFA secretary Ivo Schricker thought having England's participation would add some credibility to the tournament. After all, the English, who had invented and exported the game, defeated Italy, 3–2, in 1934 during a frenzy later dubbed "The Battle of Highbury." The game proved what many had already suspected: England was the better team. Meanwhile, Spain, who had fielded a strong lineup four years earlier, was in the midst of a civil war and did not participate. Mexico also withdrew and was replaced by Cuba, which would create quite a stir at the tournament. With Argentina and Uruguay out, Brazil was South America's lone representative. An Asian team made its debut at a World Cup: the Dutch East Indies. Japan, Asia's only other team to show interest, decided not to participate and forfeited its place because it was in the midst of a war with China. FIFA offered to pit the Dutch East Indies team against the U.S. team in a playoff for a World Cup spot, but this time the Americans—who had been successful against Mexico four years earlier under similar circumstances—declined. The Dutch East Indies earned the dubious distinction of gaining a berth to the finals without ever playing a qualifying game.

The tournament, which was played from June 4 to 19, again featured a knockout format. The formula was a cruel way to go about the tournament and forced teams that had spent four years training to go home after just one game. The tournament was played in nine cities—Paris, Toulousse, Rheims, Strasbourg, Antibles, Le Havre, Lille, Bordeaux, and Marseilles—with France automatically qualifying for the finals. FIFA also tightened its rules regarding team rosters and tie games: Each team had to present a list of twenty-two players on the eve of the tournament and if the final were to end in a tie, the teams would be declared co-champions. The seeded teams were France, Italy, Germany, Czechoslovakia, Hungary, Cuba, and Brazil, ensuring that none of them would meet each other in the first round.

The Italians were favored to recapture the trophy—and this time didn't have the pressure of Mussolini breathing down their necks. Nevertheless, Pozzo's team did feel Il Duce's ominous presence. Mussolini did his best to get into the players' heads, sending the team a telegram on the eve of their opening game against Norway with a short, but clear, message: "Win or Die."[9]

## Group Play

Germany and Switzerland opened the tournament on June 4 at Parc de Princes Stadium in Paris. The game ended 1–1 after overtime, forcing a replay that was scheduled five days later. The second game was played at the same venue and featured a tough German side with players of Austrian birth. An early 2–0 Germany lead created the illusion that this would be a cakewalk for them. The Swiss had other plans. Down 2–1 at halftime, Switzerland proved that its performance in the first game was no fluke and in the 64th minute tied the score, thanks to a goal by Alfred Bickel. Switzerland sealed the 4–2 victory with goals by Abegglan in the 75th and 78th minutes. The humiliated Germans were going home early once again.

Italy, meanwhile, opened at Velodrome Stadium in Marseilles June 5 against Norway. Unlike the home crowd that had cheered them on four years earlier, the Azzurri were greeted with a chorus of jeers after they gave the crowd the fascist salute before kickoff. The Italians ignored the crowd and got off to a brilliant start, taking a 1–0 lead on a goal by Ferrari after just two minutes. The Italians defended the lead, while Norway tried to tie the game with a series of counterattacks. The Norwegians went on to hit the woodwork three times and had a goal disallowed for having a player offside. It would take eighty-three minutes before Norway's best efforts were rewarded with a goal by Arne Brustad. The game went to overtime. Piola ensured an Italian victory when he was able to get away from Nils Eriksen, who had shadowed him throughout the match. Piola tapped in a rebound off a shot that had been deflected by goalkeeper Rolf Johansen. The Italians had cleared the first hurdle.

On the same day at Chapou Stadium in Toulouse, Cuba made its first World Cup appearance and took on an experienced Romanian team. Cuba's two stars, strangely enough, were its goalkeepers Benito Carvajeles and Juan Ayra. Both teams played to an entertaining 3–3 tie in front of 6,000 fans. Overtime failed to provide a winner. On June 10, a crowd of 5,000 showed up for the rematch. Cuba sidelined Carvajeles and replaced him with Ayra. Romania was able to take the lead with Stefan Dobai after nine minutes. In the second half, Cuba tied the score with Héctor Socorro, who had netted two goals in the first game. Once again, the game was tied and headed to overtime. With ten minutes remaining in extra time, the Cubans capped off a remarkable game when

Carlos Maquina netted the winner. The goal looked to be offside and the linesman even had his flag raised, but German referee Alfred Birlem overruled the call and the goal stood. The Cubans had miraculously pulled off a 2–1 upset.

On June 5, Czechoslovakia, runner up at the last World Cup, was pitted against Holland in Le Havre. What was supposed to be an easy game for the Czechoslovakians almost turned into another tournament upset. Czechoslovakia, which featured four players from its 1934 team, tried in vain to take the lead, but the Dutch were able to hold them off for ninety minutes. When the scoreless game went to overtime, the Dutch suddenly wilted under the pressure. Six minutes into extra time and Josef Kosˇt'álek was able to score the game's first goal. The Czechoslovakians added two more in the second overtime period, first with Nejedlý and another from Josef Zeman, for the 3–0 win. On the same day at Colombes Stadium in Paris, home team France, which was riding a ten-game winning streak going into the tournament, opened against rivals Belgium. The teams had not played each other since 1904 and both featured experienced lineups. French captain Etienne Mattler and midfielder Edmond Delfour were appearing in their third straight finals as was Belgium's Voorhoof. France wasted little time taking the lead, scoring in the first minute with Émile Veinante. Eleven minutes later, Jean Nicolas's goal made it 2–0. Belgium appeared finished, that is, until seven minutes before the half when Henri Isemborghs cut France's lead, making it 2–1. But Nicolas put the hosts—energized by the incessant cheering of the home crowd—ahead in the 69th minute, lifting France to a 3–1 win. The victory meant a meeting against Italy in the quarterfinals.

In Reims, meanwhile, Hungary was matched against the Dutch East Indies. The Hungarians had built a powerful team, which had routed Greece 11–1 in a World Cup qualifier just three months earlier in Budapest. Hungary was far too talented for its opponents and were ahead 4–0 by halftime. The scoring spree began in the 18th minute with Vilmos Kohut. Five minutes later, Gejze Toldi made it 2–0. Sarosi put Hungary ahead, 3–0, in the 28th minute and Gyula Zsengellér netted his team's fourth goal seven minutes before the end of the half. The Hungarians picked up where they left off in the second period when Zsengellér scored his second goal of the game after just seven minutes. Hungary ended the scoring spree in the 77th minute when Sarosi netted his second to complete the 6–0 romp.

In Strasbourg, Brazil and Poland put on an offensive display. Brazil fielded four players who had never played in an international game, while the Poles were making their World Cup debut. The first half belonged to Brazil and star striker Leônidas, who put his team ahead after eighteen minutes. Four minutes later, Poland's Ernst Willimowski tied the score. Leônidas, who ran circles around the Polish defense, was able to put Brazil back on top in the 25th minute. He completed the hat trick a minute before the break to put Brazil up, 3–1. Leônidas, affectionately called the Black Diamond, was one of Brazil's first superstars. Leônidas, who was twenty-five at the time of the 1938 World Cup, had started his career in Brazil before moving to Uruguay to play with Penarol in 1933, a year after scoring two goals against Uruguay in his international debut. He returned to Brazil a year later and led Vasco de Gama to the Rio Championship. After playing in the 1934 World Cup, Leônidas was a key player in Botafogo's Rio title a year later. In 1936, he signed with Flamengo, where he would play until 1942. Even with Leônidas doing all the scoring, the Brazilian defense still needed to protect the lead, but that effort failed. Down 3–1 after the first half forced the Polish attack to go into overdrive. Leonard Piontek scored in the 50th minute and Willimowski tied the game ten minutes later. Peracio gave Brazil a 4–3 lead, but with just two minutes remaining, Willimowski completed the hat trick to push the game into overtime. The goals didn't end there. Brazil took a 5–4 lead three minutes into overtime when, who else, Leônidas netted his fourth—the first player to record more than three goals at a World Cup tournament. Twelve minutes later, Romeo made it 6–4. But Poland refused to give up and Willimowski scored his fourth goal of the game, but it came too late. The Brazilians had put on an electrifying performance and were rewarded with a 6–5 win, which meant they would play Czechoslovakia in the quarterfinals.

## Quarterfinals

The field of eight teams—with the inclusion of Sweden who had been given a bye after Austria dropped out of the finals—was set. The quarterfinals were played on June 12 in four different venues. The biggest game of the round was the contest between France and Italy. Colombes Stadium in Paris was filled to capacity with 58,000 spectators gathered to root on the hosts. Seven month earlier, the French had held the world champions to a scoreless tie in a friendly game—and this time their fans were hoping for a victory. For this game, the Italians ditched their traditional blue jerseys (The French, as the home team, were allowed to wear their blue shirts) for an all-black outfit in tribute to fascism. Though the uniforms were also meant as a taunt at the largely antifascist French fans, Italy wasted no time establishing its dominance on the field and took the lead after ten minutes on a fluke goal by Colaussi. The left-winger crossed the ball hoping a teammate in the box would head it in, but French goalkeeper Laurent Di Lorto misjudged the ball and the pass turned into a goal. Italy's lead was short lived. France was able to tie the score a minute later when Oscar Heisserer slotted the ball past goalkeeper Aldo Olivieri. The second half featured an attacking Italian team; the French were unable to keep up. France's defense loosened its chokehold of Piola and the gifted striker was able to make a lot of his newfound freedom. With the French defense flung wide open, Piola was able to put Italy ahead, 2–1, in the 58th minute. The French tried to tie the score once again, but with its defense in disarray, Piola, left unmarked by Gusti Jordan, was able to head in his second goal of the game in the 78th minute off a Amedeo Biavati pass to grant Italy a 3–1 win.

In Antibes, Sweden defeated Cuba, 8–0, to end the Caribbean island's Cinderella run. The Swedes were fresh going into the game after not having played in the first round, while the Cubans were still nursing their tired muscles following a grueling two games against Romania. Sweden got four goals from striker Gustav Wetterstrom with Carvajeles back in net.

In Lille, Hungary took on Switzerland. Hungary jumped out to a 1–0 lead on a goal by Zsengellér with three minutes left in the half. Zsengellér added a second tally in the 68th minute to lift Hungary to a 2–0 win.

In Bordeaux, the 25,000 fans who gathered to watch Brazil play Czechoslovakia were treated to a savage contest. The hostility started early when Brazilian defender Zezé Procópio kicked Nejedlý to the ground and Hungarian referee Paul Van Hertzka gave him a red card for the violent foul. Brazil, now down a player, took the lead on a goal by Leônidas, his fifth of the tournament, in the 30th minute. Tempers flared once again, this time a minute before halftime, when Jan Říha and Arthur Machado got into a fistfight. Both players were red carded. The second half featured more scoring and violence. In the 64th minute, Brazilian defender Domingos handled the ball in the box. Hertzka called a penalty shot in Hungary's favor and Nejedlý scored from the spot. The game ended 1–1, though Nejedlý would go on to break his right leg and be forced to leave the game. Plánička, who played part of the game with a broken right arm, left the field in pain. Both teams—reduced to nine players each—were unable to score in overtime. A replay was scheduled two days later—the last rematch ever to be played during a World Cup tournament.

Everyone expected another violent affair between the Czechoslovakians and Brazilians in their second game. Instead, the game was a milder version of their previous encounter. Czechoslovakia, without Nejedlý and Plánička, featured six new players in the starting lineup. Brazil made nine changes to its pre-game lineup, the only exceptions being goalkeeper Walter and striker Leônidas. Czechoslovakia took the lead in the 30th minute with Vlastimil Kopecký only to have Leônidas tie the score in the 56th minute. The Czechoslovakians came close to taking the lead, again with Kopecký, but French referee Georges Capdeville ruled that Walter had saved the ball on the goal line. On the very next play, Roberto capped off his international debut with a volley that beat Karel Burket to give Brazil a 2–1 victory. Brazil had suddenly emerged as the toughest team at the tournament. Fate pitted them against Italy in a showdown that would feature Leônidas and Piola, two of the tournament's deadliest scorers. The clash, however, never happened. While Piola was fit and ready to go in Marseilles on June 16, Brazilian coach Ademar Pimenta made the controversial decision to leave Leônidas on the bench. An overconfident Pimenta defended his nutty decision with an even nuttier reason: He was saving Leônidas for the final.[10]

The Brazilian defense double-teamed Piola in a bid to shut him down. While Brazil's Domingas—whose son Ademir would play for Brazil at the World Cup thirty years later—shadowed Piola, the Azzurri were able to create plays without him, scoring in the 55th minute with Colaussi. Five minutes later, Piola again was inadvertently involved in Italy's second goal. Domingos brought down Piola in the box and Swiss referee Hans Wuthrich called for a penalty shot. Meazza converted the kick, just before his ripped shorts fell down, and Italy was up 2–0.[11] Brazil scored three minutes from the end with Romeo, but it was too late. The Italians, ever so resilient and methodical, had reached its second straight final, proving once again that Pozzo was a master at putting together lineups that could adapt to any situation.

## GIUSEPPE MEAZZA

The sport's first true superstar, Giuseppe Meazza was born in Milan, Italy, in 1910 and spent most of his professional career with his hometown team of Inter. He scored 243 goals in 361 games for the club and is still considered one of the best Italian-born players of all time.

Meazza still holds the record for most goals scored in a debut season in Serie A with 31 goals in his first season in 1930. The year before, when Serie A did not exist in its current form and the Italian Championship was composed of two leagues (split between north and south) with playoffs, Meazza, just eighteen at the time, played 29 games and scored a staggering 38 goals. He went on to win three league titles with Inter in 1930, 1938, and 1940 and an Italian Cup in 1939. On a personal level, he was the league's top scorer three times in 1930, 1936, and 1938. He spent the latter part of his club career with AC Milan, Juventus, and Atalanta.

For Italy, Meazza played in the 1934 and 1938 World Cups, winning both tournaments in the process. In 1934, Italian coach Vittorio Pozzo converted Meazza to an inside-left after playing as a center-forward for Inter. Meazza made a huge contribution to Italy's successful World Cup campaign. Against Spain, Italy needed a replay to defeat their great rivals with Meazza scoring the winning goal.

Four years later, Meazza became the team captain and partnered with striker Silvio Piola in the new-look Italian attack and the country successfully retained the trophy. In one of the most memorable World Cup moments, Meazza stepped up to take a penalty kick against Brazil at the 1938 tournament when his shorts fell down. Meazza held his shorts up and coolly shot the ball into the net. Meazza, who played 53 times for Italy, was one of only two players who appeared in both 1934 and 1938 World Cup–winning teams.

Meazza died in 1979 at age sixty-nine. Milan's soccer stadium, called the San Siro and home to both Inter and AC Milan, was renamed the Giuseppe Meazza Stadium following his death in tribute to the legendary forward.

### World Cup Career Statistics

Tournaments played: 2
Games: 9
Goals: 3

At Colombes Stadium in Paris, Hungary and Sweden played out the other semifinal on June 16. The game was coincidentally played on the 80th birthday of Hungary's King Gustav V and the Hungarians wanted to put on a good show. The Swedes—beneficiaries of having played one less game—pinned their hopes on the talents of striker Arne Nyberg, who put them ahead after less than a minute. The goal was timed at 35 seconds, making it the second fastest goal at a World Cup. The Hungarians tied the game 1–1 with the always-reliable Zsengellér in the 18th minute when the ball made its way into the net after a light deflection off defender Ivar Eriksson. The scoring didn't stop there. The Hungarians scored twice more, with Pál Titkos in the 26th minute and another from Zsengellér in the 38th minute. The team was able to pad its 3–1 lead in the second half, scoring a fourth goal with Sarosi in the 61st minute. Zsengellér added another thirteen minutes from the end to lift Hungary to a resounding 5–1 win. The Hungarians had put on a spectacular display, cruising to the final while scoring thirteen goals in three games.

Before the final match, the consolation game between Brazil and Sweden was contested on June 19 in Bordeaux. This time, Leônidas started for the Brazilians, scoring two goals in the second half, his seventh and eighth of the tournament, after Sweden had taken a 2–1 lead at halftime. Peracio scored ten minutes from the end to give Brazil a 4–2 victory. Leônidas's two goals guaranteed him top spot on the list of tournament top scorers.

## Final

The Italians, meanwhile, prepared for their second straight final. Pozzo and his players spent the days leading up to the game in the total seclusion of the Parisian suburb of St. Germain. The Italian players—all smiles as they walked onto the field—exuded the confidence needed to win a big game. The stadium was filled with 55,000 fans, not a sellout crowd since the French had lost interest in the tournament once their team had been eliminated.

Pozzo's lineup featured Foni and Rava anchoring the defense with Meazza, Piola, Ferrari, and Colaussi energizing the four-man attack. Throughout the tournament, Pozzo's team had gradually jelled with the passing of each game and were so comfortable together that they

*Italian dictator Benito Mussolini poses with members of Italy's 1938 World Cup team that won the trophy (Credit: EMPICS).*

could have beaten any team that day. The Italians scored first with Colaussi after six minutes. Hungary responded immediately, tying the game with Titkos two minutes later when his powerful shot found the back of the net. Italy regrouped and took the lead with Piola in the 16th minute, finishing off an elaborate four-player pass sequence that left the helpless Hungarian defense motionless. The Italians added a third goal ten minutes before the half when Colaussi scored his second of the game. Up 3–1, the Italians packed its defense in the second half. Hungary tried on several occasions to score and successfully did in the 70th minute with Sarosi. But the Italians were just too good for the Hungarians. Piola added a fourth goal eight minutes from the end with a wicked 12-yard shot that was too powerful for Szabo to stop. The Italians won, 4–2, and were again crowned world champions.

Pozzo had pulled off an amazing feat of molding two different teams to two successive titles. He also remains the only man to coach a team to back-to-back Olympic and World Cup winners' medals. This time, Meazza could lift the trophy free from critics who argued that the outcome in 1934 had been influenced by Mussolini. Sadly, the 1938 tournament would also mark the end of something special. Hitler had petitioned FIFA to host the 1942 World Cup, but that tournament would never be played. Ironically, fourteen months after the final, Hitler's tanks rolled into Poland. Europe, and soon the rest of the world, headed to war and the World Cup would go on a twelve-year hiatus.

## NOTES

1. Andres Cantor, *Goooal: A Celebration of Soccer* (New York: Simon & Schuster, 1996), 20.

2. Cantor, *Goooal: A Celebration of Soccer*, 20.

3. Ian Morrison, *The World Cup: A Complete Record* (Derby, UK: Breedon Books Sport, 1990), 22.

4. Cantor, *Goooal: A Celebration of Soccer*, 27.

5. FIFA World Cup/Germany 2006, "Classic Coaches," *Classic Moments from FIFA World Cup History* 2006. Retrieved from www.fifaworldcup.yahoo.com/06/en/p/cc/ita/pozzo.html (February 25, 2007).

6. FIFA World Cup/Germany 2006, "Classic Coaches."

7. FIFA World Cup/Germany 2006, "Classic Coaches."

8. Cantor, *Goooal: A Celebration of Soccer*, 42.

9. Cantor, *Goooal: A Celebration of Soccer*, 47.

10. Morrison, *The World Cup: A Complete Record*, 54.

11. Brian Glanville, *The Story of the World Cup* (London: Faber and Faber, 1997), 39.

# 3

# BRAZIL IS BORN

**1950**

World War II had left Europe in ruins. Throughout, FIFA Vice-President Ottorino Barassi hid the Rimet Trophy in a shoebox under his bed and saved it from falling into the hands of the Nazis.[1]

FIFA, which had canceled the 1942 and 1946 tournaments, was keen on resurrecting the competition in 1949. With Europe lying in ruins and under growing political turmoil, FIFA looked to stage the tournament in South America. Brazil, who along with Germany had wanted to host the 1942 tournament, was the only country to submit a bid in 1949. Until that lone bid came in, FIFA had some difficulties finding a country interested in hosting the competition. The tournament may have even been canceled altogether if Brazil hadn't made its intentions known in July 1946 that it wanted to host the soccer extravaganza, even if the one condition was that the competition be delayed a year to give organizers more time to prepare. FIFA announced Brazil as the World Cup host and the choice couldn't have been better. FIFA was banking on the country's growing appetite for soccer and carnival-like atmosphere to serve as a perfect backdrop for the event. FIFA also decided that the World Cup trophy be renamed the Jules Rimet Cup (although it was subsequently referred to as the Jules Rimet Trophy) to mark the French visionary's 25th anniversary as head of FIFA.

Construction crews had started work on a new stadium that would eventually host the final. Located on the outskirts of Rio de Janeiro, the Estádio do Maracanã—named after a small river that runs near it—would seat 200,000 spectators. To this day, it remains the largest stadium in the world. The Maracanã, which features a moat separating the crowd from the field, was quickly nicknamed the "Eighth Wonder of the World" for its size and majesty. Like the Centenario in Montevideo twenty years earlier, the Maracanã would not be completed in time for the start of the World Cup. The design proved too ambitious and construction was soon running behind schedule. Though the oval-shaped stadium officially opened in June 1950 with a game between Brazilian clubs Rio and São Paulo, scaffolding was clearly visible for much of the tournament. The Maracanã exemplified the country's soccer ambitions and yearning for rebirth. The game had emerged over the past few decades as Brazil's number one passion. Hosting, and potentially winning, the World Cup would consolidate the country's soccer supremacy and give it a chance to rally around something positive. Brazil had declared a new democratic constitution in 1946 following a dictatorship that had lasted more than a decade. The World Cup represented all of the people's hopes and dreams, even though the nation's newfound optimism wasn't enough to get organizers any closer to completing the infrastructure to flawlessly pull off the tournament. Brazilian organizers found themselves overwhelmed by the situation and FIFA decided to enlist the help of Barassi, the same man who had organized the 1934 tournament in Italy. Though the Maracanã went on to successfully host the final, the stadium was not totally completed until 1965.

When organizers crunched the numbers and figured out they were on their way to spending more than they could possible make, they proposed that FIFA abandon the single-elimination format, which only allowed for sixteen games, and replace it with four groups of four teams. The winner of each group would qualify into a final round-robin group. The winner of that group would then be awarded the trophy. This way, organizers argued, they would be guaranteed thirty games. FIFA did not favor the proposal at first. Brazil threatened to withdraw as host and FIFA caved in to the pressure. The format was controversial, but at least teams would be guaranteed a minimum of two games, particularly for European squads who had to endure a longer plane trip to get to Brazil. The controversy surrounding the new format did have some negative outcomes. Delaunay, who had been Rimet's collaborator from the start, resigned in disgust over FIFA's decision to go ahead with the round-robin format to determine a champion.

Getting Italy, which had won the last World Cup in 1938, to defend its title was not easy. Though the Italians would eventually field a team, their chances of winning the trophy had declined following a tragedy the year before. In 1949, a jet carrying the entire Torino club team crashed near Turin. In all, twenty-eight people were killed, including eighteen players, twelve of whom were regulars on the national team. The club—commonly referred to as *Il Grande Torino* (The Great Torino) because it had dominated the county's domestic league for a large part of the 1940s—had emerged as Italy's greatest club team during that decade. The team set several records, including winning five straight Italian League titles from 1943 to 1949 and amassing ninety-three consecutive home wins between January 1943 and April 1949. The team featured some of the country's most talented players, such as goalkeeper Valerio Bacigalupo, midfielder Romeo Menti, and striker Valentino Mazzola (father of Sandro Mazzola, who would go on to play for Italy at the 1966, 1970, and 1974 World Cups).

The death of Valentino Mazzola and his teammates was a giant blow to Italian soccer. He was a gifted playmaker who bore all the qualities of a team leader. Mazzola could also pass, score, defend, and tackle—a tough task considering the heavy leather ball weighing upwards of 900 grams that was used in those days. In comparison, balls currently weigh half that once inflated. Mazzola was born in Cassano d'Adda, a town near Milan, in 1919. He began his playing career as a teenager with the Alfa Romeo Milano factory, where he worked just before the start of the war. In 1939, Mazzola was drafted into the Italian navy and was stationed in Venice. While there, he tried out for Venezia and earned a spot on the team. Mazzola made his national team debut in 1942, the same year he signed with Torino. He emerged as a goal-scoring threat at Venezia and caught the eye of Torino owner Ferruccio Novo. Mazzola wasted no time once he was signed by Novo's team, leading Torino to the 1943 and 1944 league titles. By 1949, Mazzola had become one of Europe's most talented players, scoring 109 goals over eight seasons. He also played twelve games and scored four goals for Italy, although he never played at a World Cup. The *Azzurri's* starting lineup throughout much of the decade had consisted almost entirely of Torino players. On May 11, 1947, Italy defeated Hungary, 3–2, with a lineup that included ten Torino players. Unfortunately, on May 4, 1949, the team traveled home after a friendly match against · Portuguese club Benfica in Lisbon, when their plane crashed against the Cathedral of Superga on a hill overlooking Turin. The catastrophe was a national tragedy; a generation of remarkable players had been cut down in their prime. The deaths resonated across the country as it struggled to rebuild following the war. Italy would eventually send a team to compete in the 1950 World Cup, but understandably decided to travel to Brazil by boat.

FIFA had seventy-three members by 1946, but because of the war's aftermath only thirty-one teams entered the qualifying tournament. Germany and Japan were not allowed to participate and the Soviet Union, Hungary, and Czechoslovakia decided not to take part. Britain's four associations finally rejoined FIFA in 1946 for good and the affair was honored at Hampden Park in Glasgow with a game between Great Britain and a group of international All-Stars dubbed the "Rest of the World." Britain won, 6–1, and the 135,000 fans that packed into the stadium guaranteed that FIFA's share of the ticket revenues would put it on the road to fiscal stability for the first time in its history. It appeared that Britain and FIFA both needed each other after all. FIFA decided that the 1949–1950 Home International Championship would be used as a qualifying tournament with the top two teams moving on to the World Cup finals. England won the round-robin group with a 1–0 win over Scotland. But the Scottish, not satisfied with finishing second, refused to participate in the finals.

Scotland's withdrawal was just the beginning of a mass exodus of teams that pulled out of the tournament. The Philippines and Indonesia both forfeited any chance of going to Brazil by refusing to field teams ahead of the qualifying draw in January 1949. Argentina withdrew because of an ongoing dispute with the Brazilian Football Association, which meant that Chile and Bolivia—the other two teams in the group—would automatically qualify for the finals. Ecuador and Peru also decided to withdraw, which meant that Uruguay and Paraguay earned automatic spots without having to play a game. Austria also missed the tournament, claming the team was too inexperienced. Belgium's withdrawal led to the automatic qualification of Turkey, which subsequently decided to pull out. The qualifying tournament had devolved into a sham and FIFA was increasingly worried that it could not get sixteen teams to take part in the finals. Indeed, getting enough countries to play in the tournament had become a tricky proposition. FIFA was desperate to fill the spots left vacant by Scotland and Turkey and invited Portugal and France, who had both been eliminated, to fill their places. The Portuguese declined, but the French, who had lost 3–2 in overtime to Yugoslavia during a playoff game in Florence, accepted the invitation. In one of the most controversial qualifiers, Sweden defeated Ireland, 3–1, but not without some drama when Carl Erik Palmer scored his third goal of the game, even though the Irish defenders had stopped their pursuit of the nineteen-year-old player. The Irish claimed they had heard a whistle. Instead, the sound had come from someone in the crowd—not the referee. The goal stood and Sweden was through to the finals.

The United States clinched its third World Cup finals spot after finishing second in Group 9 during a qualifying tournament played from September 4–25 in Mexico City. The Americans, coached by Scottish-born William Jeffrey, finished with three points after recording a win and tie, both against Cuba. Mexico, who had won the group with eight points, had defeated the United States 6–0 on September 4 and 6–2 on September 18. The U.S. team that played in Mexico featured seven players who would go on to gain a spot in the finals the following year, including goalkeeper Frank Borghi and midfielder Walter Bahr. The chances of the U.S. team pulling off a third-place finish as it had in 1930 appeared remote. The team featured midfielder Eddie McIlvenny as its only professional and his claim to fame was having played seven games for Wrexham in England. Before a final roster could be put together, the U.S. team had lost 5–0 to Turkish club Besiktas in St. Louis, a soccer hotbed in the 1940s and the place where five U.S. players hailed from. The team also lost 1–0 to a group of English all-stars in New York. The World Cup would surely be an uphill fight.

## Group Play

The final draw was conducted in Rio on May 22, 1950. The fifteen teams that had reached the finals were placed into four groups with Brazil, Italy, England, and Uruguay heading each of their respective groups:

Pool 1: Brazil, Mexico, Switzerland, and Yugoslavia
Pool 2: England, Chile, Spain, and the United States
Pool 3: Italy, India, Paraguay, and Sweden
Pool 4: Uruguay, Bolivia, and France

FIFA breathed a sigh of relief—but the withdrawals didn't end there. India pulled out of Pool 3 after FIFA refused to let them play barefoot. India had caused a sensation playing without shoes at the 1948 London Olympics and during World Cup qualifying, but FIFA decided to impose the ban at the tournament. The Indian Football Association would eventually require its players to wear shoes after several of them suffered frostbite at the 1952 Helsinki Olympics. France pulled out of Pool 4 when they saw how much traveling was involved between games. There wasn't enough time for FIFA to re-place India and France and the tournament got started a month later with four groups of just thirteen teams. Some of the blame could be laid at the feet of organizers, who had scheduled teams—with the ex-ception of Brazil—to travel great distances between venues scattered across the vast country. The tournament was played from June 24 to July 16 in six cities: Rio, São Paulo, Porto Alegre, Belo Horizonte, Curitibia, and Recife. The biggest problem was that teams could play in hot and humid Rio one day and then have to travel 350 miles a few days later to mountainous coal-mining town of Belo Horizonte for another game.

Brazil kicked off the World Cup on June 24 against Mexico at the Maracanã Stadium before a crowd of 81,649. The Maracanã was still not complete, but that didn't stop the Brazilians from putting on a spec-tacular opening ceremony that featured the release of 5,000 pigeons and with the Brazilian players greeted by a twenty-one-gun salute. Ademir got things started for Brazil, putting the hosts ahead, 1–0, in the 30th minute. In the second half, Brazil went up 2–0 with Jair in the 66th minute. Goals by Baltazar and Ademir completed the scoring. Brazil had overcome its first hurdle and the crowd loved it.

The following day, Yugoslavia played Switzerland at Sete de Setem-bro Stadium in Belo Horizonte. The Yugoslavian team, runner up to Sweden at the 1948 Olympics, was led by its captain Zlatko Ciakowski. Yugoslavia's superiority was too much for the Swiss. Two goals in a span of six minutes by Kosta Tomasevic in the first half put the

Yugoslavs ahead, 2–0, at the break. A goal by Tihomir Ognjanov in the 82nd minute sealed the 3–0 win.

Excitement around the Brazilian team reached an all-time high with 42,000 fans turning out for the game against Switzerland on June 28 at Pacembu Stadium in São Paulo. Brazil coach Flávio Costa, who also coached club team Vasco de Gama, tinkered with the lineup that had defeated Mexico, selecting several São Paulo players to the delight of the home fans. Costa's team was one of the first to utilize a 4–2–4 formation, which combined strong defense and offense. The relatively empty midfield, which only featured two players, forced Brazil's players to not only have to steal the ball, but also pass it and start an attack. The aim of the formation was to score many goals, something that would go on to typify the Brazilian game over the next few decades. Against the Swiss, Alfredo put Brazil on the board after just two minutes, but Switzerland equalized with Jacques Fatton in the 16th minute. Baltazar set things right just before halftime and Brazil went into the locker room with a 2–1 advantage. Brazil tried to hold on to the lead, but the Swiss never gave up and that determination paid off when Fatton scored two minutes from the end to tie the score 2–2. Costa was nearly attacked by a small crowd that stormed the field. The Brazilian fans were not prepared to accept anything but a victory. The pressure was on Costa now to deliver a win against Yugoslavia.

On June 29, Yugoslavia played Mexico at Beira-Rio Stadium in beautiful Porto Alegre. Brazil's tie against Switzerland gave Yugoslavia a chance to top the group if it could muster a win. The Yugoslavs brought in Zlatko's brother, striker Zeliko Ciakowski, who went on to score two goals. Stjepan Bobek scored after nineteen minutes to give Yugoslavia the 1–0 lead. Ciakowski made it 2–0 three minutes later and scored his second in the 62nd minute. Tomasevic netted his second of the tournament nine minutes from the end. Mexico scored a consolation goal with Horacio Casarín on a penalty kick in the 88th minute. Yugoslavia won, 4–1. The victory meant the winner of Pool 1 would be determined by the Brazil-Yugoslavia game.

On July 1, Brazil and Yugoslavia met in front of 142,409 screaming fans at the Maracanã. The Brazilians couldn't have gotten off to a better start, scoring after three minutes with Ademir. The crowd wanted more, but would have to wait another hour before Brazil scored its second with Zizinho, who was making his World Cup debut. A tie would only benefit Yugoslavia's passage to the final round but Zizinho's goal sealed the victory for the hosts and passage to the final round. Zizinho, who had led Flamengo to three consecutive Rio championships starting in 1942, instantly became a national hero.

Pool 2 opened on June 25 with the match between England and Chile at the Maracanã. The English, who along with Brazil were favored to win the tournament, made their World Cup debut and fielded an impressive lineup that included Alf Ramsey, Stanley Mortensen, and Tom Finney. Chile, on the other hand, featured one full-time professional, George Robledo, a player known to the English because he played for Newcastle United in the country's First Division. What was supposed to be cakewalk for England almost turned into a nightmarish display. England struggled for much of the contest until it was finally able to take a 1–0 lead on a goal by Mortensen. England sealed the 2–0 win seven minutes after the interval when Wilf Mannion scored off a pass from Finney. England had earned its first World Cup finals win, but needed to play better against the United States if it hoped to advance to the final round.

On the same day, the U.S. team took on Spain at Brito Stadium in Curitiba. The Americans, who had not played in a World Cup since 1934, took the lead with John Souza in the 18th minute. The American defense, anchored by Belgian-born defender Joe Maca, successfully fended off one Spanish attempt after another for the next sixty-two minutes. Maca, who had played in his native country for Third Division club La Forestoise in Brussels, kept the Americans in the game. The U.S. hung on to the slim lead until Spain's Estanislao Basora tied the score in the 80th minute. The Americans were demoralized. Spain was able to capitalize, scoring again with Basora two minutes later. Telmo Zarra completed the rout three minutes later, capping off a dreadful five-minute span for the Americans. They had put together a valiant effort for most of the game until it fell apart in the final ten minutes. The Americans now had to take on the mighty English in a game everyone thought they were sure to lose.

On June 29, Spain and Chile met at the Maracanã. The Spanish team, which had made three changes to its lineup, was met with little resistance. Basora's goal in the 19th minute and one by Zarra in the 35th minute lifted Spain to a 2–0 win.

While Spain delighted the crowd in Rio, the United States and England prepared to do battle at Mineiro Stadium in Belo Horizonte in front of 10,151 spectators. England had flown 300 miles for the game and fatigue had started to set in. The English had won twenty-three out of its last thirty games since the end of the war, and its impressive record earned them the moniker "Kings of Europe." England also had Stanley Matthews, considered one of the world's best players, on the team, although he took his seat in the stands after joining the team late. Matthews had just wrapped up a tour of North America with a team of English stars, which had included a 1–0 win over the U.S. team at Downing Stadium in New York. Matthews was left out of the lineup and coach Arthur Drewry—who would come to regret that decision by the end of the game—opted to keep the same formation that had barely beaten Chile.

England won the coin toss and wasted no time playing the ball in the U.S. half. In the first twelve minutes alone, England unleashed five shots on goal, with two slamming against the post, another two spectacularly saved by Borghi, and the other sailing over the crossbar. The Americans, who were captained by McIlvenny, struggled to get out of

*The U.S. team that defeated England 1-0 during a shock result at the 1950 World Cup (Credit: EMPICS).*

their own half of the field. The English were able to use the counter-attack to their advantage and tried on three separate occasions with two Mortensen shots that went over the crossbar and a Tom Finney header in the 32nd minute that was tipped away by Borghi. Then the unthinkable happened. In the 37th minute, Walter Bahr, who had played for the U.S. team at the 1948 Olympics, launched a shot from 25 yards. Joe Gaetjens, who had come to the United States from Haiti on an accounting scholarship to attend Columbia University, dove headlong and grazed the ball for the stunning 1–0 advantage. On first glance, it appeared that Gaetjens had ducked to get out of the way. Had he headed the ball in intentionally or had the ball simply hit him and deflected into the net? No matter. The goal was valid and the crowd erupted into cheers. The Americans were astonishingly ahead, 1–0. The Americans played tougher in the second half and with a renewed feeling of confidence on their side, they attempted to score again. The goal never came. But England threatened the U.S. goal every chance it got. When U.S. midfielder Charles Colombo brought down Mortensen with a rough tackle at the edge of the box with eight minutes left to play, the English players crowded around Italian referee Generoso Dattilo, pleading for a penalty kick. Dattilo ruled it was outside the box and awarded a free kick. On the ensuing kick, James Mullen headed the ball on goal, but Borghi's acrobatic save denied England its chance to tie the score. "As the game went on, we got a little bit better and they got a little bit more panicky," said Bahr. "Nine times out of 10 they would have beaten us. But that game was our game."[2]

The final whistle blew and for the English the loss was humiliating—only to be overshadowed by the country's first-ever defeat at the hands of the West Indies in cricket the same day. The first reports that filtered back to London weren't believed at first. Several newspaper editors had at first assumed it had been 10–1 in favor of England when the score was transmitted via newswires. The American players, who were carried off the field by Brazilian fans who had stormed the field, had pulled off the greatest upset at a World Cup—and perhaps in all of American sports history—a little-known feat remembered by just a few Americans today. In fact, the only American newspaper to publish an article of the game was the *St. Louis Post-Dispatch*. The victory went unnoticed and so did most of the players on that team. Bahr, who worked as a Philadelphia high school teacher at the time, and his teammates only earned widespread recognition for their colossal feat in 2005 with the release of the movie, *The Game of Their Lives.*

"The only one at the airport to meet me was my wife," recalled Bahr, better known as the father of National Football League field-goal kickers Matt and Chris Bahr. "Nobody made anything of it. We didn't expect anything to be made of it."[3] Other players on that team weren't so lucky. Gaetjens, who scored the winning goal against England, played soccer for a few more years in France before returning to his native Haiti, only to be arrested. Gaetjens' family openly opposed the country's ruthless dictator, Francois Duvalier. Although he was not politically active, Gaetjens was arrested and never seen again. He has been presumed dead ever since.

The demoralized English, meanwhile, traveled back south to Rio in time for the July 2 game against Spain at the Maracanã Stadium. Matthews was not in top shape, but Drewry started him after his team's lackluster showing against the Americans. The English looked like their former selves in the first half, even scoring a goal with Jackie Milburn in the 12th minute—but it was disallowed by Italian referee Giovanni Galeati. Spain scored the only goal of the game with Zarra in the 49th minute to win not only the game, 1–0, but also the group. Both teams were booed off the field by the Brazilian crowd. Spain had played a miserable game, crowding its own half after scoring the goal in a bid to preserve the lead. England had been unable to show how great it was able to play and as a result crashed out of the competition much earlier than anyone had expected. The U.S. team closed the tournament the same day with a 5–2 loss to Chile at Ilha do Retiro Stadium in Recife after a hat trick by Atilo Cremaschi. The Chileans, who had been outplayed by Spain and England, put on a brilliant display and were ahead 2–0 at the half. The Americans were able to tie the score in the first four minutes of the second half with Gino Pariani and Ed Souza off a penalty kick. The Americans finished the tournament with one shocking win and two losses. It would be another fifty years before they would play in a World Cup finals.

Top-seeded Italy, which was without Pozzo due to his resigning in 1948 and now played under Hungarian-born Lajos Czeizler, opened the three-team Pool 3 on June 25 at Pacaembu Stadium in São Paulo against Sweden. Following the death of the Torino team the previous year, Italy decided to travel to Rio by boat and the long trip didn't give them enough time to adequately prepare for the tournament. The Swedish team was the reigning Olympic champion and had featured Gunnar Gren, Gunnar Nordhal, and Nils Liedholm. The trio signed with AC Milan, where they were nicknamed "Gre-No-Li" after the first syllable of each player's last name. The Swedes would prove to be Serie A's deadliest collection of forwards for much of the 1950s. But Gren, Nordhal, and Liedholm were not present in Brazil since Sweden's soccer federation refused to include professional players. As a result, Sweden decided to field a team comprised entirely of amateurs, claiming there was no room at the World Cup for pros. That didn't seem to hurt the Swedes one bit. Sweden went on to defeat Italy, 3–2, with two goals by Hans Jeppson and one by Sune Andersson. All Sweden needed against Paraguay was a tie to advance—a result that would also eliminate Italy. The Swedes did just that—four days later at Brito Stadium in Curitibia, playing Paraguay to a 2–2 tie. On July 2, Italy defeated Paraguay, 2–0, in São Paulo, but the outcome was meaningless. The Italians had been ousted and now had nothing to look forward to but the long boat ride back home.

Pool 4 only featured Uruguay and Bolivia after France withdrew from the tournament. That meant the *Celeste* had to play one game for a shot at the final round. The Uruguayans, who were competing for the first time at a World Cup since 1930, cruised to victory, dismantling Bolivia, 8–0. They also tied the record for most goals scored in one game, a record that had been set by Sweden against Cuba in 1938. Uruguay's slender star, Juan Alberto Schiaffino, scored four goals, while Oscar Ernesto Miguez netted two and Ernesto Vidal and Alcides Ghiggia each added one. Schiaffino's World Cup debut—and his four-goal performance—gave the Brazilian crowd a taste of what he had been showcasing over the last seven years in Uruguay with club team Peñarol. Schiaffino, who also held an Italian passport, was born on July 28, 1925, in Montevideo. He made his national team debut in 1946 and, along with Miguez and Ghiggia, known for his ferocious right foot, formed one of the deadliest trios of attackers ever assembled at a World Cup. Whether they could lift the *Celeste* to a second world title remained to be seen.

## Round-Robin Elimination Round

The stage was set for the final round-robin pool. The format would be the first—and only time—that a world champion would be crowned without an elimination-style tournament. That ensured there would be no real final, though the decisive game between Brazil and Uruguay would have all the feeling and emotion of a championship game. Brazil was bubbling with confidence coming into the final pool. The team had gelled over the two weeks leading up to this stage and Ademir had become the most feared goalscorer at the tournament. Brazil's opponent Sweden had knocked off Italy, but few expected the Swedes to defeat Brazil. A crowd of 138,886 packed into the Maracanã on July 3 to root on the hosts. They were in for a good time. The Brazilians, who played an attack-minded 4–4–3 formation against Sweden, looked unstoppable, playing with panache and constructing a 3–0 lead by halftime. Ademir put Brazil ahead in the 17th minute and added a second goal nineteen minutes later. Chica scored the third goal in the 39th minute and Brazil was well on its way to victory. But the goals didn't end there. In the second half, the Brazilian barrage continued and the Swedes could not keep up. Ademir scored two more goals to put Brazil comfortably ahead, 5–0, before Andersson netted a penalty kick to score the lone Swedish goal. Brazil added two more goals in the final five minutes with Maneca and Chico to cap off the 7–1 win.

Six days later, Uruguay played Spain at Pacaembu Stadium in São Paulo. Uruguay got off to a flying start, getting on the board with Ghiggia in the 30th minute. But two quick goals by Basora put Spain ahead, 2–1, at halftime. The Spanish defense was too tenacious for Uruguay to crack and an upset appeared to be in the works. While Brazil had demolished Sweden, the *Celeste* pushed forward, tying the score with Obdulio Varela in the 73rd minute. A tie was better than a loss, but for Uruguay it meant it had to beat Sweden in the hopes of setting up a decisive match against Brazil in the group's last game.

Brazil was back at the Maracanã on July 13 and was greeted by a crowd of 152,772 fans. The Brazilian attack put on another spectacular performance despite Spain double-teaming Ademir, who had scored seven goals at the tournament. The sloppy Spanish defense was no match for Brazil as Ademir and Chico went on to add two tallies each.

Zizinho and Jair also scored in Brazil's 6–1 win. The hosts looked unstoppable. The crowd had even taunted the Spanish players, waving white handkerchiefs—as to say "surrender"—after Brazil's third goal. The Brazilians, who had the benefit of playing before a home crowd and physically rested following a favorable travel itinerary, had scored thirteen goals in their last two games. The trophy was clearly within their grasp.

On the same day, Uruguay took on Sweden before a far less energetic crowd of 7,987 at Pacaembu Stadium. The *Celeste* made two changes to its lineup: goalkeeper Aníbal Paz replaced Gastón Máspoli and Schubert Gambetta came in for Juan Carlos Gonzalez. The changes didn't seem to help as Uruguay struggled from the get-go. After only five minutes, Palmer put Sweden ahead, 1–0, before Ghiggia leveled the score in the 39th minute. Uruguay's joy was short-lived and Sweden took the lead again a minute later, this time with Stig Sundqvist putting the ball past Paz, setting the score at 2–1. Uruguay came out more determined in the second period, knowing it needed a win to keep up with the Brazilians in the standings. Miguez tied the score for Uruguay in the 77th minute—and then netted the game-winner with only five minutes left for the 3–2 final score. The victory ensured that only Uruguay could challenge Brazil for the trophy. Their head-to-head match would determine the champion.

## The Final

In the group's final game on July 16, a crowd of 172,772 packed the Maracanã to celebrate Brazil's first World Cup title, which to this day remains a record attendance for a soccer game anywhere in the world. Organizers tried to limit the capacity to 150,000 for safety reasons, but keeping fans away from the stadium proved an impossible task. The lead-up to the game sparkled with celebration. The Brazilian fans were expecting a victory and plans for a large post-game celebration were in the works. Team photos with the phrase "Brazil World Champions" emblazoned across the top were printed and posted around Rio. Uruguay had scored only five goals in its two previous games and had struggled against its opponents. Uruguay was clearly the underdog, though an aura of overconfidence had crept into the Brazilian camp.

*The Brazilian players line up for the playing of their national anthem in the 1950 final round-robin game against Uruguay that would go down as one of the worst days in the history of Brazilian soccer (Credit: CFB).*

True, the Brazilians, who had been able to combine discipline and skill, only needed a tie to clinch the title, but it was in the team's nature to initiate an attacking game and play to win. Uruguay, to its credit, was able to use its defense to sew up the backline and keep Ademir off the scoreboard. The first half ended scoreless. Though the burden to score fell squarely on Uruguay's shoulders, Brazil, with the triangular strikeforce of Ademir, Jair, and Zizinho, again showed off its free-flowing, attacking style. The Brazilians were rewarded for their attacks when Ademir was able to slip a pass to Albino Friaça, who scored the game's first goal in the 47th minute. The crowd roared with joy as the players celebrated under the Brazilian sun. The frenzy appeared to give the team all the adrenaline it needed to win the game. Destiny truly appeared to be on Brazil's side. Uruguay had no choice but to push forward.

Uruguay refused to lie down. Aided by the skill and leadership of Varela, Uruguay was able to capitalize on some sloppy Brazilian plays in the back. On one such instance, newsreel images show that Brazilian defender Bigode gave Ghiggia too much room, allowing the Uruguayan player to pick up a pass from Varela. Ghiggia crossed the ball to Schiaffino, who headed it past Moacir Barbosa in the 66th minute for the 1–1 tie. The Brazilian goalkeeper had not been tested too often during the tournament and the goal proved a psychological blow. The crowd fell silent. But the Brazilian players didn't let the goal stop them. Still, Uruguay had other plans. The constant fusillade of Brazilian shots were systemically smothered by Máspoli, who had returned as the team's starting goalkeeper, after being benched against Sweden. At the same time, Brazil's defense appeared insecure each time the ball came its way, with Bigode the weakest link in the back. He had already made a mistake that led to the first goal—and he made a second key error eleven minutes from the end. Ghiggia was able to successfully dribble the ball past Bigode once again, and this time, opted not to send in a cross. Instead, he went on one of his trademark runs and blasted a shot from close range that lifted with it a cloud of dust. When the smoke cleared, the ball had made its way between Barbosa and the near post for the 2–1 lead. The angle was tight and Barbosa did not appear alert at the time. The Brazilian carnival had come to a sudden halt. The samba drums became silent. The unthinkable had occurred and Brazil was unable to do anything about it.

The final whistle brought with it Brazilian tears. Fans openly wept inside the stadium and across the country. The three-week buildup to this game did not end as everyone had envisioned: with Brazil lifting the cup. In an improvised trophy presentation, Rimet walked onto the field alone because no one from the Brazilian Football Association wanted to join him at the moment he handed Varela the cup. The fans walked out of the stadium as Varela and his teammates paraded around the field. Some Brazilian players stayed to watch. Others ran into the locker rooms with Costa, who needed a police escort when some in the crowd blamed him for the loss and tried to assault him. He said,

> We were crushed, ashamed, full of guilt. While I was [in the locker room] with the players, I could not wait to just get home. I would have liked to escape without speaking to anyone, but it was impossible. We had to wait a good while before we could leave the Maracanã.[4]

The 2–1 loss has been dissected and talked about so many times—particularly by Brazilians—that the "Maracanã Shocker" remains one of soccer's legendary matches. The loss was Brazil's version of Waterloo and the country was thrust into deep mourning. Brazil, who would never win a World Cup on home soil, would go on to achieve glory in the decades to come, although Ghiggia's goal remains the most infamous in Brazilian soccer history. Over the years, Brazilian players claimed to receive crank calls every now and then from angry fans.

Uruguay was crowned a two-time champion—along with Italy—and remained unbeaten in its two World Cup appearances. The final game also concluded what could be defined as a disorganized, but very entertaining, tournament. The competition also signaled the rebirth of the World Cup after a twelve-year respite and brought with it a newfound passion that would go on to define it for years to come. This was also a tournament of firsts. This was the first finals ever in which no players received red cards. Attendance for all twenty-two games reached 1.34 million—topping the million mark for the first time ever—and proving that the event had surpassed the Olympics as the most popular sporting spectacle on the planet.

## 1954

The competition moved over to Switzerland following the passion and agony witnessed at the Maracanã. The 1946 decision to choose Switzerland to host the upcoming 1954 competition was symbolic because that year marked the 50th anniversary of FIFA, which was based in Zurich. The World Cup was slowly entering the modern era and this tournament was the first to receive television coverage. Though it was limited, some games were broadcast live on televisions across Europe—the first real sign that the tournament would someday grow into a global commercial event. The Swiss also showed the early signs of marketing savvy—something that would come to dominate the tournament in the coming decades—by issuing the first-ever World Cup coins.

### Qualifying Tournament

Forty-five countries entered the qualifying tournament. Both Switzerland and Uruguay qualified automatically as hosts and champion, respectively. For the *Celeste*, it would be their first-ever World Cup appearance on European soil. Uruguay, still considered South America's most talented team, had spent the four years leading up to the tournament on an emotional high after having beaten Brazil. The roster remained largely the same with Máspoli, Andrade, Rodriguez, Schiaffino, and Varela—who had turned 37 on the eve of the competition—still on the roster. Brazil, on the other hand, fielded a completely revamped lineup and replaced Costa with Zezé Moreira.

The biggest upset of the qualifying tournament was Spain's failure to reach the finals after losing to Turkey. This is interesting since FIFA had already seeded Spain in the event to earn a spot in the finals. Fate had other plans. In the last game of a three-game series played in Rome on March 17, 1954, Spain tied Turkey, 2–2. An Italian boy, Luigi Franco Gemma, was chosen to pick a ball out of a drum to determine the winner. The blindfolded boy reached in and chose Turkey. Spain had been eliminated.

In other qualifying results, the United States, who had to win Group 11 for a spot in the finals, finished second to Mexico after losing to them twice, 3–0 and 4–1. Mexico, who recorded four victories in four games, scored eighteen goals and conceded just one during its qualifying run. In Britain, the Home International Championship once again served as the qualifying tournament. Again, England won, with Scotland finishing second. Unlike their decision in 1950, Scotland decided this time to participate in the finals. The South Koreans qualified at the expense of Japan, spurring a continental rivalry that continues to this day. Egypt, the only applicant from Africa, lost a playoff game to Italy.

## Group Play

FIFA's new president, Rodolphe Seeldrayers, and the sport's governing body found it necessary to change the tournament's format, combining an opening pool round with a knockout system. The sixteen qualifying nations were divided into four groups, with two teams seeded in each pool. That meant the two seeded teams—even though in the same group—would not play each other in the opening round. Oddly, tie games, even in the first round, would go to overtime but declared a draw if a winner was not found after the extra thirty minutes. The four group winners would advance to one bracket while the four runners-up in each group met in another. Goal differential (meaning the overall quantity of goals scored) was not used as a tiebreaker, like it is today, and teams battling for a qualifying spot that were tied on points in the group stage would have to meet in a playoff for a place in the knockout round. The tournament would then feature an elimination round with quarterfinals, semifinals, and a final.

Turkey, who had eliminated Spain, were seeded instead, while the unseeded West Germans were put in the same first-round group. The four pools were made up of the following teams (the first two teams listed were seeded and would not face each other in the first round):

Group 1: Brazil, France, Mexico, and Yugoslavia
Group 2: Hungary, Turkey, South Korea, and West Germany
Group 3: Austria, Czechoslovakia, Scotland, and Uruguay
Group 4: Belgium, England, Italy, and Switzerland

The most feared team entering the tournament was Hungary. The tiny European nation had produced a generation of players that was quickly emerging as a world soccer power. The Hungarians had demolished England, 6–3, in 1953 at Wembley Stadium, becoming the first team from outside Britain to defeat the English at home. The Mighty Magyars, as they were nicknamed, defeated England again in Budapest, 7–1, on the eve of the tournament. The Hungarian attack was spearheaded by striker Ferenc Puskás, who possessed the most lethal left foot in Europe. Puskás also had a supporting cast, which included Sándor Kocsis, Zoltán Czibor, Nándor Hidegkuti, and József Boszik.

But Puskás stood out. Born in 1927, he began his career in 1943 with Budapest-based club Kispest, where his father was the coach. The club was eventually taken over by the Communist Party and transformed into an army team called Honvéd, Puskás soon earned the nickname the "Galloping Major." He was an unusual-looking player—squat and stocky, and he even sported a bit of a belly. On the field, though, he possessed one of the most accurate shots in the game, able to rip balls past goalkeepers with unerring precision. Puskás's skills put Hungary, who had not lost a game since May 1950, on most people's list to win the tournament.

Group 1 opened on June 16 in Le Pontaise Stadium in Lausanne with France taking on Yugoslavia. This time, the tournament opened with a shocker. The seeded French team lost, 1–0, to Yugoslavia on a

# FERENC PUSKÁS

Widely considered Hungary's finest player ever, Ferenc Puskás spearheaded the groundbreaking Hungary team that dominated world soccer throughout the 1950s. He never lifted the World Cup, but the "Galloping Major" played for two different national teams at the tournament.

Puskás was born in 1927 in Budapest and started his pro career as a teenager, playing for his father's club team Kispest Budapest. By age 16, the stocky striker became a starter. He made his international debut two years later against Austria. Puskás was the unlikeliest of soccer stars. He was short, overweight, and not particularly strong in the air. His skills, however, were not in doubt. In 84 national team appearances, Puskás scored an astonishing 83 goals.

Puskás's club team Kispest became an army-run team in 1948 and renamed Honvéd. The star striker earned the nickname "Galloping Major" in recognition of his army rank. He played for Honvéd until 1956. In 1952, Puskás captained Hungary to an Olympic gold medal in Helsinki and the Mighty Magyars arrived at the 1954 World Cup finals in Switzerland as the team to beat. Hungary's biggest win came in November 1953 at Wembley Stadium, where England had never lost to a team from outside of Britain. Hungary won the game, 6–3. This Hungarian team, built around Puskás, played a type of soccer never seen before. Puskás was the team's fulcrum, scoring two goals against England, while his strike partner Nandor Hidegkuti netted himself a hat trick.

After losing the 1954 World Cup final to West Germany, the Hungarian team gradually disintegrated, although Puskás's career went on. He continued to play for Honvéd in Budapest, with whom he traveled to Bilbao in Spain with historic consequences. The 1956 European Cup game coincided with a period of national uprising in Hungary, and Puskás and a number of his teammates defected, taking sanctuary in Austria. Following an eighteen-month break, Puskás, out of shape and now 30 years old, appeared past his prime.

However, Puskás's old friend, Emil Oestreicher, who managed him at Honvéd, brought the striker to Real Madrid, where he would play alongside striker Alfredo Di Stefano. The duo went on to forge one of the most famous strike partnerships in history, making Real Madrid one of the most feared club teams in Europe. The club won six Liga titles and two European Cups. Puskás's finest hour came in the 1960 European Cup final in front of 130,000 fans at Glasgow's Hampden Park

(continued)

when Real beat Eintracht Frankfurt, 7–3. Di Stefano scored a hat trick, but the night belonged to Puskás, who scored four goals and ended the season with a remarkable 35 goals in 39 matches.

In 1962, Puskás was called up by the Spanish national team in time for the World Cup in Chile. But Puskás's appearance failed to ignite the Spanish attack and the team finished in last place with just a solitary victory. Puskás played for Real Madrid until 1966, before ending his career at age 39. He later coached a Greek team named Panathinaikos to a European Cup final. Puskás, who developed Alzhiemer's disease in 2000, died in 2006 at age 79 of pneumonia.

## World Cup Career Statistics

Tournaments played: 2
Games: 6
Goals: 4

goal by Miloš Milutinović in the 15th minute. On the very same day, in Geneva, Brazil defeated Mexico, 5–0, in a decisively one-sided game. The Brazilian avalanche included two goals from Pinga, and one each from Baltazar, Didi, and Julinho.

Three days later in Lausanne, Brazil and Yugoslavia played one another in what would be the most entertaining game of the group. A scoreless first half did nothing to dampen the mood of the Yugoslavians, who came out strong in the second half. Branko Zebec scored in the 48th minute after giving himself more room to operate after switching from the left wing to the middle of the field. Yugoslavia created several more scoring chances, but it was the Brazilians who leveled the score with Didi in the 70th minute. Overtime failed to produce any more goals and the tie automatically eliminated France and Mexico. The Brazilians, who hit the post on two occasions against Yugoslavia, played a brilliant game. Didi's performance—and that of the entire team—put Brazil firmly in the driver's seat to become the first South American team to lift the trophy on European soil.

Group 2 opened with favorites Hungary taking on South Korea in Zurich. The South Koreans were no match for the talented Hungarians. Two goals by Kocsis and one each from Mihaly Lantos and Puskás put Hungary ahead, 4–0, in the first half. Kocsis completed his hat trick in the 50th minute and Czibor added another tally ten minutes later to put the game away at 6–0. That wasn't enough to satisfy the Hungarians, who added three more goals in the final fifteen minutes. Andras Palotas scored twice and Puskás netted another in the final minute to clobber the South Koreans, 9–0, putting together a new record score at a World Cup. The Hungarians, so strong and flawless entering the tournament, had sent a clear message that they had their sights set on the Rimet Trophy.

At Wankdorf Stadium in Berne, the West German team, back after missing the 1950 World Cup—and for the first time not competing as a unified country—overcame seeded Turkey, 4–1. The West Germans, coached by Sepp Herberger, cruised to victory after initially falling behind 1–0 on a goal by Mamat Suat after just two minutes. Hans Schafer tied the score in the 14th minute and the first half ended 1–1. The West Germans turned on the pressure in the second half and Bernhard Klodt put his team ahead in the 52nd minute, before Ottmar Walter made it 3–1 in the 60th minute. Maximilan Morlock added a fourth with nine minutes remaining to win the game and become level with Hungary in the standings.

The Hungarians looked ready for the challenge set forth by the West Germans. On June 20, at Jakob Stadium in Basel, the 56,000 fans—only one of three games to crack the 50,000-attendance mark at that year's tournament—watched the clash between two of the strongest teams in the world. The Swiss crowd may have been expecting lots of goals. They would not go home disappointed. West Germany knew a loss to Hungary would mean playing a playoff against Turkey or South Korea for a chance to advance, but Herberger gambled that a loss could still ensure passage to the knockout round. His strategy was to see what the Hungarians could do without risking the health of his best players. As a result, Herberger revamped his lineup and purposely fielded a weaker team, starting only four of the players who had defeated Turkey. Hungary, once again, wasted no time getting on the scoreboard. Kocsis put Hungary up, 1–0, after just three minutes. Puskás scored in the 18th minute and Kocsis scored his second two minutes later to take a commanding 3–0 lead. The scoring spree didn't end there. The Hungarians padded the result in the second half with Hidegkuti, who scored two goals in a two-minute span. Kocsis made it 6–1 in the 67th minute to become the first player to ever score two hat tricks at a World Cup tournament. The West Germans tried in vain to fend off the Hungarian fusillade, but their defense was no match for Puskás and his teammates. József Tóth made it 7–1 with seventeen minutes remaining and Helmut Rahn added a second German goal in the 77th minute. The Hungarians continued to raid the West German half and they capped off the feast of goals when Kocsis scored his fourth tally, with nine minutes left, for the 8–3 win.

Turkey's 7–0 drubbing of South Korea set up the playoff game between Turkey and West Germany on June 23 in Zurich. This time, West Germany's Herberger fielded his usual starters. Turkey was never in it after West Germany built a 3–1 lead in the first half. The West Germans, fearing a potential Turkish comeback, padded its lead with Morlock in the 50th minute. The game, like so many others in this group, turned into a lopsided contest. Fritz Walter made it 5–1 two minutes later. Morlock completed his hat trick with two goals in a span of two minutes and Schafer added another tally to make it 7–1, but Kucukandonyanides Lefter was able to net a consolation goal for the Turks in the 82nd minute. Herberger's gamble of sitting most of his starters against Hungary to push a playoff had paid off.

Group 3 opened on June 16 with Scotland making its World Cup debut against Austria in Zurich. Austria, one of Europe's strongest teams before the war, had failed to produce a new generation of players worthy of any comparisons to the *Wunderteam*. Scotland entered the tournament at a disadvantage after the Glasgow Rangers team refused to release its players. Scotland played well, but fell behind in the 33rd minute on a goal by Eric Probst. The Austrians were able to defend the narrow lead in the second half, holding on for the 1–0 victory. In Berne, the defending champions, the Uruguayans, undefeated after two appearances in the finals, won their tenth World Cup game, defeating Czechoslovakia, 2–0. The win was not an easy one, but the Uruguayans were able to finally take the lead in the 70th minute with Miguez and added another with Schiaffino twelve minutes later. The *Celeste* had taken their first steps toward recapturing the title.

On July 19, the seeded Austrians wasted no time in Berne showing the Czechoslovakians who was the better of the two teams. A hat trick from Probst and a goal by Ernst Stojaspal put the Austrians ahead, 4–0, at halftime. Stojaspal scored his second of the game for the 5–0 win. In Basle, meanwhile, Uruguay had no problems disposing of Scotland under a scorching sun. A hat trick from Carlos Borges and two goals each from Miguez and Julio Abbadie gave Uruguay the 7–0 win and first place in the group. Austria finished second and also made it to the quarterfinals.

Group 4 opened on June 17 in Basle with England looking to record a win against Belgium. England, still reeling from its loss to Hungary in a friendly match, fell behind 1–0 when Leopold Anoul scored after five minutes. England tied the score with Ivor Broadis in the 25th minute and took the lead ten minutes later with Nat Lofthouse. In the second half, Broadis scored his second goal in the 63rd minute to give England a 3–1 lead. But Belgium mounted a comeback. Anoul scored again in the 71st minute and Henri Coppens made it 3–3 with twelve minutes left to play. Overtime was needed, even though the outcome would not change. England scored with Nat Lofthouse in the first minute of extra time. Belgium tied the game again; this time Jimmy Dickinson inadvertently deflected a free kick by Marcel Dries into his own goal. England had squandered a first-half lead and now needed to prevail over Switzerland if it hoped to advance.

In Lausanne, Switzerland played Italy in what turned out to be a game marred by vicious tackling. The hosts took the lead with Robert Ballaman after seventeen minutes. The *Azzurri* tied the score with Giampiero Boniperti right before the half to make it 1–1. In the second half, the game got out of hand. Brazilian referee Mario Viana failed to keep the players in line following a series of fouls that took away from the entertaining soccer that had been on display in the first period. Switzerland pulled off the upset with Josef Hugi, who stabbed the ball past goalkeeper Giorgio Ghezzi with twelve minutes left to play to grab a 2–1 win. When Benito Lorenzi had a goal disallowed in the game's waning minutes because he was whistled offside, the Italian players questioned Viana's decision. Lorenzi was so adamant in his protests that he was lucky not to be red carded. When Viana whistled the end of the game, the Italian players charged toward him, chasing him off the field and into the tunnel.[5]

On June 20, England squared off against Switzerland in Berne. The Swiss exuded confidence against the English and, with a crowd of 43,500 out in force to support them, another upset seemed possible. The English had other plans, however, even though they were missing Matthews, who had pulled a muscle in the match against Belgium.

Switzerland introduced to the world a new tactical system that relied heavily on a strong defense called *catenazz*, a precursor to Italy's *catenaccio*, which was a tactically defensive system that relied on counterattacks for creating scoring chances. The Swiss were able to fend off the English attack, which was spearheaded by captain Billy Wright, for most of the first half. But England was able to score with Jimmy Mullen in the 43rd minute and added another when Dennis Wilshaw tallied in the 69th minute. England topped the group with four points. Switzerland had to hope in a Belgium win over Italy, otherwise it would have to face the *Azzurri* in a playoff.

Italy needed a win to stay alive and was able to do just that on June 20 in Lugano. This time, the *Azzurri* decided to abandon their rough tackling for a more skillful performance. The plan worked and the Italian defensive attack sprung to life. Egisto Pandolfini gave Italy the lead in the 40th minute. The Italian offense came roaring back to life in the second period. The *Azzurri* scored three goals in a span of thirteen minutes with Carlo Galli, Amleto Frignani, and Lorenzi to take a 4–1 lead. Belgium netted a consolation goal with Anaul, who scored his third of the tournament, in the 81st minute. The win pushed a winner-take-all game between Italy and Switzerland.

The playoff game was played on June 23 at St. Jakob Stadium in Basle. The Swiss had stunned Italy just a week before and were hoping to duplicate that result. Indeed, Switzerland's winning attitude carried over and Italy ultimately paid the price. Josef Hugi put Switzerland in the lead, 1–0, after fourteen minutes. The Italians were unable to counter, scrambling to put together a real scoring opportunity. Three minutes into the second half and Ballaman made it 2–0, but not before Fulvio Nesti was able to cut the lead in half in the 67th minute. Two goals in the final five minutes—one from Hugi and another by Josef Fatton—gave the hosts a 4–1 victory and a place in the quarterfinals. The embarrassed Italians, no longer the soccer power they once were, would embark on a rebuilding program that would take nearly two decades before it would again be competitive at the World Cup.

## Quarterfinals

The quarterfinals began on June 26 with 31,000 fans turning out at the sun-drenched La Pontaise Stadium to watch Austria play Switzerland.

The game would not only feature the most goals ever in a World Cup game—nine of them in the first half alone—but also featured one of the tournament's greatest comebacks. Switzerland scored three goals in the first twenty-three minutes with Ballaman in the 16th minute, followed by Hugi in the 17th and 23rd minutes. The Austrians countered with three goals of their own—in a span of just three minutes—twice with Theodor Wagner and one from Alfred Korner. The goals didn't end there. Ernst Ocwirk's shot found the back of the net in the 34th minute and Korner added another two minutes later to put the Austrians firmly ahead, 5–3. But Ballaman scored right before the end of the first half, cutting the deficit to one goal. Austria would not be outdone and came out strong in the second half. Wagner completed his hat trick in the 52nd minute, making it 6–4, but not before Hugi completed his own hat trick six minutes later, bringing it to 6–5. Austria finally put the game away with Erich Probst in the 76th minute to win the match, 7–5, which remains the highest-scoring game in World Cup history.

In Basle, Uruguay was able to maintain its unbeaten World Cup winning streak, outscoring England in their quarterfinal matchup. The defending champions first got on the board after five minutes when Borges drilled a shot past goalkeeper Gil Merrick. The English regrouped and were able to tie the score with Dennis Wilshaw in the 16th minute. The *Celeste* took the lead for the second time after Varela's long-range effort beat Merrick. Uruguay led 2–1 at halftime. In the second period, Schiaffino was able to give the *Celeste* a 3–1 lead, deflecting in a shot born from a Varela free kick. England cut the lead down to one with Finney in the 67th minute. Matthews nearly tied the score, but his shot slammed against the post. Uruguay was able to put the game away for good with Javier Ambrois in the 78th minute to round out the 4–2 win. The English had put forth a valiant effort, but the Uruguayan juggernaut appeared unstoppable.

On June 27, Wandorf Stadium in Berne was the site of the quarterfinal matchup between Hungary and Brazil. Both teams were expected to record lots of goals, but it would become a contest known more for its fouling and red cards. Hungary, without Puskás who had injured himself against West Germany, hoped the rain that was falling just as the game got underway would favor their aerial style. Brazil, who liked to play a passing game, appeared to be at a disadvantage on the wet turf. The game turned into an affair English referee Arthur

Ellis would never forget. Some credit him with preventing an explosive situation from getting worse. Others argue the opposite, claiming Ellis and his calls escalated the violence. From the sidelines, Puskás watched as Hidegkuti scored after just three minutes. The Hungarians doubled their lead four minutes later when Kocsis headed in a Hidegkuti cross. They looked well on their way to going to the semifinals. Brazil's desperation grew following the second goal, sparking an orgy of violence. Just before the stroke of halftime, a foul on Indio led to a penalty kick, which Djalma Santos converted. That's where the scoring ended and the violent tackling picked up again. Both sides were responsible for a series of malicious fouling that carried over into the second half. Though no ejections had been issued in the first period, the second half would feature three expulsions. The Magyars still maintained a 2–1 lead and were able to score again when Ellis awarded them a controversial penalty kick. That call changed the course of the game. The Brazilian players argued Kocsis had taken a dive in the penalty box, but Ellis was not swayed and Lantos slotted the ball past Castilho.

The infuriated Brazilians tackled even harder and were able to pull one back with Julinho in the 65th minute. Hungary defended its 3–2 lead, but Ellis seemed to lose control of the game in the 70th minute when a fight erupted between Boszik and Nilton Santos. Both were promptly ejected. With just four minutes left to play, Humberto was sent off for intentionally kicking Gyula Lóránt. Kocsis headed the ball home in the 89th minute to clinch the 4–2 win. Hungary had handed Brazil a beating, but the final whistle wasn't enough to put an end to the hostilities. Players on both teams threw punches as armed guards escorted Ellis off the field. The fighting even spilled over into the locker rooms and the game was later dubbed the "Battle of Berne" following the rough-and-tumble display.[6] Puskás got into a confrontation with Pinheiro in the locker rooms, breaking a water bottle over his head.[7] FIFA blamed the riot on the Brazilians but, like Pontius Pilate, washed its hands of the affair. Puskás and Boszik were pardoned by FIFA and allowed to play in the semifinals against Uruguay, even though Ernst Thommen, president of the World Cup organizing committee, claimed to have witnessed Puskás's attack on Pinheiro, who left the stadium with his head bandaged. Puskás wouldn't play in the game because he was still nursing an injury.

On the same day at Les Charmilles Stadium in Geneva, West Germany took on Yugoslavia in the last quarterfinal game. The West Germans caught a break after nine minutes when Ivan Horvat mistakenly put the ball into his own net following a scramble in the box. The West Germans, who packed its defense after taking the lead, scored against the run of play in the 85th minute with Rahn, lifting his team to a 2–0 win and leading to a meeting against rival Austria in the semifinals.

## Four Teams Remain

In the first semifinal, Hungary and Uruguay faced off on June 30 in Lausanne. Despite what had transpired against Brazil, the Hungarians were expected to pull off their usual offensive display. Uruguay, meanwhile, had yet to lose a World Cup game and had proven it could win in Europe. Both teams were greeted by a fierce rainstorm and the 37,000 spectators who decided to show up that day would be treated to one of the tournament's most entertaining games. Given what had happened against Brazil, the Swiss authorities decided not to risk anyone's safety and surrounded the field with armed guards.[8] Hungary scored first with Czibor in the 13th minute; he beat Máspoli following a head pass from Kocsis. The Magyars padded their lead a minute into the second half when Hidegkuti headed the ball into the net. Ahead 2–0, the Hungarians played a cat-and-mouse game with Uruguay, passing the ball around the field to the delight of the crowd.

A trip to the final was all but secured, until Juan Eduardo Hohberg, a Argentine native who had been naturalized a Uruguayan citizen, scored in the 75th minute off a well-placed Schiaffino pass. With only four minutes remaining, Uruguay was able to tie the game on a similar play with Schiaffino once again feeding Hohberg, who beat Hungarian goalkeeper Gyula Grosics. The game may have been deadlocked, 2–2, but the *Celeste* wilted under the fatigue. Hohberg, who was physically overcome with emotion after scoring the second goal, collapsed on the field and had to be revived on the sidelines by team doctors with the help of smelling salts.[9] The game went to overtime. The opening extra time session ended scoreless, though Hohberg, who was back on the field, could have given Uruguay the lead after his shot struck the post. An injured Schiaffino limped up and down the field, but was ineffectual as the Hungarians turned up the pressure. With nine minutes left to play in the second overtime period, Kocsis put the Magyars ahead with one of his trademark headers. The Uruguayan defense was unable to keep up with the speedy striker and paid the ultimate price for it. Five minutes later, Kocsis put the game away with another magnificent header for his record eleventh goal of the tournament. The Hungarian team had clawed its way back to a 4–2 victory and was in the final. The *Celeste*, who had suffered its first-ever World Cup loss, had been unable to defend its title away from South America.

The other semifinal, played on June 30 in Basle, pitted West Germany against Austria before a crowd of 58,000 fans, many of whom had come from nearby Germany and Austria to cheer on their respective teams. The West Germans, keen on winning the Cup after getting this far, trampled all over the Austrian defense, scoring six goals, including two penalty kicks from Fritz Walter, to secure a 6–1 victory. Nearly every West German attack resulted in a goal with Ottmar Walter, Schafer, and Morlock all finding the back of the net. Probst scored Austria's only goal in the second half.

## Third Place

Before the final could be contested, Austria captured third place on July 3 after defeating Uruguay, 3–1, in Zurich. The Austrians got on the board with Stojaspal after sixteen minutes, only to watch their lead disappear five minutes later thanks to a tally by Hohberg. Austria sealed the win in the second half when Uruguayan Luis Cruz scored his own goal in the 59th minute and Ocwik's 30-yard blast in the 79th minute found the back of the net.

## Last Team Standing

The final was played on July 4 at a sold-out Wankdorf Stadium. A crowd of 60,000 ignored the rain that had pelted Berne for much of the day and filled the stadium to watch what would be one of the finest finals ever. The Hungarians were favored to win the game after Puskás returned to the lineup. West Germany responded with Rahn and Morlock. For sure, this would not be a replay of the 8–3 trouncing the Magyars had inflicted on the West Germans just two weeks earlier during group play. Herberger had purposely fielded a weaker team on that occasion.

## JUAN SCHIAFFINO

One of the many South American players to flee to Europe, Juan Schiaffino, who was born in Montevideo, Uruguay, in 1925, played for Uruguay but later became an Italian citizen. As a result, Schiaffino played for two national teams. He played with Uruguay from 1946 to 1954 and later with Italy from 1954 to 1958. He amassed 21 appearances with Uruguay (and 8 goals) and four appearances for Italy.

Schiaffino broke into the Peñarol youth team at age 17 and a year later was a first-team member. Two years later, he was a member of Uruguay's Copa America–winning team. With Peñarol, he won four Uruguayan League titles in 1949, 1951, 1953, and 1954. Schiaffino also played at the 1950 World Cup with Uruguay, scoring a goal—one of five he netted at the competition—in the final round-robin group game against Brazil to take the trophy. He played at the tournament four years later, helping Uruguay reach fourth place after injuring himself in the semifinals against Hungary.

Following the tournament, Schiaffino went to AC Milan. Six months later, he played his first game for Italy and then helped his club to win three league titles in 1955, 1957, and 1959, and helped them reach the European Cup final in 1958, which AC Milan lost to Real Madrid. Schiaffino won an Italian Cup with AC Milan in 1956. He played 149 games for AC Milan and scored 47 goals. At age 33, he moved to Roma and spent two seasons with them before retiring in 1962. He won a UEFA Cup with Roma in 1961.

In 1976, after nearly fifteen years away from the game, Schiaffino took charge of Penarol and later had a brief spell as Uruguay coach. Schiaffino died in 2002 at age 77.

## World Cup Career Statistics

Tournaments played: 2
Games: 9
Goals: 5

This time, he put his strongest players on the field, hoping to outwit the perennially overconfident Hungarians. The game pitted the West Germans, a team of individual talent, against the Hungarians, who epitomized the strengths of a cohesive unit. The West German team was counting on its solid defense, while the Hungarian team hoped to get the best of its opponent with its overpowering offense. On the morning of the final, Puskás awoke with pain to his right knee. The battle against Uruguay had taken its toll and he begged his coach Gustav Sebes to leave him on the bench.[10] Sebes ignored his plea.

Puskás was in the starting lineup later that day. The Hungarians took a 2–0 lead with a Puskás goal in the sixth minute and one from Czibor two minutes later. The Rimet Trophy seemed destined to go to them. But West Germany retaliated, pulling one back with Morlock in the 10th minute. Another eight minutes and Rahn was able to equalize directly off of a corner kick. The West Germans had mounted a comeback—a trait of so many games at this tournament—and the game was tied, 2–2, at halftime.

Hungary almost took the lead again after the break, but a Hidegkuti shot hit the post and a Kocsis blast bounced off the crossbar. In the 84th minute, with overtime looming, Rahn picked up a poorly punted Lantos kick, raced toward the Hungarian goal and placed a low shot into the net. The goal was a spectacular individual feat—the very thing Herberger was banking on to win the game—and the West Germans were ahead, 3–2. Victory appeared to be within reach. But Puskás tried to put Hungary back in the game, even putting the ball into the net with two minutes left to play, but English referee Bill Ling correctly called him offside. Ling's final whistle gave West Germany its first World Cup title and snapped Hungary's thirty-game unbeaten streak.

Like Uruguay four years earlier, the tournament had produced a surprise winner. Overall, the competition had been a success, even though the average attendance of 37,720 was lower than anticipated. The lack of spectators was more than made up for when it came to goals. The tournament averaged 5.38 goals per game, which to this day remains the highest average for a World Cup tournament.

Rimet presented Walter with the trophy as a steady rain continued to fall on the soaked field. Puskás walked off the field as soccer's uncrowned king as the West German players celebrated. The triumph marked the first outburst of German nationalism since the war and helped boost the morale of a people looking to rebuild their country on the ashes of Hitler's treacherous regime. The game, still referred to by German fans as the "Miracle of Berne," to this day is remembered as one of the country's greatest sporting triumphs.

## 1958

FIFA awarded the hosting duties of the 1958 World Cup to Sweden in June 1954. The original promise to alternate tournaments between Europe and South America was broken. Sweden, who had remained neutral during World War II, seemed like a perfect choice. The country had not been attacked and therefore was not in the midst of a reconstruction phase. Sweden had also emerged as a soccer power with many of its stars going over to play in Serie A. Soccer fever had just begun to sweep across the Scandinavian countries and now the World Cup was coming to their backyard.

This was also the first tournament since Rimet's death in 1956 at the age of 83, but it would also be the first tournament since the creation of the Union of European Football Associations, more commonly known as UEFA. The association's first plan of action was to create a continental club championship, known as the European Champions Cup (renamed the Champions League in 1992), in order to boost the profile of Europe's club teams. Initially, many of UEFA's founders appeared more concerned with forming a national team competition. Only the French sports daily *L'Equipe* and its editor at that time, Gabriel Hanot, were trying to establish a cause for a European club competition. He came up with a plan for a tournament to be played on Wednesday nights since league games were played on weekends. The first tournament was by invitation only and based on a club's popularity. The sixteen team representatives met in April 1955 and approved the rules set out by *L'Equipe*. Teams would play a home-and-home series, with a first leg at the home of one team and the return match at the other team's stadium. The combined goal total over two games would determine the winner. The first game was played between Sporting Clube of Portugal and FK Partizan of Yugoslavia in Lisbon. The Portuguese were held to a 3–3 tie and the second leg in Belgrade saw FK Partizan go through to the next round following a 5–2 win. The competition flourished over the years, thanks largely to clubs like Real Madrid. The Spanish club won the first five championships and gave the tournament legitimacy in its early years. The Champions League is now the most coveted trophy in all of club soccer and second only to the World Cup in prestige.

## Qualifying Round

Fifty-three countries, a new record, applied for the chance to be one of the fifteen finalists, with the addition of host Sweden, to play in what would be the first World Cup broadcast live on TVs across the planet. The qualifying rounds would include the elimination of two-time champions Uruguay, at the hands of Paraguay, and Italy, who lost to Northern Ireland. The Italians were a step away from qualifying. The Northern Ireland team had to defeat Italy in Belfast if it wanted to advance to the finals. A dense fog caused Hungarian referee Istvan Zsolt to be stuck in London. Unable to arrive in Belfast in time for the game, the Italians inexplicably refused to play unless Zsolt officiated the match. The game went ahead—and dubbed a friendly—with no bearing on who would qualify. The game ended, 2–2, and Italy would have qualified had the game counted. Instead, the match was played a month later in January 1958 with Zsolt. The Italians went on to lose, 2–1.

The Hungarian team was back, but was only a shadow of its former self following the Soviet invasion in 1956, which led to the defections of Puskás, Kocsis, and Czibor. In fact, Puskás's career lay in ruins. Only after arriving at Real Madrid in 1958, overweight and out of shape, Puskás was able to put his career back on track. He teamed up with Alfredo Di Stefano and initiated what is widely regarded as a golden era for the Spanish club. His four-goal performance in the European Cup final against Eintracht Frankfort, won by Real Madrid, 7–3, has become legendary.

The Iron Curtain may have been drawn over half of Europe, but the Soviets finally decided to join the rest of the continent, and the soccer world, and qualified for its first finals. All of Britain's four federation members—England, Northern Ireland, Scotland, and Wales—also qualified together for the first time, though chances of an English triumph had been severely hampered following the Munich air disaster in February 1958 that killed eight Manchester United players on a return flight from Belgrade. The team, coached by Matt Busby, tied Red Star Belgrade 3–3 and qualified for the semifinals of the European Cup. The plane that was carrying "Busby's Babes," the nickname given to the team by its adoring fans, crashed through a fence on its third attempt to take-off in Munich. The catastrophe eliminated any chance England had of winning its first World Cup.

Across the Atlantic Ocean, the U.S. team was paired off in CONCACAF's Group 2 with Mexico and Canada. The group winner would qualify for the finals. The Americans couldn't even muster a tie in its two games, scoring just five goals and giving up twenty-one. Mexico finished in first place with eight points—four more than Canada—and once again reached the finals. The Mexicans were joined by Group 1 winners Costa Rica. In South America, Argentina, who had not played at a World Cup since 1934, qualified for the finals and were coached by Stabile, one of the heroes of the inaugural tournament. The Argentineans had won the Copa America in 1957, but were at a disadvantage after several of their star players were lured away to Serie A. The Argentine FA retaliated, refusing to recall those players for national team duty.

Also making a return to the World Cup was Brazil. Nilton Santos and Didi were back, but poised to make his debut was a virtually unknown seventeen-year-old young man named Edson Arantes do Nascimento, better known by his nickname Pelé. His appearance in Sweden introduced the world to the sport's next superstar and his skill would forever change the game. After the final championship debacle of 1950 on Brazil's home turf and lackluster performance four years later, Brazilian soccer was in a period of transition. The Brazilians had the skill to win the World Cup, but seemed to lack the emotional stability to overcome the pressures of the tournament. In March 1958, João Havelange took over as president of the Brazilian Football Association (Havelange would be president until 1974 when was elected head of FIFA). Havelange invited Paulo Machado de Carvalho to head the national team program, including the responsibility of hiring a new coach. Paulo Machado was a successful businessman and owner of radio and TV stations. Machado's approach would forever change the way Brazilians prepared for the World Cup—he added a nutritionist, psychologist, and a dentist to the team's medical staff. Moreira was replaced by Oswaldo Brandão, who was fired after finishing runner-up to Argentina in the 1957 Copa America. For the first time ever, the Brazilian FA even considered replacing Brandão with a non-Brazilian coach, most notably Flamengo's Paraguayan-born Manager Fleitas Solich. Havelange ultimately decided not to gamble with a foreigner. Two months before the World Cup, Vicente Feola was named as the Brazil coach. Feola brought a fluid and offensive approach to the team, utilizing a 4-2-4 formation with Garrincha, Vavá, Pelé, and Zagallo making up the team's frontline.

## Group Play

Once again, FIFA changed the tournament's format. The sixteen finalists were placed in four groups of four teams in a round-robin format. The top two finishers in each group advanced to the knockout rounds. The teams were divided into the following four pools:

> Group 1: Argentina, Northern Ireland, Czechoslovakia, and West Germany
> Group 2: France, Paraguay, Scotland, and Yugoslavia
> Group 3: Hungary, Mexico, Sweden, and Wales
> Group 4: Austria, Brazil, England, and the Soviet Union

More than 1,500 journalists applied for credentials and a global audience of 40 million tuned in on June 8, 1958, to watch the opening ceremonies on live television from Rasunda Stadium in Stockholm. The ceremony was followed by a Group 3 matchup between Sweden and Mexico. The opener couldn't have gone any better for the hosts with a crowd of 34,107 showing up for the game. Sweden had assembled a powerful team with hopes of reaching the final. Liedholm was back on the roster after the Swedish FA lifted its ban on pro players, even though it was Agne Simonsson, with a goal in each half, who spearheaded the scoring. Liedholm added a penalty kick goal in the second half for the 3-0 win.

Group 1 also got underway the same day with a pair of games. In Halmstad, Northern Ireland took on Czechoslovakia. Northern Ireland, making its World Cup debut, managed a 1-0 win thanks to a goal by Wilbur Cush. In the other game, defending champion West Germany played Argentina in Malmö. West Germany had no problems dismantling Argentina. The West Germans fielded four players from its 1954 team, including Rahn, whose heroics helped defeat Argentina. But before the West Germans cruised to victory, it was Argentina who took the lead with Orestes Corbatta. West Germany leveled the score with Rahn in the 32nd minute, then took the lead three minutes later with Uwe Seeler. Rahn made it 3–1 in the final minute.

Argentina needed a win to keep its chances of advancing to the next round alive. Northern Ireland had put on a solid display in its first game and was working hard to pull off the upset on June 11 in Halmstad. The shock result appeared to be in the works after striker Peter McParland put Northern Ireland ahead after just three minutes. Argentina threw everything at Northern Ireland and was able to win a penalty kick after Dick Keith handled the ball in the box and Corbatta converted from the spot in the 38th minute. The second half featured an aggressive Argentine team and a defensive Northern Irish one. Argentina took a 2–1 lead with Norberto Menéndez in the 55th minute and put the game out of reach with Ludovico Avio five minutes later for the 3–1 win.

On the same day at Olympia Stadium in Halsingborg, West Germany again put on a great display of attacking soccer, though it was the Czechoslovakians who jumped out to a 2–0 lead in the first half on goals from Milan Dvořák and Zdeněk Zikán. The West Germans came back to life after the break, scoring with Hans Schafer in the 60th minute. Rahn leveled the score ten minutes later, his third goal of the competition, with a shot that beat goalkeeper Břetislav Dolejší. The tie gave West Germany three points in the standings and temporarily in control of first place, with Argentina and Northern Ireland tied at two and Czechoslovakia with one. The group was still wide open, but the West Germans still looked like the team to beat.

Northern Ireland had to defeat West Germany on June 15 in Malmö Stadium if it wanted to advance to the next round. Though it appeared to be a tall order at first, Northern Ireland was up to the task, especially after taking the lead with McParland in the 17th minute. The defending champions tied the score with Rahn three minutes later, but McParland restored the lead in the 58th minute. The upset was in the works, until Seeler netted the 2–2 equalizer with ten minutes left to play. The tie ensured West Germany's passage to the next round. Czechoslovakia, who had thrashed Argentina, 6–1, in Halsingborg, would now have to play Northern Ireland in a playoff game for second place and a spot in the quarterfinals.

On June 17, Northern Ireland and Czechoslovakia squared off in Malmö Stadium. Northern Ireland appeared at a disadvantage following an injury to goalkeeper Harry Gregg, which forced coach Peter Doherty to go with backup Norman Uprichard. The goalkeeper change hurt Northern Ireland as Czechoslovakia jumped out to a 1–0 lead when Zikán put the ball in the net on a shot that should have been saved by Uprichard. McParland scored—his fourth goal in three games—in the 44th minute to tie the match, 1–1. The game went to overtime and McParland's heroics were once again on display. He latched on to the ball following a Danny Blanchflower free kick. McParland was able to unleash a shot that went into the roof of the net and over Dolejš'í for the 2–1 win. Northern Ireland had done the unthinkable: advance to the quarterfinals.

Group 2 opened on June 8 at Arosvallen Stadium in the city of Vasteras with a 1–1 tie between Yugoslavia and Scotland. Yugoslavia got on the board first with Aleksandar Petakovic after six minutes. Scotland, who was makings its second-ever World Cup appearance and looking for its first win at the finals, tied the score in the second half with Jim Murray.

In Norrkoping, France and Paraguay played a high-scoring and spirited game, but it would be the French who would walk away with the win. The Paraguayans had eliminated the Uruguayans in the qualifiers and traveled to Sweden confident of a good showing. How wrong they would be after the French team, spearheaded by Moroccan-born striker Just Fontaine, put on a dazzling display of attacking soccer. Fontaine began his pro career with USM Casablanca, where he played from 1950 to 1953. He was recruited by French club Nice in 1953, where he went on to score forty-four goals in three seasons. He had made his national team debut in December 1953, scoring a hat trick in France's 8–0 win over Luxembourg. Fontaine was ready to show off his scoring heroics on a grander stage.

Paraguay took the lead with Florencio Amarilla in the 20th minute. Four minutes later, Fontaine scored, then added another in the 30th minute, to give France the lead. Paraguay tied the score with Amarilla on a penalty kick in the 44th minute and the teams ended the first half tied, 2–2. Paraguay scored the go-ahead goal with Jorgelino Romero in the 50th minute. It would be all France from that point on. Roger Piantoni made it 3–3 two minutes later and the French players, *Les Bleus*,

---

### JUST FONTAINE

Fontaine still holds the record for most goals scored at a single World Cup and is third on the list of all-time tournament scorers. Just Fontaine was born in Marrakech, Morocco, in 1933 and took on French citizenship as an adult. Fontaine began his pro career in his native Morocco at USM Casablanca, where he played for three seasons starting in 1950. He was recruited by French club Nice in 1953, where he went on to score 44 goals in three seasons for the club.

In 1956, Fontaine moved to Stade de Reims, where he scored an impressive 121 goals over six seasons. Fontaine, a clinical finisher who possessed pinpoint passing abilities and perfect ball control skills, scored 165 goals in 200 games in the French League and won the domestic title in 1958 and 1960.

Fontaine was equally impressive when he played for France. In his national team debut in 1953 against Luxembourg, Fontaine scored a hat trick to cap off an 8–0 win. Over seven years, he scored 30 goals in 21 games for France. However, Fontaine is best remembered for his performance at the 1958 tournament in Sweden, where he scored 13 goals in six matches—a feat that included scoring four goals against West Germany. Fontaine played his last match for France in July 1962, forced to retire at age 28 after breaking his left leg on two separate occasions.

Fontaine briefly coached France in 1967, but was replaced after only two games when both matches ended in losses.

### World Cup Career Statistics

Tournaments played: 1
Games: 6
Goals: 13

---

because of their blue jerseys were able to take the lead with a goal from Maryan Wisnieski in the 61st minute. Fontaine recorded a hat trick in the 67th minute; a minute later, it became 6–3 with Raymond Kopa, who had been named European Player of the Year the previous year. Jean Vincent added another goal in the 84th minute as France toppled Paraguay, 7–3.

On June 11, Paraguay, still reeling after giving up seven goals, made a few changes before playing Scotland. The lineup featured a new goalkeeper, Samuel Aguilar, with the hopes that they had enough defensive firepower to get by Scotland's sturdy defense. Juan Aguero put Paraguay on the board after four minutes, but Scotland tied the score with Jackie Mudie in the 24th minute. Cayetano Re put Paraguay ahead, 2–1, at the stroke of halftime and Jose Parodi added a third goal in the 71st minute to put Paraguay ahead, 3–1. Bobby Collins scored a minute later, but Paraguay would wind up with the victory.

At Arosvallen Stadium in Vasteras, France continued to look strong, but wound up on the losing end against Yugoslavia. Fontaine opened the scoring after four minutes, but Petakovic made it 1–1 in the 15th minute. The Yugoslavs took the lead with Todor Veselinovic in the 61st minute, before Fontaine netted his second of the game, and fifth of the tournament, in the 84th minute to make it 2–2. The French appeared content with the tie, but Yugoslavia pushed forward. Veselinovic scored the game-winner after breaking through the French defense in the final minute for the 3–2 win.

France now needed a victory against Scotland to reach the quarterfinals, though that result would also eliminate Paraguay, who had to hope for a win over Yugoslavia combined with a French loss. The French entered the game favored with Fontaine in top shape. Goals from Kopa and Fontaine, who scored his sixth of the competition, put France ahead, 2–0. Scotland pulled one back with Sammy Baird in the 58th minute, but the goal was not enough for them to make a comeback. The 2–1 win—coupled with Paraguay's 3–2 victory over Yugoslavia—guaranteed the French four points in the group standings and a spot in the quarterfinals. Yugoslavia, despite the loss, also finished with four points, good enough for second place.

Group 3 had opened with a Swedish triumph over Mexico. In the other group game, Wales and Hungary played to a 1–1 tie. Hungary took the lead with Boszik, one of just three returning players from four years earlier, with a goal after five minutes. Wales tied the game in the 27th minute with Juventus striker John Charles, who had joined his teammates just the day before the game. The 15,343 spectators at Jernvallen Stadium in Sandviken expected Hungary to go on its usual scoring spree. Instead, this Hungarian team was devoid of the attacking soccer that made it so great in 1958 and the game ended 1–1.

On June 11 at Rasunda Stadium in Stockholm, Wales once again played to a 1–1 tie, this time against Mexico. Wales took the lead with Ivor Allchurch in the 30th minute. The Mexicans pushed forward in an attempt to tie the game and finally did when Jaime Belmonte headed in the ball past Jack Kelsey in the 89th minute. The following day, the same venue played host to Sweden and Hungary. The hosts were looking for another win and a spot in the quarterfinals, while the Hungarians needed at least a point to keep their hopes alive. More than 38,000 fans packed into Rasunda Stadium to root on the home side and the Swedish players did not disappoint. The Hungarians dropped Hidegkuti, now 38, from the lineup and moved Boszik, a defender, to the midfielder in a playmaking role. The move was made to beef up the Hungarians offense, but proved futile against the hard-nosed Swedes. Kurt Hamrin put Sweden in the lead in the 38th minute and ended the half ahead, 1–0. In the second period, Lajos Tichy, part of a new generation of Hungarian players to emerge since 1954, tied the score in the 55th minute. Once again, a Hungarian goalfest was expected. It never happened and Hamrin scored the game-winner a minute later when his shot deflected off Grosics and into the net. Sweden had qualified for the quarterfinals. Hungary, Wales, and Mexico were left to battle it out for the second spot.

On June 15 in Stockholm, Sweden rested five starters, including Liedholm, against Wales, who needed at least a tie to push a playoff game. The Welsh were lucky not to lose the game and had Jack Kelsey to thank for keeping the Swedes off the score sheet. The game ended 0–0, while Hungary defeated Mexico, 4–0, in Sandviken to set up a playoff match against Wales. Tichy's two goals helped the Mighty Magyars back to their old goal-scoring ways.

The playoff between Wales and Hungary took place two days later in Stockholm. A sparse crowd of 2,832 gathered at Rasunda Stadium to see which of these two teams would advance to the quarterfinals. Tichy scored once again, his fourth goal in three games, in the 33rd minute. The Hungarian goal-scoring machine appeared to be in full swing, until Wales was able to tie the game in the 55th minute with Allchurch, his 35-yard shot beating Grosics. The Magyars had put on a dismal defensive showing and it wasn't over. A misplayed pass from Grosics to one of his defenders was intercepted by Terry Medwin, who slotted the ball past the unlucky goalkeeper for the 2–1 winner. The upset was complete and the Magyars were sent home packing. Any doubt that the Hungarians were not what they used to be was put to rest after the loss.

Group 4, meanwhile, opened on June 8 at Rimnersvallen Stadium in the city of Uddevalla with a match between Brazil and Austria. The

Brazilians had fielded entertaining teams during the postwar years and the team coached by Vicente Feola was even more fun to watch with its innovative 4–2–4 formation. Brazil's use of four strikers would guarantee another offensive team—one that would be difficult to defeat. The Austrians tried to do just that, but Brazil—which featured a new generation of stars—would prove to be too formidable for the Austrians. Those new stars, which included Garrincha and Zagallo, delighted crowds. The Brazilians blanked Austria, 3–0, with two goals from Mazola and one from Nilton Santos.

In Göteborg, England and the Soviet Union played to a 2–2 tie at Nya Ullevi Stadium. England's lineup was confident of at least a tie after tying the USSR 1–1 during a friendly in Moscow just three weeks before the start of the tournament. Nevertheless, England coach Walter Winterbottom knew he was taking a depleted roster to his third World Cup finals after the 1958 Munich air crash had tragically robbed him of Manchester United's stars Duncan Edwards, Tommy Taylor, and Roger Byrne. Against the USSR, England went down early when Nikita Simonian opened the scoring after thirteen minutes when he unleashed a powerful shot that goalkeeper Colin McDonald was not able to stop. The Soviets made it 2–0 with Alexander Ivanov in the 55th minute, but the undeterred English mounted a comeback. Midfielder Derek Kevan headed the ball past a diving Lev Yashin following Billy Wright's free kick to put England on the scoreboard. The English were able to tie the game when Johnny Hayes was brought down in the box with five minutes left to play. Tom Finney converted from the spot to tie the score at 2–2. Winterbottom was apprised of more bad news following the game when Finney was ruled out of the rest of the tournament with a right knee injury.

The Soviet Union went on to defeat Austria, 2–0, on June 11 at Ryavallen Stadium in Boras. A goal in each half, one from Anatolyi Ilyin in the 15th minute and another from Valentin Ivanov in the 62nd minute, gave the USSR three points in the standings. Yashin, who recorded his first World Cup shutout, was spectacular in goal. Yashin, just four months shy of his 29th birthday, had emerged as the world's greatest goalkeeper. Famous for his all-black uniforms—a style that distinguished him from his red-shirted teammates—gave him the appearance of a hulking spider. His ability to reach for the ball, when so many others in the same position likely couldn't, made him a standout shot-stopper. Yashin's acrobatic style, panther-like reflexes, and poise under pressure

*Soviet goalkeeper Lev Yashin (center) soars into the air to make a save in the USSR's game against England in 1958 (Credit: EMPICS).*

made him a joy to watch—and a torment for opposing strikers who often tried in vain to get balls past him.

In the group's other showdown, between Brazil and England in Göteborg, a crowd of 40,895 flocked to Nya Ullevi Stadium to watch this clash of soccer titans. Instead, the fans witnessed two teams of contrasting styles that ultimately resulted in a scoreless game. The offensive-minded Brazilians controlled the pace in the first half, while the English defense did a solid job fending off those plays. In the second half, the teams appeared to switch roles and the Brazilians were the ones on defense. The 0–0 tie meant England had to defeat Austria for a spot in the quarterfinals.

On June 15, Brazil, which featured Pelé in the starting lineup for the first time, took on the Soviet Union in Göteborg before 50,928 spectators at Nya Ullevi Stadium. Pelé had been suffering from a right knee injury and was unfit to play in the two previous games. Team captain Bellini, along with Dida and Nilton Santos, met with Machado and Feola to express their concerns with the starting lineup. The players complained that midfielders Dino Sani and Joel Antonio Martins lacked the flair that was needed to win games. Sani and Zito played a more European-style game, which focused more on strength and stamina rather than individual verve and skill. Feola agreed and, after the team's lackluster performance against England, decided to start Pelé, Zito, and Garrincha. *Jogo bonito*—the "Beautiful Game" the Brazilians play with such skill, joy, and delight—was born. The alliance between skill, imagination, and discipline would forever transform the way teams played the game and put Brazil on the path to becoming the most successful national team ever. The changes worked and the Brazilians got on the board after just three minutes with a goal from Vavá. The Brazilian striker added another in the 77th minute to down the Soviet Union, 2–0. Brazil finished first in the group and was off to the quarterfinals. Brazil had played with such flair and pizzazz, that Soviet coach Gabriel Katchalin was dumbfounded following the game. "I can't believe that what we saw this afternoon was soccer. I have never seen anything so beautiful in my life," he said.[11]

While the Brazilians marched forward, England tied Austria, 2–2, in Boras to set up a playoff game against the USSR. The teams tangled with each other on June 17 at Nya Ullevi Stadium in front of 23,182 fans. The English team, looking for some offense, fielded Peter Brabrook and Peter Broadbent. A budding player named Bobby Charlton, who had survived the Munich air disaster, sat on the bench, while Brabrook and Broadbent sparked the offense and created several scoring chances. Yashin and the Soviets were lucky on several occasions, particularly after two Brabrook shots hit the post. It appeared to be just a matter of time before England would score. In the 63rd minute, however, a poor throw from Colin McDonald was stolen by Ilyin, who blasted a shot that smacked against the post and rolled over the line. The goal proved to be the game-winner for the USSR, which marked its World Cup debut with a berth to the quarterfinals.

Pelé had finally made his World Cup debut against the USSR. Though he had failed to score, the skinny teen had made his presence felt on the field. Pelé was dwarfed by his larger, more muscular teammates and even joked about his short stature. He said that he was sure that "some of those in the stands are faintly amused to see a child on the field in a World Cup match and some are probably outraged that an important event such as a World Cup match should be reduced to parody by having an infant on the field. The more sentimental, however, probably feel pity for a team so reduced in talent as to face the need to bring children along with them."[12] Pelé's modesty aside, he was an assertive player, even at such a young age, who knew he had every right to play along side the world's best. He maintained his composure against the Soviets—even during his beloved national anthem before the start of the game—and never once appeared to lose control of his confidence. "All of us are living a dream, but none more so than me. I try not to waste time trying to analyze this strange feeling. I know this is no time to be distracted," he said.[13]

Pelé had grown up like many Brazilian boys, impoverished and playing soccer in the dusty streets with a ball made of rags. In 1956, Pelé, with the help of World Cup veteran Waldemar de Brito, traveled to São Paulo to try out for Santos. Pelé signed his first pro contract with the Brazilian club and went on to score four goals in his first game. A year later, Pelé earned a call up to the national team. The World Cup was just the beginning for the blooming star.

## Quarterfinal Action: Eight Teams Remain

The four quarterfinal games were all played on June 19 at four different venues. In Malmö, West Germany faced Yugoslavia in a game that quickly turned into a dreary defensive display. The only goal of the game was scored by Rahn in the 12th minute.

In Rasunda Stadium, Sweden was able to defeat the Soviet Union, 2–0, in front of 31,900 fans. The Soviets, who had played England for a spot in the quarterfinals just forty-eight hours earlier, appeared sluggish and tired for much of the contest. The Soviets were able to keep Sweden from scoring in the first half, clogging the midfield and relying on Yashin to do the rest. The Swedes reaped the rewards of their offensive push in the second period when Hamrin scored in the 49th minute. Agne Simonsson's goal two minutes from the end sealed the win. Next for Sweden was a date against West Germany in the semifinals.

In Norrkopping, France breezed by Northern Ireland, 4–0, as Fontaine added two more goals to his overall tally. Northern Ireland had also come off a grueling week, playing two games in three days and having to endure a daylong, 210-mile bus ride from Malmö. Uprichard didn't start in goal because of an injury and was replaced by Harry Gregg. Tom Casey was still nursing an injury after having had his left shin stitched up just a few days earlier. With Northern Ireland ailing, France was able to take the lead with Maryan Wisnieski in the 43rd minute. The French added two more with Fontaine in the 55th and 63rd minutes, before scoring a fourth goal with Piantoni in the 70th minute.

In Göteborg, Brazil and Wales clashed for the final semifinal spot. Pelé, who had become the media darling in the days leading up to the game, once again started. Vavá was injured and Feola replaced him with Mazzola. Wales put on a strong defensive showing in the first half, shutting down the Brazilians for the entire forty-five minutes. Wales held out for another twenty-five minutes in the second half until Pelé took a perfect pass from Didi, kicking the ball straight at Kelsey. The potent shot rolled off the goalkeeper and in for his first World Cup goal. "I have no idea how many times I ran and jumped, ran and jumped, all the while screaming 'Goooooooaaaaaaalllll!' like a maniac. I had to get rid of that tremendous pressure of relief and joy. I don't know what was inside me. I was crying like a baby, babbling, while the rest of the team pummeled me, almost suffocating me," said Pelé.[14] Brazil won 1–0 and Pelé had finally become a star. Next up for Brazil was a semifinal clash with France and the uncontrollable Fontaine.

## Semifinals: Final Four

On June 24, Sweden and West Germany faced off for a shot at the final at Nya Ullevi Stadium. A crowd of 49,471 fans packed the stands to watch their national team. Sweden and its fans began to believe that they could reach the final, just as coach George Raynor had predicted at the start of the tournament. The home team's other games lacked the patriotic atmosphere that had been such a staple of past World Cups. Indeed, the Swedish fans had showed apathy toward the team for much of the competition, but now seemed to rally around them, especially after organizers bussed in cheerleaders to help the crowd out. On paper, the West Germans were the stronger team and Rahn and Seeler were the most feared players in the lineup. Zsolt, considered one of the greatest referees at the time, escorted both teams onto the field as the crowd cheered on the hosts. That high level of patriotism seemed to propel Raynor's team, even though the West Germans scored first:

Hans Schafer put the ball past Kalle Svensson off a cross from Seeler. The Swedes tied the game 1–1 going into halftime with Lennart Skoglund, who played for Serie A club Inter Milan.

In the second period, Sweden attempted a comeback and got Zsolt's help when the referee red carded Erich Juskowiak in the 58th minute—Juskowiak had retaliated after he was fouled by Hamrin. Several players argued with Zsolt following the call, which did nothing to change his mind, and West Germany was down to ten players. That wasn't the only trouble for the defending champions. The team lost Walter for ten minutes while he received medical attention on the sidelines. Sweden used the two-man advantage to open up more space, allowing the hosts to control the pace and flow of the game and taking the lead for the first time with Gunnar Gren's goal in the 81st minute. The crowd went wild. With the West German defense flung wide open, Hamrin was able to dribble right into the box to put Sweden ahead, 3–1, with two minutes left to play. The Swedes knocked off the champions and were one game away from winning the trophy.

At Stockholm's Rasunda Stadium, Brazil and France squared off in a game that promised a high-level of skill and scoring. The French were led by Fontaine and Kopa, while the Brazilians featured the budding Pelé and a collection of stars. Brazil wasted no time taking the lead when Vavá blasted a volley past Claude Abbes in the first minute. France tied the score with Fontaine seven minutes later, putting the ball past Gilmar, who gave up his first goal of the tournament. The fast-paced game included so many individual talents that every foray in the penalty box could have resulted in a goal. On one of those plays, Didi put Brazil ahead, 2–1, in the 39th minute. The French were at a disadvantage after Robert Jonquet was injured in the 35th minute following a collision with Vavá. The French defender limped around the field for the rest of the game. The Brazilians had caught a huge break and the French played the remainder of the game with virtually ten players. The second half was the all-Pelé show. The teen sensation scored three goals in a span of twenty minutes. His third goal was perhaps the most spectacular, lofting a volley from the edge of the box that was unstoppable for Abbes. Piantoni scored for France seven minutes from the end, but what had started out as a close game ended in a 5–2 win for Brazil.

## Final

The final match between Sweden and Brazil was slated to be played on June 29 in Stockholm. Organizers now hoped that the country's new-found love for their national team would create an atmosphere of ardor and enthusiasm worthy of a World Cup final and, more importantly, be able to unnerve the Brazilians. Before the final could be played, France defeated West Germany, 6–3, on June 28 in the third-place game in Göteborg. The game featured four goals by Fontaine, bringing his total at the tournament to thirteen—a record for a single World Cup tournament that stands to this day. The record appeared to be a remarkable feat for a player who traveled to Sweden as a reserve with a small chance of playing in any games. With the third-place match wrapped up, preparations for the final were in full swing. Havelange, who had flown back to Rio on the eve of the game, called organizers and wanted assurances that the referee chosen for the game—which would be Maurice Guige of France—would be impartial, not succumbing to the home crowd's desire for victory. Havelange also gained a psychological edge when he asked organizers not to allow the cheerleaders to attend the game. The organizers obliged and the Swedes went back to their subdued demeanor. The Brazilian fans who made the trip, however, would be as loud as ever. The Swedish camp, however, remained optimistic. Raynor, who had correctly predicted a trip to the final, was confident that winning the trophy was a possibility. "If the Brazilians go down a goal, they'll panic all over the place," he said.[15]

Nearly 50,000 spectators showed up for the final with millions more watching on TV. The Brazilians had improved with every game and had found a new star in Pelé. Sweden had the home-field edge and King Gustav watched from the stands. A heavy rain the day before the game ensured that the match would be played on a slick surface, something that Sweden hoped would dampen Brazil's razzle-dazzle offense. Raynor's team took the lead with Liedholm after just four minutes with a low shot that beat Gilmar to his right. Pelé and his teammates trailed for the first time in the competition, but Raynor's prediction that straggling behind would result in a Brazilian downfall never materialized. Garrincha was a force on the flanks, but his efforts early on were fruitless. Brazil, however, tied the game in the ninth minute when Garrincha overcame two Swedish defenders and crossed the ball to a waiting Vavá, who put it past Svensson. With the game tied 1–1, the

Brazilians exuded the confidence that had made them so hard to beat in previous games. Garrincha was unstoppable and the Brazilians took the lead in the 39th minute with an almost identical play as their first goal. Garrincha—nicknamed the "Little Bird"—flew down the wing and crossed the ball to Vavá, who scored his second of the game. Brazil took the lead into the locker rooms.

The second half belonged to Pelé much like in the semifinal clash against France. Pelé left his mark on the game in the 55th minute when he trapped the ball at the edge of the box, hooked the ball over his own head, rounded a defender and blasted the ball past Svensson. The Swedes were finished, but not the Brazilians. Zagallo beat four defenders and rammed in a fourth goal in the 68th minute. The goal unleashed tears of joy from Zagallo as the carnival-like atmosphere that emanated from the Brazilian cheering section.

The Swedish fans had something to celebrate when Simonsson pulled one back and notched another goal, but Brazil made it 5–2 with Pelé, who headed in a well-placed Zagallo cross after he had back-heeled the ball to him. Even on the wet grass, the Brazilian team was able to pull off *jogo bonito*, weaving its series of magical passes and scoring goals, to win its first World Cup.

Pelé and his teammates were in tears when Guige blew the final whistle. The ghosts of 1950 had finally been exorcised and Brazil was finally world champion after six failed attempts. Pelé clasped his hands and covered his face as tears flowed down his face while his teammates crowded around him. The indelible image of Pelé crying portrayed the elation of an entire nation. The image was a perfect ending to a tournament highlighted by Brazil's passionate and artistic performance, which grew to a crescendo with each game and culminated when Bellini lifted the Rimet Trophy amid a sea of reporters and photographers. In a sign of ultimate sportsmanship, the Brazilian players paraded around the field carrying a Swedish flag, much to the delight of the home fans and Pelé received a standing ovation from the crowd. The players were feted as national heroes upon their arrival in Brazil the following day. Pelé, who had left his hometown with a train ticket just two years earlier in the hopes of making it big, returned home on a plane as a world champion. "'Playing [Pelé] would be like sending a lamb to the slaughter,'" Havelange recalled being told by people in the Brazilian FA before the tournament.[16] "It's certainly true that soccer was a much tougher game back then, but I stood my ground. Pelé came with the squad and was a revelation." Pelé had lived up to his billing. Now he was expected to deliver a second title.

## NOTES

1. Quoted from fifaworldcup.yahoo.com/06/en/p/pwc/1950.html.

2. BBC News, "Their Finest Footballing Hour," news.bbc.co.uk/sport3/worldcup2002/hi/history/newsid_1749000/1749379.stm (April 2, 2002).

3. Bob Ford, "Soccer Underdogs Top Dogs At Last," *Philadelphia Inquirer* (April 27, 2005), E01.

4. Cantor, Andres, *Goooal: A Celebration of Soccer* (New York: Simon & Schuster, 1996), 64.

5. Morrison, Ian, *The World Cup: A Complete Record* (Derby UK: Breedon Books Sport, 1990), 97.

6. Morrison, *The World Cup: A Complete Record*, 104.

7. Cantor, *Goooal: A Celebration of Soccer*, 74.

8. Morrison, *The World Cup: A Complete Record*, 106.

9. Cantor, *Goooal: A Celebration of Soccer*, 75.

10. Cantor, *Goooal: A Celebration of Soccer*, 77.

11. Cantor, *Goooal: A Celebration of Soccer*, 84.

12. Harry Harris, *Pelé: His Life and Times* (London: Robson Books, 2000), 39.

13. Harris, *Pelé: His Life and Times*, 40.

14. Harris, *Pelé: His Life and Times*, 43.

15. Harris, *Pelé: His Life and Times*, 46.

16. Havelange, Joao, "My World Cups," 2005, Retrieved from www.fifaworldcup.yahoo.com/06/en/p/havelange/5058.html (January 2, 2006).

# 4

# PELÉ THE KING

## 1962

FIFA controversially awarded the 1962 tournament to Chile at a meeting in Lisbon in 1956. Two other countries had put together bids (West Germany and Argentina), but FIFA agreed the competition couldn't be held in Europe for a third consecutive time. West Germany's application was rejected and Chile's candidacy eventually beat out Argentina. The Chilean people embraced the chance to host the competition and looked forward to the world's greatest sporting event coming to their country. However, that dream was almost shattered when on May 22, 1960, the country's idyllic coast was rocked by one of the worst earthquakes of the twentieth century. The epicenter, located approximately 400 miles south of the capital, Santiago, shook the ground when a plate of the earth's crust had slid beneath the South American continent. Fifteen minutes after the quake, the tremors created a tsunami. The disaster brought with it 75-foot waves that slammed against the Chilean coast and reverberated across the Pacific Ocean. Thousands had fled the quake by jumping into boats, but that proved a deadly decision. The tsunami wiped out villages and obliterated a great deal of the country's infrastructure. The death toll reached 5,700 worldwide due to the earthquake and tsunami, which caused destruction around the entire Pacific. Most of Chile was in ruins.

The country's bid risked elimination, but FIFA decided to stick with its choice despite the destruction. Chilean FA president Carlos Dittborn, who spearheaded the move to get the World Cup to his country, uttered these famous words: "We must have the World Cup because we have nothing."[1] That phrase gave Dittborn the drive to put on the greatest tournament ever. The Chileans built new stadiums, including the magnificent National Stadium in Santiago at the foot of the Andes Mountains and, despite being a poor nation, Chile vowed not to disappoint as hosts. Unfortunately, Dittborn never saw his dream come to fruition. In April 1962, a month before the tournament was to kick off, Dittborn died of a heart attack at age thirty-eight. Understandably, the stress that came with organizing such a large event had gotten to him. The country was once again heartbroken. Dittborn's death was another tragic reminder that misfortune could strike at any moment. But Dittborn's encouraging words following the earthquake resonated with the people. The stadium in Arica, near the Chilean border with Peru, was renamed in Dittborn's honor. Along with this venue and the National Stadium in Santiago, games were also slated to be played in Rancagua and in the newly built Sausalito Stadium in picturesque Viña del Mar.

Fifty-six countries—a new record—attempted to be one of the sixteen countries to qualify for the tournament. South America would be represented by five countries: hosts Chile and champions Brazil, along with Uruguay, Argentina, and Colombia. CONCACAF was once again represented by Mexico, while Europe had ten entrants: Hungary, Czechoslovakia, Yugoslavia, Bulgaria, Soviet Union, Italy, West Germany, Switzerland, England, and Spain. Sweden and France, who had finished as runners-up and third, respectively, four years earlier, failed to qualify this year. Their absence would deprive the tournament of two of the world's most entertaining teams, ushering in a new era of pragmatic and defensive-minded tactics. The new mindset would ensure a low-scoring tournament.

## Group Play

The finalists were placed in the following groups with Brazil, Italy, England, and Uruguay as the seeded teams. The draw, held in Santiago on January 18, 1962, came up with the following first round:

Group 1: Colombia, Uruguay, Soviet Union, and Yugoslavia
Group 2: Chile, Italy, Switzerland, and West Germany

Group 3: Brazil, Czechoslovakia, Mexico, and Spain
Group 4: Argentina, Bulgaria, England, and Hungary

Chile prepared for the tournament with enthusiastic displays of patriotism as nationalism reached an all-time high. The tournament began on May 30 with the opening ceremonies in the National Stadium. The ceremony, however, was tinged with sadness—the 65,000 fans who crowded inside the stadium to watch Chile play Switzerland recalled Dittborn's determination to bring the World Cup to his country. Two of Dittborn's sons raised the flags of Chile and Switzerland in a sign of unity and a marching band delighted the crowd.

At this game, the world was introduced to a new era of cynical soccer. Swiss manager Karl Rappan was one of the original exponents of this style with his so-called door bolt system that was the predecessor to Italy's infamous *catenaccio*, a method that relied heavily on a potent defense and abandoned attacking. First utilized by the Swiss at the World Cup in 1954, the defensive system saw the Swiss take the lead with Rolf Wuthrich after seven minutes. The Swiss sat on their hands and enjoyed the 1–0 lead, hoping to defend it for the remainder of the game. The plan failed and Leonel Sanchez scored two goals, the equalizer in the 44th minute right before halftime on a penalty kick and the second six minutes into the second half. Hernan Ramirez scored again in the 55th minute as the hosts won, 3–1. The result made everyone sit up and take notice.

Italy came to the competition with a winning attitude. The *Azzurri* had spent the last decade rebuilding and brought with them a budding star in Gianni Rivera and a new batch of *oriundi*—a new generation of naturalized South Americans who had come in handy during the 1930s. This time, the team featured Brazilian-born José Altafini and Argentine-born Omar Sivori and Humberto Maschio. They were viewed by most South Americans as traitors, selling out to wealthy Italian clubs who were more than happy to open their checkbooks to buy them and then have them masquerade as Italian citizens. The Chileans particularly viewed this as treasonous and had nothing but contempt for the *Azzurri*. The tensions between the Italians and Chileans was worsened by the Italian press, which had sent several reporters to Chile a few weeks before the start of the tournament to report on the country's political and social conditions following the earthquake. Corrado Pizzinelli, a reporter with the Florence-based newspaper, *La Nazione*, managed to outrage Chileans when he wrote that the country was plagued by a series of problems, including prostitution, illiteracy, and wretchedness.[2] Italian journalists bemoaned the country's poverty-stricken conditions and expressed disappointment that Italy had to play in such a grim setting. As a result of the criticisms, the game between Chile and Italy—who were both placed in Group 2—became a tense affair. No one could imagine the violence and chaos that would ensue once the teams walked onto the field.

Group 1, meanwhile, provided some upsets and near upsets as Uruguay narrowly defeated Colombia, 2–1, on May 30 at Dittborn Stadium after taking the lead in the first period. Colombia shocked the Soviet Union four days later, coming back from a 3–1 deficit to tie the game, 4–4. The usually reliable Yashin had a terrible game, even letting in a goal directly off a corner kick. The USSR team had emerged as one of the toughest teams in Europe after winning the inaugural European Championship in 1960, but had opened the World Cup on the wrong foot. The country's Communist regime had pumped lots of money into various Olympic programs in an attempt to show the world its superiority. Soccer was no different. The Soviets were out to show their supremacy as a world power, both on and off the field, and there was no better way to do that than winning the World Cup. By the time the tournament came to an end, the Soviets, once comparable to fine caviar, would become a World Cup leftover. Before the tie against Colombia, the USSR and Yugoslavia had played a brutal game on May 31 highlighted by vicious tackling, even though no players were ever red carded. The players who did leave the field had to be carried off on stretchers after Muhamed Mujic broke Eduard Dubinski's left leg. The Soviets won, 2–0, and qualified for the quarterfinals. Yugoslavia, who defeated Uruguay, 3–1, on June 2, went on to trounce Colombia, 5–0, five days later to also qualify for the quarterfinals.

Group 2 produced a series of less exciting games, although the matches were not lacking in controversy. West Germany played Italy to a scoreless tie on May 31 in Santiago. Six days later, the West Germans defeated Chile, 2–0. While Switzerland lost all three of its games, the match that got the most attention was played June 2 between Chile and Italy. The game took on added meaning, considering all that was written about the host country in the Italian press in the weeks leading up to the game. The Chilean players, like many other people in the country, had taken offense to the insults and expressed their displeasure against the Italian players. The *Azzurri* retaliated. The violence resulted in two Italian players, Giorgio Ferrini and Mario David, getting red cards. The Italian player and "traitor" Maschio had his nose broken in a now-infamous incident when he was punched in the face by Chilean Raul Sanchez. The incident was captured by TV cameras but was never seen, or punished, by English referee Ken Aston. The Italians were reduced to nine players and unable to keep up with the Chileans. Striker Jaime Ramirez scored Chile's first goal in the 74th minute, putting in a header off a free kick. Chile added another goal fourteen minutes later with Jorge Toro to make it 2–0. The Italians, beaten and battered, were eliminated in a match that is infamously known as the "Battle of Santiago." The hosts, along with West Germany were off to the quarterfinals.

In Group 3, Brazil's 2–0 triumph over Mexico on May 30 at Sausalito Stadium was highlighted by Pelé's second-half goal. Unfortunately for the Brazilians, the goal would also be Pelé's last of the competition. *O Rei*, Pelé's Portuguese nickname meaning "The King," suffered a groin injury three days later in a 0–0 tie against Czechoslovakia. Pelé had been playing hurt even before the World Cup and compounded the injury when he failed to tell the team's medical staff about it. Pelé would spend the rest of the tournament struggling to nurse himself back to health, spending most of his time in a hot tub trying to get healthy. With Pelé on the sidelines, the country's hopes of winning a second World Cup rested on Garrincha. The "Little Bird" had been one of Brazil's best players in Sweden four years earlier and now was given the responsibility to spearhead the team's bid for another title. If most Brazilians regard Pelé as the most gifted player to ever wear the yellow jersey, then Garrincha will always be remembered for his spirited style and inventiveness. Garrincha, who grew up in the slums of Rio, had been born with his right leg bent inwards and nearly two inches shorter than the other. Garrincha possessed amazing dribbling skills, along with being an effective crosser and shooter. Garrincha was also a flamboyant figure off the field. He had a drinking problem, something that would lead to his premature death in 1983 at age 49.

# GARRINCHA

Another in the fine line of Brazilians to play at the World Cup, Manoel Francisco dos Santos, more famously known as Garrincha ("The Little Bird"), is considered one of the best dribblers in soccer history. Garrincha was born in Pau Grande, a district of Mage, in the state of Rio de Janeiro, in 1933. He suffered several birth defects, including a deformed spine and a deformation in his right leg that was two inches shorter than his left and curved outward.

The success he had on the playing fields were contrasted by the demons he dealt with in his private life. A heavy drinker, he was involved in several serious car accidents, most notably a crash into a lorry in April 1969 that killed his mother-in-law. He was married twice and had eight daughters, but records show that he fathered fourteen children as a result of several affairs.

Garrincha's talents were not discovered until his late teens. He signed with Brazilian club Botafogo in 1953. He helped Botafogo win the Brazilian Championship in 1957, and his talents on the wings convinced the national team selectors to name him to the 1958 World Cup team. Garrincha, who had made his national team debut in 1955, did not start in Brazil's first two games at the tournament, but did play in the third match against the USSR. Brazil won the game, 2–0. In the final against Sweden, Brazil fell behind 1–0, but equalized after Garrincha beat a defender on the right wing and sent a cross to Vavá, who scored. Before the end of the first half, Garrincha made a similar play, again setting up Vavá to put Brazil ahead, 2–1. Brazil won the game and its first World Cup trophy with Garrincha one of the best players at the tournament.

Garrincha put on weight after the World Cup as a result of his heavy drinking, so he was dropped from the national team for a friendly in Rio against England in 1959. Three years later, Garrincha lost the weight and found a place on the 1962 national team. With Pelé injured, he emerged as the team's leader. Garrincha played a leading role in Brazil's triumph and was voted as the tournament's best player. Following the 1962 tournament, Garrincha returned to Rio and led Botafogo to victory in the 1962 Brazilian Championship. Garrincha played for Botafogo for twelve seasons, scoring 232 goals in 581 games. In 1966, with his career on the decline, he was sold to Botafogo's rivals, the Corinthians. Two years later, he signed with Colombian club Atletico Junior. That same year he went back to Brazil and joined Flamengo, where he would play for two seasons, until his retirement in 1969.

*(continued)*

Garrincha played 50 games for Brazil between 1955 and 1966, and appeared at the 1958, 1962, and 1966 World Cups. Brazil only lost one game with him on the field during those three tournaments. He died in 1983 at age 49 from cirrhosis of the liver.

## World Cup Career Statistics

Tournaments played: 3
Games: 12
Goals: 5

Without Pelé, the Brazilians struggled. On June 6, the defending champions needed two late goals from Amarildo, who had replaced Pelé in the lineup, to beat Spain, who—despite having the powerful Real Madrid team as its backbone—finished at the bottom of the group. The Spanish had entered the tournament without the services of Alfredo Di Stefano, who was out with an injury. Furthermore, the *catenaccio* system used by Argentine-born coach Helenio Herrera was put to the test; the presence of Francisco Gento and Luis Del Sol and the enlistment of Hungarian-born Puskás did little to help their chances. The Czechoslovakians, who had defeated Spain, 1–0, on May 31, lost to Mexico, 3–1. Despite the loss, the Czechoslovakians finished second in the group behind Brazil for a spot in the knockout round.

Group 4 opened on May 30 at Braden Stadium in Rancagua with Argentina edging Bulgaria, 1–0, on a Hector Facundo goal after just four minutes before a paltry crowd of 7,134. The following day, Hungary pulled off a 2–1 upset of England. The Hungarians still had Grosics in goal—the sole survivor of the team that reached the final in 1954—and a new goalscorer in Florian Albert, who netted the game-winner in the 75th minute. On June 3, Hungary slaughtered Bulgaria, 6–1, and three days later tied Argentina, 0–0, to win the group. England defeated Argentina, 3–1, on June 2, with goals from Ron Flowers on a penalty kick, Bobby Charlton, and Jimmy Greaves. The English managed a scoreless tie against Bulgaria on June 7 to clinch the last remaining spot in the eight after beating out Argentina in the group standings on goal differential.

## Quarterfinals

In the quarterfinals, England came undone on June 10 at Sausalito Stadium in Viña del Mar against Brazil and the talented Garrincha. The Brazilians were uncontrollable. Garrincha made a mockery of his marker Ray Wilson, who struggled to keep up with the speedy Brazilian throughout most of the game. Garrincha's ability to fake players and move the ball past them with ease was dizzying for the English. Brazil won 3–1 and moved on to the semifinals.

The carnival continued for Chile the same day at Dittborn Stadium in Arica when Eladio Rojas scored the game-winner in a 2–1 victory over the Soviet Union, which featured another poor performance by Yashin. The hosts took to the field on the same day that Dittborn's widow gave birth to a boy and the tiny stadium was filled to capacity with 17,268 fans cheering on Chile. A Leonel Sanchez free kick in the 11th minute took Yashin by surprise and Chile was ahead, 1–0. The joy of the crowd, however, was short lived. The Soviets tied the score with Igor Chislenko in the 26th minute. Rojas hit the ball from 30 yards out a minute later to give Chile the 2–1 win. A few dozen Chilean fans rushed onto the field following the goal in a premature celebration, but the game resumed a few minutes later and played out once referee Leo Horn of Holland was able to restore order. Brazil and Chile made it through and were slated to meet in an all-South American semifinal. There was still European representation at the tournament, though, as the Czechoslovakians ousted Hungary on June 10 in Rancagua and Yugoslavia downed West Germany at the same time in Santiago—both games ending 1–0.

Chile's remarkable run came to an end on June 13 against Brazil at Santiago's National Stadium. Garrincha and Vavá each scored twice to down the hosts. Brazil, not playing the entertaining brand of soccer that had made the green and yellow famous four years earlier, was still the most potent and talent-filled team at the tournament compared to the negative exhibited by other nations. Chile did make a fight of it with Jorge Toro and Sanchez each scoring a goal in the 4–2 loss. More worrisome for the Brazilians, Garrincha was fouled by Eladio Rojas. He retaliated and was shown a red card, which meant he had to sit out the final. Brazil's opponents in the final would be the Czechoslovakians, who for the first time in the competition scored more than one goal, downing Yugoslavia, 3-1, in the other semifinal played the same day in Viña del Mar.

With the National Stadium in Santiago filled to a capacity crowd of 67,000, the hosts beat Yugoslavia, 1-0, on June 16 in the third-place game. Rojas scored a last-minute goal to give Chile the win. Rojas, who finished the tournament with two goals, was hailed a national hero and celebrations in the streets across the country lasted into the night. For the Chilean players and people, the victory was as sweet as winning the Rimet Trophy. Dittborn's dream of getting the country to host the World Cup had come true and now Chile had finished third—higher than anyone had predicted before the start of the competition. The country finally had found something positive to rally around.

## Final

The days leading up to the final exemplified both chaos and hope. There was a surprise reprieve for Brazil as Garrincha was ruled eligible to play in the final after the Brazilian government put pressure on FIFA not to punish him. The situation was made easier when the opposing Czechoslovakians made the unusual request that Garrincha be allowed to play—a petition that flew in the face of convention—and the Brazilian star was prepared to lead Brazil to a second title. Pelé, who had been working to recover, wanted to play in the final. Team doctors, putting aside their national pride, chose to err on the side of prudence and ruled that Pelé was in no condition to kick a ball. The team's coach, Aimore Moreira—brother of Zezé Moreira that coached Brazil in the 1954 World Cup—agreed and Pelé was out of the lineup.

The final was played on June 17 in Santiago in front of 68,679 spectators. For the second successive final, Brazil fell behind early, this time thanks to a Josef Masopust goal after fifteen minutes. The Czechoslovakian strategy was to maintain possession of the ball for as long as possible: without the ball, the Brazilians couldn't create plays. Such a smart strategy did not last, though, and like in Sweden four years earlier, the Brazilians responded immediately. Amarildo equalized just two minutes later when Czechoslovakian goalkeeper Viliam Schrojf was slow to react off his line and the ball breezed past him. The first half ended, 1-1.

The Czechoslovakian team held its own until midway through the second period when its defense fell apart under the weight of the Brazilian attack. On one of their many forays in the Czechoslovakian zone, Amarildo crossed the ball to Zito, who headed it into the goal for the 2–1 lead. The Brazilians didn't need Garrincha, who was double-teamed by defenders Jozef Jelinek and Ladislav Novak, as Zagallo did all the work in the midfield. With thirteen minutes left to play, Brazil virtually ended the game when Schrojf fumbled a high ball from Djalma Santos. That allowed Vavá, who was standing in the box, to tap the ball into the empty net for the 3–1 victory. The game may have lacked the incertitude of the 1950 final, but even without Pelé, Brazil had retained the World Cup. "We had been dealt a hard blow with Pelé's injury in the second game against Czechoslovakia, and the team felt it greatly. The loss of a player of his caliber at the start of the tournament caused me to think that things would go badly for us," recalled Zagallo.[3] The combination of Garrincha and Vavá, who both finished the tournament atop the scorers' table with four goals apiece, had proven too tough for the Czechoslovakians. Zagallo said the team worked as a unit and that "nothing was achieved by individuals alone."[4]

Brazil had finally established itself as a world soccer power and the rivalry that had developed between South America and Europe at this World Cup would be renewed at future tournaments.


## 1966

The World Cup was finally awarded to the sport's ancestral home when FIFA decided to name England host of the next tournament. The World Cup had entered the modern era and the 1966 tournament was the first to be broadcast in color to an international television audience. Marketing forces also descended upon the World Cup when FIFA unveiled a mascot and official logo for the first time. The mascot was a cartoon lion named "World Cup Willie" and his likeness was featured on the tournament's official poster. The English FA had prided itself over its organization in the year leading up to the start of the tournament and the World Cup was set to feature some of the greatest stadiums ever used for the competition. Everything appeared to be on schedule when the unexpected occurred four months before the start of the tournament. The Rimet Trophy, on display at Westminster's Central Hall as part of an exhibition to generate hype for the World Cup, was stolen on March 20, 1966. Embarrassed organizers tried their best to find the coveted trophy and enlisted the help of Scotland Yard inspectors. A nationwide hunt for the trophy ensued. A week later, a police dog named Pickles, a black and white mongrel, sniffed out the trophy, which was wrapped in a bundle of newspapers under some bushes in a London garden. Hours later, British authorities proudly hoisted the trophy in front of TV cameras, showing the world that it was back in safe hands. This wouldn't be the last time someone from England would lift the cup that year.

The tournament's format remained the same as in 1962 with sixteen finalists divided into four groups of four. The top two teams in each group advanced to the quarterfinals. Seventy teams entered the qualifying tournament, even though fifty-one teams eventually took part. England automatically qualified as hosts and Brazil joined the field as reigning champions. South Africa, who had an apartheid government, was disqualified in 1964 for violating antidiscrimination laws as outlined in FIFA's constitution. The U.S. team, in the meantime, recorded its first win in eleven years, defeating Honduras, 1–0, on March 21, 1965, in CONCACAF's Group 3 qualifier. Despite the win, the U.S., once again, finished behind Mexico and failed to clinch a spot to the final qualifying group. Mexico eventually won that group and moved on to the finals.

## Group Play

The World Cup draw was held on January 6, 1966, at London's Royal Garden Hotel and was the first ever to be televised. The participants placed as follows:

Group 1: England, France, Mexico, and Uruguay
Group 2: Argentina, Spain, Switzerland, and West Germany
Group 3: Brazil, Bulgaria, Hungary, and Portugal
Group 4: Chile, Italy, North Korea, and Soviet Union

The tournament opened five months later on July 11 with England taking on Uruguay at Wembley Stadium in London. The two-time world champions played defensively throughout most of the contest, with as many as eight players in their own half. The Uruguayans held the English to a scoreless tie. England, making its fifth-ever World Cup appearance, picked up the pace in its next two games, defeating Mexico, 2–0, on July 16 and France, 2–0, four days later to win the group. Roger Hunt scored three times in those two games (twice against France and once versus Mexico), but the English were hit with a bit of misfortune when Jimmy Greaves suffered a leg injury against France. He was forced to skip the quarterfinal game and was replaced with Geoff Hurst. The English didn't know it at the time, but the injury to Greaves would be a blessing in disguise. Meanwhile, Uruguay finished second in the group standings after defeating France, 2–1, on July 15 and playing Mexico to a 0–0 tie four days later.

Group 2 appeared to be the most competitive before the tournament started. West Germany, which featured defender Franz Beckenbauer, trounced Switzerland, 5–0, on July 12 at Hillsborough Stadium in Sheffield. A scoreless tie against a rough-and-tumble Argentina on July 16 at Villa Park in Birmingham and a 2–1 victory over Spain four days later gave West Germany first place in the group. Argentina, who had been reprimanded by FIFA for its violent play, defeated Switzerland, 2–0, on July 19 in Sheffield to assure itself a spot in the quarterfinals.

Group 3 featured the incumbent Brazilians, who were looking to win a third straight Rimet Trophy. In its way stood three European teams: Bulgaria, Hungary, and Portugal. On July 12, Brazil defeated Bulgaria, 2–0, at Goodison Park in Liverpool. The Brazilians had emerged victorious, but were definitely showing signs of aging. Feola was still in charge and Pelé was back in peak form. The Bulgarian defenders, unable to keep up with the flashy Brazilians, did whatever they could to stop them, including targeting their knees and ankles in an attempt to bring them down. Bulgarian defender Dobromir Zhechev, who played with Bulgarian club Spartak Sofia, engaged in a series of rough tackles as the incensed Brazilians tried their best to play around the rough play. Pelé spent most of the game limping as he played in agony. Zhechev's attempts succeeded and Pelé would have to miss the next game. The injury came after Pelé scored his team's first goal, a swerving shot on a free kick from outside the box, in the 15th minute. Garrincha scored

Brazil's other goal in the 63rd minute for the 2–0 win. The victory would be the only highlight for Brazil. A 3–1 loss to Hungary on July 15 at Goodison Park (without Pelé) and another defeat by the same score at the hands of Portugal (with Pelé) four days later ensured that the world champions would be eliminated. An incensed Pelé announced he would never play at a World Cup again, complaining that the referees had not done enough to protect him and his teammates. "I don't want to finish my life as an invalid," he said.[5]

Meanwhile, Portugal, who would go on to win the group, started the tournament off on the right foot, defeating Hungary, 3–1, on July 13 at Old Trafford in Manchester with two goals from Benfica midfielder Jose Augusto. Three days later, Portugal suited up against Bulgaria at Old Trafford, blanking them, 3–0. The World Cup's new star, Benfica forward Eusebio, had made it 2–0 in the 38th minute. The goal would be the first of nine he would score at the tournament to temporarily dethrone Pelé as the best player in the world. The Portuguese icon, known as the "Black Pearl," was born on January 25, 1942, and joined Benfica in 1961 at the age of 19. Born in Mozambique, Eusebio was made a Portuguese citizen and made his debut for the national team in October 1961 in a 4–2 loss to Luxembourg. Known for his dribbling and fierce right foot, Eusebio showed the world what a tremendous striker he was at the World Cup. In Portugal's 3–1 win over Brazil on July 19, Eusebio showed that he was better than Pelé, though in fairness *O Rei* was playing hurt and was again subjected to some rough treatment—this time at the feet of Portuguese defenders. Eusebio scored two goals that day in Liverpool. Pelé, meanwhile, hobbled off the field in defeat. Brazil's hopes had fallen with him. In the other group game played the following day, Hungary overcame Bulgaria, 3–1, in Manchester to reach the quarterfinals.

In Group 4, the Soviet Union—ever so efficient and technically superior to most teams in the world at the time—cruised to the quarterfinals. The USSR opened on July 12 at Ayresome Park in Middlesbrough, disposing of North Korea, 3–0, edging out Italy, 1–0, four days later at Roker Park in Sunderland, and defeating Chile, 2–1, on July 10 at the same stadium.

The remaining three teams in the group—Italy, Chile, and North Korea—battled for second place with the *Azzurri* the favorites to advance. Italy played Chile on July 13 at Roker Park in a rematch of the

"Battle of Santiago." The game was not as violent as the one played four years earlier, and the Italians were able to hold on for the 2–0 win.

The *Azzurri* needed a victory over North Korea to clinch a spot in the quarterfinals. What appeared to be a manageable feat turned into a nightmare. Both teams met in Middlesbrough on July 19 in what the Italians thought would be an easy victory. Forward Gianni Rivera, who had sat out the first two games, was ready to light up the scoreboard. The North Koreans, a team with no soccer pedigree, refused to play the role of sacrificial lamb. The game would turn into the biggest World Cup shocker since the United States beat England in 1950. The local crowd cheered on the underdogs, chanting "Ko-re-a! Ko-re-a!" every time the Italians touched the ball. The North Koreans knew that they were less experienced and smaller than the Italians, and made up for that by putting on a fast-paced display. The North Koreans tackled at every opportunity and fought for every ball. The Italians were dealt a major blow when defender Giacomo Bulgarelli was fouled by Pak Seung-zin in the 34th minute and was forced to leave the game. Seven minutes later the unthinkable occurred.

North Korean goalkeeper Lee Chan-myung cleared the ball and picked up by Pak Seung-zin, who beat Rivera and headed the ball toward the Italian goal, which was guarded by goalkeeper Enrico Albertosi. Pak Do-ik gathered the ball at the edge of the box and unleashed a shot from 15 yards out that made its way into the net. The rest of the game time ticked down and the Italians were unable to score. The North Koreans had to wait a day—and rejoice in Chile's 2–1 loss to the USSR—before it could celebrate reaching the quarterfinals.

As for the Italians, the loss was the ultimate humiliation. The team flew back to Genoa in the wee hours of the night in the hopes of avoiding the wrath of the fans. The move failed. Fans threw tomatoes and rotten fruit at the players as they made their way through the airport. Italy's national team, two-time world champions, was at its lowest point ever. Only time—and future success—would cancel the embarrassment of that day. The Italian players were taunted with chants of "Pak Do-ik" wherever they went, including when appearing for their club teams. "That was a name that I couldn't shake off for two years," recalled Albertosi. "Every time I played, and I was on the road, the name Pak Do-ik was mentioned. It was a name I wanted to forget, but the fans always reminded me of it."[6]

## Quarterfinals

The quarterfinals featured the eight most-talented teams at the tournament. The four games were simultaneously played at four different venues on July 23. Hosts England took on Argentina at Wembley Stadium in front of 90,584 fans in a game that would become better known for its brutality rather than its beautiful plays. The game pitted one of the strongest teams in Europe against one of the toughest from South America in yet another intercontinental clash. The Argentines, once again, used a series of rough tackles in an effort to choke England's attack. The game disintegrated into mayhem. Argentina's relentless brutality was punished by West German referee Rudolf Kreitlein, who rushed around the field flashing yellow cards and scribbling down names and numbers in a bid to bring the fouling to an end. The punishments didn't stop Argentina from executing foul after foul, though they did put on a marvelous display of short passes when they weren't aiming for Bobby Charlton's ankles. Antonio Rattin, who played for famed Argentine club Boca Juniors, was finally sent off in the 36th minute, not for a foul, but for getting in Kreitlein's face following a booking of a teammate. Rattin was sent off, but he refused to leave the game. What followed was eight minutes of embarrassment, which included FIFA officials and police trying to get Rattin off the field. The expression on Kreitlein's face spoke volumes. He could not communicate with the players in Spanish, but the annoyed look that took over his face was understood by people of all languages. Rattin finally walked off the field, though he took his time, exchanging insults with the crowd and occasionally looking behind him to watch the game. The Argentineans, down to ten players, played a better game despite the numerical disadvantage. The English were unable to penetrate the Argentine midfield and anticipation turned to exhaustion for the players under the baking London sun. England persevered, partly due to the crowd's encouragement, and Hurst was able to net the game's only goal with thirteen minutes left to play. A Peters cross was met brilliantly by Hurst's head for the 1–0 win.

Meanwhile, West Germany played Uruguay in Sheffield in another European–South American clash. The Uruguayans, who had played so defensively in the first round, also employed roughness to bog down the West Germans. The plan failed. The West Germans, who had taken a 1–0 lead with midfielder Helmut Haller, caught a break in the 50th minute when Uruguay's captain, defender Horacio Trouche, was kicked by Lothar Emmerich. Trouche returned the favor, kicking Emmerich in the stomach. Emmerich lay on the ground as the Uruguayan players surrounded English referee Jim Finney, claiming he was faking. Nonetheless, Trouche was shown a red card. On his way off the field, he got into Uwe Seeler's face, slapping it for good measure, as he walked into the locker room. Five minutes later, Uruguayan midfielder Hector Silva brought down Haller and Finney showed him a red card. Uruguay was down to nine men. The West Germans capitalized and Beckenbauer, solid on defense throughout the game, pushed forward. He had revolutionized the sweeper position and was showing exactly how to get it done against Uruguay. The West Germans scored three more goals—with Beckenbauer, Seeler, and Haller—to win 4–0.

In Liverpool, the Portuguese took on the feisty North Koreans. Riding high from their victory over the Italians, the North Koreans jumped out to a 3–0 lead in the first half. The scoring had all started with Seung-zin scoring in the first minute with a left-footed shot from the edge of the box. Lee Dong-woon made it 2–0 in the 21st minute after goalkeeper Jose Pereira misjudged the ball. A minute later, Yang Seung-kook scored North Korea's third goal—to the delight of the many English fans who had adopted the team when they played in Middlesbrough during the group stage. Rather than pack its defense, the North Koreans continued to attack. Unable to understand that a giant lead had to be defended, especially with the likes of Eusebio on the other team, the North Koreans left room in the back and exhausted themselves late in the first half. The astute Portuguese handed the reigns over to Eusebio, who single-handedly mounted a comeback. He scored in the 27th minute and added another in the 42nd minute off a penalty kick. Down 3–2 at halftime, Portugal came out attacking in the second period, tying the score, again with Eusebio, who slammed in a shot at the 55th minute from the edge of the six-yard box. Eusebio could have made it 4–3 following a great solo run, but he was brought down in the box. Israeli referee Menachem Ashkenasi pointed to the penalty spot. Eusebio got his goal after all—his fourth of the game—to give Portugal the lead. Augusto ended the scoring spree with twelve minutes left to play, putting the ball in past Chan-myung off a Eusebio corner kick. Portugal won 5–3 and was through to the semifinals and

Eusebio had consolidated his role as the most talented striker of his generation.

The Soviet Union played Hungary in Sunderland. The clash of Eastern European soccer powers turned into a one-sided affair with the USSR taking the lead after just five minutes when Eduard Malafeev's shot was mishandled by goalkeeper József Gelei and Igor Chislenko was just a step away, pouncing on the ball and placing it in goal for the 1–0 lead. The Soviet Union's second goal also came off a defensive error. Once again, a shot by Malafeev appeared to be sailing wide when Valeri Porkujan headed the ball past Gelei. Though Gelei failed to react quickly enough, the Hungarian defense was to blame for not foiling the play. Striker Ferenec Bene scored for Hungary, but the Soviets held on for the 2–1 win. •

## Semifinals: Four Teams Do Battle

The first semifinal was played between West Germany and the Soviet Union on July 25 at Goodison Park. The teams put together a poor game. The fear of losing loomed larger than the ambition needed to score goals. The physical game grew rougher with each passing minute and Igor Chislenko paid the price when he was red carded. West Germany took the lead in the 44th minute when Haller tapped in a cross from AC Milan defender Karl-Heinz Schnellinger. The Soviets played with ten men—and then actually nine after Iosif Sabo injured himself in the first half following a failed foul attempt on Beckenbauer. Yashin was in good form, but that didn't stop the West German team from doubling its lead. A Beckenbauer blast in the 68th minute fooled its way past Yashin. The USSR got onto the board with Valery Porkujan in the 88th minute to make it 2–1, but it was too late. The win booked West Germany a trip to the final.

In the other semifinal, England played Portugal on July 26 at Wembley Stadium in front of 94,493 fans. With all their games at Wembley Stadium, England got through to the final with little trouble. The game was free of the malicious fouling that had characterized some of the earlier games. England defender Nobby Stiles did a good job marking Eusebio and avoided fouling the Portuguese striker, almost going out of his way to play a clean game. Bobby Charlton made all the difference for England that afternoon, scoring two goals to lead his team to the final. Charlton scored his first goal in the 30th minute when he kicked the ball from 20 yards out Charlton's second goal came in the 79th minute when the Manchester United star scored from outside the box. The goal was so beautiful that several Portuguese defenders shook Charlton's hand after the ball landed in the net.

The English, leading 2–0, spent the remaining minutes trying to stifle Eusebio, double-teaming him each time he collected the ball, although they were smart enough not to foul him. But the vivacious Portuguese striker was able to score—this time from the penalty kick spot in the 82nd minute after Bobby's older brother Jackie Charlton batted the ball with his hand to prevent it from going into the empty net. Unable to score the equalizer, Eusebio and his teammates walked off the field losers and it was England, who won the game 2–1, who got the chance to play in the World Cup final.

**Final**

The final was played on July 30 at Wembley Stadium in front of 96,924 spectators, which included Queen Elizabeth and Prince Phillip. Another 400 million people around the world, including in the United States for the first time and broadcast on a two-hour tape delay on NBC, watched the hard-fought game on television via the BBC's feed. Both the English and West Germans entered the game confident they could win the Rimet Trophy and the teams put on an attractive, attacking display—a repudiation of the dour, defensive tactics that had characterized the rest of the tournament. When it was over, the game featured six goals, with the English taking a staggering 45 shots on net to West Germany's 35. The loud English crowd was silenced when Haller gave West Germany the lead after thirteen minutes. Bobby Moore's awareness helped England to a quick equalizer. Within six minutes, the crowd was back on its feet after Moore was fouled midway inside the German half. Rather than head back to defend, he picked himself up quickly and delivered an instant free kick on to Geoff Hurst's head to tie the game. The first half ended, 1–1. England came out determined after the break and put itself on the path to World Cup glory in the 77th minute when Martin Peters scored the go-ahead goal.

## BOBBY MOORE

One of the greatest English players ever, Bobby Moore was born in 1941 and captained England to the 1966 World Cup title. He also captained English club West Ham United for over a decade and is widely regarded as one of the greatest central defenders ever.

Moore joined West Ham as a teenager in 1956. He was eventually called up to the national team in 1962 as final preparations were being made for the World Cup. Moore had never played for the national team when he flew to Chile with the rest of the team, but made his debut in England's final pre-tournament friendly, a 4–0 win over Peru. Moore proved so impressive that he stayed with the team, but England was eventually eliminated in the 1962 quarterfinals against Brazil. A year later, and for the first time, Moore captained England in just his twelfth appearance in England's 4–2 victory over Czechoslovakia. In 1964, Moore lifted the FA Cup after West Ham defeated Preston North End, 3–2. That same year, Moore also overcame testicular cancer and was named as the English Football Writers' Player of the Year.

In 1965, Moore added more silverware to West Ham's trophy cabinet, lifting the European Cup Winners' Cup after defeating German club 1860 Munich 2–0 in the final. In 1966, England hosted the World Cup and Moore emerged as the team's leader to become one of the country's greatest sports icons.

Four years later at the 1970 World Cup, Moore was again named team captain. England's title defense was dealt a blow before the start of the tournament when an attempt was made to implicate Moore in the theft of a bracelet from a jewelry store in Bogota, Colombia, where the English were training prior to the World Cup. The accusation turned out to be fictional. Moore was arrested and then released. He traveled with the England team to play another match against Ecuador in Quito. He played in the friendly, but when the team plane returned to Colombia, Moore was detained and placed under four days of house arrest. The charges were eventually dropped and Moore joined his teammates in Mexico to prepare for the World Cup. The English team was eliminated in the quarterfinals at the hands of West Germany.

Moore joined Fulham in 1974, where he played for two seasons. He played for two teams in the North American Soccer League (NASL) for

(continued)

the San Antonio Thunder in 1976 and the Seattle Sounders in 1978. In his first year in the United States, he also made a final appearance on the international field for Team USA in games against Italy, Brazil, and England in the U.S.A. Bicentennial Cup. Moore retired in 1978.

Moore died from stomach cancer in 1993. A bronze statue was erected in 2007 outside the main entrance of the new Wembley Stadium to honor his memory.

## World Cup Career Statistics

Tournaments Played: 3
Games: 14
Goals: 0

A West German free kick with fifteen seconds to play gave Wolfgang Weber a close-range shot, tying the score, 2–2. The exhausted teams headed to overtime. Hurst's dubious goal, which glanced off the line after hitting the crossbar and awarded by Swiss referee Gottfried Dienst, put England ahead, 3–2 in the 98th minute. Hurst's goal and Dienst's decision generate controversy to this day. Photography and video technology have been unable to offer viewers decisive evidence on whether or not the ball crossed the line. Nonetheless, Hurst went on to score again 22 minutes later, his third goal of the game, to become the first player—and the only thus far—to record a hat trick in a World Cup final. The goal gave England the 4–2 win and the trophy—the first time a host nation had won the World Cup in thirty-two years. Moore walked up to the royal box to collect the trophy from Queen Elizabeth. Finally, the country that had invented the game was crowned the best team in the world.

## 1970

The World Cup returned to the Americas in 1970 after FIFA, six years earlier, decided to award the tournament to Mexico. Argentina had also vied for hosting rights, but lost its bid due to the country's precarious economy. The altitude and scorching heat, which topped 100 degrees in the summer, were the two main concerns when Mexico was named

*Pelé walks off the field a defeated man after Brazil's elimination at the 1966 World Cup (Credit: EMPICS).*

host. Mexico City, host of the 1968 Summer Olympics, already had a showpiece venue in the Azteca Stadium. The withering Mexican heat and thin air that came with playing at high altitudes were expected to wreak havoc on the health of players. Games were scheduled to be played at midday—in order to coincide with primetime TV hours in Europe—and players spent months leading up to the tournament training for such adverse conditions. Could a team from Europe win the World Cup in temperatures reaching an unbearable 100 degrees, or would it be a South American team accustomed to such a climate that would lift the Rimet Trophy? Champions England left nothing to chance and traveled to South America in May, a month before the tournament began, and set up camp in Bolivia and Colombia in the hopes of training under circumstances similar to what the players would face a few weeks later. But their South American sojourn ran afoul in Bogota when Bobby Moore was accused of shoplifting a bracelet from a jewelry store inside the Tequendama Hotel. Moore was subsequently charged with theft and placed under house arrest, apparently unaware of the Colombian pastime of accusing tourists of crimes they had never committed. England's preparations hit a temporary snag. Moore was released in time to play at the World Cup after a series of tense negotiations between English FA officials and Colombian police. Two years later, the store's owners were charged with conspiracy. Clearly, the accusations against Moore had been fabricated. The charges against him were later dropped.

On the other hand, Brazil was optimistic of its chances of winning the trophy for a record third time, though its preparations for the finals, underwritten by Havelange, were compromised in March, just three months before the finals. The team's coach, João Saldanha, was replaced by Zagallo, who had so successfully won the World Cup for Brazil as a player in 1958 and 1962. The switch in coaches was tinged with irony since Zagallo had been Saldanha's protégé while at Brazilian club Botafogo. Saldanha had given the team a new direction, but storm clouds began to gather over the team a year before the finals, culminating with his firing after he had contemplated dropping Pelé from the lineup. Saldanha and Pelé had locked horns, a power struggle that appeared to doom the team. With Zagallo at the helm, optimism was high again. A third trophy would mean the Brazilians would keep it forever: FIFA had determined in 1930 that a country that won the trophy three times could retire it and keep it forever. The Brazilians were eager to oblige and the rivalry between European and South American teams would intensify over the next month.

The biggest surprises were the absence of perennial contenders Argentina, Hungary, and Spain, not to mention Yugoslavia, who finished runners-up to Italy in the 1968 European Championship, and Portugal, who had placed third at the World Cup four years earlier, from the field of sixteen nations after all of them failed to qualify. Though the qualifiers went off without a hitch (and featured a record seventy-one countries), one game between Honduras and El Salvador triggered a war.

Known as the "Soccer War," the nations engaged in a tense, six-day conflict in 1969 that was enflamed by a riot that had broken out during the game, which El Salvador won, 3–0. The political situation in Honduras deteriorated. The government placed the blame on the nation's fledgling economy and on the 300,000 undocumented Salvadoran immigrants working in Honduras. In January 1969, the Honduran government refused to renew the 1967 Bilateral Treaty on Immigration with El Salvador that had been designed to regulate the flow of migrants. Three months later, the government announced it would expel those who had acquired property under agrarian reform without fulfilling the legal requirement that they be Honduran by birth. As tensions mounted, the World Cup qualifier between the two nations increased the hostilities. Violence broke out during the first game in Tegucigalpa, but the situation worsened during the second match in San Salvador. Honduran fans were roughed up. Meanwhile, an unknown number of Salvadorans were killed in Honduras as thousands began to flee the country. On June 27, Honduras broke diplomatic relations with El Salvador. On July 14, military action officially began. The Salvadoran air force attacked Honduras while the army launched a major offensive along the main road connecting the two nations. At first, the Salvadorans made rapid progress. The Salvadorans began to experience fuel and ammunition shortages after the Honduran air force crippled El Salvador's oil storage facilities. The war ended on July 20 after officials negotiated a cease-fire. When it was all over, 2,000 people had been killed. The process of qualifying for the World Cup went forward and El Salvador clinched a World Cup berth for the first time.

The tournament format witnessed two key changes. Per the usual, the sixteen finalists were placed into four groups with each playing the other one time in a round-robin format. The top two teams in each group advanced to the quarterfinals. The draw was held on January 10, 1970, in Mexico City. One change in the format was the tossing of a coin to determine a winner in the event teams were tied after overtime. Fortunately, such a maddening method was never needed.

## Group Play

Another departure from tradition was that there were no seeded teams. Instead, FIFA decided to separate countries based on geography and allowed for each group to have a mix of teams. The teams were grouped as follows:

Group 1: Belgium, El Salvador, Mexico, and Soviet Union
Group 2: Israel, Italy, Sweden, and Uruguay
Group 3: Brazil, Czechoslovakia, England, and Romania
Group 4: Bulgaria, Morocco, Peru, and West Germany

A significant rule change was the allowing of player substitutions during a game, which would be both a blessing and curse. The tournament kicked off on May 31 with a Group 1 game that pitted Mexico against the USSR. A capacity crowd of 112,000 packed into the boiling cauldron known as the Azteca Stadium, but first had to watch the opening ceremonies, which featured the release of 50,000 colorful balloons. The tedious game ended scoreless, but for the hosts it was a hard-fought point. The Mexicans were missing midfielder Alberto Onofre, who had broken his left leg four days earlier during practice. The Soviets had played cautiously and defensively for much of the contest, another sign that European teams might wilt under the adverse conditions. The game's only highlight came when team captain Albert Shesterniev was replaced by Anatoli Pusatch at halftime, becoming the first player to substitute another in the history of the tournament.

The Mexicans would live up to the expectations of an impatient country by advancing to the knockout phase, along with the Soviet Union, even though Mexico's 1–0 win over Belgium on June 11 at the Azteca Stadium resulted from a questionable penalty call. With 105,000 screaming fans inside the stadium, Argentine referee Angel Norberto Coerezza felt the pressure of the fans. The game's only goal came in the 15th minute when Javier Valdivia collided into Belgium's Leon Jeck in the penalty area. Jeck, who had successfully cleared the ball, was still on the ground after completing the play. Remarkably, Coerezza whistled a penalty kick in favor of the Mexicans and Gustavo Peña scored from the spot kick. Mexico was through to the quarterfinals for the first time ever.

Group 2 saw Uruguay and Italy prevail over Sweden and Israel after a series of dull games. The *Azzurri* defeated Sweden, 1–0, on June 3 at Luis Dosal Stadium in Toluca, which at nearly 8,800 feet above sea level was the highest altitude of any of the venues. Rivera was left out of the lineup and his role in the midfield went to Sandro Mazzola, although it was Angelo Domenghini who scored the game-winner. The Italians, anchored in the back by defender Giacinto Facchetti, played Uruguay to a scoreless tie three days later at Cuauhtemoc Stadium in Puebla, and garnered another 0–0 result on June 11 against Israel in Toluca. The *Azzurri* only needed a tie to advance and again Italian coach Ferruccio Valcareggi started Mazzola in the midfield. Rivera would only come in later, to replace Domenghini. The duel between Mazzola and Rivera over who would start had dogged Valcareggi before the start of the World Cup and only intensified once the tournament began. With the group stage complete, the Italians were through, but Valcareggi was no closer to deciding whether Mazzola or Rivera would start in the quarterfinals.

In Group 3, Brazil was pitted against England and two other traditionally strong teams in Czechoslovakia and Romania. In Brazil's opener against Czechoslovakia, Pelé audaciously attempted to lob a shot over goalkeeper Ivo Vikto from the midfield line, missing the goal by the slimmest of margins. The so-called "Clash of the Champions" between Brazil and England on June 7 at Jalisco Stadium in Guadalajara was one of those unique contests that lived up to all the pregame hype. A year before, the Brazilians had scraped by England, 2–1, in a friendly played at the Maracanã. This time, Brazil won again, 1–0, though the English were lucky not to lose by more. Goalkeeper Gordon Banks pulled arguably the greatest save ever on a Pelé header when he stopped the ball near the foot of the post. Emotions ran high throughout the game and featured a capacity crowd of 66,000, most of whom rooted for the Brazilians. The game's only goal came from the muscular Jairzinho in the 59th minute, following a pass from Tostão on the left side of the penalty area that resulted in a well-executed Pelé pass. Zagallo, famous for his luck, continued to shine. Tostão's recovery from a severe left eye injury on the eve of the tournament was a testament to that lucky streak. A ball had hit Tostão in the eye during practice, detaching his retina in the process. Two operations later and Tostão's vision was restored and so were Brazil's chances. The Brazilians clinched a spot in the quarterfinals on June 10 as a result of a 3-2 win over Romania in Guadalajara.

The next day, England joined the two-time champions after dispatching Czechoslovakia, 1-0, in Guadalajara. The only goal of the game came when Allan Clarke converted from the penalty spot following a handball by Vladimir Hagara in the box.

In Group 4, Peru made its World Cup debut by edging Bulgaria, 3-2, on June 2 at Guanajuato Stadium in Leon. The Peruvians trailed 2-0 at halftime, but put their offensive attacks into overdrive in the second period to mount a comeback. Peru, who went on to defeat Morocco, 3-0, on June 6, advanced to the quarterfinals along with West Germany. Runners-up four years earlier, the West Germans played its usual well-organized style, featuring a combination of hard-nosed defense and high-flying offense. The team featured the leadership of veterans like Seeler and Beckenbauer, not to mention the offensive abilities of striker Gerhard "Gerd" Müller, who had netted ten goals during the qualifying round. By the time his career came to an end, Müller set several records that remain unchallenged today. The Bayern Munich star scored 365 goals in 427 games in the Bundesliga and 68 goals in 62 games for West Germany. Despite their talent level, West Germany only narrowly defeated Morocco, 2-1, on June 2 in Leon with Müller scoring the game-winner twelve minutes from the end. West Germany went on to trounce Bulgaria, 5-2, on June 7 in Leon and a 3-1 victory over Peru three days later in the same stadium guaranteed them a spot in the knockout round.

## And Then There Were Eight . . .

The quarterfinals took place on June 14 and featured four teams from the Americas and four from Europe. The rivalry between the two continents would reach a boil at this point of the competition. Though some games featured regional rivalries—like Brazil versus Peru, and West Germany against England in a rematch of the 1966 final—the other two matchups pitted continent against continent in an all-out battle for world supremacy. Italy was pitted against Mexico, while Uruguay took on the Soviet Union.

The *Azzurri* took on Mexico in Toluca, turning on the pressure against the hosts after getting off to a slow start in their three group-stage matches. The Italians, who had played like they were in shackles in the first round, freely created plays. Down 1–0 after just twelve minutes the Italians tied the score when a shot by Domenghini found the back of the Mexican net. Teams were allowed for the first time at this World Cup to substitute players and Valcareggi found the task arduous, particularly when it came to choosing Mazzola or Rivera. The compromise was to start one of them, then replace him with the other. This controversial decision would ultimately come to haunt the Italians. Against Mexico, Mazzola played the first half, and was replaced by Rivera after the break. Rivera's uncanny ability to control the ball and create plays energized the *Azzurri's* attack. Rivera's cross allowed Gigi Riva to beat two Mexican defenders and put the ball in the goal for the 2–1 lead. Rivera also scored, putting in a rebound off a shot by Domenghini. The fourth Italian goal was another Rivera creation, sending in a pass to Riva for the 4–1 win. The goal silenced the Mexican crowd. The Italians had played a spirited game, though the players had been unable to sleep the night before—since dozens of Mexicans decided to sing and dance in the streets and on the roof of the hotel where they were staying. Following the loss to Italy, the celebrations that had enraptured Mexico were over. The North Korean monkey was finally off Italy's backs. The victory also ensured the Italians would be jeered by Mexican fans for the rest of the tournament.

The USSR and Uruguay played a tough game at the Azteca. The *Celeste*, the two-time World Cup winners, were in the midst of rebuilding its soccer reputation while the Soviet team, a formidable opponent with a biting attack, did its best to penetrate the Uruguayan defense. The match ended scoreless and went into extra time. With the clock winding down, a cross by Luis Alberto Cubilla, which clearly went over the end line, made its way into the penalty area. Midfielder Victor Esparrago latched onto the ball and scored in the 117th minute, although Dutch referee Laurens Van Ravens failed to see that Cubilla's pass was out of play. The goal stood. Again, the mighty Soviets had failed to reach the final.

Brazil, who had been the crowd's favorite from the start, played an entertaining game against Peru. Roberto Rivelino's left foot gave Brazil the lead. His teammate Tostão made it 2–0, but Peru was able to pull one back. But Brazil's energetic and free-flowing attack took advantage of Peru's relatively weak defense. Pelé's long shot was assisted into the goal by Tostão, bringing Brazil up 3–1. Again, Peru responded in the 70th minute. Teófilo Cubillas scored to cut Brazil's lead to 3–2. Jairzinho ended any dream of a Peruvian comeback when he scored in the 75th minute, giving the South American giants a 4–2 victory.

The last quarterfinal pitted England against West Germany. Ahead 2–0, England appeared to have West Germany beaten. England coach Alf Ramsey had committed a tactical blunder and decided to take out Bobby Charlton so as to rest him for the semifinals. The move, though necessary because of the intense heat, hurt the English. Without Charlton as playmaker, England lost its ability to create plays and was unable to fend off the waves of German attacks. After Beckenbauer made it 2–1, West Germany tied the score with eight minutes remaining with a Seeler header. The English defense had not been able to catch the chubby midfielder in the offside trap and the perfectly taken header was able to slip in past backup goalkeeper Peter Bonetti, who hesitated on the play. Bonetti had replaced Banks, who had suffered from a bout of food poisoning on the eve of the game, and the English, for once, were vulnerable in the back. The game ended 2–2. The West Germans avenged their 1966 final loss after Müller scored the game-winner in the 108th minute following another Bonetti blunder.

## Semifinal Match-ups

On June 17, Italy and West Germany faced off at the Azteca. Most Mexicans stayed away from the game after their beloved team had fallen to Italy; the 80,000 who did attend not only rooted against the *Azzurri*, but also were in for a goal-filled afternoon. The Italians featured Mazzola in the starting lineup, while Rivera, who had proven a key component in previous games, sat on the bench. The *Azzurri* took the lead after seven minutes when Roberto Boninsegna scored off of a rebound. The Italians would hunker down and employ the *catenaccio* to fend off the West German onslaught that highlighted the remainder of the game. The West Germans controlled the rhythm of the match. The game became a tense affair with Beckenbauer playing the last thirty minutes of the second half with a dislocated shoulder. Beckenbauer refused to be substituted and played with a thick white bandage around his shoulder. His decision to stay was a courageous one, but added to West Germany's woes. Müller had been shut down by Italy's defense and was unable to create any chances. Italy appeared on its way to the final for the first time since 1938, but not before Schnellinger snatched the dramatic equalizer in the second minute of injury time. The Italians—just seconds from reaching the final—had to start over. "It wasn't that good a game in the first 90 minutes," Riva said. "The extra time was where things really got exciting."[7]

Five minutes into extra time, the tiring Italian defense allowed Müller to find the space he needed following a Seeler header that wasn't cleared in time. Müller got the ball and blasted it past Albertosi. Down 2–1, Italy persevered and quickly reversed the tide. Defender Tarcisio Burgnich tied the game and then, two minutes before the end of the first overtime session, Domenghini broke through on the right and passed the ball to Riva, who slotted the ball into the far corner. Italy was back on top, 3–2. Five minutes after the start of the second overtime, Müller netted his tenth goal of the competition, tying the score 3–3. The Italians immediately regrouped and, from the restart, Boninsegna went on another run into the West German half. His cross reached Rivera, who side-footed the ball into the net in the 111th minute. Rivera's goal marked the end to the afternoon's scoring spree. The 2½-hour battle had proven to be an epic struggle between two of Europe's strongest teams. The Italians, who had been accused of playing defensively, showed that they could react to any situation, even scoring when need be. The *Azzurri* had become a better team compared to their opening-round displays and were now off to the finals. The game lives on as one of the greatest achievements in Italian sports history. A plague mounted outside the Azteca Stadium refers to the match as the "Game of the Century."

The same day in Guadalajara's Jalisco Stadium, Brazil and Uruguay squared off in an all-South American semifinal. The rivalry between both countries had been born in 1950 during Brazil's ill-fated attempt to win the trophy. Now, the Brazilians were a far better team. Again, the Brazilians had the advantage of the huge Mexican crowd behind it. Brazil's *jogo bonito* was once again on display against the defensive-minded Uruguayans. However, the attack-minded Brazil everyone had become accustomed to seeing fell behind after nineteen minutes when Cubilla scored from a narrow angle with Felix off his line. The Brazilians tied the score just before the end of the first half with Clodoaldo. The teams played evenly for much of the second period until Brazil snatched the lead in the 76th minute with Jairzinho, whose goal came off a great sequence of passes that had begun with him in midfield. Jairzinho passed to Pelé, who flicked the ball to Tostão. He then passed it to Jairzinho who slammed the ball into the goal. Brazil was on its way to another final, but not before another magical Pelé pass, this time to Rivelino, who scored in the final minute for the 3–1 win.

## Third Place

The third-place game played on June 20 at the Azteca Stadium was unlike past consolation games. The game was a feisty affair between West Germany and Uruguay. Midfielder Wolfgang Overath did a good job anchoring the defense following the absence of Beckenbauer, even scoring what would turn out to be the game-winner in the 27th minute. Müller, who finished as the tournament's top scorer with ten goals, failed to score. The Uruguayans had done a superb job shutting down the West German offense, but for the first time at this competition were not afraid to come out of their defensive shell. Uruguay would fail to get on the board and to the dismay of the 104,000 spectators who had crammed into the stadium, the West German team would only score once for the 1–0 victory.

## The Championship Match

The setting for the final between Brazil and Italy on June 21 at noon was the pleasantly cool temperatures that enveloped the Azteca Stadium. The 107,000 people inside were in for a show. The contrast in soccer styles featured the Brazilians with their flamboyant, attacking style against the Italian team's defensiveness, although the *Azzurri* had astonishingly scored eight goals in the tournament's knockout phase. Exactly which Italian team would show up on the field that day was anyone's guess. The Italian camp was divided between whether Mazzola or

# PELÉ

Call him "The God of Football," or "The King," or just simply "Pelé." Whatever you call him, the memories remain the same. With every touch of the ball, Pelé was capable of conjuring up something new—and beating his opponents in the process. A killer instinct near the goal, Pelé was as close to perfection as any athlete could get. If the Brazilian teams of the 1960s and 1970s came to represent the best there was in world soccer, then Pelé can largely be credited for providing those breathtaking skills.

Pelé is still the most recognizable soccer player in the world, even though more than thirty years have passed since he retired. Edson Arantes Do Nascimento is known to many as the best to ever play the sport. He was raised in a poor family in the coastal village of Tres Coracos, Brazil. He first learned to play the game from his father, Dondinho, who played professionally as a striker until his career was halted by a fractured leg. Pelé was discovered at the age of 11 by Waldemar de Brito, one of Brazil's most popular players, who brought Pelé to São Paulo for a tryout with Santos four years later. At age 16, Pelé made his professional debut, scoring a goal for Santos against Corinthians.

Blessed with bursts of speed and a powerful shot, Pelé earned a spot on Brazil's World Cup team in 1958. Just 17, Pelé became an instant star. He scored six goals, including two in the final against Sweden, to help Brazil win its first World Cup. Four years later, Pelé played on Brazil's World Cup team in Chile, but an injury sidelined him after the first game. Brazil retained the title, but Pelé had very little to do with it.

Several European clubs made multimillion-dollar offers to sign Pelé, but the Brazilian government declared him an official national treasure in a bid to prevent him from being transferred out of the country. At the 1966 World Cup in England, Pelé was the victim of a series of brutal tackles and left the tournament a defeated man once again.

Pelé would get his revenge four years later at the 1970 finals in Mexico. Pelé, then 29, led one of the greatest teams ever assembled to win Brazil's third World Cup. In the 4–1 triumph over Italy in the final, Pelé scored a glorious goal en route to glory. The day after the final, the *London Sunday Times* headline summed it up: "How do you spell Pelé? G-O-D."

Pelé's personal statistics are staggering. During his club and national team career, he scored 1,280 goals in 1,360 games, second only to another Brazilian, Arthur Friedenreich, who recorded 1,329 goals in

*(continued)*

1,239 games from 1909 to 1934. Pelé, who made 93 appearances for Brazil, scored an average of one goal in every international game he played—the equivalent of a baseball player hitting a home run in every World Series game. He also shattered records at the club level: 127 goals for Santos in 1959, 110 in 1961, and 101 goals in 1965. He also led the club to two World Club championships.

Pelé retired from the sport in 1974, but came out of retirement the following year to play in the North American Soccer League with the New York Cosmos for two seasons. His appearance in the NASL jumpstarted a national soccer craze never before witnessed in the United States. His star quality gave instant credibility to a sport largely ignored by the masses and, for the first time, made millions of Americans aware of the sport.

On Oct. 1, 1977, Pelé's NASL mission came to an end, but not without a memorable experience. His last game was an exhibition match between the Cosmos and Santos at Giants Stadium, which was sold out six weeks beforehand and broadcast in forty countries. Pelé played the first half for the Cosmos—even scoring a goal on a powerful shot from 30 yards away—and the second period for Santos. In 1993, Pelé was inducted into the National Soccer Hall of Fame in Oneonta, New York.

## World Cup Career Statistics

Tournaments played: 4
Games: 14
Goals: 12

Rivera should start in the final. Exactly which player would start would also be anyone's guess. Italy, which featured Mazzola and not Rivera from the start, managed to keep Pelé off the scoreboard in the opening minutes. The tactical move appeared to work, but the Italians would be proven wrong by game's end. The Brazilians picked up the tempo and began making runs into the Italian half. After nineteen minutes, Pelé flew high above Burgnich and headed down a Rivelino cross from a Tostão throw-in that made its way into the goal. "We jumped together, then I came down, but he stayed up there," said Burgnich.[8] Brazil had scored its 100th goal at a World Cup and, fittingly, Pelé marked the milestone. The well-organized Italians did not give up. Eight minutes before halftime, a defensive mishap allowed Boninsegna to steal the ball in the midfield and beat Felix to tie the score. The teams headed into the locker rooms tied, 1–1. "Pelé really wanted to win that World Cup," recalled teammate Carlos Alberto. "When you have a player like him on your team, then you're halfway to achieving such a goal. It was a great time to be playing the game."[9]

In the second half, Brazil was able to put the game away and Italy bowed down to Pelé's offensive pressure. The Brazilians were clearly the better of the two teams, able to move the ball great distances across the field while running very little. This conservation of energy— particularly after a short tournament played at such high altitudes and hot temperatures—gave the Brazilians an advantage over the exhausted Italians. In the 65th minute, Gerson fired off a marvelous shot from outside the area to give Brazil a 2–1 lead. The *Azzurri*, out of breath and outmatched, tried to keep up. Mazzola was unable to produce any scoring chances as the Brazilians continued to dictate the flow of the game almost unimpeded. Five minutes later, Gerson's long ball was headed down by Pelé, who instead of going for the goal, created a pass that Jairzinho was able to put into the net. Jairzinho, who scored seven goals at the tournament, became the first player to net a goal in every game of the World Cup, a feat that has never again been equaled. Up 3–1, Brazil did not stop there. The Brazilians added to the lopsided lead when Pelé fed the ball to Carlos Alberto, who fired off a shot that blew past Albertosi in the 86th minute for the 4–1 final score.

The game was over, but Valcareggi made a move that stunned everyone. Six minutes from the end and with the game seemingly out of reach, Domenghini was replaced by Rivera. The move proved fruitless. Brazil had won and the victory allowed the team to forever retire the Rimet Trophy. Zagallo became the first man to win the trophy as both a player and coach, proving that the South American style of attack was more powerful than Europe's defensive-minded approach. Pelé's dream of winning another World Cup completed a dream he had set for himself following his team's early exit four years earlier. This was to be Pelé's last World Cup and he capped off the tournament in style. When East German referee Rudolf Glockner blew the final whistle, a sea of Mexican fans ran onto the field. Pelé was lifted and carried around the field on their shoulders. A black sombrero was placed on his head while the crowd reveled in the victory. In Brazil, 90 million people celebrated in the streets for days. The somber Italian players, meanwhile, arrived in Rome believing the fans would give them some credit for reaching

*Pelé celebrates his goal against Italy in the 1970 World Cup final (Credit: EMPICS).*

the final. They couldn't have been more wrong. Some 20,000 people awaited them at the airport in Rome, many tossing tomatoes at them while others brandished sticks in an effort to beat them. Several players were assaulted as they made their way onto the team bus. For the Italians, the loss was an embarrassing end to a tournament that they had no hope of winning at the start, but had come so close to conquering in the end.

## NOTES

1. Quoted from www.sportingnews.com/archives/worldcup/1962.html.

2. Filip Bondy, *The World Cup: The Players, Coaches, History, and Excitement* (New York: Mallard Press, 1991), 20.

3. Andres Cantor, *Goooal! A Celebration of Soccer* (New York: Simon & Schuster, 1996), 105.

4. Cantor. *Goooal! A Celebration of Soccer*, 106.

5. Ian Morrison, *The World Cup: A Complete Record* (Derby, UK: Breedon Books Sport, 1990), 200.

6. Personal interview, February 24, 2003.

7. Personal interview, February 24, 2003.

8. Harry Harris, *Pelé: His Life and Times* (London: Robson Books, 2000), 121.

9. Personal interview, April 8, 2006.

# 5

# TOTAL FOOTBALL

## 1974

The World Cup entered a new era. West Germany, chosen to host the tournament by FIFA in 1966, would put on a fine show. After the Rimet Trophy had been won outright by Brazil, FIFA unveiled a new one, designed by Italian sculptor Silvio Gazzaniga, which weighed 11 pounds and was nearly 20 inches in height. Though names like the Stanley Rous Trophy and Churchill Cup, in honor of Britain's Winston Churchill, had been considered, FIFA decided to keep it simple and named it the FIFA World Cup.[1] A new trophy was not the only change. A new FIFA president was elected days before the 1974 finals. Sir Stanley Rous stepped down after thirteen years and was replaced by Havelange, the first non-European to hold the post since FIFA was founded in 1904. The tournament also featured a format change. A second group phase replaced the knockout rounds after the first round. The new system guaranteed half of the teams at least six games, a ploy to create more games. The first round featured sixteen teams divided into four groups of four teams. The second round would become two groups of four teams. The winners of the second phase groups would play in the final.

Security became a priority on the eve of the competition following the Munich Olympics massacre in 1972 where eleven Israeli athletes were murdered by a group of Palestinian terrorists. Though organizers did a thorough job when it came to security, it never became an issue and the tournament went ahead violence-free. Unlike Mexico 1970, a competition where players baked under the sun, this World Cup would be plagued by heavy rain. Many games were played in awful weather, particularly the match between West Germany and Poland, which would determine a place in the final. The field in Frankfurt was so drenched that the city's fire department had to be called in to soak up the water. The effort proved fruitless.

The hosts were favored to win the tournament after taking the European Championship in 1972. Two other countries no one expected to be competitive were Holland and Poland, but they were the teams that would feature the most entertaining brand of soccer at the tournament. The Dutch, led by Johan Cruyff, would play some of the best soccer ever seen in a World Cup, leaving behind a tactical legacy known as "Total Football." The Dutch battle plan was simple. It called for all the players on the field to either attack or play defense, their positions interchangeable at any moment depending on the flow of the game. What emerged was a fluid, attacking style. Cruyff had already won the Golden Ball, given to the European Player of the Year, in 1971, 1973, and 1974. Tall and slim, Cruyff had been a star with club team Ajax Amsterdam from 1964 to 1973. He signed with Spanish club Barcelona in 1973, where he would go on to play for five seasons. Cruyff's fantastic dribbling skills, which featured bursts of acceleration and imagination, dazzled crowds and left opposing defenders scratching their heads. His signature move, the "Cruyff Turn," was an infallible way of getting past defenders. The move included faking a pass in one direction, then sliding the ball behind his standing foot and speeding off in the other direction. Only twenty-seven years old at the time of the 1974 World Cup, Cruyff was in his prime.

Poland, meanwhile, also featured a talented group of individuals. The team, winner of the Olympic gold medal two years earlier, was led by striker Grzegorz Lato and midfielder Kazimierz Deyna. Other contenders included Italy, runners-up four years earlier, a team that once again featured the much-maligned *catenaccio* and rested its hopes on goalkeeper Dino Zoff's heroics and Mazzola's offensive spurts. Reigning champs Brazil was still a strong team, but lacked the talents of Pelé to inspire them. The three-time World Cup champion had retired from the national team in 1971. Four years later, he would take on a new mission, signing with the New York Cosmos and becoming the sport's ambassador in an effort to make soccer a game Americans could fall in love with.

Ninety-four countries—a new record—were involved in the qualifying rounds, though the usual sixteen qualified. The qualifying tournament did feature some surprises, including East Germany, Australia, Haiti, and Zaire, who all made their World Cup debuts. Once again, the United States failed to qualify, finishing third behind regional powerhouse Mexico and Canada in CONCACAF's Group 1 standings. Mexico's 3–1 win at home over the United States on September 3, 1972, all but ended the Americans' chances of reaching the finals. Another loss to Mexico, a 2–1 defeat in Los Angeles, meant the U.S. team would finish last in the three-team group and would have to wait another four years for a shot at the finals. The Americans were in good company that year since England also failed to qualify.

Reaching the finals took on a bizarre twist after the Chilean military, led by Augusto Pinochet, stormed the presidential palace on September 11, 1973, and seized power from President Salvador Allende, who was found dead soon after. A junta headed by Pinochet was established, which immediately suspended the constitution and imposed strict censorship, particularly over leftist parties that had constituted Allende's Popular Unity coalition. On September 26, the Soviet Union and Chile played to a scoreless tie in Moscow. But the Soviet Union refused to fly to Chile to play the second leg because of Pinochet's coup d'état. FIFA subsequently disqualified the USSR. Chile automatically qualified for the finals.

Every World Cup game was broadcast live via satellite to homes across the globe for the first time. German clothing maker Adidas— realizing the money-making opportunities of having the tournament played in Germany—printed up shirts in conjunction with what had increasingly become an extremely marketable event. The World Cup draw was held on January 5, 1974, in Frankfurt. The organizers had chosen a group of boys from a choir in Berlin to pick the balls out of a bowl containing the names of each country. To everyone's surprise, West Germany and neighbors East Germany were drawn in the same group. Organizers not only feared a potential terrorist attack in the wake of Munich, but now they also had to worry about the political fallout that could occur once these two countries met on the field. The rest of the draw resulted in the following:

Group 1: Australia, Chile, East Germany, and West Germany
Group 2: Brazil, Scotland, Yugoslavia, and Zaire
Group 3: Bulgaria, Holland, Sweden, and Uruguay
Group 4: Argentina, Italy, Haiti, and Poland

## Group Play

The tournament opened June 14 with a change. The opening match would no longer feature the home team, but the reigning champions. The opener, played under a driving rain, pitted Brazil against Yugoslavia in Frankfurt and the result was a scoreless tie. Organizers didn't seem to mind that no one scored since they had been preoccupied with the heavy security that surrounded the stadium. Police thoroughly searched passengers at airports and tanks were parked near runways. The West Germans did not want a repeat of what had occurred at the Munich Olympics and did everything to make sure security was tight. As for the game, Brazil—who had neither Pelé, Tostão, Gerson, nor Clodoaldo to rely on this time around—did not look like the team that had steamrolled its way to the trophy four years earlier. The only threat was a series of long-range free kicks from Rivelino, but they never materialized into goals. The rain also made it impossible for the Brazilians to employ the *jogo bonito*. In other words, any chance of putting together a string of pretty plays had been out of the question. The Yugoslavs, on the other hand, came close to scoring and argued with Swiss referee Rudolf Scheurer for failing to blow a penalty kick in their favor after midfielder Jovan Acimovic was tripped in the box.

Group 1 opened the same day in Berlin's Olympic Stadium with West Germany taking on Chile. There was a lot of pressure on the West Germans to win the trophy, though they did little in the opener to convince the 83,168 attendees that they could do just that on home soil. A long-range, cannonball of a shot by Paul Breitner in the 17th minute landed in the back of the net and was enough to get the win. The West Germans hung on to the narrow lead and were assured of the result, especially after Chile's Carlos Caszely was red carded in the 67th minute following a hard tackle on Berti Vogts.

At Volkspark Stadium in Hamburg, meanwhile, East Germany squared off against Australia in a clash of World Cup newcomers. The East Germans put pressure on the Australian defense from the start, but to no avail. The first half ended scoreless and the Australians were hoping to get a point out of the game. The East Germans, however, were able to score—one off an own goal in the 58th minute when Australian Colin Curran deflected the ball into his own net and the second in the 72nd minute with Joachim Streich—for the 2–0 win. Four days later, the Australians were officially eliminated after receiving a 3–0 walloping at the hands of West Germany in Hamburg. At that game, the hosts looked unstoppable—overcoming a resilient Aussie defense with a series of attacks that resulted in an Overath goal in the 13th minute and another from Bernhard Cullmann in the 35th minute. The West Germans turned off the pressure, probably in an effort to conserve energy for its upcoming game against East Germany, but was able to score a third goal with a trademark header from Müller in the 53rd minute off a Uli Hoeness corner kick.

West Germany took on East Germany on June 22 in Hamburg. The first-ever meeting between these countries produced inevitable political tensions and even-tighter security. Some 3,000 East Germans were granted permission to cross the Berlin Wall and attend the game, but only after some heavy scrutiny from West German police. West Germany had four points in the standings and a guaranteed spot in the second round, while the East Germans needed at least a tie to advance. The first half failed to produce a goal. In the second half, however, East Germany caught a break when Jurgen Sparwasser was able to settle a ball off a long pass from Erich Hamann. Sparwasser then rounded a defender and beat goalkeeper Sepp Mair in the 77th minute for what turned out to be the game-winner. The East Germans won the group with five points and clinched a spot in the next round.

The Group 2 battle between Brazil and Yugoslavia that had failed to produce a goal allowed Scotland to take an early lead in the standings after defeating Zaire, 2–0, on June 14 at the Westfalen Stadium in Dortmund. The Zairians, like many teams from Africa that would qualify for the finals in the decades to come, were a very fit and athletic team, but were no match for Scotland's talent and organization. Scotland got on the board when Peter Lorimer scored off a Joe Jordan header in the 34th minute. Seven minutes later, Jordan's header slipped through the hands of goalkeeper Muamba Kazadi. The game took an unexpected twist when the power in the stadium went out for five minutes in the second half, but Scotland emerged as the winner, 2-0.

On June 18, the 62,000 spectators that had gathered to watch Brazil play Scotland at Wald Stadium in Frankfurt were in for a shock. The Brazilians were unable to again score with Scottish goalkeeper David Harvey putting on one of his best performances in his career. The scoreless tie allowed Scotland to maintain its group lead—along with Yugoslavia after it had defeated Zaire 9-0—with three points. The Brazilian team, which only had two points, needed a win over small fish Zaire if it wanted to move on to the next group round. Although that was not expected to be a problem, a feeling of panic nonetheless had crept through the Brazil camp.

Scotland and Yugoslavia, meanwhile, played to a 1-1 tie on June 22 in Frankfurt. Scotland needed a win to progress to the next round and had to rely on the remote chance that Brazil only beat Zaire by two goals. Scotland's failure to score more than two goals against Zaire had come back to haunt the team. Now it had to wait to see if Brazil could falter against Zaire later the same day. Instead, Brazil came out of its cocoon, finally ending its scoring drought at Park Stadium in Gelsenkirchen. Brazil needed to win by at least three goals—and it was able to do just that. Jairzinho gave Brazil the lead after twelve minutes with a low shot that beat Kazadi. A 25-yard shot from Rivelino in the second half made it 2-0. Brazil was still not through to the second round, that is, until eleven minutes from the end when a shot by Valdomiro slipped past Kazadi, who at first appeared to stop the shot. Instead, Kazadi's blunder, his second of the competition, turned into Brazil's good fortune. Brazil's 3-0 win kept its title defense hopes alive. Although Zaire would not record a point, it's interesting to note that every team's game against the Africans ultimately determined the outcome of the group.

Group 3 was highlighted by the presence of Holland and "Total Football." Dutch coach Rinus Michels had assembled a group of the country's great individual talents and transformed them into the most skillful team at the tournament. Unfortunately, Holland was unable to show off most of that artistry on June 15 at the Niedersachsen Stadium in Hanover because of some brutal fouling by Uruguay. Holland, which had returned to the World Cup for the first time in forty years, took the lead after seven minutes when Johnny Rep headed in a pass from Ajax defender Wim Suurbier. Uruguay did little, other than engage in a series of vicious tackles. In the 70th minute, Uruguay was reduced to ten players when Julio Montero-Castillo was red carded for punching forward Rob Rensenbrink in the stomach. Holland won the game, 2–0, in the 87th minute when Rep netted his second goal.

Four days later, Holland tied Sweden, 0–0, in Dortmund. The Swedes, who had played Bulgaria on June 15 to a scoreless tie, could have scored if not for Cruyff's masterful management of the Dutch midfield. In fact, his abilities could have given Holland the lead, but that never materialized.

At the same time, Bulgaria and Uruguay tied 1–1 in Hanover. The Group 3 standings were as follows: Holland 3 points, Sweden and Bulgaria 2, and Uruguay 1. It was anyone's guess which two teams would qualify to the next round, although the Dutch were fancied by most. On June 23, Holland showed why it was one of the strongest teams at the tournament, downing Bulgaria, 4–1. The Dutch jumped out to a 2–0 lead in the first half on two penalty kicks from Johannes Neeskens. In the 71st minute, Rep scored his third goal of the competition, but seven minutes later, Bulgaria reduced the deficit when Ruud Krol inadvertently put the ball in his own net while trying to clear it after smacking the crossbar. In the 87th minute, midfielder Theo de Jong scored off a Cruyff pass.

The Dutch were joined in the next round by Sweden, who blanked Uruguay, 3–0, on the same day at Rhein Stadium in Dusseldorf. A scoreless first half marked 225 minutes that Sweden had not scored at the tournament. Uruguay, who only needed a tie to move on, did its best to keep the Swedes off the scoreboard. Uruguay's dreams, however, crumbled in the second half. A minute into the period and Sweden took the lead on a goal by striker Ralf Edstrom. Roland Sandberg scored in the 74th minute and Edstrom added his second of the match four minutes later for the 3–0 win. Like Brazil, Sweden had gotten off to a slow start, but like the reigning champions, had not given up a goal in the first round.

Group 4 opened on June 15 when Italy took on Haiti in Munich. The Italians were favored to win the game—and the group—but found itself down 1–0 on a goal by Emmanuel Sanon in the 46th minute. The Italians, plagued by the nightmare of losing to North Korea just eight years earlier, had to deal with being behind. Zoff, who was celebrating his 32nd birthday, had conceded his first goal in 1,142 minutes. The *Azzurri* didn't let the goal get to them and were able to tie the score six minutes later with Rivera. Italy then took the lead with midfielder Romeo Benetti in the 66th minute following a blunder by the Haitian defense. The Italians didn't sit on the 2–1 lead. Striker Piero Anastasi, who had come in the game for Giorgio Chinaglia, scored with twelve minutes left to cap off a 3–1 victory. Chinaglia, Italy's star player, had played horribly. When he was pulled off the field by Valcaraggi in the 70th minute, Chinaglia responded by insulting him as he stormed past the bench, then proceeded to smash several water bottles in the locker room. Chinaglia, who had won the Italian League title with Rome-based club Lazio just before the start of the World Cup, would sign with the Cosmos in 1976 and go on to become one of the NASL's biggest stars.

On the same day, Poland pulled off a shocker, defeating Argentina, 3–2, at Necker Stadium in Stuttgart. Poland was up 2–0 after eight minutes on goals by Lato and Andrzej Szarmach. The first goal came with the complicity of Argentine goalkeeper Daniel Carnevali, who dropped the ball after making what should have been a routine save off a corner kick. It would not be Carnevali's only mistake that day. In the second half, Argentina cut the lead after defender Ramon Heredia scored in the 62nd minute off a pass from striker Mario Kempes. Two minutes later, Poland restored its two-goal lead: Lato scored after Carnevali tried to clear the ball and misjudged it, throwing the ball to the feet of the Polish striker. Like Holland, Poland also played a style similar to "Total Football." The entertaining game came to a close when Carlos Babington scored Argentina's second of the game. Poland won, 3–2, sending a warning to everyone in the group that they were for real.

Italy and Argentina battled each other on June 19 in Stuttgart. Babington did a great job in the midfield, sending an array of passes that cut the Italian defense in half. One of those Babington passes in the 19th minute allowed Rene Houseman to waltz past the defense and unleash a shot that beat Zoff. The Italians—with Chinaglia on the bench the entire match—tied the game fifteen minutes later on a Roberto Perfumo own goal. At first, Benetti's pass looked like it had been saved by Carnevali, but Perfumo intercepted the ball and put it past his own goalkeeper. The game ended 1–1. Both Italy and Argentina needed a win in their last games, against Poland and Haiti, respectively, if either hoped to get through to the next phase. Poland, meanwhile, took first place in the group after demolishing Haiti, 7–0, in Munich. Szarmach scored a hat trick and Lato added two goals.

The other team from the group that would advance to the next round was decided on June 23 when Argentina defeated Haiti, 4–1, in Munich. Argentina did its best to run up the score, knowing that the goal differential would determine who gained passage to the second round. The Italians, meanwhile, needed at least a tie against Poland. Any hope the *Azzurri* had to get through to the next round crumbled in the first half when two Polish goals—one from Szarmach and another from Deyna—ended the dream. Chinaglia played the first period, but was pulled at halftime in favor of Boninsegna. Fabio Capello, who would go on to become a successful coach with AC Milan, Real Madrid, and Juventus, was able to pull one back late in the game, but it wasn't enough. The Italians were eliminated.

## New Style of Second-Round Play

The second phase featured two pools. Brazil, East Germany, Holland, and Argentina were placed in Group A. Poland, Sweden, West Germany, and Yugoslavia in Group B. The winner of each group would meet in the final.

Group A kicked off with East Germany taking on Brazil on June 26 in Hanover. The East Germans did their best to contain the Brazilians, utilizing their solid defense to try and stifle them, but a Rivelino goal in the 50th minute off a free kick gave Brazil the 1–0 victory. The group's second game was played the same day and featured Argentina—without Babington who was suspended after accumulating two yellow cards in the first round—and Holland in Gelsenkirchen. Cruyff continued to put his skills on display, scoring two goals to help lead the Dutch to a resounding 4–0 win. Krol and Rep scored Holland's other two goals. In its next group game, Holland defeated East Germany 2–0 on June 30 in Gelsenkirchen. The East German team put on its usual defensive display in the hopes of attaining a tie against the mighty Dutch. East German defender Konrad Weise was given the arduous task of marking

Cruyff. Though Weise did a good job—better than any other defender at the tournament had before him—Cruyff was still able to create scoring chances. "Total Football" was all about interchanging players, and even though Cruyff was taken out of the game, Neeskens was the one who put Holland in front, 1–0, after eight minutes—his fourth goal in five games. Holland put the game away fifteen minutes into the second half when Rensenbrink scored for the 2–0 win.

In Hanover, meanwhile, Brazil and Argentina met for the first time at a World Cup, renewing a continental rivalry that had been created throughout the decades at the Copa America. Brazil took the lead with Rivelino in the 31st minute, but that advantage lasted just three minutes when Miquel Brindisi's superbly taken free kick flew over the wall and caught Leao out of position. The goal—the first conceded by Brazil at the tournament—motivated the Brazilians offensively. Jairzinho's header, off a cross by Ze Maria in the 49th minute, proved to be the game-winner.

The winner of Group A would be decided by the outcome of the July 3 match between Holland and Brazil, two impressive teams. On the one hand, Brazil had steadily progressed over the course of the tournament. On the other hand, Holland had been consistently solid from the start. The first half ended scoreless, highlighted by a series of ferocious fouls on both sides. In the second period, the Dutch managed to break down the Brazilian defense. Five minutes into the half, Neeskens was able to put Holland ahead, 1–0, off a Cruyff pass. Holland further sank Brazil's hopes fifteen minutes later when Cruyff volleyed the ball past Leao off a Kroll cross to make it 2–0. Luis Pereira was red carded in the 84th minute after tackling Neeskens, bringing to an end any chance of Brazil repeating as champions and winning a fourth title. The Dutch were in the final.

Group B opened on June 26 with Poland playing Sweden in Stuttgart. The wet field hampered play between the teams. The only goal of the game came in the 43rd minute when Lato headed the ball past Ronnie Hellstrom to break Sweden's stretch of 313 minutes without having given up a goal.

In Dusseldorf, meanwhile, West Germany struggled against Yugoslavia for much of the first half. The West Germans were able to get on the scoreboard with Paul Breitner in the 39th minute. Beckenbauer took charge in the midfield and was back at his best, distributing balls along the wings. Müller added another thirteen minutes from the end to seal the win.

Yugoslavia's hopes of advancing to the final ended on June 30 against Poland. Yugoslavia's 2-1 loss to Poland in Frankfurt—thanks to goals from Deyna and Lato—ensured their elimination and allowed Poland to keep pace with West Germany in the Group B standings.

Nearly four hours later, West Germany won again, outpacing Sweden, 4–2. Like Group A, this group would be decided by a winner-take-all game between West Germany and Poland. The dreadful weather that plagued the competition continued to wreak havoc on the tournament in Frankfurt. On July 3, despite the awful conditions, West Germany and Poland tried their best to play attractive soccer—though both sides were handicapped by the drenched field. The West Germans only needed a tie to win the group, but did their best to take the lead. Lato was the most dangerous Polish player on the field in the first half, although he was unable to get the ball past Maier. The second half featured a more aggressive West German team. Müller, who had been invisible for much of the game, left his mark in the 76th minute when he scored what turned out to be the game-winner, lifting the hosts to the final. The trophy would be contested between Holland and West Germany.

## FRANZ BECKENBAUER

Arguably the best German player and coach ever, Beckenbauer redefined the role of the sweeper, lifting the World Cup as captain in 1974, before repeating the feat as head coach in 1990.

Beckenbauer celebrated his first international appearance for West Germany in 1965 at the age of 20 and went on to play in three World Cups. The young Beckenbauer made his first finals appearance in 1966, scoring two goals in a 5–0 win over Switzerland, but his team lost in the final to England. His second World Cup in Mexico 1970 was also memorable as he played in the semifinal against Italy with a dislocated shoulder, carrying his injured arm in a white sling. However, his dedication went unrewarded as Italy won, 4–3. The Germans had to settle for third place.

Four years later, he would relish his finest hour. By now, Beckenbauer was playing in the position he revolutionized over the years behind the

*(continued)*

defense. He organized the team from the back, but he would also come forward when his teammates mounted an attack. After a 2–1 win over Holland in the final, Beckenbauer became the first captain to lift the brand new FIFA World Cup trophy.

He began his career at the age of nine in the youth system of SC Munchen 06, before joining Bayern Munich in 1958. He made his debut for Bayern in 1964. In 1977, Beckenbauer left the Bundesliga to join the New York Cosmos. By the time he left Munich he had won every major honor with the team, which included three European Cups, four German League titles, and four German Cups. He left his country hoping to find a new challenge in the NASL. The move across the Atlantic also brought an end to his international career. Since he was playing abroad, he was no longer considered for selection by the German Football Association. He made 103 appearances for his country, becoming the first German ever to break the 100-game barrier.

In 1982, he made his comeback in the Bundesliga at age 35, playing for one season with Hamburg. He retired a year later following a second spell with the Cosmos. In July 1984, after the failure of coach Jupp Derwall at that year's European Championship, Beckenbauer was named national team coach. His first major success as coach came during the World Cup tournament in 1986 when he led his team to the final. Although Argentina won the trophy, Beckenbauer had come of age as a manager.

In 1990, West Germany went undefeated at the World Cup to win the trophy. He became the first man to win the World Cup as a player and a manager. After the World Cup, Beckenbauer became president of Bayern Munich until 1998, when he was named vice-president of the German Football Association. It was under his reign that the successful campaign to host the 2006 FIFA World Cup was launched. He took on an active role in the planning and staging of 2006 World Cup finals, where he served as chairman of the organizing committee.

## World Cup Career Statistics

Tournaments played: 3
Games: 18
Goals: 5

## Third Place

The third-place game between Brazil and Poland was played on July 6 at Munich's Olympic Stadium. With little to play for, the game lacked the intensity witnessed in the previous rounds. The 79,000 spectators spent most of the time jeering the teams rather than cheering them. The game was settled in the 76th minute when Lato, the tournament's top scorer, netted his seventh goal of the competition. Lato had broken clear of the Brazilian defense and unleashed a low shot that blew past Leao. Though the linesman's flag quickly went up to signal an offside, Italian referee Aurelio Angonese chose to ignore his collaborator and the goal stood. While Lato celebrated what would be the game-winner, Jairzinho protested the goal. His arguments fell on deaf ears and led to a yellow card.

## Championship

The final was played on July 7 in Munich between West Germany and Holland. The Dutch lineup was the same one that had been fielded in the previous four games despite the physical beating the Dutch players had suffered at the hands of the Brazilians. The game was delayed due to the lack of corner kick flags that had never been placed into the ground. Some thought the delay was created by the hosts in order to gain a psychological edge over their opponents. That may have been the case, but it didn't work. The Dutch, which were favored, took the lead  even before the West Germans got a chance to touch the ball. Cruyff picked up the ball, strolled up field with it, and with a burst of energy dashed into the penalty area. Though Vogts was in pursuit, it was Hoeness who made the desperate challenge and tackled Cruyff to the ground. The Dutchman was down and English referee Jack Taylor pointed to the spot. Neeskens struck the ball past the diving Maier to give Holland a 1-0 lead to successfully convert the first-ever penalty kick given to a team in a final.

The Germans, rather than panic, retaliated with Vogts eventually playing Cruyff out of the game. Cruyff gradually retreated into his own half—in a bid to give the midfield more support—but Rensenbrink failed to live up to his task of passing the ball and creating spaces like he had in previous games. The Germans, meanwhile, were given more space to create plays, though Müller was unable to do much offensively.

Both teams put together a series of chances, creating the perfect mix of emotion suitable for a game watched by 77,833 spectators inside Munich's Olympic Stadium and a world television audience of nearly one billion.

A second penalty kick, this time in West Germany's favor, was whistled in the 25th minute. Bernd Hölzenbein, who had a reputation as a diver, had burst into the Dutch area. Wim Jansen made contact with him after lunging toward the ball and failed to make contact with it. Hölzenbein dropped to the ground and Taylor awarded the hosts a penalty. Breitner slotted the ball past Jan Jongbloed to tie the game, 1–1. Holland was clearly rattled by the goal and momentum shifted to the West Germans. The hosts applied pressure to the Dutch defense in the hopes of taking the lead. The Dutch could have scored when Wim Rijsbergen broke up yet another German attack and fed the ball to Wim van Hanegem. His long pass caught the West German defense by surprise and both Cruyff and Rep broke through with only Beckenbauer and Maier to beat. Cruyff forced Beckenbauer to come to him, passing the ball to Rep, who wasted his chance when he kicked it straight at Maier who made the easy save. Tensions between both sides began to bubble over after Neeskens fouled Hölzenbein from behind and the Dutchman was yellow carded. Taylor was determined to maintain order and had done well up to this point. The West Germans finally took the lead just before the break. In the 43rd minute, midfielder Rainer Bonhof ran down the right with sweeper Arie Haan in pursuit. The Dutchman cut the ball back into the box, taking Rijsbergen out of the play in the process. Müller picked up the ball and ran effortlessly away from Krol, poking the ball past Jongbloed for the 2–1 lead.

The second half continued to be a spellbinding affair. The Dutch defense was unable to handle the West German offensive onslaught. Holland stuck to its task of defending, hoping that in the process it would be able to carve a hole in the West German defense. Substitute René van de Kerkhof only occasionally persuaded Rep to switch sides and the fluidity of "Total Football" appeared to have reached its limit. In the meantime, Cruyff did not possess the usual freedom that had characterized his previous performances. West Germany could have extended its lead when Jurgen Grabowski beat Krol down the right side and dished the ball off to Müller, who found the net—only to have the goal disallowed for being offside. Though the players did not argue the call, replays later showed the goal was valid. In the dying minutes, Holland could have forced extra time when Neeskens' shot appeared to beat Maier, but the ball was off the mark and glanced off the side netting. The Dutch had been defeated, 2–1, and West Germany could celebrate its second World Cup. The home fans rejoiced as Beckenbauer lifted the new trophy into the sky. The Dutch team, who had played so well throughout the tournament, had to be content with second place—and with an eye toward attaining revenge in four years' time.

## 1978

The World Cup returned to South America for the first time in sixteen years. FIFA finally awarded the tournament to Argentina. Organizing the competition grew complicated after the country was plunged into a precarious political situation under the brutal military dictatorship headed by Jorge Videla. Thousands of people had been killed at his orders; even Omar Actis, president of the World Cup Organizing Committee, was assassinated. Skepticism spread around the world about whether the government could pull off the tournament. Many nations that qualified for the finals feared for their safety, but the junta, who dealt with its critics with imprisonment and torture, guaranteed there would be no violence during the tournament.

When the military junta took control in March 1976, not one thing had been done to prepare for the World Cup, even though the tournament had been awarded to Argentina in 1966. With a new government in place, an organizing committee was created and no expense was spared. From an organizational point of view, the country worked hard preparing for the crush of fans from around the world expected to arrive. Argentina went through an overhaul. Streets were modernized and airports fixed. The government wanted to give the world an image of Argentina that made it appear modern.

At the same time, stadiums were refurbished, though many of the playing fields looked shabby by the time the World Cup kicked off. Three stadiums—the Antonio Liberti "Monumental" in Buenos Aires, Rosario Central's Gigante de Arroyito, and Velez Sarsfield Stadium— were remodeled. Another three stadiums were built in Mendoza, Cordoba, and Mar de Plata at a combined cost of $700 million. Though the expense of staging the tournament began to spiral out of control, organizers embarked on a massive marketing campaign to raise money. The Argentina '78 logo was plastered everywhere, including T-shirts and other trinkets, in what would become a marketing model for future World Cups. Security was once again a huge concern. Shortly before the start of the tournament, a bomb killed a policeman in Buenos Aires and an Amnesty International protest of the junta signed by a dozen players added to the controversy swirling around the competition. Similar to the security concerns faced by West Germany four years earlier, Argentine authorities were also concerned, but eased up on the eve of the games after the Mononeros, a left-wing terrorist group, vowed that violence would not disrupt the competition.

In the end, the World Cup would go off without a hitch. Nevertheless, some of the sport's greatest stars missed out on the tournament. Cruyff and Breitner refused to travel with their respective national teams because of Argentina's record on human rights. Beckenbauer had quit the international game shortly before the start of the tournament and was playing soccer for the Cosmos.

The North American Soccer League garnered credibility around the world when Pelé signed with the Cosmos in 1975. As a result, players from all over the globe lined up to join the upstart league. Although the NASL was hardly a world-class league, it now had enough marquee talent to draw crowds in excess of 70,000 at Giants Stadium. In 1976, the league and the USSF staged the Bicentennial Cup. Brazil, Italy, and England were invited to come to the United States in May of that year to face Team America, a group of NASL all-stars, which included Pelé. Team America went on to lose both its games, but the publicity generated by the tournament was slowly making soccer as popular as baseball in this country. Pelé retired from the game in 1977 with a farewell match at Giants Stadium that drew 75,646 fans—a near sellout—for his final sojourn that was part traveling circus, part missionary work. After twenty-two years of brilliance and 1,281 goals on the professional level, the Brazilian ended his journey with a game between the Cosmos and his former club, Santos. Pelé played a half for each team, even scoring a goal for New York in the first period. The emotional goodbye, however, didn't signal the end of soccer in this country—at least not quite yet. The NASL's popularity had become so big that even Cruyff could not escape the chance to play here. In 1979, he signed with the Los

Angeles Aztecs. He went on to play with the Washington Diplomats a year later before joining Spanish club Levante in 1981.

The problem with the NASL was that it was filled with foreigners and American-born players were hard to come by. At the same time, the USSF—unable to lure a world-class foreign coach to take over the national team—hired Walter Chyzowich, a former American Soccer League star, who was given the uphill task of qualifying for the World Cup for the first time since 1950.

Ultimately, the 1978 tournament qualifiers would be a complicated series of games in CONCACAF that saw Mexico qualify for the finals once again. The Mexicans were lucky to come out of the preliminary round after posting a better goal differential over the United States and Canada. Though the Americans were eventually eliminated after losing a playoff against Canada, 3–0, in Port-au-Prince, Haiti, the group did feature another series of firsts. On September 24, 1976, in Vancouver, the Canadian team beat the U.S. team, 1–0, in the first-ever World Cup qualifying game played on artificial turf. Four weeks later, on October 20 in Seattle, the United States defeated Canada, 2–0, on goals from Julie Veee and Miro Rys. The game was played in the Kingdome, which had only opened seven months earlier, and was the first time that a qualifier had been played in an indoor venue.

The 1978 World Cup was not aired on network TV in the United States, but was instead relegated to forty-five cities across the country, and further limited still to closed-circuit outlets including Madison Square Garden in New York and the Aladdin Hotel in Las Vegas. Some games were shown on local television in eleven U.S. markets, but the World Cup still had a long way to go before it would be embraced by American networks.

### Group Play

The World Cup finals format remained the same as in 1974 with a record-breaking ninety-nine nations entering the qualifying fray. The qualifying tournament lasted a record twenty-one months with Brazil, Holland, West Germany, Italy, Poland, and Spain all on the shortlist of teams to fear in the finals. Joining them were Iran and Tunisia, which qualified for the first time, and Austria, which made its return to the tournament after a twenty-year absence. There was also a batch of high-profile countries that failed to make it. For the second straight time, England was a no-show. In addition, Yugoslavia and the Soviet Union, countries who had regularly reached the finals over the past two decades, also failed to qualify.

The final draw was held on January 14, 1978, at the Teatro San Martin in Buenos Aires. FIFA determined that Argentina, West Germany, Brazil, and Holland would not meet in the first phase. The teams were grouped as follows:

Group 1: Argentina, France, Hungary, and Italy
Group 2: Mexico, Poland, Tunisia, and West Germany
Group 3: Austria, Brazil, Spain, and Sweden
Group 4: Holland, Iran, Peru, and Scotland

Argentina were favored to win the World Cup and featured Valencia striker Mario Kempes, a veteran of 1974 tournament and the only European-based player on the national team. In fact, the chain-smoking forty-year-old coach, Cesar Luis Menotti, did not call up any other players based in Europe and was criticized for it. Menotti, nicknamed *El Flaco* (The Thin One) because he was skinny, also angered the public when he selected no players from Argentina's most-beloved club, Boca Juniors. As a result, Menotti earned another nickname, *El Loco* (The Crazy One), for his inexplicable choices. But Menotti could count on the talents of striker and team captain Daniel Passarella, playmaker Osvaldo Ardiles, and Kempes's partner on attack, Leopoldo Luque. He even had the luxury of leaving seventeen-year-old superstar Diego Armando Maradona—who some compared to Pelé—off the roster. The move was controversial, but Maradona would have plenty of time to shine in the decade to come.

The tournament opened on June 1 between trophy holders West Germany and Poland—which had finished in third place four years earlier—in front of 77,000 spectators at Monumental Stadium in Buenos Aires. Like previous openers, the game was a dreary contest and predictably ended 0–0. Both teams kicked around the ball back and forth with little imagination. The pressure of opening the competition may have proved too nerve-wracking for both teams. In fact, this was the fourth straight World Cup opener to finish scoreless. The crowd let the teams hear it after only twenty-five minutes when jeers filled the cavernous stadium. Those jeers accompanied the players for much of the game and past the final whistle.

The remainder of the games in Group 2 didn't fare much better. Despite West Germany's and Poland's poor start, both teams advanced to the second round at the expense of Tunisia and Mexico. The group did feature a first: Tunisia defeated Mexico, 3–1, on June 2 at New Rosario Stadium in Rosario. Tunisia, a 1000–1 shot to win the tournament, became the first African nation to win a World Cup finals game. West Germany, meanwhile, proved it could score and trounced Mexico, 6–0, on June 6 in Cordoba Stadium in Cordoba. West Germany jumped out to a 4–0 lead at halftime and finished on a high note, thanks to the prowess of Karl-Heinz Rummenigge, an outstanding dribbler who finished the game with two goals. The win was enough to send the West Germans through to the next round, though they played Tunisia to a 0–0 tie just four days later in the same stadium. It was the Polish, however, who won the group. Their 1–0 win over Tunisia on June 6 and a 3–1 victory over Mexico four days later earned them the top spot—a quite lackluster group that featured as its only bright spot a gutsy Tunisian team that had come very close to advancing.

Italy and France opened Group 1 on June 2 in Mar de Plata Stadium. The group, widely considered the toughest, was hard to predict. No one was guaranteed success, not even the favored Argentines and Italians. The *Azzurri*, made up almost entirely of Juventus players, had again hoped to utilize the *catenaccio* to squeak by its opponents. Those plans had to be changed when France took the lead after only thirty-one seconds. Bernard Lacombe scored off a pass from Didier Six. The Italians were forced to attack—and attack they did. The team played an imaginative style not seen at a World Cup since the 1930s and were rewarded in the 29th minute when the pint-sized Paolo Rossi scored his first national team goal. The Italians didn't stop there. Renato Zaccarelli, who came into the game at halftime following an injury to Giancarlo Antognoni, didn't waste any time. His goal in the 52nd minute proved to be the game-winner, lifting the Italians to a 2–1 win and injecting the team with a huge dose of morale.

The first obstacle for Argentina was Hungary. The challenge proved no easy task. Contrasted to the apparent ease with which the Italians had squeezed by the French, Karoly Csapo put Hungary ahead after ten minutes, a goal accompanied with a deathly silence by the 77,000 fans sitting inside the Monumental Stadium. The silence didn't last long. The chanting that ensued fueled the Argentine players and that encouragement allowed Luque to tie the score. The flag-waving crowd did not stop there and neither did the Argentine players. Daniel Bertoni scored the winner seven minutes from the end to give Argentina a hard-fought 2–1 victory. The drama that characterized Argentina's opening game would carry throughout the competition. Menotti's game plan was simple: feed off the energy of the crowd. If they did that, the victories would follow.

Italy had an easier time than Argentina against Hungary on June 6 in Mar de Plata. Juventus star Roberto Bettega put on a one-man show, scoring a goal, setting up another, and hitting three shots on goal. Rossi put the *Azzurri* ahead in the 34th minute, deflecting a Marco Tardelli shot into the net. Bettega made it 2–0 soon after, getting by two defenders before unleashing a shot that wound up in the back of the net. Benetti scored Italy's third goal in the 60th minute, but Hungary was able to put one past Zoff when Andreas Toth converted a penalty kick in the 81st minute. Italy's performance sent a message to Argentina: the *Azzurri* were going to challenge the hosts for a spot in the next round.

In Buenos Aires, Argentina played France and again had a difficult time. The French, which featured speedy playmaker Michel Platini, outplayed the Argentines in the first half. Though a France goal appeared to be on the horizon, it was Argentina that took the lead. After tackling Kempes, French sweeper Marius Trésor tripped himself up on the ball. Swiss referee Jean Dubach inexplicably whistled a penalty kick in Argentina's favor, which Passarella converted in the dying seconds of the half. France's bad luck didn't end there. Ten minutes into the half, goalkeeper Jean Paul Bertrand-Demanes had to be carted off the field after colliding into the post trying to make a save. He was replaced with backup Dominique Baratelli. The goalkeeping change didn't hurt the French, who tied the game with Platini. The crowd once again began to incite the Argentine players and the repeated chanting of "Ar-chen-tina! Ar-chen-tina!" appeared to wear the French players down. With Menotti nervously pacing back and forth along the sidelines with a cigarette in one hand and a serious scowl on his face, Argentina was able to grab the win when Luque scored against the run of play with eighteen minutes to play. The unlucky French had been ousted. The Argentineans were through to the next round, but still needed to beat the Italians for a chance to finish first and continue to play in Buenos Aires.

On June 10, the Monumental buzzed with emotion. The confetti-filled stadium was packed with 77,260 spectators. Once again, the flag-waving fans were there to cheer on Argentina. They knew Italy was no pushover. Both teams had qualified to the next round, but what developed over the next ninety minutes was a rugged contest that lacked imagination and flair. That was nothing new for the hosts, who, even without having played their best soccer, had still been able to win two games thanks to a series of scrappy plays. The Italians, on the other hand, had relied heavily on Rossi to create chances.

Rossi was Italy's best player. He had developed into a formidable goal-poacher and was spotted at an early age by Juventus scouts. He was loaned to Como in a bid to toughen him up. Rossi eventually switched to fellow Serie B team Vicenza. He scored twenty-one goals during the 1976–1977 season and helped the club win promotion to Serie A. Rossi performed even better the season after, scoring twenty-four times to lead the team to second place behind Juventus. Italy coach Enzo Bearzot called him up to the national team that same year. The twenty-one-year-old Rossi had emerged as Italy's biggest star since Rivera. Standing just 5'7" and weighing 146, Rossi was not much of a physical presence. What made him so strong was the ability at being in the right place at the right time. His first-ever goal for the *Azzurri* against France was a perfect example of his artistry: After ricocheting around the box, the ball rebounded off Rossi's leg and into the back of the net. Rossi—dubbed "Pablito" by the Argentine press, a name that would stick with him at the next World Cup in Spain—truly possessed a striker's instinct. Those same skills would come in handy for Italy four years later. Against Argentina, however, Rossi was not able to show off any of those instincts that had made him so popular back home. If that wasn't enough, tempers began to flair in the second half after Benetti and Ossie Ardiles were involved in a clash. The argument left Ardiles holding his face, but whether he was really hurt was anyone's guess. Bettega once again proved decisive, scoring a brilliant goal in the 67th minute that silenced the noisy crowd. His one-two with Rossi was superb. Bettega finished the play with a strong shot from the edge of the penalty area for the 1–0 result.

On June 3, the Brazilians, the uncrowned kings of the game, opened Group 3 in Mar de Plata with a disappointing 1–1 tie against Sweden. The Brazilians were a shadow of their former selves. Gone was the style that had characterized the team since Pelé's playing days. Zico was the only player on the field who showed any glimmer that Brazil was still an entertaining and attacking team. Rivelino, the team's sole survivor from the 1970 squad, was now the captain, but long gone was his leadership and creativity. The Swedes were more persistent and took the lead in the 37th minute with Thomas Sjoberg. The Brazilians managed to tie the game with Reinaldo at the end of the first half.

The group's other opening game also produced a shocking result when Austria beat Spain, 2–1, at Jose Amaliftani Stadium in Buenos Aires. Walter Schachner left the Spanish defense with dropped jaws in the 10th minute to give Austria the lead. The goal—one of the best ever scored at a World Cup—originated in the midfield when Schachner got the ball on the halfway line, then wiggled through two defenders before unleashing a potent shot that beat goalkeeper Miguel Angel Gonzalez. Spain was able to tie the score with Dani in the 21st minute, but the Austrians pressed forward. The second half was dominated by the Austrians, who were rewarded in the in the 78th minute when Hans Krankl banged in a left-footed shot into the net for the game-winner.

On June 7, Spain and Brazil played to a scoreless tie in Mar de Plata, while Austria won the group—and passage to the next round—following a 1–0 triumph over Sweden at Jose Amaliftani Stadium. A penalty kick converted by Krankl in the 43rd minute was enough to defeat Sweden. The Brazilians, who had recorded two ties and scored just one goal, were self-destructing. Coach Claudio Coutinho benched Rivelino against Spain, following a spat in which the captain had publicly lashed out against the coach. Brazil's final group game on June 11 against Austria, while Spain played Sweden at the same time, would determine who would take second place.

Brazil needed a win and knew Austria was assured passage to the next round. That, however, didn't stop the Austrians from playing the way they had in the group's previous two games. Once again, the Brazilians lacked the flair and imagination that fans had been accustomed to seeing from the yellow-shirted magicians. Rivelino was again benched and all he could do was watch from the sidelines as his teammates struggled against the gritty Europeans. The Austrians ultimately paid the price for a defensive error they committed. The only goal of the game came in the 40th minute when Austrian defender Bruno Pezzey misjudged a cross and Roberto Dinamite, who was standing in the box, kicked in the game-winner. The 1–0 victory was enough to get Brazil through to the next round. Brazil's victory had made Spain's 1–0 win over Sweden irrelevant when it came to the group standings. The Spanish team had only themselves to blame for not being able to secure the points they needed against Austria and Brazil in the group's previous two encounters.

Spain wasn't the only European team struggling at the tournament: teams in Group 4 suffered the same fate. Holland found itself also hoeing a tough road to the next round. Despite a 3–0 shellacking of Iran on June 3 in Mendoza, a scoreless tie against Peru four days later showed that the Dutchmen's 3-5-2 formation wasn't good enough to pierce the Peruvian defense. The Dutch players later blamed the poor field conditions. The tie had given Peru—3–1 winners over Scotland on June 3—passage to the next round. The Dutch were also on the verge of clinching a spot to the next round, but had to avoid a loss to Scotland on June 11 in Mendoza. The game did not go well for the Dutch, losing to Scotland 3–2 on two goals from Archie Gemmill and one from Kenny Dalglish. Scotland needed to beat the Dutch by two goals to maintain its World Cup survival. The win wasn't enough and for the second straight tournament, Scotland was ousted on goal differential. Holland had dodged a bullet. The team now had almost a week to regroup and work on a strategy to get back to the final.

## Second Round Group Play

The final eight teams were drawn into two groups of four. The round-robin format featured Italy, Holland, West Germany, and Austria in an all-European Group A, while Group B featured Argentina, Peru, Poland, and Brazil. The situation really heated up in the second round. The Dutch were reunited with the West Germans in a rematch of the 1974 final. The teams took to the field on June 18 in Cordoba. West

Germany led 2–1 until a goal from Rene van der Kerkhof with seven minutes left to play helped give the Dutch a hard-fought tie. Holland, who had defeated Austria 5–1 on June 14, sat atop the group with 3 points.

The group's real threat, however, were the Italians. The scoring partnership of Bettega and Rossi had proven lethal in the first round and was now prepared to do the same in the second. The *Azzurri* opened the group on June 14 with a 0–0 tie against West Germany at the Monumental and needed a victory over Austria to win the group. Ultimately, the *Azzurri* were successful, but not without complicating their lives.

On June 18, the Italians appeared tired and sluggish against Austria at the Monumental. The crowd of 50,000 jeered both teams for much of the game after expecting a slew of goals from Rossi and his teammates. The game's only goal came in the 13th minute with Rossi—the tiny striker intercepted the ball and then in a moment of sheer brilliance, back-heeled the ball to Franco Causio. Rossi continued his run toward the Austrian goal and Causio finished the play by flicking the ball back to him. Rossi grabbed the pass and scored his third goal of the competition. The goal silenced the critical crowd, if only temporarily, as the *Azzurri* locked down its defense and defended the 1–0 lead up until the final whistle. The crowd had wanted more. The Italians gave them just enough.

The fight for a spot in the final came down to the last game on June 21 between Holland and Italy at the Monumental. The game proved to be one of the tournament's hottest tickets, attracting 70,000 spectators. The heckling that had accompanied the Italians in the previous game was surely still ringing in the ears of the players and Bearzot wanted to make sure that the goalscoring duo of Rossi and Bettega would not disappoint. The Italians had to commit themselves to attacking and abandon the *catenaccio* if they hoped to reach their first final in eight years. An own goal gave the *Azzurri* the lead after Holland's Willy Brandts put the ball into his own net in the 19th minute. Rossi and Bettega had beaten the offside trap and with the ball heading into the goal, Brandts, who was giving chase, slid into the ball and at the same time crashed into goalkeeper Piet Schrijvers. Brandts made amends for his error in the 50th minute when his 20-yard thunderbolt beat Zoff. The Italians were once again guilty of trying to defend a slim lead and had paid the price for their defensive approach. The long-range shot once again proved to be Zoff's weakness that day. This time it was Haan's 30-yard shot that beat Zoff. The Dutch had effectively executed its "Total Football" style with every player effectively covering the field. The Dutch had reached their second straight final. Once again, Bearzot and his team were done in by the *catenaccio*.

Group B opened on June 14 with Brazil's 3–0 drubbing of Peru in Mendoza. The Brazilians had scored more goals in this game then their combined total in the previous three matches. The win, of course, was facilitated by Brazil's ability to revert back to its dynamic offensive style. Dirceu, who started in place of Rivelino, wasted no time getting on the scoreboard, netting the game's opening goal in the 14th minute with a 20-yard free kick that curved around the Peruvian defense and into the goal guarded by Ramon Quiroga. Dirceu scored again in the 27th minute and the Brazilians finally put the game away in the 70th minute when Zico converted a penalty kick. Suddenly, the same Brazilian team that had been so maligned by its fans and had played so terribly in the first round were now favored to reach its fifth championship game.

Host Argentina was forced to play in Rosario against Poland after losing to Italy and finishing second in the group. The Argentineans had to do without the heroics of Luque, who was out with a shoulder injury, and had to rely instead on Kempes. Up until that point, Kempes—known for his flowing brown hair and ability to convert free kicks from long distances—had done little to show why he deserved to be in the starting lineup. The game on June 14 served as a homecoming for Kempes, who had played for Rosario Central before hopping over to Valencia in Spain. He celebrated his return to his former stadium by scoring in the 15th minute for the 1–0 lead. The goal was Kempes's first goal of the tournament. Deyna botched a penalty kick when his weak shot was easily saved by goalkeeper Ubaldo Fillol in the 37th minute. Ardiles's midfield prowess and Kempes's ability to dance around the sluggish Polish defense allowed Argentina to control the pace of the game. Kempes, left unshackled by the Polish defense, scored the winner in the 70th minute. The crowd of 40,000 was ecstatic and celebrated the win into the night. Kempes had finally turned into the national hero that Menotti—and the country's regime—had wanted him to be on the eve of the tournament. Kempes's first burst onto the international scene happened four years earlier. Just 19 at the time of the World Cup in 1974, Kempes had failed to live up to expectations. He squandered an easy chance to score in Argentina's first-round game against Poland and never recovered. He would go on to finish the tournament without a goal. He signed a five-year contract with Valencia in 1976 and in his first full season in Spain was able to score twenty-four goals. The following season, Kempes increased his total, this time netting 28 goals, marking the highest total in a Spanish League season since Di Stefano's 31 in 1957.

## MARIO KEMPES

With the exception of Diego Maradona, nobody shines brighter in the pantheon of Argentine soccer than Mario Kempes. His father, who had been an amateur player, encouraged the young Kempes to play soccer when he was nine. Seven years later, Kempes led his local team to the regional championship. He made his pro debut in 1973 for Instituto de Córdoba in a game against Newell's Old Boys.

Kempes' biggest achievements came with the national team. His first national team appearance came in 1973 when he was only 19, during the South American qualifying rounds for the 1974 World Cup. "El Matador" would play in three World Cups (West Germany 1974, Argentina 1978, and Spain 1982), making a total of 18 appearances. The team from Argentina performed disastrously in 1974, where it was knocked out in the first round after being on the wrong end of a thrashing by Johann Cruyff–inspired Holland team. Kempes was unable to make his presence felt, failing to score in the tournament. Three years later, Kempes was the new darling of Valencia fans. Prior to the move, he had become all-time leading goal scorer at Rosario Central, hitting 100 goals in two seasons. Kempes' record in Spain's Liga is impressive too: two Spanish Cups, two European Cup Winners Cups, one European SuperCup, and twice as leading goal scorer in 1977 with 24 goals and again a year later with 28.

Kempes was called up by coach Cesar Luis Menotti for the 1978 World Cup. Argentina's first-round wins over Hungary and France were enough to see his team through to the next round. However, on a personal level, Kempes noted that it felt like a disappointment being unable to score.

*(continued)*

In the end, Kempes would break out of his slump, finishing as the tournament's leading goalscorer with 6 goals. Argentina went on to defeat Poland (Kempes scored twice) in the first round, tie Brazil and defeat Peru (another two goals from Kempes) in the following round, and qualify for the final against Holland. In the final, Argentina beat Holland, 3–1, with Kempes scoring two goals.

Argentina went into Spain 1982 as one of the favorites—with many of the 1978-winning side still on the team. The team, however, was knocked out of the competition. Though he came to be known for his goals, Kempes is also remembered for his fair play: he was never yellow carded or sent off during his international career.

## World Cup Career Statistics

Tournaments played: 3
Games: 17
Goals: 6

While Poland beat Peru 1–0 on June 18 in Mendoza in a game marred by four yellow cards, all eyes that day were on Argentina's game against rivals Brazil. The 46,000 fans that filled Rosario Stadium were anxious to see an Argentine victory. Though they would be disappointed, they would be entertained for ninety minutes. The game turned into a savage confrontation—and the six fouls in the opening three minutes. Brazil controlled the midfield even though Menotti had ordered Kempes to play in the middle in an effort to regain control. Argentina was dealt another blow when Ardiles had to leave the field injured and was replaced by Ricky Villa. Coincidentally, both players would sign with English club Tottenham Hotspur later that summer. The game ended 0–0, therefore leaving the group wide open for either team to win. Both Argentina and Brazil were tied in the standings with 3 points. Brazil's game against Poland and Argentina's match with Peru would determine who would reach the final.

The Brazilians were upset that their game against Poland on June 21 in Mendoza kicked off a few hours before the Argentina–Peru game. The players argued that it would give the hosts an unfair advantage because it allowed Argentina to do exactly what it needed to reach the championship game. Organizers felt that fans would not attend the other matches if they were played at the same time. The excuse may have been lame (especially because, conversely, so many first-round games had been simultaneously played, thus hurting the chances of attaining the maximum live TV audience worldwide), but Brazil knew it had to win and run up the score. Goal differential would come into play in the case of a tiebreaker. But the Brazilians were worried by half-time. Just seven minutes into the game, Zico had to leave because of an injury. A successful Nelinho free kick gave Brazil the lead in the 12th minute. That came as some relief. The Brazilians played their usual pretty style, but that couldn't stop Poland from tying the score with Lato in the 44th minute. With the teams tied 1–1 after the first period, Brazil feared elimination.

The second half featured a Brazilian explosion of goals. The three-time World Cup champions took the lead in the 57th minute when Roberto made a shot that smacked off the post and then put in his own rebound. With the Polish defense in tatters, Roberto scored again five minutes later after the ball bounced off the post and crossbar. Brazil won, 3–1, and temporarily led the group with five points and a goal differential of five. They were in the final—unless Argentina could win and score at least four goals. What emerged was one of the World Cup's most controversial games.

Argentina knew what it needed to do. Peru had nothing to play for. Argentina had the weight of the country—not to mention the military junta—and its fervent fans on them. A trip to the final was Menotti's goal from the start. The only thing that separated his team from that dream was Peru. Argentina made its intentions known from the opening whistle. Menotti pushed his men forward and put four other players around Kempes on attack. The 40,567 fans that had packed Rosario Stadium encouraged the team with its rabid chanting and flag-waving. The Peruvian defense had stretched itself thin in order to keep up with its opponents, something that created huge gaps in the back and allowed Kempes to maneuver the ball with ease. Argentina's midfield was working wonders, moving the ball forward at will.

On one of those plays, Passarella was able to execute a 20-yard pass in the 21st minute to Kempes, who scored his third goal of the tournament with a left-footed shot that was too potent for the Argentine-born goalkeeper Ramon Quiroga to handle. Argentina could have scored at least three more times while the Peruvian defense frantically tried to clear the ball. Albert Tarantini was able to give Argentina a 2–0 lead in the 43rd minute. His header, off a corner kick from Bertoni, sailed into the net. Argentina was two goals away from clinching a spot in the final. The second half proved decisive. Kempes scored again in the 48th minute. A minute later, Luque headed the ball into the net off a pass by Bertoni. Argentina was in the final. The crowd chanted away as the players took no chances. Menotti encouraged them to continue going forward and Rene Houseman scored in the 66th minute. He had come in for Bertoni just two minutes earlier and had now been able to give his team a 5–0 lead. Omaro Larrosa, who was playing for the injured Ardiles, created a chance that Luque was able to put away in the 72nd minute for the 6–0 win. Argentina was in the championship game. The victory enraged the Brazilians, who accused Quiroga of throwing the game. They went as far as to accuse Peruvian officials of accepting bribes from the junta to ensure Argentina's victory, but no wrongdoing was ever proven.

## Consolation Round

On June 24, Brazil and Italy met at the Monumental for a shot at third place. The crowd of 76,600 booed the Brazilians. Italy—without Tardelli and Benetti, who both had to sit out after accumulating two yellow cards during the course of the competition—took the lead in the 38th minute when Causio scored off a Rossi pass. Brazil was able to win the game in the second half. In the 63rd minute, Nelinho's 35-yard blast mesmerized Zoff, again unable to stop the swirling kick from far away. Zoff had been weak when it came to long-range shots and the Brazilians had capitalized on it. A minute later, Dirceu put in a 20-yard volley that beat Zoff. Once again, Zoff had been unable to stop the long ball. The 2–1 win gave Brazil third place—a fitting way for Rivelino to finish his World Cup career—while the Italians had to wait another four years to get their revenge.

## The Final Match

The passion the Argentine crowds had exuded throughout the tournament was ready to explode into joy on the day of the final. Standing in the way of that happiness was a vastly experienced Dutch team. Even without Cruyff (who would end up playing briefly in the NASL with the Los Angeles Aztecs and Fort Lauderdale Strikers), Holland was favored to win its first World Cup. The team had lost a heartbreaker four years earlier. This time, the Dutch had brave the potent Argentine attack and its raucous crowd. The final itself was not without controversy. The game was delayed while Argentinean officials complained about a lightweight cast on van der Kerkhof's arm. The 71,000 fans that packed into the Monumental on June 25 greeted the players with a spectacular shower of confetti and toilet paper streamers that littered the field. The frenzy had begun even before any of the players touched the ball.

Fillol showed why he was one of the world's best goalkeepers when in the 25th minute, he managed to get an outstretched hand onto the ball kicked by Rep. Fillol had sent a clear message to the Dutch: they would have to produce a spectacular play to get the ball past him that evening. By the end of the night, he would be named the best goal-keeper of the tournament. As the first half came to a close, Argentina was able to score. In the 37th minute, Ardiles took the ball from a Luque pass. The wily Argentine striker found Kempes unguarded and dished the ball off to him. Kempes managed to wiggle through several Dutch defenders and tapped the ball into the goal. Kempes' goal wasn't the prettiest, but it was good enough to give Argentina a 1–0 lead. The second half was similar to the first with play limited to a midfield stalemate. The only chances came off defensive errors or from an oc-casional spark of individuality. The noise in the stadium grew louder with each passing minute. The coveted trophy appeared—for now—to belong to the host team. The Dutch, however, weren't going to leave without a fight. Substitute Dirk Nanninga's spectacular header found the back of the net with eight minutes left on the clock. The crowd at the Monumental was silenced. If that wasn't enough, the Dutch could have won the game in the last minute, but Rensenbrink's shot hit the post. The game ended 1–1.

What stood between Argentina lifting the trophy was 30 minutes of extra time and a Dutch team that appeared to be getting stronger with each passing minute. Menotti's pep talk appeared to work wonders and his players came out strong. Kempes, who had been limited to a few touches of the ball in the second half, made his presence felt in extra time. In the 105th minute, Kempes recovered a loose ball in the penalty area, managed to get past two defenders, and put the ball into the net for the goal. Kempes ran toward the corner kick flag in jubilation. His outstretched arms as he ran toward the crowd ultimately become the symbol of Argentina's victory. The Dutch never recovered. Holland, in desperate need to tie the game, left itself open in the back. Argentina capitalized on that weakness in the 116th minute. A Kempes pass to Bertoni, left unmarked in the box, allowed him to slam the ball into the net from close range. The goal gave Argentina a 3–1 win and the title. The Dutch had again come so close, but failed at the last hurdle. The crowd erupted at the sound of the final whistle and even more confetti and streamers poured onto the field. Passarella was carried off the field carrying the trophy. A new champion was crowned, sending a clear message to everyone that Argentina was the world's newest soccer power. The World Cup had been staged with virtually no hiccups, but the schedule needed to be modernized for the next World Cup, which would feature 24 teams. FIFA had plenty of new challenges over in the coming years as the tournament became an even larger spectacle.

## 1982

The two biggest changes FIFA made in time in time for España 1982 was the format and the number of teams. The World Cup was expanded to twenty-four countries, and if that wasn't enough, the formula was also changed. For the first time, the teams were divided into six groups (1 through 6) of four teams; the top two teams in each group advanced to the second round. From that point forward, the teams were split into four groups of three (numbered 1 to 4). The winners of each group would advance to the semifinals. It would be the only World Cup to be played with this format, but the decision to expand the tournament allowed FIFA to give it broader representation. Ironically, the underdogs at this tournament would turn it in a grand performance. Once again, the World Cup was dominated by unbearable heat. To make matters worse, organizers had to deal with a number of mishaps, including a ticket scandal (the first of many that would plague practically every tournament from this point forward) and a botched draw five months before the start of the competition.

The draw was held in Madrid on January 16, 1982, and was immediately followed by controversy. For starters, a dispute erupted after En-gland was named one of the six seeded teams. Belgium and France were the outraged nations and rightfully so. England, who had not qualified for a World Cup since 1970, had barely made it to the finals after finishing second to Hungary in Europe's Group 4. FIFA stood by its decision and decided to keep England a top seed, along with Argentina, Spain, Brazil, Italy, and West Germany. That was only the start of what would become a debacle of a day for Spanish organizers. FIFA concocted a scheme to avoid having South American teams drawn into the same group. To make sure Chile and Peru did not end up in the same group as Argentina and Brazil, the miniature balls that contained their names were supposed to be added to the rotating cages only *after* Argentina and Brazil's group had been decided. But, someone forgot to remove the balls containing Peru and Chile and those countries were in it from the start, confusing the millions of people around the world who watched the draw live on television.

The confusing formula didn't end there. Scotland was mistakenly placed in the Argentina group and only afterward did FIFA officials realize that Belgium too had been drawn too early in the draw, defeating the complicated formula of trying to keep certain teams apart. As a result, Scotland was transferred to Brazil's group and Belgium rightly placed with Argentina. The comedy of errors didn't end there. The revolving drum-shaped cages that continually released the balls jammed at one point, while another ball cracked in half. Organizers were red-faced. A dark cloud lingered over the draw and many inside FIFA feared Spain was not up to the task of hosting such a high-profile event. Though Spanish officials took the heat for the foul-ups, ultimately it was FIFA who had put the draw together. What would happen in five months when the expanded tournament was set to begin was anyone's guess.

The only FIFA official who appeared upbeat—at least at the start of the proceedings—was Havelange. The Brazilian, who was elected to the top of the FIFA food chain in 1974, had spearheaded the move to expand the tournament after a block of African and Asian nations supported his nomination. It was a no-brainer that the tournament would be made larger to accommodate more nations from outside

Europe and South America. Asia and Africa were rewarded by FIFA and given two slots each at the 1982 World Cup. Some argued that more nations would produce more defensive games and tedious 0–0 ties, but that would be far from the truth. The inclusion of Cameroon, Algeria, Kuwait, and New Zealand, for example, coincided with the fact that there was no clear favorite to win the title on the eve of the competition. And such a scenario not only would go on to produce more excitement, but it also created lots of suspense, particularly when Cameroon, Algeria, and Kuwait gave some of the world's more established powers a scare in the first round. Despite the emergence of smaller nations, and the success of the NASL, the United States again failed to reach the finals. This time, the Americans were eliminated in the first round of CONCACAF after being placed in the same group with Mexico and Canada, both of whom also failed to reach the finals. In the end, the region would be represented by Honduras and El Salvador. In general, it was a bleak time for the game in this country. The U.S. played no games in 1981, and only one a year later (a 2–1 win over Trinidad and Tobago) and one in 1983 (a 2–0 victory over Haiti).

## Group Play

The two-year qualifying process, which featured 106 nations, was reduced to 24 finalists placed in the following pools:

Group 1: Italy, Poland, Peru, and Cameroon
Group 2: West Germany, Austria, Chile, and Algeria
Group 3: Argentina, Belgium, Hungary, and El Salvador
Group 4: England, France, Czechoslovakia, and Kuwait
Group 5: Spain, Yugoslavia, Northern Ireland, and Honduras
Group 6: Brazil, Soviet Union, Scotland, and New Zealand

As far as the favorites were concerned, Argentina, the reigning champions, looked strong once again. Menotti again coached the team and he now had a new weapon in his arsenal: Maradona. The squatty player with legs like tree trunks had been overlooked four years earlier. This time, the former Boca Juniors playmaker was prepared to make his World Cup debut. Maradona was not the only player from the youth ranks to graduate to Menotti's team. Ramon Diaz was also called up to the national team; with him was Ardiles, who, back from his experience playing with Tottenham, reinforced the team's much-feared midfield. Kempes was also back, but this time the team star was Diaz. Kempes was there to serve in a supporting role after being the star in 1978. West Germany, as usual, also looked potent, though it would be without the services of Barcelona striker Bernd Schuster, who was plagued by a knee injury. The West Germans, winners of the European Championship two years earlier, looked poised to add another World Cup to their trophy case.

Brazil also was on the list of favorites; out was Coutinho as coach and in was Tele Santana. Unlike Coutinho, Santana encouraged his players to attack and put constant pressure on opposing defenses. Though the famed *Selecao* didn't appear to have a genuine goalscorer after Careca had to sit out the tournament because of an injury, Santana's team did feature a plethora of midfielders such as Zico (who many at the time considered the best Brazilian player since Pelé), Cerezo, and Socrates, all of whom were adept at creating plays and scoring goals. The absence of a true scorer—a problem worsened by Santana's insistence that Zico play deep in the midfield—forced the Brazilians to rely on set pieces and penalty kicks for its scoring. The Brazilians, however, were a fun bunch to watch compared to other teams, who were too often restrained by paint-by-numbers defensive tactics that had proven effective but created games that were awful to watch.

The tournament kicked off on June 13 with a Group 3 clash between Argentina and Belgium in Barcelona. The game not only featured something the previous four opening games had failed to accomplish (a goal), it also produced an upset. The curtain-raiser marked Maradona's World Cup debut. Ironically, it was held at the Nou Camp Stadium, home to the same Barcelona team that had signed Maradona on the eve of the tournament for a $7 million transfer fee. The Belgians flooded their own half with players—at times, the entire team stayed back to play defense—and Maradona was crowded by defenders each time he tried to get a touch on the ball. A solid Belgian defense would ultimately beat Argentina's offense when striker Erwin Vandenbergh's left-footed blast from outside the box in the 60th minute proved to be the winner. Kempes, so brilliant four years earlier, was invisible for most of the game, while Diaz looked out of shape in the midfield. The

1-0 loss marked the first time since Italy in 1950 that a reigning champion had lost its first game.

Speculation ran rampant that the Argentines were distracted by the Falklands War. Argentina, already in the midst of an economic crisis and led by an ever-growing unpopular military junta led by General Leopoldo Galtieri, decided in March 1982 to launch what it thought was a quick and easy war to recapture the Falkland Islands from the British. The decision to launch the offensive, a bid to spur nationalism, backfired. Once they overcame the surprise of being attacked, the British launched its own offensive and the naval assault resulted in the death of 635 Argentineans. The British eventually prevailed and the Argentines surrendered on June 14, a day after Argentina's opening loss.

Back in Spain, Group 1 opened June 14 with a 0-0 tie between Italy and Poland at Balaidos Stadium in Vigo on Spain's Atlantic coast. Zoff, always reliable for the Italians, marked his 100th national team appearance with a series of saves, but the *Azzurri's* attack lacked the firepower needed to pierce the Polish defense. Though the Italians came close on several occasions, they blew a chance to collect two points in the 80th minute when Tardelli's empty net shot went off the crossbar.

Cameroon and Peru, the two other teams in the group, squared off the next day at Riazor Stadium in La Coruna. The game ended 0-0. Italy returned to action June 18 against Peru in Vigo. The *Azzurri* desperately needed a win to break away from the rest of the group and quell the Italian press, which was calling for Bearzot's head. Italy also had to break free of its defense-dominant style if it wanted to win. Though Bearzot knew his team had to take the offensive initiative, the players seemed reluctant to make forays into the Peruvian half. The Italians, however, did score first with Roma winger Bruno Conti in the 19th minute. The Italians were unable to do anything after that and Paolo Rossi, a phantom in the first half, was substituted by Causio at halftime.

The second half saw the Peruvians put on a mix of solid defending and spectacular attacking. Peru was rewarded in the 84th minute after Ruben Diaz tied the score. The Italians had failed to get a win and there was no doubt that something was wrong with Bearzot's team.

Rossi was not playing the same way that had brought him prominence at the World Cup four years earlier. His skill as a goal poacher had fizzled. In fact, Bearzot's decision to call up Rossi had come under intense scrutiny in the weeks before the start of the competition. He had been affectionately called *Pablito* at the last World Cup. Now the once-beloved Rossi was considered by many to be nothing but a cheater. Serie A had been rocked by a game-fixing scandal that had tarnished the league's reputation. The shame that had befallen Italian soccer grew even larger when Rossi, on loan to Perugia from Vicenza, was one of the players implicated.

## PAOLO ROSSI

If any one player has ever demonstrated innate opportunism when it came to scoring goals, it was Paolo Rossi. A born goalscorer, Rossi burst onto the international scene at the 1978 World Cup and solidified his reputation in leading Italy to the 1982 tournament.

Rossi's career ran the risk of ending prematurely in 1979. After his great showing at Argentina 1978, Rossi returned to Serie A to spearhead Perugia's attack. He was having a brilliant season until December 1978 when his team could only muster a 2–2 tie with Avellino. After an investigation, Rossi and several of his teammates were convicted of fixing the game. Rossi claimed his response to a question posed to him by an Avellino player was wholly innocent: "Two-to-Two. Only if you want." Despite the denials, the punishment was a severe one: a three-year suspension, which was later commuted to two on appeal. Only 22 at the time, Rossi's career appeared over.

Rossi was born in Prato in the Tuscany region on September 23, 1956. Juventus scouted him at an early age and loaned him to Serie B club Como in an effort to toughen him up. Only after moving to Serie B team Vicenza, did he prove to be an exceptional goalscorer. His 21 goals during the 1976–1977 season helped Vicenza earn promotion to Serie A. He did even better the following season, scoring 24 goals to help Vicenza to second place in the standings behind Juventus.

Italy coach Enzo Bearzot gave Rossi his first national team appearance in 1977. The Rossi scoring juggernaut was ready to kick into high gear. Only 21, Rossi had an excellent World Cup in 1978, displaying a poacher's instinct and a knack for being in the right place at the right time each time the ball was played to him. His small stature earned him the nickname *Pablito* from the Argentine press. His three goals, however, boded well for his future and that of Italy's national team at the next World Cup.

*(continued)*

The glory came to an abrupt end with his suspension. By the time his two-year ban came to an end in the spring of 1982, Juventus again snapped up Rossi, but this time decided to keep him. His return to the game in April 1982, just weeks before the 1982 World Cup in Spain, meant that he had little chance of winning a spot on Bearzot's roster. But Bearzot showed faith in Rossi's abilities and called him up to national team duty.

The Italian media were skeptical, even more so after Italy's dismal first round. The *Azzurri* scraped through on goal differential after recording three ties in three matches. Rossi, who started all three games, failed to score. In the second round, the *Azzurri* found themselves grouped with Brazil and Argentina. Rossi fired blanks against Argentina, but Italy won anyway, 2–1. Despite failing to score, Bearzot gave Rossi another chance against Brazil, a game Italy needed to win in order to advance to the semifinals. The match turned out to be an epic encounter with Rossi scoring a hat trick in a 3–2 victory. The Rossi goalscoring machine was back on track and it would be his heroics from this point forward that landed Italy in the final.

He scored two goals against Poland in the semifinals, before netting his sixth strike against West Germany in the final. He finished the tournament as top scorer with six goals, winning the World Cup for Italy and in the process silencing the critics. He was named European Player of the Year later that year.

The accolades didn't end there for Rossi. With Juventus, he won the Italian Cup in 1983, the Serie A title and European Cup Winners' Cup in 1984, and the European Cup in 1985. He left Juventus in 1985 for rival AC Milan. Again, Bearzot picked him to play for Italy at the 1986 World Cup, although he never played a single minute at the tournament.

Rossi, who made 48 appearances for Italy and scored 20 goals, ended his career with Verona in 1987. He currently works as an entrepreneur.

## World Cup Career Statistics

Tournaments played: 2
Games: 14
Goals: 9

The Italian soccer scandal erupted in February 1980 after Italian police charged 38 players with fraud. Two gamblers claimed they had paid players to fix games. The charges were eventually dropped against all the players for lack of evidence. Rossi was never accused of taking any money in return for throwing games, but his failure to cooperate with prosecutors to testify against other players landed him in hot water. The Italian FA, however, conducted its own investigation, which eventually led to the suspension of 17 players, including Rossi. The federation had determined that Rossi's actions before Perugia's 2–2 tie against Avellino was enough to get him banned. He vehemently denied being involved, though federation officials pointed to an off-the-cuff comment he made to an opposing player during the game that included the phrase, "Two-to-two? Only if you want."

Rossi was suspended for three years (a ban that was eventually reduced to two years on appeal) and he returned to the playing fields with his new club Juventus in April 1982 with just three weeks left in the season. Bearzot called him up for national team duty and put him on Italy's 22-player World Cup roster. If Rossi's fitness wasn't enough of a debate, the Italian camp was rife with turmoil. Despite the popularity of the players with Spanish women, who packed the training sessions in Barcelona to catch a glimpse of the dark-haired Don Juans, Bearzot had a tough time hiding the internal bickering that appeared to get worse with each game. The Italians experienced something similar at the 1978 World Cup, but on that occasion the federation's public relations machine, coupled with a series of decent results, had kept the unrest a secret from prying reporters. This time, the secret was out and the results weren't there to hide behind. If anything, the poor results unmasked the trouble that was brewing among the players. The only thing going in Italy's favor during the first round was Poland's inability to win games.

On June 19, Cameroon and Poland also played to a tie, this one a scoreless, defensive affair in La Coruna. The opening half featured a polished Polish offense against the defensive-minded Africans. Cameroonian goalkeeper Thomas N'Kono and his quick reflexes were able to keep Poland off the scoreboard. In the second half, the Polish defense suffered and Cameroon's ability to take advantage of the counterattack served as a warning, but striker Roger Milla was unable to hit the target during one of his many runs. The result was the third match of the group to end scoreless. After four games, all four teams were tied at two points.

The group's low-scoring run ended on June 22 when Poland trounced Peru, 5–1, in La Coruna. The first half had ended 0–0 and the 25,000 fans who gathered at Rainor Stadium were probably expecting another scoreless tie. But the avalanche of goals began in the 55th minute with Wlodzimierz Smolarek after a Peruvian mixup in the midfield allowed Poland to steal the ball and make a run up the field. Three minutes later, a pass from Zbigniew "Zibi" Boniek to Lato, who was playing in his third World Cup, allowed him to score his tenth all-time World Cup goal. Boniek scored one of his own in the 61st minute to make it 3–0. Andrezj Buncol, who had assisted on Boniek's goal, scored one of his own seven minutes later to cap off a four-goal run in thirteen minutes. The Peruvians were down for the count and the tired defense gave up another goal in the 76th minute when Wlodzimierz Ciolek—who had entered the game just three minutes before in place of Smolarek— scored to make it 5–0. Peru netted a consolation goal with Guillermo LaRosa in the 83rd minute. The win clinched Poland a spot to the next round.

Italy, meanwhile, only needed a tie against Cameroon the following day in Vigo to advance. Both teams had two points apiece, but Italy had scored one extra goal and led in the goal differential tiebreaker. Italy squandered a host of chances from the start, including one by Conti in the 11th minute with the goal wide open. N'Kono put in another great show between the posts and prevented the frustrated, and sometimes nervous, Italians from putting the ball past him. A scoreless first half was fine for Italy. The *Azzurri* took the lead with Francesco Graziani in the 60th minute. A minute later, Cameroon tied it up when Gregoire M'Bida knocked in the ball past Zoff on a play the Italians argued was offside. The Italians were able to get another tie—the third in three games—and joined Poland in the next group stage.

African soccer, which had been written off by many as a hopeless cause, had threatened the traditional powers at the World Cup. Although Cameroon had been eliminated, it had given everyone a taste of the raw talent and unabashed enthusiasm. For the Italians, reaching the next stage did nothing for their morale. The players decided after the first round to stay mum and not grant interviews following harsh criticism from the media. The term *silenzio stampa* (media blackout) was born and would last the entire length of the tournament. The relationship between the players and the Italian press reached a breaking point in Barcelona when Rossi and Cabrini, who were roommates, were accused of being more than that when both players were spotted bare-chested on the balcony of their hotel room. The players elected team captain Zoff to represent the team at news conferences. Only he would talk to reporters after games. The choice was an odd one. After all, Zoff's polite demeanor and shyness made him a weird spokesman. Zoff, of course, was more famous for being one of the world's greatest goalkeepers and, at age 40, the oldest player at the World Cup. Zoff, who possessed an effortless dive and fists capable of successfully stopping cannonball shots, started his pro career in 1961—at a time when many players at the World Cup were toddlers—playing with Italian clubs Napoli and later Juventus, where he set a league record by going nine straight games, a total of 1,145 minutes, without conceding a goal. During a seven-year stretch with Juventus, he played every minute of every league game. But Italy's version of the Iron Horse often gave up dumb goals, particularly on long-range shots and had some people wondering whether he was too old to guide a team to the title.

Group 2 opened on June 16 with an upset when West Germany lost to Algeria 2–1 at El Molinon Stadium in Gijon. The Algerian victory, one of the biggest surprises in World Cup history, seemed improbable on the eve of the match. Algeria, a 1000–1 shot to win the cup, dominated the game from the opening whistle, deflating the West Germans' morale almost from the start. The West German players melted under the intense heat while the Algerian attack, led by African Player of the Year Lakhdar Belloumi and inspired by a Brazilian style of play, capitalized on that weakness. Algeria took the lead in the 54th minute when striker Rabah Madjer was in place to kick the ball into the net following a shot from Belloumi that had bounced off West German goalkeeper Toni Schumacher. The lead only lasted fourteen minutes. That's how long it took for the West Germans to regroup and, thanks to a goal by Rummenigge, they tied the score. Algeria wasn't done. A minute later, Belloumi scored the winner. The incredulous West Germans walked off the field in dismay as the jubilant Algerian players raised their arms in celebration as the 42,000 fans cheered them. All of Spain appeared to be rooting for the underdog Algerians. But the good fortune that had befallen the North Africans against West Germany disappeared on June 21 against Austria in Gijon. The Austrians, 1–0 winners over Chile four days earlier at Carlos Tartiere Stadium in Oviedo, also appeared to suffer against the Algerians at first. Then were able to take the lead in the 56th minute with Schachner after the Algerian defense failed to clear the ball. The Austrians added an insurance goal eleven minutes later when Hans Krankl's left-footed shot ended Algeria's dreams of another upset. Elsewhere, the previous day, in Gijon, West Germany avenged its loss against Algeria and took its frustrations out on Chile, defeating the South Americans, 4–1, thanks to a Rummenigge hat trick.

On June 24, the attacking Algerians pulled off another upset. This time, the venue was Oviedo and the opponent was Chile. The flair that the Algerians had been able to put on the field was too much for the sluggish Chileans. The Algerians wasted no time getting on the scoreboard. Much to the amazement of the 18,000 fans, the Algerians jumped out to a 3–0 lead after thirty-four minutes with two goals from Tedj Bensaoula and one by Salah Assad. The Algerians, spent of energy in the second half, focused on defending their lead. The Chileans mounted a comeback and pulled a goal back in the 60th minute when Miguel Neira converted a penalty kick. With sixteen minutes remaining, Chile scored again when Juan Carlos Letelier beat three defenders before scoring. The game, which in the first half had appeared to be a forgone conclusion, was anyone's to win. The Algerians fended off everything the Chilean players threw at them to hold on to the 3–2 victory. The win was big, but eventually proved meaningless. If Algeria wanted to be the first African team in World Cup history to qualify out of the first round, it had to wait for the decisive West Germany–Austria game in Gijon. Though unbeknownst to the Africans, the Europeans were about to orchestrate the most shameful display in soccer history.

If the Austrians won or the game ended in a tie, then Algeria would qualify to the next round. But that never came to be because of what is now remembered as the greatest farce in the history of the game. A 1–0 win for West Germany ensured that both teams would go on to the next round (and leave the Algerians out) and that is exactly how the game ended. Instead of playing the match, the Austrians waited for its European neighbors to take the lead. And the West Germans did just that after ten minutes when Horst Hrubesch headed the ball into the goal. Following the goal, the teams stopped playing. Content with the score, the contest turned into something of a scripted play. The ball was kicked around aimlessly for the next seventy-nine minutes and the crowd of 41,000 who had come to watch the game began to jeer and whistle. Some Algerian fans in the stands tried to storm the field at one point, but were thwarted by police officers who were vigilantly patrolling the sidelines. The players appeared unfazed by the reaction of the crowd and continued to kill the clock in what ultimately became a black eye for the game. When Scottish referee Bob Valentine whistled the end of the game, West Germany had won. FIFA was helpless. There was nothing they could have done to end the charade. A chorus of boos accompanied the players off the field, but they cared very little. The result had put West Germany, Austria, and Algeria all in first place with four points, but the two European nations were the ones to advance due to better goal differential. The outraged Algerians filed a complaint with FIFA the following day, arguing the game had been rigged. FIFA rejected Algeria's pleas, but introduced a revised system at future World Cups in which the final two games in each group were to be played simultaneously in order to end any machinations.

Group 3 had opened with an Argentine defeat at the hands of Belgium. In the other group game played on June 15 at Nuevo Estadio in Elche, Hungary put on an offensive display against El Salvador that gave fuel to the argument that allowing smaller nations into the tournament would result in lopsided outcomes. Hungary showed no mercy, taking a 3–0 lead by halftime and scoring seven more goals after the break to lambaste El Salvador, 10–1, to record the largest margin of victory ever in a World Cup finals game. The naïve El Salvadorians were nothing more than a sparring partner for the astute Hungarians, who turned the game into a scrimmage as Havelange looked on from the stands. Laszlo Kiss, who entered the game in the 55th minute, netted a hat trick to become the first and only substitute to score three goals in the finals.

Hungary's next game against Argentina on June 18 in Jose Rico Perez Stadium in Alicante would not be a cakewalk. Argentina's defense was much more experienced than El Salvador's and the Hungarians knew it. Hungary also knew that Argentina had Maradona, a playmaker who could, with the flick of the foot, change the outcome of a game. Though Maradona had yet to prove those skills on the World Cup level, he used the game against Hungary as his coming-out party. Argentina attacked from the beginning and found the back of the net in the 26th minute when Maradona headed down a Passarella free kick that Bertoni was able to score. Two minutes later, Maradona was able to head the ball into the net for his first World Cup goal. The stocky Argentine added another goal ten minutes into the second half and Ardiles made it 4–0 in the 60th minute. The Magyars were unable to respond, though they were able to score a consolation goal with Gabor Poloskei with fourteen minutes left to play. Argentina had avenged its loss to Belgium and with a 4–1 win and, with Maradona in top form, the team appeared to have the advantage over the rest of the teams in the group.

Belgium, however, would win the group after posting a 1–0 win over El Salvador on June 19 and a 1–1 tie versus Hungary three days later. The Belgians were outsiders to win the World Cup, but they were picked by some, replacing Holland, as the most entertaining team in Europe. The Red Devils had talent in every part of the field with Jean Marie Pfaff guarding the goalposts, Eric Gerets marshalling the defense, and Jan Ceulemans scoring the goals, though he had failed to net one in the first round.

Argentina, meanwhile, was able to secure second place and a spot in the next round on June 23 with a resounding 2–0 victory over El Salvador. The Argentineans didn't run up the score on the lowly El Salvadorians like Menotti and his men may have wanted, but the 32,000 fans in Alicante didn't appear to mind. The El Salvadorian team employed the same tactic it had against Belgium and featured eleven players in the back. The frustrated Argentines threw everything they could at them and were able to score twice thanks to a penalty kick by Passarella in the first half and Bertoni's goal in the second. The 2-0 win was enough to get Argentina through, but Menotti had to deal with Maradona's sudden inability to quickly resolve games. In fact, a huge dose of criticism was heaped on Maradona by Argentina's press for not being able to score against the weak Central Americans. Doubts were beginning to swirl around him. Maradona appeared unfazed. Menotti had left a then-seventeen-year-old Maradona out of the 1978 World Cup team. Now, Menotti was being criticized for bringing the twenty-one-year-old blossoming star and making him a starter.

Maradona's journey to stardom had been uphill from the start. Born in a shantytown in the outskirts of Buenos Aires, Maradona grew up very poor. At age ten, Maradona was spotted by a talent scout while playing for his neighborhood team. Maradona was given a chance to play with the Cebollitas ("Little Onions"), which served as a youth team for pro club Argentinos Juniors. As a ball boy, Maradona amazed fans by endlessly juggling the ball during halftime intermissions. In some cases, he earned a larger chunk of the applause than the team did during games. Maradona made his debut with Argentinos Juniors at age fifteen, playing for the club between 1976 and 1981 before his transfer to Boca Juniors. A year later, he won his first Argentine League title. Maradona was quickly showing everyone that he was a burgeoning star on the national level and was able to prove that on a global stage when, as an eighteen-year-old, he led Argentina to the World Youth Championships in Japan.

Group 4, meanwhile, also featured lots of drama, but the Spanish authorities were more concerned about the off-the-field troubles. The group was played in Valladolid and Bilbao and featured England and its infamous hooligans, whose violent behavior at games had become notorious and created security concerns among organizers. Those same organizers braced for the worst as English fans made their way to both cities. The hooligans had terrorized other cities during past competitions with their mix of drinking and vandalism. Extra police were stationed in the streets and at stadiums, but the violence was limited and failed to pose the massive problems authorities had predicted.

On the field, England locked horns with France on June 16 at San Mames Stadium in Bilbao. The English players braved the 100-degree heat and got off to a flying start when Bryan Robson scored after twenty-six seconds to record the fastest goals in finals history. *Les Bleus* tied the score in the 26th minute when Gerard Soler's kick breezed past a diving Peter Shilton. Robson made his presence felt again in the second half, putting England ahead, 2–1, with another goal in the 66th minute. His goal, a towering header off a cross from Trevor Francis, was no match for the French backline. Paul Mariner made it 3–1 for England with eight minutes to play, scoring from close range.

The following day, Czechoslovakia and Kuwait played to a 1–1 tie at Nuevo Estadio Jose Zorrilla in Valladolid. The Czechoslovakian team found the Kuwaitis to be a tougher opponent than previously expected. Kuwait, coached by Brazilian Carlos Alberto Parreira, played a South American style that proved too difficult for the Europeans to handle. Kuwait's soccer federation had pumped millions of dollars into the national team program with the aim of turning the tiny Arab country into a soccer power. Parreira had the benefit of training the players for nearly a year after qualifying. Preparations aside, Czechoslovakia got on the board first after referee Benjamin Dwomoh, who hailed from Ghana, awarded a dubious penalty kick and Antonin Panenka converted in the 21st minute. Kuwait tied the game with Faisal Al Dakhil in the 58th minute.

Czechoslovakia's luck didn't get any better on June 20 in Bilbao. A 2–0 loss to England exposed the Czechoslovakians' limitations both defensively and offensively. Robson was once again the most effective player on the field for the English, that is, until he suffered a groin injury in the second half that led to his leaving the game. England's first goal came in the 63rd minute after Francis knocked the ball in from five yards out. Three minutes later, the leaky Czechoslovakian defense showed how porous it really was when a low Mariner cross was accidentally deflected into the net by an opposing defender.

In the other group game played the next day, France routed Kuwait, 4–1. The four goals were only part of the story that day in Valladolid. Ahead 3–1, Soviet referee Miroslav Stupar awarded *Les Bleus* a fourth goal in the 79th minute when Alain Giresse's shot made its way into the net, while the Kuwaiti defenders stood motionless. The Kuwaiti players argued they had heard a whistle and stopped, tricked by someone blowing a horn from the stands. Stupar ignored their pleas until a man in a turban and white tunic ran onto the field. The man, Kuwaiti FA president Prince Sheikh Fahid Al-Ahmad, so incensed with the call, had scurried from his seat to give Stupar a piece of his mind. Al-Ahmad continued to protest the call as the French players looked on in amazement. At this point, the Kuwaiti players began to walk off the field. Al-Ahmad had gotten to Stupar, who feared the Kuwaiti players would abandon the game. He immediately disallowed the goal, as if it had never happened. Police officers had to restrain French coach Michel Hidalgo and the game was suspended for eight minutes. Stupar would never referee an international game again, while Al-Ahmad was later fined $12,000 by FIFA. (In an odd footnote to the story, Al-Ahmad was killed by Iraqi soldiers during the 1991 Gulf War.) Meanwhile, France, which only needed a tie to advance to the next round, played Czechoslovakia to a 1–1 tie on June 24 in Valladolid. The following day in Bilbao, England, playing its worst game of the tournament, defeated Kuwait 1–0. The only goal of the game came off a long kick from Shilton that Mariner was able to control at the other end. Mariner then flicked a fancy back-heel pass to Francis, who shot the ball into the net to win the game and top the group.

In Group 5, hosts Spain, a 5–1 shot to win the cup, kicked off the tournament on the wrong foot June 16 at Luis Casanova Stadium in Valencia, tying Honduras, a 500–1 shot, 1–1. The pressure put upon the team by the 49,562 fans in the stadium—which included King Juan Carlos—and the millions watching on TV around the country proved too immense. That pressure got to the Spaniards after just seven minutes. That's all the time it took Honduras to get on the board with Hector Zelaya. The stunned crowd was silenced just as the cheering had begun to grow to a crescendo. Spain was able to level the score in the 65th minute after Argentinean referee Arturo Ithurralde awarded the hosts a penalty. Roberto Lopez-Ufarte converted the kick, which allowed the king and everyone else in the country to breathe a sigh of relief. In the other group game played the next day, Northern Ireland and Yugoslavia played to a scoreless tie at La Romereda Stadium in Zaragoza. The only highlight of the game was the presence of Norman Whiteside, who at seventeen years and forty-one days old became the youngest player to ever make a World Cup debut. The previous record had been held by Pelé.

On June 20, Spain, in need of a good showing, defeated Yugoslavia, 2–1, in Valencia before 48,000 fans. The win was just what Spanish fans were looking for, though the hosts had struggled for much of the contest. Yugoslavia scored first and took the lead with Ivan Gudelj after ten minutes. Spain appeared to catch a break two minutes later when Danish referee Herning Lund-Sorenson whistled a penalty kick in their favor. The Yugoslavs argued that the foul had occurred outside the box. The referee thought otherwise and awarded the kick. Lopez-Ufarte, who had scored from the spot against Honduras, missed the kick. The referee ordered it to be retaken because goalkeeper Dragan Pantelic had moved off his line before the ball had been kicked. This time, Juan Juanito lined up for the kick and scored to make it 1–1. In the second half, Yugoslavia appeared stronger than Spain, but was unable to take the lead. Against the run of play, the hosts were able to catch another break. A defensive error led to a corner kick that eventually turned into Spain's game winner. Enrique Saura had given Spain the victory and a shot at advancing to the next round.

In Zaragoza the following day, Honduras stunned the world again. This time, the Central Americans were able to tie Northern Ireland, 1–1. The Europeans, which featured a mix of English-based club players, had taken the lead after two minutes with striker Gerry Armstrong. The goal appeared to signal the start of a defeat. The Hondurans had other plans and continued to push forward, tying the score with Antonio Laing in the 60th minute. They had given another team in its group a headache and had every intention of making a run into the next round. The only thing standing in Honduras' way was Yugoslavia, who had to hope in a Spanish loss against Northern Ireland to reach the second round.

On June 24, Honduras's dream of advancing came to a crashing halt after losing to Yugoslavia, 1–0, in Zaragoza. The Hondurans had held the Europeans scoreless up until the 87th minute. It was then that Chilean referee Gaston Castro awarded Yugoslavia a penalty kick, which Vladimir Petrovic was able to convert. Yugoslavia's hopes of advancing now hinged on the outcome of the Spain–Northern Ireland game slated to take place the next day. Northern Ireland had to win the game in Valencia in order to advance, while the hosts could also move on in the event of a loss, but by no more than a one goal. Spain again felt the pressure and its early exit from the tournament became a real possibility after Northern Ireland took the lead with Armstrong in the second half. The 49,500 Spanish fans made their presence felt in Luis Casanova Stadium as they chanted and cheered for ninety straight minutes. The support from the crowd fueled the team, but veteran Northern Ireland goalkeeper Pat Jennings had a stellar outing, thwarting several shots that had been peppered his way by the Spanish attack. Northern Ireland's 1–0 win meant it had booked its pass to the second round. Though they had lost, the Spaniards, who were tied in the standings at three points with Yugoslavia, were able to qualify thanks to a better goals-against-average. Though few people were celebrating in Spain, the Honduran players were feted upon their arrival in Tegucigalpa. The airport was packed with 50,000 of their flag-waving countrymen ecstatic with how the players had performed against three of Europe's strongest teams.

Group 6 became the stage for Brazilian skill and elegance. The team had been rebuilt and again boasted an offensive firepower that promised a return to the glory days. The three-time world champions lived up to all the pre-tournament hype, defeating the Soviet Union, the other favorite in the group, 2–1, at Sanchez Pizjuan Stadium in Seville. The game, which featured Brazil's *jogo bonito* accompanied by the samba beat of its yellow and green–clad fans, was one of the most exciting matches of the opening round. The 68,000 spectators cheered on the Brazilians in unison until they were silenced in the 33rd minute when Andrei Bal squeezed in a goal after Waldir Peres, continuing the Brazilian tradition of bad goalkeepers, failed to grab the ball, which slowly trickled past him. The USSR maintained the lead until the 75th minute when Socrates netted a magnificent goal, sidestepping two defenders and unleashing a potent shot from outside the penalty box. The Brazilian attack didn't end there at 1–1. The Soviet defense did its best to keep up, but in the 88th minute, Eder scored the game-winner, leaving the Soviets nothing to show for its gritty effort.

Four days later, Brazil squared off against Scotland, who had trounced New Zealand 5–2 on June 15 at La Rosaleda Stadium in Malaga. The Scots had shown everyone that they could score at will, even if the New Zealand team had been no match for them. Brazil, on the other hand, was hardly intimidated. Once again, a 43,000, pro-Brazilian crowd packed Benito Villamarin Stadium in Seville. The carnival-like spectacle in the stands was a reminder of how much fervor the World Cup could generate, particularly by the Brazilians. Scotland took the lead with midfielder David Narey in the 18th minute after releasing a swerving shot from the edge of the penalty area that was too much for Waldir Peres to stop. Brazil tied the score fifteen minutes later when a 25-yard Zico free kick made its way over the Scottish wall and landed in the net past goalkeeper Alan Rough. The Brazilian juggernaut continued in the second half when a header from Oscar, off a curling Junior corner kick, gave Brazil the 2–1 lead in the 48th minute. Brazil was not done. Eder scored Brazil's third goal in the 64th minute, mesmerizing Rough with a fantastic chip shot. Brazil closed the scoring with Falcao, nicknamed the "King of Rome" for his club exploits with Italian club

AS Roma, sending a 25-yard rocket for a goal in the 86th minute to cap off the 4–1 drubbing.

While Brazil had won big, the USSR was trying to get its act together and overcome the psychological blow that had accompanied the players following its opening loss. The Soviets were able to do just that against New Zealand on June 19 in Malaga, shutting out the Kiwis 3–0. The USSR remained on course to at least finish second and qualify for the second group phase. Standing in its way, however, was Scotland, who needed a win against the Soviets if it wanted to advance. Both sides butted heads on June 22 in Malaga and the result was not exactly what Scotland had in mind. The 2–2 result did nothing for Scotland and for the second straight time had been bounced out of the tournament on goal differential.

Brazil, on the other hand, continued to impress. New Zealand, the next victim on Brazil's hit list, was no match for the South Americans when the two teams met on June 23 in Seville. New Zealand had made several runs at the Brazilian goal, but those opportunities proved fruitless. Predictably, Brazil took the lead with Zico in the 29th minute after connecting on a bicycle kick off a Leandro cross. Two minutes later, the chemistry between Leandro and Zico led to another goal: Leandro's cross across the box allowed Zico to put the ball past goalkeeper Frank Van Hattum. The Brazilians then put together a series of passes that got the 43,000 fans in the stadium chanting with each touch of the ball. In the second half, Zico decided it was his turn to play the role of setup man, assisting once on a Falcao goal in the 55th minute and then again on one by Serginho fifteen minutes later. Brazil won the game, 4–0, and the group in impressive fashion. They scored thirteen goals in three games and gave up just two. Brazil appeared destined to hoist the trophy for a fourth time, but before they could celebrate, they had to endure a tougher second-round group that would truly test the talent of Santana's team.

## Second Round Group Play

The second round would feature four groups with Group C as the toughest of them all. The winners of each group would advance to the semifinals. The groups stacked up as follows: Group A had Poland, Soviet Union, and Belgium; Group B included England, West Germany, and Spain; Group C was composed of Brazil, Argentina, and Italy; and Group D consisted of France, Austria, and Northern Ireland.

The second round opened on June 28 with the Group A clash between Poland and Belgium in Barcelona. The Poles didn't miss a beat and continued to show opponents why their strikers were some of the deadliest on the planet. Juventus-bound Boniek put Poland ahead after just four minutes. Once again, his partnership with Lato proved decisive. It was Lato's defense-cutting pass from the right that allowed Boniek to connect with the ball and blast it into the net. Boniek struck again 22 minutes later, this time heading the ball into the goal. Though Boniek had scored twice, it had been Lato's agility and deft passing that powered the Polish counterattack. Belgium's defense tried in vain to keep up, but was caught napping on several occasions. Poland's great form continued seven minutes after the break when a Lato pass set up Boniek, who rounded goalkeeper Theo Custers and slotted the ball into the net for the hat trick and the 3-0 win.

Three days later, Belgium, which made four changes to its lineup, took on the USSR in Barcelona. Those changes—which included the debut of third-string goalkeeper Jacques Munaron—proved fruitless. The Soviets played harder and scored the 1-0 win with Khoren Oganesyan in the 49th minute. The loss sent Belgium packing, while the Soviet Union's final game against Poland would determine the winner of the group and the first semifinalist. Poland, knowing it only needed a tie to advance, put on a defensive display against the Soviet Union on July 4, banking instead on Lato's abilities to make the most of the counterattack. The USSR, in turn, was unable to break down the Polish defense and the game ended scoreless. Poland had reached the semifinals for the second time in World Cup history, while the USSR had fallen short once again.

Group B featured three of Europe's toughest teams and opened on June 29 with a rematch of the 1966 World Cup final between West Germany and England in Madrid. Both teams lacked the inventiveness and offensive stamina to produce an exciting game. As a result, the 75,000 spectators that packed the Bernabeu Stadium were treated to an uneventful contest. The English, who produced several scoring chances early in the game, had their best chance with Robson in the 38th minute. Sadly, that was also the last time the English would produce a scoring chance. The West Germans didn't do much better, although they did put together a final assault in hopes of grabbing a goal. Rummenigge's 25-yard blast hit the crossbar in the 85th minute, but it would have been an injustice for anyone to come away with a win. The game ended 0–0.

West Germany's next game against Spain three days later in Madrid was a different story. The Spaniards, who had showed how fragile they were in the first round, were no match for West Germany. Spain appeared content with having gotten this far. The West Germans opened the scoring in the 49th minute with Pierre Littbarski, who had been left on the bench against England. Littbarski was also part of the second goal in the 75th minute when he latched on to the ball following a pinpoint pass from Paul Breitner, who passed it to Klaus Fischer for the empty-net goal. The two-goal lead was good enough for the West Germans, who had a temporary lapse in concentration down the stretch. That mistake allowed Spain to score in the 81st minute when Jesus Maria Zamora headed the ball past Schumacher to the delight of the 91,000 fans. In the end, West Germany won 2–1. Following England's scoreless tie on July 5 against Spain, West Germany was able to seal its place in the semifinals.

Group C, meanwhile, was dubbed the "Group of Death." The trio of heavyweights had won a combined six World Cups with Brazil leading the way with three. Italy, twice a World Cup winner, and Argentina, the defending champions, rounded out the group. The three group games, all scheduled at Sarria Stadium in Barcelona, would feature numerous goals and the most attractive soccer played at the tournament. The group opened on June 29 with Argentina and Italy battling for a chance at securing the first points of the group. Italy—battered by the press, unimpressive in the first round, and the worst team still playing in the tournament—decided the best way to stop Argentina was by employing a very physical game against Maradona. The first half was a brutal encounter with tough-guy defender Claudio Gentile shadowing Maradona every step of the game. The Libyan-born Gentile, who did not live up to his name, tackled Maradona every time he got the ball. Repeatedly chopped down by Gentile, Maradona was forced to endure a series of rough tackles. The contact may not have been personal, but it was hardly friendly. Maradona, who had been a target by defenders throughout the competition, could do nothing but get up and try again. Argentina responded with its own rugged brand of soccer, but the Italians, once again, played like a group of strangers who had come together at the last minute for a pickup game in the park. The first half ended 0–0. In the second half, Bearzot changed the game plan and decided to ease up on Maradona and instead initiate an offensive drive. Argentina never saw it coming. Menotti's men appeared surprised each time the *Azzurri* grabbed the ball and made a run toward their goal. A series of passes that began in midfield resulted in a Marco Tardelli goal in the 56th minute. After a Maradona free kick hit the post, the team's Juventus-based players decided it was time they pull their act together and secure the win. The result was another goal. This time, Rossi's shot was blocked by Fillol, but Tardelli was able to grab the rebound and dish it off to Cabrini, who slammed the ball into the roof of the net with a powerful left-footed shot in the 68th minute. Argentina did not sit idly by, however, and Passarella tried with all his strength to get his team on the scoreboard. With its title defense slipping away, Passarella pulled one back in the 83rd minute off a powerful free kick that left Zoff rooted to the turf. The goal was too little too late, and Italy had come out on top, 2–1.

If Argentina wanted to retain its title it had to defeat their rivals, Brazil. The July 2 encounter between the South American powerhouses—the only two teams left in the competition from outside Europe—would not go Argentina's way. For now, the Brazilians, who had played the most offensive soccer of any team at the tournament, didn't skip a beat. This was also Maradona's chance to compare his skills against the best in the world. Unfortunately for him, Maradona would fall flat on his face. The Brazilians were just too fast and flashy for the Argentines, putting on a display of one-touch soccer that would have made the Harlem Globetrotters jealous for both their artistry and effectiveness. Zico gave Brazil the lead after twelve minutes, putting the ball past Fillol on a rebound after Eder's swerving free kick dipped over the wall and ricocheted off the crossbar. The Brazilians took advantage of every inch of the field, creating spaces in the midfield that forced the Argentineans to open up and leave their defense vulnerable to Zico's speed and prowess. Maradona was unable to do anything, rendering him insignificant for much of the first half. Brazil, on the other hand, squandered a host of chances and the first half ended with the three-time champions in the lead, but not by much, at 1–0.

The second half was more of the same. Brazil continued to put on the offensive pressure in search of an insurance goal. That security net came in the 67th minute in the form of a goal from Serginho when he headed the ball past Fillol off a Falcao cross. Five minutes later, Junior broke through the Argentine midfield and was able to score on a breakaway with the helpless Fillol looking on in horror as the ball blew past him and rolled into the net. The Argentines—frustrated with the score—turned to brutality in order to halt the Brazilian attack. Maradona was red carded in the 85th minute following a hard tackle on Batista, who had come in for Zico. Mexican referee Mario Vazquez witnessed Maradona's vicious foul that ended with his studs slamming into Batista's groin. Argentina, now down to ten men, retaliated with a goal in the 89th minute when Diaz was able to score with a hard shot that sailed into the net past a diving Waldir Peres. The goal was pretty, but Argentina was out of the competition. Maradona had been taught a lesson from the Brazilian masters. But Argentina's problems did not end there. The players flew home, only to have their luggage held at the airport in Buenos Aires until $18,000 in overweight baggage costs were paid. The team had seen better days, and though no one knew it at the time, Maradona's time to shine would come four years later when he would turn the disappointment of this World Cup into his finest hour.

On July 5, the Brazil–Italy game would determine which team would earn a place in the semifinals and, in the process, became the most exciting game of the tournament. The Brazilians could have settled for a tie in order to advance, but not playing for a win was not part of their philosophy. The Brazilians were clearly the favorites to win, while the Italians had to break out of their defensive shell like they had against Argentina if they had any hope of winning the game. Surprisingly, the *Azzurri* took the lead with Rossi, playing in only his eighth game since coming off his suspension, when a Cabrini pass allowed him to head the ball into the net for his first goal of the competition. The Brazilians drew clear battle lines while in search of the tying goal. Seven minutes later, Socrates was able to penetrate down the right side of the Italian defense and from the narrowest of angles put the ball past Zoff at the near post. Momentum again swung Italy's way. In the 25th minute, Rossi was able to steal the ball from Cerezo. Rossi was able to make a clear run at the goal for his second strike of the game. In the meantime, the Italian defense did a solid job containing the Brazilians. Gentile, so effective against Maradona, marked Zico with the same efficiency.

The *Azzurri* created several more scoring chances and clearly were in control of the game.

A pep talk from Tele Santana at halftime worked wonders on his players and Brazil was back in control in the second period. In the 68th minute, Falcao, who roamed free in the midfield, used his right foot to take the ball into the box, and then used his left to unleash a shot that Zoff tried to block with his outstretched arms. Though contrary to their philosophy, the Brazilians decided to go on a reckless run, playing in search of another goal when they should have tried to preserve the score. Again, Rossi was the biggest threat to Brazil's World Cup survival. Rossi scored in the 74th minute to complete the hat trick and defeat Brazil, 3–2, to oust them from the tournament. It was rather ironic that Brazil's fantastic run had come to an abrupt end because of the team's unwillingness to sit on the ball and kill the clock. Brazil's wide-open style, the kind fans around the globe had come to enjoy, ultimately did them in. The Italians, perfectionists defensively, had come out of hibernation. The *Azzurri* were now serious contenders to win a third title. Bearzot, who had placed his faith in Rossi from the start, was partially vindicated after being abused by the press.

*Brazil's Zico takes a shot at the Italian wall at the 1982 World Cup (Credit: CFB).*

Meanwhile, Group D kicked off on June 28 with France defeating Austria, 1–0, at Vicente Calderon Stadium in Madrid. This group was the least balanced of the four, with France proving it was a soccer power thanks to a new generation of players who had finally begun to gel. The French, far superior than the Austrians, grabbed the game-winner with a Bernard Genghini free kick in the 39th minute. *Les Bleus*, who were without the services of the injured Platini, showed how strong they could play against an Austrian team—which many were rooting against after its first-round plot with West Germany that earned them a spot in the second round.

Three days later, Austria was able to earn a 2–2 tie against Northern Ireland after making five changes to its lineup, including leaving out Krankl. Northern Ireland had taken the lead with Billy Hamilton in the 27th minute on a wonderful header. The Austrians responded in the second half with two goals, one from Bruno Pezzey in the 50th minute and the other with Reinhold Hintermaier, who fired off a free kick from outside the box in the 67th minute. The Austrian team enjoyed its first lead of the game. Hamilton, who had established himself as one of the tournament's unlikeliest stars, equalized seven minutes later. A well-played lob by Jimmy Nichol forced goalkeeper Friedl Koncilia to come out of his goal, allowing Hamilton the time to head the ball into the empty goal. The diving header was one of the prettiest goals of the tournament and solidified the twenty-four-year-old's place as one of the most outstanding players of the competition.

On July 4, France played Northern Ireland for the fourth and final spot in the semifinals. The game had all the makings of an upset, but once the players stepped onto the field at Vicente Calderon Stadium, *Les Bleus* were able to show why they were one of the world's most talented teams. France outclassed Northern Ireland both offensively and defensively, even though Martin O'Neill had been able to make a run at the French goal in the seventh minute, only to have his goal disallowed. France was ahead 1–0 with Alain Giresse in the 33rd minute. The French padded that lead a minute after halftime when Dominique Rocheteau put the ball past Jennings following a solo run. Rocheteau scored again in the 67th minute when he grabbed the ball outside the penalty box, danced his way past four defenders, and unleashed a shot past Jennings for the 3–1 lead. At the other end, an error by French goalkeeper Jean Ettori, who was unable to grab a Whiteside cross, allowed Armstrong to score. Armstrong's goal once again put a smile on his red-cheeked face and allowed his teammates to celebrate what had certainly become a World Cup that had exceeded all expectations. The French, however, were not done. Giresse added another goal in the 80th minute to cap off the 4–1 victory. France was the only European team to emulate the Brazilian style and was the only team at the competition able to entertain and get results at the same time. The French not only deserved a spot in the semifinals, but a place in the final.

## Final Four: Semifinals

The semifinals featured a quartet of Europeans with Italy pitted against Poland in a first-round rematch and West Germany playing France. Both matches were played on July 8 with Italy versus Poland in the afternoon and West Germany against France in the evening. For the first time since 1966, the semifinals failed to feature a team from South America, who had a tradition of faltering on European soil. Brazil's 1958 triumph in Sweden was the only exception to this rule. The tournament had also lacked individual star power. In the past, the World Cup had often been dominated by a handful of players. Maradona, hyped as a possible superstar-in-the-making on the eve of the competition, said before the start of the second round that the tournament would be dominated by a team, rather than an individual. "This won't be Maradona's, Zico's or Rummenigge's World Cup. This will be the World Cup of a team. Only if a good team has a particularly talented player will he be able to do anything special."[2]

One of those players able to achieve superstar status had been Boniek. Poland—now without the services of its star striker who was out for suspension after amassing a second yellow card against the USSR—saw its chances of reaching the final severely hampered. Italy, which featured Rossi, played Poland at the Nou Camp in Barcelona with the knowledge that a good performance from the Juventus striker would ensure passage to the final. The *Azzurri*, riding high from after their wins against Argentina and Brazil, took the lead with Rossi in the 22nd minute. The goal was the result of a perfectly executed free kick by Giancarlo Antognoni. The kick opened up the Polish defense and Rossi, always present in the penalty area, headed the ball in for his fourth goal of the tournament from only six yards out. The Poles had expected Antognoni's kick to transform into a high cross, but instead he had chipped the ball low for Rossi. The pro-Italian crowd of 50,000 chanted and waved flags, but had its joy temporarily halted when Antognoni had to exit the game in the 28th minute after he was injured going for a loose ball. With temperatures in the stadium hovering near 90 degrees, the Polish tried to tie the score, but the task proved difficult without a finisher like Boniek on the field. Without him, Poland could not crack open the Italian defenders, who were missing the services of Gentile, who had also amassed two yellow cards and an automatic game suspension. Once again, the *Azzurri* used the counterattack to their benefit, adding an insurance goal when a Conti cross in the 73rd minute allowed Rossi to head the ball in again. This time, Rossi's fifth goal of the competition made him the tournament's temporary top scorer, catapulting Italy into the final with the 2–0 win. The likelihood of Italy reaching the final had been a dream just a month earlier. Now, the Italians had solidified a place in the championship game with a real shot at being crowned world champions for the first time in forty-four years.

In the other semifinal, West Germany and France faced off in what would become an epic clash—a potpourri of scoring, strength, and stamina. The West Germans countered France's flashy style in the only way they knew how: by featuring a very organized defense and midfield. The teams traded goals in the first period and went on to play ninety grueling minutes, another thirty of overtime, and ultimately a penalty kick shootout. For the first time ever at a World Cup tournament, a shootout would be used as a tiebreaker.

Littbarski put West Germany ahead in the 17th minute, but Platini was able to tie the score nine minutes later on a penalty kick. With the score deadlocked at one, both teams put together a series of scoring opportunities and employed a wide-open style of play that showed, at least for once, how European teams were also able to play entertaining soccer.

The hard-fought match continued until the middle of the second half when a long ball sent French defender Patrick Battiston racing clear toward the German goal. Moments after Battiston had headed the ball toward the goal from inside the German penalty area, Schumacher thrust himself upon the French player feet first, knocking Battiston unconscious and breaking a few of his teeth in the process. The ball went wide of the post and Dutch referee Charles Corver awarded a goal kick amid the vociferous protests of the French players. The game was interrupted for several minutes while Battiston, who laid motionless on the emerald-colored grass, was carried off the field on a stretcher. Schumacher did not even receive a yellow card for his karate-style assault and the game continued.

*Les Bleus* could have won the game in the final minute after defender Manuel Amoros sent a thundering kick crashing onto the West German crossbar. The humid conditions and end-to-end pace favored the French. *Les Bleus* jumped out to a 3–1 lead on goals in the 92nd minute from Trésor, who had moved up field in a rare offensive display, and from Giresse six minutes later. The never-say-die West Germans countered with a goal from Rummenigge in the 102nd minute. Fischer tied the game, 3–3, five minutes later with a bicycle kick from just six yards out. Ettori's inconsistent, often sloppy goalkeeping, had caught up with him. France risked elimination. The game was headed to penalty kicks.

The shootout was a dreadful way to produce a winner, but after such a hard-nosed game, the players limped off the field exhausted. The shootout—soccer's equivalent of Russian roulette—would determine Italy's opponent in the final. The shootout may not have been fair, as some critics argued, but at least it was exciting. The tension in the stadium reached unbearable levels. With France ahead, 3–2, in the shootout, everyone's attention turned to Uli Stielike of West Germany. French goalkeeper Ettori guessed correctly and saved his kick. The West German player collapsed to the ground in agony. With his head buried in his hands, Littbarski walked up to his West German teammate and tried to console him. While this took place in the midfield circle, West German goalkeeper Schumacher blocked a shot by Six. His brilliant save cancelled Stielike's error, ensuring that the teams were once again even. Littbarski himself scored, as did Six and Platini for France and Rummenigge for West Germany. The shootout went to sudden death. Maxime Bossis, who had been the most consistent French player at the tournament, saw his shot saved by Schumacher. The miss was decisive. Hrubesch, the top scorer in the Bundesliga the previous season, smashed in the winner, lifting West Germany to a 5–4 victory for a place in the final. The French, so close to reaching a World Cup final for the first time ever, had been eliminated. The shock defeat would linger for several years, though the French would go on to win the European Championship two years later and qualify for the 1986 World Cup. To this day, however, some of the French players on the field that night still refuse to set foot in Sanchez Pizjuan Stadium.

The French players could not even find consolation playing for third place on July 10 when Poland got the better of them, 3–2, in Alicante. The game was decided in the 47th minute by a splendidly executed free kick by Janusz Kupcewicz.

## The New Champs Are Crowned

In the final, the Italians were led by Rossi, who over the course of a few weeks went from villain to national hero. A sellout crowd of 95,000 packed the Santiago Bernabeu Stadium on July 11. A sea of flashbulbs greeted the players as they walked across the perfectly manicured green field. Both sides spent the opening minutes trying to figure out the best way to threaten each other's goal. Goalkeepers Zoff and Schumacher became spectators as ball possession remained bogged down in the midfield. The Italians, however, threatened on the counterattack and caught a break: Brazilian referee Arnaldo Coehlo awarded the *Azzurri* a penalty kick in the 24th minute after Conti was fouled just three yards from the goal. Cabrini took the penalty kick, but his powerful shot went wide to the left. The botched kick went down in the record books as the first missed penalty shot ever in a World Cup championship game. The West Germans used the right flank to their benefit with Rummenigge and Wolfgang Dremmler employing a series of short passes meant to outsmart the Italian defense. But the Italians were able to outmaneuver the West German attack and tried to use the counterattack to their benefit. A series of fouls undermined the fluidity of the match and the first half ended scoreless.

In the second period, the Italian counterattack kicked into high gear. It took just twelve minutes for Rossi to score his tournament-leading sixth goal. The goal was reminiscent of Rossi's previous goals at this competition. Gentile, back from his one-game ban, sent the ball into the box. Three Italian players—Rossi, Conti, and Gabriele Oriali—charged toward the goalmouth in a mad scramble. Stielike tried to clear the ball, but was unsuccessful. Rossi lunged toward the ball and was able to head it in past Schumacher. West German coach Jupp Derwall said afterward that the goal sunk his team's hopes of winning the cup. "Any team has a problem when Italy is ahead, 1–0, and this was a goal shot very quickly and very well. After that goal, it was more difficult to get through the very strong and tight Italian defense."[3]

*Marco Tardelli wears his emotions on his sleeve after scoring against West Germany in the 1982 World Cup final in Madrid (Credit: EMPICS).*

West Germany tried to mount a comeback, but the Italian defense suffocated any attempt. The West German team, desperate to tie the game, left its defense vulnerable to Italy's shrewd counterattack. Rummenigge, hobbled by a sore leg, had a clear chance to score in the 56th minute when his hard shot found its way into the Italian box—and even got behind Zoff for a second—but the ball was swatted away by the defense. In the 59th minute, the Italians went up 2–0 when Tardelli scored what turned out to be the game winner with a blistering shot off a play that had been set up by Conti and Rossi. Tardelli, who did not have a reputation as a finisher, scored a goal that will forever be etched in the minds of Italian fans. Following the goal, Tardelli ran toward his bench where Bearzot and a gaggle of players waited to hug him as police officers tried to keep them from walking onto the field. Tardelli's raw emotion, punctuated by a liberating scream as he ran toward the Italian bench, became so famous that ABC's *Wide World of Sports* used it for years in its opening sequence. The West Germans were finished and Italy scored a third goal in the 81st minute. Conti dribbled the ball down the right side with no West German players even bothering to challenge him. Conti passed the ball off to a waiting Alessandro Altobelli, who beat Schumacher with a powerful shot to put the game away. The worn-out West Germans, demoralized by Italy's 3–0 lead, scored two minutes later with Breitner, but there wasn't enough time to do much else. The Italians were able to pull out the win in convincing fashion and were crowned World Cup winners for the third time. Zoff led his teammates to the podium to receive the trophy. The players then took a victory lap around the stadium, hoisting aloft the World Cup and basking in their newfound glory.

**NOTES**

1. Ian Morrison, *The World Cup: A Complete Record* (London: Breedon Books Publishing, 1990), 249.

2. Joe Ritchie, "Stars Take Back Seat in the Latest World Cup." *Washington Post*, D2, July 9, 1982.

3. Joe Ritchie, "Italy is the World Cup Champion, 3–1." *Washington Post*, D1, July 11, 1982.

# 6

# THE HAND OF GOD

## 1986

The World Cup returned to Mexico for a second time, and in doing so became the first country to host the tournament more than once. Originally awarded to Colombia in 1974, the South American country announced in 1983 that it could no longer afford the costs attached with hosting the tournament. FIFA named Mexico as the new host in May 1983 during a meeting in Stockholm, beating out the United States, Canada and Brazil, who had all hastily put together bids. Brazil had inexplicably dropped out before the vote. That wasn't such a surprise considering that the Mexican TV network, Televisa, which spearheaded the effort to bring the World Cup to Mexico, was headed by Havelange's friend, Amilio Azcarrage. One of Televisa's senior executives was Guillermo Cañedo, president of the country's World Cup organizing committee, so it became very clear what backroom deal had transpired to ensure that Mexico would get to host the competition for a second time in sixteen years. The World Cup was supposed to jumpstart the Mexican economy, which was at its worst levels in fifty years. If that wasn't enough, a replay of what happened to Chile before the 1962 World Cup occurred in Mexico. An earthquake in September 1985, only eight months before the tournament was set to begin, rocked Mexico, killing 20,000 people. Once again, doubt was cast over whether the hosts could organize the event. When organizers deemed that the stadiums had not been damaged in the quake—downplaying fears that the tournament may have to be moved elsewhere or canceled—FIFA again gave the country the thumbs up. Mexico would pick up the pieces and go on to stage a fine tournament.

Another controversy to cloak the event was FIFA's decision to allow Camel cigarettes to be an official sponsor of the tournament. Allowing the cigarette maker to display its ads around the field during games was another sign of the commercialism that had come to dominate the World Cup. Havelange defended the decision, saying he was not a smoker and that FIFA needed the money in order to pull off such an expensive competition. Another RJ Reynolds product, Winston, had appeared as an on-field sponsor four years earlier, also a decision that had been criticized by antismoking groups. But the Camel ads went even further in Mexico, as evidenced by the large, yellow Camel balloon floating outside the Azteca Stadium on the day of the final. It would be the last time a cigarette company would officially sponsor the World Cup.

Again, FIFA tinkered with the tournament's format. Using two group rounds was dropped and replaced with a knockout formula. The twenty-four finalists were arranged in six groups of four. After group play, the four best third-placed teams would join the six group winners and six runners up into the single-game elimination bracket. FIFA made other changes. In response to the controversial match four years earlier in which West Germany and Austria produced exactly the result both teams knew beforehand would advance them to the next phase at the expense of Algeria, FIFA scheduled the final two games in each group to be played simultaneously. One thing FIFA could not fix was the altitude and weather. Like in 1970, the games would be played at extremely high altitudes and in the sweltering afternoon sun in order to favor Europe's primetime TV schedule. Sixteen years earlier, Mexico City had crowned Pelé the world's greatest player. This time, the World Cup was prepared to anoint his successor. Once again, Brazil and Argentina were favored to win the tournament. France, Denmark, Hungary, and the Soviet Union rounded up the list of favorites from Europe. Algeria qualified for the second straight tournament, another sign that soccer in the developing countries was narrowing the gap, while Canada qualified for its first finals ever after overpowering Honduras and Costa Rica in CONCACAF's final round. A 2–1 win over Honduras in St. John's, Newfoundland, proved to be the decisive match.

The United States meanwhile, failed to qualify for the finals even though the NASL and USSF had joined forces in order to bolster the team's chances. In order to make the Americans competitive, the USSF and the league created a team in 1983 called Team America. Based in Washington, D.C., the team of Americans played the 1983 season as a NASL franchise. The team fielded the best American players (although several U.S.-born stars like Ricky Davis decided to stay away) and a handful of naturalized Americans like Alan Green and Alan Merrick. The team was coached by Greek-born Alkis Panagoulias He, too, had been naturalized, although he had experience coaching in Europe with Greek club Olympiakos. Panagoulias had also led the New York Greek-Americans to three straight U.S. Open Cup titles in the late 1960s and would eventually go on to coach Greece at the 1994 World Cup.

The impetus behind the creation of Team America was to prepare the national team for the qualifying rounds of the 1986 World Cup. Although unprecedented in the soccer world, the experiment failed after the team went 10–20 and failed to make the playoffs. The USSF and the league pulled the plug on the franchise after just one season. The Americans' 1–0 loss to Costa Rica in Torrence, California, ended their chances of advancing to the finals and suffocated the league's longevity. In 1967, the NASL formed after the United Soccer Association and the National Professional Soccer League merged. In a span of 17 seasons, a staggering 62 teams had played in the league over that time. Despite having a league loaded with superstars, the United States had failed to reach the World Cup finals during the NASL's existence. In 1984, the NASL folded and the sport all but disappeared from American consciousness. All that remained to keep the sport alive in this country was college soccer and the Major Indoor Soccer League, a version of the game played in arenas on hockey rink-sized artificial turf fields. It would be another twelve years before the MLS would come into existence.

The World Cup draw took place on December 15, 1985. Mexico, Argentina, West Germany, France, Brazil, and Poland were the six seeded teams. The televised draw took place at the Televisa television studios with a majestic Aztec décor serving as a backdrop. The twenty-three-minute draw was not only efficient, but produced several very competitive first-round groups. The teams were divided as follows:

Group A: Argentina, Italy, Bulgaria, and South Korea
Group B: Mexico, Belgium, Iraq, and Paraguay
Group C: France, Canada, Hungary, and The Soviet Union

Group D: Brazil, Algeria, Northern Ireland, and Spain
Group E: West Germany, Denmark, Scotland, and Uruguay
Group F: Poland, England, Morocco, and Portugal

## Group Play

Mexico's stadiums would serve as ideal venues just like they had in 1970. Organizers bragged that the Azteca Stadium, site of the final, could be emptied in twelve minutes if need be. The hot weather and altitude, however, remained an issue, though FIFA tried to downplay those concerns. The Azteca was the venue with the second-highest altitude, located 7,390 feet above sea level. Though the Azteca would serve as an ideal showpiece, many Mexicans would never get a chance to watch a game from its stands. The massive unemployment that plagued the country continued to paralyze the local economy on the eve of the tournament and locals were unable to afford the price of tickets. Thanks to Televisa, TV coverage was ample and large screens were installed in poor neighborhoods throughout the country, a goodwill gesture and also a deterrent to dissuade those who thought they could gain admission to games without a ticket. The players, meanwhile, were concerned with conquering the dizzying effects that came with competing at such soaring altitudes. Toluca, the highest altitude, was located 45 miles west of Mexico City at 8,500 feet above sea level. The Brazilians had set up training camp in Toluca just to adjust to the rigors of playing at such a high level in the event they would have to play there in the later rounds. The Belgians had tried to duplicate the experience by setting up a pre–World Cup camp in the cozy Swiss ski resort town of Ovronnaz. Once in Mexico, they faced other problems. Days before the start of the tournament, the team played a friendly against Mexican club Universidad Catolica. A rough tackle on Nico Claesen led to a brawl, which included the players sitting on both benches. Police officers broke up the mayhem after several tense minutes that included punching and kicking. For the Belgium team, the climate was anything but ideal.

The opening ceremony on May 31 before the clash between Italy and Bulgaria was a colorful celebration inside the Azteca, though the 95,000 fans who had packed the grounds jeered politicians as they tried to deliver their welcome speeches. Italy entered the tournament on a low note, failing to qualify for the 1984 European Championship and losing to Norway and Poland in warm-up games during preparations. The *Azzurri*—as always, criticized by the national press—were an older team, and Bearzot had made the mistake of holding on to many of the same players. Rossi had embarked on another of his famous scoring slumps—he would never see a minute of action in Mexico. The Bulgarians almost arrived late to the stadium after the 100,000 cars that had been parked in and around the sprawling complex created a large traffic jam. Once the Bulgarians did make it to the game, they were surprised to find that Bearzot had left Rossi on the bench and replaced him at the last minute with striker Giuseppe Galderisi. Gaetano Scirea and Antonio Cabrini, both playing in their third World Cups, anchored the defense. It was Scirea's free kick in the 43rd minute that allowed Altobelli to give the *Azzurri* the lead. The Bulgarians equalized five minutes from the end when Nasko Sirakov's header beat goalkeeper Giovanni Galli for the 1–1 tie.

The group's other game was played two days later in Mexico City's other stadium, the Estadio Olimpico '68, between Argentina and South Korea. Diego Maradona, who had ended the World Cup four years earlier with a red card, was back on the world's stage with a vengeance. He wanted revenge for all that had happened to him four years earlier and in the two ensuing years he had spent with Barcelona. His Spanish sojourn had been a disaster and the player once touted as the best in the world had not lived up to that billing. A year after Argentina's World Cup elimination, Maradona led Barcelona, coached by Menotti, to the Copa del Rey, beating rivals Real Madrid in the final. That would be the only bright spot for Maradona. He had an unhappy tenure with Barcelona following a bout with hepatitis; then an ill-timed tackle by Atletico Bilbao's Andoni Goikoetxea could have put an early end to Maradona's career. He recovered from the ankle injury and returned four months later. Unknown to many, Maradona had also picked up a cocaine habit, an addiction that would plague him throughout his life. Barcelona's management was not satisfied with Maradona and in 1984 transferred him to Italian club Napoli, where he immediately became an adored star. Though the southern Italian club had never won a domestic league title, Maradona's arrival generated widespread optimism. The little Argentine had finally found a place he could call home and the peace of mind that came with that gave Maradona a renewed sense of optimism entering the World Cup.

Argentina, coached by Carlos Salvador Bilardo, had injected some changes into the lineup compared to Menotti's 1982 squad. For starters, Maradona was surrounded by a supporting cast that took some of the pressure off him. The game against South Korea was a brilliant example of this strategy. For every pass Maradona was able to put together, the South Koreans responded with a series of harsh tackles and fouls. The fouling was reminiscent of Gentile's coverage of Maradona four years earlier and this time Spanish referee Victoriano Sanchez Arminio did the same thing past match officials had done: turn a blind eye. This time, Argentina's tactics allowed other players to pick up the slack with Jorge Burruchaga also creating plays in the midfield and Real Madrid striker Jorge Valdano poised to finish them. Argentina's first goal came after only five minutes when Maradona's free kick rebounded off the South Korean wall. Maradona grabbed the rebound and put in a pass for Valdano who was able to score. Goal number two came twelve minutes later when Maradona floated in a pass off a free kick for Oscar Ruggeri, who headed the ball into the net. Maradona's skillful passing and ability to create goals off set pieces had paid off. Kim Pyung-suk, the defender given the task of guarding the world's greatest player, was substituted three minutes after Argentina's second goal. Argentina put the game away in the 46th minute when Maradona's cross created chaos in the South Korean area, which allowed Valdano to tap the ball in for the 3–0 win.

The Maradona show continued against Italy on June 5 at Cuauhté-moc Stadium in Puebla before a crowd of 32,000. Bearzot's team was old and the relentless Mexican sun was too much for them to handle. The other force too hot for the Italians to handle was Maradona. The *Azzurri*, who had found scoring so difficult against Bulgaria, took the lead after six minutes when a handball in the Argentine box resulted in a penalty kick. Altobelli scored the ensuing kick and Italy was ahead, 1–0. The Argentines tied the score twenty-nine minutes later when Maradona, who was being covered by his Napoli teammate Salvatore Bagni, raced up field to get into position to score. Once he had left Bagni behind him, Maradona received a long pass from Burruchaga up the left flank. Maradona raced Scirea to the ball. Instead of waiting for the ball to drop, Maradona's left foot connected with the sphere in midair. Scirea and Galli were both stunned as the ball trickled across the penalty area and into the right side of the net past Galli. Maradona jumped up and down in celebration as his teammates ran toward him. The game ended 1–1 and the Italians had once again gotten off to a sluggish start.

Five days later, Argentina defeated Bulgaria, 2–0, at the Estadio Olimpico '68 to win the group. A Valdano goal after three minutes and one from Burruchaga in the 78th minute, born from a pinpoint Maradona cross, made the difference that afternoon. The Maradona juggernaut had finally taken off. Bilardo's squad not only had the tactical commonsense to outright steamroll opponents, but the players also exuded confidence never before seen at a major competition since Kempes and his crew won the World Cup eight years earlier. With the Falklands War behind them and democracy finally returning to Argentina, the players also appeared to have the psychological edge going into the competition. Little did they know that they would be confronted with their past demons later on in the knockout round.

Italy, meanwhile, took second place in Group A following a hard-fought 3–2 victory over South Korea in Puebla. Altobelli scored his third goal of the competition in the 18th minute. He could have made it 2–0 in the 26th minute, but his penalty kick slammed against the post. The ghosts of Korea that hung over Italian soccer made a brief return when South Korea tied the game in the 60th minute with Choi Soon-ho off a 25-yard blast. The goal had come against the run of play and the composed Italians were able to retake the lead in the 73rd minute when Altobelli scored his second goal of the game from a free kick. In the 82nd minute, Altobelli scored again, but FIFA officially credited it as an own goal from Cho Kwang-rae and the Italian striker was denied the hat trick. The South Koreans pulled one back in the final minute with Cha Bum-keun, but it was too little, too late. Italy's defensive supremacy and Altobelli's abilities to spark the offense was all the *Azzurri* needed to win 3–1 and secure a spot in the next round. Bulgaria, who had finished third, also moved on to the knockout phase as one of the four best third-place teams, though it had failed to win a game.

Group B, also based in Mexico City and Toluca, featured host team Mexico, coached by Yugoslavian Velibor "Bora" Milutinovic. The Mexicans had trained for the competition like never before and featured a blend of veterans and young stars. Striker Hugo Sanchez, who played with Real Madrid, returned to his homeland for one last stint with the national team. Sanchez had also played in the NASL with the San Diego

# DIEGO MARADONA

Argentines are proud of their famous sons and daughters—especially the trinity of Evita Peron, Ernesto "Che" Guevara, and Diego Maradona. Indeed, with the possible exception of Pelé, Maradona is widely regarded as the greatest soccer player ever. Born in the shantytown of Villa Fiorito on the outskirts of Buenos Aires, Maradona learned to play the game in the streets and alleyways near his home.

Short and stocky, Maradona, known as "El Pipe de Oro" (The Golden Boy), possessed exceptional ball-handling skills. During halftime at Boca Juniors games, he often delighted crowds by juggling the ball with his feet without it ever hitting the ground. Maradona signed his first professional contract with Argentinos Juniors in 1976, before moving on to play for Boca Juniors for a season in 1981. He led Argentina to the 1979 World Youth Championship in Japan and played his first game for the senior team that same year. Like many South American players during the 1980s, Maradona moved to Europe after signing with Spanish club Barcelona. Following two seasons in Spain marred by an injury that threatened to end his career, Maradona signed with Napoli in Italy in July 1984. Napoli, a team that had never won an Italian League title, was taken to new heights. Maradona led the team to two titles (1987 and 1990), an Italian Cup in 1987, a UEFA Cup in 1989, and an Italian SuperCup in 1990.

No stranger to success, he also courted controversy. Apologists spoke of his honest nature. Critics could not find excuses for his erratic behavior. In Naples, where he is still beloved, Maradona also faced a scandal regarding an illegitimate son and was the object of some suspicion over his friendship with the Camorra, the local mafia. Maradona left Napoli in 1992, after serving a fifteen-month ban for failing a drug test, and played for Sevilla (1992–1993), Newell's Old Boys (1993), and Boca Juniors (1995–1997). He also attempted to work as a coach on two short occasions, leading Mandiyú of Corrientes (1994) and Racing Club (1995).

If Maradona's club career was stellar, then his World Cup appearances were equally successful. At the 1982 World Cup in Spain, Maradona failed to live up to the hype. Argentina lost its opening game to Belgium, and then went on to beat Hungary and El Salvador. Maradona scored twice against the Hungarians, but was unable to repeat the dose against Italy and Brazil in the second round. In fact, he grew so frustrated with his markers that he was red carded and Argentina crashed out of the competition. At Mexico 1986, Maradona, who was in his prime, had an exceptional tournament. His five goals—one against Italy and two a piece against England and Belgium in the quarter and semifinals—took Carlos Bilardo's team to the final. He sealed his reputation in the final when his assist led to the game-winner in a 3–2 win

*(continued)*

over West Germany. At this tournament, he became notorious for a goal in the quarterfinals against England, which video evidence later clearly revealed he had scored with the aid of his hand. He later claimed it was the "Hand of God" that had caused him to score the goal—a claim to the general derision of the English public and in particular the tabloid newspapers, who still resurrect the incident occasionally even today, branding him a cheat. However, Maradona showed the other side of his nature just a couple of minutes later in the same match, by running half the length of the field and beating almost the entire English team along the way, to score what is widely regarded as the most exceptional goal of all time.

Four years later, Maradona assumed a different role in Argentina's title defense. The 1986 tournament took place in Italy, where Maradona was nearing the end of a seven-year spell with Napoli. Though his physical powers had been greatly diminished by a serious ankle injury, Maradona remained as strong and feared as ever. That reputation alone carried the team through against Brazil, Yugoslavia, and Italy in the knockout stage. However, there was nothing he could do about Andreas Brehme's game-winning penalty kick for West Germany in the final. In tears, Maradona watched as West Germany lifted the trophy.

The last chapter in Maradona's World Cup career was also the darkest. The controversy that appeared to follow Maradona unfolded at USA 1994, in which he helped Argentina triumph over Greece and Nigeria. The news came out, however, that he failed a drug test, which showed signs of the banned stimulant ephedrine; he was thrown out of the competition. His national team career was over after 34 goals in 91 appearances. Without Maradona, Argentina lost to Romania and was eliminated from the tournament.

Maradona returned to Boca Juniors once his 15-month ban ran out. His club career ended after 21 seasons with Boca Juniors' 2–1 defeat of River Plate in October 1997. Argentina celebrated Maradona's career in November 2001 with a testimonial game at La Bombonera Stadium, home of Boca Juniors. The No. 10 captained the national team to victory over a group of world all-stars. In 2000, Maradona was voted FIFA's "Player of the Century" in an Internet poll, garnering 53.6 percent of the votes. In a reconciliatory gesture, in order to settle his reputation, FIFA appointed a committee to vote on its "Player of the Century," which gave the award to Pele. He went on to coach Argentina at the 2010 World Cup.

## World Cup Career Statistics

Tournaments played: 4
Games: 21
Goals: 8

Sockers in 1979 and 1980. He also played for the Dallas Burn of Major League Soccer in 1996, making him the only player to ever kick a ball in both leagues. Playmaker Manuel Negrete, responsible for orchestrating plays from the midfield, was one of the world's best at that position.

The players also had the crowd backing them—like previous World Cup hosts—but the Mexican fans this time exuded an energy and enthusiasm never before seen at a World Cup. The crowds also showed the world a new way to cheer and introduced everyone to the wave. The coordinated movement of the fans would become a stable of the competition—and future sporting events around the planet. As for the Mexicans, they trounced the competition in the first round. In the team's first game against Belgium on June 3 at the Azteca Stadium, the passion of the 110,000 home fans—coupled with Sanchez's abilities—resulted in a 2–1 win. Sanchez, nicknamed "Hugol," scored the game-winner in the 38th minute. Four days later, the Mexicans tied Paraguay, 1–1, before an even bigger crowd at the Azteca Stadium. This time, 114,600 fans packed the palatial stadium. What the crowd witnessed was a game littered with fouls. The contest also featured five yellow cards, one of which was handed out by English referee George Courtney to Sanchez. The card was Sanchez's second of the tournament, which meant he had to miss the crucial final first-round game against Iraq.

While anxious Mexicans bit their nails with anxiety, Paraguay and Belgium were also looking to move to the next round. Paraguay, who had defeated Iraq 1–0 on June 4 in Toluca, played Belgium to a 2–2 tie seven days later. The result in Toluca gave Paraguay four points and Belgium three. Mexico, who also had three points, could win the group with a victory over Iraq, which had become the group's punching bag. The Mexicans were almost certain of a place in the next round, but the crowd wanted to see another triumph. The players obliged. The Azteca was once again packed to the rafters with 104,000 cheering fans. Iraq packed its defense as Mexico tried to score. The excitement generated by the Mexican attack eventually turned to frustration as Milutinovic ordered his players to hit the Iraqis on the flanks. That frustration ended in the 54th minute when Negrete's free kick made its way over the Iraqi wall. The ball appeared headed for a goal kick, but Fernando Quirate was quick enough to put his head on the ball, which deflected into the net. Mexico had not only secured passage to the next round, but had also won the group following the 1–0 victory. Paraguay and Belgium joined them in the next round.

In Group C, played in Leon and Irapuato, France blanked Canada, 1–0, on June 1 in Leon. The Canadians had been able to hold France goalless for much of the contest, but Jean-Pierre Papin made up for earlier missed chances and netted the winner in the 33rd minute. The following day, the Soviet Union trounced Hungary, 6–0, in Irapuato. The match featured two teams with an outside chance of winning the World Cup. The USSR's performance against Hungary was as shocking as it was entertaining. In the end, the unbridled Soviet attack proved too powerful for the Hungarians. The win was even more impressive since the reigns of coaching the USSR had been handed to Valeri Lobanovski, who had successfully managed Dinamo Kiev on the club level, just three weeks before the start of the tournament. The Soviet offensive had also taken pressure off its defense and goalkeeper Rinat Dasaev, who had spent the day before the game in a hospital following a bout with food poisoning. He played the whole game, spending most of it alone like a spectator at the other end of the field.

France and the Soviet Union, the two strongest teams in the group, battled on June 5 in Leon. Platini gave the Soviet defense plenty of headaches, particularly in the first half, when he blasted a 30-yard shot that slammed against the crossbar. The USSR picked up the offensive pace after the interval and Vasili Rats was able to put them ahead in the 53rd minute. *Les Bleus* tied the score eight minutes later with Luis Fernandez, who put the ball past Dasaev off a well-placed lob in the box from Jean Tigana. The one-all tie was a fair result and allowed both teams to stay focused on their quests of advancing past the group stage. On June 9, France defeated Hungary 3–0 in Leon, while the Soviet Union outlasted Canada 2–0 at the same time in Irapuato.

Hungary, 2–0 winners over Canada three days earlier in Irapuato, needed a win to guarantee them a place in the second round. The French team could afford a tie, knowing that it could move on as one of the best third-place teams. But *Les Bleus* didn't settle for anything less than a victory and applied pressure on the Hungarian defense. Platini once again settled into his role as the team's inspirational leader. France took the lead in the 41st minute with Yannick Stopyra, who headed the ball into the net from six yards out. The Hungarians also got several shots off, including one from Lajos Detari that hit the bar, but nothing could get past goalkeeper Joel Bats. In the second half, France doubled its lead with Tigana in the 62nd minute. Platini got involved in France's third goal, laying off a weak-looking pass to Dominique Rocheteau, who put the ball past Hungarian goalkeeper Peter Disztl. The Soviet victory over Canada, meanwhile, was good enough for them to win the group over France, who placed second, following the goal differential tiebreaker. Hungary, who only had two points, was sent home packing.

Group D, played in Guadalajara and Monterrey, featured a Brazilian team that once again felt at home playing under the Mexican sun. Sixteen years later, Pelé, Tostao, and Gerson had been replaced by Careca, Alemao, and Socrates, but the Brazilians still featured a good dose of *jogo bonito*. While Spain, Algeria, and Northern Ireland all cringed at the prospect of having to play Brazil, the South Americans were a relaxed bunch as they practiced their juggling skills for hours as if they were about to perform at a circus. The Brazilians opened against Spain on June 1 at the Jalisco Stadium before a crowd of 35,748. It wasn't the biggest crowd of the competition, but the pro-Brazilian throng and its samba drums made enough noise to generate the sort of enthusiasm everyone had come to expect to see and hear at a World Cup match. The Brazilian team was once again favored to win its group, but appeared to lack motivation and stamina in the early going against Spain. Brazil, however, could always find a way to win and did just that with Socrates in the 63rd minute, putting the ball past Andoni Zubizarreta when a Careca shot rebounded off the Spanish goalkeeper. The goal gave Brazil 1–0 win.

Two days later, Algeria and Northern Ireland played to a 1–1 tie at Trez de Marzo Stadium. The clash, between two countries that had shocked onlookers at the last tournament, was marred by long stretches of vicious tackling. Algeria's unsportsmanlike conduct may have hampered Northern Ireland, but Brazil would not be so easily intimidated.

At the Jalisco Stadium on June 6, Brazil took on Algeria and spent much of the first half creating chances. The Brazilians even had a goal by Casagrande disallowed after Guatemalan referee Romulo Mendes Molina ruled that he had committed a foul before scoring. No matter. The Brazilians spent the second period firmly in the Algerian half and were able to win the game with a goal by Careca in the 66th minute. The goal wasn't the result of Brazil's spectacular ability to score, but off an Algerian mistake. Muller's low cross shot created a scramble in the box. Unable to clear it quickly enough, Careca latched on to the ball and unleashed a shot that went into the back of the net. The two victories shot Brazil to the top of the group with four points.

The Spaniards, who had edged out Northern Ireland 2–1 on June 7 at Trez de Marzo Stadium, locked horns with the Algerians five days later in the final game of the group. Spain booked a spot to the knockout round following a 3–0 win over Algeria at Technologico Stadium in Monterrey. Both teams employed a physical game, but in the end it was Spain who was through to the next round.

Simultaneously, Brazil played Northern Ireland. Brazil, already set to head into the second round, played its best game of the first round. Santana's players had finally hit their stride and the fluid passing was a sign of good things. The 51,000 fans that had filled the Jalisco Stadium wanted to see goals scored—and they got their wish after Careca scored in the 15th minute. Brazil increased its lead with Josimar in the 41st minute. Socrates and Junior were superb in the midfield, distributing passes down the middle and on the flanks that kept the out-of-breath Northern Ireland players out of the game. Careca made it 3–0 off a perfect back-heeled pass from Zico with three minutes left to play. Certainly, this had to be the year Brazil would win an unprecedented fourth World Cup. The game was also symbolic for another reason, as it was Northern Ireland goalkeeper Pat Jennings's 119th, and final, appearance for the national team. Brazil's three goals were a heartbreaking end to what had been a fine career for him. In tribute, the entire Brazilian team signed the game ball and presented it to Jennings after the game.

By the time the first round came to an end, FIFA found itself on the verge of a problem: Spain's Ramon Maria Calderé, who had been hospitalized with salmonella poisoning a few days before the game against Northern Ireland, had been treated with several medicines forbidden under FIFA doping regulations. FIFA had tightened its doping controls on the eve of the competition and the results had started to show. Players had been randomly tested in the first thirty-eight games and only Calderé had failed. The Spanish federation was fined $12,000 and its team doctor, Jorge Guillen, was cautioned. "We are confident the player did not know the composition [of the medication] and therefore cannot be punished," FIFA spokesman Guido Tognoni said in a statement. "But the team doctor must have known and therefore he and the Spanish delegation must bear full responsibility."[1] Scotland striker Willie Johnston was the last player who had failed a drug test at the World Cup—that happened eight years earlier and he was booted from the tournament after his test came back positive for banned substances. FIFA later suspended Johnston for a year.

Group E, played in Neza and Queretaro, was the tournament's "Group of Death." The real question was which team out of West Germany, Denmark, Scotland, and Uruguay would have an early funeral. West Germany and Uruguay each had tradition on their side—a psychological edge at every World Cup—while Denmark and Scotland had become two of Europe's toughest teams over the last decade. In the end, three teams would move on and one would leave early.

West Germany and Uruguay opened the group on June 4 at La Corregidora Stadium in Queretaro. The West Germans had ended the previous year without a win in six games. The West Germans, coached by Beckenbauer, tussled with Uruguay, but an error would put the South Americans in the lead. A misplayed ball by defender Thomas Berthold allowed Antonio Alzamendi to gain possession and fire off a shot that bounced off the underside of the crossbar and into the goal. The only attacking that took place following the goal was on West Germany's part, using the long ball and runs down the middle to infiltrate Uruguay's defense. The result was several tense moments for the defense, but the West Germans were unlucky. Beckenbauer replaced defender Andreas Brehme with Littbarski in the second half. The move was a piece of coaching genius and resulted in some much-needed offensive firepower. Beckenbauer was forced to replace midfielder Lothar Mattaeus in the 73rd minute with Rummenigge, who was playing in his third World Cup. Rummenigge's presence proved decisive and his assist with six minutes remaining allowed Klaus Allofs to give the West Germans a tie.

On the same day, at Neza 86 Stadium in Neza, Denmark defeated Scotland, 1–0, before a small crowd of 18,000 fans. The humid weather may have been the reason why so many people stayed away that afternoon, but those who did brave the heat witnessed a hard-fought contest and a Scottish team lacking the offensive needed to win games. Scotland, coached by Alex Fergusson, could not rely on the services of striker Kenny Daglish, who was forced to pull out of the tournament with a knee injury a few weeks before it was set to start. Scotland squandered several chances in the first half, but it would be the Danes in the second period that provided the offensive fireworks. Preben Elkjaer scored their lone goal in the 58th minute, a win that gave them first place in the group.

Four days later, La Corregidora Stadium in Queretaro was the site of West Germany's clash against Scotland. West Germany, yearning for a win, played a fast-paced game despite the unbearable heat. Scotland hit back, scoring first after seventeen minutes when Gordon Strachan put the ball past Schumacher. The lead only lasted five minutes. Allofs was able to cut past the Scottish defense and lofted a cross into the box that allowed Rudi Voeller to win the aerial battle with a bunch of Scottish defenders, heading the ball in for the 1–1 tie. The West Germans won the game in the second half—again a combination play between Allofs and Voeller made the difference in the 50th minute. This time, Voeller provided the decisive pass, allowing Allofs to slot the ball past goalkeeper Jim Leighton. The win assured West Germany a spot in the round of sixteen.

On the same day in Toluca, Denmark routed Uruguay, 6–1. The Danish offense, lead by Elkjaer's hat trick, allowed the team to book a place in the next round. The group's final two games were a meaningless exercise. Denmark defeated West Germany 2–0 on June 13 in Queretaro in a shocking result between two teams who had earned berths to the next round even before the ball had been kicked. At the same time in Toluca, Uruguay and Scotland played a game plagued by hard tackles and time wasting. Uruguay went into the game needing a win—or at least a tie—in the hopes of keeping its World Cup dreams alive. The Uruguayans got off on the wrong foot, reduced to ten men following a hard tackle by Jose Batista on Strachan. French referee Joel Quiniou ejected Batista and the Uruguayans had to face an uphill battle. Despite having the numerical advantage, Scotland failed to score. Uruguay was able to hold on to the scoreless tie and the result was enough to see them through to the round of sixteen. The Uruguayan team may have earned a second round berth but, in the process, it had cemented its image as a hard-tackling team that would resort to dirty tricks to get a positive result.

Group F, played in Monterrey and in Guadalajara, was also hard to predict. The Mexican fans—anxiously waiting to see some exciting soccer from Morocco, England, Poland, and Portugal—would be left disappointed. The group saw a surprise winner with Morocco finishing first after they compiled two scoreless ties—one against Poland on June 2 and another versus England four days later. The game that won the group for Morocco was a 3–1 victory over Portugal on June 11 at the Jalisco Stadium in Guadalajara. In that game, the Moroccan team played with the killer instinct that made it one of the most entertaining teams to watch at the tournament. Abderrazak Khairi put Morocco ahead in the 18th minute, picking up a lose ball and blasting a 25-yard shot that was too fast for Abdelkarim Damas to get a hand on. Nine minutes later, Khairi was able to make another run in the Portuguese half and, with a low shot, beat Damas for a second time. The Moroccans added an insurance goal with Abdelkarim Krimau in the 63rd minute, completing the rout and the most improbable result seen at the tournament thus far. Diamantino Miranda pulled one back for Portugal with ten minutes left to play, but it wasn't enough to deter the Morocco from winning the game, 3–1.

England, 1–0 losers to Portugal on June 3, needed a win over Poland. England's 0–0 tie against Morocco had left its lineup in disarray following injuries to striker Ray Wilkins and team captain Bryan Robson. Wilkins had received a red card against Morocco and was forced to sit the game out, while Robson had dislocated his shoulder and had to leave the game late in the first half. Against Poland on June 11, the English team needed to play with speed and skill if it hoped to get the win. The team also needed a leader on the field, someone who could outsmart the Polish defense. That man turned out to be Gary Lineker. By the time the first half was complete, England had taken an insurmountable 3–0 lead thanks to Lineker's three goals. His first goal after eight minutes allowed England to open the floodgates. Lineker's second goal, a perfectly executed half volley, came five minutes later. His third goal in the 35th minute brought the game to an end. Lineker had become the first Englishman to score a hat trick at a World Cup since Hurst in the 1966 final. Reaching the round of sixteen—which had appeared so unlikely before kickoff—was a reality thanks to Lineker's heroics. Poland, who finished with three points, qualified as one of the tournament's best third-place teams.

## Round of Sixteen

The round of sixteen featured eight very competitive match-ups: Mexico–Bulgaria, Belgium–Soviet Union, Brazil–Poland, Argentina–

Uruguay, France–Italy, West Germany–Morocco, England–Paraguay, and Spain–Denmark. Traditional powers Brazil, Argentina, and West Germany appeared favored to advance, though Mexico, France, and England went into the elimination round with all the confidence needed to reach the final.

Mexico opened the round of sixteen against Bulgaria on June 15 at the Azteca. The stadium was teeming with 115,000 fans, waving flags and chanting incessantly. The noise became deafening at one point, and for the Bulgarians it would prove to be the end of their World Cup journey. The Mexicans, who had reached the World Cup quarterfinals sixteen years earlier on their own soil, repeated that feat, defeating Bulgaria, 2–0. Bulgaria had reached the knockout stage without a win and, against Mexico, put on a feeble series of scoring chances. Milutinovic had his offensive weapon back and Sanchez did not disappoint. Mexico took the lead with Negrete in the 35th minute. Negrete was involved in Mexico's second goal, lofting a corner kick into the Bulgarian box that was met by Raul Servin, whose well-timed run allowed him to knock the ball into the net. An entire nation reveled in the victory.

On the same day in Leon, 32,227 spectators witnessed Belgium outlast the Soviet Union 4–3 in overtime. The Belgians, who came back twice, were able to knot the score at two and send the game to extra time. Belgium took its first lead in overtime. A Stephane Demol header in the 100th minute beat Dasaev for the 3–2 lead. Belgium scored its fourth goal eight minutes later with Claesen. The Soviets, however, were not done. Igor Belanov, who had already scored two goals that afternoon, completed the hat trick in the 111th minute on a penalty kick. Belgium had pulled the first shock result of the knockout phase.

On June 16, Brazil played Poland at Jalisco Stadium in Guadalajara. Poland's players, hoping to pull off an upset, wasted no time creating chances. Boniek menaced the Brazilian defense, showing glimmers of the greatness similar to the ones he had displayed four years earlier in Spain. Whatever defensive setbacks the Brazilians may have had to deal with in the opening fifteen minutes were offset by their tenacious offense. After Careca was brought down in the box, Brazil was awarded a dubious penalty, which Socrates converted in the 30th minute. The goal was a prelude of more to come. The Polish team missed several scoring chances, but the Brazilians capitalized on theirs. Josimar made a mockery of Poland's defense, using his speed to move swiftly past defenders, to make it 2–0. Edinho made it 3–0 in the 78th minute following a back-heel pass from Careca. The assist, a piece of artistry only a Brazilian could pull off, entertained the crowd. The Brazilians had not only defeated Poland, but had also managed to overcome the heat in a fashion far better than their opponents. Poland, unable to do anything other than watch as the Brazilians played the ball, gave up a fourth goal. Zico, who had come in for Socrates, was tripped in the box. Careca scored from the spot in the 82nd minute to complete the 4–0 rout.

The Brazilians weren't the only South Americans to put their talents on display that day. One of the continent's biggest rivalries—Argentina versus Uruguay—landed at the World Cup for the first time since the hotly contested final of 1930. The game also marked another milestone: the 400th game ever played a World Cup. The game was expected to be a defensive, and possibly even violent, affair. All eyes were once again affixed on Maradona, though it was Italian referee Luigi Agnolin who became the protagonist for all the right reasons. His superb officiating kept the players in check and allowed for the match to proceed without incident. Maradona was a bundle of energy that afternoon, distributing balls to his teammates with precision and rigor. Maradona created two excellent scoring chances in the first half. The first, a pass to Valdano, went wide. The second was a personal effort, curling a 35-yard free kick that hit the crossbar. In the end, Argentina won the game—not because of Maradona's passing or Valdano's shooting—but because of a defensive error. A poor clearance by the Uruguayan defense allowed Pedro Pasculli to steal the ball and score in the 41st minute to win the match. Bilardo's men had disposed of their rivals and were another step closer to the final.

On June 17, France took on champion Italy at the Estadio Olimpico '68 in Mexico City. France's midfield domination and Platini's class assured there would be a new World Cup champion. His goal in the 14th minute, a clever flick over Galli, put France in the lead, 1–0. The play not only exposed Italy's weak defense, but also confirmed Platini's reputation as one of the greatest players on the planet. The Italian offense was no better than its defense, rarely threatening the French goal. France was able to double their lead with Stopyra in the

57th minute. A 2–0 victory landed France in the quarterfinals against Brazil.

European teams went on to win the remaining three games in the round of sixteen. West Germany, playing drab and dour, struggled against Morocco on June 17 at Universitario Stadium in Monterrey. Only a well-executed free kick from Mattaeus in the 87th minute allowed the West Germans to win, 1–0. The next day at the Azteca, England, on the verge of elimination a week earlier, steamrolled over Paraguay, 3–0, thanks to two goals from Lineker. The pair of goals brought his tournament tally to five. The third European team to book a spot in the quarterfinals was Spain, whose 5–1 drubbing of Denmark was as remarkable as it was extraordinary. Real Madrid star Emilio Butragueño scored four goals on June 18 in Queretaro.

## Quarterfinals

A European country had never won a World Cup in the Western Hemisphere. The eight teams in the quarterfinals included five Europeans nations—France, West Germany, England, Belgium, and Spain—and only three from the Americas—Brazil, Argentina, and Mexico. A place in the semifinals was at stake with four games that produced one of the most exciting rounds ever played at a World Cup. First up, there was a clash between Brazil and France on June 21 in Guadalajara, in which one of them would have to go home and in what would be an epic do-or-die game. The teams were equally strong. The French lacked a world-class finisher, but had gotten plenty of production out of its midfield. The Brazilians, on the other hand, had Careca and Muller. The game would come down to more than just who had the best goalscorers. The players defied the ferocious temperatures, which touched 120 degrees at field level. More than two and a half hours—including the wretched necessity of those spell-binding penalty kicks—were needed to determine a winner. The game swung from one end of the field to the other for the first 120 minutes. With intense speed and superhuman strength, the players were able to sustain the momentum in their fifth match for the third straight week, despite the heat and high altitude. Brazil was able to get sixteen shots on goal, compared to France's fifteen. The game was a duel between Brazil's attack and France's midfield. France, so adept in the middle of the field, became increasingly worried by Brazil's one-touch passing. *Les Bleus* had cause for concern. After seventeen minutes, Brazil scored a breathtaking goal. After another seventeen minutes, a ripple of passes between Socrates, Branco, and Josimar, a one-time exchange between Junior and Muller, and a final thrust by Junior fed Careca the ball. The Brazilian striker cut through the French defense for the goal.

The French team, which had not been down a goal since playing the Soviet Union, regrouped its midfield and mounted a response. In the 40th minute, the team regained its rhythm. Giresse slipped a pass to Rocheteau clear on the right and his low pass deflected off Brazil's Edinho. Stopyra's goalmouth dive confused the Brazilian defense, and the ball rolled free as Platini stole it and, with all the calm of a training game, tapped the ball into the net. The second half contained enough scoring chances for a few games. Zico replaced Muller in the 70th minute and Santana's decision almost paid off instantly. Four minutes later, Zico's first touch of the ball sent his Brazilian teammate Branco on a run toward the goal. Out rushed Bats, spreading himself across Branco's path in an effort to steal the ball, but the play resulted in a Brazilian penalty kick. Zico was ready to take the shot, but his decision to take the kick proved hasty. Behind Zico's back, Platini signaled to Bats that he should dive left. The French goalkeeper took the hint and the advice resulted in a save. Brazil had just lost its chance to win the game in regulation. Twenty-two tired and sweat-soaked jerseys, with tired legs to match, headed to overtime.

Team doctors frantically rushed to the aid of the players, quickly massaging their legs to avoid them from cramping up. Some players dropped to the ground upon hearing Romanian referee Ioan Igna whistle the end of regulation. Others walked over to the sidelines to get a sip of water with all sluggishness, as if anchors were tied to their ankles. Surprisingly, the extra session produced another thirty minutes of fast-paced, heart-stomping action. Both sides continued to hurl themselves forward in search of the winning goal, but physically they were crumbling. A Platini pass in the 116th minute sent Bruno Bellone clear—only for him to be manhandled off the ball a yard outside the Brazilian penalty area by Carlos. No foul or card was given. Igna had committed a blunder. He had granted France the advantage rule, but Bellone had lost the ball in the process. Clearly, it was no advantage at all.

Overtime finally came to an end and for a second straight World Cup, France was headed to penalty kicks. The players assembled in the center circle waiting to be called up to the spot to take their kick. Exhausted and drained, many sported blank faces as the shootout got underway. France had the advantage from the start after Bats punched away the first 12-yard penalty kick by Socrates. The French kept the advantage only because their third kick, by Bellone, rebounded off the post and the back off Carlos's head to score. Even then, the French could not escape memories of their elimination at the hands of West Germany on penalty kicks four years earlier. Platini, of all players, shot high over the bar, giving Brazil a chance to tie. Each team had converted three of four kicks when Julio Cesar slammed Brazil's fifth off the left post. Fernandez, stoic and composed, atoned for Platini's miss and scored the winner for France. *Les Bleus* were off to the semifinals for the second straight tournament. The scoreboard read: France 4, Brazil 3. Once again, the Brazilians had come up short. In the face of such humiliation, Santana resigned.

The French win put them on a collision course with rivals West Germany. Before France could meet West Germany, the two-time world champions had to overcome Mexico on June 21 in Monterrey. Following a scoreless 120 minutes, this match, too, went to penalty kicks. Schumacher stopped a pair of shots while none of his teammates missed their kicks. Alternating kicks began with the West German side: Allofs began the shootout with a goal, which was canceled out by Mexico's Negrete. Then Brehme scored, but Schumacher got his leg on Quirarte's weak kick. Mattaeus blasted his shot into the lower left corner, while Schumacher's diving save allowed him to block Servin's low shot. Littbarski also scored, lifting West Germany to a 4–1 win, and the shootout was over. Both teams had played an extremely cautious game. For the Mexicans, their World Cup was over. The West Germans moved on and were in the World Cup semifinals for a record eighth time.

The match between Argentina and England on June 22 at the Azteca Stadium was one of the most tension-filled games ever played at a World Cup. The two nations had last clashed four years earlier. Not on a field, but during the Falklands War. Argentina suffered a crushing defeat, which eventually led to the downfall of the country's brutal military junta. For Argentina, the quarterfinal clash was reason for revenge. Though none of the players or coaches admitted to it publicly, it was common knowledge that the anxiety of playing in a World Cup game was heightened because of the tense history between the two nations. The Mexican authorities, fearing the worst, assembled 20,000 police officers in and around the stadium to diffuse any trouble that might arise from the potentially explosive match. Though several skirmishes occurred before the start of the game between individual fans from both teams, there was no mass violence. The midday sun was once again too much for the players to handle, but Argentina seemed to fare a lot better than the English. The sharp black shadow cast in the middle of the field by the ornate loudspeaker suspended above the center circle was an indication of how hot the sun was when the game kicked off at noon.

The high temperatures had done little to stop Maradona, who would score two goals by the time the game was over. When Tunisian referee Ali Bennaceur blew the final whistle, Shilton led a posse of teammates over to the match official to complain about the legitimacy of Argentina's first goal. The players had already angrily protested the goal when it was scored in the 51st minute, demanding a handball decision. Those complaints were ignored. TV replays confirmed everyone's suspicion: Maradona had surreptitiously used his left hand to give Argentina the 1–0 lead. England had suffered at the hands of Maradona—literally. Bennaceur should have known the goal was a metaphysical improbability. Maradona, standing only 5'4", could have never out-jumped Shilton. In the end, Maradona's controversial goal did not make the difference that afternoon. England had been solidly defeated by a superior team.

In the second half, England's coach, Bobby Robson, was forced to resort to an attacking 4-4-2 formation by bringing on Chris Waddle and John Barnes. Robson's fears that Maradona would overpower his defense came to fruition as the game went forward. The English defense, along with the 114,580 spectators buzzing like bees and blowing horns inside the Azteca, trembled in anticipation every time Maradona gained possession of the ball. Maradona dazzled the English players, along with the crowd, with every run he made, weaving and twisting the ball as if it was securely attached to his left foot. Maradona's gliding runs were too fast for the English players to handle, though the defense did an efficient job of breaking up plays in the midfield and clearing the ball up the field. Bilardo also suspected that the game could be won or lost in the midfield. He sacrificed a striker, Pasculli, and replaced him with the more defensive Hector Enrique. The move worked and Argentina's reinforced defense was able to shut down Lineker, who, with five goals, was the tournament's top scorer and most dangerous striker. The controversy erupted six minutes into the second half. Maradona's first goal is probably one of the most talked about at a World Cup. The goal was born in the midfield, like so many of Argentina's plays, with Maradona playing the ball to Valdano on the right. Defender Steve Hodge broke up the play, slicing the ball safely back to Shilton. That's when Maradona rose to meet the ball in the air with his head and seconds later the ball bounced into the net. Maradona had cheated, punching the ball into the goal with his fist. Shilton argued Maradona had scored with his hand. On first glance, the goal appeared legitimate.

Maradona's second goal was scored with such beauty and finesse that it is often considered the greatest piece of individuality in the sport's history. Maradona, who had swerved and swayed his way past English defenders for much of the game, went on a run that began in his midfield and culminated with him celebrating with his teammates near the corner kick flag. Maradona took the ball and beat out defenders Kenny Sansom, Terry Butcher, and Terry Fenwick, who were all moving so slowly compared to the Argentine that they looked like glaciers. With effortless ease, Maradona slid the ball past Shilton for the goal. Maradona's unflappable run had been too much for the English players to handle and Argentina were ahead 2–0. Maradona had left his indelible mark on the tournament, even though it was Lineker who was able to score his sixth goal of the competition in the 80th minute, but it was Argentina who won the game, 2–1. The England goal, stabbed into the net past goalkeeper Nery Pumpido from close-range, proved meaningless but gave Lineker the title of tournament top scorer.

But the player everyone was talking about was Maradona. The first goal had angered the English. His second, a piece of genius, had eliminated them. Maradona was asked by reporters to explain the contentious goal. "That goal was scored a little bit by the hand of God and another bit by Maradona's head," he told reporters.[2] From that point on, the play was forever known as the "Hand of God" goal.

On June 22, Spain versus Belgium in Puebla, the last of the four quarterfinal games, had its moments, but was basically an uninspiring blend of fouling and defensive soccer that ended in a shootout. The teams traded goals in regulation. Belgium took the lead when Jan Cuelemans deposited a header into the near post in the 34th minute. Spain, who did most of the attacking in the second half, got the equalizer with five minutes left to play when second-half substitute Juan Antonio Señor struck a 25-yard free kick into the back of the net. Overtime failed to produce a goal and the two weary teams went to a shootout. Belgium scored all five of its kicks to win the game, 5–4. Belgium was through to the semifinals, but as a reward had to face Argentina and Maradona.

## Semifinals

The game between Argentina and Belgium on June 25 was no replay of the opening match of the 1982 World Cup. In that game, Belgium's

*Diego Maradona tries to get past two English defenders during an epic win for Argentina during the 1986 World Cup quarterfinals (Credit: EMPICS).*

defense had been able to subdue Maradona, but this time would be different. The Belgian defense appeared terrified as Argentina was able to control the ebb and flow of the game by maintaining possession in the midfield with Maradona occasionally sending lethal passes into the Belgian box for the waiting feet of Burruchaga and Valdano. Argentina, however, had been unable to create any offense (with the exception of a disallowed Valdano goal in the 10th minute scored with his arm). Belgium was content with clearing the ball as the players tried to preserve their strength under the intense sun beating down on the Azteca Stadium. Maradona was too quick and clever for the Belgian defenders despite their attempts to chop him down. But Belgium had hung on and the first half ended scoreless. With his teammates unable to do anything offensively, Maradona decided it was up to him to leave his stamp on the game. He did an efficient job of ripping apart Belgium's defense in the second half and, in the process, put on a show of individuality not seen since the days of Pelé. Maradona's first goal came in the 51st minute when Enrique crossed the ball from the right. Maradona was able to pick it up, beat out two defenders, and deposit the ball past goalkeeper Jean-Marie Pfaff. Ten minutes later, Maradona was able to put on another delightful individual display. This time, he went on a solo run, leaving three Belgian defenders in the dust, before slotting the ball past Pfaff. The goal was reminiscent of his second strike against England. Argentina won, 2–0. Maradona had single-handedly taken his team to the final.

Two hours later in Guadalajara, West Germany and France met in a grudge match reminiscent of the 1982 semifinals. Unlike four years earlier in Spain, now France was playing its best soccer in history. The game was also a reunion of sorts between Schumacher and Battiston, who had been injured in that infamous collision. Thankfully, there was no repeat of that incident. Unfortunately, the game also lacked the intensity that took place in Seville. West Germany had played cautiously for much of the competition, but its solid defense and ability to outlast teams had become its calling card. *Les Bleus* were aware that the West Germans were capable of all kinds of tricks and had to find a way to avoid falling behind. But fall behind they did, by a score of 1-0. Brehme's free kick after eight minutes streaked under the body of Bats, who dove to make the save but could do nothing to stop the ball. France had a chance to tie the game three minutes later when Platini's header turned into an assist for Giresse, who volleyed the ball wide. France's clearest chance to tie the game came in the 15th minute when Platini, once again, struck a potent volley that was too hard for Schumacher to handle. The ball rebounded off the goalkeeper's hands and ended up in front of Bossis. The goal was empty. The ball was at his feet. But Bossis, pressured by the situation, shot the ball over the crossbar. France also had a slew of scoring chances in the second half, but Platini was effectively taken out of the game by Wolfgang Rolff's tight man-to-man marking. Against the run of play, Voeller scored on a breakaway in the 89th minute to win the game, 2–0, and lead West Germany to its second straight championship game. France would find some consolation by taking third place on June 28 in Puebla, beating Belgium 4–2 in overtime.

## The Final

The championship game was billed as a battle between two continents. The game was played on June 29 before 114,580 fans and featured all the color and pageantry worthy of a coronation. Matthaeus had been given the responsibility of marking Maradona—a double gamble on Beckenbauer's part. Matthaeus remained the most creative player on a team known more for its efficiency than beauty. With Matthaeus busy moving from the midfield to defense, the West Germans would be deprived of their most offensively gifted player. At the same time, Argentina wasted no time getting on the board, taking a 1–0 lead thanks to a goal by Jose Luis Brown in the 22nd minute. Although the West Germans were able to keep Maradona from finding the back of the net, it often meant that he was double-teamed, leaving his teammates wide open for passes. The only way for West Germany to stop Maradona was to foul him. One of those fouls, which resulted in a free kick, gave Argentina the lead. Matthaeus, who had earned a yellow card from Brazilian referee Romualdo Arpri Filho for his foul on Maradona from behind, could do nothing but watch as Burruchaga took the free kick and sent a cross in front of Schumacher, who was unable to catch the ball. That's when the ball reached Brown, who headed it into the net. The crowd was back on its feet in the 56th minute when a Maradona pass found Enrique, who dished it off to Valdano. Schumacher came out of his goal to try and cut off the shot and Valdano slipped the ball past him at the far post for the 2-0 lead.

Brown hurt his right shoulder with thirty minutes left in the game, but Bilardo refused to take him out of the game. Brown played the rest of the contest with his arm strapped to his body, bringing back memories of Beckenbauer playing in a sling against Italy in the 1970 World Cup semifinals. For all intents and purposes, the game appeared over. Argentina was bracing itself for a massive celebration. Beckenbauer replaced Felix Magath with Dieter Hoeness five minutes after the second Argentine goal and picked up some momentum from that switch. The West Germans rallied and got a goal from Rummenigge in the 74th minute off a Brehme corner kick that allowed the veteran striker to poke the ball in past Pumpido from three yards out. The West Germans continued to attack and amazingly tied the score seven minutes later when an unmarked Voeller headed it past Pumpido for the 2-2 tie.

The West Germans had played their best stretch of the tournament in the second half and it could not have come at a better time. Matthaeus, whose job appeared done, deserted Maradona in the game's dying minutes. What a tactical error that would turn out to be. If the West Germans expected Argentina to become complacent and gamble in overtime, they were sadly mistaken. Instead, Bilardo's team stayed focused and with six minutes remaining, Maradona, alone in the midfield, fed a pinpoint pass to Burruchaga on the right side. The Argentine striker, pressured by Hans-Peter Briegel, moved the ball into the penalty area and waited for just the perfect moment to unleash a strong kick that beat Schumacher for a third time that afternoon. Argentina won, 3-2, and Argentina had its hands on its second World Cup trophy. The final whistle ushered with it an invasion of fans onto the field. They hoisted Maradona onto their shoulders—like they had with Pelé sixteen years earlier—and paraded him around the field. A fan even tried to put a sombrero on Maradona's head, like what had happened to the Brazilian legend, but it fell off in the confusion. Finally, the Argentine people had something to rejoice about and the Mexican fans, who had adopted the South Americans as their team, got the celebrations off to a wild start on the field. If Argentina was the best team in the world, then Maradona, a one-man highlight reel, was undoubtedly the best player the planet had seen since Pelé. What he could do with a mere touch of the ball was comparable to what Frank Sinatra did with a microphone and Pablo Picasso with a paintbrush. His dream of winning the World Cup had finally come true.

## 1990

Fittingly, the soccer universe converged upon Italy in 1990. In doing so, Italy became the first European nation to host the World Cup twice. Serie A clubs had gone on massive spending sprees throughout the 1980s, attracting the world's most talented players and transforming Serie A into the planet's greatest domestic league. The best would once again play in Italian stadiums, only this time it was for a chance to be crowned world champions. The format remained the same as in Mexico with the twenty-four finalists eventually whittling themselves down to sixteen for the start of the knockout stage. The United States, named hosts in 1988 of the 1994 World Cup, put together a rag-tag team of college stars to qualify for its first finals in fifty years. The Americans struggled through CONCACAF qualifying, but were able to pull through. Part of their success was thanks to the absence of the Mexicans, who had been excluded from participating after FIFA found them guilty of deliberately fielding overage players in youth tournaments. A 35-yard left-footed goal by midfielder Paul Caligiuri allowed the Americans to beat Trinidad and Tobago, 1-0, on November 18, 1989, in Port-au-Prince, to reach the finals, stunning the crowd and the soccer world in the process. The goal—dubbed the "the shot heard 'round the world"—was worth millions of dollars. The USSF and FIFA breathed a collective sigh of relief. Commercial interested surrounding the 1994 World Cup was saved and the USSF could finally embark on trying to revive soccer in this country.

The qualifying rounds once again featured a slew of upsets and controversy. A record 112 nations played for two and a half years for a shot at the 1990 finals. Brazil played at home on September 3, 1989, against Chile in front of 141,000 fans at the Maracanã Stadium. The Brazilian team was expected to cruise to the finals until, when in the 65th minute, a spectator hurled a flare onto the field. Brazil was leading 1-0 at the time. Chilean goalkeeper Roberto Rojas crashed to the ground, claiming the flare had exploded and blinded him. Rojas lay on the grass bleeding as team doctors tended to him. The game was halted. Brazil, who had played in every World Cup finals, ran the real risk of missing out on the big show for the first time because the tossing of the flare by one of its fans could have resulted in their automatic disqualification. Brazilians cried at the prospect of having to ban Brazil from the tournament because of fan violence. World Cup organizers cringed. What would a World Cup be without Brazil? Instead, television replays and a FIFA investigation uncovered that Rojas had faked his injury in an effort to get Brazil disqualified. Rojas was banned for life and Chile was disqualified from all FIFA-sanctioned tournaments for two years. The Brazilians were automatically awarded a 2–0 victory, which saw them through to the finals.

England, who had been humiliated at the 1988 European Championship after losing all three first-round games, qualified behind Sweden in Europe's Group 2. Scotland disposed of the likes of France and Norway to finish second behind Yugoslavia in Group 5. Ireland, coached by Englishman Jackie Charlton, reached the finals for the first time after finishing second to Spain in Group 6. The toughest group in Europe, which featured West Germany, Holland, Finland, and Wales, saw the Germans and Dutch make the cut. Europe was also represented by hosts Italy, Austria, Belgium, Czechoslovakia, Romania, and the Soviet Union. The South Americans featured Brazil, along with trophy-holders Argentina and first-timer Colombia, whose domestic league had been temporarily suspended after the government uncovered that drug money had been used to bankroll clubs. The Africans were represented by Egypt and Cameroon, who was back after putting on a dazzling performance in 1982. South Korea and the United Arab Emirates, also first-time qualifiers, emerged from Asia.

## Pre-Tournament Analysis

The final draw for *Il Mondiale*—the World Cup—was held on December 9, 1989, at Rome's Palazzo dello Sport. A galaxy of stars, including tenor Luciano Pavarotti and actress Sofia Loren, ushered the unofficial start of the tournament. Argentina, Italy, Brazil, West Germany, Belgium, and England were the six seeded teams. Retired stars such as Pelé and Rummenigge took part in the elaborate ceremony and ever-complicated draw of trying to avoid mixing teams from the same geographic regions in the first round. The first round groupings were as follows:

Group A: Italy, Austria, Czechoslovakia, and the United States
Group B: Argentina, the Soviet Union, Romania, and Cameroon
Group C: Brazil, Costa Rica, Scotland, and Sweden
Group D: West Germany, Yugoslavia, the United Arab Emirates, and Colombia
Group E: Belgium, South Korea, Spain, and Uruguay
Group F: England, Holland, Ireland, and Egypt

The final group was without a doubt the "Group of Death" with England and Holland, two of Europe's strongest teams, mixing it up with Ireland and Egypt. Holland, winners of the 1988 European Championship following a spectacular 2–0 win over the USSR, featured three of the world's greatest players. Strikers Marco van Basten and Ruud Gullit plied their club trade at AC Milan, leading the Italian team to a number of international and domestic titles during the late 1980s. (Van Basten and Gullit were also the two goalscorers in the aforementioned championship game against the Soviets at Euro 1988.) They were joined at AC Milan by central defender Frank Rijkaard, also a national team regular, whose goal against Benfica in the European Champions Cup a month before the start of the World Cup lifted AC Milan to the title. The Dutch were clearly prepared to do battle in Italy, hoping that club success would translate into wins for the national team.

West Germany, meanwhile, had its own trio of superstars playing in Italy. Matthaeus was playing with AC Milan's intra-city rivals Inter Milan and, along with Brehme, led the team to the Italian League title in 1989. In the season leading up to the World Cup, Matthaeus and Brehme were joined at Inter by Jurgen Klinsmann, a talented striker whose aerial abilities instilled fear in the hearts and minds of defenders across the peninsula. The German trio was also looking to be crowned world champions on familiar Italian soil.

Italy, Brazil, and Argentina were also favored to win the tournament. The Italians had the home crowd behind them and could rely on their hard-nosed defense, anchored by AC Milan's Franco Baresi and Paolo Maldini. The team's offense remained much of a mystery. Gianluca

Vialli had developed into one of the country's strongest strikers, but whether he was totally fit remained a question after injuring his right foot. Italy's coach Azeglio Vicini also had to contend with where to put rising star Roberto Baggio and whether Juventus striker Salvatore "Toto" Schillaci, who had burst onto the national team scene late in his career, was even worth keeping on the roster.

The enthusiasm typically reserved for the *Azzurri* took on a violent twist a month before the start of the tournament. On May 6, the team's first practice at Coverciano, in the suburbs of Florence, turned into mayhem when twenty people surrounded Schillaci's car and pounded on the roof and hood, kick in the taillights and shouting racial slurs against the Sicilian-born striker. Schillaci was an easy target. After all, he played with Juventus, a team fans in Florence have always loved to hate. The rivalry had reached a boiling point on the eve of the World Cup after Fiorentina played Juventus in the first-leg of the UEFA Cup final in Turin. The game was marred by fouls on the field and violence in the stands. Juventus wound up wining the trophy two weeks later in the return leg. Tensions flared further after Fiorentina sold Baggio to Juventus. Schillaci was also a southerner, something that also made him easy prey for racist hoodlums who typically cause trouble at soccer games in Italy. Italian soccer federation president Antonio Matarrese tried to downplay the incident at a news conference that afternoon, saying, "It is obvious that with all the passion that surrounds our league, a few fans are bound to lose control."[3] Whether the fans would pick on Schillaci in front of a global audience remained to be seen.

The Brazilians, meanwhile, were once again going through a transformation. Coming up short at the 1982 and 1986 World Cups had taken a psychological toll on the team. Brazil coach Sebastião Lazaroni decided to abandon the traditional tactics surrounding *jogo bonito*, opting instead for a more European, defensive-minded approach meant to win games—similar to how the West Germans and Italians had been able to do with success the previous decade. If playing attacking-minded and stylish soccer meant losing games, Lazaroni was more than happy to change the team's tactical mindset. Efficiency won the day, but whether the Brazilians would win the cup was seriously in doubt.

Brazilian rivals Argentina still had Maradona and he remained a threat. Maradona had led Napoli, characterized as a symbol of Italy's underprivileged and blue-collar south, to two Italian League titles and a

## SALVATORE SCHILLACI

The music world has one-hit wonders and the World Cup has Salvatore Schillaci. Born in 1964 in Palermo, Italy, Schillaci, nicknamed Toto, grew up in a poor family. He played soccer in the streets and eventually signed for Sicilian club Messina in 1982. He played with Messina until 1989 and then joined Juventus. He made his Serie A debut in August 1989 and coach Azeglio Vicini selected him to play on Italy's 1990 World Cup team.

Despite his lack of international experience, Vicini gambled on Schillaci's astuteness and eye for the goal. In Italy's first game against Austria, Schillaci sat on the bench, but replaced Andrea Carnevale in the second half. The Schillaci fairytale was about to take off. He scored the winner against Austria in Italy's 1–0 win. Against the United States, Schillaci again made an appearance as a substitute. In the next match, against Czechoslovakia, Vicini placed Schillaci in the starting lineup alongside Roberto Baggio. Italy won, 2–0, with Baggio and Schillaci scoring. In the round of sixteen and quarterfinals, against Uruguay and Ireland, respectively, Schillaci scored in each game. In the semifinals against Argentina, Schillaci was once again a starter. The game ended 1–1, with Schillaci scoring for the Italians. Argentina eventually eliminated Italy on penalty kicks.

In the third-place match against England, Italy won, 2–1, with Schillaci scoring on a penalty kick to bring his tournament tally to six. He finished as the tournament's top scorer, but his national team career ended shortly after the competition. Schillaci would only make sixteen appearances for Italy and score seven goals.

After the 1990 World Cup, Schillaci played two more seasons for Juventus, before joining rivals Inter. Following two lackluster seasons where he was plagued by injuries, Schillaci became the first Italian in 1994 to sign with Japan's new league, the J-League, when he joined Jubilo Iwata. Schillaci retired in 1999 and today runs a youth soccer academy in Palermo.

### World Cup Career Statistics

Tournaments played: 1
Games: 5
Goals: 6

UEFA Cup. Maradona had pulled off an amazing feat, particularly for a club that had never won a major tournament since its creation in 1926. Maradona's supremacy within the Italian League also angered the rich northern Italian clubs, who vowed at the start of every season to knock Maradona off his throne.

Things, however, were not going so well for Argentina. The defending champions were an older team and Bilardo, like so many coaches before him, failed to notice the cracks that had begun to form around his roster. Bilardo became a target of the country's government officials, most notably flamboyant President Carlos Menem, who couldn't understand why Ramon Diaz had been left off the team. Diaz's exclusion was Maradona's doing. Once friends, the two players had become bitter enemies after Diaz had supposedly criticized him to other teammates.

## Group Play

Argentina opened the tournament on June 8 at the refurbished Giuseppe Meazza Stadium in Milan against Cameroon. The game, which had been proceeded by a spectacular opening ceremony, would go down as one of the World Cup's biggest upsets. The crowd of 73,780, filled with AC Milan and Inter Milan fans, jeered the Argentine anthem—a knock at Maradona because he played with rival club Napoli. The crowd embraced the Africans, applauding Cameroon and cheering for them each time they gained possession of the ball. In the opening ten minutes, Argentina appeared to be on its way to putting Cameroon away. Every failed chance at goal by Argentina turned into a confidence boost for the Cameroonians. The game wore on as Maradona put together a string of great plays, but his teammates didn't appear to be on the same page. Striker Claudio Caniggia came in at the start of the second half, hoping that Maradona could put through a magical pass to him that would result in a goal. That would never happen. Argentina caught a break in the 60th minute when French referee Michel Vautrot red carded Kana Biyik for a foul on Caniggia. However, subsequent replays showed that Caniggia's heel had made contact with Biyik. The Cameroon team, nicknamed the "Indomitable Lions," played with ten players, and even played better despite the numerical disadvantage.

Five minutes after Biyik's dismissal, Francois Oman-Biyik rose into the air and headed the ball down toward goal. The ball hit the grass hard and rolled under Pumpido's body for the goal. The crowd roared as the players piled on top of Biyik in celebration. Maradona knew that time was running out and a loss would be an embarrassment. Argentina was not capable of much as Cameroon, who ended the game with nine players following the sending off of Benjamin Massing in the 88th minute, fouled its way to victory. Caniggia and Maradona bore the brunt of Cameroon's fouling and the duo became ineffectual as a result. Massing's foul on Caniggia earned him a second yellow card that afternoon, but still Argentina had come up short. For Cameroon, a berth to the second round appeared a possibility, although red cards would become a problem down the stretch.

The following day, Rome's Olympic Stadium was the site of Italy's first game of the tournament. The Group A favorites took on Austria in front of 72,302 fans. The Italians were under tremendous pressure, but Vicini's team fed off the enthusiasm created by the crowd. They kept up their momentum and, after the 78th minute, Schillaci, who had entered the game just four minutes earlier for Napoli striker Andrea Carnevale, headed in the game winner after connecting with a Vialli cross. The Italians won 1–0 and could breathe a sigh of relief.

On June 10, the United States made its World Cup return at Florence's Communale Stadium against Czechoslovakia. The 33,266 fans in the stands, many of whom were Americans vacationing in Italy or stationed at nearby military bases, would see six goals. Unfortunately for the Americans, five of those goals would come against them. To their credit, the one goal they did score was a beauty. In the 61st minute, striker Bruce Murray passed the ball through the Czechoslovakian defense to Caligiuri, who beat his marker for a breakaway that left him one-on-one with goalkeeper Jan Stejskal. Caligiuri faked a shot on goal, leaving Stejskal on the ground, then dribbled the ball around him and with a right-footed shot blasted the ball into the net from 12 yards out. The U.S. team, whose odds of winning the World Cup stood at 50,000-to-1, was losing 3–1 at that point, though the goal seemed to stun the Czechoslovakians. The goal did little to change the flow of the game. Czechoslovakia played target practice against the Americans for ninety minutes, taking twenty-three shots on goal, compared to just seven by the United States.

Czechoslovakia took the lead in the 26th minute when striker Tomas Skuhravy put the ball in from close range past goalkeeper Tony Meola following a give-and-go with Lubomir Moravcik. The Americans, outmatched in every part of the field, didn't let the goal get to them until the 40th minute when defender Mike Windischmann fouled Ivan Hasek in the penalty area. The foul set up a penalty kick that was converted by Michal Bilek for a 2–0 lead. The second half would only get worse for the Americans. Czechoslovakia took a commanding 3–0 lead with Hasek in the 50th minute. Three minutes later, the U.S. team was reduced to ten players after striker Eric Wynalda was red carded following a push on a Czechoslovakian player following a throw-in. Swiss referee Kurt Rothlisberger wasted no time pulling out the red card. The call seemed absurd and would be the first in a string of refereeing errors to mar the competition. The Caligiuri goal—the only highlight of the game for the Americans—did nothing to stop the Czechoslovakian attack. Skuhravy scored his second of the game in the 79th minute and a goal by Milan Luhovy in the 89th minute brought the game to an end. A minute before the fifth goal, Meola had prevented another goal, saving a penalty kick by Bilek after defender Steve Trittschuh's fouled Hasek in the box. Nevertheless, Czechoslovakia had managed to humiliate the United States 5–1. "We were a very young team. It didn't matter how much we tried to prepare for that World Cup," Meola recalled. "We had no clue what that first game would really be all about."[4]

On June 14, the United States had the tough task of playing Italy in Rome. A raucous crowd of 73,423 fans cheered on the *Azzurri*. The Americans had one goal in mind: concede the fewest goals possible. The Italians appeared to open the floodgates after eleven minutes when Giuseppe Giannini sliced through John Harkes and rifled the ball past goalkeeper Meola for the 1–0 lead. The Italians would control the pace of the game, applying pressure on the American defense for the next eighty minutes, but to no avail. The Italians would not score again. The *Azzurri* had a chance to make it 2–0 in the 33rd minute when defender Nicola Berti was upended by Caligiuri in the box. Vialli took the ensuing kick, fooled Meola who darted to his left, but the ball hit the base of the right post and bounced away. The Americans, who had displayed tremendous fortitude, had been lucky to give up just one goal. The Italians had earned another two points and a second round berth.

The Italians finished group play with a game against the Czechoslovakians, who had been 1–0 winners over Austria on June 15 in Florence. The June 19 game once again attracted more than 73,000 fans to the Olympic Stadium. Italy won, 2–0, after its two newest stars, Schillaci and Baggio, scored. The Italians dominated the game for long stretches and opened the scoring with Schillaci after nine minutes, heading the ball into the net after Giuseppe Giannini missed his shot. Baggio's goal—one of the prettiest ever scored at a World Cup—was a work of art. The Juventus-bound player, who left Fiorentina for a record $14 million transfer fee on the eve of the tournament, gathered the ball in the midfield, played a one-two with Giannini, and then embarked on a superb solo run. He strode into the Czechoslovakian half, beat three defenders and unleashed a shot that found the back of the net. The Italians won the group, but the Czechoslovakians also moved on after finishing in second place.

At the same time, the U.S. team, looking for its first World Cup win in forty years, played Austria in Florence. Before the game, USSF President Warner Fricker gave reporters an update on the preparations for the 1994 World Cup. It was common knowledge that professional soccer was all but dead in the United States. The only thing to take its place was the MISL, which many claimed was a bastardized version of the world's game because it was played indoors on a green rug. Though the MISL was criticized by soccer purists, it was the only version of the sport that remained alive during the 1980s. Some had expressed doubt that the Americans could host the tournament. "We will look to FIFA, we will look to Italia '90—but in the form of advice," said Fricker. "It's our job [to organize the tournament] and we will do it, and do it well."[5] Fricker's blunt approach was meant to quell the critics. Fricker, however, would never get a chance to organize USA 1994. He would be defeated by Alan Rothenberg, a Los Angeles lawyer backed by FIFA, two months later in a contentious USSF election. The shakeup—which began when FIFA urged Rothenberg to join the race three weeks before the vote—allowed the USSF not only to embark on the arduous task of building up its national team in order to make it worthy of competing with the rest of the field in four years, but also to organize a World Cup that could withstand criticism. Many people feared that America's lack of soccer tradition would not enable it to pull off such a massive event. For FIFA, the tournament was a chance to get its hand into a previously untapped market. The commercial opportunities were endless.

The United States' match against Austria gave everyone at the USSF a glimpse of just how much work needed to be done to build up its national team. Austria won 2–1 after scoring two second-half goals. The Austrians were down a player after Peter Artner was red carded in the 33rd minute following his tackle intended to injure U.S. striker Peter Vermes. Even before Artner's sending off, the game had degenerated into a rumble. A minute before the red card, Austrian defender Robert Peci took down Murray with a hard tackle that resulted in a yellow card. Murray waited for referee Jamal Al Sharif of Syria to turn his back before punching Peci in the face. The referee never saw the punch. Murray almost got away with another ridiculous foul nine minutes later. Murray brought Peci down with a move that would have won him a belt at Wrestlemania. The referee allowed Austria's medical staff to enter the field and tend to Peci while the linesman recounted the details of the foul to Sharif, who showed Murray a yellow card. The Americans gave it their all, but that wasn't enough.

In the second half, Austria turned on the pressure. A right-footed shot by Andreas Ogris in the 49th minute planted itself in the right corner of the net past Meola. Windischmann had a chance to close in on Ogris, but the Austrian was too quick for him. The Americans, like in the previous two games, lost their composure after falling behind. As a result, the Austrians scored again in the 63rd minute when Michael Streiter centered a pass in the box to Gerhard Rodax, who was left unmarked by Windischmann. His right-footed shot blew past Meola for the 2–0 lead. The U.S. team's defensive lapses had led to both goals. When they were down by 1–0, coach Bob Gansler had replaced Desmond Armstrong, a defender, with Wynalda, a striker, in the hopes of generating some offense. Despite giving up the goal, the move did bear some fruit. The Americans scored their second goal of the tournament in the 83rd minute when midfielder Tab Ramos, the most impressive U.S. player at the World Cup, beat Austrian defender Ernest Aigner in the penalty area and slipped in a pass to Murray, who slipped the ball through the outstretched hands of goalkeeper Klaus Lindenberger. The Austrians won 2–1, but hadn't scored enough goals to make it to the round of sixteen as one of the first round's best third-place teams. The Americans, meanwhile, walked off the field with their heads held up high despite going 0–3 against Italy, Austria, and Czechoslovakia. Their revenge would come four years later at home.

Group B, played in Naples and Bari, featured more fireworks after Cameroon's stunning upset of Argentina. Romania recorded a 2–0 victory over the USSR on June 9 at Bari's San Nicola Stadium with two goals by Marius Lacatus. Four days later, Argentina rebounded at the San Paolo Stadium in Naples against the USSR. Both teams made changes to their lineups, though the absence of Dasaev from the Soviet goal was the most notable. If things had gone bad for Argentina in the opener, they took a turn for the worst after just ten minutes when Pumpido suffered a double leg fracture after colliding with teammate Julio Olartichoachea. Pumpido was replaced with second stringer Sergio Goycochea. The Soviets took advantage of the momentum that had swung their way and almost scored a few minutes later, but were deprived when once again the "Hand of God" reared its ugly head. Off a corner kick, Oleg Kuznetsov's header was aimed right at goal when Maradona, standing a few feet from the line, stuck out his right hand and stopped the ball from going in. Referee Frederickson was standing only 10 feet away, but never whistled a penalty kick in the USSR's favor. Once again, a missed call had marred a World Cup game. Maradona took his defensive tricks and translated them into offensive magic that made the 56,000 fans jump to their feet in a stadium that had become Maradona's adopted home. Maradona took a corner kick on the left side in the 27th minute that was cleared to Olartichoachea, who ran toward the Soviet defense with the ball before unleashing a pass that allowed Pedro Troglio, unmarked in the center of the box, to hit a powerful header into the net. Argentina eased off after taking the lead, allowing the USSR to get back into the game. Argentina caught another huge break in the second half when Frederickson ejected defender Vladimir Bessonov in the 48th minute after the Soviet player was spotted pulling Caniggia's jersey. In the 79th minute, Burruchaga intercepted a sloppy back pass by Kuznetsov, pounced on the ball, and deposited it into the net for the 2–0 victory. Argentina again now had a real shot of getting through to the second round.

On June 14, the "Indomitable Lions" pulled off another upset, defeating Romania, 2–1, in Bari. The game appeared headed for a tie—a result useful to both teams—but thirty-eight-year-old Roger Milla changed the course of the game. Milla, who had played the waning minutes against Argentina, entered this game in the 58th minute. Milla, a member of Cameroon's 1982 team, had come out of semiretirement on the eve of the tournament and would become one of the World Cup's biggest stars at an age where most players are retired. His goal in the 76th minute gave Cameroon the lead and allowed him at the time to become the oldest player to ever score at a World Cup. The Africans didn't stop there. A mix of hard tackling and counterattacking allowed Cameroon to increase its lead. Ten minutes after Milla scored, the veteran star added another goal. Cameroon appeared to be coasting to a win when Romania notched one goal with Gavrila Balint, who had come on for Raducioiu in the 63rd minute. Cameroon held on for what became an astonishing 2–1 win and a trip to the knockout round—the first time an African team advanced past the group stage at a World Cup. On June 18, the San Paolo Stadium in Naples was once again the backdrop for Argentina as 52,733 spectators rabidly cheered on Maradona in Argentina's 1–1 tie versus Romania. The result allowed both teams to advance to the next round. Pedro Monzon put Argentina ahead in the 61st minute, but Balint was able to draw the game level seven minutes later. In the meantime, the Soviet Union, who had no chance of advancing out of the group stage, routed Cameroon, 4–0, in Bari. The loss exposed a number of defensive weaknesses that had dogged the Africans through much of the competition, but it didn't do anything to stop them from advancing to the round of sixteen. The Soviets had earned only two points in three games and again suffered an early World Cup exit. In the years following the tournament and the subsequent collapse of communism, the USSR split into Russia and fourteen smaller independent states, although eleven of the former Soviet republics fielded a team called the Commonwealth of Independent States, or CIS, at the 1992 European Championship.

Group C, played in Turin and Genoa, was dominated by the presence of Brazil. In the group opener on June 10 at the newly built Delle Alpi Stadium in Turin, Brazil defeated Sweden, 2–1, on two goals from Careca in the 40th and 57th minutes. Careca, who played with Napoli since 1987, sent a signal to his teammate Maradona that Brazil was also a contender for the trophy. Sweden pulled one back with Tomas Brolin in the 78th minute, but to no one's surprise, the Brazilians had come out on top. The next day, Costa Rica, coached by Milutinovic, stunned Scotland, 1–0, at Marassi Stadium in Genoa. Juan Cayasso scored the game winner in the 49th minute. On June 16, Brazil got the best of Costa Rica, 1–0, in Turin, which assured them of a trip to the second round. That night in Genoa, Scotland beat Sweden, 2–1; the Scottish clinched the win when Mo Johnston converted a penalty kick with nine minutes left to play.

Scotland was again alive, but needed at least a tie against Brazil if it hoped to move on. Sweden and Costa Rica—both knotted at two points in the group standings—both had an equal chance of advancing. Their head-to-head match in Genoa would determine which one, if not both, would keep its World Cup dream alive. While Brazil eliminated Scotland following a 1–0 win on a goal by Muller in the 81st minute at the rain-soaked Delle Alpi Stadium, Costa Rica pulled off another upset and the small nation became the unlikeliest team to advance to the round of sixteen. The feat was no fluke. Everything appeared to be going according to script as Sweden, clearly favored to win, took the lead in the opening half. Milutinovic, who had worked his tactical magic with Mexico four years earlier, made a move that changed the course of the game. In the 62nd minute, Milutinovic brought on forward Hernan Medford, who energized his team's attack. Costa Rica tied the score with Roger Flores in the 75th minute after taking advantage of a Swedish defensive lapse to head in the ball into the net. Then the improbable occurred with three minutes left to play: the sluggish Swedish defense, unable to stop Medford from the time he had walked onto the field, allowed the Costa Rican striker to run 40 yards untouched before he was able to slot the ball past goalkeeper Thomas Ravelli. Costa Rica had come from behind for the 2–1 victory and produced a shocker of seismic proportions.

Group D, played in Bologna and Milan, produced few surprises. West Germany, enjoyed the same benefits Argentina had in Naples. Playing in Milan allowed Matthaeus, Brehme, and Klinsmann to enjoy the crowd support. The West Germans wasted little time against its first-round opponents, outclassing Yugoslavia, 4–1, on June 10 and trouncing the United Arab Emirates, 5–1, five days later. Colombia took on the United Arab Emirates on June 9 at Bologna's Renato Dall'Ara Stadium. Colombia's superiority was rewarded with goals from Bernardo Redin in the 52nd minute and the blond, pompom-haired midfielder Carlos Valderamma with five minutes remaining. The Colombians, however, suffered a setback on June 14 in Bologna, losing 1–0 to Yugoslavia. The match appeared headed for a scoreless tie, but Davor Jozic changed that in the 73rd minute, volleying the ball past flamboyant goalkeeper Rene

Higuita for the winner. The Colombians needed at least a tie against the West Germans if they hoped to achieve the point needed to go through as one of the competition's four best third-place teams. The Inter Milan faithful once again came out in force with 72,510 spectators filling the Meazza Stadium. West Germany, already assured a spot in the round of sixteen, did not display the attacking killer instinct that had characterized its previous two games. The West Germans controlled the pace of the game with the Colombians content with playing the ball in the midfield and running out the clock in the hopes of attaining a 0–0 tie. The South Americans became a victim of their own time-wasting tactics when the West Germans, always deadly on the counterattack, took the lead with Pierre Littbarski in the 89th minute. The goal, set up by Voeller, deflated any hopes Colombia had of advancing. But in the second minute of stoppage time, the Colombians pulled off the unthinkable. Valderrama, who had done little throughout the game, put through a crisp, rolling pass that cut the West German defense, allowing Freddy Rincon to get off a shot that went like a missile through goalkeeper Bodo Illgner's legs. The Colombian players pounced on top of Rincon in jubilation. Colombia and Yugoslavia both assured themselves a trip to the next round.

Group E, played in Verona and Udine, offered few surprises. Spain, Belgium, and Uruguay—all favored to advance—got the best of South Korea and the group finished in that order. Belgium, favored to win the group, opened with a 2–0 win over South Korea on June 12 at the Bentegodi Stadium in Verona and a 3–1 victory over Uruguay five days later. The only minor surprise of the group was the all-European clash between Spain and Belgium that would determine which of the two would move on to the next round in first place. Belgium needed a tie to finish first, while Spain, in need of a win, put on an entertaining display in Verona. Spain took the lead in the 27th minute when Luis Miguel Michel converted a penalty kick after Michel Preud'homme brought down Julio Salinas in the penalty box. The Spanish lead was short-lived when Patrick Vervoot's free kick bounced off the Spanish wall and into the net. Spain got the win with a goal six minutes before halftime. Alberto Gorriz was able to head the ball past Preud'homme from a Michel corner kick that caught the Belgian defense by surprise. The three-goal, first-half fireworks were followed by a failed chance for Belgium to tie the game in the second half. Enzo Scifo's penalty kick slammed against the post in the 61st minute after Argentine referee Juan Carlos Loustau whistled a penalty kick in Belgium's favor. Spain was victorious, 2–1, and finished first in the group. Belgium and Uruguay, finished second and third, respectively.

Group F, which included England, Holland, Ireland, and Egypt, was intentionally played on the islands of Sicily and Sardinia in order to keep the threat of hooliganism off the Italian mainland. The move was controversial, but deemed necessary by the police who were expecting the worst. Group play opened on June 11 with a clash between England and Ireland at the Sant'Elia Stadium in Cagliari. Lineker took over from where he had left off in Mexico four years earlier and opened the scoring after eight minutes. Lineker's goal was a great display of individuality. After receiving a pass from Chris Waddle, Lineker played the ball off his chest—under pressure from two Irish defenders—and poked the ball past the advancing Pat Bonner. The Irish goalkeeper, unable to close the angle on Lineker, could only watch as the ball trickled into the net. If that splendid goal wasn't enough to get English fans excited, then the bright lightning, followed by a torrential rain, did the trick. The field conditions made it harder for both teams to create any real scoring chances. However, Ireland tied the game in the 73rd minute when Kevin Sheedy took a pass from Steve McMahon—and fired off a left-footed shot at the edge of the box that whisked past Shilton. The English goalkeeper was making his 119th international appearance—tying a record first achieved by retired Northern Ireland goalkeeper Peter Jennings—wasn't to blame. The shot was too potent. The game ended 1–1.

The following day at the La Favorita Stadium in Palermo, Holland and Egypt played to a 1–1 tie. The Egyptians, making their return to the tournament for the first time since 1934, had defeated Scotland and Czechoslovakia in pre–World Cup friendlies, but a tie against the Dutch was a shock result. The star-studded Dutch had underestimated the Egyptians and it cost them dearly. A goalless first half had Holland, picked by some to win the tournament, frantically trying to score in the second period. The Egyptians built several scoring chances but the Dutch, disorganized offensively, were fortunate to take the lead against the run of play in the 59th minute. Van Basten crossed the ball from the left side, allowing second-half substitute Wim Kieft to unleash a shot past goalkeeper Ahmed Shobeir. The Egyptians did lock down their defense following the goal, but striker Ahmed El Kas spurred his teammates offensively. The Egyptians were once again moving the ball dangerously into the Dutch half and had three chances to tie the game. Goalkeeper Hans van Breukelen did a great job guarding the Dutch goal, making up for the many mistakes committed by his defense. He couldn't smother every shot and, in the 82nd minute, the Egyptians were awarded a penalty kick. Ronald Koeman pulled down Hossam Hassan in the box, even though TV replays later showed that it had occurred just outside the area. Referee Emilio Soriano Aladren of Spain didn't hesitate and pointed to the spot. Magdi Abedelghani's perfectly executed conversion on the penalty ensured that Egypt would earn a hard-fought 1–1 tie.

If Egypt had proven to be a formidable opponent, then the Dutch had a lot to worry about when they played England on June 16 in Cagliari. Robson employed the sweeper system for the first time in his managerial career, using Mark Wright, who played with English club Southampton, in that lone position between the defensive line and the goal. The strategy worked, though England couldn't do better than a scoreless tie against Holland. The Dutch were lucky to earn another tie after the English had given them heaps of trouble, particularly with Lineker and midfielder Paul Gascoigne, whose speed and hustle allowed his team to move the ball up field with relative ease. Shilton broke the international cap record with his 120th appearance and celebrated the milestone with a shutout.

Egypt's 0–0 tie against Ireland a day later in Palermo threw the group into chaos. All four teams were tied with two points. It was anyone's group to win and both remaining games took place concurrently. The Egyptians had a real chance of becoming the second team from Africa to advance to the round of sixteen after Cameroon. The only thing standing in their way was England; the teams were deadlocked, 0–0, in the first half in Cagliari. Elsewhere, the other group game between Ireland and Holland in Palermo had ended with the Dutch in front 1–0 on a goal by Gullit in the 11th minute. Back in Cagliari, Mark Wright and Gascoigne connected for what turned out to be the game's only goal. A Gascoigne free kick allowed Wright to rise above the Egyptian defenders and head it in. The win allowed England to win the group. Back in the other game, Ireland was able to tie the score with Niall Quinn in the 72nd minute when van Breukelen failed to hold on to a back pass by Dutch defender Berry van Aerle, allowing Quinn to kick the ball over the line. Both Ireland and Holland ended with identical records. FIFA ordered that lots be drawn to determine second and third place. The luck of the Irish allowed them to finish second (and play Romania in the round of sixteen), while Holland had to face West Germany.

## The Round of Sixteen

The round of sixteen featured a number of dream match-ups: Brazil–Argentina, England–Belgium, and West Germany–Holland. The other games included Cameroon–Colombia, Czechoslovakia–Costa Rica, Ireland–Romania, Italy–Uruguay, and Spain–Yugoslavia. The first game of the round took place on June 23 between Cameroon and Colombia in Naples. Before the start of the tournament, few would have picked either of these two teams to get this far. The growth of Colombian soccer—fueled by the explosion of drug-trafficking during the 1980s that had helped pump much-needed money into the coffers of the country's club teams—and the sudden rise of Cameroon were the first signs that traditional European dominance had been threatened. At the San Paolo Stadium, before a crowd of 50,000, Cameroon and Colombia put on a no-holds-barred, lively contest that had generally been rare in much of the first round. The carefree style of both teams led to a number of defensive errors, but goals failed to materialize. The match ended scoreless and headed into overtime. Cameroon's Milla, who had come in at the 54th minute, once again changed the outcome of the game, scoring the go-ahead goal in the 106th minute. Two minutes later, he put on another offensive exhibition that allowed Cameroon to move on to the quarterfinals. Higuita, who was known for taking penalty kicks and dangerously coming out of the penalty area to play the ball, committed an error that cost his team. Higuita—10 yards away from his goal—never expected that Milla would try to steal the ball away from him. Milla did, running toward the empty net before easily placing the ball into the goal. Milla, who now had four goals in the tournament, celebrated with a dance around the corner kick flag. The Colombians pulled one back in the 115th minute with Redin, but it turned out to be nothing more than a consolation goal. The "Indomitable Lions" were in the quarterfinals.

The second game of the day between Czechoslovakia and Costa Rica in Bari was another contest between two teams that few people expected much out of at the start of the tournament. Ultimately, Czechoslovakia proved too tough for the Costa Ricans. Skuhravy's hat trick—all three goals were scored on headers—was too much for Costa Rica, who lost 4–1. Early on, Skuhravy put his team ahead in the 12th minute, but Costa Rica briefly stunned the crowd of 47,700 spectators when it tied the score with Ronald Gonzalez in the 55th minute. Czechoslovakia broke the tie eight minutes later. Once again, the Sparta Prague striker's aerial supremacy was too much for Costa Rica's defense. Lubos Kubik scored Czechoslovakia's third goal in the 78th minute, before Skuhravy completed his hat trick in scoring the team's fourth goal in the 82nd minute. The goal, his fifth of the tournament, temporarily placed him atop the scorers' table. The goals also paid off in other ways. Italian scouts had been tracking Skuhravy's progress. As a result, he was offered a contract to play with Genoa at the end of the World Cup. Costa Rica, on the other hand, had pulled off the impossible and Milutinovic was hailed as a miracle worker. The wily Yugoslavian would weave the same sort of magic four years later with the United States.

The all–South American clash between Brazil and Argentina in Turin had everyone salivating at the thought of what tension and beauty such a game could produce. The result, however, ended up as a dull contest that was decided with a single flash of brilliance. Careca and Alemao were reunited with Maradona—all teammates at Napoli—but this time found themselves on opposite sides of the ball. The Brazilians dominated the game for eighty minutes, but were unable to score. If Brazil had abandoned the *jogo bonito* style so many craved to see again, then Argentina's performance was as melancholy as a tango. Maradona, invisible for much of the game, played like any ordinary midfielder. That all changed with a flick of the foot. Against the run of play, Maradona was able to stab the ball up field to a waiting Caniggia, who beat the offside trap, calmly rounded the Brazilian goalkeeper Taffarel and placed the ball into the goal for the game-winner. All Taffarel could do was stare to the ground, immobile for several seconds, with his head slumped low as Caniggia embraced his teammates in celebration. Maradona, his arms in the air triumphant, ran over to Caniggia to congratulate him. The goal stunned the

*Brazil's Branco (wearing the number 6 jersey) tries to put the ball past a wall of five Argentina players—which includes Diego Maradona (the third man in)—off a free kick during a Round-of-16 game at the 1990 World Cup (Credit: CFB).*

Brazilians, who lost their temper in the game's dying minutes. Team captain Ricardo Gomes was red carded by referee Quiniou and Brazil, who had lost to Argentina for the first time at a World Cup, had to deal with another early exit. Maradona had delivered the game-winning play, even though he was playing with ankle pain—and he was the only bright spot on a team that many thought had no business being in the quarterfinals.

That night in Milan, an all-European clash took place. West Germany and Holland tangled for a place in the quarterfinals. Though no one expected these two powerhouses to meet this early in the knockout stage, many were hoping it would generate enough excitement given that the tournament had thus far been dominated by low-scoring games. The game was barely twenty-two minutes old when a series of ugly events resulted in two players—Voeller and Rijkaard—getting red carded. The ejections unfolded rather surprisingly. Voeller dribbled the ball down the left side when he was tackled by Rijkaard. Argentine referee Juan Loustau whistled for the play to stop and showed Rijkaard a yellow card. The warning, Rijkaard's second of the tournament, would make him ineligible to play the next game if Holland were to advance. As the Dutch players lined up for West Germany's subsequent free kick, Rijkaard walked over to Voeller and spat at him. Voeller said something back to the Dutchman and got himself yellow carded in the process. On the ensuing free kick, the ball bounced toward the goal, but van Breukelen was able to quickly break up the play before Voeller could get his foot on the ball. Voeller, not able to stop fast enough, tumbled over van Breukelen. The Dutch goalkeeper, not happy with Voeller's actions, had a few choice words for the West German striker as he lay on the ground. When Voeller responded, Loustau flashed him a red card. At that very moment, Rijkaard came over to the referee and gave him a piece of his mind. Loustau wasted no time pulling out another red card and the Dutchman joined Voeller for an early shower.

The game, still scoreless, continued to delight the 75,000 fans. Beckenbauer readjusted his midfield—leaving Klinsmann alone up top as the team's sole striker after moving Matthaeus and Littbarski further back—now that the team had to deal with the loss of Voeller. The move allowed Klinsmann twice as much space as usual to move the ball. He took every chance he had to break toward goal, but the plays were effectively broken up by the Dutch defense. The first half ended, 0–0. The West German offense grew livelier in the second period with Klinsmann able to score his fourth goal of the tournament in the 51st minute for the 1–0 lead. The Dutch response was weak with van Basten virtually invisible on the left flank and Gullit only occasionally getting a shot off after one of his runs down the middle. The West Germans padlocked their defense in a bid to maintain the lead. Brehme, always powerful defensively and occasionally powerful offensively, scored West Germany's second goal in the 82nd minute to put the game away. The match, however, was not over and the Dutch were able to pull one back when Loustau awarded Holland a penalty kick. Ronald Koeman was perfect from the spot, but the goal provided little comfort for Holland. Dutch coach Leo Beenhakker had put forth a poor offensive plan and did nothing, once Rijkaard was sent off, to stem the barrage of West German attacks. On the other hand, the 2–1 score proved West Germany was capable of defeating tougher opponents. The win also fueled the West Germans' confidence. "I don't think that there are other teams in this World Cup who can beat us. Why should we not become world champions?" said Beckenbauer.[6]

The round of sixteen rolled on in Genoa with Ireland and Romania doing battle on June 24 in what turned out to be a very defensive-minded game. The match, locked in a scoreless struggle for 120 minutes, was decided on penalty kicks. The first four kickers for both teams managed to successfully score, but Ireland goalkeeper Pat Bonner stopped a shot by Daniel Timofte to put his team in position to win the game. David O'Leary lined up to take what would be the decisive kick, beating goalkeeper Silviu Lung with a high kick to his left for the 5–4 victory. The Irish players jumped all over O'Leary, while Timofte's teammates tried to console him. All Timofte could do was stand there with his head buried in his hands. Ireland, who had not won a game at the tournament, advanced. "The pubs will sell more booze tonight than they have all year," Charlton joked at the post-game news conference. "I am delighted for the Irish people."[7]

Ireland would play the winner of the Italy–Uruguay match. The Irish players waited and watched as the *Azzurri* beat Uruguay 2–0 in Rome. The Italians were on a roll and goalkeeper Walter Zenga hadn't given up a goal in four games. Vicini tinkered with his lineup after a scoreless first half, inserting striker Aldo Serena in place of Nicola Berti in order to jazz up the offense. Serena assisted on Italy's opening goal, sending in a ground pass to Schillaci, who broke through two defenders and blasted a long, left-footed shot that dipped into the goal past Fernando Alvez. Vicini's other substitution also paid off: defender Pietro Vierchowod, who was playing in his third World Cup. Vierchowod made an unusual run down the right flank, but was tackled to the ground. The call resulted in a free kick taken by Giannini, who lofted up a hooking, right-footed kick that allowed Serena to deflect the ball past Uruguay's Alvez.

The Uruguayan team did little in the second half, though it had done an effective job of keeping the ball out of its own half in the opening forty-five minutes. Uruguay's defensive strength was comparable to a swarm of mosquitoes, both bothersome and disruptive to Italy's offense. The Italians had found a way to win the game, 1–0, and Vicini's deep bench was the reason why the hosts were widely favored to win the trophy for a fourth time.

The round came to a close on June 26 in Verona with Yugoslavia defeating Spain, 3–2, in overtime with two goals from Dragan Stojkovic, who scored the winner in the 92nd minute to set up a clash with Argentina. The winning goal, a curling free kick that defied the law of physics and made its way around the Spanish wall, was splendid.

In the other game of the day, England edged out Belgium, 1–0, in an overtime thriller in Bologna. David Platt, on the bench for all of England's group games, was given a chance to play in the second half. He responded by scoring a high-flying volley in the very last minute of the extra session—his first goal for his country—to send England through to the quarterfinals. The result was a tremendous for the English, whose club teams had overcome a five-year ban from playing in European club competitions. The ban was instituted after a riot at the 1985 European Champions Cup final between Liverpool and Juventus; the riot caused the death of thirty-nine fans at the Heysel Stadium in Brussels and was blamed on English thugs. The ban was also expected to cripple the English game on the national team level. However, the World Cup had rendered a rather different verdict. The threat of hooliganism still loomed large. Confrontations between Italian police and English fans in the coastal town of Rimini, in the days leading up to England's game against Belgium, ended with 246 Brits expelled from the country. There had also been minor skirmishes involving English fans and police in Sardinia before and after England's first-round games against Ireland and Holland. Worry spread across Italy that as England progressed, troublemakers would follow.

## Eight Teams Scramble in the Quarterfinals

On June 30, both Argentina and Yugoslavia failed to score in their quarterfinal clash in the suffocating heat of Florence. Yugoslavia, reduced to ten players after thirty minutes when Refik Sabanadzovic received his second yellow card of the game, was able to keep up with Argentina, who could not take advantage of the one-man advantage. Maradona was not a factor, unable to create any scoring chances for his teammates. The marathon game dragged on. A penalty shootout would once again be needed to determine a winner. Argentina had taken luck to a whole new level, despite Maradona failing to score his kick—another sign that the world's greatest player was unfit despite having lost nearly twenty pounds on a crash diet just two months before the start of the tournament. Argentina's hero that afternoon was Goycochea, who saved two shots, one by Dragoljub Brnovic and another by Faruk

Hadzibegic, to scrape by, 3–2, and reach the semifinals. The defending champions were still alive—but barely. As an interesting historical note, this would be the last time Yugoslavia put forth a team as a unified country. The nations that comprised the federation would secede and Yugoslavia as it was known would soon dissolve into the independent nations of Croatia, Slovenia, Bosnia and Herzegovina, and Serbia and Montenegro.

Italy's 1–0 victory over Ireland in Rome set up an emotional semifinal clash between Argentina and Italy, to take place later in Naples. In the Italy–Ireland game, Schillaci had once again scored the winning goal against Ireland. Schillaci's fourth goal of the competition in the 37th minute was a mixture of opportunism and determination. Once again, the little Sicilian was in the right place at the right time. Schillaci pounced on a rebound following a hard shot by AC Milan midfielder Roberto Donadoni and kicked the ball into the opposite corner of the net. At the other end, Zenga reveled in his fifth consecutive shutout, keeping the Irish offense off the scoreboard.

On July 1, West Germany continued its winning ways, surpassing Czechoslovakia, 1–0, in Milan. The West Germans put on a sizzling performance en route to a tournament team record ninth semifinal appearance. The West German juggernaut appeared unstoppable. The team's performance against the scrappy Czechoslovakians was capped off by Matthaeus, who converted a penalty kick in the 25th minute. The 1–0 score was no true measure of how dominant the West Germans had been for much of the game. Defender Guido Buchwald could have put West Germany on the board in the 20th minute, but the attempt was thwarted by goalkeeper Jan Stejkal. On the ensuing corner kick, Ivan Hasek cleared the ball off the line. After the penalty kick, Klinsmann came close to making it 2–0 in the first half of stoppage time, but Hasek cleared the ball off the line once again.

The quarterfinal nightcap between England and Cameroon was a clash of temperaments. The question before the start of the game was whether Cameroon could knock off England without the services of four starters. The Africans had defeated Argentina in the opener with only nine men and went on to defeat Romania without two of their starters. Against England, the "Indomitable Lions" were missing sweeper Victor N'Dip, defender Jules Onana, and midfielders Emile Mbouh Mbouh and Andre Kana Biyik, all of whom had accumulated two yellow cards during the course of the tournament and were forced to sit out a game. Not a good sign for a team that lacked depth. Cameroon, however, had become one of the most popular teams with Italian fans and many of the 55,200 fans who watched from the stands of the San Paolo Stadium in Naples were rooting for the underdog Africans. The teams also featured dueling veterans: Cameroon's Milla, who was thirty-eight, and England's Shilton, who was two years older and was appearing in his 123rd national team game.

The match took on epic proportions when Cameroon—with its blend of physical and creative soccer—nearly knocked off the English. The embarrassment was spared when Lineker scored two goals, both penalty kicks, to lead England to the semifinals for the first time since 1966. England had gotten off on the right foot, actually ahead, when David Platt connected with the ball off a cross from Stuart Pearce in the 26th minute. The English defense was having all sorts of problems against Cameroon. Des Walker and Terry Butcher, both playing hurt, had a tough time keeping up with the Africans' offense. The English defense gave Cameroon all sorts of room to move the ball, but any attempt to tie the score was stopped by Shilton. England was also lacking the leadership of Robson, who had been sent home with a sore foot, but Butcher did a good job wearing the captain's armband. In the second period, Cameroon coach, the Soviet-born Valery Nepomniachi, inserted Milla, who was resting a sore leg following a fall in practice, and hoped the veteran could come through once again. The move proved a good one when Milla, in an attempt to maneuver the ball in the England box, was brought down by Gascoigne. Referee Edgardo Codesal Mendez whistled a penalty kick. Emmanuel Kunde scored from the spot in the 61st minute, although Shilton had come close to making the save. The goal appeared to energize the Africans.

Four minutes later, the unthinkable occurred. Milla moved the ball up the field, quickly played a nifty one-two to the other substitute, Eugene Ekeke, who put the ball in the net past Shilton. England was down, but not out, and mounted a desperate attempt to get a 2–2 tie. England did just that when Lineker was upended in the box with nine minutes left to play. Cameroon's lack of discipline had come to haunt them once more. Lineker scored from the spot to push the game into overtime. The frustrated Africans lost their cool in extra time and goalkeeper Thomas N'Kono's foul on Lineker in the box was rewarded with another penalty kick. Lineker converted the kick in the 105th minute to lift England to a 3–2 win and set up a semifinal clash with West Germany in Turin. Cameroon had been bounced out of the tournament, but the players were rewarded with a long applause from the crowd and handshakes from the English players. African soccer had finally left its imprint on the World Cup and Cameroon's strong showing against England was proof that its quarterfinal appearance had been no fluke.

## Semifinal Action

England's progression to the semifinals was a nightmare for Italian authorities, who had been secretly hoping for the team's early exit. Five years after the Heysel tragedy (where 39 fans were killed) had touched off an emotional Juventus victory over Liverpool in Brussels to be crowned European champion, the city of Turin was not looking forward to hosting large amounts of English fans. The mayor of Turin, Maria Magnani Noya, asked FIFA to invert the semifinal venues and have England play West Germany in Naples. FIFA was stern in its warning and in a statement said that the English crowds had been "under control" and that the games would not be switched.

The other semifinal between Italy and Argentina sparked another controversy. Maradona tried to lobby the Neapolitan fans into cheering for Argentina, reminding them that northern Italians often regarded southerners as foreigners. Maradona had tried to take advantage of an age-old rift within the country that had pitted the industrial north against the agrarian south. But Maradona had gone too far in his attempt to get fans in Naples to cheer for him like they had for the last seven years on the club level. In a public plea—another in a long line of controversial statements uttered by Maradona—the Argentine captain did a bit of trash-talking. "Naples is suddenly part of Italy and the entire country is begging for its support," Maradona told reporters at a news conference. "Don't forget that you are southerners. You have been treated like Africans."[8] Northern fans had jeered Maradona while he was at Napoli and fans in Milan had booed his national anthem during the tournament opener. Sarcastically, Maradona, who appeared visibly upset at the time, tried to put a new spin on the situation, saying, "The people of Milan aren't that racist after all. They rooted for Cameroon in that game."[9] Countering Maradona's theory that Naples should cheer for Argentina was Schillaci. He had become Italy's unlikeliest star and as a Sicilian had been able to unite the country. Schillaci, now a starter, had replaced Vialli in Vicini's lineup. Maradona, or his comments, did not appear to be an issue for the Italian players in the days leading up to the July 1 game. Italy's goalkeeper Zenga was closing in on two records—records that on the eve of the tournament had appeared impossible even for a goalkeeper of his immense talent. Zenga had played all 450 minutes and was only seven minutes away from breaking the record of consecutive minutes played, which was recorded by Brazil's Leão in 1978. The record of scoreless minutes at a World Cup, recorded by Shilton in 1982 and duplicated by him four years later, was 499 minutes. Zenga, unfazed that he was on the verge of rewriting the record books, also had his defense to thank. The Italian backline had not made any mistakes. Maradona had not posed much of a threat thus far in the competition, appearing quite ordinary in Argentina's previous five games. He had failed to score and had played poorly against Yugoslavia. Despite that, not a day went by without Maradona appearing central to the World Cup's evolving plot.

Maradona's adopted hometown was buzzing the day of the game. A banner that hung from the San Paolo's upper deck appeared to sum up the city's mood: "Diego, you are always in our hearts—but we are Italian!" But something did appear and feel different that evening. The 60,000 fans weren't nearly as noisy as the crowds had been at the Olympic Stadium. It even seemed that some were waving blue and white Argentine flags. The sea of red, white, and green was not there. On the field, both teams fought it out, producing an entertaining game. Argentina played with skill and determination—the first time it had done so at the tournament—while Italy used its midfield to try and generate opportunities for Schillaci. Vicini had fielded an anomalous lineup, inserting Schillaci along with Vialli, while Baggio inexplicably sat on the bench. The move appeared to pay off in the early going when Schillaci scored his fifth goal of the tournament. The goal involved three players and developed in the 17th minute when Giannini flicked a back header to Vialli. The Sampdoria striker took the pass and unleashed a powerful shot. Goycochea only partially stopped it and Schillaci, ever the opportunist, avoided the offside trap, scooped up the rebound and slammed the ball into the net. The fans were elated. Italy appeared poised, almost destined, to reach the final.

The Italians sat on the 1–0 lead, hoping their suffocating defense could drown out Argentina's chances. The plan was not a bad one, but Vicini's move to switch over to the *catenaccio* was a mistake. Maradona didn't give up and sent shivers down the spines of Italian fans every time he played the ball. The game's momentum shifted toward Argentina in the second half and a Zenga error resulted in the tying goal. The Italians were starting to fall apart and Argentina's offside trap had stopped Schillaci from doing anything. Argentina equalized in the 67th minute when Maradona fed the ball to Olarticoechea, who sent in a floating cross from the left that allowed Caniggia to head the ball past the advancing Zenga. The Inter Milan goalkeeper had finally been beaten after 517 minutes, although he had surpassed Shilton's record by eighteen minutes. Zenga should have made the routine catch, but he had come up empty and allowed Caniggia, so lethal in the air, to score. The game was tied 1–1.

The occasional foray into the Italian half had paid off for the South Americans. All Argentina had to do was hold on and hope penalties would get them through once again. Argentina, so gritty in the second half, became more conservative in overtime. Baggio had come in for Giannini in the second half, but had done little to spark the *Azzurri's* offense. Baggio, however, was involved in a play that gave Italy a numerical advantage. The first overtime session was in its fourth minute of injury time when Ricardo Giusti slapped Baggio in the head. Referee Vautrot was losing control of the game. He hadn't seen the incident, but the linesman who was a few feet away relayed what happened to the Frenchman. Vautrot pulled out a red card and Giusti was out of the game. Maradona argued against the call as the clock dragged on for another three minutes. Vautrot appeared to have lost of track of time, but he finally blew his whistle to signal the end of the first overtime period. The second overtime session produced nothing and penalty kicks were needed once again to determine a winner.

Baresi scored Italy's first kick. Jose Serrizuela responded with a goal for Argentina. Goycochea almost saved Baggio's shot, but it went in. Burruchaga scored his kick for the 2–2 tie. Luigi De Agostini converted Italy's third kick, while Olarticoechea made it 3–3. This is where the Italians lost the game: Donadoni shot his kick to the right, but Goycochea guessed correctly and made a two-handed save. Donadoni fell to his knees in desperation. Maradona, who had missed against Yugoslavia, scored his shot to take the lead. Italy's chances of staying alive hinged on Serena, who had come in for Vialli in the second half. He shot to his right, but Goycochea guessed correctly once again and stopped the ball. The Argentineans, who had scored just five goals at the tournament, won 4–3 on penalties and reached their third final ever. Italy's World Cup dream was over. The team who had never lost a game at the tournament was forced out by Argentina's cynical, yet effective, game plan. "If we had played all our games in Rome, I don't think we would have ever lost. We would have won the World Cup," Maldini recalled. "Naples was Maradona's hometown. There definitely was a feeling that had been broken between us and the Italian fans." Not everyone on the team agreed. Donadoni took the blame for the defeat. "We can't blame the fans. That's no excuse," he said. "We lost that game on the field and because Argentina was better than us in the shootout. We did everything we could to win the game."[10]

The following night in Turin, West Germany and England met in a game widely considered the most entertaining of the tournament. England—playing its best soccer in decades—went on the attack from the start. The West Germans responded with a strong defense. The West Germans also had some luck on their side, taking the lead off a Brehme free kick in the 59th minute. Shilton had been tricked by the ball's trajectory when the ball was deflected by defender Paul Parker. The English defender found redemption ten minutes from the end of the game when his cross found Lineker in the box. The striker, surrounded by two West German defenders, wasted no time and slotted the ball past Illgner with a powerful left-footed shot. The tying goal was Lineker's tenth all-time goal at a World Cup. The game went to overtime where both teams squandered several scoring chances. This game would also go to penalty kicks—the first time that both semifinal games hinged on a shootout. Lineker, Beardsley, and Platt scored the first three for England, while Brehme, Matthaeus, and Riedle scored for West Germany. The fourth kick is where England's dream crumbled. Stuart Pearce's shot was deflected by Illgner's leg, while Olaf Thon put the West Germans ahead, 4–3. Waddle's shot went high over the crossbar and West Germany was through to the final for the third straight time, setting up a rematch of the 1986 final against Argentina.

## Third Place

Italy's only consolation came in the shape of a 2–1 defeat of England on July 7 in Bari in the third-place game. Schillaci scored his sixth goal of the competition in the 85th minute on a penalty kick after Parker brought him down in the box. The goal was good enough for the Sicilian to become the tournament's top scorer. It was also Shilton's final game for England. The graying goalkeeper called it quits after 125 international appearances and his teammates crowded around him once the game drew to an end. The crowd of 51,426 fans cheered on both teams, but naturally reserved its loudest cheers for the home team. A banner inside the San Nicola Stadium summed up the sentiment of an entire country: "Thank you, *Azzurri*. You are the real champions."

## Final

The championship game took place the following day at the Olympic Stadium in Rome before a crowd of 73,603 spectators and was watched by more than one billion people around the world. Maradona and his teammates were jeered as they emerged from the tunnel and onto the field. The Italians had not forgotten that Argentina had eliminated their beloved team. Maradona had become public enemy number one across Italy. The fans jeered him loudly as the band played Argentina's national anthem. The Italians felt betrayed. Maradona was visibly furious, muttering to himself in disgust as the booing rained down on him. The excitement usually generated by a championship game disappeared quickly. Instead, the game was largely a bore with Argentina using its usual theatrics and time wasting to try and push the game to penalty kicks. *Inept, appalling, boring,* and *loathsome* were some of the adjectives used to describe Bilardo's team that evening. Without a doubt, the game was the worst of the competition. The West Germans also didn't look as energized as they had in previous games, but that was understandable. Four weeks of games had taken its physical toll on the players, but that didn't stop the players from occasionally pushing the ball up field against Argentina's barricaded defense. Argentina was without Caniggia, who was forced to sit the game out after accumulating a second yellow card against Italy. With an unfit Maradona on the team, Argentina was unable to do anything offensively. The West Germans employed a simple strategy: Thomas Hassler and Matthaeus controlled the midfield and moved the ball to Voeller and Klinsmann, both of whom misfired time and time again. Defensively, the plan was equally uncomplicated with Buchwald shadowing Maradona and keeping him under control. The game took on a twist in the 68th minute when referee Mendez flashed Monzon a red card for clobbering Klinsmann. Monzon earned the dubious distinction of becoming the first player to ever be booted from a World Cup final.

West Germany prevailed when Mendez awarded them a penalty kick. Defender Stefan Reuter brought the ball up the right side, and then sent a pass to Voeller in the box about 15 yards in front of the goal. An instant later, Voeller, no stranger to the Olympic Stadium since playing for AS Roma, was brought down by defender Roberto Sensini, and Mendez pointed to the spot. Brehme converted the penalty in the 84th minute, drilling a low shot that went in between the right post and Goycochea's outstretched arm. With time running out, the frustration among the Argentine team grew, reaching a low point when striker Gustavo Dezotti, who was playing for Caniggia, lassoed Kohler around the neck with his arm and brought him to the turf. That led to a red card, leaving Argentina two players short for the final four minutes. Maradona also earned a yellow card for arguing the call. In the end, Brehme's penalty kick proved to be the winner. In joining Brazil and Italy as the only other countries to win the World Cup three times, West Germany had been able to outshoot Argentina 16–1. The final whistle brought joy to the West Germans and tears to Maradona's red eyes. An upset Maradona refused to shake Havelange's hand at the trophy presentation. Afterwards, Maradona announced he was retiring from the national team.

Across Germany, meanwhile, wild celebrations erupted in the streets, the likes not seen since the collapse of the Berlin Wall seven months earlier. The victory also marked the last time West Germany would play at a World Cup. German reunification, in the works on the eve of the competition, would allow East Germans to play for the team four years later. The infusion of new talent would ensure the country's soccer competitiveness into the next decade. While the West German players paraded around the field with the trophy to the loud cheers of the crowd, the stadium's scoreboard displayed a message: "*Ciao Italia. Hello USA.*" Indeed, a new era was dawning for the sport and the previously untapped market of the United States, site of the next World

Cup—and the commercial interest that came with it—represented the future of the game. Would Americans embrace the world's most popular sport? The surprising answer would come in four years' time.

## NOTES

1. FIFA press release, June 13, 1986.
2. Internet Soccer Fans Association, www.isfa.com/news/?id=20495.
3. News conference, Coverciano, Italy, May 6, 1990.
4. Interview, April 8, 2006.
5. News Conference, Florence, June 19, 1990.
6. Michael Janofsky, "West Germans Eliminate Dutch," *The New York Times*, June 24, 1990, C3.
7. News Conference, Genoa, June 24, 1990.
8. News Conference, Naples, July 1, 1990.
9. News Conference, Naples, July 1, 1990.
10. Interview, July 31, 2005.

# 7

# A NEW FRONTIER

## 1994

The World Cup finally came to America's shores after six years of planning. Similar to the 1970 and 1986 World Cups played in Mexico, players would be forced to play in extreme temperatures. But the heat wasn't only on the players. The question was whether the United States could generate enough interest in its own country worthy of such a grandiose event. Many had their doubts. The NASL had disappeared ten years earlier and, with no pro domestic league to replace it, soccer was relegated to the periphery of the American sporting conscience. A World Cup on U.S. soil, the soccer-hating critics said, would be a dismal failure with international stars—unknown to the vast majority of American sports fans—resulting in games being played in half-empty stadiums. FIFA officials knew the United States lacked a soccer tradition, but were quickly impressed when the USSF put in a bid to host the 1994 World Cup. At the time, the United States emerged as favorites after FIFA delegates—impressed with this country's stadiums and home to corporations with money to spend—deemed the bid superior to those put together by Brazil and Morocco. Sure, Brazil had the soccer pedigree, but lacked everything else: FIFA delegates found disorder during an inspection and stadiums in dire need of modernization. Similarly, Morocco, with just two modern stadiums, lacked the facilities to host the tournament. FIFA, not satisfied with Brazil's bid, made the unprecedented decision in July 1988 to award the tournament to the United

States, who received 10 of the 19 votes. Morocco got 7 and Brazil only 2. A member of Brazil's bid, Guimaraes Octavio Pinto, told reporters afterward that the decision to award the World Cup to the Americans was like "giving the World Series to Brazil."[1]

The twenty-four nations competing for a spot in the finals would make history. The competition would be played in nine cities—Boston, New York, Washington, Orlando, Chicago, Detroit, Dallas, San Francisco, and Los Angeles—and for the first time would be played in a country with four time zones. The format remained the same, but the schedule was put together in such a meticulous manner as to cut down on teams having to crisscross the country, particularly in the first round, with just a few days rest between games.

## Preparations: The Qualifying Draw, New Rules, and Generating Interest

In the meantime, USA '94 organizers wasted no time getting the ball rolling on the tournament. The 1991 World Cup qualifying draw was held in New York's Paramount Theater at Madison Square Garden amid the glitz usually reserved for other top-notch events. Millions around the world watched to see where the 141 nations who had entered the qualifying fray would be placed. The record number of entrants was another sign of soccer's growing popularity—and the world's ever-changing map. The Soviet Union had collapsed, allowing Estonia, Lithuania, and Latvia to field their own national teams. The genie was literally out of the bottle with actress Barbara Eden hosting the event. Of course, most Americans were not aware the draw was even going on or why more than 600 journalists had packed a theater usually reserved for boxing matches and dance troupes. Instead, they were there to watch men pull ping-pong sized balls out of plastic urns for an hour on a Sunday afternoon. Although ESPN only found the time on its twenty-four-hour all-sports cable channel to televise the final thirty minutes of the event, Spanish-language network Univision broadcast the draw in its entirety.

World Cup organizers also sensed it was their duty—not to mention FIFA's mandate for them—to promote the sport. The organizers launched Legacy Tour '94, a series of fan festivals held across the country with the purpose of generating interest in the game and creating a base of soccer fans for years to come. By the end of the tour, more than one million people—many of whom had never before kicked a ball—had participated in the 200 Legacy Tour '94 events in 110 cities. "World Cup USA '94 wants the dream to continue after the games are over to ensure that future generations will experience the joy of the world's greatest sport," said Rothenberg.[2]

While organizers worked on generating interest with the American public—mounting a nationwide advertising campaign unprecedented in U.S. sports history—FIFA had spent the four years leading up to the 1994 World Cup cracking down on the sort of defensive tactics that had allowed Argentina to advance to the final the last time around. Short of enlarging the goals and breaking games into four quarters (both of which were mulled over), the sport's organizing body decided to quell criticism from purists and make only minor rule changes. Italia '90 and the abysmal 2.21 goals-per-game average—the lowest ever at a World Cup—sent a signal to FIFA that it had to do something to discourage teams from wasting time. Amidst talk of rule changes, some feared the "Americanization" of the world's game, but FIFA was cautious and the changes did improve the quality of play. FIFA decided to modify the rule that allowed a player to pass the ball back to his own goalkeeper. Widely used as a time-wasting technique, the goalkeeper was no longer allowed to pick up the ball with his hands if a teammate passed it back to him. Instead, he would have to play the ball with his feet. The other change was the introduction of three points for a win rather than two in a bid to cut down on teams settling for a tie. The fact that England, Denmark, Portugal, France, and Poland failed to qualify for the finals had little bearing on the level of play that would be on display in the finals. The rule changes didn't end there. FIFA had produced another last-minute change. FIFA's International Board decided in March 1994 that a tackle from behind should be punished with an automatic red card. Originally, FIFA had wanted every tackle punished with an automatic expulsion, but common sense prevailed and the rule makers backed off the ridiculous punishment.

Organizers, meanwhile, were lucky not to have to worry about the threat of hooliganism after England failed to qualify. Soccer-haters hoping to see rioting and mayhem in the streets to prove that soccer was a sport that Americans had no business being involved with must have been severely disappointed. Organizers did have the chore of convincing what appeared to be an apathetic American public that the World Cup was coming to their shores. A Harris poll conducted three weeks before the start of the World Cup did little to quell fears that the tournament could be played in desolate stadiums. Although ticket packages had sold out six months earlier, it was anyone's guess what the atmosphere would be like. The poll found that 56 percent of those surveyed said they were not interested in watching any World Cup games on TV with 65 percent saying they were not interesting in attending. If that wasn't bad enough, only 38 percent knew that the World Cup was a soccer tournament. But USA '94 organizers tried to put a spin on the results, claiming that those who didn't know the World Cup would be played in this country had decreased from 80 percent in February and 87 percent the year before. "We had to literally create something out of nothing," recalled Rothenberg, who as head of the USSF also assumed control of the organizing committee. "It wasn't easy."[3]

## The U.S. National Team

The USSF was also working to build up its national team program. With no pro league, staging friendlies against other nations was the only way for American players to gain any experience. Milutinovic was named the U.S. team's new coach in March 1991. Could the miracle worker who coached Mexico in 1986 and Costa Rica in 1990 to the World Cup's elimination rounds do the same with the United States? A host nation had always advanced past the first round and the United States didn't want to be the only country to have the distinction of not moving on at least to the round of sixteen. With no Americans playing on club teams, Milutinovic set up a training base in Mission Viejo, California, and selected thirty players to join him there. Featuring a mix of World Cup veterans, college players, and MISL stars, Milutinovic began the arduous process of building the national team from the ground up. By 1993, the U.S. team had played 34 internationals, posting 10 wins, 13 losses, and 11 ties. Not a terrific record, but the ability to get experience before the tournament was Milutinovic's goal. Two years after Milutinovic had set up camp, a number of American players had gotten the chance to play abroad. Eric Wynalda, Tab Ramos, and John Harkes had all inked deals with European clubs and were now testing themselves on a weekly basis in league games. Wynalda signed with FC Saarbrucken in Germany, Ramos spent time at Real Betis in Spain, and Harkes had a successful run at Sheffield Wednesday in England.

The USSF, now renamed U.S. Soccer, also organized an annual summer tournament starting in 1992 called the U.S. Cup with the excuse of inviting national teams to this country while testing American facilities and getting playing time for its players. In 1992, the inaugural U.S. Cup was staged as a four-team, six-game round-robin tournament. The first tournament featured the United States, Portugal, Ireland, and Italy. The Americans surprisingly claimed the trophy, defeating Ireland, 3–1, and Portugal, 1–0, before tying Italy 1–1 at Chicago's Soldier Field. The Americans had finally proven that they could play soccer against the best teams in the world. A year later, the Americans made history at U.S. Cup '93, which served as a prelude to the World Cup. The tournament featured Brazil, Germany, and England, although it was the U.S. team that grabbed the headlines: it notched a stunning 2–0 win over England at Foxboro Stadium on the outskirts of Boston—the first time the Americans had been able to beat the English since the 1950 World Cup. The televising on ABC of the U.S.–Germany game on June 13 from Chicago's Soldier Field was the first time that an English-language network had broadcast a soccer game commercial free. Though Germany won the round-robin tournament, the Americans held their own, losing to Germany 4–3 in a nail-biter. There was room for improvement, but Milutinovic had done a lot to bring respect and credibility to a program that just a decade earlier was in shambles. Never before in the history of American sports had so much pressure been put on a team. The future of soccer, the pundits argued, depended on whether or not the U.S. team could make a decent showing. If winning the World Cup was an impossible goal, the least the team could aim for was a shot in the round of sixteen. On June 4, just two and half weeks before the start of the tournament, the United States played Mexico in Pasadena, California, site of the World Cup final, in front of a crowd of 93,000, mostly Mexican, fans. The U.S. team played with its full squad for the first time that year, upsetting the Mexicans, 1–0. The game meant nothing, but for the first time the Americans showed everyone that they were for real.

## The Final Draw

The World Cup 1994 officially came to life on December 19, 1993, in Las Vegas, site of the final draw. The six seeded teams—Germany, Italy,

Brazil, Argentina, Belgium, and the United States—were placed in six groups of four teams. The outcome was as follows:

Group A: The United States, Romania, Switzerland, and Colombia
Group B: Brazil, Sweden, Russia, and Cameroon
Group C: Germany, Spain, Bolivia, and South Korea
Group D: Argentina, Bulgaria, Greece, and Nigeria
Group E: Italy, Ireland, Norway, and Mexico
Group F: Belgium, Holland, Morocco, and Saudi Arabia

Like at every World Cup, USA '94 featured a "Group of Death." At this tournament, the luck of the draw had made Group E the toughest with Italy, Ireland, Norway, and Mexico set to lock horns in the group stage. Italy's opening game against Ireland at Giants Stadium in East Rutherford, New Jersey, was one of the most anticipated matches of the first round and tickets sold out months in advance. Also, the Northeast's Italian and Irish communities would not only guarantee a capacity crowd, but an atmosphere worthy of a World Cup. Italy was coached by former AC Milan manager Arrigo Sacchi, who had triggered loads of controversy despite his success on the club level. Sacchi never fully abandoned the *catenaccio* style that had become such a staple of the national team's style and mixed it with a zone 4-4-2 formation that featured lots of midfield pressing. His critics argued that Sacchi's tactics amounted to a basketball-style deployment of players where the long ball reigned supreme and individuality was squashed. When he coached AC Milan, pundits and fans also doubted his style. But Sacchi proved them wrong, winning an Italian League title and two European Champions Cups. While Italian club teams continued to play a conservative defense with the occasional counterattack, Sacchi demanded versatility and enthusiasm from his players.

Sacchi's problems didn't end there. Two months before the start of the tournament, Sacchi had not even decided on which players would make up the team's core. He had called up 73 players since he was appointed coach in 1991 and appeared no closer to making a decision. Only a handful of players appeared assured of a spot, including Paolo Maldini, Franco Baresi, and Roberto Baggio. The rest was an enigma. The *Azzurri* had also lost games to France and Germany in the months leading up to the finals, but it had been unforgivable that Italy suffered a 2–1 loss at the hands of Pontedera, a team in Italy's fourth division, during a practice session. Italian newspaper *La Gazzetta dello Sport*, the largest of Italy's three sports dailies, took a tongue-in-cheek approach to the situation in a front-page headline that read: "Let's send Pontedera to the World Cup." The situation wasn't any better for Sacchi on the other side of the Atlantic. Italian-Americans anxiously awaited the team's arrival, but *America Oggi*, an Italian-language daily, called for Sacchi to be fired. "Sacchi must go now before it is too late," the newspaper demanded.[4]

Sacchi didn't let the critics get to him. The team booked the entire 111-room Somerset Hills Hotel in New Jersey through July 14, the day after the semifinal at Giants Stadium. The team set up camp at the Pingry School in Martinsville, New Jersey, where the Italian federation upgraded the facilities and installed a state-of-the-art grass field. Off the field, the Italian players were a classy bunch, often spotted dressed in dark Armani suits, Gucci shoes, and stylish sunglasses while signing autographs and posing for pictures with female fans and children outside the training grounds. As for the difficulty of Italy's group, Sacchi was optimistic. "Our group and the one that includes Brazil are the most difficult," he said. "I'm not worried that it went this way. Actually, it will motivate us to do well from the start."[5] But Italy's pre-World Cup friendlies, particularly the one played against Costa Rica at the Yale Bowl in New Haven, Connecticut, a week before its opener against Costa Rica, exposed a series of weaknesses. The defense, for starters, showed a certain tinge of grey, particularly with AC Milan's Baresi and Tassotti, both now thirty-four years old. The Italians won 1–0 on a goal from Giuseppe Signori after a dribble from Roberto Baggio set him up. Once again, Sacchi used the game to experiment, providing fresh ammunition to his critics that he continued to be indecisive. Sacchi shot back after the game, saying, "I have 22 players at my disposal and depending on who is fit or not, I will determine which lineup to go with. I still don't know which team I will field against Ireland, but all I do know is that we will be ready that day."[6] Those were words Sacchi would come to regret seven days later when the Italians looked anything but ready to beat Ireland or contend for a fourth title.

Brazil, on the other hand, was once again everyone's favorite to win the trophy, though it had come up short since 1970. Less than a year before the finals, Brazil had been desperate and staring at the real possibility of not reaching the finals. Although Brazil's absence would have hurt the quality of the tournament and attendance, it would have been devastating back home. "If what we do on the field can give people in Brazil some happiness, then it is our duty to win [the World Cup] every time," said Brazil coach Carlos Alberto Parreira of his team's attitude entering the tournament.[7] Originally, Parreira did not want to call up striker Romário, but eventually caved to popular pressure. His two goals against Uruguay in a 2–0 win put Brazil back on the path to qualification following a loss to Bolivia—the first time the Brazilian team had ever lost a World Cup qualifier. Romário first developed his reputation as a pampered athlete when he scored 73 goals in 123 games for Brazilian club Vasco de Gama. He won three Dutch titles with PSV Eindoven in 1989, 1991, and 1992, but drove the club crazy when he often decided to fly to Brazil without notifying the team. Romário had even insisted that Parreira call up another temperamental star, Edmundo, to join him on attack in place of Muller, but Parreira ignored his pleas. Edmundo never made the World Cup roster.

### Group Play

The opening ceremony at Soldier Field was styled as a Super Bowl halftime show event, replete with streamers, balloons, and loud music. But the start of the World Cup was anything but flawless. Talk-show host Oprah Winfrey, who was the ceremony's emcee, began the festivities by falling off a platform and bruising her leg. Singer Diana Ross blew her choreographed penalty kick from five feet away, kicking the ball wide, and President Bill Clinton's entrance into the stadium was welcomed by boos. After the Hollywood-style ceremony, the Germans, competing as one nation for the first time since World War II, got off to a flying start. Klinsmann proved once again what a great scorer he was when Germany opened the tournament on June 17 against Bolivia. Klinsmann's goal in the 61st minute, a play initiated by a Matthaeus long ball that had rebounded off Thomas Hassler, was the winner. Klinsmann didn't stop there. His goal in a 1–1 tie with Spain four days later, and a two-goal performance in a 3–2 victory over South Korea on June 27 at the Cotton Bowl in Dallas, helped the reigning champions win Group C. Spain finished second and also earned a berth to the round of sixteen after tying South Korea, 2–2, on June 17 in Dallas and squashing Bolivia, 3–1, on June 27 in Chicago. Two goals from José Caminero assured Spain a place in the next round.

All eyes, of course, were on Group A. The United States presented a rebuilt team and Milutinovic, known as a World Cup miracle maker, hoped to make believers out of a skeptical American public. Soccer had struggled to make it in this country and a successful national team could certainly reverse that trend. Americans love to root for a winner and Milutinovic's team was prepared to deliver wins. The United States opened on June 8 at the Pontiac Silverdome outside Detroit against Switzerland before 73,425 spectators in the first World Cup game ever played indoors. More than 2,000 trays of natural grass grown in California were installed in the Silverdome, an experiment organizers had put into use the previous year at U.S. Cup '93 when Germany and England played the tournament's final game there. However, for the U.S.–Switzerland game, the suffocating heat inside the un-air-conditioned dome reached 106 degrees, but that didn't stop the teams from putting on a good game. Things didn't look good for the Americans early on when the Swiss took a 1–0 lead after only five minutes. Defender Thomas Dooley brought down Alain Sutter just outside the box and Georges Bregy converted the 19-yard free kick with a curling shot that made its way over the American wall and over Meola's head in the right corner of the net. The U.S. response was feeble at first, but grew more convincing as the half wore on. In the 45th minute, Harkes was taken down by Swiss midfielder Ciriaco Sforza, setting up a free kick for the Americans about 30 yards away from the Swiss goal. Wynalda, who had woken up that morning covered in hives after suffering an allergic reaction to something he had eaten the day before, lined up to take the kick. Wynalda's wicked shot curled over the wall and hit the underside of the crossbar before finding the back of the net just as goalkeeper Marco Pascolo tried to put a hand on it. The crowd cheered and the U.S. players rejoiced. The U.S. striker, drained of energy after a night of being ill, had scored one of the biggest goals in American soccer history. The Americans, although not totally impressive, had earned a 1–1 tie and a point.

Next up for the Americans was mighty Colombia at the Rose Bowl. The Colombians—picked by Pelé to win the World Cup—had lost to Romania, 3–1, on June 18 in Pasadena and were desperate to get at least a point to stay alive. The Americans knew it would be an uphill battle, but had the support of the home crowd behind them. The 93,194 fans who attended the game that afternoon were mostly decked out in the red, white, and blue, with only a few yellow and blue-clad supporters bothering to make the trek to the stadium. By the time the game was over, the crowd was chanting, "U-S-A, U-S-A," at decibel levels unheard of for a soccer game in this country. To everyone's surprise, the Americans took the lead in the 32nd minute when Harkes, sent a hard cross from the left across the middle of the field about 15 yards away from the goal. Harkes's pass, intended for the speedy Earnie Stewart, never got to him. Instead, the ball was intercepted by the leg of Colombian defender Andreas Escobar, who mistakenly deflected the ball into his own net. Goalkeeper Óscar Córdoba, who had moved to his right to stop Stewart, never had a chance to stop the ball. The own goal left Escobar and his teammates stunned while the Americans celebrated. Milutinovic's team had caught the break they needed to beat such a strong team and were now safely in control of the game. The most indelible image of the match, if not the tournament, was Marcelo Balboa's bicycle kick. The shot didn't go in, but that didn't matter to the pro-U.S. crowd who went bonkers at everything the Americans did that afternoon.

The Colombians attempted a comeback in the second half, but Valderrama, who did a good job controlling the midfield, could not get his teammates in the game. The U.S. team had momentum on its side and Stewart, unstoppable on the right flank, made it 2–0 in the 52nd minute after outrunning two defenders to the ball, including Escobar, and hit a hard shot that bounced into the goal. Dooley, who had played sweeper against Switzerland and got himself involved offensively, hung back on defense this time, while Balboa and Alexi Lalas, with his red mop hair and goatee, shut down the Colombians' feeble effort to get off any shots on goal. The Colombians could do nothing until the 89th minute when Adolfo Valencia scored. But the goal was ultimately little consolation for the Colombians, who were officially eliminated. The Americans had pulled off a 2–1 upset and now had a real chance of advancing to the round of sixteen. The crowd erupted at the sound of the final whistle and the Americans celebrated on the field like they had won the trophy. Meola danced around the field waving an American flag, while his teammates waved to the crowd and hugged each other. The win was the first World Cup victory since the United States' defeat of England in 1950. If that win had been a fluke that barely got any attention at home, this victory was for real and expected to help soccer become a major sport in this country. "We played with a lot of heart that day," Meola recalled. "I have many great memories of that game."[8]

The Americans were poised to win the group with a win, but lost to Romania, 1–0, on June 26 before 93,869 at the sun-baked Rose Bowl. The pesky Romanians attacked from the start and were rewarded in the 18th minute when defender Dan Petrescu put the ball past Meola. Harkes received a yellow card, his second in three games, rendering him unavailable for the next game. Harkes's card did not sit well with Balboa, who went over to the New Jersey native and reprimanded him. Balboa even shoved Harkes, who then pushed him back. The 1–0 scene wasn't pretty and a sign that team unity had begin to fall apart. The loss was only a minor setback, and the Americans qualified for the round of sixteen.

Meanwhile, Colombia's 2–0 win over Switzerland turned out to be a bittersweet one for the South Americans. Colombia was already out of the competition before the game, but played their hearts out. The Colombians had finally come to life, but ultimately went home in disgrace. A few days after the team returned to Colombia, Escobar was gunned down following a fight with a group of men outside a restaurant in Las Palmas, a suburb of Medellin. Escobar was shot twelve times as the men shouted "Goal!" each time the gunman pulled the trigger. Several men were later arrested in connection with Escobar's murder, but the reason behind the assassination remains a mystery.

In Group B, Brazil cruised past Russia, 2–0, on June 20 at Stanford Stadium in Palo Alto, California and trounced Cameroon, 3–0, four days later in the same stadium to set up a game against Sweden that would determine the winner of the group. Sweden had posted a 2–2 tie against Cameroon at the Rose Bowl. Down 2–1 in that game, the Swedes earned the tie thanks to a goal from Martin Dahlin with fifteen minutes left to play. In their next game, the Swedes beat Russia, 3–1, at the Silverdome in Detroit when Dahlin scored two goals.

Sweden had to defeat Brazil if it wanted to top the group and wasted little time against the fast-paced Brazilians on June 28 at the Silverdome. Sweden took the lead with Kennet Anderrson in the 24th minute. Brazil responded, tying the game with Romário in the 47th minute. The Brazilian striker, who had scored a goal against Russia and Cameroon, impressed the crowd of 77,217 with his dribbling skills and quick cuts into Sweden's penalty box. The Brazilians lacked the quality players in the midfield needed to carry the team and relied heavily on the individual brilliance of Romário and Bebeto to score the goals. The tie gave Sweden a berth to the next round and allowed Brazil to win the group.

Brazilian fireworks aside, the most exciting game of the group was played between Russia and Cameroon at Stanford Stadium. Milla, back for another spell at age forty-two, scored for the "Indomitable Lions," but Russian striker Oleg Salenko would also make history that afternoon, netting a World Cup–record five goals in a game to lead Russia to a 6–1 win. Salenko, who had also scored in Russia's 3–1 loss to Sweden, was now the tournament's top scorer with six goals.

Over in Group D, Argentina was favored to advance past the group stage and again featured Maradona, who had come out of retirement. Maradona had vowed to never play again for the national team after losing to West Germany in 1990. But he was forced out of retirement eight months before the 1994 World Cup with Argentina in the midst of almost failing to qualify for the tournament. Maradona had had a tumultuous three years in between World Cups. After Italia '90, Maradona returned to play for Napoli, but was suspended for fifteen months in 1991 after a drug test found cocaine in his blood stream. The Maradona soap opera didn't end there. He left Naples under the cover of night amid the flashbulbs of the paparazzi. His friendship with the *Camorra*, the local mafia, tarnished his reputation and placed him in a heap of legal trouble. He also admitted that he had an illegitimate son, though he refused to take a DNA test. The Italian courts ruled in 1993 that Maradona was the boy's father. After his suspension, Maradona refused to return to Napoli to finish out his contract and instead signed with Sevilla in June 1992. But Bilardo, who now coached the Spanish club, could not inspire the former superstar to greatness. A year later, Maradona moved back to Argentina and signed with Newell's Old Boys, where he played for just one season. In February 1994, the team dumped him after Maradona skipped too many practices, a problem that echoed his behavior at Napoli. With Maradona's career once again in ruins, he attacked a group of journalists who were camped out outside his home, firing a compressed air-rifle and injuring five of them slightly. Maradona's playing days appeared over. That is, until he was convinced to join the national team to help Argentina qualify for the 1994 World Cup finals.

Argentina, coming off a humiliating 5–0 loss to Colombia in Buenos Aires, was on the verge of elimination. Instead of going through automatically to the finals, Argentina had to play a two-game playoff series against Oceania winners Australia. A 1–1 tie in Sydney put Argentina, which featured Maradona with the captain's armband, in good shape for the return leg scheduled for Nov. 17 at the Monumental Stadium in Buenos Aires. Argentina went on to win 1–0 at home to make the finals. Maradona was not back to his former self in either game, but Argentine fans were happy to have him back. In the months leading up to USA '94, Maradona made great progress getting his body back into shape. It seemed unbelievable, but Maradona was poised to return to the World Cup—and perhaps lift it one more time. Caniggia, who had also served a brief suspension for illegal drug use, was also back on the roster. Midfielder Fernando Redondo, who had been ignored by Bilardo four years earlier, was on the team this time after getting a call from the team's coach Alfio Basile. Redondo's inclusion had been opposed by Maradona after the two clashed during a Spanish league game when Redondo played with Tenerife, but Basile ignored Maradona's request.

Argentina, Nigeria, which replaced Cameroon as the Cinderella team from Africa, and Bulgaria, led by Barcelona striker Hristo Stoitchkov, all finished their group matches tied for first place with six points. All three advanced, though Nigeria was the group winner thanks to goal differential, while Argentina placed third. Greece, who was making its World Cup debut, lost all three games and crashed out of the tournament much to the dismay of thousands of Greek-Americans who had attended the team's games. Argentina won its first two games and looked like an early favorite to win the tournament. Against Greece on June 21 at Foxboro Stadium, Argentina scored two goals in each half, including a hat trick from Gabriel Batistuta and a bullet of a shot from Maradona in the 60th minute to win 4–0. Maradona, slimmer than ever, was back to playing like his former self and appeared ready to guide his team to a third consecutive final. Maradona's goal against Greece unleashed celebrations throughout Argentina and Naples, where the fans never stopped loving him. Four days later, Argentina defeated Nigeria, 2–1, at Foxboro, thanks to two goals from Caniggia. The team was finally gelling, but problems lurked ahead.

Just as Argentina prepared for the round of sixteen, Maradona failed a drug test administered after the win against Nigeria. A cocktail of drugs, which included five variants of the stimulant ephedrine, were found in his urine sample. Banned by FIFA, ephedrine is typically used by asthmatics to help clear the respiratory system but is also a stimulant that can also enhance a player's performance. Maradona, who had lost 26 pounds for the tournament, had told reporters on the eve of the World Cup that he had accepted Basile's call because he "wanted to retire in style."[9] Now, he found himself disgraced—once again—and out of the competition. Argentina's soccer federation suspended Maradona from the tournament on June 30, just hours before his team's final group game against Bulgaria. "It's with great sadness that we have to say that Maradona is suspended and will not play," a somber Havelange said at a news conference in Dallas. "I was always praying that the result would be different."[10] To make matters worse, a preliminary FIFA investigation found that Argentina's team doctor Pedro Ugalde denied knowing if Maradona took any drugs. Maradona faced a possible lifetime ban, though FIFA never followed through on that threat.

Maradona's absence cost Argentina dearly that afternoon at the Cotton Bowl in Dallas. Bulgaria beat Argentina, 2–0. Argentine fans, many wearing replicas of Maradona's famous number 10 jersey, left the stadium worried about their team's chances. Argentina was going to the next round, but the team's morale was not where it should be. Argentina was not the same without Maradona. The disgraced star would not go quietly. Maradona complained to whomever would listen that FIFA, with whom he had never had a great relationship, had done him in just as Argentina was gaining momentum. In other words, Havelange had a vendetta against him, Maradona claimed, and that was the reason for his suspension. The embattled star refused to take responsibility for his actions. His reputation was ruined and his team was left in disarray.

In New York, the Group E match-up between Italy and Ireland on June 18 was billed as the biggest first-round game of the tournament. Tickets with a face value of $75 were going for upward of $700 from scalpers. Sacchi's team expected a large reception from a pro-Italy crowd. Instead, the Italian fans were in the minority and Giants Stadium could have easily been confused with a stadium in Dublin. Traffic was tied up for miles from the Lincoln Tunnel in New York to East Rutherford as thousands of cars waving orange, white, and green flags out their cars made their way to the stadium. The banners that hung inside the stadium, filled with 74,226 fans, recalled places close to the hearts of Irish fans, like Cork City and Derry. Chants of "You'll never beat the Irish, You'll never beat the Irish," reverberated across the stands, silencing the few thousand attendees donning blue. The Irish players responded with a 1–0 victory over a stunned Italy. The game, a rematch of the 1990 quarterfinal that saw the Italians victorious 1–0, was played under the stinging sun and highlighted by a host of missed chances on both ends. Ireland scored after twelve minutes when Ray Houghton lobbed the ball from 20 yards out, just making it over the outstretched arm of Italian goalkeeper Gianluca Pagliuca, who was too far out of his net. The ball was able to just squeak under the crossbar for the goal. "It was a lucky shot," Italian defender Billy Costacurta said of Houghton's goal. "They were lucky and we were not."[11]

Sacchi had promised his team would play to win. Instead, the *Azzurri* found themselves trying to tie the score. The defense did a poor job of clearing the ball on several occasions and failed to control the tempo. The Irish, much more physical on the ground and in the air, played the long ball down the wings and forced the Italians to expend plenty of energy. Fatigue set in and the incessant chanting from the Irish fans seemed to bother the *Azzurri*. The Italians outshot the Irish, 14–12, but it was Ireland who had the clearest chance to score again in the 71st minute when John Sheridan fired a strong shot from inside the box, only to see it slam off the crossbar after beating Pagliuca. At the other end, Baggio did very little as the Irish defense double-teamed him. After the game, the Italian press went after Sacchi, already under pressure for his dubious decisions, and blamed him for the loss. Italy's next game against Norway was a necessary win. For Ireland, the victory was cause for celebration. The Irish players spent the night barhopping in New York, drinking beer and feting coach Jack Charlton, who smoked a cigar in the locker room to mark the momentous win.

On June 23, Italy squared off against Norway at Giants Stadium. The Norwegians had defeated Mexico, 1–0, at RFK Stadium in Washington,

D.C., four days earlier and were in search of another win. This time, the Italian fans did get a large share of the tickets and the atmosphere was that of a home game for the *Azzurri*. Once again, the Italians got off on the wrong foot after Pagliuca was red carded for handling the ball outside the box in the 21st minute in a bid to stop a breakaway attempt by Øyvind Leonhardsen. Reduced to ten men, Sacchi was forced to make a tactical switch. To everyone's amazement, he took off Roberto Baggio and put in backup goalkeeper Luca Marchegiani. Baggio, who had been named 1993 FIFA World Player of the Year, did not take kindly to the move, muttering, "Is this guy crazy?" as he walked off the field and toward the Italian bench. Baggio and Sacchi had reached a breaking point and now the Italians were not only down a player, but were in a must-win situation without their star. The *Azzurri* looked dead. Afterward, Sacchi explained the move by saying Baggio was nursing an injured Achilles tendon and could not be counted on to help out on defense. But Baggio had other words for his coach. "I have never in my career been substituted in this manner," he said. "I do not really know how I should react to any of this."[12]

The Italians persevered, while the Norwegians weren't much of a threat. Norway's coach, Egil Olson, and his insistence that his team rely on the long ball to move the ball about the field did nothing to scare Baresi and Maldini. Norway's hockey-style dump-and-chase approach made for awful soccer. Unlike Brazil's *jogo bonito*, which focused on individual talent and flair to create an eye-appealing game, Norway's insistence on using the long ball left little room for individual plays. Following a scoreless first half, there was more bad news for the Italians. Baresi hurt himself in the second period and was forced to abandon the match. The Italians eventually won, in typical dramatic fashion, when Dino Baggio came to the rescue. His header in the 69th minute lifted the Italians to victory. The jubilation, however, was short lived. Baresi's knee injury was worse than first expected. The Italian captain had to undergo surgery and would have to miss the remainder of the tournament. The *Azzurri*, battling to avoid the national disgrace that would have come with being eliminated, were still alive. A 1–1 tie against Mexico at RFK Stadium, while Ireland and Norway played to a scoreless draw at Giants Stadium, ensured that all four teams were deadlocked with four points after three games. In the end, Norway would be the odd team after losing to group winner Mexico and second place Ireland on goal differential. The Italians were lucky to advance, moving on as one of the tournament's four best third-place teams.

Meanwhile, Group F also became a hotly contested affair. Holland beat Saudi Arabia, 2–1, on June 20 at RFK Stadium, then followed that up with a 1–0 loss to Belgium five days later at the Citrus Bowl in Orlando. Holland won the group on goal differential, ahead of Saudi Arabia and Belgium, after beating Morocco, 2–1, on June 29 in balmy Orlando on goals from Dennis Bergkamp in the 43rd minute and Bryan Roy with twelve minutes left to play. The upset result of the group occurred when Saudi Arabia defeated Belgium, 1–0, on a goal from Saeed Owairan after just five minutes. His solo run down the field—reminiscent of Maradona's second goal against England at Mexico '86—stunned the Belgian defense and later proved to be the most spectacular goal of the tournament. Owairan's goal won the game for the Saudis, putting them in the knockout stage of the competition for the first time ever. Belgium, on the other hand, had failed to impress, but moved on as one of the four best third-place teams.

## Round of Sixteen

The round of sixteen featured eight match-ups with a mix of traditional powers and several World Cup newcomers. Brazil–United States, Holland–Ireland, Sweden–Saudi Arabia, Romania–Argentina, Germany–Belgium, Bulgaria–Mexico, Spain–Switzerland, and Italy–Nigeria were the eight games that opened the knockout stage.

Germany beat Belgium, 3–2, on July 2 in Chicago with three first-half goals. Voeller, who scored two of those goals, put Germany ahead as Klinsmann added a third to close out the first half. The game wasn't without controversy. Belgian forward Josip Weber ran into the box in an attempt to grab onto a long pass from Georges Grun in the 69th minute that had gone deep in the German box. Closely marked by Brehme, Weber was bumped from behind by Thomas Helmer as he ran toward the goal and went sprawling to the ground. Weber got up in protest and was stunned when referee Roethlisberger waved play to go on. The decision unleashed a chorus of boos from the crowd and protests from the Belgian players, who were losing 3–1 at that point. The decision made a difference after Belgium's mustachioed defender Philippe Albert scored in the 90th minute to make it 3–2. Though the Belgians attacked relentlessly during the two minutes of stoppage time—even bringing goalkeeper Michel Preud'homme forward—the Germans would come out on top that afternoon.

Spain blew past Switzerland, 3–0, on the same day in Washington, D.C., while Sweden downed Saudi Arabia, 3–1, in July 3 in Dallas. The surprise result of the round came later that day when Romania beat Argentina, 3–2, at the Rose Bowl. Maradona's absence cost Argentina dearly. All Maradona could do was watch from the stands and sit there with tears in his eyes as his teammates walked off the field losers. On July 4, Holland defeated Ireland, 2–0, in the stifling humidity of Orlando with Bergkamp scoring his second goal of the competition after eleven minutes and Wim Jonk adding another in the 41st minute.

That afternoon in Palo Alto, the 84,147 fans in attendance at Stanford Stadium wore clothing covered in red, white, and blue. For American soccer fans, it was no better way to root on their team and celebrate Independence Day at the same time. Even though Brazilian fans were also out in force, chants of "U-S-A! U-S-A!" filled the stadium once the game got underway. The Americans gained a one-man advantage in the 43rd minute after Leonardo's bone-crunching elbow found Ramos' face. Ramos went down like a prizefighter who had been knocked to the ground, while Leonardo was shown a red card by Quiniou. The Brazilians pressured the U.S. goal the entire time until Bebeto, off a sensational pass from Romário, managed to score in the 72nd minute, despite being down a player. Bebeto's goal—the only one of the game—ensured Brazil's passage to the quarterfinals. On Bebeto's goal, Lalas missed a sliding tackle on the Brazilian striker following a pass from Romário. Bebeto followed up the pass with a shot that beat Meola at the far post. The Brazil bench erupted into celebration. That was the only goal Brazil needed to win the game.

Milutinovic and his players received cheers as they walked off the field. The Americans had put on too much of a defensive display against Brazil, but criticisms were muted by praise. Milutinovic had pulled off another miracle. The team had triggered the passion of American sports fans and, for the first time in a long time, the United States was a soccer-loving country, too. In the process, American players also won some respect. In some cases, they were rewarded with contracts from foreign clubs. Lalas, originally a long shot to make the U.S. team, signed with Padova in Serie A, becoming the first American in nearly sixty years to play in Italy. Others, like Meola, tried their hand, err, foot, at something new. He ditched soccer, a move criticized by many, in order to become a place kicker for the New York Jets. He had a decent tryout, but was only given a chance to play on the team's practice squad once the season got underway.

The Italians, meanwhile, played Nigeria on July 5 at Foxboro Stadium. The contest was considered a huge mismatch with the Italians expected to dominate. The match quickly became a physical affair with the Africans fouling the *Azzurri* every chance they got. The Italians, playing in their white away jerseys, responded with their own brand of dirty play. Mexican referee Arturo Brizio Carter gave out eight yellow cards and sent off Gianfranco Zola in the 76th minute—twelve minutes after he had come in for Signori—for an innocuous foul that at worst could have be punished with a yellow card. The Italians struggled to get on the scoreboard and the Nigerians took the lead with Emmanuel Amunike in the 26th minute. Italy, as usual, struggled offensively as Sacchi spent much of the game barking orders from the sidelines. The Italians pressured the Nigerians the rest of the game—even playing with ten players—but could not find the back of the net. Baggio, who was shadowed the entire game by nineteen-year-old defender Sunday Oliseh, was unable to hit his stride and every time the ball came to him, a Nigerian player was ready to swat it away. Italian reporters sitting in the press box anxiously waited for the final whistle so that they could bombard Baggio and Sacchi with questions as to why the *Azzurri* had done so poorly. They never got their chance.

Before Italy could say *arrivederci* to USA '94, Baggio, nicknamed the "Divine Ponytail" because of his Buddhist beliefs, showed everyone why he was such a lethal player. With the clock winding down, the ball played into the Nigerian box just yards away from the net. Roberto Mussi found the ball at his feet and passed it to an unmarked Baggio. The Italian one-timed the ball and slotted it past goalkeeper Peter Rufai. The Italians had tied the game. The goal unleashed celebrations in the stands and joy on the field. The Italians had pulled off a miracle and forced overtime. In the extra session, the Italians caught another break. The referee awarded them a penalty kick in the 102nd minute that Baggio converted. The Italians won, 2–1, and were off to the quarterfinals.

"This team was on its way to the airport," Baggio told reporters at a news conference afterward. "I brought them back from the plane."[13]

That afternoon, Bulgaria continued to stun everyone with Hristo Stoitchkov netting his fourth goal of the tournament against Mexico at Giants Stadium after just six minutes. Mexico, another team that enjoyed the advantages of playing at "home" thanks to the large Mexican turnout, rallied. The *Tricolores* tied the score ten minutes later when Alberto Garcia Aspe converted a penalty kick. The game ended, 1–1, after overtime and went to a shootout. Mexican goalkeeper Jorge Campos, wearing one of his usual colorful jerseys, was no match for the Bulgarian kickers that day. Bulgaria advanced after winning the shootout, 3–1.

## And Then There Were Eight

The tournament moved to the quarterfinals, where a lopsided representation of the soccer world was on display. Of the eight remaining teams, seven hailed from Europe with Brazil as the only country from South America. This part of the competition could have easily been dubbed "Brazil versus the world," but since the *Selecao* was the only team from South America to win the World Cup outside its own continent, the time seemed ripe for a European team to win the competition in the Americas for the first time.

Italy opened the round with a clash against Spain in Boston. The Italians had reached the brink of physical exhaustion versus Nigeria, but were still alive thanks to Roberto Baggio's late-game heroics. Sacchi was banking on Baggio to come through for the team once again on July 9. The *Azzurri* took the lead with Baggio after the 25th minute, but Spain responded with a goal from José Luis Caminero in the 58th minute. The game appeared headed for overtime, but the Italians managed one last play with Signori. The Lazio striker, alone on the counterattack, fed the ball to Roberto Baggio, who rounded Barcelona goalkeeper Andoni Zubizarretta and deposited the ball into the net for the 2–1 victory. Baggio, with his flapping ponytail behind him, raised his arms in celebration. Victory belonged to Italy once again. In injury time, Luis Enrique had his nose shattered when he was elbowed in the face by Tassotti in the box. With blood pouring from his face and tears streaming down his cheeks, the Spanish midfielder cried out in search of a penalty. Hungarian referee Sandor Puhl ignored his pleas and the match continued. Puhl never saw the foul, otherwise a penalty kick would have been whistled and a red card issued to the Italian defender. After the game, FIFA's Disciplinary Committee, aided with TV replays, spotted the foul and handed Tassotti a seven-game ban. His World Cup tournament was over.

On the same day in Dallas, Brazil and Holland tangled with one another for a spot in the semifinals. As usual, Bebeto and Romário took it upon themselves to lead the team. Romário put Brazil ahead in the 52nd minute and Bebeto added a second goal eleven minutes later to give Brazil a commanding 2–0 lead. The Dutch fought back. Bergkamp cut the lead to one in the 65th minute and Aaron Winter tied the score ten minutes later. The Brazilians, masters of individual flair, earned the win thanks to a free kick shot by defender Branco in the 80th minute just outside the penalty box. Brazil won, 3–2, and remained most people's favorite to win the competition.

The biggest upset of the quarterfinals came in the Bulgaria–Germany game on July 10 at Giants Stadium. Germany's aging stars had done a good job getting the defending champions this far, but fatigue and the hot weather had taken its toll on Berti Vogts's team. Stoichkov's speed cost Germany in the end, though Matthaeus had put the three-time champions ahead in the 50th minute off a penalty kick. The Bulgarians tied the score with Stoichkov in the 75th minute, unleashing an in-swinging free kick that made its way over the German wall and into the back of the net. Five minutes later, the unexpected occurred when Yordan Letchkov headed in a goal. There was a collective grasp inside the stadium as the few hundred Bulgarian fans cheered. Bulgaria's 2–1 win put them in the semifinals for the first time ever. The World Cup had its surprise team. Now, how many more surprises the Bulgarians had left in them depended on whether they could defeat Italy.

In the last quarterfinal match played later in the day, Sweden bounced Romania out of the tournament on penalty kicks in Palo Alto. The game ended, 1–1, after Romania scored in the 89th minute when Florin Ra˘ducioiu knocked in the ball off a free kick by Gheorghe Hagi. Romania led 2–1 in overtime after a goal from Ra˘ducioiu in the 101st minute. Once again, the Romanian striker was in the right place at the right time when Swedish defender Patrick Andersson blocked a shot with his body, but the rebound rolled straight to Răducioiu's right foot. The exhausted Romanians—who had a man advantage after Swedish defender Stefan

Schwarz was red carded in the 102nd minute—were unable to put the game away. Instead, Sweden tied the score for a second time on a header by Kennet Andersson off a 25-yard pass from Roland Nilsson in the 115th minute. In the shootout, Sweden goalkeeper Thomas Ravelli stopped two shots to put Sweden in the semifinals for the first time in thirty-six years and set up a Group B rematch against Brazil.

## Semifinals

Roberto Baggio came through again against Bulgaria in the first semifinal played on July 13 at Giants Stadium. Baggio was at the top of his game. He effortlessly tore apart the Bulgarian defense with a pace never before shown by the striker at the tournament. He put Italy ahead, 1–0, in the 20th minute and added a second goal five minutes later. Stoitchkov was able to pull one back on a penalty kick just at the stroke of halftime for his sixth goal of the competition. The Bulgarian and Salenko would finish tied for the honor of tournament top scorer. The Italians, physically drained and emotionally exhausted, clung on for the 2–1 win. Baggio hobbled off the field a hero and was met at midfield by Gigi Riva. The former Italian great, a member of Italy's coaching staff, hugged Baggio as the they walked off the field. Baggio began to weep as the duo headed into the locker rooms. "Once again, Baggio was the difference for us," Maldini said. "For all the criticisms before the World Cup, he was our leader."[14]

Three hours later at the Rose Bowl, Brazil had a tough time eliminating Sweden in the other semifinal. The Swedes kept Romário and Bebeto from getting the ball for most of the contest, but as the game wore on, the Brazilians were relentless in their pursuit. In the 80th minute, Romário was finally able to score to give the *Selecao* a place in the championship game. Three days later, Sweden captured third place with a 4–0 win over Bulgaria at the Rose Bowl.

## The Final

Attention was focused on the final, which pitted soccer superpowers Brazil and Italy against each other, both biding to win an unprecedented fourth title. The final also pitted Baggio against Romário in an all-out duel over who was the best player in the world. The Italians

# ROMÁRIO

Another talented Brazilian to lead his country to a World Cup title, Romário de Souza Faria was born in 1966 in Rio de Janeiro. Discovered by scouts at a young age after he was spotted playing on the dirt fields near his home, Romário began his pro career with Brazilian club Vasco de Gama, where he won two championships in 1987 and 1988. He followed that by signing with Dutch powerhouse PSV Eindoven, where he played until 1992, winning three Dutch League titles in 1989, 1991, and 1992. He moved to Spain's Barcelona in 1993 and helped the club win the league title. He also finished as Liga top scorer with 30 goals in 33 matches. Romário was named FIFA World Player of the Year in 1994, after finishing second in the voting the previous year.

In 1995, Romário returned to Brazil to play for Flamengo. He spent the next year at Valencia, before returning to Flamengo in 1998. He played for Vasco de Gama again in 2000, winning the Mercosur Cup—South America's version of the UEFA Cup—and the Brazilian League title. From 2002 through 2004, Romário played with Brazilian club Fluminese. In October 2004, the club fired Romário after he got into a conflict with the team's coaching staff over playing time. He returned to the team that gave him his start, Vasco da Gama and, in 2005, Romário scored 22 goals in the Brazilian Championship to make him the league's top scorer.

In 2006, Romário joined Miami FC and helped the American team reach its first-ever United Soccer League playoffs, netting 18 goals in 23 appearances. In the fall of 2006, Romário signed on to a four-game guest stint in the Australian A-League with Adelaide United FC.

A journeyman on the club level, Romário, often a controversial figure known for his combative nature and lack of discipline, became a permanent fixture of the Brazilian national teams of the 1990s. He won the silver medal at the 1988 Olympics, scoring seven goals. He was part of the Brazilian team that participated in the 1990 and 1994 World Cups, leading the team to success at USA '94. He scored five goals at the tournament and was named the World Cup's MVP that year. Romário was left off of the 1998 and 2002 World Cup teams. He scored 55 goals in 70 games for Brazil, making him the third highest scorer in the history of the Brazilian team behind Pelé and Ronaldo. Romário played in his last game for Brazil in April 2005, scoring a goal in a 3–0 win over Guatemala in an exhibition match.

## World Cup Career Statistics

Tournaments played: 2
Games: 7
Goals: 5

found themselves in a crisis. Baggio had suffered a pulled hamstring in his left leg and was at risk of missing the game. "There is no status as to the certainty of whether I will play the final," a resigned Baggio told reporters at a news conference following the match against Bulgaria. "I am very happy for Italy. I hope I gave people plenty of joy."[15] Zola, who was coming off a red card suspension, was set to replace Baggio after team doctors would only say that his chances of appearing in the final were 50–50. Sacchi had fielded six different starting lineups over the course of six games, forced to deal with injuries and red cards on a scale never before endured by a team that had reached the World Cup final. In the Brazil camp, injuries were not an issue. The *Selecao* had dominated its six previous matches with an overpowering offense. Romário and Bebeto provided the one-two punch along the way, with the midfield and defense acting as support.

The final on July 17 took place in front of 94,194 spectators inside a sun-drenched Rose Bowl. Another two billion watched on television. The game was a stalemate; the rhythm was bland. Players on both teams were slowed down by the heat with Baggio gingerly playing the ball, but never really able to jumpstart the Italian offense. The Brazilians came closest to scoring in the 76th minute when Pagliuca almost made a blunder, bobbling a shot by Mauro Silva that bounced toward the goal. Instead, the ball softly rolled off the post. Pagliuca grabbed the rebound, kissed his hand, and then thanked the post by patting it. Baresi returned to the lineup, making a miraculous recovery three weeks after undergoing arthroscopic knee surgery. The AC Milan sweeper was everywhere on the field, foiling one Brazilian attempt after another.

The game ended 0–0. The thirty-minute overtime failed to produce a goal and the final went to a shootout for the first time in World Cup history. The Rose Bowl was shrouded in silence as both teams prepared to take the five decisive kicks. Italy's Baresi went first, but his shot went high over the crossbar. Pagliuca made up for the missed kick with a diving save on Brazil's Marcio Santos. Italy's Demetrio Albertini and Brazil's Romário connected on their kicks as did Alberigo Evani and Branco. Then came the mistakes that allowed Brazil to win the cup. Italian Massaro's kick was saved by Brazil's Daniele Taffarel. Then Dunga put Brazil in the lead, 3–2, to set up Roberto Baggio for the decisive kick. The Italian superstar ran toward the ball with the hopes and dreams of an entire nation resting firmly on his shoulders. But his kick sailed high over the bar and into the bright blue sky as Taffarel dropped to the ground, pointing to the sky in celebration. There would be no more late-game heroics for Baggio. Brazil could finally claim its fourth World Cup. Sacchi tried to console Baresi as he wept. The Italians had put on an intrepid effort, playing with perseverance and spirit, but it wasn't enough in the end. Many thought the shootout had been an unfair way to settle the game, but the Italians didn't complain. Donadoni, who was on the team that had lost to Argentina four years earlier in a shootout, was once again on the losing end. "I don't look back at Italia '90 or USA '94 with any disappointment," he said. "You only get one, maybe two, chances in a lifetime to play for a World Cup."[16]

Dunga raised the trophy as the Brazilian players saluting their fans, putting an end to one of the most successful and entertaining tournaments in World Cup history. The fans chanted, *"Ole, Ole, Ole, Ole, Bra-sil, Bra-sil,"* as the players circled the field. Brazil had clearly been

*Italy's Roberto Baggio moves the ball past Brazil's Dunga (wearing number 8) on his heels during the 1994 World Cup final at the Rose Bowl in Pasadena, Calif. (Credit: EMPICS).*

on a mission from the onset and never wavered from it. Parreira made several controversial decisions along the way, but in the end he was proven correct. He had faith in Taffarel when no one else did, even after he was dropped by Italian club teams Parma and Reggiana in the years since the 1990 World Cup. Parreira dropped Rai from the midfield, a player expected to emerge as a team leader. Rai, wearing the famed No. 10 jersey and the younger brother of former Brazilian star Socrates, played poorly once the tournament began. Although it was strange not to see a No. 10 jersey on the field for Brazil, it was also possible that Rai, named South America's Player of the Year in 1992, could not handle the burden of wearing the same number made famous by Pelé. Parreira benched Rai in favor of a midfield that included Dunga, Mauro Silva, and Zinho. The trio, who kept to a short-passing, free-flowing system, had been too strong for opponents to handle. Up front, Bebeto delivered the passes and Romário scored the goals. Parreira, who went on to coach the New York/New Jersey MetroStars in Major League Soccer, was happy with the feat. "In Brazil, finishing second is the same as being in last place," he joked.[17]

## Postgame Wrap-Up

USA '94 had allowed Americans to relish in the joy that comes with a World Cup. FIFA hoped the tournament's success would unleash a new-found passion for the game on U.S. soil. The creation of a new national league, one of the requirements FIFA imposed on the United States when it was awarded the World Cup, would certainly be the start of something new. More children were playing soccer in the suburbs than ever before and the U.S. team had showed it could compete with the game's other powers. The World Cup was a huge success, shattering World Cup records for total attendance (3.58 million spectators) and average attendance per game (68,991). Prior to the start of the tournament, Rothenberg had stated: "The mission statement adopted by the World Cup Organizing Committee is twofold: to put on the greatest World Cup in history and to leave a legacy for soccer in the United States."[18] Staging the greatest tournament ever had become a reality. Whether it left behind a legacy strong enough to sustain the sport remains a question to this day.

## 1998

The World Cup returned to France after a sixty-year absence. The tournament bore little resemblance to the one staged in 1938. The World Cup had become a marketing bonanza with corporate sponsors pumping millions of dollars into the tournament. A record 174 countries tried to earn a spot to France '98 as FIFA expanded the field of entrants to include eight more teams, bringing the first round to thirty-two contenders. The expanded field meant a new format with the finalists equally divided into eight groups of four. Only the top two finishers in each group moved on to the knockout stage. Brazil, Italy, Germany, Argentina, and England were once again favorites to win the trophy with France, playing in its first World Cup since Mexico '86, joining the mix because it was the beneficiary of being the home team. *Les Bleus* featured an impressive roster of veterans, which included Zinedine Zidane, Didier Deschamps, and Marcel Desailly. The team also had an infusion of young talent, including Thierry Henry, David Trézéguet and Youri Djorkaeff. Brazil, meanwhile, had its usual mix of veterans and rising stars. One of those youngsters, twenty-one-year-old Ronaldo—maintaining the tradition of Brazilian players to go by one name—led the way. The Inter Milan striker, who had sat on the bench at USA '94 and never saw any playing time, was going to get his chance to shine in front of billions. He had dazzled crowds in his native Brazil and Serie A, where he earned the nickname *Il Fenomeno* (The Phenomenon). While an injured Romário sat in his living room watching the tournament on TV after he was excluded from the team, it was up to Ronaldo to pick up where the Brazilian great had left off four years earlier.

### Group Play

The World Cup draw was held for the first time in a stadium on December 4, 1997. Nearly 38,000 people packed the Stade Velodrome in Marseilles to watch the ceremony. Argentina, Germany, Italy, Spain, Romania, and Holland joined defending champions Brazil and hosts

France as the seeded teams. The thirty-two finalists were placed as follows:

Group A: Brazil, Norway, Scotland, and Morocco
Group B: Italy, Austria, Chile, and Cameroon
Group C: France, Denmark, Saudi Arabia, and South Africa
Group D: Spain, Bulgaria, Paraguay, and Nigeria
Group E: Holland, Belgium, Mexico, and South Korea
Group F: Germany, Yugoslavia, the United States, and Iran
Group G: Romania, England, Colombia, and Tunisia
Group H: Argentina, Croatia, Japan, and Jamaica

The World Cup kicked off with the Brazilians recording a hard-fought 2–1 victory over Scotland on June 10 at the Stade de France in St. Denis, a suburb of Paris. Brazil followed that up by posting a 3–0 win over Morocco six days later at Parc Lescure in Bordeaux. Norway, who finished second in Group A, stunned the Brazilians on June 23 in Marseille when Kjetil Rekdal converted a penalty kick in the 88th minute for the unexpected 2–1 win. The Brazilians later criticized American referee Esse Baharmast for awarding the kick, but replays clearly showed he had made the right call. Brazil and Norway both advanced to the round of sixteen.

The Italians performed on par with the Brazilians, salvaging a 2–2 tie against Chile in the Group B opener on June 11 in Bordeaux with a Baggio penalty kick in the 85th minute. His kick exorcised the ghosts that had haunted him the last time he was at the World Cup and missed a penalty kick, that time costing Italy a World Cup title. The *Azzurri* improved their points during the next two games, blanking Cameroon, 3–0, on June 17 at the Stade de la Mosson in Montpellier, and outlasting Austria, 2–1, six days later in St. Denis to finish first in the group ahead of Chile. Christian Vieri was at the top of his game, scoring four of Italy's seven total goals—two against Cameroon and one each against Chile and Austria. The Chileans finished runners-up after recording three ties.

In Group C, France had an easy time winning the group. *Les Bleus* trounced South Africa, 3–0, in Marseille on June 12 in front of 55,000 fans with goals from Christophe Dugarry in the 34th minute, an own goal in the 77th minute, and a third from Thierry Henry in stoppage time. The scoring did not end there. Six days later, France defeated Saudi Arabia, 4–0, in St. Denis with Henry scoring two goals, unleashing celebrations across the country. France had never bestowed such public affection on its national team. In a country where the love of soccer was relegated to the lower socioeconomic classes, for once it appeared that an entire country was cheering on *Les Bleus*. The players responded by delighting the crowds with even more victories. On June 24, France, who had already clinched a berth to the round of sixteen, edged Denmark, 2–1, at the Stade Gerland in Lyon with Emmanuel Petit scoring the winner in the 56th minute. France won the group, but the Danes also moved on after South Africa could only manage a 2–2 tie against Saudi Arabia at the same time in Bordeaux.

Group D saw the shock elimination of Spain, who could only finish third behind Nigeria and Paraguay. Spain began the tournament on the wrong foot, losing 3–2 to Nigeria on June 13 at the Stade de la Beaujoire in Nantes. The Nigerians, playing with the same determination that landed them in the round of sixteen at USA '94, won the game thanks to a goal by Sunday Oliseh in the 78th minute. Spain could only go as far as a scoreless tie against Paraguay on June 19 at the Stade Geoffrey-Guichard in St. Etienne as Nigeria edged out Bulgaria, 1–0, at the Parc de Princes in Paris to top the group.

Nigeria, who had six points, was through to the next round. Paraguay had two points with Spain and Bulgaria each at one with a game left to play. On June 24, Paraguay squared off against Nigeria at the Stade de Toulouse in Toulouse for a chance to reach the next round. At the same time, Spain played Bulgaria at the Stade Félix Bollaert in Lens. Both had to hope for a win, coupled with a Paraguay loss, in order to move on to the next round.

But Paraguay wasted no time getting on the board, scoring after a minute with Celso Ayala. The Nigerians tied the score with Wilson Oruma ten minutes later. Paraguay scored in the 59th minute with Miguel Benitez and a third time with José Cardozo with four minutes left to play to seal the 3–1 win and a spot in the second round. Spain, meanwhile, also won, but it no longer mattered. In the end, Spain's 6–1 defeat of Bulgaria was a meaningless result. Spain, a country with an outstanding soccer tradition, had again come up short to the chagrin of the many fans who had traveled across the border to watch their beloved team.

In Group E, Holland and Mexico finished first and second, respectively. The Dutch were in great shape after outscoring its opponents 7–2 in the first round, while Mexico also put on a scrappy performance following a 3–1 defeat of South Korea on June 13 in Lyon and a 2–2 tie versus Holland on June 25 in St. Etienne. The Holland–Mexico game turned out to be the most exciting of the group. The Dutch took the lead after four minutes with Phillip Cocu, then doubled their lead with Ronald de Boer in the 18th minute. But Mexico mounted an extraordinary comeback late in the second half, cutting the lead in half in the 75th minute with Ricardo Palaez to 2–1 and then tied it in stoppage time with Luis Hernandez. Belgium finished third after recording three ties.

In Group F, Germany finished first thanks to goal differential after finishing in a tie with Yugoslavia at seven points. The United States had never won a World Cup game on European soil and kept that awful streak alive at France '98. This time, the U.S. team was coached by Milutinovic's assistant Steve Sampson. The team was looking to improve on the results set four years earlier at home. A tough group stood in the way, but Sampson was set on the possibility of a second-place finish and a berth to the round of sixteen. Sampson could have never imagined in 1994 that he would ever be head coach of the U.S. team at a World Cup. Sampson, the first American-born coach to lead the team to a World Cup finals, had never professionally played or coached before. Sampson wasted no time changing the team once he took the helm.

He controversially removed Harkes, who had served as team captain, from the roster and benched defensive mainstays like Balboa and Lalas. U.S. Soccer did not interfere with Sampson's tactical decisions. After all, it was his scouting report that was widely credited for the stunning 2–1 win over Colombia at the 1994 World Cup. Sampson spoke fluent Spanish and used that to court Hispanic-Americans, long ignored by American soccer officials. Sampson was born in Salt Lake City and played college soccer at San Jose State and UCLA, but tore the cartilage in his knee and never embarked on a pro career. Sampson was hired to work as a member of the 1994 World Cup Organizing Committee, but a suit and tie wasn't his thing. When Milutinovic announced he wanted to hire an assistant coach, U.S. Soccer officials demanded he be an American. Not before long, Sampson found himself sitting on the bench and reviewing videotapes of opponents. Milutinovic was fired in 1995, claiming that the U.S. Soccer Federation had accused him of not taking a larger role in developing youth players, and Sampson was named interim coach. Few expected Sampson to be hired full-time with coaches such as Parreira courted by federation officials. When Parreira refused the position, Sampson was given the job. "I'm just having a great time," Sampson said shortly after taking over. "We had a great World Cup, but there's so much more we can achieve."[19] Unfortunately, Sampson would never achieve further World Cup success.

Major League Soccer, which began in 1996 as the first pro soccer league in this country since the NASL, was only in its third season. Sampson, scrambling to put together the most competitive team he could, called up a combination of MLS players and those who plied their trade in foreign leagues. Sampson's twenty-two-man roster also included several players born outside the United States that had been naturalized—a decision that would turn out to be a controversial and not sit well with some of the team's veterans. Clearly, with MLS still in its infancy, Sampson could not solely rely on American-born players to lead the team. On the eve of the finals, Sampson put defender David Regis on the roster. Regis, who was born in France, had become a citizen just five weeks before the start of the tournament. Regis became eligible for citizenship because his wife was American. Regis wasn't alone. Thomas Dooley, who had played at USA '94, was back and this time was named captain. He was a German native and the son of a deceased American soldier. Roy Wegerle, a native of South Africa, became a citizen because he was married to an American, while Preki Radosavljevic—who was born in Yugoslavia and became a U.S. citizen in 1996 after playing for nearly a decade in the MISL—also made the team.

The Americans opened the tournament on June 15 against Germany in front of 43,815 fans in Paris. They were looking for at least a tie—and their first World Cup point on European soil—but the Germans had other plans. The Americans never had a chance, generating little offensively and playing too naïvely defensively. Germany walked all over Sampson's team, taking the lead after just eight minutes with Andreas Moller, only to double the score with Klinsmann in the 64th minute. Frankie Hejduk produced the only scoring chance for the Americans, nearly tying the game in the 52nd minute. Regis sent a cross to Hejduk, whose shot was headed just inside the right post. German goalkeeper

Andreas Köpke dove to his right and made the save. Claudio Reyna followed up with a shot, but it bounced off Köpke's knees. The Germans' win propelled them to the top of the group standings in a tie with Yugoslavia, who had defeated Iran 1–0 in St. Etienne the day before.

The U.S. team needed a victory against Iran to stave off elimination. Ironically, the Iranian team was coached by Jalal Talebi—an Iranian national who had lived in California for seventeen years—who had taken over the team just two weeks before the start of the tournament. But the game also had political implications. The United States' relationship with Iran had been strained by nearly two decades of conflict that stemmed from the Islamic Revolution of 1979. The game, however, was a chance to make amends between "The Great Satan" and the Iranians, but the U.S. players had bigger things on their mind. They needed a win. Sampson was losing control of the team after Balboa and Lalas publicly stated that they were dissatisfied with sitting on the bench. Sampson decided to change his formation against Iran, scrapping his 3-6-1 lineup against Germany in favor of a 3-5-2 with Brian McBride and Roy Wegerle on attack and moving Hejduk to the midfield. The U.S. played Iran on June 21 in Lyon only days after President Bill Clinton called for improved relations with the Middle Eastern nation. The teams also heeded the call. The Iranian players shook hands with the Americans before kickoff, even handing them white flowers and posing together for a group photo. The pleasantries ended there.

On the field, the Iranians outplayed the Americans, winning 2–1 and knocking Sampson's team out of the World Cup. FIFA knew the game was a high security risk and French police made sure to quash any protesters bent on disrupting the game in front of a worldwide audience. The match went off without incident, except for a peaceful protest against Iran's Islamic regime. Several thousand Iranian expatriates living in France smuggled T-shirts and banners into Gerland Stadium displaying the picture of Massoud Rajavi, head of an opposition group called the National Council of Resistance. French police in riot gear tried on several occasions to take away the banners, but the fans just kept displaying new ones.

The Americans were aggressive from the start. McBride's shot hit the crossbar in the third minute and another shot slammed against the post twelve minutes later. A Reyna shot also hit the post in the 33rd minute. Luck was clearly not on the team's side. The Americans, in their zeal to take the lead, left their defense vulnerable to the Iranian counterattack. Iran exploited those weakness in the 40th minute when Hamid Estili, poorly covered by Reyna, headed the ball past goalkeeper Kasey Keller for the 1–0 lead. The crowd of 39,000—made up largely of Iranian fans—erupted into cheers as Estili kissed the ground in celebration. The second period was no better for the Americans. A shot by Regis in the 68th minute hit the post, once again denying the Americans a goal. Mehdi Mahdavikia sprinted past the disheveled American defense and drilled a shot past Keller in the 83rd minute to seal the win, the first for Iran at a World Cup. The Americans would only score five minutes later when McBride's header made its way into the back of the net. Sampson, under pressure for losing against Germany, had no good excuse for the loss, even saying he would put the same lineup on the field against Yugoslavia despite criticisms as to why he left Wynalda on the bench. Sampson had no answer. All that remained was to fire Sampson. U.S. Soccer did no such thing, even though the team could not duplicate its success of four years earlier.

The U.S. team, which had lost two games and scored just one goal, had to now play Yugoslavia in its last game. Four days after losing to Iran, they took on Yugoslavia in a game they needed to win to salvage some pride. Sampson's team couldn't even do that in Nantes, though Hejduk, one of the few bright spots on the team, saw his header hit the post just twenty-four seconds into the game. Three minutes later, Yugoslavia took the lead when Slobodan Komljenovic's header beat Friedel off a rebound from Siniša Mihajlovic's curling 35-yard free kick. The goal proved to be the winner, even though the Americans had played well and created more chances than their opponents.

At the same time, Germany's 2–0 win over Iran in Montpellier assured it first place in the group. Yugoslavia, which had finished second, also advanced.

The Americans finished the tournament 0–3. Wynalda was given a chance to shine late in the game against Yugoslavia, but the effort proved meaningless. Critics charged that Sampson had benched his best players, some of which had openly criticized him during the tournament. Sampson refused to respond to those complaints, only to say that he wished that those who were angered by his moves would keep their disapproval private. On June 29, four days after the United States' exit from the World Cup, Sampson announced his resignation. An interesting parallel to note: When Milutinovic left three years earlier, Rothenberg announced he had resigned; Milutinovic later admitted he had been fired.

"We at the federation thank Steve for his tremendous service to our national team program and to soccer in the USA," Rothenberg said in a statement. "His tireless work has helped advance sport and, on balance, it was an era of growth."[20] The mood, however, felt like everything but one of growth. The last-place finish at the World Cup (the team would place 32nd overall out of 32 teams) was proof to the world that the United States was still a soccer lightweight. Sampson was replaced with D.C. United coach Bruce Arena, though Parreira, who had coached Brazil to the 1994 World Cup title, had again been rumored as a candidate. Arena had garnered lots of success with the University of Virginia and later in MLS. Now, his mission was to make sure the national team program was on track to qualify for the 2002 World Cup.

Five months after the World Cup debacle and poor finish, Sampson broke his silence and spoke publicly about what had ailed the team during the tournament. He engaged in a round of finger pointing, blaming the creation of MLS for why his players had lost their competitive edge.

> Returning to the U.S. gave [the players] a level of comfort that was impossible to enjoy in Europe or Mexico. Returning to the U.S. made them instantly stars of their teams. From a promotional standpoint, the "star" factor was crucial to the success of the league. From the personal development and preparation for the World Cup qualifying, it was highly detrimental.[21]

He also blamed strained labor relations between U.S. Soccer and the team after the players hired a lawyer and formed an association in an effort to reap the marketing benefits of participating at a World Cup. "Labor negotiations drove a wedge between players and management that created an atmosphere of mistrust," Sampson said.[22] Following the World Cup, U.S. Soccer created Project 2010, a program with a stated goal of winning the World Cup by 2010. The project's aim was also to recruit top youth players from around the country and give them a place to train and develop their skills. The project would have mixed results over the coming decade.

In Group G, the Romanians excelled against all of their opponents. They beat Colombia 1–0 in Lyon on June 15 and tied Tunisia 1–1 on June 26. The Romanians stunned England, 2–1, on June 22 in Toulouse to win the group, with the game-winning goal scored in the final minute by Petrescu. Charging into the goal area to chase down Constantin Gâlca˘'s pass, the Romanian defender tangled with his Chelsea teammate Graeme Le Saux, putting his left foot around the English defender to poke the ball between the legs of goalkeeper David Seaman. Petrsecu's goal was a lovely finish to a hard-fought game. England, however, finished in second place, setting up a round of sixteen clash against rivals Argentina. England, who only needed a tie against Colombia to guarantee a place in the final sixteen after beating Tunisia 2–0 on June 15 in Marseilles, got goals from Darren Anderton in the 20th minute and David Beckham eight minutes later. Beckham scored off a curling 30-yard free kick that found the back of the net, much to the delight of English fans at the Félix Bollaert Stadium.

Argentina, meanwhile, won Group H in style, going 3–0 in its first World Cup without Maradona after twenty years. The South Americans defeated Japan, 1–0, on June 14 in Toulouse on a goal by Batistuta in the 28th minute. Seven days later, Argentina beat World Cup first-timer Jamaica, 5–0, in Paris with Batistuta netting a hat trick, bringing his tournament tally to four. Argentina's reward was a date with England in the round of sixteen. Croatia, wearing the stylish red-and-white checks on their jerseys, finished second after posting two wins: 3–1 over Jamaica on June 14 in Lens and 1–0 against Japan six days later in Nantes.

## The Round of Sixteen

The round of sixteen featured ten European teams, four from South America, and one apiece from North America and Africa. The matchups were as follows: Italy–Norway, France–Paraguay, Germany–Mexico, Romania–Croatia, Brazil–Chile, Nigeria–Denmark, Holland–Yugoslavia, and Argentina–England.

Italy opened the knockout round with a win over Norway on June 27 in Marseilles. Norway, a team that had been riding a seventeen-game unbeaten streak that included a victory over Brazil in the previous round, lost 1–0. Vieri scored his fifth goal of the competition and the Italian defenders stymied Norway's long-ball attacks for much of the second half. Vieri's goal came after eighteen minutes on the counterattack. Luigi Di Biagio sent a long ball through to Vieri, who outran defender Dan Eggen to drive a right-footed shot past goalkeeper Frode Grodas. Italy's barrel-chested defender Fabio Cannavaro kept close guard on striker Tore André Flo, sticking to him like glue each time he went for a high ball. Pagliuca made a spectacular diving save on Flo's close-range header in the 71st minute to preserve the win.

Later that day, Brazil crushed Chile, 4–1, in Paris, leaving no doubt that the South Americans wanted to retain the title. Two goals from Cesar Sampaio in the first half—the first in the 11th minute and the second fifteen minutes later—silenced the few thousands. Chilean supporters who had gathered at the Parc de Princes. Ronaldo added a third goal in stoppage time to put Brazil ahead 3–0 at the half. The Chileans pulled one back, but the Brazilians sealed the victory with another goal from Ronaldo, who had spent the better part of the game roaming free in the Chilean half.

France, meanwhile, prepared for the round of sixteen amid growing support across the country. France's game against Paraguay on June 28 at Felix Bollaert Stadium brought out a sea of blue, white, and red. France, without the suspended Zidane, who had amassed a two-game ban after receiving a red card against Saudi Arabia, had a tough time against Paraguay. The hosts came close to taking the lead after sixteen minutes when Bernard Diomede's shot was batted away by goalkeeper Jose Luis Chilavert. Three minutes later, Chilavert, a goalkeeper in the tradition of Higuita, just watched as a 20-yard shot from Djorkaeff sailed wide of his net. France's best scoring chance came five minutes before halftime when Henry put up a nifty chip shot that sailed over the defense and out of reach of Chilavert, only to see the ball bounce off the post. Paraguay, on the other hand, created few scoring chances, resorting to rough tackles and time-wasting techniques. The move earned them jeers from the crowd of 38,000 flag-waving French fans.

The second half featured more of the same with the Paraguayans more than happy to push the game into overtime. They were successful. In the extra session, *Les Bleus* did their best to try to defeat Paraguay, but Zidane's absence showed. With penalty kicks looming, defender Laurent Blanc finished off Paraguay with an historical goal in the 114th minute. The "Golden Goal"—FIFA's version of sudden-death overtime—had only been introduced earlier in the year to settle tie games during the knockout rounds of a competition. Blanc's volley from point-blank range was so powerful that even Chilavert couldn't put a hand on it. The goal ended the match and put Blanc in the history books as the first player at a World Cup to score such a goal.

That evening, the Nigerians also yearned to make history, trying to become only the second African nation since Cameroon in 1990 to reach the quarterfinals. Standing in their way was Denmark, surprise winners of the 1992 European Championship. Danish striker Peter Moller wasted no time leaving his mark three minutes into the match, giving his team the lead after unleashing a powerful shot from the top of the penalty box. Moller also had a hand in Denmark's second goal nine minutes later, blasting a free kick from nearly 25 yards out that forced goalkeeper Peter Rufai to block the ball with two hands. The ball rebounded back into play where Brian Laudrup was able to gain possession and score. Denmark led 2–0 at the half. Nigeria attempted a comeback in the second period, but Denmark held strong. Substitute Ebbe Sand scored Denmark's third goal in the 60th minute, less than a minute after he had come in for Moller. Rufai's inability to hold on to another shot resulted in a fourth Danish goal: Martin Jorgensen drilled a low shot in from the right that Rufai failed to grab in the 76th minute for the 4–0 lead. Nigeria attempted to claw its way back, but all they could do was score a goal with Tijani Babangida in the 78th minute. The Danes defeated Nigeria, 4–1, and were off to the quarterfinals.

On June 29, Germany outclassed Mexico, 2–1, in Montpellier with two goals in the final fifteen minutes. Down 1–0 after Hernandez had put the *Tricolores* ahead in the 47th minute, the Germans staged a rally that ended Mexico's hopes of putting up the biggest upset of the tournament. Klinsmann tied the score in the 75th minute, but with temperatures hovering around 90 degrees, the Germans appeared sluggish, while the Mexicans, no strangers to such heat, controlled the pace. The Germans' never-say-die attitude helped them win the game when Oliver Bierhoff's perfect header from 12 yards out with four minutes left to play won the game for Germany. Bierhoff, who had previously scored three goals in the first round, out-jumped defender Raul Lara for the ball off a pass from Ulf Kirsten for the goal. Later that day in Toulouse, Holland defeated Yugoslavia, 2–1, on Edgar Davids's stoppage time goal in the 92nd minute. Davids's goal was a fitting way for the gusty midfielder to make amends with Dutch coach Guus Hiddink. Davids had been recalled to the team following a two-year absence. He had originally been left off the squad after hurling insults at Hiddink following Holland's poor showing at the 1996 European Championship.

Croatia advanced to the quarterfinals on June 30 following a 1–0 win over Romania thanks to Davor Suker's penalty kick goal in the first period of stoppage time. The goal came off a disputed call by Argentine referee Javier Castrilli, who whistled a foul on midfielder Gabriel Popescu inside the box after his leg became tangled with that of Aljosa Asanovic as both tried to chase the ball. Popescu protested, but there was no changing Castrilli's mind. Another bad call had determined the outcome of a World Cup game.

That evening, the showdown between old foes Argentina and England in St. Etienne was the most anticipated game of the round. The teams had not played each other at a World Cup since that infamous game in 1986. With the Falklands War a distant memory and Maradona not there to stir controversy, the game was free from the tumult some had expected in the days leading to the kickoff. Both sides traded penalty shot goals with Batistuta scoring for Argentina after six minutes and Alan Shearer for England four minutes later. The goal of the game—and possibly the tournament—was scored in the 16th minute when England striker Michael Owen, just eighteen years old, went on a solo run, something reminiscent of Maradona's second goal against England twelve years earlier. Owen then slotted the ball past goalkeeper Carlos Roa for the 2–1 lead. The Argentineans didn't let the goal get them down, tying the score with Javier Zanetti in the first half of stoppage time. The half ended, 2–2, but the fireworks did not end there. Beckham was red carded by Danish referee Kim Milton Nielsen for kicking Diego Simeone. The Argentine exaggerated by falling to the ground like he had been shot. The game ended 2–2 following overtime. On penalty kicks, Roa's save on David Batty's kick gave Argentina the 4–3 win. Once again, England had been bounced out of the tournament on penalty kicks.

## The Quarterfinals

The quarterfinals opened on July 3 with France playing Italy in St. Denis. The game ended scoreless after a thrilling 120 minutes in which

Zidane, back from suspension, did everything but score. The French outshot the Italians, 31–10, but the *Azzurri* had been able to put on a superb defensive display to push the game into a shootout. The Italians tried to reverse the curse of the shootout that had plagued them over the last two World Cups. The third time, however, would not be the charm. Goalkeeper Fabian Barthez's save on Italy's second kick by Demetrio Albertini was crucial as France scored its next three kicks. When Luigi Di Biagio's shot crashed onto crossbar, the crowd of 77,000 erupted into cheers. France won the shootout, 4–3, to earn a spot in the semifinals. The Italians left the field in defeat. The World Cup had ended early for them once again.

Two hours later in Nantes, Brazil outlasted Denmark, 3–2, thanks to two goals from Rivaldo. At the outset, the Danes took the lead after two minutes with Martin Jorgensen. The Brazilians reacted and nine minutes later, Ronaldo, in his new role as playmaker, fed the ball to Bebeto. The veteran unleashed a shot that found its way into the lower left corner to tie the score, 1–1. Ronaldo didn't stop there. The Inter Milan striker found Rivaldo in the 27th minute on the left side. Rivaldo's chip shot over goalkeeper Peter Schmeichel made it 2–1. The Brazilians looked firmly in control for the first time that evening, but the game got nastier as the game progressed. Aldair brought down defender Thomas Helveg in the 37th minute, which drew a yellow card from Egyptian referee Gamal Ghandour. Two minutes later, Soren Colding was given a yellow card for fouling Roberto Carlos after slamming the Brazilian midfielder in the neck with his forearm. The Danes put on the pressure, which made for a riveting game. In the 50th minute, Roberto Carlos attempted to clear the ball from his own box with a bicycle kick. He missed the ball, which dropped to Laudrup's feet. The Danish striker was unforgiving, firing a shot into the net to make it 2–2. Brazil then scored the game-winner in the 61st minute when Rivaldo stole the ball in the midfield, ran up the left flank and blasted a shot from 30 yards out that found the far corner of the net. Brazil was one step closer to successfully defending its title.

Holland also won in exciting fashion on July 4, eliminating Argentina, 2–1, in Marseilles with a goal from Bergkamp in the 90th minute. Frank de Boer's 60-yard pass was controlled masterfully by the Dutch striker, who brought the ball down to his feet, played it around defender Roberto Ayala in the box and unleashed a shot past Roa. The victory set up a semifinal date against Brazil.

But the biggest upset of the tournament took place that evening in Lyon when Croatia crushed Germany, 3–0. The aging Germans ran out of comebacks after Croatia took the lead in the first half of stoppage time with Robert Jarni. The Croatians put the finishing touches on the win with two late goals. Goran Vlaovic scored in the 80th minute and Suker added another five minutes later to complete the rout. The Croatian players celebrated on the field after the final whistle as the majority of the 39,000 fans at the Stade Gerland cheered them on. Croatia was in the semifinals and had to play France for a shot at the final.

## Semifinal Action

The first semifinal was contested between Brazil and Holland on July 7 in Marseilles. The Brazilians were favored to win, but for the first time faced a formidable opponent. That didn't stop Brazil coach Mario Zagallo from predicting that his team would advance to the final. For every decision he had made up until this point, there were 160 million second-guessers back home dissecting his every decision. Zagallo's gutsy prophecy also did little to get his players energized. Brazil's clearest scoring chance came in the 74th minute when Ronaldo—tightly marked by Frank de Boer the entire game—missed on a breakaway. The game ended scoreless and the thirty-minute sudden-death overtime failed to produce a goal. Brazil's reputation, and Zagallo's prediction, hung in the balance. In the shootout, Brazil scored its first three kicks with Taffarel saving Cocu's shot. The save gave Brazil a temporary 3–2 edge. Dunga scored Brazil's fourth and Taffarel's save on Ronald de Boer helped Brazil prevail 4–2. Taffarel lifted his arms, pointing to the sky in relief. The save touched off wild celebrations on the Brazil bench and among the yellow-and-green-clad fans that made up the majority of the 54,000 spectators inside the Velodrome Stadium that night. Brazil had once again reached a World Cup final.

In the other semifinal played the following day, France and Croatia met in St. Denis. A scoreless first half opened the doors to an electrifying second period. Suker's goal in the 46th minute gave Croatia a 1–0 lead. The Croatian scoring machine took the ball on his left foot, let it bounce once and drilled it past Barthez, who was charging out of the net in an attempt to smother the shot. Unfortunately for Barthez, he missed the block and the shot went in. Then the unlikeliest of players stepped up and tied the game: defender Lilian Thuram, who had never scored in thirty-seven appearances for France. A minute after Suker's goal, the French defender scored off a Dorkaeff pass. French coach Aimé Jacquet had started Thuram in all eighteen games *Les Bleus* had played between the 1996 European Championship and the World Cup finals. Thuram, one of the greatest defenders at the tournament, added goalscorer to his resume twice when, in the 70th minute, he stole the ball from Jarni before curling a left-footed shot for the 2–1 winner. France maintained the tempo until Blanc was shown a red card in the 74th minute following a push on Slaven Bilić that the Croat defender claimed had faked a punch to the head, fooling Spanish referee Jose Garcia-Aranda. Even with that penalty, France had booked a place in the final for the first time in tournament history. The only thing standing in the way of *Les Bleus* lifting the trophy was Brazil. "We played

*Brazil's Ronaldo goes head first toward the goal as the Dutch defense tries to stop him during the 1998 World Cup quarterfinals (Credit: EMPICS).*

really well that day," Thuram recalled. "I knew we could win the World Cup after that game."[23]

For Croatia, reaching the semifinals punctuated a stirring run for them. In the end, the Croatians, an underdog that turned themselves into title contenders, had to settle for third place on July 11 after defeating Holland, 2–1, in Paris. Suker scored the game-winner in the 35th minute to finish as the tournament's top scorer with six goals.

## The Final

France was abuzz with expectation in the days leading up to the July 12 final. The intrigue intensified hours before kickoff in St. Denis when reporters were amazed to learn that Ronaldo had been scratched from Zagallo's starting lineup. Ronaldo had been playing with a bad knee, so that was the reason given, but it was revealed after the game that the Brazilian star had suffered a seizure the night before. Roberto Carlos, who shared a room with Ronaldo, awoke at 4 a.m. to find Ronaldo suffering a seizure and quickly alerted the team's medical staff. Ronaldo was taken to a Paris hospital, and although doctors there could not find anything physically wrong with him, Brazil's team spokesman Nelson Borges later insisted that the player had felt dizzy, suffered a 30-second convulsion, and eventually vomited. Ronaldo later declared himself fit to play, but it was likely that he had buckled mentally under the pressure in the form of a panic attack. The revelation that Ronaldo had not been fit to play was just one of several that depicted a Brazilian locker room in disarray in the hours before kickoff. Ronaldo arrived at the stadium the afternoon of the game, along with his teammates, and although there were some concerns regarding his health, Zagallo agreed to play him. Nike, which sponsored the Brazilian team and had used Ronaldo in its World Cup advertising campaigns, denied that it had put any pressure on Ronaldo to play. "With regard to rumors circulating about presumed pressures Nike put on the Brazilian national team so that Ronaldo would play, Nike wants to emphasize that the report of such involvement is absolutely false," said Nike spokesman Massimo Giunco.[24]

It was obvious from the opening minute that something was wrong with Ronaldo and Brazil would ultimately pay the price for his sub-par performance. The Brazilians could barely string together a series of

## RONALDO

Nicknamed "The Phenomenon," Ronaldo Luis Nazário de Lima, known simply as Ronaldo, has enjoyed tremendous success on the World Cup level, winning the 1994 and 2002 tournaments. His 15 career goals at the World Cup makes him the tournament's all-time leading scorer.

Ronaldo was born in Rio de Janeiro in 1976. Like many Brazilian children, he began to play soccer in the streets. Ronaldo's abilities were first discovered at age 14 when he was recommended to the Brazilian youth team by Jairzinho, who was a former teammate of Pelé and a World Cup champion in 1970. Jairzinho also arranged for his former club, Cruzeiro, to sign him. Ronaldo scored 12 goals in 14 games in the Brazilian Championship. Ronaldo made his international debut for Brazil in 1994 in an exhibition game against Argentina. He was named to Brazil's 1994 World Cup roster as a 17-year-old, but never got a chance to play. Like many Brazilians, the teen sensation moved to Europe to play with PSV Eindoven that same year, scoring 54 goals in 57 games.

In 1996, Ronaldo attracted the attention of Barcelona, where he went on to score 34 goals in 37 games during the 1996–1997 season. He was transferred to Inter the following year. Ronaldo burst onto the World Cup scene in 1998 when as a starter under coach Mario Zagallo, he led Brazil to the final against France. The night before the game, Ronaldo suffered a convulsive fit, which almost forced him to miss the match. Despite Ronaldo recovering in time for the game hours later, many blame the incident on Brazil's 3–0 loss to France.

A year after the 1998 World Cup, he severely injured his right knee when playing for Inter during a league match against Lecce and was sidelined for four months with a ruptured tendon. During his first comeback in 2000, he played only seven minutes during an Italian Cup game against Lazio before injuring himself for a second time when he twisted his recently repaired knee. After two operations and twenty months of rehab, Ronaldo returned in time for the 2002 World Cup, scoring two goals against Germany in the final. Ronaldo finished as the tournament's top scorer with eight goals, helping Brazil win its fifth World Cup title. He was named FIFA World Player of the Year in 2002 for the third time, after having won the award in 1996 and 1997. Also in 2002, he was transferred from Inter to Real Madrid after failing to lead the Milan-based club to a Serie A title.

At the 2006 World Cup, Brazil won its first two group games, but Ronaldo was repeatedly jeered for being overweight. Nonetheless, coach

*(continued)*

Carlos Alberto Parreira kept him in the starting lineup. His two goals against Japan allowed him to become the 20th player ever to score in three different World Cups. He broke the all-time World Cup scoring record of 14, held by Germany's Gerd Muller, after scoring his 15th goal in a match against Ghana in the round of sixteen. Despite the player's impressive records, Brazil was eliminated by France in the quarterfinals.

## World Cup Career Statistics

Tournaments played: 3
Games: 19
Goals: 15

passes. Simply trying to make any serious threats to the French goal appeared an arduous task. The French, with the support of the home fans, dictated the pace of the match, frequently playing the ball in the Brazilian half with little resistance. Zidane, the player France was counting on to make the difference, cemented his place as the greatest player in the world when he scored on a header in the 27th minute off a corner kick taken by Emmanuel Petit. Zidane did not stop there. In the 45th minute, Djorkaeff put up a high ball in the box off a corner kick that Zidane again headed into the net past Taffarel for a goal that was a carbon copy of the first. France led 2–0 at halftime. "Zidane was just spectacular," Djorkaeff recalled. "Everything had come together for us."[25]

The stunned Brazilians did even less in the second period with Ronaldo roaming the field in a zombie-like state. Brazil gained an edge when French defender Marcel Desailly was red carded for an appalling foul on Cafu in the 68th minute. However, the one-man advantage did little to breathe new life into Zagallo's team. *Les Bleus* sealed the victory with a goal from Petit in the 90th minute after Patrick Vieira sent a pass that split open the Brazilian defense. Petit ran the ball into the box and past Taffarel to make it 3–0. French captain Didier Deschamps collected the trophy amid loud applause from the emotional crowd of 75,000 that had filled the Stade de France. France celebrated in style with nearly a million people dancing in the streets along the Champs Elysées. The win was a jolt of glory for millions across France, many of whom had cared very little about the outcome of the competition just a month earlier. France, the country that helped start the World Cup, was finally a world champion. *Les Bleus* had also been able to arouse an indifferent nation on the eve of the finals to embrace them in the end. Only after winning the trophy did Zidane admit how tough the feat had been. "There was huge pressure on us, especially before the big games," he recalled. "Not too many people believed in us, but we always believed in ourselves. We really wanted to accomplish something great—and we did."[26]

## 2002

The World Cup entered the new millennium and uncharted territory. In May 1996, FIFA decided for the first time that the tournament would be played outside of the Americas and Europe after jointly awarding the competition to Japan and South Korea. The joint bid, also a first, meant that both countries received automatic spots to the finals. The co-hosts made interesting bedfellows. At odds historically, Japan and South Korea had to overcome centuries of tension if they wanted to pull off a great tournament. At first, South Korea and Japan were competitors in a bitter bidding war. At FIFA's urging, the two nations combined their bids. That was just the first hurdle. Even after FIFA awarded both countries the tournament, problems persisted. Who would host the opener and the final was just one of the issues that needed to be settled. The other was what name would be given to the competition. Following the English alphabetical order, Japan wanted "World Cup Japan/Korea 2002." The South Koreans argued to go with the French alphabet, with the excuse of keeping with FIFA's French origins, and have their country named first in the tournament's official name. FIFA intervened and a compromise was reached after months of bickering. "Korea/Japan" was the name both sides agreed to go with in the end. South Korea was awarded the opening game and Japan given the responsibility of hosting the final.

### The Final Thirty-Two Teams

A record 199 countries played for a chance to be one of the 30 teams (along with Japan and South Korea) to play in the finals. France, Argentina, and Portugal were all touted as pre-tournament favorites, although all three would be in for a surprise finish once the competition got underway. France, the reigning champions, had retained the bulk of its roster and hoped the same players could deliver once again. Argentina and Portugal both featured an array of stars that had reached their peak that summer. The final draw, held on December 1, 2001, in the Korean city of Busan, featured the following eight seeded teams: France, Brazil, Spain, Argentina, Germany, Italy, South Korea, and Japan. Groups A through D were to play in South Korea, while games involving teams in Groups E through H would play in Japan. This is how the eight groups looked:

Group A: France, Denmark, Uruguay, and Senegal
Group B: Spain, Slovenia, Paraguay, and South Africa
Group C: Brazil, Turkey, Costa Rica, and China
Group D: South Korea, Portugal, Poland, and the United States
Group E: Germany, Ireland, Cameroon, and Saudi Arabia
Group F: Argentina, England, Sweden, and Nigeria
Group G: Italy, Croatia, Ecuador, and Mexico
Group H: Japan, Belgium, Russia, and Tunisia

Like previous tournaments, there was a "Group of Death" and this time that honor went to Group F. The game between Argentina and England was clearly the biggest first-round game of the competition and stood as a rematch of the 1986 and 1998 quarterfinals, both of which saw the English eliminated. The England–Sweden game was also an interesting match-up because it pitted England coach Sven-Goron Erikkson against his native Sweden. Nigeria had put together solid showings in 1994 and 1998 and was clearly the strongest team to emerge from Africa in the last decade.

## Group Play

The African nation to turn heads, however, was Senegal. The West African nation made its tournament debut on May 31 in the opener against France at Seoul Stadium in Seoul, defeating the reigning champions, 1–0, and marking the first of what would be a series of upsets over the course of the next month. Like at Italia '90, an African team had upset the defending champions. Senegal was coached by Frenchman Bruno

Metsu, who had twenty-one players on his team playing for French clubs. No one expected such a shocking outcome before kickoff. The uninspired French were unable to create a solid scoring chance as the Senegalese frustrated *Les Bleus* every chance they got. They used their speed and creativity to move the ball into the French half and continued to apply pressure as the game wore on. The barrage paid off, and Senegal took the lead after thirty minutes when El Hadji Diouf beat defender Frank Leboeuf on the left and sent the ball into the French box. Petit was unable to clear it and the ball wound up in the direction of Barthez who was unable to put his hands around it. The loose ball allowed midfielder Pape Bouba Diop to knock it into the net. Diop took off his jersey during a wild goal celebration that included his teammates dancing with joy near the corner kick flag, evoking memories of Cameroon twelve years earlier. *Les Bleus* had been unlucky. Just before the goal, Trézéguet's shot hit the post. France had also come close in the second half when Henry's shot struck the crossbar. Senegal held off a late French onslaught for the win.

*Les Bleus* were in trouble. The loss against Senegal had revealed a number of weaknesses. Without Zidane, who sat the game out with a thigh injury, France was not the powerful force it had been in 1998. Christophe Duggary had not been up to the task of replacing Zidane, unable to do what his countryman had so aptly done so many times before. France's second game showed little improvement. On June 6, *Les Bleus* were still unable to score after being held to a 0–0 tie in Asiad Stadium in Busan by Uruguay, who had lost 2–1 to Denmark just five days earlier. Only a win by at least two goals against Denmark in its last game could see France through to the round of sixteen.

Zidane was forced to come off the bench in the hopes of jumpstarting the French attack, but his presence wasn't enough on June 11 against the Danes at Incheon Munhak Stadium in Incheon. France was denied the space to move the ball with Denmark putting on a magnificent defensive display. Scoring two goals against the Danes proved an impossible task. Then Denmark took the lead after twenty-two minutes when midfielder Stig Tofting crossed the ball to striker Dennis Rommedahl, who put the ball in the back of the net with a powerful half volley that beat Barthez. Jon Dahl Tommasson made it 2–0 in the 67th minute after tapping the ball into the goal following a low crossing pass from Jesper Gronkjaer. Similar to the match against

Senegal, France could not score, but hit the woodwork several times. Desailly's header slammed against the crossbar and Trézéguet did the same from four yards out. France had not been able to score a goal in three games and was eliminated in disgrace. Denmark won, 2–0, to top the group. France's loss also gave it the distinction as the first World Cup champion to be booted from the group stage since Brazil in 1966.

While Denmark had its way against France, Senegal and Uruguay played to a 3–3 tie at Suwon Stadium in Suwon. Uruguay, who had been the last team to qualify for the finals after defeating Australia in a two-game playoff the previous November, was also eliminated. The two-time champion Uruguayans needed a win to move on to the next round, while Senegal only needed a tie. The Africans, who had stunned the world with their victory over France and 1–1 tie against Denmark on June 6, would move on to the round of sixteen after scoring three goals in a span of eighteen minutes. Senegal took the lead in the 20th minute when Khalilou Fadiga converted a penalty kick. Then Diop scored two goals, one in the 26th minute and again in the 38th minute, to put Senegal ahead, 3–0. Both goals were a mix of speed and acrobatic skill. For the first goal, Diop side-footed the ball off a cross from Henri Camara, sending it into the roof of the net. The second goal was just as beautiful. Diop once again met a cross from Camara, only this time he volleyed the ball into the goal just under the crossbar. Down 3–0 at the half, Uruguay coach Victor Pua made a few changes, including dropping a defender and putting striker Diego Forlan into the game. The changes worked. Only twenty-seven seconds into the second half and Uruguay was on the board. Midfielder Richard Morales, a second-half substitute for Marcelo Romero, scored from close range. Forlan cut the lead to one in the 69th minute and Álvaro Recoba, who had come close to scoring on several occasions, made it 3–3 on a penalty kick in the 88th minute. Uruguay was awarded the penalty after Morales tried to go for the ball only to find defender Habib Beye in his way. Morales made contact and tumbled to the ground. The fall was a dive, but the penalty had been called. Recoba followed up that piece of acting by slotting the ball into the net. Uruguay came close to winning the match in stoppage time when a botched defensive clearance allowed Morales to head the ball toward the net. The ball sailed wide past the Senegal goal and the game ended, 3–3. Though the Uruguayans had put on a great second half show, it wasn't enough to carry them through, and the tie allowed Senegal to move on to the next round.

In Group B, Spain, historically the World Cup's biggest underachievers, beat Slovenia, 3–1, on June 2 at Gwangju Stadium in Gwangju to record its first victory in a World Cup opening game since 1950. Spain then rattled off another win by the same score five days later against Paraguay at Jeonju Stadium in Jeonju to become the first team to reach the round of sixteen. Spain won the group following a tough 3–2 win over South Africa on June 12 at Daejeon Stadium in Daejeon. Spain had been down 2–1, but was able to mount a comeback with goals from Real Madrid's goalscoring sensation Raul González in the 56th minute and one from Gaizka Mendieta in stoppage time. The loss eliminated South Africa, giving Paraguay, 3–1 winners over Slovenia in Seogwipo, the edge in the standings on goal differential.

Brazil, meanwhile, in Group C, entered the tournament, as not one of the favorites. The team had had a tough time qualifying for the finals, but the players turned on the pressure once they arrived in South Korea and a trio of R's—Ronaldo, Rivaldo, and Ronaldinho—ultimately proved impossible to stop. The Brazilians opened with a 2–1 win over Turkey on June 3 at Munsu Cup Stadium in Ulsan. Rivaldo's penalty kick with three minutes left to play won the *Selecao* the match. But Rivaldo garnered lots of attention for another reason a few minutes after netting the goal. He aptly won a corner, but delayed taking the kick in an effort to waste time. A frustrated Hakan Unsal kicked the ball at Rivaldo in an attempt to get him to restart the match. The ball hit Rivaldo in the knees, but that didn't stop the Brazilian from clutching his face and rolling on the ground in pain. South Korean referee Kim Young-Joo fell for Rivaldo's theatrics and showed the Turk his second yellow card of the game. Unsal was automatically red carded and any chance Turkey had of a late comeback had ended. FIFA, after reviewing replays of the incident, fined Rivaldo $7,300 for his unsportsmanlike conduct. Rivaldo apologized, but seemed unfazed by the whole thing. "These things happen in football," he said.[27]

On June 8 in Seogwipo, Brazil tore apart China's defense with Roberto Carlos putting his team ahead, 1–0, after fifteen minutes. The Chinese, playing in their first-ever World Cup, were astutely coached by Milutinovic, who had pulled off miracles at the last four tournaments with Mexico, Costa Rica, United States, and Nigeria. Though he had coached all four of those countries to the knockout rounds, a loss to Brazil would mathematically eliminate his team. Rivaldo made it 2–0 in the 32nd minute. Then a Ronaldinho penalty kick in the first half of stoppage time and a goal from Ronaldo in the 55th minute put the *Selecao* on top, 4–0. Brazil won the group on June 13 in Suwon with a whopping 5–2 victory over Costa Rica with two goals from Ronaldo in the span of three minutes starting in the 10th minute. Edmilson, Rivaldo, and Junior added to team's tally.

If the Brazilians were for real, so was Turkey, who were playing in the finals for the first time since 1954. A narrow loss to Brazil, followed by a 1–1 tie against Costa Rica on June 9 in Incheon, and a convincing 3–0 rout of China four days later in Seoul, ensured their passage to the round of sixteen.

Group D, on the other hand, became fertile ground for upsets. South Korea stunned Poland, and 49,000 of its hometown fans, at Asiad Main Stadium in Busan with a 2–0 win. Goals from Hwang Seon-Hong in the 26th minute and Yoo Sang-Cheol in the 53rd minute lifted the team to victory. The upsets didn't end there.

The day after South Korea's shocking victory, the United States, coached by Arena, defeated Portugal, 3–2, at Suwon Stadium in Suwon. The Americans took the lead after four minutes with John O'Brien after goalkeeper Vitor Baia failed to clear a McBride header. The ball fell to O'Brien, who was standing just a few yards from the Portuguese goal, and buried it in the back of the net. The U.S. served up a one-two punch in the 29th minute when a Landon Donovan cross was deflected off defender Jorge Costa for the unfortunate own goal. The Americans were leading 2–0 and flying high. The Americans had more in store for Portugal's lackluster defense. Defender Tony Sanneh crossed the ball in the box for McBride with nine minutes left in the half, who put the ball past Baia with a diving header near the far post, bringing the score to 3–0. But the Portuguese ended the first half on a positive note. In the 39th minute, off a corner kick, O'Brien's clearance fell to the feet of Beto, who put the ball past goalkeeper Brad Friedel for the goal. Portugal pressured the U.S. defense in the second half, forcing the Americans to lock themselves down in their own half of the field. The visible problem was that Portugal's finishing was questionable after squandering several opportunities. Portugal was able to get a goal in the 71st minute, but only after Jeff Agoos put the ball into his own net. Unable to gain possession, the Americans were forced to soak up the pressure in the final nineteen minutes, but the Portuguese were unable to create any real chances over that time. The Americans were able to let the clock run out to record one of the biggest upsets in tournament history. Afterward, Arena told reporters at a news conference that the victory was "probably the biggest win in the modern era" for American soccer.[28] Now a win against South Korea would put the Americans through to the second round for the first time since 1994.

On June 10, the U.S. team squared off against South Korea in Daegu. The Americans picked up where they left off against Portugal, playing aggressively and moving the ball forward in the hopes of taking the lead. Arena's offensive-minded strategy paid off in the end. In the 24th minute, O'Brien's long pass from midfield found striker Clint Mathis near the edge of the South Korean box. Mathis unleashed a left-footed shot into the lower-left corner of the net for the lead. The South Koreans had their chance to tie the match when Agoos pulled down Hwang Sun-Hong in the penalty box. Friedel's spectacular save denied Lee Eul-Yong from the spot. Kim Nam-Il's follow-up attempt off a rebound went wide of the left post. The South Koreans applied more pressure in the second half despite Friedel's ability to save everything that was thrown at him. But South Korea got the equalizer with twelve minutes left to play when Lee Eul-Yong served up a free kick from midfield into the box where striker Ahn Jung-Hwan was able to out-jump the U.S. defense and head the ball past Friedel, who stood motionless on his line, and into the right side of the net.

South Korea could have won the game in the final minute, but Choi Yong-Soo's kick was too potent and the ball sailed high over the crossbar. The game ended 1–1. "It was a difficult game, but I am happy with the point," Arena told reporters.

Korea's fitness is outstanding. Most people, a month ago, would not have believed the United States would get four points in our first two matches. One hundred percent of the people would have said no. It was a very difficult opener with Portugal and a draw with Korea. It's a good feeling to get four points.[29]

The Americans were close to the round of sixteen, but had to defeat Poland, or hope in a Portugal loss against South Korea, to earn a trip to the next round.

Portugal, meanwhile, responded to its loss to the U.S. with a 4–0 rout of Poland under a driving rain in Jeonju. A Pauleta hat trick and goal from Rui Costa—who entered the contest in the second half—in the 88th minute capped off the win. The Polish defense could not keep up with Portugal's offensive onslaught. Portugal upped the tempo with every passing minute and it showed. Pauleta was unstoppable for stretches of the game, resulting in goals in the 14th, 65th, and 77th minutes.

Portugal looked like the team everyone had expected on the eve of the tournament. Now they still had the chance to save face and earn a berth to the next round. But Portugal fell short of that goal. South Korea, supported by a boisterous crowd of 50,000 in Incheon on June 14, proved too skillful and fast for Portugal. The South Koreans only needed a tie to move on to the round of sixteen, but it was obvious from the start that the co-hosts and their fans were in search of a win. South Korea's coach, Dutchman Guus Hiddink, had physically prepared his team for the rigors of the tournament. That peak physical conditioning proved pivotal against the disorganized Portuguese defense. Lee Young-pyo frustrated Figo for much of the first half, stealing the ball from him five times in the first twenty minutes. In another one-on-one duel, Lee outplayed the ball around Figo, leaving the Portuguese star on his butt. Figo was having a bad game and his teammates knew it. Joao Pinto took his anger out on Kim Tae-young in the 27th minute, tripping him to the turf. Argentine referee Angel Sanchez red carded Pinto for the rough challenge. A swarm of Portugal players protested the decision, but the card stood. The first half ended scoreless. After the game, Sanchez alleged that Pinto punched him in the stomach after showing him the red card.[30] FIFA suspended Pinto from all competitions for four months after reviewing the incident.

Portugal's antics continued in the second period. Beto's second yellow card in the 66th minute after tripping Lee brought Portugal down to nine players. South Korea wasted no time taking advantage of the numerical advantage. Four minutes after Beto was red carded, Park Ji Sung trapped the ball on his chest, beat midfielder Sérgio Conceicao with a deft flick and then volleyed a left-footed shot through Baia's open legs. Facing elimination, Portugal regrouped and attempted to mount a comeback. Figo's free kick attempt curled close to the post in the 75th minute, but went wide. Portugal wasted three other chances. The first missed chance came in the 85th minute when Nuno Gomes failed to make contact with the ball from a few yards out. Then Conceicao's shot was deflected off the inside of the post in the 89th minute with Lee Won-jae beaten. Finally, Conceicao's shot in the third minute of stoppage time was smothered by Lee, ending Portugal's dreams of advancing. South Korea had pulled off the 1–0 win and another upset.

At the same time, the United States lost to Poland, 3–1, in Daejeon. No matter. South Korea's shock result against Portugal allowed the Americans to advance to the round of sixteen. Poland, which was eliminated from the tournament before the game, was up 2–0 after five minutes. The U.S. team appeared to buckle under the remaining pressure and could not string together enough passes to create a decent scoring chance. The problem was exacerbated in the 36th minute when Agoos was replaced with DaMarcus Beasley after pulling a muscle. Poland didn't stop its attacking ways in the second period and went up 3–0 in the 66th minute when substitute Marcin Zewlakow scored after coming in a minute earlier. The Americans put hope in a South Korean win, but in the meantime, Friedel saved his second penalty kick of the tournament, outguessing Maciej Zurawski after Sanneh had brought down Pawel Kryszalowicz in the box. The U.S. team, knowing that South Korea was winning, scored a consolation goal thanks to Donovan in the 83rd minute. The Americans had lost, but more importantly, they had finished second in the group to South Korea and made it through to the final sixteen. "Nobody would have picked out the results in this group," Arena told reporters at the postgame news conference. "It was an unusual World Cup. There will be interesting results ahead of us."[31]

In Group E, Germany finished on top after manhandling Saudi Arabia, 8–0, on June 1 at the Sapporo Dome with striker Miroslav Klose recording a hat trick. After tying Ireland 1–1 four days later at Saitama Stadium thanks to another Klose goal, Germany defeated Cameroon, 2–0, on June 11 at Ecopa Stadium in Shizuoka. Against Cameroon, Klose scored his fifth goal of the tournament. However, the match degenerated into a physical free-for-all. Spanish referee Antonio López Nieto tried his best to maintain order, but his record sixteen yellow and two red cards turned the game the most ill-disciplined contest in tournament history. The bookings beat the previous mark of twelve recorded the same day in the Group A game between Senegal and Uruguay. The flurry of cards had also beaten the previous record of ten set at USA '94 between Mexico and Bulgaria.

Against Cameroon, the Germans had grown frustrated as the game wore on even though they were assured a spot to the next round. That's when tempers flared. With five minutes left to play in the first half, German defender Carsten Ramelow was red carded after collecting his second yellow card in the span of three minutes. The ejection didn't seem to hurt Germany. German goalkeeper Oliver Kahn, who had been busy stopping shots in the first half, was a spectator for much of the second period as the "Indomitable Lions" appeared unable to mount an attack. In the 73rd minute, Cameroon had a clear chance to tie the score, but Patrick Mboma's sliding shot, after the ball had rebounded off the post, was stopped by Kahn. López continued to pull out yellow cards out of his chest pocket faster than a Las Vegas poker dealer. The teams were finally level when Cameroon's Patrick Suffo was red carded in the 77th minute. At even strength, Germany continued to put on the pressure until Klose scored again. Germany won the game and a second-round berth.

Ireland, who had tied Cameroon 1–1 on June 1 at Niigata Stadium in Niigata and earned a second draw against Germany four days later, blanked Saudi Arabia, 3–0, on June 11 at International Stadium in Yokohama under a steady rain. The win allowed Ireland to finish second in the group and advance to round of sixteen. The Irish took the lead with Robbie Keane after seven minutes on a blistering shot off a cross from Gary Kelly. The Saudis attempted to tie the score, but Ireland coach Mick McCarthy had a few tricks up his sleeve. In the second half, McCarthy strengthened his attack after bringing in Niall Quinn for defender Ian Harte and moving Damien Duff over to the right. Keane was now in position to score once again, while the Saudi Arabians fell apart in the face of McCarthy's tactical changes. Gary Breen made it 2–0 in the 61st minute off a volley. The goal ensured passage to the next round. For good measure, Ireland added a third with three minutes left to play when Duff rifled a shot that found the back of net—Saudi goalkeeper Mohammed Al-Deayea could not handle the wet ball as it slipped through his fingers.

In Group F, widely referred to as the "Group of Death," Argentina defeated Nigeria, 1–0, at Kashima Stadium in Ibaraki. The South Americans faced an uphill battle from the start after defender Roberto Ayala pulled a muscle minutes before kickoff during pregame warmups. Without the defensive stalwart starting in the back, coach Marcelo Bielsa hoped for a productive performance from midfielder Juan Sebastian Veron. Unfortunately for Argentina, that never happened. Veron's game was full of sloppy passing, which allowed Nigeria's Jay-Jay Okocha to use his velocity to try to create scoring chances for his team. That didn't work either and both sides headed into halftime deadlocked at 0–0. In the second half, Bielsa made changes to his lineup, benching striker Claudio López in exchange for Kily González. But Nigeria's defense stood firm, swatting away every offensive assault Argentina made at their goal. Those missed chances included close-range headers from Juan Sorín and Mauricio Pochettino. Argentina finally cracked the Nigerian defense in the 63rd minute when Batistuta headed in the ball near the far post following a well-taken Veron corner for the 1–0 win.

On the same day, England and Sweden played to a 1–1 tie in Saitama. But England's thoughts quickly focused on the June 7 match against Argentina in Sapporo. In that game, England finally had the opportunity to exorcise the ghosts of Maradona and Beckham turned in an amazing performance and the only goal of the game. Beckham converted from the spot a minute before halftime after Michael Owen was tripped in the box by Pochettino. In the second half, England suffered under Argentina's offensive strain, conceding possession to the South Americans. A series of crosses and the stamina of Pablo Aimar sent Erikkson into a tizzy. Erikkson removed Owen, a striker, and replaced him with defender Wayne Bridge in the 80th minute. Luck was on England's side, however, with Argentina failing to convert in the dying minutes. England now led the group with four points, followed by Argentina and Sweden—2–1 winners over Nigeria on June 7 at Wing Stadium in Kobe—tied at three. The Nigerian team, which had zero points, was officially eliminated.

Argentina needed a victory over Sweden to assure itself a spot in the round of sixteen. But for Argentina, it wasn't meant to be, despite the fact that Bielsa's team was stacked with talent. Veron watched from the sidelines as Sweden and Argentina played to a 1–1 tie on June 12 at Miyagi Stadium in Miyagi. Sweden's defense did a magnificent job crowding the box and clearing nearly every ball. At various stages of the game, all eleven Swedish players were in the box defending, foiling every chance the Argentineans could put together in the opening forty-five minutes. Tensions were riding high on the Argentina bench. The game was tied 0–0 in the waning minutes of the first period with Argentina playing nowhere near its capabilities. Any chance by Bielsa to jumpstart his offense in the second half with the inclusion of Caniggia had to be scraped—especially after the veteran striker, who was sitting on the bench, got himself red carded just before halftime for shouting insults at Referee Ali Bujsaim of the United Arab Emirates. Bielsa went with Crespo in place of Batistuta in the 58th minute, but the change did nothing to ignite his attack. If anything, it hurt. Sweden took the lead a minute later when Anders Svensson's 25-yard free kick found the back of the net. Argentina now needed to score two goals in thirty minutes if it hoped to advance. Veron entered the game in the 63rd minute, but his presence did little for the two-time champions. Argentina tied the game in the 88th minute when Crespo's penalty kick was saved by goalkeeper Magnus Hedman, but the Argentine striker was able to grab his own rebound and slam it in the net. The goal had come too late and the contest ended 1–1. That result, coupled with England's scoreless tie against Nigeria at Nagai Stadium in Osaka, allowed Sweden to win the group on goal differential. England finished second. Argentina was out of the tournament.

Group G featured some of the biggest refereeing blunders ever seen at a World Cup. The Italians, known as slow starters, had to get past their group opponents Ecuador, Croatia, and Mexico and bad calls from the referees to get into the round of sixteen. The *Azzurri* opened with a 2–0 victory over Ecuador on June 3 in Sapparo. Two goals from Vieri crushed Ecuador's hopes of earning a win in its first World Cup game ever. Mexico's 1–0 win over Croatia on the same day at Stadium Big Swan in Niigata was highlighted by Cuauhtémoc Blanco's game-winner off a penalty kick in the 60th minute.

Italy's second game versus Croatia did not go so well for the *Azzurri*. The Italians were dealt a 2–1 loss thanks to two bad calls from English referee Graham Poll. To be fair, Poll wasn't the only one to blame. Danish assistant referee Jens Larsen raised his flag on two occasions, calling back goals that were not only legitimate, but would have won Italy the game. Before those incidents, things had looked up for the *Azzurri*. Vieri scored a goal that was called back in the 50th minute after Larsen raised his flag, ruling him offside. TV replays showed that Vieri was clearly onside. That didn't stop Vieri from trying again. Five minutes later, he put Italy in front with a header off a cross by Cristiano Doni in the 55th minute. Italy's Coach Giovanni Trappatoni ordered that his team shut down the Croatian defense, like it had done so effectively at past tournaments, but the Croatians were not going to give up so easily. Croatia coach Mirko Jozic replaced midfielder Davor Vugrinec with striker Ivica Olic in the 57th minute. The move changed the course of the game. Sixteen minutes after he had come on, Olic headed the ball into the goal to make it 1–1. Italy no longer looked in control. Croatia exploited Italy's sudden lapse in concentration and took the lead three minutes later. Milan Rapajic's long kick was blocked by defender Marco Materazzi, who had replaced Alessandro Nesta following an injury in the 24th minute. But Materazzi's deflection allowed the ball to sail into his own net past a stunned, and motionless, goalkeeper Gianluigi Buffon. Croatia was ahead, 2–1.

The Italians, staring at the prospect of an unexpected loss, tried to tie the score, but Francesco Totti's attempted free kick hit the post. The *Azzurri* thought they had managed to snag a point in the waning minutes after Materazzi's long ball pass rolled forward, untouched, and past goalkeeper Stipe Pletikosa. But Larsen once again raised his flag, claiming striker Filippo Inzaghi, who was in the box, had fouled defender Josip Simunic as the ball entered the goal. The contact appeared minimal, but Poll agreed. "For some reason, the referee and the linesman really didn't like us that day," recalled Vieri. "My goal should have stood. I really think it's the referee's job to correct the linesman. I really think we could have won the game. We were unlucky. That loss set the tone for us for the rest of the World Cup."[32]

The Italians had suffered a 2–1 loss to Croatia and now needed a miracle in the final game against Mexico, 2–1 winners over Ecuador on June 9 in Miyagi, to advance. On June 13, Italy tied Mexico, 1–1, in Oita thanks to a goal from Alessandro Del Piero with five minutes left to play. The tie allowed Mexico to win the group and Italy to advance as the second-place team only because Ecuador upset Croatia, 1–0, simultaneously in Yokohama. "We played very well the entire game. We certainly didn't deserve a loss against Mexico," said defender Gianluca

*Christian Vieri is one of Italy's all-time leading World Cup scorers (Credit: Courtesy of the author).*

Zambrotta. "I think we worked hard to score and we were rewarded in the final minutes."[33]

Group H produced another series of stunning results when co-host Japan bid *sayonara* to mediocrity after spending four years preparing for the finals. Winners of the 2000 Asian Cup and second place at the Confederations Cup a year later, losing to France 1–0 in the final, Japanese soccer was slowly emerging as a world power. The national team's fortunes were similar to those of the United States, growing largely out of the creation in 1993 of the country's first pro league. Though Japan was not expected to lift the World Cup, the expertise of French-born coach Philippe Troussier gave momentum to a young and ambitious squad that had set its sights on showing everyone—including its own people—that it could compete with the rest of the world. Troussier was named coach in September 1998 and the Japanese Football Association was at first wary of giving him much power. In fact, Troussier was criticized for being power-hungry when it came to scheduling games and choosing players. The criticisms came to an end once Troussier started delivering results. Japan's desire to be a soccer power dated back to 1986 after the team failed to qualify for the World Cup finals.

The Land of the Rising Sun, known more for its love of baseball, enacted a revolutionary program aimed at developing young players. Many Japanese officials openly joked at the time that the only way their team would qualify for the World Cup finals was as hosts. But the team played at France '98, setting the stage for this World Cup. The engine the country needed to jumpstart the development of players was the J-League—much like USA '94 did for MLS—and suddenly world-class players were flooding into the country. Clubs rushed to build state-of-the-art training facilities. One of them, the J-Village in the city of Fukushima, became a national-team training camp where school-age players could develop their skills. The focus on cultivating homegrown talent had an immediate impact. In 1993, at home, Japan's Under-17 team reached the quarterfinals of the World Youth Championships. In 1999, Japan lost in the final of the World Under-20 tournament. A year later, the team was eliminated in the quarterfinals at the Summer Olympics after losing to the United States on penalty kicks. Some Japanese players have even moved abroad. Striker Hidetoshi Nakata became the first Japanese-born player to win Italy's Serie A title with AS Roma in 2000.

At the World Cup, Troussier's men continued to shine. The team tied Belgium 1–1 on June 4 in Saitama and beat Russia 1–0 five days later in Yokohama to lead the group standings. Japan was helped by the fervor of the crowds, unleashing a wave of nationalism never before seen. In its last group game against Tunisia on June 14 in Osaka, Japan won again, this time 2–0, on goals from second-half substitute Hiroaki Morishima in the 48th minute and Nakata fifteen minutes from the end. Japan not only advanced, but had also won the group. The victory set off wild celebrations among the 45,000 fans inside Nagai Stadium—and across the country. "We have written a new page in Japanese football history," Troussier said, "and the World Cup is not over yet."[34] Belgium, thanks to a 3–2 victory against Russia on June 14 at Ecopa Stadium in Shizuoza, finished in second place ahead of the Russians and Tunisians.

## Round Two: The Sixteen Teams

The stage was finally set for the round of sixteen. Though the tournament had featured a number of upsets, the knockout phase had gotten off to a predictable start when Germany defeated Paraguay, 1–0, in Seogwipo. Oliver Neuville scored with two minutes left in the game to notch the win. The match, one of the most boring so far at the competition, seemed to be heading hopelessly into overtime until the German striker blasted a shot past Chilavert off a cross from his Bayer Leverkusen teammate Bernd Schneider. Germany's win came as little surprise—even though the three-time champions did not get a shot on goal in the first half—but what did shock FIFA and the organizers was the small turnout. Only 25,176 spectators showed up at Jeju Stadium, way short of the 42,000 capacity. The poor attendance was in part due to the venue's location (on Jeju Island, which required a plane ride from Seoul) so that many fans never bothered to buy tickets. Hours before kickoff, organizers began giving tickets to local schoolchildren and their families, but that wasn't enough to fill the stadium.

Five hours later, England cruised to a 3–0 victory over Denmark in Niigata, and the English wasting no time showing the Danes who was the better team that evening. After five minutes, a poor clearance from Denmark's Martin Laursen allowed Beckham to gain control of the ball and direct it into the box from the left side. Rio Ferdinand headed the ball directly at goalkeeper Thomas Sorensen, who played with English club Sunderland. The Danish goalkeeper tried to hang on to the ball, but dropped it past the line for the goal. Owen made it 2–0 in the 22nd minute as his shot from six yards out beat Sorensen for the second time. Rain started to fall midway through the second half, but that didn't stop England from scoring a third, and final, goal. A poor clearance from Niclas Jensen allowed Beckham, ever the opportunist, to steal the loose ball and dish it off to striker Emile Heskey, whose one-time shot squeaked into the net off Sorensen's left elbow.

On June 16, Senegal pulled the first shocking result of the knockout round in Oita, downing Sweden, 2–1, in overtime when Henri Camara scored a "Golden Goal" in the 103rd minute. Camara had scored in the 37th minute to tie the score, after Sweden had taken the lead with Larsson after eleven minutes. On the same day, Spain ousted Ireland 4–3 after penalty kicks in Suwon. The match had ended tied at 1–1. In the shootout, Spain goalkeeper Iker Casillas emerged as the hero when he saved David Connolly's and Kevin Kilbane's shots, before Mendieta bagged the winner. The Spanish team, who had broken the hearts of its fans so many times before at the World Cup, was in the final eight and had its sights set on the trophy.

The United States started the round of sixteen on June 17 in Jeonju against a very familiar opponent: Mexico. The all-CONCACAF match-up was expected to be thrilling given the bad blood that had developed between the neighboring countries over the last decade. The Mexicans put pressure on the American backline from the start, but it was the Americans who took the lead. Against the run of play, Reyna ran the ball down the right flank and crossed it to striker Josh Wolff. Wolff then passed the ball to McBride, which gave him just enough space to release a wicked shot that beat goalkeeper Oscar Perez for the 1–0 lead after just eight minutes. The Mexicans dominated possession after the goal and nearly tied the score on a number of occasions, but Friedel was having another top-notch performance. The first half ended with the U.S. team in the lead.

The *Tricolores* upped the ante in the second half, but that much-needed goal never arrived. In the 52nd minute, a free kick from Braulio Luna at the corner of the U.S. box had Friedel scrambling to push it over the crossbar and out for a corner. The Americans played tough defensively, using the counterattack to their advantage. The U.S. players once again scored against the run of play in the 65th minute when a run and cross from Eddie Lewis found Donovan near the far post. Donovan coolly headed the ball past Perez for the 2–0 lead to seal the win. Mexico attempted a comeback in the final twenty minutes, but Friedel was able to thwart those efforts. The Americans emerged victorious and—to the shock of the soccer world—had reached the quarterfinals. "There has been a lot of bad blood over the years [against Mexico]," Arena said at a news conference after the game, "but when the game is over, we're friends again. Mexico is a great team and I'm proud of my guys. It is a great day for U.S. soccer."[35]

U.S. striker Brian McBride dribbles the ball against Mexico during the 2002 World Cup (Credit: EMPICS).

The United States had not earned everyone's respect. Critics of Arena's team—possibly uncomfortable with them knocking off some of the planet's more established soccer powers—had called them a lucky team. But Arena didn't let the skeptics get to him. He knew that the U.S. team had outclassed Portugal in the first round and had now successfully eliminated rivals Mexico in the elimination round. "I don't know if we were lucky," Arena said. "We beat the winner of the group with Italy."[36] Back in the United States, soccer fever was growing despite the fact the games aired live in the wee hours of the night. For the first time since 1930, the United States looked like a World Cup contender.

On the Japan side of the bracket, Brazil took on Belgium in Kobe. The game was another example of the increasingly poor officiating that marred the tournament. The Brazilians were extremely lucky to get the victory after Jamaican referee Peter Prendergast committed a number of mistakes. In the 36th minute, Marc Wilmots jumped in the air over Brazilian defender Roque Junior to head Belgian Jacky Peeters's cross past goalkeeper Marco, but Prendergast disallowed the goal. Prendergast argued that Wilmots had pushed Roque Junior, but subsequent TV replays showed that he had made a bad call. Wilmots later said Prendergast had admitted to him at halftime that he had made a mistake. The *Selecao*, knowing that they had been the recipient of a favorable call, used the second half to put the game away. In the 67th minute, Ronaldinho floated the ball across the penalty box to Rivaldo, who, initially with his back to the ball, controlled it on his chest and sent a spectacular volley off his left foot for the goal and the lead. The Brazilians reinforced their lead twenty minutes later when substitute Kleberson ran the ball down the right flank, then put a pass in the path of Ronaldo who side-footed it past goalkeeper Geert De Vlieger for the 2-0 score. Brazil had showed some signs of offensive brilliance with its two goals, but had shown too many weaknesses on defense and in the midfield. Up next for the holders was a quarterfinal clash versus England. For Brazil, there would be no more room for mistakes.

On June 18, Japan's fairytale tournament, and all the enthusiasm that had carried the team to the knockout round, came to an end in Miyagi. Turkey scored the game's only goal in the 12th minute when Unit Davala rose above the Japanese defense to head the ball into the net. Perhaps Troussier's mistake was changing his lineup before the start of the game, dumping strikers Atsushi Yanagisawa and Takayuki Suzuki and going with Akinori Nishizawa as a sole forward. That tactic stifled the Japanese attack and didn't give them the firepower they needed to put Turkey away in the early going. Even in defeat, Troussier expressed optimism, saying, "We have shown with our youth system, dynamism and ambition that we can play with the best."[37]

While the Japanese team was gracious in defeat, the South Korean team was hoping to knock off Italy in Daejeon. What may have seemed like an impossible task before the match became reality after bad refereeing decisions once again dogged the *Azzurri*. The red-clad crowd of 39,000 South Korean fans transformed Daejeon Stadium into one of the most hostile places ever for an opponent. Trappatoni knew that relying on the *catenaccio* would be risky and decided to go with a more offensive-minded formation with Del Piero playing alongside Vieri. Totti was behind them in the role of playmaker and was expected to move the ball upfield for his teammates. The experiment appeared to work and the *Azzurri* took the lead after eighteen minutes when Vieri headed in a Totti corner kick. What happened after the goal is what ultimately did the Italians in. Up 1–0, Del Piero moved back into the midfield with Vieri operating as a sole striker. Alongside Del Piero was the gritty Gennaro Gattuso, whose job it was to neutralize the South Koreans in the midfield. The hosts were not prepared to surrender. Despite Buffon's save on Ahn Jung-Hwan's penalty kick in the first half, Hiddink's team refused to give up. The Italians, who were missing Nesta and Cannavaro because of injuries, were trying not to let the ghosts of 1966 get to them. The South Korean fans had other plans.

The South Korean players grew bolder as the crowd cheered their every pass. The fans even held up posters with the dreaded message "Remember 1966?" And even though none of the Italian players had been born when North Korea shocked Italy 1–0 in England, the players were well aware of Italy's most humiliating loss ever at a the World Cup. To be reminded of it—again—and allowing that thirty-six-year-old loss to get to them somehow showed how mentally weak the Italians were over the course of the game. But Italy's biggest mistake was taking a defensive posture. The *catenaccio*, which had been effective in the past, would only help the South Koreans. Hiddink had taught his side not only confidence, but immense physical stamina. Those had been South Korea's ingredients to success.

The South Koreans made the Italians pay for a rare defensive lapse in the 88th minute. A cross from the right side bounced off the legs of defender Christian Panucci, putting the loose ball into the path of Seol Ki-hyeon, who drilled it past Buffon for the 1–1 equalizer. A minute later, Vieri had the chance to put the game away, but the Inter Milan striker put the ball over the crossbar from just six yards out. The game was headed to overtime. The South Koreans had defied the doubters in the opening round. Now, they were poised to do it again in the knockout stage. In extra time, South Korea continued to play with its typical upbeat tempo as the Italians struggled to keep up. The game's chubby referee, Ecuadorian Byron Moreno, who rarely made a call in Italy's favor, became the game's protagonist. He red carded Totti thirteen minutes into overtime after giving him a second yellow on the night for diving in the box. TV replays showed that the decision was too harsh, but Totti's argument that he should get a penalty kick helped earn him his second yellow. Trappatoni was livid on the sidelines, complaining and gesturing to the FIFA officials near his bench that the call was bogus. Even after Totti was sent off, the Italians did not give up. Gattuso came close to netting the winner, but his attempt was smothered by goalkeeper Lee Woon-jae.

The game then became a live flashback reminder of the 1966 game—with three minutes left in overtime, South Korea pulled off the biggest upset of the tournament. Ahn, who played with Serie A team Perugia, beat Maldini in the air for the ball and headed it past a diving Buffon for the winner. The crowd erupted into cheers as Ahn celebrated the goal with his teammates. "That was the worst loss of my life," said Maldini. "I was totally exhausted. We weren't prepared to lose, but we did."[38] Like in 1966, the Italians went home humiliated by a Korean team. Hiddink's team was in the quarterfinals.

The Italians were disappointed with the outcome, blaming the loss not on their poor finishing, but Moreno. Trappatoni openly complained that the referee had favored the home team. "Korea definitely had a few advantages," Trappatoni said at a news conference afterward. "I don't understand why we had to become a victim of bad decision-making. I think the winner should have been Italy."[39] A day after the loss, Perugia dumped Ahn, saying he had ruined Italian soccer. Not too many people at the tournament sympathized with Italy's version of events. In reality, the conspiracy theories put forward by the Italian press in the days following the loss were an excuse to mask Trappatoni's inept tactics and failure to field a more attacking squad. The whining had reached a crescendo, but back in South Korea, the critics' dissent had been drowned out by a country swept by World Cup fever and the realistic belief that their team could reach the final. In the days following the loss, FIFA's website was inundated with emails from angry Italian fans complaining of Moreno's refereeing.

## Quarterfinal Match-Ups

The quarterfinals included four teams—South Korea, United States, Senegal, and Turkey—that few had predicted would get this far. The biggest clash of the round took place June 21 and pitted Brazil against England in Shizuoka. Erikkson's team was aware that it had to apply lots of offensive pressure on Brazil from the start or risk losing the game. Owen did just that, scoring in the 23rd minute after faking a hard shot that forced Marcos to fall to the ground. The England striker then put the ball in the goal with ease to Marcos's right for the 1–0 lead. England defended the advantage as defenders Rio Ferdinand and Sol Campbell kept Ronaldinho and Rivaldo from scoring. But that didn't last long. In the first half of stoppage time, Brazil equalized when Ronaldinho's run down the middle forced the English defense to come apart. Ronaldinho's pass to Rivaldo on the right allowed him to place the ball past Seaman. Building on the 1–1 score, Brazil won the match in the second half on a rocket from Ronaldinho. The Brazilians won a free kick 30 yards from the England goal after midfielder Paul Scholes fouled Kleberson. The distance seemed even too much for Ronaldinho, but that didn't stop him from putting all the power he could on the ball, lofting it over the England wall and hitting the net after hitting the underside of the crossbar.

In the second game of the day, the U.S. was aiming to reach the World Cup semifinals for the first time since 1930. In order to achieve that, the Americans had to overcome Germany in Ulsan. Arena knew defeating Germany would not be easy, but after overcoming Mexico, the team was confident a victory was not impossible. Another upset could happen. It almost did. The Americans entered the game with nothing to lose, having exceeded expectations. The win against Mexico landed Donovan on the cover of *Sports Illustrated*, relegating the Los Angeles Lakers and Detroit Red Wings—winners of the NBA Championship and Stanley Cup, respectively—to the inside pages. Germany, meanwhile, was aiming to make its tenth appearance ever at a World Cup semifinals. The Germans, who had been criticized back home by the national media for their inability to dominate games, suffered a barrage of U.S. attacks in the first half. In the 17th minute, a dazzling solo run by Donovan down the right side ended with a curling shot that was tipped away by Oliver Kahn. Thirteen minutes later, Donovan was once again scampered down the field, beating the German offside trap following a pass from Claudio Reyna, but Kahn was again there to block the shot. While the Germans threatened from set pieces, it was the Americans who came close to scoring again. McBride broke down the left flank in the 36th minute, feeding a pass to Eddie Lewis, whose shot was too weak, and Kahn was there to make the save. The Germans did not give up. Against the run of play, Ballack headed the ball past Friedel in the 39th minute off an in-swinging corner by Christian Ziege from the right side to take a 1–0 lead.

The Americans continued to test Kahn in the second period, but the German goalkeeper was unbeatable between the posts. The U.S. team was able to score in the 50th minute, but Scottish referee Hugh Dallas made a bad call after a shot by defender Gregg Berhalter crossed the line. Cheers erupted among the 38,000 fans inside Munsu Cup Stadium, but the shot was then deflected by Kahn, ricocheting off the forearm of German defender Torsten Frings and back toward the German goalkeeper. Berhalter looked at the referee, thinking it was a handball, which if called by Dallas, would have resulted in a penalty kick. The call never came, though some of the players argued that it should have been a goal because the ball had initially crossed the line. TV replays supported that argument. Another game had been marred by a bad call.

The Americans persevered. Donovan had another fine chance in the 55th minute following a clever one-two with McBride, but his shot was low and Kahn once again smothered the shot. The Americans tried everything, but the stingy German defense was too tough to beat. The game proved entertaining but unproductive for the U.S. players. It wasn't until the final minute when a Mathis cross from the right was headed by Sanneh toward Kahn, but the ball hit the side netting. The Americans were unlucky, even against a German team not in top form, to lose, 1–0. Germany may have gotten the win, but the crowd cheered for the Americans. "We were pretty confident that we could pressure them and create some chances," Arena said at a postgame news conference.

> I think we did that. The difference in the game, besides the goal by Ballack, was Kahn. He came up with some great saves and kept them in the match in the early going, and he came up with some saves in the second half that kept us off the board.[40]

Arena's team had proven that the United States could compete with the world's best teams, erasing the painful memory of their last-place finish four years earlier in France. "I'm really proud of our team," Arena said. "We were a bit unlucky, because if we got a break or two, we could have been in the semifinals of the World Cup."[41]

On June 22, South Korea faced Spain in Gwangju, trying to topple another European soccer power and keep the miracle alive. Hiddink's team did just that, outlasting Spain 5–3 on penalty kicks after playing to a scoreless tie. The result, however, was once again conditioned by controversial officiating. This time it was Egyptian referee Gamal Al-Ghandour. After having two Spanish goals called back in regulation, Al-Ghandour nullified a third in overtime. The first officiating error occurred in the 43rd minute when Morientes headed the ball into the goal, but at that very moment the referee whistled Enrique Romero, who had provided the pass, offside. In the fourth minute of the second half, Al-Ghandour disallowed another goal that had been headed in, this time by Ivan Helguera, noting that he had tugged on the jersey of a South Korean player. Both of those calls could be debated. The third call against Spain, however, could not.

The goal that could have won the game for Spain a minute into extra time became another opportunity for Al-Ghandour to a make the most scandalous call of the game. Midfielder Sanchez Joaquin strode past the South Korean defense near the right end line, then crossing the ball to the middle where Morientes, once again, headed the ball into the net. Al-Ghandour disallowed the goal because his assistant had raised his flag to signal that the ball had been dribbled over the end line before Joaquin crossed it. TV replays later showed that the ball was in play before the pass. The game went to penalty kicks and Joaquin suffered more bad luck in the shootout when his kick, Spain's fourth, was saved. The South Koreans converted all five of their kicks to pull off another upset. South Korea was in the semifinals thanks to Hiddink's master coaching and some help from the refs.

In the last quarterfinal match-up, and the second game of the day, in Osaka, Senegal—the first African country to reach the quarterfinals since Cameroon in 1990—saw its dreams of advancing to the semifinals shattered by Turkey. The Europeans won, 1–0, on a "Golden Goal" by Ilhan Mansiz just four minutes into overtime. Mansiz had entered the game in the 67th minute for ineffective striker Hakan Sukur. The Turks were in the World Cup semifinals for the first time, setting up what was to become an epic match against Brazil.

## Semifinals

The first semifinal pitted South Korea against Germany on June 25. The controversial refereeing decisions that had helped carry South Korea into the semifinals fueled conspiracy theories—particularly in Italy and Spain—that FIFA had gone out of its way to ensure that the co-hosts went far in the competition. True, South Korea's appearance in the semifinals ensured interest in the tournament continued into the later rounds, but it was also true that Hiddink had put together a tough and experienced team. The conspiracy theories did nothing to dampen the enthusiasm of the South Korean people, who embraced the game like never before. In Seoul, Germany ended the South Korean party, defeating the co-hosts, 1–0, to reach the final. Ballack's goal on the counterattack with fifteen minutes left to play ended South Korean hopes of reaching the final. The victory also proved costly as Ballack picked up his second card of the tournament, which ruled him out for the final.

The following day, Brazil reached the final, edging out Turkey, 1–0, in Saitama. Ronaldo's goal in the 49th minute—his sixth of the tournament—put the *Selecao* in the final for the seventh time in tournament history.

A final featuring Brazil and Germany turned out to be quite a surprise. The tournament had been characterized by a group of emerging nations having their way with the game's established powers. In the end, none of the game's newcomers were able to reach the final. In the third-place game played on June 29 in Daegu, Turkey outlasted South Korea, 3–2. Hakan Suker's goal—recorded 10.8 seconds after the opening kickoff—was the fastest goal ever scored at any World Cup. The final score aside, both countries had plenty of reasons to be proud. South Korea became the first Asian country to reach the semifinals, while Turkey could legitimately call itself an emerging European soccer power.

## The Final

The final on June 30 in Yokohama was billed as a contrast in styles: Brazilian flair versus German pragmatism. Although the teams had won seven World Cups between them, Germany and Brazil had never before met in a final. Many expected Brazil to do all the attacking with Germany soaking up the pressure and expected to use the counterattack. It turned out to be the other way around. The Germans dominated possession—even though Ballack was sitting the game out—and moved the ball across the field with the style and grace that had been more typical of the Brazilians at the tournament. However, it was the Brazilians who created more scoring chances in the opening half. Brazil had a clear chance to take the lead in the waning seconds of the first period when Kleberson fired off a shot that bounced off the crossbar. Germany's only attempt on goal had come four minutes earlier when Neuville's cracking shot flew high over the crossbar. The second half was all Brazil. Ronaldo had three clear chances to give Brazil the lead, but his first shot went wide of the net and the other two

*Cafu lifts the World Cup trophy in 2002 following Brazil's 2–0 victory over Germany in the final (Credit: Empics).*

were thwarted by Kahn. The German goalkeeper had come up with an outstanding foot save in the first half of stoppage time following a Ronaldo shot.

The Brazilians were determined to take the lead; they did, in the 67th minute. Ronaldo stripped Dietmar Hamann of the ball and made a quick pass to Rivaldo who cracked a low, driving shot toward the net. Kahn failed to hold on to the ball, allowing it to spill back into play where a charging Ronaldo grabbed the rebound and converted for the 1–0 lead. The Brazilians scored again twelve minutes later when Rivaldo sent a right-wing cross from Kleberson into Ronaldo's path. The Brazilian grabbed possession, then gracefully slipped it past Kahn to make it 2–0. The outcome was Ronaldo's revenge for a humiliating 3–0 loss to France in the 1998 final four years earlier. Ronaldo had clearly been the best player at the tournament, scoring eight goals in seven games to win the Golden Boot award as top scorer—the best tally at a tournament since Muller in 1970. Kahn had been magnificent in goal scoring, but it hadn't been enough to carry his team to victory. Cafu accepted the World Cup trophy amid a snowstorm of confetti as his teammates partied on the field. Brazil had its fifth World Cup title.

**NOTES**

1. News Conference, Zurich, July 4, 1988.
2. Interview, April 13, 1996.
3. Interview, April 13, 1996.
4. Jere Longman, "A Controversial World Cup Coach Keeps Them Guessing," *The New York Times*, May 1, 1994, Section 8, Page 13.
5. News conference, Las Vegas, December 18, 1993.
6. News conference, New Haven, Conn., June 11, 1994.
7. Personal interview, June 26, 1997.
8. Personal interview, April 8, 2006.
9. News conference, Buenos Aires, June 1, 1994.
10. News conference, Dallas, July 3, 1994.
11. Personal interview, May 16, 2002.
12. News conference, East Rutherford, N.J., June 18, 1994.
13. News conference, Boston, July 5, 1994.
14. Personal interview, July 31, 2005.
15. News conference, New York, July 15, 1994.
16. Personal interview, April 8, 2006.

17. Personal interview, June 26, 1997.

18. News conference, Chicago, June 17, 1994.

19. Interview, East Rutherford, N.J., August 1, 1995.

20. Press release, U.S. Soccer, October 27, 1998.

21. John Haydon, "Sampson Cites Reasons for Bad Cup Showing," *The Washington Times*, C8.

22. Haydon, "Sampson Cites Reasons."

23. Interview, August 12, 2006.

24. Press release, Nike Italia, July 13, 1998.

25. Interview, April 1, 2006.

26. Interview, August 8, 2002.

27. Gavin Hamilton, "Spot on Rivaldo Spoils His Cards," *World Soccer*, July 2002, 34.

28. News conference, Suwon, South Korea, June 5, 2002.

29. News conference, Daegu, South Korea, June 10, 2002.

30. Gavin Hamilton, "Figo and Co. Humbled by Vibrant Hosts," *World Soccer*, July 2002, 40.

31. News conference, Daejeon, South Korea, June 14, 2002.

32. Interview, July 31, 2005.

33. Interview, August 12, 2006.

34. Mike Plastow, "Party Gets into Full Swing," *World Soccer*, July 2002, 56.

35. News conference, Jeonju, South Korea, June 17, 2002.

36. News conference, Jeonju, South Korea, June 17, 2002.

37. Mike Plastow, "Troussier's Tactics Go Astray," *World Soccer*, July 2002, 64.

38. Interview, July 31, 2005.

39. News conference, Daejeon, South Korea, June 18, 2002.

40. News conference, Ulsan, South Korea, June 21, 2002.

41. News conference, Ulsan, South Korea, June 21, 2002.

# 8

# "FOUR"-ZA ITALIA!

## 2006

The World Cup returned to Germany, but the decision wasn't without controversy. The decision in July 2000 to award the tournament to the Germans came after a series of high-pressuring lobbying tactics. On July 3, 2000, three days before FIFA's twenty-four-member executive committee would vote, Brazil withdrew its bid, leaving only Germany, South Africa, England, and Morocco in the mix. Many were predicting a South African victory, which would mark the first time that a World Cup would be held in Africa. Asia's four members hinted that they planned to vote for Germany, making the heavily favored South African and German bids tied, 11–11, with two votes still up in the air. The swing votes belonged to Scotsman David Will and Oceania president Charlie Dempsey.

## FIFA Votes on 2006 Location

The vote was held on July 6, 2000, in Zurich. The bid that garnered the most votes would be awarded the tournament. The bid with the fewest votes would be eliminated after each round. After the first round, Germany led with 10 votes, South Africa 6, England 5, and Morocco 3. The North Africans, who had put together failed bids in 1994 and 1998, were out. The second round saw Germany and South Africa tied with 11 votes apiece and England with only 2. England, who had only hosted the finals once, was eliminated. Round three saw Germany win the right to host the tournament with Germany 12 votes, South Africa 11, and one abstention. The single non-vote by Dempsey guaranteed that the World Cup would return to Europe. A 12–12 vote would have been a victory for South Africa since FIFA President Jospeh "Sepp" Blatter, an open supporter of South Africa's bid, would have cast the tie-breaking ballot. Blatter, who had been elected FIFA boss in 2002 after Havelange retired, had spearheaded the move to move the World Cup outside of Europe and South America.

Dempsey later said he abstained because a vote for either bid would have hurt Oceania's eleven members, although he never explained why that would be the case. There had been an understanding that Dempsey would vote for South Africa, but the intense lobbying on the part of the Germans had gotten to him. Dempsey admitted he had originally supported England's bid, but refused to vote in the final ballot after they were eliminated. Amid all the speculation over why Dempsey had abstained, there was another wrinkle: a German magazine, *Titanic*, sent a hoax latter to eight FIFA executive members the morning of the vote, asking FIFA members to award the finals to Germany. The letters, faxed to the officials at their Zurich hotel and placed under their doors, promised gifts in return for their votes. Some of those "gifts" included a smoked ham and a cuckoo clock. None of the delegates who received the fake letter, which included Dempsey, called the phone number printed on them.

The official announcement, made in front of the 500 reporters gathered inside Messe Congress Hall on July 6, brought with it shock and cheers. Blatter walked up to the podium and proclaimed "Deutschland" the winner. The head of Germany's bid, the legendary Beckenbauer, was hailed a hero back home. His two-year lobbying effort to promote the bid had paid off.

South Africa would have to wait until May 2004 when they were awarded the right to host the 2010 finals over Morocco, Libya, and Egypt after FIFA only accepted bids from African nations.

## Marketing and Broadcasting Deals

In the United States, the World Cup had finally become a big deal with networks paying millions to broadcast the tournament. Calling it the "biggest TV deal in a single country in FIFA's history," the sport's world governing body announced in November 2005 that a $425 million deal was reached to broadcast games in the United States through 2014.[1] Under the agreement, the 2006, 2010, and 2014 World Cups, the 2007 and 2011 Women's World Cups, and the 2009 and 2013 Confederations Cups would be broadcast in English by Disney-owned ABC and ESPN and in Spanish by Univision. In a joint bid, ABC/ESPN paid $100 million for the rights, while Univision doled out $325 million for the Spanish-language rights. In a news release, FIFA said the two networks had been

> awarded the TV rights to all FIFA events for the U.S. territory from 2007 to 2014, including the two FIFA World Cup final competitions within this period. This impressive new agreement covers a wide range of media categories, including multimedia broadband Internet and mobile telephony.[2]

Only four years earlier, there had been a real possibility that only Spanish-language broadcasts of the 2002 World Cup would be available in this country. On that occasion, Soccer United Marketing (SUM), MLS's marketing arm, paid $40 million for the U.S. English-language rights to the 2002 and 2006 World Cups. Under the pact, SUM had actually purchased the rights from German media giant Kirch, which was near bankruptcy when the deal was struck. SUM then entered into the revenue-sharing agreement with ABC/ESPN to ensure the games would be broadcast.

Germany '06 got off the ground amid marketing controversy as well. Budweiser, the official beer of the World Cup, agreed not to advertise as "Bud" because another German brewer, Bitburger, protested that the word "Bud" sounded too much like its nickname, "Bit." Anheuser-Busch, which owns Budweiser, had paid $40 million to be one of the tournament's fifteen official sponsors. Adding to the dispute was Germany's resentment that an American company had the exclusive rights to sell beer inside stadiums in a country that had invented beer. Budweiser agreed to allow Bitburger to sell its beer at World Cup sites, albeit in unmarked plastic cups. Budweiser would sell its own beer in cups that has its logo emblazoned across it. But the marketing wars didn't end there. Adidas, the tournament's official sponsor, splashed its three-stripes logo all over Germany. But Nike, which was the official sponsor of the Brazil and U.S. teams among others, didn't give up without a fight. The squabble between the sportswear giants reached a crescendo on the eve of the tournament, with Nike plastering its swoosh logo everywhere it could—an amazing feat since the American company had never shown any real interest in soccer until the 1994 World Cup—angering the German sportswear giant. Adidas called on FIFA to crack down on any company who would do anything to drag attention away from Adidas' role as an official sponsor. Another German brand, Puma, also entered the fray. If Nike sponsored eight national teams, and Adidas six, then Puma could boast twelve teams on its side outfitted by them, including Italy. Although Adidas claimed it outfitted more likely winners—including Germany, France, and Spain—in the end, Puma would have the last laugh when it came to who was dressing a winning team.

## Group Play

The World Cup draw took place on December 9, 2005, in Leipzig with 198 entrants amid the usual pageantry reserved for such FIFA events. Model Heidi Klum and Pelé were on hand as the eight groups were put together. Germany, England, Argentina, Mexico, Italy, Brazil, France, and Spain were the seeded teams and would not meet in the first round. Here were the results:

Group A: Germany, Poland, Ecuador, and Costa Rica
Group B: England, Sweden, Paraguay, and Trinidad and Tobago
Group C: Argentina, Holland, Serbia and Montenegro, and the Ivory Coast
Group D: Mexico, Portugal, Angola, and Iran
Group E: Italy, Czech Republic, Ghana, and the United States
Group F: Brazil, Croatia, Australia, and Japan
Group G: France, Switzerland, South Korea, and Togo
Group H: Spain, Ukraine, Tunisia, and Saudi Arabia

Germany opened the tournament on June 9 at Allianz Arena in Munich against Costa Rica. Klose celebrated his 28th birthday by scoring two goals, picking up where he left off at the last World Cup, and Philipp Lahm and Torsten Frings scored one apiece to lead Germany to a 4–2 win. "Obviously, we're very satisfied with the performance, but with it being the opening game we were a little nervous, both before and during the match," Klinsmann said during a news conference following the game.[3]

That night in Gelsenkirchen, Ecuador, a team many had argued could only win when playing in the altitude of Quito, stunned Poland, 2–0. "We're not going to win the cup, but as a minimum we must get to the second round. That would be a great achievement for us," Ecuador coach, the Colombian-born Luis Fernandez Suarez, said before the start of the tournament. "It would be a sign that progress has been made."[4]

In Germany's second game five days later, this time against Poland, the match appeared on its way to ending in a scoreless tie. Before the game, German police arrested 300 German and Polish hooligans. German fans had greeted the Poles with the Nazi salute—a crime in Germany and a grim reminder of Poland's suffering during World War II. Fortunately, none of that violence and intolerance affected the game itself. On the field, the Germans' never-say-die attitude paid off in stoppage time when Oliver Neuville latched on to a cross from David Odonkor to slot the ball past Polish goalkeeper Artur Boruc. The goal set off wild cheers in Dortmund's Westfalenstadion and on the streets in all parts of the country. The Germans were in the second round.

The next day, Ecuador joined the hosts in the round of sixteen, downing Costa Rica, 3–0, in Hamburg. Poland defeated Costa Rica, 2–1, on June 20 in Hanover, while Germany and Ecuador locked horns in Berlin for a shot at first place. It wasn't much of a game as Germany, backed by an enthusiastic crowd of 72,000, took the lead after just four minutes with Klose. The German striker scored again in the 44th minute to put Germany ahead, 2–0, at halftime. The Germans clinched the win and the topped the group in the 57th minute with Podolski. The Germans and their brand of swift, attacking soccer unleashed celebrations across the country and for, the first time, the belief that Klinsmann's team could win the trophy.

England got things started in Group B on June 10, defeating Paraguay, 1–0, in Frankfurt. The game-winner came after just three minutes when Beckham sent a dangerous curling shot into the box from the left side that was mistakenly headed by Paraguay defender Carlos Gamarra past his goalkeeper Justo Villar and into his own net.

That evening, Trinidad and Tobago, making its World Cup debut, played Sweden to a scoreless tie. The result was shocking considering that Trinidad and Tobago were playing with a man down following Avery John's red card a minute into the second half. In the net, Trinidad and Tobago goalkeeper Shaka Hislop had a great outing, stopping shot after shot in what turned out to be a thrill-a-minute contest.

Five days later, England played Trinidad and Tobago in Nuremberg. The English were looking for a convincing win after a poor performance against Paraguay. Instead, Eriksson's team played another disappointing game. If winning was all that mattered at this stage, then England had done its job. A goal from Liverpool striker Peter Crouch in the 83rd minute off a cross from Beckham gave England the lead. The lanky striker, who had all the coordination of Big Bird, rose above defender Brent Sancho to head the ball past Hislop. TV replays later showed that Crouch had grabbed onto Sancho's dreadlocks. Steven Gerrard scored England's second goal in stoppage time to give his side the 2–0 victory. Hislop was fantastic between the posts once again, but could do nothing to stop England from finding the back of the net. The only promising thing going for England, aside from a spot in the round of sixteen, was the return of Wayne Rooney. The Manchester United striker, who had not played since suffering a cruciate ligament injury, came on in the 58th minute—earning loud applause from the 41,000 spectators—but never got into the game. His return had been rushed, but the hope was that he could be fit for the knockout stages.

Later that day, Sweden finally earned a win, beating Paraguay, 1–0, in Berlin with a goal from Freddy Ljungberg in the 89th minute. On June 20, England played Sweden in Cologne. Sweden needed at least a tie to get to the round of sixteen, while England needed to finish first in the group if it wanted to avoid playing Germany in the knockout stage. The game ended 2–2. Both teams got the points each needed, although England's chances of going far into the tournament suffered a devastating blow following an injury to Michael Owen. The Newcastle United star fell awkwardly in the first minute when he tried to pass the ball. His right knee buckled underneath him as he fell to the ground in agony. Owen was substituted with Crouch, who did little during the game. England had recorded another sub-par performance after the defense failed to clear the ball in 90th minute, which allowed Barcelona striker Henrik Larsson to poke it into the net for the tie.

Group C opened on June 10 with Argentina playing the Ivory Coast in Hamburg. With Maradona watching from the stands, Juan Riquelme, wearing the number 10 jersey did his best impersonation of the Argentine legend, setting up both goals in a 2-1 win over the Africans. Riquelme, who played with Spanish club Villareal, showed why he was one of the best playmakers in the world, single-handedly dictating the flow of the game and cutting through the impotent Ivory Coast defense with his pinpoint passes. The Ivory Coast, making its World Cup debut, struggled to control Riquelme and both of Argentina's goalscorers, Hernan Crespo and Javier Saviola.

The next day in Leipzig, Holland tangled with the team from Serbia and Montenegro—known as Yugoslavia just four years earlier—in front of 43,000 fans, many of whom were wearing orange and rooting for the Dutch. (By the time the 2006 tournament came to an end, the players would come to represent a nation that no longer existed after the now-independent countries of Serbia and Montenegro came to an amicable split.) In the meantime, Serbia and Montenegro played far too cautiously with the Dutch, wasting little time getting on the board. Chelsea striker Arjen Robben scored on a breakaway in the 18th minute, with his speed and dribbling abilities forcing goalkeeper Dragoslav Jevric to come out of his net, to record the winner.

On June 16, Argentina toppled Serbia and Montenegro, 6-0, in Gelsenkirchen. Maradona was back in the stands with his posse of family and friends, screaming at the top of his lungs and encouraging the two-time world champions. Argentina's second goal was not only an amazing display of individual skill, but a sign that the team's separate parts could work together. The Argentineans strung together twenty-three uninterrupted passes among eight players en route to the goal. The play went like this: Riquelme to Maxi Rodriguez to Juan Pablo Sorin back to Rodriguez, back to Sorin to Javier Mascherano to Riquelme to Roberto Ayala to Esteban Cambiasso to Mascherano to Rodriguez to Sorin, back to Rodriguez, to Cambiasso to Riquelme to Mascherano to Sorin to Saviola to Rodriguez, back to Saviola to Cambiasso to Hernan Crespo, who back-heel passed it back to Cambiasso, who hammered the ball in the net for an amazing goal. Argentina was through to the round of sixteen.

On the same day, Holland also booked a place in the knockout round, edging Ivory Coast, 2-1, in Stuttgart. Five days later in Frankfurt,

Argentina and Holland played for a shot at first place. The most anticipated game of the tournament turned out to be little more than a training session, given that both teams had advanced to the next round. The game ended, 0–0, and the stalemate allowed Argentina to win the group on goal differential. The tie was also a chance for Argentina to rest several of its starters while showing just how deep its bench was when strikers Carlos Tevez and Lionel Messi—who could be starters on any other team—started for the first time. The tie also suited the Dutch, who in finishing second avoided Germany in the round of sixteen. Argentina, judging from the way it had played in the first round, appeared to fear no one.

The clash between Mexico and Iran on June 11 in Nuremberg opened Group D. The Mexicans were coached by Argentinean Ricardo Lavolpe, who bore an uncanny resemblance to Al Pacino in the movie *Scarface*. They opened the scoring after twenty-eight minutes with Omar Bravo. The Mexicans gave up an equalizer eight minutes later when Yahya Golmohammadi slammed the ball into the net after the defense failed to clear the ball off the corner kick. The Iranians, looking for their second win ever at a World Cup, could do little as Lavolpe reshuffled his lineup, changing from a 3-4-3 to a 3-5-2. The Mexican attack came to life after the move as the Iranians spent the remainder of the first half soaking up the pressure. While the Mexicans picked up steam in the second period, the Iranians ran out of it: Bravo scored again in the 76th minute and Antonio Naelson, known by the nickname "Zinha," added a third goal eleven minutes from the end to give Mexico the 3–1 victory. The team dedicated the win to goalkeeper Oswaldo Sanchez's father, who had died just a few days prior to the game. Sanchez had flown to Mexico for the funeral after arriving with the team in Germany, then flew back in time to start against Iran. As for the chain-smoking Lavolpe, who dealt with the stressful game by lighting up on the bench, FIFA warned him the following day that smoking on the sidelines was against the rules. Lavolpe's cigarettes may have been burned out, but not his teams chances of advancing to the round of sixteen.

That evening, Angola made their World Cup debut against its former colonizer, Portugal, in Cologne. What appeared to be a mismatch turned into a riveting contest despite the bad blood between the nations. The last time the two teams had met on the soccer field was five years earlier in a friendly in Lisbon. On that occasion, the Portuguese led 5–1, but the game had to be suspended after Angola had a fourth player red carded and the game degenerated into a brawl. The only other previous encounter between both teams was in 1989 when Portugal blanked Angola, 6–0. The Portuguese were expecting a similar result, but Angola put in a fine performance. In the end, Portugal was only able to win by a score of 1–0. Angola might have lost the game, but won many admirers that evening. The game's only goal came after five minutes when Figo galloped past defender Jamba (who went by one name in tribute to the Brazilian players he idolized), then passed the ball to an open Pauleta who side-footed the ball into the goal.

On June 16 in Hanover, the Angolan players put on another surprise showing, only this time they were able to snatch a point from Mexico. The goalless tie, which put Mexico's qualification to the next round in jeopardy, gave the Angolans cause for celebration.

The next day, Portugal beat Iran, 2–0, in Frankfurt with Figo, who was now thirty-three years old and playing his best soccer in years. The Iranian defense, which had looked so lackluster against Mexico, also had to contend with Deco, who missed the game against Angola because of a foot injury. But it was Figo's crosses and series of passes for his teammates to feast on that allowed Portugal to dominate the game. Figo's pass to Deco gave Portugal the lead in the 64th minute. Another Figo play, this time resulting in a take-down in the box, gave Portugal a penalty kick with ten minutes left to play and Cristiano Ronaldo was impeccable from the spot.

Portugal won the group on June 21 after defeating Mexico, 2–1, in Gelsenkirchen, while Angola's dreams of advancing died following a 1–1 tie versus Iran in Leipzeg. Angola could have edged out Mexico for second place on goal differential, but the Africans were unable to score more goals.

While Group C was universally thought of as the "Group of Death," Group E would be the tightest group with all four teams (Italy, Czech Republic, Ghana, and the United States) vying for spots in the final round of matches. Following the draw, the Americans, who had argued they should have been a seeded team and not Mexico by virtue of their FIFA ranking (number 5 in the world going into the tournament by FIFA's much-criticized computer system) and CONCACAF Gold Cup title won a year before, were confident they could finish at least second. "It sets the tone for the World Cup. For everybody, the first game is very important," Beasley said. "You don't want to lose. You don't want to come out of the first game and have zero points."[5]

The meeting between the Czech Republic and the United States on June 12 was a clash of soccer superpowers. Yes, the word *superpower* applied to the Americans and the Czechs, number 2 in the FIFA rankings, but the match was far from a clash of great teams. The Czechs did their part, but the Americans never showed up for the contest in Gelsenkirchen. The bar had been set high for Arena and his team after reaching the quarterfinals in 2002. Eager to prove they were among the sport's elite, Arena brought his most-talented team ever to Germany and it featured a mix of MLS stars and those who played abroad. The Americans even got a pregame pep talk from President George W. Bush, who called the team from Washington to wish them well. Those well wishes did little for the players. The Czechs got on the board after five minutes when the American defense was too slow to react to defender Zdenek Grygera, who went on a furious run down the right flank. Grygera's cross was met by the towering Jan Koller—all 6'7" of him—who headed the ball into the net past Keller. The Czechs doubled their lead with Tomas Rosicky in the 36th minute. Another Rosicky goal in the 76th minute humiliated the Americans, who looked bewildered for much of the 3–0 game. The Americans, who could only muster a single shot on goal, showed once again that it could not compete on the world stage, particularly at a World Cup on European soil. The Americans' record fell to 0–8 in World Cup games played in Europe. "I really think the biggest part of the game was the early goal," Arena said. "For the most part, I thought we defended really well. Give Rosicky credit—that was a great second goal he scored. The third goal in the second half came a little bit against the run of play." The loss was reminiscent of the Americans' 5–1 drubbing at the hands of Czechoslovakia at Italia '90. Arena, who sat in the seats that day in Florence as a fan, said the losses were not comparable. "I don't think we looked like that 1990 team," he said.[6]

The Italians, traditionally slow starters at the World Cup, broke with tradition, defeating Ghana, 2–0, on June 12 in Hanover. The Italian players, distracted by a match-fixing scandal brewing back home, started the game on the defensive, but then emerged as an offensive threat as the game wore on. Even the Italians' traditionally ironclad defense did not resemble the old-style *catenaccio*. Instead, it was more fluid and selfless with Cannavaro, who won every ball on the ground, swatting away any chance Ghana tried to put together. Italy's initial nervousness gave way to unbridled attack—even though Totti, who had suffered an ankle injury two months earlier, started in the midfield but was far from top form. Totti would be eventually replaced in the second half by Argentine-born Mauro Camoranesi. The Italians led 1–0 at halftime following an Andrea Pirlo goal in the 40th minute. Pirlo timed his shot perfectly, blasting the ball from 20 yards out. Ghana's midfield trio of Sulley Muntari, Michael Essien, and Stephen Appiah were expected to excel on the eve of the game, but poor finishing let the team down, particularly in the second half when they needed the equalizer. The Italians finished off their opponents with seven minutes left to play when substitute Vincenzo Iaquinta, who had come in for AC Milan striker Alberto Gilardino, stole the ball following a weak back pass by defender Samuel Kuffour. Iaquinta was off to the races, rounding goalkeeper Richard Kingston and tapping the ball into the empty net for the 2–0 win.

Five days later, Ghana stunned the Czechs, putting on a sparkling display en route to a 2–0 win. The Ghanaians, in the second match of their World Cup debut, had finally played with the flair many had expected to see from them, while the Czechs lacked the pace and power that they had used to defeat the Americans. Asmoah Gyan put Ghana in front after two minutes. The Czechs failed to respond and with lone striker Vratislav Lokvenc could do little to threaten Ghana's defense. Koller was out due to injury and the Czech team that had dismantled the U.S. never showed up. Essien created chance after chance in the midfield. Gyan even missed a penalty kick in the 65th minute, but Ghana got that second goal with eight minutes remaining when Muntari's powerful shot beat goalkeeper Peter Cech.

That evening in Kaiserslautern, the United States and Italy matched wits in a game that the *Azzurri* were expected to dominate. The Italians, however, never took charge and the plucky Americans were able to remain competitive in a game that was rich in controversy but meager in quality. In the days following the loss to the Czechs, Arena had publicly lambasted the players—DaMarcus Beasley in particular—for their poor performances. The round of finger pointing could have bred resentment in the U.S. ranks. Instead, it appeared to galvanize the team in time for the game against Italy. The Americans started strong, but it was Italy that took the lead after twenty-two minutes when Gilardino's header off a Pirlo free kick found the back of the net. The Italians could have killed any U.S. chance of a comeback, but that second goal never came. Worse, the *Azzurri* complicated matters for themselves five minutes later by giving up a bizarre own goal following a Bobby Convey free kick from the right sideline. The ball hit defender Cristian Zaccardo in the leg, then took an awkward bounce and spun into the net for the own goal. Then the game took on an even odder twist. A minute after the U.S. equalizer, the Italians were down a man after midfielder Daniele De Rossi elbowed Brian McBride in the cheek. Uruguayan referee Jorge Larrionda pulled out a red card and the AS Roma player was out of the game. De Rossi walked off the field as the U.S. team's medical staff stitched up McBride's bloody face. Seconds before the end of the first half, Larrionda pulled out his red card once again, sending off U.S. midfielder Pablo Mastroeni following a two-footed tackle on Pirlo. Both sides were even with ten men.

The second period featured more rough tackles and theatrics. Two minutes after the break, the Italians again gained the numerical player advantage after Pope was given a second yellow card and ejected after a tackle on Gilardino. The call seemed unjustified, particularly since Pope had won the ball on the play. The Italians were unable to put the one-man advantage to good use, though Italy coach Marcello Lippi responded to the situation by putting in Del Piero to replace Zaccardo and Iaquinta for Luca Toni. Del Piero had two clear chances in the last twenty minutes, but Keller saved them both. The first attempt came in the 73rd minute when Keller jumped to his right to deny Del Piero's shot. Keller would again make a big save in the 79th minute, punching out a long-range attempt unleashed by Del Piero. The game ended, 1–1. "We told our team that this group would go down to the last day," said Arena.

> Our challenge is to try to get four points and see where that takes us. I thought our effort was fantastic. I'm proud of the way my team kept their composure and got the one point. I thought we were the better team. We had a fantastic first half and certainly to get two red cards within a span of five minutes was very difficult. Not many teams would hold their composure. I thought we did a great job there and I'm really proud of the team. That's the kind of team the U.S. should be putting on the field and the kind of effort we should have.[7]

The Italians had encountered a severe setback, while the Americans had earned their first World Cup point on European soil and were still in the hunt for a spot in the round of sixteen. An Italy win over the Czech Republic, coupled with a U.S. victory over Ghana, would allow the Italians to win the group—avoiding Brazil in the second round—and the Americans to finish second and also advance to the next round.

The Italians were able to top the group and advance on June 22 in Hamburg, eliminating the ten-man Czech Republic with a 2-0 victory thanks to goals from Materazzi and Filippo Inzaghi. Italy took the lead in the 26th minute from a Materazzi header; this was before the Czechs were reduced to ten men just before halftime with the dismissal of Jan Polak, who chopped down Totti from behind and earned himself a second yellow card. The Czechs were again missing the injured Koller and it was left to Juventus midfielder Pavel Nedved to ignite the attack. He barely did. Twice in the early going did Nedved test Buffon with long-range shots, but the Italian goalkeeper did an excellent job thwarting the efforts of his Juventus teammate. Three minutes from the end, Inzaghi—who came in during the second half for Gilardino—rounded Cech to make it 2-0 just as the Czech Republic had thrown everyone forward in a bid to tie the score. "This team has terrific spirit, probably the most fighting spirit I have had in any team," Italy coach Marcello Lippi said at a news conference afterward. "We deserve to qualify. We played two great games to beat Ghana and Czech Republic. They are two very difficult teams."[8] An hour later, a cloud fell over the win as Italian federation prosecutor Stefano Palazzi recommended that Juventus, AC Milan, Fiorentina, and Lazio be demoted to Serie B for their involvement in the Serie A match-fixing scandal that was starting to overshadow everything the Italians had done on the field in Germany. After the World Cup, Juventus would be demoted to the second division. AC Milan, Fiorentina, Lazio, with the addition of Reggina, remained in Serie A, but absorbed point deductions to start the season. Many were all ready drawing comparisons between this Italy team and the one that captured the World Cup sixteen years earlier. In that instance, the team had also been under a cloud of suspicion because of a match-fixing scandal. Whether the *Azzurri* could replicate the success of 1982 remained to be seen.

The Americans, meanwhile, were no match for Ghana in Nuremberg. Knowing that the Italians were winning should have served as motivation for Arena's men—but even that wasn't enough for them to overcome the Africans, who ultimately won a place in the final sixteen with a 2–1 win to become only the fifth team from that continent to advance from the group stages of a World Cup. Appiah converted a controversial stoppage time penalty, which was handed out by German referee Markus Merk after Razak Pimpong was judged to have been pushed by U.S. defender Oguchi Onyewu just before halftime. The goal secured Ghana the triumph after Clint Dempsey had cancelled out Ghana's first goal by Haminu Dramani. The Americans struck the post midway through the second half, but otherwise were not of an offensive threat after Arena fielded a 4-5-1 formation. Ghana took the lead in the 22nd minute when Dramani dispossessed Reyna and ran into the box, curling the ball past Keller. Dempsey put the U.S. team back on equal footing two minutes from the break after Beasley unleashed a low cross from the left following a defensive mix-up by the Ghanaians. Appiah's penalty kick appeared to knock whatever momentum the Americans had amassed in the closing minutes of the half. In the second period, Arena put in striker Eddie Johnson to join Brian McBride for the final twenty-nine minutes, a move that kick-started a series of U.S. offensive assaults. McBride struck the post in the 66th minute with a header off a Lewis cross. For the remainder of the contest, the U.S. team pressured Ghana's defense, but the Africans did as well on the other end. The game opened up and provided unabashed, end-to-end action, but neither team was able to convert. "It is extremely disappointing," Keller said at a news conference following the game. "We put ourselves in position to be able to advance in the third game. Obviously, we're disappointed with the decision of the referee. But in the end, we didn't make the plays that we needed to make."[9]

Arena was not gracious in defeat, blaming the referee for the team's elimination. "We worked real hard to get back into the game. I'm very disappointed in the judgment of the referee for that penalty kick call and putting our team down at [the] half and having to chase the game for that second half," he told reporters at a postgame news conference. "I would have liked to come out at halftime even and have a chance to play the game and win that game, because I thought we were in good position at the time. The call was a big call in the game."[10] In the days following the loss, Arena verbally dumped on MLS, blaming the league for not properly preparing players for the World Cup. His comments angered the league, but that didn't stop Arena—who was fired by U.S. Soccer officials after they refused to renew his contract—from taking a coaching job a month later with the New York Red Bulls, an MLS team previous known as the New York/New Jersey MetroStars. The decision to dump Arena was no surprise and came on July 13 following a five-hour meeting at LaGuardia Airport in New York between U.S. Soccer President Sunil Gulati, Arena, and U.S. Soccer Secretary General Dan Flynn.

In Group F, all eyes were on Brazil, a nation that had participated in all of the previous seventeen World Cup tournaments. If you believed all the hype (and the Nike ads) surrounding Brazil, then the *Selecao* was favored to conquer a sixth title. Indeed, in an environment of such high expectations, there was no room for error. Anything short of winning the trophy would be seen as a defeat. Winning another title was possible given Brazil's roster. Roberto Carlos and Cafu were back, forming the core of a team many were comparing to the one that had won the World Cup in 1970. Parreira was back coaching the team after the triumph at USA '94 and was relying on the so-called "Magic Quartet" with two-time FIFA Player of the Year Ronaldinho, Kaka, Ronaldo, and Adriano forming the frontline. "Brazil is considered the favorite because of the success it has had in the past," Parreira told a news conference before the start of the World Cup. "But the tournament is treacherous. Being the favorite off the field doesn't count for much. On the field, everyone is equal. We have to be careful that we're not taken by surprise."[11]

Brazil would soon learn that eleven solo artists did not necessary make an orchestra. Problems were evident in the Brazil camp even before the tournament began. Ronaldo had injured himself midway through the season with Real Madrid. He reported to Brazil's training camp overweight and sluggish. Ronaldo's own website listed his weight at 190 pounds—21 pounds more than he weighed four years earlier. The twenty-nine-year-old striker had also complained of blisters—five of them on his left foot—in his never-ending saga of excuses for why he was in such poor shape. Ronaldo was also not pleased with the Brazilian media's fascination with his problems, lashing out at them at a news conference on the eve of the tournament, saying his weight was of "interest to nobody."[12] Despite Ronaldo's weight problems, Parreira was ready to add another trophy to Brazil's ever-crowded collection of accolades. Standing in its way were Group F opponents Croatia, Australia, and Japan. Parreira had employed a conservative playing style twelve years earlier and was once again playing the pragmatist, much to the dismay of most Brazilians. But as long as the team kept winning—while showing a few glimpses of the country's famed *jogo bonito*—then Parreira could do no wrong. Ronaldo was another story.

In Brazil's debut on June 13 against Croatia in Berlin, the five-time world champions were far from peak form. While Kaka and Ronaldinho appeared in top shape, Ronaldo and Adriano were not. What resulted was a lethargic game in which the Croatian attack showed plenty of potential, but ultimately never threatened the Brazilian goal. The only goal of the game came from a fierce shot fired by Kaka in the 44th minute from long range that beat Pletikosa. Despite the loss, Croatia's fans lit red flares in honor of their team's positive performance. Brazil had won—but barely.

The previous day, Australia, marking its return to the finals following a thirty-two-year absence, used its stamina to defeat Japan, 3–1, in Kaiserslautern. Hiddink had imposed a tough regimen on the team all in the hopes of developing the players' stamina in time for the finals. Hiddink's plan worked and the Socceroos were able to come from behind in the second half. Japan, playing in its third consecutive World Cup, was down 1–0 at halftime. Hiddink made a series of key substitutions in the second half, removing striker Mark Bresciano and replacing him with Tim Cahill in the 53rd minute, then took out defender Craig Moore for striker Josh Kennedy eight minutes later. Hiddink's battle plan paid off as the Socceroos created a slew of chances. His final move occurred fifteen minutes from the end of the game when striker John Aloisi entered the game in place of forward Luke Wilkshire. The Aussie front-line cranked up the pressure, determined to earn at least a tie. The Socceroos did just that in the 84th minute when Cahill, who was coming off a knee injury, put the ball in the goal off a right-footed shot. Five minutes later, Cahill was the hero once again, scoring from 20 yards out on a screamer of a shot that bounced off the post and into the net. If that wasn't enough, the Aussies, knowing full well that goal differential would determine who would advance to the second round, scored a third goal in injury time, this time Aloisi sealing Japan's fate following a fabulous solo run.

The Japanese, seeking a win after falling apart to Australia over the course of the final six minutes, were looking for a victory against Croatia. The teams squared off on June 18 in Nuremberg with the Croatians also in desperate need of a win if they wanted to remain in contention for a spot in the final sixteen. Japan, coached by former Brazilian great Zico, ran out of steam early and so did the Croatians. The game ended scoreless, but Croatia could have won the game in the first half after Darijo Srna saw his penalty kick blocked by Japan goalkeeper Yoshikatsu Kawaguchi. His heroics kept Japan in the game and Croatia off the scoreboard, though Croatia watched another near miss, a Niko Kranjcar shot in the 28th minute that beat Kawaguchi but slammed off the crossbar.

That evening in Munich, Brazil played Australia in another game that would end in a victory for the five-time champs. Brazil's 2–0 win gave it the points needed to advance, but was unconvincing. Australia's Hiddink fielded a six-man midfield in an attempt to cancel out Kaka and Ronaldinho. The plan worked with the Brazilian duo finding little space to maneuver the ball, while Cafu and Roberto Carlos, known for their effortless runs forward down the flanks, could do little. The aging stalwarts were past their prime and it showed against Australia. The loss of Roberto Carlos and Cafu's speed made Brazil vulnerable in the back and failed to ignite their attack. Alas, Ronaldo once again looked far from fit, sluggishly trying to move the ball and often attempting to shield it, as Australian defenders stuck close to him. Brazil's ineptness aside, the *Selecao* were able to take the lead in the 49th minute after Ronaldo for once held onto the ball while drawing three defenders. He dished the ball off to Adriano, who used the space to unleash a potent shot from the edge of the box that went through defender Scott Chipperfield's legs and past goalkeeper Mark Schwarzer. Down 1–0, Hiddink was forced to make a tactical change and Harry Kewel was brought in for Cahill. The move never really paid off and Brazil scored again. This time, the Brazilians made it 2–0 in the 90th minute when Kaka's shot bounced off the post, and Fred, who had come in just two minutes earlier for Adriano, was first to touch the ball and tap it in for the goal.

Parreira rested five players against Japan on June 22 in Dortmund after having secured a spot in the round of sixteen. Brazil only needed a point to top the group. Japan needed a win and it showed, taking the lead after the 34th minute with Keiji Tamada, who unleashed a powerful shot past AC Milan goalkeeper Dida. Ronaldo, however, put on his most convincing outing of the tournament and silenced the critics—at least temporarily—with a fine performance. Although he still looked pudgy and sported a gut under his tight-fitting yellow jersey, Ronaldo scored two goals, equaling Gerd Muller's record and surpassing Pelé to become Brazil's leading all-time World Cup scorer with fourteen goals. Zico, coaching against his country, could do little to prepare his players for the Brazilian offensive onslaught. As Brazil moved the ball forward, the intimidated Japanese defenders began to give their opponents more room. Ronaldo's first goal came in the 45th minute when Ronaldinho flicked the ball to Cicinho, who headed the ball across the goalmouth, allowing the burly striker to put the ball in the net with ease for the 1–1 tie. In the second half, Juninho gave Brazil the lead in the 53rd minute and Gilberto made it 3–0 six minutes later. Ronaldo's record-tying goal came nine minutes from the end when he curled a right-footed shot past goalkeeper Yoshikatsu Kawaguchi. After the game, Nakata, Japan's twenty-nine-year-old star striker, retired in disgust following his national team's abysmal showing. Nakata also wept in the locker room following the 0–0 tie against Croatia. His club, Fiorentina, confirmed his retirement, saying that his contract with the club, which still had another year left on it, had been annulled.

Simultaneously in Stuttgart, Australia and Croatia played an intense match—and participated in yet another World Cup game where the protagonist turned out to be the referee. Australia needed Brazil to beat Japan and at least a tie against Croatia to advance to the round of sixteen. Englishman Graham Poll, one of the most respected referees in the world, had a lousy day. He failed to award Australia two penalty kicks, and he red carded Croatia's Australian-born striker Josip Simunic in stoppage time after showing him a *third* yellow card just three minutes after he had been booked a second time, an offense that should have gotten the player booted from the game. Australia played a strong game, but the match descended into anarchy in the final ten minutes thanks to Poll's abysmal performance. Croatia took the lead after two minutes when Darijo Srna's superbly executed free kick was too much for backup goalkeeper Zeljko Kalac to handle. Hiddink's decision to bench Schwarzer—the hero six months earlier when he led Australia to a win over Uruguay after penalty kicks to clinch a World Cup berth—was controversial, but justified. Schwarzer looked far from impressive in the first two games and Hiddink decided to shake things up in the back with the presence of the former AC Milan goalkeeper. Hiddink would come to regret the decision by game's end.

Down 1–0, the Socceroos regrouped, tying the score in the 38th minute when Poll correctly whistled a penalty kick after Stejpan Tomas handled the ball in the box. Australia's Craig Moore's powerful kick beat Pletikosa and tied the score. The second half brought with it more goals and further frustration. The Aussies cranked up the pressure, but the Croatians endured the offensive ambush. Croatia was able to regain the lead, this time against the run of play, in the 56th minute when Kalac allowed Niko Kovac's kick to slip threw his fingers and into the goal right below the crossbar. Down 2–1, Australia looked finished. Poll was no help, failing to award the Socceroos a penalty kick when Stjepan Tomas handled the ball in the box. Croatia then saw Simic red carded in the 85th minute, only to have the teams even again with ten players when Brett Emerton was ejected after receiving two yellow cards. The Aussies battled back, like they had against Japan, and the stamina and determination infused in them by Hiddink came through in the end. Kewell scored eleven minutes from the end off a Bresciano cross to tie the score, 2–2. Aloisi looked offside on the play, but Poll let the goal stand and the yellow-clad Australian fans, which made up a majority of the 52,000 in attendance at Gottlieb-Daimler Stadium, cheered the goal. Australia was through to the second round. Croatia and Poll were sent home.

Group G, with France, Switzerland, South Korea, and Togo, opened June 13 with South Korea downing Togo, 2–1, in Frankfurt. Ahn Jung-hwan scored the game winner in the 72nd minute for the South Koreans, who looked anything like the powerful and hard-running team that had finished fourth four years earlier on home soil. Togo, playing in its first World Cup finals, had seen its preparations undermined by a pay dispute with the country's soccer federation that forced the German-born Togo coach Otto Pfister to walk off in frustration a day before the match, only to return hours before the game and resume his place on the bench.

The following day, France and Switzerland squared off in Stuttgart. Both sides conspired to play what turned out to be one of the dullest games at the tournament. The teams had played each other in the qualifying rounds, tying each other on both occasions—0–0 in Paris and 1–1 in Berne—and could do no better at the World Cup. France, who had not scored in four straight World Cup games dating back to the 1998 final against Brazil, would have to score goals if it hoped to get far. Five days later in Leipzig, Raymond Domenech's team finally had something to cheer about that evening. France got on the board with Henry after nine minutes, but *Les Bleus'* failure to score again hurt them in the end when Park JI-sung grabbed the equalizer nine minutes from the end to earn a 1–1 tie. Zinedine Zidane's indolent style appeared to stifle the team's midfield, but Domenech insisted on keeping the Real Madrid midfielder in the game even though he seemed to be hurting the team. Trézéguet, on the outs with Domenech, replaced Zidane in the 90th minute, but there was no time for France to do anything more to win the game. Worse yet, Zidane, who had announced a few months earlier that he would retire after the tournament, collected a second consecutive yellow card and was out in France's next game against Togo. A place in the next round seemed highly doubtful for France, while the South Koreans had three points and were in very good position to advance.

Switzerland eliminated Togo on June 19, beating them 2–0 in Dortmund. Pfister's resignation over bonuses, followed by his swift return on the eve of the Togo–South Korea match, had created an unsettled mood in the Togo camp. This time, the players threatened not to show up against Switzerland. FIFA intervened and settled the dispute, trying to avoid the embarrassment a no-show could cause. Togo certainly could have played better, but a series of wasted chances and off-the-field pay-dispute shenanigans were too much for any team to endure. A goal from Alexander Frei in the 16th minute and a strike by Tranquillo Barnetta with two minutes left to play was enough for the Swiss to win the game and tie South Korea with three points at the top of the group standings.

France finally showed what it was made of in its next match, blanking Togo, 2–0, in Cologne. Without Zidane, Domenech's team appeared more likely to score, although a 0–0 first half was anything but promising for *Les Bleus*. The second period was another story. France grabbed the lead in the 55th minute with Patrick Vieira, who celebrated his 30th birthday with a goal. Trézéguet got the start alongside Henry and the French imposed their game on the Africans. Vieira was impeccable in the back, pushing forward in a manner reminiscent of the way Rijkaard did for Holland. Vieira added to his birthday gift six minutes after he scored, heading the ball in for Henry, who made the final score 2–0. France finished second in the group and clinched a berth to the round of sixteen, joining first-place Switzerland, who had defeated South Korea, 2–0, in Hanover.

Meanwhile, Spain dominated Group H, which also included Ukraine, Tunisia, and Saudi Arabia. The perennial World Cup underachievers blanked Ukraine, 4–0, on June 14 in Leipzig, then followed up that performance with a 3–1 drubbing of Tunisia five days later in Stuttgart thanks to two goals from Fernando Torres. Whether Spain would be finally able to break from the shackles of early elimination and reach the final remained a mystery. For now, the team was playing to the potential that head coach Luis Aragones had expected in the months leading up to the tournament. On June 23, Spain cruised to its third straight win, edging Saudi Arabia, 1–0, in Kaiserslautern. The winner came via a header from Juanito in the 36th minute. Spain was off to the round of sixteen.

The fight for second place between Ukraine, Tunisia, and Saudi Arabia wasn't much of a contest. After losing to Spain, Ukraine, playing in its first World Cup finals ever, recovered and downed Saudi Arabia, 4–0, after AC Milan striker Andriy Shevchenko, back in top form after his abysmal showing against Spain, ignited his team's attack, even scoring a goal. The Saudis, coming off a 2–2 tie against Tunisia five days earlier in Munich, could do little in the face of such offensive intensity, especially after the Ukrainians switched from a standard 4-4-2 to a 3-5-2. Ukraine sealed a berth to the round of sixteen on June 23, defeating Tunisia, 1–0, in Berlin. Once again, Shevchenko came up big, scoring a penalty kick in the 70th minute.

## The Round of Sixteen

Unlike 2002, the knockout round featured few surprise teams, although several nations like Ghana, Ukraine, Ecuador, and Australia were all vying to become the tournament's Cinderella team. The traditional powers had asserted their dominance with six teams—Brazil, Italy, Germany, Argentina, France, and England—winning a combined fifteen World Cups between them. FIFA had also done away with the "Golden Goal," replacing it with the old system that called for two fifteen-minute overtime periods regardless of whether a team scored first.

The knockout stage began on June 24 with Germany defeating Sweden, 2–0, in Munich. Podolski scored in the 4th and 12th minutes, while Swedish defender Teddy Lucic was sent off in the 35th minute after accumulating his second yellow card. Things only got worse for Sweden. Hennich Larsson missed a penalty kick in the 53rd minute, ending any hope of a comeback. German fans had real reason to believe that a trip to the final was not out of the question. The win brought joy across Germany and the newfound belief the team could reach the final.

In Leipzig that evening, Argentina took on Mexico in what would be one of the most thrilling games of the competition. The winners would earn themselves a quarterfinal clash with Germany. Argentina was expected to cruise past Mexico, but that assumption proved wrong from the onset. In the end, it was the individual skill and brilliance of Rodriguez that made the difference. Rodriguez's goal—a spectacular volley—gave Argentina a 2–1 win in overtime. His goal in the 98th minute ousted Mexico from the round of sixteen for the fourth straight tournament. Rodriguez scored after settling a long cross from Sorin off his chest and striking it powerfully with his left foot from the edge of the penalty box. The Mexicans had played very well until that point, dominating possession and imposing their game on Argentina. Rafael Marquez's goal after six minutes was evidence of that, putting Argentina behind for the first time at the tournament. Argentina tied the score four minutes later when Riquelme's corner from the right side was mistakenly headed into his own goal by Jared Borgetti as he tried to beat out Crespo for the ball. The goal was awarded to Crespo despite replays that showed it was a Borgetti own goal.

On June 25, England and Ecuador squared off in Stuttgart. England was looking for another brilliant performance, but Eriksson's insistence on fielding a cautious lineup with five midfielders and Rooney as a lone striker did little to encourage an attacking game. The 4-1-4-1 formation meant that the English created few scoring chances, relying on the sporadic Ecuadorian blunder in the back. The Ecuadorians, in their typical 4-4-2 formation, tried to exert some pressure, but the clogged midfield was impossible for the South Americans to penetrate. The only goal of the game came, predictably, off a set piece. Beckham became the first England player to score at three separate World Cups, unleashing a kick that sailed over the Ecuadorian wall and just inside goalkeeper Cristian Mora's right post in the 60th minute. Rooney, playing in his first full game since returning from injury, found more space to move the ball in Ecuador's half following the goal, but none of his chances materialized. The heat, with temperatures reaching 90 degrees, and humidity of that day was too much for some players, including Beckham, who became ill and vomited near the sidelines. He was eventually substituted by Eriksson and replaced with Aaron Lennon with three minutes left to play.

A day after Argentina and Mexico mesmerized crowds with the very best of Latin soccer, powerhouses Portugal and Holland put on a display typical of all the ugly qualities that had come to dominate the European game in recent years. The game grew from a scrappy affair into one that degenerated into a kicking match with each passing minute thanks to the complicity of card-happy Russian referee Valentin Ivanov. Although Ivanov had blown his whistle more times than a traffic cop, the players did not help matters. By the end of the game, Ivanov had handed out a record-tying sixteen yellow cards and a record-setting four red cards, which were given to Portuguese midfielders Deco and Costinha and Dutch defenders Khalid Boulahrouz and Giovanni van Bronckhorst. In the end, Portugal won, 1–0, with Maniche scoring the only goal in the 23rd minute, firing the ball into the top corner. The goal was the fruit of some clever passing by the Portuguese. Cristiano Ronaldo started the play, putting through an effortless pass to Deco down the right wing. The Barcelona midfielder then crossed the ball to Pauleta, who tapped it back to Maniche for the easy goal. Nothing but violence ensued following the goal.

Costinha picked up a red card in the 45th minute after handling the ball near the midfield line. He had picked up his first yellow card after taking down Phillip Cocu earlier in the match. Boulahrouz was the next player sent off in the 63rd minute after aiming for Figo's nose during a violent confrontation. Barcelona teammates Deco and van Bronckhorst were also ejected, in the 78th and 90th minute, respectively, for violent offenses. The image that encapsulated the mood of the evening was Deco and van Bronckhorst sitting side-by-side in the stands after getting red cards. Both looked unhappy with Ivanov's decision. As for the game, Portugal had been able to defeat Holland—along with the tactical shortcomings of Dutch coach Marco van Basten's 4-5-1 formation—but things would be uphill against England in the quarterfinals. Portugal manager Luiz Felipe Scolari had taken his perfect record at the World Cup to eleven games after winning seven as coach of Brazil in 2002 and added four wins with Portugal at Germany '06. The Portuguese also reached the quarterfinals for the second time in their history and for the first time since 1966.

The showdown between Italy and Australia on June 26 in Kaiserslautern was a rematch of sorts for the *Azzurri*. Eliminated in the knockout round by the Hiddink-coached South Koreans four years earlier, the Italians were looking to exact some revenge on the Dutchman. Hiddink had pulled off the upset in 2002 and was looking to repeat that feat with the Socceroos. In 2002, the talk after Italy's defeat had been about conspiracy theories aimed against the sport's established powers. This time, the talk would be about referees trying to restore soccer's nobility to their just position at the top of the world. The first half ended scoreless with both countries coming close to taking the lead. Schwarzer, back in net after the Kalac experiment had gone awry against Croatia, kept the Australians in the match as Toni's speed and Gilardino's agility kept the defense on its toes and Italy's hopes alive. In the second half, Lippi beefed up his attack and replaced a tired Gilardino with Iaquinta. Lippi's 4-3-1-2 formation suffered a blow in the 50th minute when Materazzi was given a straight red card by Spanish referee Luis Medina Cantalejo after bringing down Bresciano. The call was harsh and the Italians were forced to withdraw. Toni was replaced with Barzagli, a defender, and Totti replaced Del Piero. Although he was far from fit, Lippi was banking on Totti to spark the Italian offense.

All the while, the Socceroos were the ones who controlled the pace of the game, dominating possession and creating chances. Buffon was solid, as usual, and kept the Aussies off the scoreboard. Cannavaro played masterfully, like he had in Italy's three first round games, anticipating his opponents and reading plays before they occurred. The game appeared headed for overtime when the Italians attempted one last foray into the Australian box. Fabio Grosso forced his way down the left flank in the last minute of the game and ran toward the box where defender Lucas Neill fell to the ground following a missed challenge. Grosso seized the opportunity and tumbled over Neill as he tried to regain possession of the ball. Cantalejo pointed to the spot and the Italians were saved. Totti lined up for the kick, blasting it into the net without hesitation, for his first World Cup goal and the 1–0 victory. The Italians had been lucky, winning the game and avoiding a possible penalty kick shootout that had condemned them at three previous tournaments. Blatter angered Italian fans a few months later when he said Italy did not deserve to win the game.

In the other game of the day, Ukraine and Switzerland, by far the weakest two teams left at in the competition. The game ended scoreless with the Swiss—who had gone beyond the group stage for the first time since hosting the tournament in 1954—and Ukraine playing a contest devoid of any entertainment. The players, even Shevchenko, did not appear up to the task of competing in a knockout round; it was as if neither side expected to get this far in the tournament. The Swiss, at times, appeared to employ a 6-3-1 formation with no ambition to score. The game reached a virtual standstill late in the second half and in the ensuing two overtime periods. In the penalty kick shootout, the Swiss missed three kicks in three attempts, while Ukraine netted three goals in the shootout for the 3–0 win. The Swiss earned the dubious distinction of being the first team eliminated from the World Cup to never score a goal during the course of the tournament. It was also the first team to miss all of its penalty kick opportunities since shootouts were used as tiebreakers.

Everyone was expecting the Brazilians to finally put together one of those displays worthy of the players who had donned the yellow jersey in the past. Prior to the game, a fuming Parreira went after his critics who claimed the team was not playing an entertaining enough brand of soccer. Parreira's answer that *jogo bonito* wasn't the only thing that mattered made headlines. "History doesn't talk about the beautiful game—it talks about champions," he told reporters at a news conference. "Why do we have to play beautiful soccer when no one else does?"[13] But Brazil did play beautifully on June 27 against Ghana in Dortmund. It wasn't the prettiest effort of all time, but the Brazilians freely moved the ball against the Africans, particularly in the midfield. Ghana, Brazil's toughest opponent in the competition thus far, suffered a setback when Ronaldo beat the offside trap in the fifth minute, dancing around Kingston, then sidestepping him to tap the ball into the empty net. Ronaldo's step-over move was reminiscent of Garrincha, who tormented defenders by repeatedly putting one foot over the ball and back again, causing them to flinch, and in the process able to move the ball past them. With his tally now at fifteen goals, Ronaldo became the World Cup's leading all-time scorer. Brazil went up 2–0 in the 45th minute with Adriano, who started in place of Robinho, although he appeared to be offside. The Brazilians scored again in the second period, this time, Ze Roberto beat the offside trap and Kingston in the 84th minute to walk the ball into the empty net to make it 3–0. There was no dispute that Brazil had won, but questions over why Ronaldinho continued to play so poorly and the vulnerability of the defense were issues Parreira needed to fix in the quarterfinals.

That evening, France took on Spain in Hanover. The Zidane farewell tour had reached the knockout round, but whether it would continue depended on Spain. Zidane played arguably his best game at the tournament until this point, leading the attack and energizing his teammates in the process. France's 3–1 win was a testament to Zidane's skills and hard work. The Frenchman wasn't the only ageless star on the team that night able to roll back the years. Barthez had a stellar game in net and Thuram won most of the balls that came his way. Spain, meanwhile, put on its usual World Cup underachieving act. Spain had played well in the first half, winning a penalty kick in the 28th minute when Thuram tripped defender Pablo in the box. Striker David Villa struck the ball hard against Barthez for the 1–0 lead. Though the French players spent most of the first half chasing around the Spanish players, they were able to tie the score in the 41st minute when Vieira fed the ball to Franck Ribéry, who beat Casillas for his first international goal. Ribéry, only twenty-three and lauded by many as Zidane's successor, was unstoppable on the flanks. Easily identifiable by the large scar that traces down the right side of his face—a reminder that he survived being thrown through the windshield of a car at age 2 years old—Ribéry had all the finesse of a world-class soccer player and the rugged looks of a boxer. Ribéry, like Zidane, embodied the combination of class and toughness to make him one of the team's most feared offensive weapons.

The Spanish attempted to regain the lead in the second half, but the French were the ones able to control the midfield. The French defense tightened its hold in the back, winning balls in the midfield and relying on Ribéry and Zidane to burst forward. Seven minutes from the end and France took the lead. Zidane floated a free kick that made its way into the box where Vieira was able to head the ball into the net. Spain was defeated, but that didn't stop the French from pushing forward. Deep into stoppage time, Zidane used his elegance to play the ball into the Spanish half, unleashing a low, but powerful shot, that beat Casillas for the 3–1 win.

## Quarterfinal Match-Ups

The quarterfinals opened on June 30 with Germany hosting Argentina in Berlin. Argentina had played well in the first round, but appeared humbled against Mexico in the round of sixteen. Against the hosts, Argentina looked authoritative, even taking the lead in the 49th minute with Ayala's header off a corner kick. However, the South Americans endured some trouble down the stretch. Goalkeeper Roberto Abbondanzieri was replaced in the 71st minute with backup Leo Franco following an injury. Seven minutes earlier, the Boca Juniors goalkeeper had received a blow to his hip from Klose and, despite extensive treatment, was forced to come off.

The game changed after that. The Germans attacked with a larger sense of urgency, needing a goal to push the game into overtime. Cheered on by the 72,000 fans in the stands at the Olympiastadion, the Germans used the flanks to their advantage, winning a series of corner kicks in the process. In the 80th minute, on one such play, a corner was cleared to Ballack, who crossed the ball to Tim Borowski. The Werder Bremen midfielder passed the ball to Klose, who then directed his header past Franco to tie the score. Overtime came and went and the game went to penalty kicks. The Germans proved once again that they have no equals when it came to winning a shootout, scoring all four of the kicks they took. Argentina missed two of them as Ayala and Cambiasso saw their kicks saved by Jens Lehmann. Following the game, a melee erupted on the sidelines. As the punches flew, Argentina's Leandro Cufre was shown a red card. Torsten Frings was also later suspended for his involvement in the fracas. The incident was an unfortunate end to an enthralling game.

In Hamburg that evening, Italy had little trouble eliminating Ukraine. The Italians took just six minutes to score when Gianluca Zambrotta picked up a cheeky back-heel from Totti, blasting it into the net with a low shot from outside the box. The Ukranians were never in the game. Instead, the Italians, playing a 4-4-1-1 formation with Toni as the lone striker, turned the match into a cakewalk. Toni scored two goals in the second half in the 59th and 69th minutes to lift Italy to a

3–0 victory. The players dedicated the win to former Italy defender Gianluca Pessotto who had survived a fall from a fourth-story window at Juventus' Turin headquarters on June 27, three days before this game. Since he was holding a rosary, it was widely believed to be a suicide attempt. The plunge coincided with widening investigations regarding the match-fixing allegations. Though not implicated in the scandal, Pessotto was said to be depressed and unhappy with his role as the club's team manager. He suffered multiple fractures and internal bleeding from the fall. He was released from the hospital a month later. The five Juventus players on Lippi's team were badly affected by the incident, and some of them flew to Pessotto's bedside before the Ukraine game. At the end of their June 30 quarterfinal clash against the Ukraine, the entire Italian team posed behind a banner expressing support for their friend with the message: *Siamo con te Pessottino* ("We are with you, little Pessotto").

On July 1, England and Portugal met in Gelsenkirchen for a shot at the semifinals. Penalty kick tiebreakers had been a disaster for England in the past and when the game ended scoreless, a look of despair came over the players' faces. Once again, history repeated itself. England had played with ten players for much of the second half after Rooney was red carded in the 62nd minute. Perhaps Rooney's foul on Ricardo Carvalho came from his frustration at his inability to score. The England striker stomped on Carvalho's groin as the Portugese player lay on the ground. Referee Hector Elizondo of Argentina had no choice but to show him a red card, although some of the players later contended that Rooney's Manchester United teammate, Cristiano Ronaldo, had pointed out the offense, jogging 40 yards to Elizondo in order to discuss the punishment. Rooney's exit was another blow to England's effort after Beckham was forced to leave the game just ten minutes earlier following an injury to his right ankle. The game ended 0–0 after 120 minutes characterized by fatigue and desperation. In the shootout, goalkeeper Ricardo was able to save three of England's kicks as Portugal prevailed, 3–1, to reach the semifinals at a World Cup for the first time since 1966. After the game, Rooney issued a statement contending he was not angry at Ronaldo. "I bear no ill feeling to Cristiano, but I am disappointed that he chose to get involved," he said. "I suppose I do, though, have to remember that on that particular occasion we were not teammates."[14] Rooney was eventually fined $4,000 by FIFA and suspended for two games. The loss was so devastating for Beckham, who had left the game in tears after injuring his right ankle, that he resigned as the team's captain. Six months later, Beckham signed to play for the Los Angeles Galaxy of Major League Soccer in a five-year deal, which included bonuses and commercial endorsements, worth $250 million.

Following the Portugal–England match, Brazil and France squared off in a rematch of the 1998 World Cup final. *Les Bleus* exuded confidence following Zidane's masterful performance against Spain, while Parreira changed things around, putting together a 4-3-1-2 formation with Ronaldo and Ronaldinho on attack. Adriano was dropped and Juninho was positioned in the midfield. The changes did nothing to inspire the Brazilians. France, on the other hand, played with a sense of purpose that night in Frankfurt with Zidane, who had turned thirty-four just a week earlier and played like a youngster again. The Brazilian defense labored in its efforts to keep up with Zidane and Ribéry. It was just a matter of time before France would score. That moment came in the 57th minute when Zidane floated a free kick into the penalty box from the left. Henry somehow broke away from the Brazilian defense and volleyed the ball past Dida from close range. The goal won France the game and the Zidane farewell tour continued into the semifinals. France had beaten Brazil at its own game, playing its own version of *jogo bonito*. For Parreira, the loss meant widespread humiliation and his subsequent resignation.

## Semifinals: Four Teams Remain

Germany's own dreams of winning a fourth World Cup vanished in the last ninety seconds of its game on July 4 against Italy in overtime. German fans were banking that Klinsmann's team would complete its improbable run to the final. The *Azzurri*, however, had never lost to Germany at a World Cup and had come to the tournament off of a 4–1 drubbing of the Germans March 1 in a friendly in Florence. That Germany loss had been the low point of Klinsmann's tenure, but all had been erased by the team's impressive run at the World Cup. Frings' suspension had put a damper on Germany's hopes prior to kickoff. He was banned for his part in the brawl that followed the shootout win over Argentina, a game where Frings had played a key role in shutting down the Argentine attack. FIFA had decided to take no action against the German player, but reversed itself when Italian satellite network Sky Italia showed FIFA the tape it had shot of Frings throwing a punch at Argentina's Julio Cruz during the fight. Frings was suspended for one game and fined $4,000.

The Germany–Italy game itself was played at a ferocious pace. The game was hardly reminiscent of Italy's 4–3 win over West Germany at the 1970 World Cup semifinals. To the contrary, the game ended 0–0 and extra time loomed. The *Azzurri* came storming out of the blocks in the first overtime period. Gilardino's shot hit the post after rounding Ballack. Then, Zambrotta whipped a shot that rattled the crossbar. Lippi wanted to avoid penalty kicks—and it showed given Italy's frenetic pace. In order to do that, Lippi brought in Iaquinta and Del Piero in place of Camoranesi and English-born Simone Perrotta. The substitutions worked wonders. With a minute left in overtime, off a corner kick, Pirlo passed the ball to Grosso in the box. The defender curled a left-footed shot that beat Lehmann at the far post. The goal stunned the crowd while Grosso celebrated with all the emotion of Tardelli's goal against West Germany at the 1982 World Cup final. Not to leave anything to chance, the Italians put an end to the game a minute later when Gilardino passed the ball in the path of Del Piero, who fired a chip shot that beat Lehmann to end the game. The 2–0 result put Italy in the final for the first time since 1994. Germany's World Cup adventure had come to an end.

France and Portugal met in the other semifinal, played the following night, in Munich. The last time these countries played a game that meant something was at the 2000 European Championship. On that occasion, Zidane's penalty kick in overtime won the game for the French. This time, the teams were again evenly matched. And once again, Zidane made the difference. His penalty kick strike in the 33rd minute proved to be the winner. Despite his age and poor showing in the group stage, Zidane had emerged as the tournament's most impressive player. The player who had grown up in the slums of Marseilles playing soccer on dirt fields with the sons of other North African immigrants was on his way to his second World Cup final in eight years. For Portugal, the loss was heartbreaking. Even the return of Deco, who was coming off a suspension, could do little to energize the Portuguese attack. Ronaldo was ineffective on the flanks, canceled out by the grittiness of Vieira. France deserved the win.

## ZINEDINE ZIDANE

The French midfielder became famous in 1998 for heading two goals in the final against Brazil to win the World Cup, and then became infamous for another header in the final against Italy eight years later.

Zidane, whose parents immigrated to France from Algeria, grew up in the predominately Arab ghetto of La Castellane in Marseilles. As a child, Zidane played on the dusty streets near his house. He eventually joined US Saint-Henri, his neighborhood team. On the recommendation of Saint-Henri's coaching staff, he was signed by Septemes Sports Olympiques. At age 14, Zidane left Septemes after Jean Varraud, a scout with Cannes, took notice of him. Zidane went to Cannes for what was intended to be a six-week tryout, but remained at the team for four years. Zidane then spent four years with Bordeaux. In 1996, he left France and was transferred to Juventus. At the Italian club, Zidane became one of the top players in the world. He helped the Italian giants to two Serie A titles and reached two consecutive Champions League finals, in 1997 and 1998, only to lose both.

Zidane earned his first cap with the French national team in August 1994, coming on as a substitute in the 63rd minute in a friendly against the Czech Republic. France was down 2–0 when Zidane entered the game and scored two goals for the 2–2 tie. At the time, France coach Aime Jacquet had planned to field the team around Manchester United star Eric Cantona. When Cantona got himself banned for a year in January 1995 after attacking a verbally abusive Crystal Palace fan during an English League match, Jacquet rearranged the team and positioned Zidane as playmaker. Despite the critics, France reached the semifinals of the 1996 European Championship. Zidane solidified his place as a world star when he helped France win the World Cup in 1998. In France's second game of that tournament, Zidane received a red card and a two-game suspension in a 4–0 win over Saudi Arabia for stomping on Saudi Arabia's Fuad Amin. He scored his only goals of the tournament in the final against Brazil—both headers off corner kicks in the first half. France won the game, 3–0, to win its first—and only—World Cup. Zidane duplicated that success two years later, leading France to the 2000 European Championship. In 2001, Zidane was transferred from Juventus to Real Madrid, finally winning a Champions League trophy when he scored the winning goal in a 2–1 win over Germany's Bayer Leverkusen in the 2002 final at Glasgow's Hampden Park.

(continued)

A thigh injury prevented Zidane from playing in France's first two games at the 2002 World Cup. He returned for the third game, but France was ultimately eliminated without ever scoring a goal. Four years later, Zidane earned his 100th cap for France on the eve of the World Cup in a 1–0 victory over Mexico at the Stade de France in Paris.

Zidane showed how instrumental he was during the 2006 World Cup—and how hot tempered. Zidane let his temper get the best of him again in the closing minutes of France's second game of the 2006 tournament against South Korea. Zidane received a yellow card for a late tackle, his second card of the tournament. As a result, he was suspended from the third and final match of the group stage. France nonetheless beat Togo, 2–0, allowing Zidane to play in the knockout round. He returned to action in the round of sixteen against Spain, setting up teammate Patrick Vieira for the second and game-winning goal. In stoppage time, Zidane scored the final goal of the match for a 3–1 victory. In the quarterfinals against Brazil, Zidane assisted on Thierry Henry's goal, giving France a 1–0 win. In the semifinals, Zidane scored on a penalty kick to down Portugal 1–0 in the semifinals.

Zidane played his second World Cup final—and final pro game—against Italy in Berlin. He scored after seven minutes on a penalty kick with a cheeky chip shot that hit the crossbar before narrowly bouncing behind the goal line. He became one of only four players to achieve the feat of scoring in two different World Cup finals, sharing the honor with Pelé, Paul Breitner, and Vavá. Zidane's final pro game was marred in the 110th minute when he head-butted Italian defender Marco Materazzi in the chest. Zidane was red carded and did not participate in the penalty kick shootout, which Italy won, 5–3. Despite the controversy over his offense, Zidane was awarded the Golden Ball as the tournament's MVP.

Zidane was also elected FIFA World Player of the Year three times (1998, 2000, and 2003) and was named European Player of the Year in 1998.

In 2018, Zidane led Real Madrid to the Champions League, his third consecutive title, becoming the only coach in history to win three straight European club titles.

## World Cup Career Statistics

Tournaments played: 3
Games: 12
Goals: 5

## Third Place

Germany capped off its jubilant World Cup in style. With the country rallying behind the team, Germany defeated Portugal, 3–1, in front of 52,000 ecstatic fans in Stuttgart and giving them one more chance to party into the night. Two goals from Bastian Schweinsteiger—the first in the 56th minute followed by another twenty-two minutes later—gave the Germans some consolation after the loss to Italy. The German striker was also involved in Germany's other goal in the 60th minute after his low shot was diverted into the Portuguese net by Benfica midfielder Petit. The Germans, written off as a weak team before the start of the tournament, had emerged as one of the strongest. Winning third place was an unexpected achievement for Klinsmann, who resigned after the game. Klinsmann, heavily criticized for living in California and traveling to Germany every few weeks to meet with his players, had been able to instill an attacking mentality in a team not traditionally known for its offense.

## The Final

The all-European final between Italy and France was a rematch of the 2000 European Championship. On that occasion in Rotterdam in 2000, Italy, just thirty seconds away from pulling off a 1–0 win, conceded the equalizer in stoppage time. A goal by David Trézéguet in sudden-death overtime won France the trophy.

The rematch of that epic final was played on July 9 in Berlin's Olympiastadion, the same site where runner Jesse Owens won four gold medals at the 1936 Summer Olympics. The Italians were favored, but Zidane's performance against Spain and Brazil made France a legitimate contender for the final prize. Many had predicted a scoreless tie—given the strong defenses—but they would be mistaken. Perhaps it was the soaring temperatures, but the knockout stages of the tournament had featured a rather cautious tactical approach. The fear of not losing had resulted in just three goals total in the two semifinals and penalty shootouts resolved four of the fourteen previous games, excluding the final and third-place matches.

France took the lead after seven minutes when Florent Malouda galloped into the box and was clumsily brought down by Materazzi.

Referee Elizondo pointed to the spot, apparently fooled by Malouda's dramatic fall. Zidane stepped up to take the shot, cheekily chipping the ball to Buffon's left, which hit the underside of the crossbar and bounced to the ground just inches past the line for the score before rolling out. A gaggle of Italian defenders raised their arms as to signal no-goal, but Elizondo was correct to award the goal. The relieved play-maker raised his arms in relief, jogging away as his teammates hugged him. The old magician had conjured up one more trick. In the process, Zidane, who was playing in his last game, had made history, joining Brazilians Pelé and Vavá, along with Germany's Paul Breitner, as the only players to ever score in two World Cup final games. The French couldn't have gotten off to a brighter start.

The Italians, down for the first time at the tournament, knew they had to quickly react. And react they did. Materazzi made amends for conceding the penalty when he headed the ball off Pirlo's out-swinging corner kick, towering over the French defense to tie the score. Materazzi's goal—his second goal of the competition—leveled the score at 1–1. The Italian attack grew bolder and threatened, like it had in previous games, in the air and off dead balls. On another play that developed off a corner kick, Pirlo expertly took another corner kick and Toni was able to meet the ball with a towering header that rattled the crossbar. Barthez, who appeared beaten on the play, was relieved to have the woodwork on his side.

If Italy dominated the first half, France dictated the pace in the second period. Zambrotta and Cannavaro had their work cut out for them with Henry using all his speed and power to move the ball into the Italian box. France was dealt a blow in the 55th minute when Vieira suffered a hamstring injury. Vieira hobbled off the field, replaced with Alou Diarra. Lippi made a few changes of his own, replacing Totti and Perrotta, in a bid to stem the French tidal wave of attacks with two pairs of fresh legs. Lippi's moves seemed to pay off immediately after Luca Toni's header found the back of the net, but one of his teammates was deemed offside and the goal was pulled back. Certainly, the goal would have been a crushing blow to France's hopes, but the call allowed the score to remain tied. Overtime, like in 2000, seemed inevitable. The Italians, purveyors of defensive efficiency, held on as Gattuso did a remarkable job of covering the entire field, stealing the ball away every time a French player tried to create something and even powering his way into the opposing penalty area that helped generate a Toni shot that Thuram was able to deflect. Henry swooped up the flanks, but Cannavaro and Materazzi broke up those plays as well. The French, frustrated at not being able to score, continued to put on the offensive pressure, but to no avail. Extra time lurked on the horizon as the sun set and nightfall began to envelop the sky.

Trézéguet, the hero in Rotterdam six years earlier, was brought in, but he was to become the villain in Berlin. Zidane came back to life in extra time, bursting into the box with a powerful header that was tipped over the bar by Buffon's fingers. The play, the stuff of highlight reels, would be overshadowed by another Zidane header just a few minutes later. In tne meantime, Henry, who had been knocked to the ground in the first minute following a collision with Cannavaro, looked too tired at this point to do anything threatening offensively. He also limped out of the game in the final minute of overtime.

Insanity entered the game when Zidane, in a moment that can only be described as utter madness, charged toward Materazzi, head-butting the Italian defender in the chest. Materazzi fell hard to the ground the moment Zidane thrust his head into him. Elizondo did not see the assault, but Buffon ran toward him to point out the offense. Elizondo consulted the linesman, who had also missed the incident, but it was the fourth official, Cantalejo, who was stationed in between the Italian and French bench, who witnessed the head-butt. However, questions arose as to whether Cantalejo had seen TV replays on a small monitor placed along the sidelines. If he had, Cantalejo would be the first referee ever to use instant replay, a method that FIFA has rejected for nearly a decade. FIFA said afterward that TV technology was never used as part of the decision that led to Zidane's red card. In fact, the majority of those in the stands had not seen the incident. How else would it be explained that the decision to eject Zidane was greeted by a chorus of jeers. FIFA later indicated that a fifth official, who is on the sidelines as a backup in the event one of the other four can no longer continue with his duties, is the only one to use a TV monitor to double-check and track times of goals and other statistics. But FIFA said the fifth official never came into contact with the referees through the headsets, which were used by the referee and his assistants for the first time at this World Cup to communicate during games.

Zidane, who had requested to be substituted late in the second half but had been ignored by his bench, did not argue the decision and slowly

*In this video sequence, France's Zinedine Zidane (wearing the white jersey) viciously head-butts Italian defender Marco Materazzi during overtime at the 2006 World Cup final after the two exchanged words (Credit: RAI).*

made his way into the tunnel to the locker rooms, his head slumped down as he strutted past the podium where the World Cup trophy was sitting. The image of Zidane walking past the trophy, so close and yet so far away from his grasp, a defeated man in his last game, was surreal. The Frenchman's brutal act ensured that he would end his career in disgrace after earning so much praise during the tournament. His performance in the tournament had earned him demigod status back in France and in the slums of Marseilles where he was raised and learned to play soccer on dirt fields. That status might now be in jeopardy. The game lost its meaning in the last ten minutes following Zidane's sendoff. The Italians could make nothing out of the man advantage and Elizondo ended the game after a grueling 120 minutes. Zidane did bask in one consolation. He won the Golden Ball award as the tournament's best player despite his shameful incident. Zidane edged out Cannavaro for the prize, earning 2,012 points compared to the Italian captain's 1,977.

The Italians were cold and ruthless in the shootout. With Cannavaro standing in the midfield with his teammates, his arms folded with his face expressionless and tense as a marble statue, Pirlo, Materazzi, De Rossi, Del Piero, and Grosso blasted the ball into the net past France goaltender Barthez. Grosso's winning kick—a ferocious left-footed shot that flew into the upper right corner of the goal—sent the Italian players into ecstasy. Grosso ran from one side of the field to the other as his teammates chased him. The game marked only the second final ever to be decided on penalties. Grosso's decisive kick brought with it celebration on the Italian bench and tears from the French. The Italians had avenged their World Cup final loss to Brazil in 1994 on penalties and the agonizing loss to the French in the final of Euro 2000. Camoranesi went over to the French bench to his Juventus teammate Trézéguet to console him, before joining his teammates on the podium, where a sea of white confetti greeted the team as Cannavaro planted a kiss on the trophy before proudly lifting it toward the sky.

Although the trophy presentation degenerated into chaos, Germany '06 was one of the best-organized soccer tournaments ever staged. The jeers that greeted the celebration didn't appear to bother the players. The German crowd, still upset at the *Azzurri* for ousting their team, may have also been influenced from what they saw, or didn't see, on the jumbo screens inside the stadium. The screens replayed the game's two goals and the shootout, but not the most controversial moments like Zidane's head-butt. Instead, the reporters sitting in the press section

# FABIO CANNAVARO

Growing up just a corner kick away from the San Paolo Stadium in Naples, Italy, Cannavaro had the privilege of serving as a ball boy during the time Diego Maradona played for Napoli. Cannavaro, a defender, was discovered by Napoli scouts as a boy and was eventually given a spot on the first team in 1992. Three seasons later, Cannavaro moved to Parma.

While at Parma, Cannavaro cemented his reputation as a talented defender. Under coach Carlo Ancelotti, Cannavaro helped the club finish second in Serie A in 1997—the club's best-ever finish, just a point behind champion Juventus. In 1998–1999, Parma won the UEFA Cup and Italian Cup to become one of the most successful Italian teams of the 1990s. In 2002, he moved to Inter Milan, where he played for two years, before he was transferred to Juventus in 2004. He won his first Italian League title in 2005 with Juventus and a second title the following season with the Turin-based club. Although Juventus was later stripped of those titles following a match-fixing scandal and relegated to the country's second division, Cannavaro was long gone. He moved to Spanish club Real Madrid in the summer of 2006, signing a three-year contract with the Spanish giants.

Cannavaro's first taste of international success came as a youngster when he helped lead Italy's Under-21 team to consecutive European titles in 1994 and 1996. That year, he also played for Italy at the 1996 Summer Olympics in Atlanta. Cannavaro graduated to the senior national team in January 1997, making his debut against Northern Ireland. He went on to play for Italy at the 1998 and 2002 World Cups and 2000 and 2004 European Championship tournaments. Cannavaro was named Italy's team captain following the international retirement of Paolo Maldini, winning over teammates with his leadership and laid-back Neapolitan approach. Cannavaro's only international goal came with the captain's armband in a 4–0 win against Tunisia in May 2004. Cannavaro captained Italy to the 2006 World Cup title, where he was considered one of the finest players at the tournament. He finished only second to France captain Zinedine Zidane in the race for the Golden Ball award as the tournament's MVP. He was personally vindicated four months later when he was named European Player of the Year and FIFA's World Player in 2006.

## World Cup Career Statistics

Tournaments played: 3
Games: 18
Goals: 0

did see Zidane's viciousness on monitors placed on their tables. Zidane's senseless act had no explanation at first. Speaking for the first time since the incident three days after the game, Zidane said in an interview on Canal Plus, a French television network, that Materazzi cursed at him and mentioned his sister. "I tried not to listen to him, but he repeated them several times," Zidane said about Materazzi's taunts. "Sometimes words are harder than blows. When he said it for the third time, I reacted."[15] For months, Materazzi vehemently denied accusations that he had insulted Zidane's mother and sister, but changed his tune two months later, saying he had made an inappropriate comment about the Frenchman's sister. The incident was a sad ending to another spectacular, emotion-filled World Cup.

For Italy, beset by a scandal back home, the victory was further evidence the country remains a perennial soccer powerhouse. The title moved Italy within one of all-time leader Brazil and helped bring joy to a soccer-mad nation. "The further we progressed in this tournament, the more we realized we could win it," Lippi said. "Our confidence grew from match to match, especially when we beat Germany."[16] Nine months later, Italy experienced a baby boom—another one of the joys that comes with winning the World Cup.

## NOTES

1. FIFA press release Zurich, November 2, 2005.
2. FIFA press release, Zurich, November 2, 2005.
3. News conference, Munich, June 9, 2006.
4. Personal interview, May 24, 2006.
5. News conference, Gelsenkirchen, June 11, 2006.
6. News conference, Gelsenkirchen, June 12, 2006.
7. News conference, Kaiserslautern, June 17, 2006.
8. News conference, Hamburg, June 22.
9. News conference, Nuremberg, June 22, 2006.
10. News conference, Nuremberg, June 22, 2006.
11. News conference, Berlin, June 12, 2006.
12. News conference, Koenigstein, Germany, June 9, 2006.
13. News conference, Koenigstein, Germany, June 28, 2006.
14. England Football Association, press release, July 3, 2006.
15. Interview, Canal Plus network, July 12, 2006.
16. News Conference, Berlin, July 9, 2006.

# 9

# VIVA ESPAÑA

The first World Cup on African soil became a reality when FIFA awarded South Africa the tournament in 2004. After losing out to Germany for the right to host the 2006 World Cup, FIFA opened the bidding process solely to African nations. South Africa won the right to host the 2010 World Cup, part of a short-lived policy—abandoned in 2007—to rotate the tournament among FIFA's six confederations. FIFA President Sepp Blatter's push to get the World Cup to take place in Africa was met with widespread admiration, although there were rumblings that the country—lacking the proper infrastructure and plagued by a high crime rate—would not be able to host such a massive event. Critics warned the tournament would have to be moved to another country. Although some FIFA executives, both publicly and privately, expressed concern over South Africa's preparations, Blatter repeatedly assured organizers they had his full support and confidence. In the end, Blatter would be proven right with the summer of 2010 turning into a coming-out party for the new, post-apartheid South Africa and the continent as a whole. Soccer had been able to not only showcase the country but open future business and tourism opportunities to a continent that had too often garnered attention from the world for all the wrong reasons. There had been 18 World Cups throughout the tournament's history: ten in Europe, four in South America, three in North America, and one in Asia. This was a first for Africa. Add to that the fact that games would be played during the winter—for the first time since Argentina hosted in 1978—and the atmosphere and feel would truly be unique. "It's hard not to cry at the sight of a World Cup right here. We have come a long way. To have the World Cup here, just 16 years after democracy, is a real achievement," said former South African player Shaun Bartlett, who worked as an ESPN analyst during the tournament.[1]

South Africa haters were given some fuel on the eve of the tournament when thousands of fans stampeded outside Makhulong Stadium, located in a Johannesburg suburb, for an exhibition match between World Cup finalists Nigeria and North Korea only five days before the start of the tournament. The chaos outside the venue, which was not part of the World Cup, left 15 people injured, including a police officer who had tried to quell the mayhem. The 12,000-seat venue became the center of violence after tickets were handed out for free outside the stadium. FIFA later said it had nothing to do with the game, in a public relations effort meant to deflect any negative attention. The rampaging crowd—which included many wearing South Africa and Nigeria jerseys—left behind with it images of disorganization and crowd violence, something that made FIFA executives cringe. The worry was all for naught. Two weeks into the World Cup and it was clear that the organizing committee had done a fine job. "There were negative perceptions. Some even suggested that we won't be able to host the tournament. We were able to deliver the stadiums in time—some of them a year before the start of the World Cup—and it's been a big success," said former South African captain Lucas Radebe.[2]

If that wasn't enough, the South African authorities basically allowed FIFA to run its country for a month. Under pressure from the sport's governing body, the South African judicial system overhauled the way it would deal with crime during the tournament. Instead of drawn-out police investigations followed by even longer trials, the courts would expedite all criminals arrested during the tournament. A man who had stolen a cell phone was sentenced to five years behind bars two days after he was arrested. He was tried in one of 56 courts set up across the country aimed at doling out swift justice. The aptly named "instant justice courts" dealt with all cases throughout the 30-day competition, putting defendants away for crimes ranging from petty theft to armed robbery. The worst case the tribunals dealt with took place on the eve of the tournament when two men were sentenced to 15 years behind bars apiece after being found guilty of armed robbery. Two days before the start of the tournament, the men, both from Zimbabwe, robbed a

Portuguese newspaper photographer in his hotel room in the middle of the night, forcing him at gunpoint to give up his cash and equipment. As a result, hotels that housed journalists across the country were given 24-hour police protection. Other hotels had already decided to hire private security firms to guard their facilities in the event armed robbers got the wrong idea. One of the most trivial cases the tribunals had to deal with was the arrest of a group of Dutch women who were accused of wearing outfits FIFA deemed to be part of an "ambush marketing campaign" aimed at promoting a beer company. FIFA was out to protect one of its main sponsors, Budweiser, by forcing the authorities to arrest the women. The women were later released and thrown out of the country. The incident, however, was more about marketing than crime.

Blatter's continued commitment to the South African bid originally came out of FIFA's willingness to rotate the World Cup across the various continents in order to use soccer's importance and popularity to help underserved areas culturally, economically, and politically. At South Africa 2010, the continent would be represented in the World Cup finals by six countries, a massive increase from one in 1970, two in 1982, three in 1994, and five after 1998. The pressure on African soccer, which had underachieved at previous World Cups, was tremendous. While the continent produced some genuine stars over the past few decades, players who would go on to earn millions playing club soccer in Europe, a lack of funding, disorganization at the federation level, and political instability all added to their woes. The 2010 World Cup did little to erase that. If anything, their troubles on the field were highlighted, much to the chagrin of local fans who adopted all the African nations participating at the tournament.

The organizing committee selected ten venues spread across nine host cities, with the final to be played at the refurbished 84,500-seat Soccer City Stadium in Johannesburg. Five new stadiums were built, with another five existing venues upgraded to FIFA's standards. South Africa spent a staggering $1.3 billion to upgrade venues, roadways, and public infrastructure—a considerable sum for a nation emerging from the days of apartheid where many of its inhabitants earn a daily wage of one dollar—in time for the tournament. And whether crime (the country averaged 50 murders a day prior to the start of the tournament) or other logistical issues would be an impediment to hosting such a grandiose event, Danny Jordaan, head of the South African World Cup Organizing Committee, said, "Fans need to rest assured that security measures have been taken into consideration. Some $90 million will be spent on procuring specialized equipment, including crowd-control equipment, command vehicles, additional helicopters, specialized body-armor, high-tech bomb disabling equipment, and mobile cameras. The mobile command centers will largely be based at the match venues but can be moved around if the need arises and will feature high-tech monitoring equipment, which will be able to receive live footage from airplanes and other cameras."[3]

An affable man who had worked alongside Nelson Mandela in the country's post-apartheid government starting in 1994, Jordaan urged fans from around the world to visit South Africa while at the same time sounding what would be a prophetic statement: "This is the year when, as a nation, we will open our doors, hearts, and sporting spirits to the world. This is our time. This is our year."[4]

South Africa had come a long way since Mandela was released from prison in 1990 after spending 27 years on remote Robben Island, located in the southern Atlantic Ocean within view of lovely Cape Town. Mandela himself had been banned from playing soccer, the only joy the 2,000 prisoners enjoyed during recreation on what had become Africa's version of Alcatraz. In 1967, the prisoners set up a 24-team league, dubbed the Makana Football Association, and used it to demonstrate to their white captors that they were not inferior, neither intellectually nor physically, to whites. Now, the World Cup, the game's premier event, was going to be played on South African soil, where whites and blacks now lived equally. Jordaan was correct. This was to be South Africa's year—on and off the field—as the nation basked in positive attention for one of the few times in its recent history. Indeed, by the time the tournament came to an end, an estimated 500,000 visitors—the majority Americans—flooded into the Rainbow Nation to witness the tournament and bask in the pageantry that is the modern World Cup.

Thirty-two finalists—including South Africa, who had automatically earned a spot in the final as host nation—began qualifying for the tournament in 2007. For the second straight time, the defending champions were not given an automatic bid, leaving Italy the task of having to endure the rigors of qualification. With 204 of FIFA's 208 members vying for the 31 remaining spots, the 2010 World Cup shared a record with the 2008 Summer Olympics in Beijing for the number of countries competing in a sporting event. As always, qualification was not without controversy. During the second game of a two-game playoff between France and

Ireland, French striker Thierry Henry handled the ball twice in the play that led to the winning goal. The outcome sparked debate that referees should have access to instant replay. Swedish referee Martin Hansson, who had failed to call the Henry handball, said the outcome left him in tears afterwards. "If you watch the rest of the game, it was maybe one of the best games in my career, except for that terrible thing."[5]

FIFA, as it had done in the past with other botched calls, rejected Ireland's petition to have the game replayed and also turned down its request to participate as a 33rd finalist. FIFA promised to look into goal-line technology to review plays—an issue that would rear its ugly head again during the finals—but Ireland was left looking from the outside in, with many branding Henry a cheater. In another controversial match, the African playoff battle between Algeria and Egypt, the game was marred by fan violence, but it was the Algerians who emerged victorious in the end in a dramatic one-game playoff held in Sudan that was resolved on a goal by defender Antar Yahia.

FIFA held the much-anticipated World Cup draw on December 9, 2009, in picturesque Cape Town. With hundreds packed into the Cape Town International Convention Center to learn the fate of the thirty-two finalists, FIFA announced that the seeded teams would be based on the October 2009 world rankings. Therefore, South Africa, Italy, Brazil, Spain, the Netherlands, Germany, Argentina, and England were seeded and would not face each other during the group stage. The ceremony, co-hosted by FIFA Secretary general Jerome Valcke and South African actress Charlize Theron, also featured Los Angeles Galaxy star David Beckham and Ethiopian runner Haile Gebrselassie. The draw yielded the following first-round groupings:

Group A: South Africa, Mexico, Uruguay, and France
Group B: Argentina, Nigeria, South Korea, and Greece
Group C: England, United States, Algeria, and Slovenia
Group D: Germany, Australia, Serbia, and Ghana
Group E: Netherlands, Denmark, Japan, and Cameroon
Group F: Italy, Paraguay, New Zealand, and Slovakia
Group G: Brazil, North Korea, Ivory Coast, and Portugal
Group H: Spain, Switzerland, Honduras, and Chile

The United States ended up in arguably the most manageable group ever in its history. Although England appeared fearsome (and favorites to win the group as per the usual pre-tournament hype), the Americans looked at Algeria and Slovenia as beatable opponents. The United States was coming off a wonderful year after finishing runners-up at the 2009 Confederations Cup, a tournament held in South Africa the year before the World Cup that served as a logistical dry run for the host nation. While the Americans had come within 45 minutes of winning their first FIFA trophy (up 2-0 at halftime against Brazil), they would go on to lose 3-2 in a heartbreaking defeat that left Clint Dempsey in tears. The loss may have hurt, but the experience of traveling to South Africa, training there, and acclimating to the chilly temperatures, time difference, and altitude would serve them well a year later at the World Cup. On top of that, the Americans had defeated then No. 1-ranked Spain 2-0 in the semifinals in one of the greatest, if not improbable, wins in U.S. soccer history.

The Americans dominated CONCACAF once again during World Cup qualifying, finishing first in the final group stage ahead of rival Mexico. Qualifying, as usual, had been a long process for the United States, including a two-game series with Cuba. The United States clinched a spot in the finals following a 3-2 win at Honduras in San Pedro Sula

*Actress Charlize Theron with a look of surprise after learning that France had been placed in the same group as her native South Africa (Credit: 2010 FIFA WC OC).*

thanks to two goals from striker Conor Casey. Ironically, Casey would not be included in the final 23-man squad named by coach Bob Bradley seven months later. Led by Landon Donovan, the United States was as prepared as it would ever be. A record number of Americans were playing in some of Europe's top domestic leagues, and even Donovan, a regular with the Los Angeles Galaxy, had completed a successful loan spell with English club Everton during the winter while Major League Soccer lay dormant. Donovan had gained the respect of the English, no small thing, ahead of what would be an epic USA-England clash. The match would reveal two things: England's weaknesses (highlighted by the usual pre-tournament hype that surrounded the home of the Premiership) and the new heights of popularity soccer had achieved in what had forever been a baseball-crazed nation like the United States. Americans had always struggled with soccer, whether it was playing or watching in large numbers. It was too low scoring for some; outright boring to others. However, the summer of 2010 would change all that thanks to the U.S. team and its exploits half a world away.

For the U.S. team, the drama wouldn't start at the World Cup but two and a half years earlier. It was during the grueling, marathon process of qualifying—when most Americans are not paying attention to the fortunes of their national team—that the drama was in full swing. On the final day of qualifying, for instance, with the Americans already in the finals, Bradley was looking for at least a draw in order to finish atop the final six-team group ahead of regional rival Mexico. The Mexicans—who had lost 2-0 to the United States on the road at Columbus Crew Stadium in Columbus, Ohio, but had defeated them at home 2-1—had also booked their ticket to South Africa. The only thing on the line for either the United States or Mexico was regional bragging rights. "We take a great amount of pride in trying to be the best team in CONCA-CAF. The competition in the final round [of qualifying] has been very strong and that's the reason everything has been very close," said coach Bob Bradley.[6]

The jubilation that had come with qualifying, however, was muted days later when promising striker Charlie Davies was involved in a car accident just outside Washington, DC, where the United States was slated to play Costa Rica in the final qualifier. Davies suffered a lacerated bladder and fractures to his tibia and femur in his right leg. He also suffered facial fractures and a broken left elbow. Davies would work hard to recover but was left off Bradley's final roster. Davies had been a standout at the Confederations Cup the previous summer, and Bradley was banking on him to spearhead the American attack at the World Cup. Against Costa Rica, the inspired Americans, playing with heavy hearts, put on a wonderful performance. Already assured of a spot in the finals, the United States let their opponents do most of the playing. Costa Rica, who had yet to qualify and would need to walk away with a victory, controlled the pace and flow of the match. They scored twice in a four-minute span to rock the Americans. In the 21st minute, forward Bryan Ruiz ran onto a pass on the left side of the penalty area, pushed past U.S. defender Oguchi Onyewu, and then cut into the six-yard box. Ruiz then squeezed his shot through Tim Howard's legs for the 1-0 lead. Three minutes later, Costa Rica made it 2-0 on an unstoppable blast from Ruiz just outside the area as the ball slammed into the upper left corner. Howard had no chance to grab it. The United States, with its never-say-die spirit, scored in the 72nd minute when midfielder Robbie Rogers crossed a perfect ball from the right wing position. The ball was headed up in the air by Bradley's son, Michael, and ultimately fell to Donovan's feet. Donovan's shot was saved, but Bradley skillfully slid to slam the rebound into the roof of the net to cut the lead in half.

The frantic finale featured the ejection of Costa Rica coach Rene Simoes and a member of his staff, who both engaged the fourth official in a heated argument on the sidelines as the game moved into injury time. Both had to be escorted from the field by security guards as the crowd jeered. If that wasn't enough drama, the U.S. team was reduced to ten players for the last seven minutes of the game after Onyewu collapsed to the ground in the Costa Rican box. He was later diagnosed with a torn patellar tendon in his left knee, suffered while he was backpedaling after a corner kick. He was stretchered off and would be sidelined for the next few months. The injury drew the ire of his new club, AC Milan, though Onyewu hadn't appeared in a single league game for them that season. The club even threatened U.S. Soccer, saying they wanted to be monetarily compensated for the injury. In the end, nothing came of it and Onyewu spent most of that season in rehabilitation.

In what appeared to be the final play of the game, more than four and half minutes of the announced five minutes of stoppage time in, Rogers took a corner kick from the right that Jonathan Bornstein was able to connect with on a header. "We won the corner kick and I was standing with Steve Cherundolo in midfield when I looked over at him and said, 'One of us should go in the box.' He just looked at me. I took it upon myself to run into the box and no one was marking me once I got there. Robbie Rogers put up a good ball off the corner kick and I just headed it. We had practiced that play 100 times," recalled Bornstein.[7]

The goal sent the American players into ecstasy, while the shocked Costa Ricans looked on with sadness. When the final whistle blew, the Americans celebrated as the Costa Rican players walked off the field in tears. The players paraded around the field waving American flags and messages of support for Davies. In the ninth minute of the match, thousands of fans sitting near the midfield at RFK Stadium had held up signs with No. 9—Davies' jersey—in his honor. The draw may have been favorable to the United States in allowing them to win the group, but it doomed Costa Rica. Instead, Honduras benefited. While the United States tangled with Costa Rica, Honduras was playing El Salvador. Holding on to a 1-0 lead, the players celebrated at the end of their match when they learned of Bornstein's goal. The country—in the midst of political turmoil following a coup—was given a reason to celebrate as Honduras returned to the World Cup finals for the first time in 28 years. Bornstein had become a household name in Honduras virtually overnight. His newfound rock-star status was clearly understood. After all, it was his goal that put Honduras through, unleashing days of celebration in the streets. Qualifying for the World Cup prompted de facto Honduran President Roberto Micheletti to declare a national holiday the day after Bornstein's goal, offering "this gringuito who scored on a header" an all-expenses-paid trip to the resort spot of Islas de la Bahia.[8] Bornstein never took him up on the offer. As for Costa Rica, it would have to face a two-game playoff against Uruguay. The two-time World Cup champions would go on to defeat Costa Rica 1-0 on the road in a tense November 14 encounter, followed by a 1-1 draw at home four days later to reach the finals. Costa Rica, finalists four years earlier, had been eliminated.

Meanwhile, the grueling club schedule that typically preceded the World Cup took a seemingly heavier toll ahead of the 2010 tournament. Many of the world's biggest stars missed the finals: players like Michael Ballack of Germany, Michael Essien of Ghana, and Rio Ferdinand of England. In March, three months before the World Cup, David Beckham's dreams of playing for England were shattered when he was injured during a Serie A game with AC Milan. Beckham, a teammate of Donovan's at the Galaxy, had also used the winter months to train and was on his second stint with the Serie A club. Beckham suffered a ruptured Achilles tendon and would end up as a spectator on England's bench in South Africa. The rash of injuries didn't end there. Didier Drogba of the Ivory Coast and Andrea Pirlo of Italy were also injured with an arm and calf injury, respectively, but traveled to South Africa with their teams in the hopes of recovering in time for the tournament. The overcrowded schedule of league and continental tournament matches had worn the players out. Marketing and television interests, however, were too big for clubs and once again the World Cup would be made to suffer for it.

Not that the World Cup and FIFA were immune to the almighty dollar. Sponsors jumped on as fast as they could, despite a global economic recession that crippled the world markets just a year earlier, and were looking to South Africa's emerging economy to promote their products. No other company did it quite as aggressively and astutely as Coca-Cola. A World Cup sponsor for nearly forty years, Coca-Cola blanketed South Africa with billboards and television commercials a year before the tournament. The soft drink–maker even paid for the erection of new street signs in poor areas across South Africa, including Soweto, but with one catch: they would all feature the red-and-white Cola-Cola logo. The marketing hit a crescendo during the tournament when small cans of soda were handed out to visitors as soon as their passports were stamped at South African airports.

Although most promotions occurred off the field, one thing that affected players was the ball used at the World Cup. Adidas, an official tournament sponsor, had the tradition of unveiling a new ball every four years. This particular World Cup ball was dubbed "jabulani," the word meaning "to celebrate" in the Bantu language isiZulu, one of the official languages of South Africa. However, some players, particularly goalkeepers, were hardly cheering, comparing it to a cheap children's plastic ball you'd buy at a supermarket. They argued that the ball's tricky trajectory made it hard to stop.

As for the South African team, it had to seriously contemplate the possibility that it could be the first host nation not to progress beyond the first round despite flashes of potential at the 2009 Confederations Cup, when it reached the semifinals before losing to Brazil. Less than a year before the World Cup, Brazilian coach Joel Santana had been fired and replaced with countryman Carlos Alberto Parreira, back for a second stint in charge of the team. Parreira, who led Brazil to the World Cup title in 1994 on American soil, quit the South Africa coaching job in 2007 because of a family illness. On the eve of the World Cup, Parreira geared up for his biggest challenge yet and held training camps in Brazil and Germany. Wins over Thailand, Guatemala, and Colombia on the eve of the World Cup were a positive sign that the team was on the right track. But South Africa would also need some luck in order to progress and took heart in South Korea's amazing fourth-place finish at the 2002 World Cup when it was able to channel the enthusiasm from the home crowd to its benefit. They needed the same recipe for success.

South Africa opened the tournament on June 11 at Soccer City Stadium in Johannesburg against Mexico before a near-capacity crowd of 84,490. The opening ceremony prior to the match, marred by the death of Mandela's 13-year-old great-granddaughter the night before in a car accident, went on as planned, although the Nobel Peace Prize winner was not in the stands to greet the teams and a worldwide television audience. Mandela, who had largely disappeared from public life, would be a no-show. "First, let me convey a message from Madiba. He would be with us to greet you. Unfortunately, there was a tragedy in the family. But he said, 'The game must start; we must enjoy the game.' We are humbled by this moment to host one of the great tournaments of this world," South African President Jacob Zuma told the crowd.

When Blatter handed the World Cup trophy to Mandela in May 2005, it was a symbolic gesture of a promising future for South Africa. Five years later, the future was now and the country was prepared to host the soccer world. "Here and now the FIFA World Cup is in Africa. The FIFA World Cup is in South Africa. Ke Nako!" Blatter told the enthusiastic crowd as fans blew on their vuvuzela horns—yes, those same horns that had annoyed players and TV commentators alike the previous year when South Africa hosted the Confederations Cup. From the Zulu meaning "to make a lot of noise," the vuvuzelas, and the buzzing din created by thousands of them blowing in unison inside a stadium, became a symbol of the tournament. When the American players traveled to the country in late May, vuvuzelas were placed in each of their rooms after they checked into the tranquil Irene Country Lodge outside Pretoria. If this World Cup had a soundtrack, it was the vuvuzela. Despite complaints from players and broadcasters, Blatter came to the vuvuzela's defense just days into the competition and declared they

*Nelson Mandela lifts the World Cup trophy after FIFA awards the tournament to South Africa (Credit: 2010 FIFA WC OC).*

*The ear-splitting vuvuzela horns became both the most annoying and most popular fan accessory at the World Cup (Credit: 2010 FIFA WC OC).*

would not be banned. Others favored the makarapa as their stadium accessory. A cut-out construction helmet decorated with team logos and colors, the makarapa was another popular item sold at airports and outside stadiums by vendors.

At the South African team's final news conference three days before the opening match, the excitement among the staff and players was palpable. The team was already being credited with unifying its country. From large cities to tiny townships, citizens were just as excited as the players. The South African team had wrapped up its preparations with a 1-0 victory over Denmark at Soccer City, the team's third consecutive win, and was looking to beat Mexico to top Group A. The loud fans that greeted the players energized the team. The players soaked up the love, and the expectations created a sense that the team could do better than even the most optimistic expectations. Midfielder Reneilwe Letsholonyane put it best: "There is always going to be pressure because we know we're not playing for ourselves. We've united an entire nation. The whole nation is behind us, and we need to repay them."[9]

Unity was one thing, but reality another. South Africa entered the World Cup ranked a lowly 83rd by FIFA—only North Korea was worse in the pecking order of any of the 32 finalists at 105th. According to a FIFA survey, only 22 percent of those polled predicted South Africa would make it past the group stage. With no world stars on the roster, South Africa had to make the best with what it had. The last-minute coaching change hadn't helped during the preparation process. The players, however, shrugged off the negativity. Instead, they basked in their newfound popularity and the joy that was sweeping the nation. "For a brief moment, the nation gets together behind one team. I think that's fantastic," said defender Matt Booth, the only white player on the team.[10]

The South African players sang and danced as they waltzed out of the tunnel and onto the field before the buzzing crowd at Soccer City in the opener. Mexico looked the better team early on, but the South African defense—seemingly nervous at first under the weight of all the pressure and glare of the crowd—settled into the game as the minutes wore on and was able to absorb the pressure of the Mexican attack. After 32 minutes, Mexico appeared to take the lead on a Carlos Vela goal, but it was ruled offside. The crowd gasped the moment the ball crossed the line, but were back to blowing their plastic horns in delight after seeing referee Ravshan Irmatov of Uzbekistan wave off the goal. Irmatov also made some history of his own that afternoon by becoming the first Uzbek official to ever referee a World Cup finals game.

Halftime ended scoreless, but it was South Africa—with the vuvuzela-tooting crowd behind it—to open the scoring when Siphiwe Tshabalala fired a superb 55th-minute strike—only fitting that the first goal recorded at a World Cup on the African continent be scored by an African player. The crowd erupted in jubilation when Tshabalala's goal, a rifling shot that hit the twine in the top of the net, beat goalkeeper Oscar Perez to his left side. Mexico coach Javier Aguirre used all three of his subs in an effort to try and level the score. Just when it appeared that the hosts would collect all three points, it was veteran Mexican defender Rafa Marquez who rescued the draw for his side with a close-range finish 11 minutes from time. The Mexicans may have been known for their attacking game, but the team would need to finish more of its chances if it had any hope of advancing to the knockout stage. The South Africans were happy with a point, with qualification to the second round still a possibility.

Although both South Africa and Mexico played a brilliant opener, Diego Forlan–led Uruguay shone in Group A. The team improved with every game thanks to its solid defense and swift counterattack. Uruguay opened on the evening of June 11 in Cape Town with a relatively dour showing—a scoreless draw against France. The game was a defensive affair—a sign of things to come in this tournament's opening round—as the stalemate lingered on. Overall, France had more scoring chances, but both sides limited their offense to a few long-range efforts and bogged down midfield play that was riddled with fouls. Even Forlan had been unable to find the back of the net. The French, meanwhile, employed Nicolas Anelka as a lone striker, and he barely saw the ball that night. On the other side of the field was Forlan who appeared the most resolute in his efforts to score, forcing French goalkeeper Hugo Lloris, one of the best young players at the tournament, to make an excellent save after just 16 minutes. Veteran Thierry Henry entered the game in the second half, but there was little even he could do to change the outcome. Uruguay's Nicolas Lodeiro, a second half sub, was red-carded following a nasty challenge on Barclay Sagna, an unfortunate ending to such a bad game.

Five days later, Uruguay showed what it was made of with a re-sounding 3-0 victory over South Africa. Two goals by Forlan and another from Alvaro Pereira recorded what could have been the worst possible outcome for the host nation. The game was played on Youth Day, a national holiday commemorating the 1976 student uprising in Soweto against the apartheid government. The day-long celebrations, however, were cut short after South Africa fell behind early in the match. Forlan opened the scoring with a dipping free kick from 30 yards out in the 24th minute that sailed past goalkeeper Itumeleng Khune. The Atletico Madrid star added a second in the 80th minute on a penalty kick after Khune received a red card for tripping Luis Suarez in the penalty box. The enthusiastic home crowd was finally silenced in stoppage time when Pereira killed off the match with a third goal. Uruguay had its ultimate weapon in Forlan. The team had also brought a piece of home to South Africa after the federation shipped a ton of beef so that the players could hold an outdoor meat roast, known as an *asado*, the previous day. "We are convinced we can win the World Cup. We can be a tough rival for any of the teams out there if we play well," said a confident Uruguay manager Oscar Tabarez, who had coached the team at the World Cup 20 years earlier in Italy.[11]

France and Mexico, both in need of a win to keep their hopes of advancing alive, faced off on June 17 in Polokwane. The French entered the game with high hopes of getting to the knockout stage, but by the time it was over they were on the verge of elimination. Mexico, limited to a single goal in its first game, finally put its offensive weapons on display with promising youngster Javier Hernandez and grizzled veteran Cuauhtémoc Blanco scoring to give their side a 2-0 victory. For Hernandez, his 64th-minute strike meant that the World Cup was now a family affair for him. Hernandez's grandfather, Tomas Balcazar, scored for Mexico at the 1954 World Cup. Hernandez was even able to one-up his father, who played at the 1986 World Cup but failed to find the back of the net.

While the French played cautiously, Mexico was much more lively with the ball and ambitious in its quest to score. Both sides went into the dressing rooms tied 0-0. Hernandez, in for Efrain Juarez in the 55th minute, and Blanco, in for Guillermo Franco just seven minutes later, changed the outcome of the game. Marquez, who left Barcelona and signed with the New York Red Bulls weeks after the tournament, was able to split the French defense with a through ball. Hernandez, having sprung the offside trap, carefully sidestepped Loris before tapping the ball into the open net. The French response was feeble. Instead, Mexico made sure it collected three points when Blanco scored off a penalty kick to the right of Loris with 11 minutes left to play. Like 2002, France was now at serious risk of not getting through to the next round, while Mexico took top spot in Group A, alongside Uruguay, with four points. For France, the loss to Mexico resulted in the team's total implosion. The undoing began during halftime when France coach Raymond Domenech harshly criticized Anelka for his poor performance. Domenech even threatened to bench Anelka, something he would go on to do in the second half. Anelka fired back, unleashing a tirade against his coach. As a result, Anelka was eventually sent home to Paris after the French federation deemed him a distraction. The soap opera did not end there; it grew and spilled over in full public view. At the team's first training session after the loss, the trouble that started in the dressing room erupted into a public feud. Domenech's bizarre management style finally got to the team. He communicated badly, often keeping his players in the dark. He also had a penchant for selecting a roster based on astrological signs and often drew the ire of French fans when the team played poorly. After a heated argument at the team's practice facility in Knysna, outside Cape Town, between captain Patrice Evra and fitness coach Robert Duverne, things got worse. Domenech had to jump in to separate the two. Domenech's involvement made things worse, just as it had during the Mexico game, and the fight ended with Duverne tossing his stopwatch and accreditation on the ground before storming off. Subsequently, the players decided to walk off the field and boarded the bus back to their hotel. As a result, team director Jean-Louis Valentin announced, before dozens of assembled cameramen from around the world, that he quit his post, effective immediately, after the players decided to boycott the training session. Asked about his seemingly hasty decision, Valentin quipped, "Ask the players. They do not want to play anymore. It's unacceptable!"

Valentin also vehemently denied he was the source of the leak to the French media, revealing the halftime argument between Anelka and Domenech. Within hours, the players released a statement saying they opposed the federation's decision to expel Anelka and complained that officials "at no time tried to protect the team" during the fracas. The first signs of trouble arose after the opening game against Uruguay, when the players implored the stubborn Domenech to play with a traditional 4-4-2 formation instead of his preferred 4-2-3-1, which left Anelka all alone offensively. Domenech appeared open to the plan prior to the Mexico match but ditched it after he learned that it had come from former French star Zinedine Zidane, who was now working as a scout for Algeria's national team. "I tried to convince them that what they were doing was an aberration, an imbecility, a stupidity," Domenech said of the players' strike, while the whole time deflecting blame from himself.[12]

On June 22, South Africa faced France in Bloemfontein, while at the same time Uruguay played Mexico in Rustenberg. A draw between Uruguay and Mexico would see both sides through to the Round of 16, bringing back bad memories of the 1982 opening-round match between Austria and Germany. In that game, both teams conspired to produce a 1-0 final score for Germany, which saw both teams through to the next round at the expense of Algeria. But the fears were unfounded this time. Instead, Uruguay and Mexico played a highly entertaining game. The outcome, a 1-0 win by Uruguay, was resolved in the 43rd minute by Suarez. The Uruguayan defense once again come through, while the offense, marshaled by Forlan, was able to find the back of the net following a cross from Edinson Cavani that found Suarez's head. Uruguay topped the group as Mexico would also advance after finishing second.

At the same time, all eyes were on the hosts, looking to avoid early elimination, and the French, who captured the headlines for all the wrong reasons in the days leading up to the game. The South Africans, propelled by the crowd and their horns, did all they could to win—and win with a large enough margin to advance. They jumped out to an early lead after 20 minutes when Bongani Khumalo tucked the ball into the net after Loris missed his chance to stop it with his fist. South Africa doubled the lead in the 37th minute after the French defense—in utter disarray—failed to clear the ball on no less than three attempts, allowing Katlego Mphela to finally score. With nothing to lose, Domenech, using his 4-2-3-1 formation, put in Henry, but it was too little too late. South Africa continued to throw caution to the wind and tried in vain to score a third goal, needing to run up its score if it wanted to advance on goal differential. Instead, France finally scored in the 70th minute with Florent Malouda. His goal ended South Africa's slim hopes of advancing to the knockout stage. The host nation's players and enthusiastic fans, however, held their heads high after finishing third in a very tough group, being eliminated only because of a goal differential. "They did not make it past the group stage, but they did what the country asked of them—they played with pride, passion, and skill. They gave their best and that's all we could have asked for," said Jordaan.[13]

For France, the goal was very little consolation for a team that not only played horribly but also lacked cohesion before totally humiliating themselves, their federation, and their country before the world. For many, France's meltdown was karma for Henry's handball against Ireland in qualifying. Domenech, who announced he was going to step down even before the tournament began, walked away in disgrace four years after he advanced his team to the World Cup final. His successor, former French defender Laurent Blanc, was given the tough task of cleaning up the team's image after the affair drew the criticism of French President Nicolas Sarkozy and other senior members of his cabinet. Henry, who joined Marquez with the Red Bulls after the World Cup, was summoned to Paris for a private meeting with Sarkozy. The controversy was behind them. Henry retired from the national team, Anelka was given an 18-game national team suspension, and Blanc was ordered to rebuild the squad.

In Group B, Argentina was not only favored to finish first, but it was also on the list to contend for the title. The team, under the stewardship of former superstar Diego Maradona, barely advanced to the finals

*Argentina coach Diego Maradona was all smiles ahead of his team's first World Cup game (Credit: Getty 2010 FIFA WC OC).*

after suffering through a tough qualifying tournament. After Argentina booked its spot to the finals, Maradona used the news conference immediately after the match, broadcast live on Argentine television, to lash out at reporters who criticized him throughout his brief tenure. In a foul-mouthed tirade, Maradona told reporters in Montevideo following Argentina's 1-0 win over rival Uruguay that he was not pleased with them. "There were those who did not believe in this team and who treated me as less than nothing. Today we are in the World Cup finals with the help of no one, but with honor. To all of you who did not believe in us, and I apologize to all the women here, you can suck it, and keep sucking it," said Maradona.[14]

The outburst become an overnight sensation on YouTube, with Internet sites selling t-shirts emblazoned with the phrase "They can keep sucking it" and ringtones playing the vulgar message becoming all the rage in Buenos Aires. Maradona, always a controversial figure, was slapped with a two-month ban by FIFA in November, meaning he could not attend the draw in South Africa. The ban, however, did not affect his ability to coach the team at the World Cup.

Argentina opened its World Cup campaign on June 12 against Nigeria at Ellis Park in Johannesburg. The Argentines swarmed the Nigerian half but got its lone goal on a header by defender Gabriel Heinze after just six minutes. The goal, off a Juan Veron corner kick, was a brilliant display of athleticism after Heinze lunged forward and struck the ball with all his might. Argentina showed some defensive vulnerability, but Nigeria did very little in the way of creating any real scoring chances. Defender Taye Taiwo, a teammate of Henize at French club Olympique Marseille, came close to tying the score when his shot came within a hair of the post with 20 minutes left to play. Striker Lionel Messi had at least four decent attempts on goal, but goalkeeper Vincent Enyeama did a solid job of keeping Argentina from running up the score. On the sidelines, Maradona put on his own show. He ditched the tight-fitting tracksuit and sneakers for a spiffy gray suit. Looking more like the best man at a wedding than a coach, Maradona also sported a beard to cover up scars sustained from an attack by his pit bull earlier in the year. He also put on a show for fans. Whenever the ball rolled toward his bench, Maradona was more than happy to tap it, even perform a brief juggling act, much to the delight of the crowd. In the group's other game, South Korea defeated Greece 2-0 at Nelson Mandela Bay Stadium in Port Elizabeth. The South Koreans earned three valuable points in the race for second place. With a goal in each half, they exposed weaknesses in the Greek defense, the bedrock on which the team was built and the reason they surprisingly won the 2004 European Championship. On the flip side, the Greek offense was totally impotent, a bad sign in a group where goal differential was seen as a major factor in trying to advance into the Round of 16. Under German coach Otto Rehhagel, the Greek team won the European Championship by frustrating opponents with its rugged, rock-solid defense and ability to score that one goal needed to gain a victory. That same strategy, however, did not work in South Africa.

On June 17, Argentina played South Korea at Soccer City before a crowd of 82,174. An Argentina victory would assure them of a spot in the elimination round. A draw would base the outcome on the group's final game. True to form, Argentina put together a dazzling performance, with Messi in the playmaker role, as the team rolled to another victory. During qualification for the finals, Maradona came under fire for playing Messi out of position and too deep for him to really matter offensively. In South Africa, Maradona put Messi, who earned $46 million annually at Barcelona, behind the two strikers in a 4-3-1-2 formation that started to yield results. The marriage between Maradona and Messi got off to a rocky start when he took over as national team manager in September 2008. At the time, Maradona branded Messi a greedy player. Under Maradona, Messi would score only one goal in ten qualifying matches.

Maradona the coach was more a motivator than a master tactician. He essentially played the role of father to the players, hugging and kissing each of them as they walked off the field following the Nigeria game. Maradona's success as a player and his World Cup triumph in 1986 cast a long pall over the country's national team program. In the time since Maradona left the national team in 1994, many players emerged who were compared to him. But Messi, above all, most resembled Maradona—both in stature and style. Argentine society had a strong emotional bond with Maradona ever since the 1982 World Cup. Still an idol, Maradona could do no wrong in the eyes of most. The bond created between an old idol like Maradona and a new one like Messi was perhaps the secret ingredient for Argentina to capture another World Cup. The similarities between the two were extraordinary. Both could go on incredible runs and deliver delicious passes; both could change direction with the ball under pressure from defenders in an intricate tango that was truly sensational to watch. Maradona had also played for Spanish club Barcelona at one time early in his career—a place where Messi made a name for himself as a global star. The comparisons were only bolstered after Messi scored two goals with Barcelona in 2007 that were eerily similar to ones tallied by Maradona—including one with his hand—that solidified his heir-apparent status to the former star.

Messi, however, continued his goal drought against the South Koreans, but the Barcelona superstar would end up playing a role in all four of his team's goals. An opportunity for a goal of his own opened the floodgates after a Messi free kick in the 17th minute took a deflection off the leg of Park Chu-young, leaving goalkeeper Jung Sung-ryong rooted to the ground. Argentina doubled the score with Real Madrid standout Gonzalo Higuain, who tucked the ball into the net after Messi fed the ball to Maxi Rodriguez. The Argentine attack was in full swing, but the defense was too wide open. It made for some entertaining play but was far too risky for any team looking to go deep at this tournament. Maradona's insistence to leave off veteran defenders Javier Zanetti and Estebian Cambiasso, both Champion League winners with Inter Milan just a month earlier, had been a huge mistake. As a result, the South Koreans were able to pull within one right before halftime when Lee Chung-young took advantage of a blunder by defender Martin Demichelis to keep the outcome temporarily in doubt.

In the second half, Argentina's attack was both relentless and unforgiving. With 15 minutes left to play, Argentina made it 3-1 when Messi played the ball to second-half substitute (and Maradona's son-in-law) Sergio Aguero, who saw his shot blocked. Although Maradona had used him sparingly during qualifying, Higuain tallied on a header five minutes later to complete the hat trick. Argentina's 4-1 win made them look like early title contenders, with Maradona suddenly one of the best managers in the world. Neither was true, of course, but in a tournament where teams are largely judged by their last game, Argentina and Maradona did indeed appear to be serious contenders.

On the same day in Bloemfontein, Greece dashed Nigeria's hopes in a scrappy 2-1 win. The Nigerians—with the backing of the South African fans in the stands—took the lead in the 16th minute thanks to a Kalu Uche goal off a free kick. Like most African teams, Nigeria was known for a physical brand of soccer—a style that would come to haunt them in the 33rd minute when midfielder Sani Kaita was red carded. The ejection came when Kaita kicked an opponent in frustration after he held on to the ball for too long. With Nigeria down to 10 men, Rehhagel, using a 3-5-2 formation, made a change and put on an extra striker. His newfound 3-4-3 worked wonders, and Diitrios Salpigidis tied the score for Greece right before halftime. Nigeria totally broke down in the second half, and Greece was able to grab the game-winner in the 71st minute with Vasilis Torosidis. Greece, therefore, was still in the hunt for a spot in the Round of 16, while Nigeria, who many considered a dark horse to win the group, was in a 0-2 hole and in last place.

Argentina brought Greece back to reality, however, dispatching the former European champions 2-0 on June 22 in Polokwane. Messi, who could have used a day off, insisted that he didn't need the rest. Goals from Demichelis and veteran striker Martin Palermo decided the outcome. Maradona rested most of his starters, but that didn't help the cautious Greeks in their efforts to crack the Argentines. Instead, Greece struggled most of the way and only rarely put together any type of offense. The game ended with plenty of hugs and kisses from the giddy Maradona and an aura of confidence heading into the Round of 16. At the same time, Nigeria and South Korea did battle in Durban in what turned out to be a drama-filled 2-2 game. With Greece losing, Nigeria knew it needed a win to advance. The feisty South Koreans, however, had other plans. A draw would put them through, but the South Koreans played to win. The back-and-forth pace of the game was incredible to watch, but the big story of the night was more about missed chances than goals scored. The Nigerians' only remorse was the failure from Ayegbeni Yakubu to tally in the 65th minute. Only five yards from the goal, Yukubu had a chance to put the ball into the empty net, but the shot went wide. Although he made a penalty kick four minutes later to tie the game 2-2, Yukubu's miss was indicative of the sort of tournament Nigeria experienced. "Everything that could go wrong for us went wrong. We had our chances to score, but we just couldn't finish them," said Nigerian midfielder Dickson Etuhu.[15]

With Argentina and South Korea emerging from Group B, the competition was much more difficult in Group C. The United States entered the World Cup with the stated goal of advancing to the Round of 16. Anything less would be a disappointment. In its opening game against England, the United States had an opponent it knew very well—loaded with players who were household names in this country, like Wayne Rooney and Frank Lampard—thanks to thousands of hours of Premiership and F.A. Cup games shown on Fox Soccer Channel and ESPN every weekend. Several Americans, like goalkeeper Tim Howard, defender Jay DeMerit, and midfielder Clint Dempsey, played in England. Donovan, the creative force behind the American attack, completed a 10-week winter loan spell with Everton and became an instant fan favorite. "I think the biggest plus for me was gaining the confidence to play at that level consistently. It's one thing to play one good game against a good team but it's much harder to do it week in and week out. I feel I am now as prepared as I'll ever be to play in a World Cup," said Donovan.[16]

The Americans prepared well for their opponents in an effort to take advantage of any possible weakness the English could exhibit at the tournament. However, the anticipated Donovan-Beckham clash would never take place since the English star was sidelined earlier in the year, relegated to the bench as part of his country's unofficial role as a team coach. "I think we are all devastated that he is missing out on his last chance to play in a World Cup," said Donovan.[17]

England was coached by Fabio Capello, an Italian, whose refined palate (he is a noted wine connisseur) and love of art (he has one of the most extensive private collections of paintings in Italy) sets him apart from the beer-drinking, blue-collar, St. George Cross–waving fans who pack into bars across England to root for their beloved nation. There was also some truth behind Capello not relating to his players. Rooney and several others on the team came from humble beginnings. There was a language barrier to overcome, although Capello had done his best to learn English as soon as he took charge two years earlier after the team failed to qualify for the 2008 European Championship. He angered the English public when he loaded his coaching staff with Italians, including his friend Franco Baldini. A former player, the 64-year-old Capello successfully coached AC Milan, Real Madrid, Roma, and Juventus to league titles. All he was missing was a World Cup title—and a possible final, pitting his English team against his native Italy—for his personal trophy case. Anything short of reaching the final would be a disappointment, if only because England had not won it since 1966. And Capello earned a staggering $9.9 million annually, the highest-paid coach at the tournament. By comparison, U.S. coach Bob Bradley, who loved attending Bruce Springsteen concerts and watching sports on TV in his spare time, pocketed a meager $600,000 a year.

U.S. coach Bob Bradley arrives in Johannesburg ahead of his team's crucial Group C match against England (Credit: Backpagepix/FIFA).

The U.S.–England game also revived memories of the 1950 World Cup match in which the Americans pulled off a shocking 1-0 victory. The team captain at the time, Walter Bahr, became a star in the lead-up to the 2010 World Cup. U.S. Soccer was more than happy to trot him out for the fans to see, possibly as a good omen for the Americans who looked forward to history repeating itself. The Americans, with the backing of Nike's marketing machine, released a new jersey ahead of the World Cup modeled after the 1950 team shirt, replete with a diagonal blue stripe across the front. "The design was nice back in 1950 and I'm glad they went with a similar jersey and used the same one at this World Cup," said Bahr.[18]

The English looked strong in every part of the field except at the goalkeeper position, where Capello was still pondering who to go with just weeks before the U.S. game. None of the three goalies called up by Capello—David James, Joe Hart, or Robert Green—inspired any real confidence in the English backline. This would end up being the team's downfall in the end. For now, the English relished the role of favorite to beat the Americans (and win the group), and they traveled to South Africa confident of a win. The United States, meanwhile, also had delicate matches against Algeria and Slovenia—teams it had never played before—in its quest to advance. Bradley set up camp at Princeton University in New Jersey, close to the media glare of New York City, and even briefly visited President Barack Obama at the White House before jetting off to Johannesburg. Optimism exuded out of the U.S. camp. "I think we have a good chance to get out of our group. As we learned last summer at the Confederation's Cup, every point and every goal are important in a tournament like this. Our focus is on the first game against England and then we will adjust accordingly," said Donovan.[19]

The United States' preparation ahead of the England game featured few surprises. The players were healthy, and the only real and ultimately trivial hiccup was when the team bus was delayed twice by hungry elephants blocking the road to snack on a few trees. Getting stuck behind an elephant on a major road is something that could only happen at a World Cup in Africa. The players laughed it off—one of the lighter moments in the days leading up to what would be a tense game. The Americans took to the field against England on June 12 in Rustenberg, in what was easily the most anticipated match in U.S. soccer history. What ensued was an inspired U.S. performance and a tough 1-1 draw that temporarily put both teams atop Group C. After a nervous start, the English scored on their first chance when Lampard played the ball into the top of the penalty area that missed Rooney but found its way to Emile Heskey, who fed the ball to Steven Gerrard. Making a diagonal run into the area ahead of Ricardo Clark, Gerrard one-touched the ball and put it past Howard in the fourth minute. The Americans feared that the floodgates had been opened. Instead, the English were put back on the defensive as the Americans regained possession and confidence. "I thought we responded well. I thought we were playing well, they were sitting back and we were creating chances," said Dempsey.[20]

Bradley's men evened the score in the 40th minute when Dempsey grabbed the ball 35 yards from the English goal, faked out Gerrard, and unleashed a powerful left-footed shot that Green failed to hold on to. Instead of making the easy save, the ball trickled over the line for a goal. Dempsey joined former U.S. striker Brian McBride as the only player in American soccer history to score at two different World Cup tournaments. "These balls move so much if you just hit them on goal you'll have a chance. It's one of those goals you always say 'Why can't I get one like that?' and I'm happy to have scored in both World Cups I've participated in," said Dempsey.[21]

The second half was a stalemate, with the United States playing to preserve the result. The frustrated English, with a noticeably irritated Capello pacing the sidelines near his bench, did little in the way of trying to regain the lead. The Americans were able to slow the game down, outmuscling the English on the ball in all parts of the field. The midfield became a large battlefield, with striker Jozy Altidore using his large frame to steal balls, while Donovan used his pace to try and create some offense. Things opened up a bit in the 70th minute when Howard was called on to preserve the draw. During a five-minute stretch, the English challenged Howard several times, but a strong defensive performance from the back four, comprised of Onyewu, DeMerit, Steve Cherundolo, and team captain Carlos Bocanegra, helped keep the game knotted at one. The four defenders took to the field together for the first time since the United States' 2-1 qualifying loss to Mexico the previous summer in Mexico City. In the 71st minute, Gerrard found Rooney unmarked in the box but could barely get his head on the ball. Four minutes later, off a quick restart, Rooney hit a shot from 20 yards that slid just past the right post, with Howard stretching out his arms to cover the net. Howard was undoubtedly the hero of the game, playing with pain for most of the contest after taking a boot from Heskey to his ribs in the 29th minute while making a diving clearance on a cross from defender Glen Johnson. At the other end, Green had very little to worry about after the Americans pulled back offensively in an effort to preserve the draw. Green, however, would never play again in the tournament after his blunder. The final score marked the first time since the 1994 World Cup that the United States had opened the tournament with a draw. "I think when you play at the highest level against the best competition, if you're up to the challenge then it will bring the best out of you. England has so many potent strikers and midfielders that you're going to have to be on your game in order to play well," said Howard afterwards.[22]

With the England game in the books (and record ratings on ESPN and Spanish-language broadcaster Univision), the United States prepared for its next match against Slovenia, 1-0 winners over Algeria in its opening game. American fans had flocked to South Africa in record numbers despite the economic recession, a 17-hour plane ride, and the high cost of airfare and hotels. More than 130,000 of the 2.8 million World Cup tickets put up for sale were purchased by Americans, the highest total of any country other than South Africa. ESPN, for its part, had invested a lot into making the World Cup a success. Aside from paying $100 million for the rights to the 2010 and 2014 World Cups—more than any other broadcaster in the world—the 24-hour sports cable network put together a staff of 300 people to work on the tournament. The ESPN compound right outside the International Broadcasting Center near Soccer City Stadium dwarfed all others. The commitment to broadcast all the games live, plus 65 hours of studio time, was truly unprecedented. By comparison, 20 of the World Cup's 64 games had been called from inside a Connecticut studio just four years earlier. An estimated 50,000 Americans would ultimately flock to South Africa by the time the tournament came to an end, in large part prompted by the images beamed to living rooms by ESPN, and ratings would reach playoff baseball and basketball-type numbers. The ticket-buying frenzy on the part of American citizens said a lot about "the growth of soccer in the United States. It also shows that Americans are indeed soccer fans," said U.S. Soccer President Sunil Gulati.[23]

Slovenia had a defense-first philosophy instilled into its players by coach Matjaz Kek. The strategy had served them well in the past since

*American fans, like the trio above, traveled to South Africa in record numbers (Credit: Gallo Images/FIFA).*

the team lacked any real stars. But Bradley knew that the heroics that occurred in the first game meant nothing if the United States could not get a result against tiny Slovenia. "We've had a good focus the whole time. We've said it so many times that we understand what the first round is about, but we were still excited to start the World Cup playing against England. It's a big game and a big night, and overall we take away positive things as we now get ready for Slovenia," said Bradley.[24]

The game against Slovenia turned out to be another epic encounter for the United States. Another hard-fought game tinged with controversy, the Americans fell behind 2-0 on June 18 at Ellis Park. American fans flocked to the game in record numbers, and the crowd support was noticeable. Not to be outdone, the Americans mounted a comeback thanks to second-half goals from Donovan and Bradley. The first half was difficult for the United States, which inexplicably struggled despite having the better team. The Americans gave up an early goal in the 13th minute when Valter Birsa hit a perfect strike into the right side of the goal from 25 yards out. Howard had no chance at making the save. With three minutes left in the half, Slovenia scored again on a fast break following a long period of U.S. pressure and possession. Striker Milivoje Novakovic beat Onyewu's futile offside trap after playing the ball to midfielder Zlatan Ljubijankic, who blasted a shot easily underneath Howard for a 2-0 lead. Donovan said the players huddled in the dressing room at halftime, optimistic about tying the score. "We all spoke about first of all believing that we could do it. . . . That was the first thing that was said, and the second was that we need to score as early as we can. We knew if we did that we'd have a chance to get back in the game," he said.[25]

The second half was a new game. The Americans, ignoring the fact they were down, continued to pressure Slovenia's defense with Donovan once again spearheading the effort in midfield. It was Donovan who tallied in the 48th minute after blasting the ball into the roof of the net from close-range—a shot that caused Slovenian goalkeeper Samir Handanovic to flinch. The goal, from just six yards out, was the culmination of a play that saw Donovan dribble the ball freely along the right flank and into the box, before shooting it into the net from a tight angle for one of the most improbable-looking strikes in World Cup history. "In the end, I decided to take a touch, aim high, and aim at his head. I don't think he wanted to get hit from there," Donovan said.[26]

Following a series of chances for the United States, the Americans scored in the 82nd minute on a toe-poke from Bradley, who was set-up on the right side by Altidore. After putting the ball into Bradley's path, the midfielder banged in the goal and caused the crowd to erupt into cheers. The U.S. comeback was complete, and the Americans looked to have salvaged a draw. Not so fast. The inspired Americans scored the go-ahead goal in the 85th minute, but Maurice Edu's volley was disallowed by Malian referee Koman Coulibaly for apparently no reason. The blown call caused confusion as celebration turned to head-scratching on the field and in the stands. When Coulibaly blew the final whistle, he was surrounded by American players looking for an answer. The referee remained tight-lipped as the players surrounded him. "Who knows what it was? I'm not sure how much English he spoke or if he spoke English. We asked him several times in a non-confrontational way. He just ignored us," said Donovan.[27]

Bradley refused to go into the details of the blown call. FIFA bestowed upon its referees ultimate power and the ability not to answer their critics for whatever calls they made on the field. For most American fans, the practice was horrific. For a country just getting interested in the game, it didn't sit well with many that a call could be made with no obvious explanation. The speculation was that the Americans had been tugging the shirts of the Slovenian players in the box the moment the goal was scored. However, the shirt-tugging—a common practice on set pieces and corner kicks—had been done by players on both sides. With no conceivable offside, the call remained a mystery. American fans watching in record numbers on ESPN were outraged. What Americans hated more than anything was injustice, and it had clearly occurred against the U.S. team. For fans used to sports with instant replay, the call was baffling. The FIFA practice of using a diverse referee pool at the World Cup was admirable, but in this case Coulibaly's only prior experience was the African Nations Cup, hardly enough to qualify him to officiate a World Cup match. A game of this magnitude had been too much for him to deal with in the end. "The duty of the referee is not to explain a call. The job of the referee on the field is to implement the laws of the game," said Jose Maria Garcia-Aranda, a former match official and head of FIFA's refeering department.[28]

FIFA eventually pulled the plug on Coulibaly and sent him home early, as it often did with referees who made blunders. The American players took the call in stride and, with two points after two games, were still in the hunt for a spot in the final 16. "I've heard a few things. Honestly, I think that on that set piece, most of what took place was that Slovenian players were holding our players. The one thing I've heard was that one player from Slovenia had his arms around [my son] Michael. Michael was trying to break loose from being held, and the foul was called. I don't know if that's accurate, but that's one version," said Bradley.[29]

In some ways, the missed call was good for the United States. The team got even more attention back home (TV ratings were proof of that), and the play became fodder for sports-talk radio shows across the county. For the first time ever, Americans cared about the fortunes of their national team. But Bradley was focused on his players' fighting spirit. "I think this team has shown that it keeps fighting until the end and we have now had the experience of pushing games when we're behind. It's a credit to the mentality of the players and to the fact that they're going to fight for 90 minutes every game. We have a third match where we still have the chance to determine our ability to move into the final round," he said.[30]

The thrilling 2-2 game put the United States' destiny in its own hands. A win in its final group match on June 23 against Algeria in Pretoria would automatically earn the Americans a spot in the knockout round.

With Algeria's shocking 0-0 draw against England in the other Group C match amid a shower of boos from fans, the Americans entered the final game in second place tied with the English on two points but ahead on goals scored (three for the United States and one for England). The United States could also draw against Algeria if England lost to Slovenia. The two draws by England prompted a crisis meeting. Capello eased his alcohol ban, and the players were allowed to relax with a beer during the private meeting meant to raise the players' spirits ahead of their crucial third game. Defender John Terry said afterwards that the purpose of the team meeting was for the players to vent their anger and frustrations. Terry said the players watched the Algeria game over again to "see where we went wrong—which is probably the whole 90 minutes."[31]

The Americans played Algeria in Pretoria, with the majority of the 35,827 fans in attendance Americans. The most notable attendee was former president Bill Clinton, who was using the trip as a chance to hob-nob with Blatter in an effort to get the 2022 World Cup to the United States. What Clinton saw would turn out to be one of the most exciting games of the tournament, replete with drama and a riveting finale. The Americans may not have given up an early goal like they had in their previous two matches, but without a reason to react it seemed like the offense had no motivation to score. In reality, the United States was on the brink of elimination at halftime. Deadlocked 0-0 against Algeria, the English were leading 1-0 on a goal from Jermaine Defoe after just 23 minutes in Port Elizabeth. The English would win their game; the Americans would continue to struggle. The Americans had squandered several chances and the frustration was starting to mount. Altidore and Dempsey came close on several occasions, but the ball just did not want to find its way into the net. As the clock struck the 90th minute, the Americans were in third place and looked to be going home early. With the game in stoppage time, Howard cleared the ball to Altidore as the Americans launched one final attack. Altidore crossed the ball into the box and an onrushing Donovan side-footed it into the net for the most dramatic of goals. Donovan celebrated by running toward the corner kick flag as his teammates, both on the field and bench, piled on top of him in jubilation. The game was over. The Americans had won Group C, with England coming in second, and were headed to the Round of 16 for the first time since 2002. Donovan became a hero overnight and America had a new soccer icon. The never-say-die Americans had done it once again. "They never quit," exclaimed Bradley.[32]

A festive atmosphere filled the U.S. locker room as Clinton joined the players in celebration. Like the rest of the country, Clinton had been sucked in by the emotion. The former president was now a soccer fan—like so many across the country—and like never before the World Cup was right up there with the Olympics as an event Americans were interested in. Clinton said he was hoarse after the game after spending 90 minutes screaming. "I lost my voice. I had to come home and drink hot tea with honey for an hour," Clinton said afterwards.[33]

Group D featured the powerhouse Germans as the favorites to advance. Not widely favored to win the Cup, the Germans traditionally fielded a strong team. The squad, under the guidance of coach Joachim Low, was one of the youngest at the tournament. Indeed, Loew, an assistant under 2006 World Cup coach Jurgen Klinsmann, put together the youngest German squad to ever play at a World Cup in 76 years. After thrashing Australia 4-0 in their opener on June 13 in Durban, the Germans took a misstep and lost 1-0 to Serbia five days later in Port Elizabeth. The loss, however, was no indication of how talented the German team was. Two questionable calls from Spanish referee Alberto Undiano resulted in the ejection of German striker Miroslav Klose eight minutes before halftime. Both fouls, misjudged tackles on the part of Klose, were by no means bookable offenses. However, Undiano made his disapproval known in the form of two yellow cards, and Loew's team was down a man. In all, the referee issued nine yellow cards. The reinvigorated Serbians took advantage of having an extra man on the field and scored what turned out to be the game-winner a minute after Klose's sendoff with Milan Jovanovic. The result put in jeopardy Germany's chances of advancing and put Serbia in position to reach the Round of 16. The Serbians had lost to Ghana 1-0 on June 13 in their opener. Coupled with a 1-1 draw between Ghana and Australia on June 19 and the group was wide open; even Australia with one point had a chance of reaching the Round of 16 with a win in its final group game.

On June 23, Germany played Ghana at Soccer City, while Australia and Serbia faced off in Nelspruit. Although Germany was able to win 1-0 on a goal from midfielder Mesut Ozil, Ghana would also advance— as what would be the only African team to reach the final 16—thanks to favorable results elsewhere. Germany won the group as a result, putting to rest any disappointment after losing to Serbia. The Germans, a blend of experience and youth, looked tough to beat. They also incorporated players from other ethnicities into their lineup. Ozil, for example, was of Turkish descent, while defender Jerome Boateng was originally a native of Ghana. In an odd twist, Boateng played against his brother, Kevin-Prince Boateng, when Germany faced Ghana, since the brothers had chosen different national teams. It was the first time in World Cup history that siblings played against one another in a game.

Ghana managed to reach the Round of 16 after Australia defeated Serbia 2-1, a result that ensured both teams were going home early. Serbia's inability to convert led to its demise. After its stunning win over Germany, the opportunity to advance was truly squandered. In another odd footnote, Serbian midfielder Dejan Stankovic completed a unique feat, becoming the first player to appear in three World Cups for three different teams. At the 1998 tournament he represented Yugoslavia, while in 2006 he was part of the Serbia and Montenegro side that also crashed at the group stage.

Group E featured the Netherlands, another traditional World Cup power that had reached the final twice but had never been able to win the tournament. In a group that also featured Denmark, Japan, and Cameroon, the Dutch looked to be the odds-on favorites to advance. The Dutch not only looked good, but they cruised to the Round of 16 after defeating Denmark 2-0 on June 14 at Soccer City and edging out Japan 1-0 five days later in Durban. Midfielder Wesley Sneijder scored the game's only goal against Japan and solidified himself as one of the most exciting players at the tournament. At the same time Japan, which defeated the Samuel Eto'o–led Cameroon 1-0 in its first game, needed a victory over Denmark to advance. The Netherlands' match against Cameroon was played at the same time with very little at stake. Cameroon, the only African team to ever reach the quarterfinals of a World Cup (it had done so in 1990), became the poster child for the continent's failure at this tournament. A loss to Japan, in addition to a 2-1 loss to Denmark, doomed Cameroon to last place with no chance of getting through to the final 16.

The Dutch were able to defeat Cameroon 2-1 on June 24 in Cape Town to finish atop the group, with a perfect 3-0 record, as Japan joined them in the knockout stage with a riveting 3-1 victory over the Danes. The Japanese dominated the match and showed their superiority on set pieces when they scored the first two goals off free kicks. Keisuke Honda put Japan in the lead after just 17 minutes, ripping a shot from 30 yards out. Yashito Endo, who was named Asian Player of the Year going into the competition, doubled the score 13 minutes later after curling a free kick into the goal. "We knew exactly which players would step up and take the free-kicks. We prepared ourselves for it but it was futile. The game was settled by the two first-half free-kicks," said Denmark coach Morten Olsen.[34]

Denmark pushed forward in search of a goal but in the end produced very little against a Japansese defense that had looked hard to beat throughout the tournament. The Danes got on the board with striker Jon Dahl Tomasson, but only after he saw his penalty kick saved by goalkeeper Eiji Kawashima and blasted in the rebound for the tally. Japan did one better, however, to clinch the win with three minutes left to play when Honda broke free and set up Shinji Okazaki for the easy finish and a 3-1 win. "The players were not afraid and fierce at the same time. It was fantastic," Japan coach Takeshi Okada said after the game.[35]

Group F saw the reigning World Cup champions Italy play in the tournament's easiest group after the luck of the draw had paired it alongside Slovakia, Paraguay, and New Zealand. The Italians had a topsy-turvy time following their World Cup win in 2006. Coach Marcello Lippi had stepped down after the win and was replaced with Roberto Donadoni. The team struggled under the former AC Milan and Italy midfielder and reached the quarterfinals of the 2008 European Championship before being eliminated by the eventual winners, Spain. Donadoni was forced out and Lippi brought back to rekindle some of the magic that had inspired the team to victory. But Lippi did very little to instill any promise that Italy could repeat as champions. He relied on the same core group of players who had won the title four years earlier and took a relatively old squad (nine players were over 30) with him to South Africa. To make matters worse, Lippi had remained loyal to a group of Juventus players who had won the Cup four years earlier. That group had not done so well in Serie A in the months prior to the start of the tournament, sounding alarm bells that Italy was in for a rough time at the World Cup.

Fabio Grosso, the left back who converted the decisive penalty kick in the final against France four years earlier, had already been cut two weeks before the World Cup after being named to the preliminary 30-man squad. Lippi never even considered picking Antonio Cassano, the temperamental Sampdoria forward, or Mario Balotelli, the similarly hot-headed 18-year-old Inter Milan striker who helped his club win the Serie A league cup and Champions League titles just a month before the start of the World Cup. He had also left off striker Giuseppe Rossi, who was born in New Jersey to Italian parents and had dual citizenship. Rossi had shunned advances from former U.S. coach Bruce Arena in 2006 and had decided to represent Italy, prompting many American fans to brand him a Benedict Arnold. He had played well for Italy at the previous year's Confederations Cup, scoring twice in the opener against the United States, but struggled during the second half of the season with his Spanish club Villarreal. Add to that woes within Italian soccer that its best team, Inter Milan, was comprised primarily of foreign players (all 11 starters in the Champions League final were non-Italians) and things did not look good for Lippi. "We are not the oldest, there are a couple of teams older than us. We have a mix, nine players from 2006 is less than 50 percent. I haven't seen a team at a World Cup that four years later turn up with 23 new players. We have the right mix with young players and those with quality," assured Lippi.[36]

The Italians opened with a 1-1 draw against Paraguay on June 14 in a heavy Cape Town rain. Six days later, the *Azzurri* played New Zealand to a 1-1 draw in Nelspruit in what was one of the biggest upsets of the first round. In both games, Italy had fallen behind, only to scrap by and claw its way to a tie. It wasn't pretty and it wasn't convincing. Even for traditional slow-starters like Italy, two draws against two considerably weak teams was telling. Lippi came under fire. Another draw in the final game, against Slovakia, would be enough to send Italy packing early. Slovakia had tied New Zealand 1-1 on June 15 in Rustenberg and had lost to Paraguay 2-0 six days later in Nelspruit. Paraguay, in first place with three points, played New Zealand in its final game. The group was still wide open going into the final match, something no one would have predicted on the eve of the World Cup. Ellis Park was the site of Italy's clash with Slovakia. The June 25 game was do-or-die for both sides. The Italians knew they needed to start strong. Going down a goal early, like they had in the previous two contests, could do them in. The *Azzurri* got off to a slow start and played poorly throughout the first half, a display worthy of the worst opening 45 minutes the team had ever played in its illustrious history. They had played the first two games without the injured Pirlo. Against Slovakia, the AC Milan midfielder was on the bench, however, prepared to enter the game if things got sticky. The Italians knew that grinding out a draw could get them through, but the Slovakians had other plans. Italy may be known for its tight defense, but the back four was at its weakest in the competition. Without veteran goalkeeper Gianluigi Buffon, injured during the Paraguay game with a back ailment and done for the tournament, the Italians had nothing securing the back. Back-up goalkeeper Federico Marchetti, who had a brilliant season at Cagliari, was out of his element and too slow to react on shots. It didn't help that captain Fabio Cannavaro was similarly slow and unsure of himself, showing his age on both goals in the Paraguay and New Zealand clashes. As in those two games, the Italian defense unraveled quickly. Slovakia's opening goal after 25 minutes typified Italy's sloppy play when midfielder Daniele De Rossi carelessly lost the ball about 30 yards from the goal, allowing Juraj Kucka to collect it, slipping a pass to Robert Vittek, whose finish on the turn was impressive. The Italian attack, spearheaded by Vincenzo Iaquinta as a lone striker, was a no-show. Lippi's redesigned 4-5-1 was not working. His 4-4-2 against Paraguay and 4-3-3 versus New Zealand had not worked. His new formation wasn't much better. The half ended 1-0 in Slovakia's favor, and the Italians were lucky not to be behind by more.

In the second half, Lippi put in striker Fabio Quagliarella, who had yet to log a single minute at the tournament, in a bid to get the attack going. It worked, but it was too late. The move would also not improve the defense, which gave up too much possession. Pirlo's entry in the 56th minute woke up the Italians, but Slovakia doubled its lead again with Vittek in the 73rd minute off a pass from Marek Hamsik. A 2-0 hole was too much for the Italians to get out of. Feisty forward Antonio DiNatale cut the lead with nine minutes left to put Italy in position to gain a draw. With the Italians pushing forward, Marchetti was left totally exposed. As a result, Slovakia put the game away in the 89th minute with midfielder Kamil Kopunek, who had entered the match just two minutes earlier. Italy responded when Quagliarella scored one of the tournament's best goals off a brilliant chip shot, but it was too late. That set up a dramatic and frantic finale, with the Italians scrambling to tie the game. Simone Pepe came close, but the ball sailed wide. The final whistle brought with it joy from the Slovakians and tears from Quagliarella. Lippi, a winner four years earlier, jogged into the tunnel after the game. He was not interested in waiting around any longer. At the news conference following the match, a somber Lippi delivered a stunning mea culpa. "I take all responsibility for what happened because if a team show up at such an important game like today with terror in their heads, hearts, and legs, and the team can't express their ability, it means the coach hasn't trained them as he should psychologically, tactically, or physically. Especially psychologically. You can't believe the Italy team is the one you saw out there," he said.[37]

Lippi was out as coach. His replacement, Cesare Prandelli, had a huge task ahead of him. The Italians had finished last with just two points in three games. The players were shaken afterward, and the 10-hour flight home to Rome would end with a handful of fans hurling insults at them. Not since the 1974 World Cup had Italy failed to get out of the first round. Not since 1970 had Italy conceded so many goals in a single game. For the first time ever, both the champions and the runners-up from the previous World Cup were gone after the first round. In the group's other game, New Zealand and Paraguay ended in a scoreless draw in Polokwane. The outcome ensured that Paraguay were group winners, followed by Slovakia, which was in the Round of 16 in its first World Cup appearance as an independent nation. For Paraguay, it was an enormous achievement and a sign that South American teams were for real at this tournament. The players were also motivated by emotion, dedicating each victory to striker Salvador Cabanas, who did not make the team after being seriously injured in January in a nightclub shooting. New Zealand, which featured a semi-pro player named Andy Barron, who earned a living as an investment banker, was eliminated after three draws but would end up with the dubious distinction of being the only team at the tournament to finish undefeated.

Group G was led by perennial favorites Brazil, outsiders Portugal, talented Ivory Coast, and the mysterious North Koreans. Dubbed the "Group of Death," the Brazilians made getting out of a tricky draw look relatively easy. Brazil topped the group after a hard-fought 2-1 win over North Korea on June 15 that took the five-time World Cup winners way too long to secure. Scoreless at halftime, the Brazilians delighted the fans at Ellis Park with a goal from Maicon after 55 minutes and a second from Elano in the 72nd minute. Until that point, the North Koreans looked poised to pull off an upset. Not entirely out of the question after beating Italy at the 1966 World Cup, the North Korean players were kept away from prying eyes of the world press. FIFA limited the team's exposure and many of the players found themselves out of place. Most had never before seen a cell phone, while others had never been exposed to another culture. The strict Communist rule the North Koreans lived under also didn't allow for traveling fans. Instead, the government paid Chinese actors to fill the stands and wave North Korean flags. Although North Korea had been able to pull within a goal in the final minute (to the delight of the actors in the stands), the outcome was never really in jeopardy for Brazil. On the eve of the tournament, Brazil coach Dunga had come under fire back home for not playing *jogo bonito* and relying too much on a European-style defensive tactic that had the stated goal of winning games, albeit in an ugly fashion. The Brazilians were used to playing pretty and winning. The two had become synonymous over the decades, but Dunga embraced a contrarian philosophy. Against North Korea, the team had played poorly but won. The similarly defensive Portuguese could do no better than a scoreless draw against the Ivory Coast on the same day in Port Elizabeth. Despite having Cristiano Ronaldo in the lineup, Portugal looked like a team that could not score.

On June 20 at Soccer City, Brazil faced the Ivory Coast in freezing 30-degree temperatures. For Brazil, the game was a chance to show everyone that it had the ability to win a game by a larger margin than it had against North Korea. A win would also clinch them a spot in the Round of 16. To Dunga's relief, both things came true. Luis Fabiano powered Brazil to a 3-1 win, scoring two goals in the process. Elano added a third as Brazil looked like contenders once again. The style was still dull, but a win was a win. The Brazilians may have lacked a showman like Ronaldinho (who had been left off the World Cup roster), but they did have tough players who hustled for every ball. "To those who complain about our style, I say there is nothing more pretty than winning," said Brazilian defender Lucio.[38] Fabiano's second goal in the 50th minute, however, was controversial after he controlled the ball with his arm before scoring. That wasn't the only injustice. French referee Stephane Lannoy may not have waved off Fabiano's goal, but he did eject Brazil striker Kaka after getting two undeserved yellow cards.

Like other African teams at the tournament, the Ivory Coast had performed well below expectations and as a result was on the brink of elimination. The following day in Cape Town, Portugal blew things open against North Korea, toppling them 7-0 in a game that looked more like a training session. Ronaldo's goal in the 87th minute ended a two-year scoring drought for him in a Portugal jersey. Five days later in Durban, Portugal and Brazil played to a scoreless draw, while the Ivory Coast put three past North Korea for a meaningless victory. Group winners Brazil and runners-up Portugal were through to the next round.

Aside from Brazil, Spain was the other team favored to reach the final. Winners of the European Championship two years earlier, the Spanish played the brand of soccer Brazil had once employed: highlighted by elegant and fluid movements combined with a short-passing game involving every player on the field. Although favored to capture Group H, Spain was forced to recover after losing its opener 1-0 on June 16 in Durban against a plucky Swiss side. The result was shocking but showed that although Spain was a tough team, it was beatable. The United States had snapped Spain's 35-game unbeaten streak a year earlier and now it was Switzerland. Spain passed and passed the ball but never found the back of the net. Instead, Switzerland's defensive 4-4-2 set-up was rewarded after Gelson Fernandes scored the game-winner in the 52nd minute after a mad-scramble in front of the Spanish goal. In the group's other game played the same day, Chile downed Honduras 1-0 in Nelspruit for its first World Cup win since grabbing third place at the 1962 tournament at home

On June 21, Spain got back on track at Ellis Park with a 2-0 victory over Honduras, eliminating the Central Americans, on two goals from David Villa. The Spanish striker had come under fire after the loss to the Swiss, but he made amends with his goals. He did miss a penalty kick—vital if the group were to come down to goal differential, but that would not be the case in the end. In Port Elizabeth, Chile downed Switzerland 1-0 on the same day to catapult itself to the top of the group. Spain played Chile on June 25 in Pretoria in a game that would decide which team would win the group and avoid Brazil in the Round of 16. The incentive was there for Chile to win, but Spain managed to snatch the victory with two first-half goals, by Villa in the 24th minute and midfielder Andres Iniesta 13 minutes later. Spain was assertive, although Chile virtually stopped playing after hearing that at the same time Switzerland and Honduras were scoreless. The Chileans pulled one back with midfielder Rodrigo Millar in the 47th minute after being reduced to 10 men in the first half following the ejection of Marco Estrada for having tripped Spanish striker Fernando Torres. Spain won 2-1 to capture the group, with Chile finishing second to also advance. The Swiss, despite the upset over Spain, could only manage a draw against Honduras and were done early.

The Round of 16 was set: Uruguay-South Korea, U.S.-Ghana, Germany-England, Argentina-Mexico, the Netherlands-Slovakia, Brazil-Chile, Paraguay-Japan, and Spain-Portugal. The United States was on

# DAVID VILLA

David Villa Sanchez is one of the most talented players to ever come out of Spain. The son of a miner who was raised in a working-class family in northern Spain, Villa almost missed out on a professional career after breaking his femur as a child. He started his pro career in 2001 with Spanish club Sporting Gijon, but moved on to Real Zaragoza after just two seasons. He joined Valencia in 2005, and his knack for finding the back of the net drew increased interest from a number of clubs across Spain, including famed side Barcelona. In a club career spanning just nine years, Villa had scored 178 goals in 219 league matches. Villa signed with Barcelona in 2010 just as his national team career was also beginning to blossom.

Villa made his international debut for Spain in 2005 and was a key member of the team that captured the 2008 European Championship and 2010 World Cup. Not a major contributor to Spain's youth teams, Villa burst onto the scene on the senior level in a big way. He scored three goals at the 2006 World Cup before Spain flamed out in the second round against France. Villa had already ousted Raul as Spain's first-choice striker and repaid Spain's then-coach Luis Aragones by scoring six goals en route to qualifying for the finals of the 2008 European Championship. He was partnered with Fernando Torres, and the duo became one of the most explosive ever at an international tournament. Villa tallied a hat trick in Spain's 4-1 win over Russia during the first round at Euro 2008. In the semifinals, Villa sustained a thigh injury after attempting a free kick. Although he went on to miss the final, Villa's four goals in four matches were a big reason why Spain landed in the final against Germany.

Villa's five goals at the 2010 World Cup propelled Spain to the title for the first time. Playing as a lone striker, he had come under fire after Spain's 1-0 loss to Switzerland in the opener. But Villa shrugged off the critics and scored two goals in the following match versus Honduras. He would score another goal in his side's 2-1 win over Chile in the final opening-stage match. The goal against Chile, Villa's sixth at a World Cup, made him his country's all-time scorer at the tournament. Villa went on to tally goals seven and eight against Portugal and Paraguay, respectively, to put Spain in the final. Although he missed out on being named tournament MVP—an honor that went to Uruguay's Diego Forlan—Villa was the 2010 World Cup's biggest star by far.

## World Cup Career Statistics

Tournaments played: 3
Games: 12
Goals: 9

the easy side of the bracket and had a chance at history by reaching the semifinals, Germany versus England looked like an early final, and Argentina was taking on Mexico in a rematch of a second round game that had taken place four years earlier. Surprise Asian sides like South Korea and Japan were hoping to pull off an upset at a tournament where it seemed like anything could happen, while all five South American representatives had made it through to the second round. Ghana remained the sole African team to emerge from the opening round.

The second round opened on June 26 with Uruguay taking on South Korea in Port Elizabeth. The South Americans were favored, but the South Koreans had bucked the odds before and outmaneuvered teams with better pedigrees. Forlan was again at the top of his game, however, as Uruguay churned out a 2-1 win to advance to the quarterfinals on two goals from Luis Suarez. His second goal in the 80th minute broke the 1-1 deadlock. The Koreans had chances to win the match, but Uruguay scored the opportunistic goal to grab the win. Uruguay would face the winner of the U.S.-Ghana game in Rustenberg before a crowd of African fans blowing the ubiquitus vuvuzelas for much of the contest. It was anyone's game to take, and the Americans could make history with a win and reach the quarterfinals, matching their exploits at the 2002 World Cup.

The Americans played Ghana on June 26 before 34,976 fans. Although the South Africans in the crowd were pulling for their Ghanain brothers, U.S. fans made up a good chunk of the crowd at Royal Bafokeng Stadium that evening. With millions watching back in the United States, the Americans, for the first time perhaps, felt the pressure of the tournament weighing on them. With noticeability came responsibility, and Bradley's men were hoping not to give up an early goal as they had in the first two group matches. Howard was again in the net, with Altidore and striker Robbie Findley up top looking for their first goals of the tournament. Donovan and Dempsey were the force in midfield, aided by Ricardo Clark. Onyewu was relegated to the bench in favor of Jonathan Bornstein, while Michael Bradley was hoping to produce similar heroics as the Slovenia match. For the Americans, the outcome was not what they had hoped. Ghana powered ahead and gave the Americans a tough game. It was a rematch of a group-stage game won by Ghana in 2006, and the Americans were out for revenge. The loss in Germany four years earlier had eliminated the United States, and the Americans did not want a repeat of history. In the end, Ghana was victorious 2-1 following an overtime goal by Asamoah Gyan in the 93rd minute. The United States went down early after Boeteng put Ghana on the board after just five minutes when Clark lost the ball in the midfield. The Americans, as usual, fought back and Donovan equalized from the penalty spot in the 62nd minute. The Americans had a chance to put the game away, but the attack came up short after Ghana's goalkeeper Richard Kingson had a stellar outing. After the game, Gulati lamented the elimination, saying going to the quarterfinals would have raised the profile of the sport back home. "You look at the way the draw worked out and you start dreaming," he said.[39]

Despite the loss, the American public had embraced the team in record numbers. The TV audience for the Saturday match between the United States and Ghana was 19.4 million, higher than all but two games at the 2009 World Series and all but Game 7 of the 2010 NBA Finals. In the game's immediate aftermath, Gulati was noncommittal about renewing Bradley's contract. In August, however, Bradley's contract was renewed for another four-year cycle, although many of the team's veterans, like Donovan, bemoaned the missed chance to go further into the tournament. "There is no guarantee that we'll ever have another opportunity like this ever again in our lifetimes," said Donovan.[40]

The two biggest games of the Round of 16 both took place on June 27. In Bloemfontein, Germany powered on by routing England 4-1. Although the final score left little doubt as to Germany's superiority, there was one problem. With Germany ahead 2-1 right before halftime, England scored what had been a clear goal. Incompetent officiating was on display once again after Lampard's shot struck the crossbar and fell behind the goal line. Neither referee Jorge Larrionda of Uruguay nor his linesman were in position to award the goal, and the chance to go into halftime tied 2-2 vanished. History had repeated itself—forty-four years after England won the World Cup on a controversial Geoff Hurst goal against West Germany when the ball bounced off the crossbar and on the goal line. The situation had now been reversed. History not only repeated itself, it also wiped the board clean. But it was Germany's superiority, spearheaded by youngsters Thomas Müller and Mesut Ozil, that did England in. The English were headed home early and Capello was surprisingly rewarded with a two-year contract extension for his abysmal efforts.

Later that evening at Soccer City, Argentina and Mexico renewed their World Cup rivalry. In a game that was also marred by a bad call, Argentina downed Mexico 3-1 on two Tevez goals, one of which was clearly offside. The game changed in the 26th minute when Tevez scored off a header into the empty net from just a few yards out. Replays showed Tevez was offside, but the referee's assistant did not raise his flag. The Mexican players vehemently argued the call, but Italian referee Roberto Rosetti, a candidate to officiate the final after Italy's early elimination, let the goal stand. When the large screens inside the stadium replayed the goal at the end of the first half, the Mexican players—pointing upwards—tried to get Rosetti's attention. The confusion caused a fracas near the sidelines, with Maradona forced to intervene to get the Mexican players away from the referee. FIFA spokesman Nicolas Maingot said afterward that showing the goal had been "a clear mistake" and replays were no longer shown inside stadiums for the remaining matches. The offside goal ended Mexico's hopes and ensured Argentina of another win, much to Maradona's delight. Afterwards, Maradona dismissed the controversy, saying referees had failed to whistle defenders who were out to injure creative players like Messi. "What's being done to Messi is a scandal! They don't look for the ball, they look for his legs and kick him," he said.[41]

The pressure was on Blatter to address the mistakes by the referees. An opponent of goal-line technology and instant replay, Blatter said it would be "nonsense" not to consider changes. Upon further review, Blatter said FIFA would look at ways to limit such mistakes in the future and ordered the International Football Association Board to consider changes. "After witnessing such a situation, we have to open this file again, definitely," said Blatter, referring to England's non-goal against Germany.[42]

On June 28 in Durban, the Netherlands downed Slovakia 2-1 thanks to the individual skills of Arjen Robben and Sneijder. Robben scored from 20 yards out in the 28th minute, but the Dutch could only seal the win when Sneijder netted a goal in the 84th minute. Vittek scored on a penalty kick in stoppage time, but there was no time left for them to mount a comeback. The same day at Ellis Park, Brazil used its usual reliance on dead balls and counterattacks to blow out Chile 3-0 to also reach the quarterfinals. Chile's fluid attack was broken up by Brazil's dogged style. Awaiting Brazil was a real test against the Netherlands, in what would be its toughest opponent to date at the tournament. Once again, the Brazilian media hounded Dunga for his unattractive style and called on him to use the pretty play of the past. Dunga countered that the nostalgia was misplaced. "My grandfather always told me that soccer was better in his day and my father told me the same thing. I will tell my son someday in the future that it was better in my time and my son will tell his boy about how beautiful Brazilian soccer was in his time," countered Dunga.[43]

On June 28 in Pretoria, Paraguay and Japan locked horns for a spot in the quarterfinals. The game ended scoreless after 120 minutes and would be the first at this World Cup to be decided on penalties. Paraguay scored all five of its kicks to win the shootout 5-3. The win pitted Paraguay against Spain, 1-0 winners over Portugal in a match played on June 29 in Cape Town. The Iberian derby was decided by a Villa goal in the 63rd minute. Although the goal would win the encounter, replays showed that the Spanish striker had been in an offside position. At the same time, Spain coach Vicente del Bosque played down his team's emergence as a favorite to win it all. "We are one of the eight best teams in the world," he said.[44]

The biggest quarterfinal match was the first held on July 2 between Brazil and the Netherlands in Port Elizabeth. The Dutch, hungry for a title, rallied to defeat Brazil 2-1. Down 1-0 at halftime, the Dutch put on an amazing display in the second half when Sneijder tied the score in the 53rd minute on a header off a corner kick. The Dutch took the lead, again with Sneijder, in the 68th minute. The Brazilians lost their composure and were reduced to 10 men in the 73rd minute when Felipe Melo was red carded for stomping on Robben. The upset was complete, and it was the Dutch who celebrated on the field at the sound of the final whistle, beating Brazil for the first time since 1974. The Dutch had won passage to the semifinals and Dunga was fired within hours. "It is sad and it is difficult. Nobody ever prepares to lose," said Dunga.[45]

Uruguay played Ghana a few hours later at Soccer City, marking the first time that these two teams had ever faced one other. Following a drama-loaded 1-1 game after 120 minutes, the match went to penalties. But Ghana lost its chance to win in the final minute of extra time when a goal-bound header nodded by Domonic Adiyiah was intentionally handballed off the line by Suarez. The Uruguayan forward was shown a red card, and a penalty kick was awarded to Ghana. Gyan, who had scored against the United States, failed to convert after the ball slammed against the crossbar. Suarez, who watched the kick from the tunnel, rejoiced by thrusting his arms into the air before running into the dressing room. In the shootout, Uruguay emerged victorious 4-2. The crowd left disappointed as Africa's lone representative at the tournament had been eliminated. After the game, Suarez boasted that the

"Hand of God" now belonged to him, while Ghana coach Milovan Reje-vac argued that his side had suffered the "ultimate football injustice."[46]

In Cape Town, Argentina and Germany faced off on July 3 in another epic World Cup encounter. Germany had eliminated Argentina four years earlier during the same stage of the tournament on penalty kicks. Another close game was expected between what had turned out to be two of the best sides at the tournament. But Argentina's lax defense was a problem as the German midfield duo of Ozil and Müller emerged as the most talked-about youngsters at the tournament. Germany had already twice scored four goals in a game and Argentina was poised to be its next victim. In the end, the Germans rolled over Maradona's side 4-0 after taking the lead with Müller just three minutes into the contest. Aided by veteran midfielder Bastian Schweinsteiger, the German offense went into overdrive in the second half when Miroslav Klose made it 2-0 in the 67th minute off a pass from Lukas Podolski. Germany's third goal came seven minutes later thanks to defender Arne Friedrich, and they completed the rout with another Klose tally off an Ozil pass. The margin of defeat was Argentina's worst since 1974. For Germany, reaching the semifinals was a just reward for having played so well over the past three weeks. The only blemish was a yellow card that would keep Müller out of the next game. As for Maradona, he was hailed a hero back in Buenos Aires, but the loss left its mark. The Argentine federation fired him weeks later after both sides failed to come to terms. Spain, meanwhile, closed out the quarterfinals that evening with another 1-0 win, this time over Paraguay, reaching the semis for the first time since 1950. No longer World Cup underachievers, Spain again got the game-winner from Villa in the 83rd minute. Both sides traded missed penalty kicks in the second half, but it was Spain that was able to avoid overtime when a shot from Pedro Rodriguez rebounded off the post, allowing Villa to tuck in an easy goal.

The semifinals were, as expected, tense affairs. With a World Cup final appearance on the line, the four remaining teams—the Netherlands, Uruguay, Spain, and Germany—were all looking to win the Cup. The Germans were no strangers to World Cup semifinals, having gotten there on home soil four years earlier, and were looking for their fourth title. The Netherlands, which had never won the World Cup, hoped history was on its side this time around.

The first semifinal, played on July 6 in Cape Town, saw the Netherlands edge past Uruguay 3-2 with Robben's strike in the 73rd minute turning out to be the game-winning tally. In the second semifinal the following day in Durban, defender Carlos Puyol, known more for his sliding tackles and his curly mop of hair than scoring goals, headed the game-winner after 73 minutes in a thrilling 1-0 win over Germany. In a rematch of the 2008 European Championship won by Spain, goalkeeper Iker Casillas bagged himself another shutout as the Germans were badly hobbled in midfield by Müller's absence. Germany would go on to capture the meaningless third-place game against Uruguay (with Forlan named tournament MVP), while Spain and the Netherlands reached the final, ensuring that a first-time World Cup winner would be crowned at a sold-out Soccer City Stadium and with a global audience of 700 million.

Soccer City, on the eastern edge of Soweto, lit up one final time on the night of July 11. The stadium—remodeled and made to resemble a large African cooking bowl from the outside—was buzzing with thousands of vuvuzelas. A global TV audience of a billion had tuned in to watch the World Cup, and the perception of South Africa would forever change for the positive in the hearts and minds of those who had watched the competition and attended the matches. The tournament had been widely considered a success by Jordaan, FIFA, the teams that had traveled there, and the fans who made the trek. "This stadium is a monument to our success. It will be here forever as a reminder of what took place in this country and how our country responded to such a large event," Jordaan boasted, as a large smile crossed his face.[47]

The 92-year-old Mandela put aside advice from his personal doctor not to leave his home because of his failing health and made a brief appearance before the start of the game—his beaming smile sending goose bumps down the spine of the fans in attendance. FIFA had wanted Mandela, the icon of South Africa, to make the token appearance. The small car that drove him onto the field disappeared into the tunnel and Mandela retreated back to his home before the game ever began. Moments later, the World Cup trophy was almost knocked from its pedestal after security guards successfully stopped a Dutch fan from trying to put a hat on it. As for the final itself, the game never lived up to the hype. Both teams played defensively and, with so much at stake, appeared afraid to attack. The game got bogged down in the midfield with both sides resorting to a series of fouls. The Dutch were the biggest offenders, tackling the Spanish players with impunity in an effort to break up the great passing game that had gotten them this far. The most egregious foul was committed by Dutch midfielder Nigel de Jong, who brought down Xabi Alonso in the 28th minute with a high-flying kick to the chest that was worthy of a straight red card. English referee Howard Webb doled out 14 yellow cards and kept the red one in his pocket during regulation play so as not to give any one team a player advantage in such an important game. "We had intended to play beautiful football, but we were facing a very good opponent," said Dutch manager Bert van Marwijk, who had studied the tape of the U.S. victory over Spain the previous year in the days leading up to the final.[48]

The Dutch did something offensively as the match wore on, but scoring efforts by Robben and his teammates were repelled by Casillas. Regulation ended scoreless and penalty kicks, the manner by which the previous final had been decided, loomed on the horizon that chilly night. Webb ejected Dutch defender John Heitinga after he violently took down Iniesta. The Dutch were forced to play down a player for the remaining 11 minutes of overtime. Spain countered the fouling by attacking and was finally rewarded with a spectacular Iniesta goal. After three consecutive 1-0 games, Spain added a fourth when Iniesta broke free and scored the game-winner with just four minutes left in extra time. The goal was indicative of the style of play the Spanish had perfected over the past three years. The winning sequence began deep in the Spanish half with Puyol winning the ball and barreling forward, initiating a 25-second build-up that featured touches by five Spanish players and just six passes before Iniesta fired a diagonal ball into the net. The Spanish had defined their playing style above all with skill and patience. All Holland could do in the face of it all was to commit fouls. Even with Torres scoring no goals at this tournament after coming off a knee injury, Spain relied on Villa to bag goals and its potent midfield to get him the ball. Defensively, Puyol provided calm and control in the back with Casillas always there to make crucial saves. A combination of endurance and grace gave Spain the World Cup, becoming the first team in history to lose its tournament opener and prevail in the final. "It just had to go in. It's amazing. I can't believe it," Iniesta said after the game.[49]

When Webb blew the final whistle, he found himself surrounded by irate Dutch players. Webb ignored them as the Spanish players exulted on the sidelines. Iniesta fell to the ground in tears. In one of the tournament's lasting images, Blatter handed Casillas the World Cup trophy and an entire nation rejoiced. Yet South Africa also had reason to rejoice. The country had pulled off the event in magnificent style. Spain may have been worthy champions, but South Africa was even worthier hosts. Another winner that evening was a German mollusk named Paul the Octopus, who became an international sensation after successfully predicting the outcome of all of Germany's games, including Spain's win in the final. Paul died three months after the World Cup, but will forever be remembered for his predictions.

The final alone was watched by a staggering 24.3 million people in the United States, making it the most-viewed soccer game in American television history. Overall, ESPN's ratings were up 30 percent compared to 2006. The next World Cup—to be held in Brazil (with games that will air in primetime on the East Coast)—is expected to be an even bigger success as Americans continue to embrace the World Cup. As the U.S. team improves, the World Cup will continue to provide fans with thrills and chills that will last a lifetime.

## NOTES

1. Personal interview, June 11, 2010.
2. News conference, June 22, 2010.
3. Personal interview, February 25, 2010.
4. Personal interview, February 25, 2010.
5. Jeffrey Marcus, "Referees Talk Openly, but Not about That One Call," The New York Times, June 21, 2010.
6. News conference, October 10, 2009.
7. Personal interview, May 29, 2010.
8. News conference, October 15, 2009.
9. News conference, June 8, 2010.
10. News conference, June 8, 2010.
11. News conference, June 17, 2010.
12. News conference, June 21, 2010.
13. Personal interview, July 7, 2010.
14. News conference, October 14, 2009.
15. News conference, June 22, 2010.
16. Personal interview, April 15, 2010.
17. Personal interview, April 15, 2010.
18. Personal interview, July 1, 2010.
19. Personal interview, April 15, 2010.
20. News conference, June 12, 2010.
21. News conference, June 12, 2010.

22. News conference, June 12, 2010.
23. Personal interview, July 8, 2010.
24. News conference, June 12, 2010.
25. News conference, June 18, 2010.
26. News conference, June 18, 2010.
27. News conference, June 12, 2010.
28. News conference, June 19, 2010.
29. News conference, June 19, 2010.
30. News conference, June 18, 2010.
31. News conference, June 20, 2010.
32. News conference, June 23, 2010.
33. News conference, June 24, 2010.
34. News conference, June 24, 2010.
35. News conference, June 24, 2010.
36. News conference, June 9, 2010.
37. News conference, June 25, 2010.
38. News conference, June 14, 2010.
39. Personal interview, July 2, 2010.
40. News conference, June 26, 2010.
41. News conference, June 27, 2010.
42. News conference, June 29, 2010.
43. News conference, June 28, 2010.
44. News conference, June 28, 2010.
45. News conference, July 2, 2010.
46. News conference, July 2, 2010.
47. Personal interview, July 9, 2010.
48. News conference, July 11, 2010.
49. News conference, July 11, 2010.

# 10

# OBRIGADO, GERMANY

The 2014 World Cup was awarded to Brazil in 2007 after Colombia—the only other nation to present a bid—withdrew its application. As a result, Brazil was named host for only the second time in history. Brazil had hosted the tournament in 1950, losing out on the title to Uruguay. For Brazil, this World Cup was a chance for redemption, an opportunity to erase the bad memories of the *Maracanazo*. While Brazil had won five World Cups, no victory had ever taken place on its home soil. Furthermore, the World Cup was returning to the "spiritual home" of soccer and marked the first time since 1978 that the tournament would take place in South America.

Brazil coach Luiz Felipe Scolari, back for another run as manager after winning the World Cup with the team in 2002, publicly exuded confidence in his players in the months leading up to the finals. In an interview with the Spanish sports daily *Marca*, Scolari took a shot at Spain, the reigning world champions and a favorite to repeat after winning the 2012 European Championship: "I believe in my team. We need to have respect for the other contenders, but there are teams that have won a World Cup and believe they're the best. We have won five."[1]

The long process of qualification began in June 2011, a year after the history-making 2010 tournament in South Africa, and featured 203 of FIFA's 208 member nations. With Brazil automatically reaching the finals as host, the 2014 tournament also featured all the previous World Cup champions: Uruguay, Argentina, Italy, Germany, England, France, and Spain. FIFA had also voted in December 2010 to award the host nations of the 2018 and 2022 tournaments—the first time two hosts had been chosen in the same day by FIFA's 24-member Executive Committee. On the eve of the vote, FIFA decided to award the 2018 tournament to one of four bids (England, Russia, and joint bids from Belgium/Netherlands and Portugal/Spain). For 2022, FIFA would consider five others (Australia, Qatar, Japan, South Korea, and the United States).

The United States had put together a strong bid. With the help of former president Bill Clinton, the federation tried to impress on the executive committee members the positive financial implications and state-of-the-art infrastructure the United States had to offer. Like in 1994, the U.S. bid featured modern venues, including several new NFL stadiums. It was a win-win for everyone. FIFA, however, had other plans. To the disbelief of many, the 2018 tournament was awarded to Russia and the 2022 World Cup to the tiny Middle Eastern nation of Qatar. No sooner had Qatar been awarded the tournament than questions began to swirl around the legitimacy of its bid, the process in which they were awarded the tournament, and whether the country could ever host games with temperatures reaching 100 degrees Fahrenheit. FIFA even considered moving the tournament to December to make it work.

*FIFA president Sepp Blatter had to deal with several scandals within world soccer's governing body in the lead-up to the 2014 World Cup finals (Credit: FIFA/Getty Images).*

Two of FIFA's 24 Executive Committee members were suspended after undercover reporters working for Britain's *Sunday Times* caught them trying to sell their votes. Over the next four years, five more members of the Executive Committee—including the U.S.'s Chuck Blazer—were either banned or forced off after charges emerged of them giving or taking bribes. Qatar's Mohamed bin Hammam was booted from the committee for corruption tied to his time as head of the Asian Football Confederation. The *Sunday Times* reported that bin Hammam had allegedly bribed fellow committee members to vote for Qatar's bid. The Qataris have repeatedly denied the allegations. With the 2018 and '22 tournaments mired in controversy, the image of FIFA and its president, Sepp Blatter, seemed forever tarnished.

As for qualification to the 2014 tournament, the United States—under new coach Jurgen Klinsmann—reached the finals for a seventh straight time, a streak that stretched back to 1990. Once again, it won the Hexagonal, amassing 22 points over 10 matches. At the same time, Mexico, a team tarnished by a string of poor results and coaching changes, finished fourth and eventually defeated Oceania's group winner New Zealand, in a home-and-home tie-breaker series to book its ticket to Brazil. Mexico, however, reached the finals with some help from the United States. Mexico had lost its final Hexagonal game to Costa Rica, 2–1, in Mexico City. Simultaneously, the United States, already through to the finals, defeated Panama 3–2 on the road following a last-gasp goal from Aron Jóhannsson. The U.S. victory was enough to put the Mexicans in the playoff.

Jóhannsson was one of the players Klinsmann had brought into the national team fold since taking over in 2011. The team had gone through a transformation from the days of Bob Bradley, who later became coach of Egypt. Klinsmann was trying to impose his own style on the squad—something that was in constant flux—and the former German international scouted several Americans with dual citizenship playing in Europe that he thought would work well in his lineup. Jermaine Jones, a midfielder, became one key contributor. Another controversial call-up was German American Julian Green, just 18, and a player who was stuck playing with Bayern Munich's reserve team. Green's inclusion in Klinsmann's final 23-man roster for the World Cup became even more shocking when it appeared to come at the expense of Landon Donovan, the team's all-time leading scorer and the symbol of American soccer for over a decade.

Donovan had taken a sabbatical from the game a year earlier—something that had irked Klinsmann. The decision proved to be his undoing. At a news conference, Donovan said he was not angry at Klinsmann. "Based on my performances leading up to camp, based on my preparation for the camp, based on my fitness, based on my workload, based on the way I trained and played in camp, I not only thought I was part of the 23, I thought I was in contention to be starting. That's why this has all been pretty disappointing." Donovan would retire from the game by the end of the year.[2]

While Donovan was on the losing end, Major League Soccer as a whole was the big winner. Twenty-two MLS players—half of them on the U.S. team—were selected to be part of World Cup rosters, an increase from six in 2010. Among some notable choices were the New York Red Bulls' Tim Cahill of Australia and Brazil's Julio Cesar, who was on loan with Toronto FC for the spring. England's Premier League was the most represented domestic competition at the World Cup with a total of 110 players, while all the players chosen to play for Russia played in the country's top pro league.

The World Cup was again a 32-team affair with eight groups featuring four teams apiece. The seven seeded teams were based on the October 2013 FIFA rankings in addition to Brazil, who was made a seed as is traditionally done with host nations. The final draw was conducted on December 6, 2013, and held in the resort town of Bahia. It produced the following groups:

Group A: Brazil, Croatia, Mexico, and Cameroon
Group B: Spain, Chile, Netherlands, and Australia
Group C: Colombia, Greece, Ivory Coast, and Japan
Group D: Uruguay, Costa Rica, England, and Italy
Group E: Switzerland, Ecuador, France, and Honduras
Group F: Argentina, Bosnia-Herzegovina, Iran, and Nigeria
Group G: Germany, Portugal, Ghana, and the United States
Group H: Belgium, Algeria, Russia, and South Korea

The United States ended up in the toughest group against three opponents with intriguing connections to the national team. Ghana had eliminated the United States from the last two World Cups; Portugal had been the team the United States had defeated in a stunning upset at the 2002 tournament, while Germany was the team Klinsmann had coached at the 2006 World Cup. "We will be meeting old friends. It is already something special to have the United States in our group. Jurgen and I have had a very good and close relationship for a long time," Germany coach Joachim Loew, who had served as Klinsmann's assistant, said following the draw.[3]

The United States, aside from being in a tough group, was also the team that had to travel the most between its three first-round matches. Furthermore, the Americans were scheduled to play Portugal in the city of Manaus, which was located deep in the jungles of the Amazon. Tropical and wet weather conditions awaited both teams. "We don't complain. We take it on. We do the traveling and we adjust to the climate. This is what a World Cup is about. It's about these challenges. It's exciting in certain ways, and a big challenge. That's what we want," said the ever-optimistic Klinsmann.[4]

This World Cup would also feature some innovations. FIFA had instituted water breaks because of the warm temperatures, the use of goal-line technology to determine whether the ball had completely

*Goal-line technology, a system that alerts the referee to when the ball has crossed the line for a goal, was used for the first time ever at a World Cup in 2014 (Credit: FIFA/ Getty Images).*

crossed the line for a score, and the use by referees of a vanishing spray to ensure that the proper distance was observed before the taking of free kicks. All three had been used at various other tournaments in the past as part of a FIFA experiment. All three would prove successful at the 2014 World Cup.

While FIFA had control over what occurred on the field, it was worried about what had been going on off it. A year before the World Cup, many Brazilians had grown frustrated and upset at the staggering amount of money the government had spent on stadiums and other infrastructure projects related to the tournament. During the Confederations Cup the year before, thousands of Brazilians had taken to the streets to decry the cost overruns and the government's neglect of schools and hospitals. At the same time, FIFA president Blatter publicly criticized the hosts, telling a gathering of Swiss reporters in January 2014 that Brazil was behind in its preparations. "No country has been so far behind in its preparations since I have been at FIFA, even though it is the only host nation which has had so much time—seven years—in which to prepare," Blatter told the Swiss newspaper *24 Heures*. When asked if Brazil understood the scale of the work involved in hosting a World Cup, Blatter was quoted in the same newspaper as saying: "No. Brazil has just found out what it means and has started work much too late."

While Brazilian officials admitted to spending $14 billion on the tournament ($4.2 billion on the twelve stadiums alone), Brazil's tourism minister, Vinicius Lages, tried to downplay the negative figures, saying that more than 3.1 million Brazilians and 600,000 foreigners were expected to travel throughout Brazil for the World Cup. That would inject $4 billion into the country's economy.[5]

Nonetheless, the enormous costs—$3 billion more than had been budgeted—highlighted the corruption and mismanagement that often comes with the staging of such a large sporting event. Despite the demonstrations, the country's sports minister, Aldo Rebelo, was confident Brazil would host a wonderful tournament. "Through the World Cup, Brazil will offer not only the material conditions to hold a great event but, above all, will show how warmly the Brazilian people welcome visitors from around the world. I believe that those who visit us during the World Cup will appreciate this distinguishing feature that is so characteristic of our people," he said.[6]

## FIRST ROUND

While the protests had reached their height the summer before the World Cup, they mostly subsided in the months that followed. But protests grew louder again in the weeks before the June 12 opener, and police in riot gear had to be called in just hours before kickoff to quell the protesters that had gathered before the Group A game featuring Brazil and Croatia at the Arena de São Paulo in the capital São Paulo. It would be the last time demonstrations of any sort would take place so close to a venue on the day of a game.

As for the game itself, Brazil opened the tournament with a 3–1 victory thanks to two goals by Neymar, while Mexico narrowly defeated Cameroon 1–0 the following day at Arena das Dunas in Natal. Brazil had not put together a convincing performance, but it won nonetheless, catching a break from the Japanese referee Yuichi Nishimura and his controversial decision to award a penalty kick after striker Fred crumbled to the ground following what looked like minimal contact from Dejan Lovren. The call changed the game's outcome, and Neymar coolly converted the penalty kick to break a 1–1 draw. The call drew the ire of Lovren. Speaking with reporters outside the team's dressing room, he lashed out at Nishimura, saying what was on the

Brazil's Neymar was expected to lead the host nation to a World Cup title, although an injury in the quarterfinals changed the team's fortunes (Credit: FIFA/Action Images).

minds of so many: "It's a scandal! This referee should not be at this World Cup."[7]

Although Brazil were heavy favorites to win the group, it was held to a scoreless draw against Mexico on June 17 as an entire nation, both nervous and riveted, watched on TV and in public squares. The hero of the game was Mexican goalkeeper Guillermo Ochoa, who thwarted all of Brazil's 14 attempts that evening at the Castelão Stadium in Fortaleza to preserve the shootout. If not for Ochoa, Brazil would certainly have won the match. "I can't remember a goalkeeper performing like that in a World Cup," observed Mexico coach Miguel Herrera, who became famous for his over-the-top sideline goal celebrations.[8]

The pressure was on Brazil and Scolari to win its final game. The team had looked out of sorts at times in its previous two matches, and Scolari's 4-3-2-1 appeared overly reliant on Neymar. His other strikers—notably Fred and Jo—had been unimpressive. It would take a third game to ensure Brazil's passage to the Round of 16, with a resounding 4–1 win against Cameroon on June 23 at Mane Garrincha Stadium in Brasilia. Neymar was again the star, scoring the first two goals to lead the team to victory. The Brazilians made it look easy when it counted most, but it had come against a relatively weak opponent. Neymar tried to reassure the Brazilian public afterward, saying, "There is no pressure [on the team]."[9]

Not to be outdone, Mexico put together a strong second-half performance at Arena Pernambuco in Recife to defeat Croatia 3–1 and advance to the second round. As Herrera performed all sorts of physical contortions on the sidelines, his players grew stronger as the match wore on. Rafa Marquez's header in the 72nd minute broke open the game for the Mexicans. The crowd of 41,212 grew louder in its support for the Mexicans, and the cheers helped carry the team to success. "You could see how happy it made the fans. It was like playing at home," Herrera commented afterward.[10]

In Group B, the much-anticipated Spain–Netherlands game, a rematch of the World Cup final four years earlier, on June 13 at Arena Fonte Nova in Salvador, quickly turned into a lopsided affair. The Dutch, looking for revenge, piled on the pressure—and the goals. The outcome was a 5–1 win for the Dutch. It was a total humiliation for the reigning champions. The highlight of the afternoon was the first of Robin van Persie's two goals. His flying header right before halftime beat Iker Casillas and set the tone for the rout. "I did not expect a scoreline like this," said Netherlands coach Louis van Gaal.[11]

The Dutch truly looked unstoppable, beating Australia 3–2 on June 18 and 2–0 against Chile five days later to win the group. While the Dutch were impressing, Spain was depressing. After losing to the Netherlands, it was Chile's turn to beat Spain—a 2–0 victory in a do-or-die match on June 18 at the Maracanã Stadium that meant an early exit for Spain. As a result, Chile advanced to the Round of 16 as the second-place team. Xabi Alonso summed up the mood best for Spain, saying, "We didn't know how to maintain our hunger or that conviction needed to win a tournament."[12]

Group C—called the "Group of Life" because all four teams had an equal chance of advancing—saw Colombia get off on the right foot by defeating Greece 3–0 on June 14 at Mineirao Stadium in Belo Horizonte. The South Americans—without star striker Radamel Falcao, who had suffered a torn ACL six months earlier—emerged as the Cinderella story. Colombia beat Ivory Coast 2–1 and Asian champion Japan 4–1 to reach the Round of 16. James Rodriguez's three goals—one in each game—put Colombia on the path to success. The 22-year-old's prowess would also work out well for him after Spanish club Real Madrid decided to sign him later that summer. "It is a huge success to see Colombia reach this level, but we can't start thinking ahead of time or what will happen later on," said Colombia's Argentine-born coach, José Pékerman.[13]

With Colombia dominating the group, the three remaining teams fought for second. Greece would be the ones to do it, qualifying for the knockout stage in dramatic style after scoring the game-winner in the third minute of stoppage time during its game against Ivory Coast on June 24 in Fortaleza. The 2–1 victory came via a Georgios Samaras penalty kick following a controversial decision by referee Carlos Vera of Ecuador. The Greeks celebrated the goal in what was one of the most dramatic finales at this World Cup.

Meanwhile, Group D turned out to be one of the more interesting groups. It featured three former World Cup winners—Italy, Uruguay, and England—along with Costa Rica. Although no one expected much from the Central American nation, it would be all everyone was talking about after stunning Uruguay 3–1 in its opener on June 14 in Fortaleza. The *Ticos* then edged out Italy 1–0 a week later in Recife to advance to the Round of 16. "It was a beautiful match. The people of Costa Rica deserve this day," rejoiced Costa Rican coach Jorge Luis Pinto following the match against Italy.[14]

With England once again putting in a sub-par showing (it would finish last in the group with two points, after recording draws against Italy and Costa Rica), second place would come down to the showdown between Italy and Uruguay. With Italy needing only a draw to advance, it had a slight advantage going into the game on June 24 in Natal. But the *Azzurri* looked slow—especially in its attack—and striker Mario Balotelli was taken off at halftime. The Italians then went down a man after midfielder Claudio Marchisio was red-carded in the second half following a high tackle on Arévalo Rios. With the Italian attack incapable of scoring, defender Diego Godin's header in the 81st minute put Uruguay ahead. It turned out to be the game's only goal, but all eyes were on Luis Suarez by the time the game came to an end. The Liverpool striker—known for having bitten opponents on two previous occasions—was caught on video sinking his teeth into the shoulder of Giorgio Chiellini. The Italy defender tried in vain to get the attention of match officials, even pulling down his jersey to show the teeth marks, but the game wore on. After the game, FIFA announced that it would launch an investigation after TV replays clearly showed the bizarre act. Uruguay went through to the Round of 16, but Suarez's World Cup would be over. He was handed a four-month ban from all competitive matches for both club and country. In addition, Suarez was suspended for nine competitive international matches, meaning he would have to sit out the 2015 Copa America.

In Group E, France was attempting to redeem itself after a poor showing and internal squabbling in 2010. With Switzerland, Honduras, and Ecuador all vying for a spot in the knockout phase, the French showed their superiority. France comfortably defeated Honduras 3–0 on June 15 at Beira-Rio Stadium in Porto Alegre (highlighted by the goal-line technology, which was used for the first time ever at a World Cup) and then Switzerland, 5–2, five days later in Salvador. The French, so flawless in their performance and featuring Karim Benzema in great form, prompting coach Didier Deschamps to say, "We were almost absolutely perfect."[15]

Meanwhile, Switzerland were runners-up, defeating Honduras 3–0 on June 25 in Manaus. The Swiss, traditionally a second-tier European team with little international success, proved tougher than its Central American opponent. A hat trick by Xherdan Shaqiri—with goals in the 6th, 31st, and 71st minutes—helped the Swiss advance. The playmaker was unstoppable for much of the game, spearheading his side's attack.

Afterward, Shaqiri thanked his teammates, saying, "I wanted to show everyone that we could play soccer. . . . I am happy about that and proud of my team."[16]

While the Swiss were impressive in Group E, Argentina was the favorite to win Group F. Messi was the one everyone was looking to once again, after a disappointing 2010 tournament. The Barcelona playmaker was still at the top of his game despite sitting out part of the Liga season with an injury. It was no surprise that Argentina became Messi-dependent from the start and needed him to score decisive goals. In the end, Argentina took all nine points, edging out Bosnia and Herzegovina 2–1 on June 15 at the Maracanã and overcoming Iran 1–0 six days later in Belo Horizonte. Messi scored the winning goal in both games. His strike against Iran in the first minute of stoppage time, a curling left-footed shot from 25 yards out, was memorable. "We have a genius who is called Messi and we are fortunate that he is Argentine. Iran made it difficult for us, but with Messi everything is possible," said Argentina coach Alejandro Sabella.[17]

Argentina's 3–2 victory over Nigeria (who went through nonetheless as runners-up) on June 25 in Porto Alegre assured the South Americans first place. Against Nigeria, Sabella switched from his 5-3-2 formation to a 4-3-1-2, with Messi as the playmaker alongside strikers Gonzalo Higuain and Ezequiel Lavezzi. Once again, two goals from Messi made the difference. As for Messi's teammates, they looked overwhelmed at times and unable to provide much support. But Messi didn't appear to need the help. His four goals in three games made him only the second Argentine since Maradona to score that many goals in a World Cup group stage. Indeed, Messi was out of this world and he was showing it. "Messi is from Jupiter. He is an amazing player," hailed Nigeria coach Stephen Keshi.[18]

Another team looking to join Argentina and Nigeria in the knockout round was the United States. The Americans needed to defeat Ghana in its Group G opener in Natal if it had any hope of advancing. It did just that. Clint Dempsey wasted no time putting the United States ahead, scoring after just 30 seconds—the fifth-fastest goal in World Cup history—following a dazzling run in the box. Needing just four touches, Dempsey got past two players before depositing the ball into the net.

The Americans were hoping the goal would be enough—especially after Jozy Altidore pulled a hamstring and had to be substituted midway through the first half—to grab the win. Instead, the U.S. defense gave up a goal in the 82nd minute when Andréw Ayew knocked the ball inside the left post and past Tim Howard to tie the score. The United States had spent much of the second half fending off attacks and struggled to create any offense. That all changed on a set piece. With four minutes left in the game, defender John Brooks, on as a halftime substitute when Matt Besler was removed from the game with hamstring tightness, headed home the winner off a Graham Zusi corner kick.

An incredulous Brooks celebrated—his hands on his head and a look of shock across his face—by lying face-down on the grass as his teammates piled on top of him. Brooks said afterward that he had dreamed of scoring the game-winner the previous day. The dream had become a reality. "I thanked God for the great moment. . . . It's unbelievable," he said.[19]

The goal unleashed wild celebrations in the stands—where a large American fan contingent had convened, including Vice President Joe Biden—and gave the team a much-needed three points to start the tournament. Klinsmann said afterward that he "was still convinced we were going to win this game even after [Ghana] got the equalizer. I had the feeling that another two or three chances would come and we would need just one of those opportunities, which then happened. This is definitely the result we wanted. The players worked hard for it."[20]

The players knew they would have to work even harder in its second match against Portugal. On June 24 in Manaus, Klinsmann's men took on a Portugal side that featured an injured Cristiano Ronaldo and little else in the way of a supporting cast. Nevertheless, Portugal took the lead with Nani after just five minutes following a poor play by Geoff Cameron, who had failed to clear the ball. Both sides appeared sluggish for stretches of the first half, and the heat and humidity of the jungle made it unbearable at times. In the 39th minute, referee Nestor Pitana of Argentina whistled for a water break—the first in World Cup history. The U.S. had struggled in the first half but dominated the start of the second. Jermaine Jones tied the score in the 65th minute when his 27-yard shot off the right post found the back of the net. "We discussed at halftime with all the players. We said, 'It's all good, guys, we're going to get this first goal, then we're going to get a second goal,'" Klinsmann recalled.[21]

With the game tied 1–1, the Americans hit their stride. Ronaldo, who had been named FIFA's Player of the Year in January, was invisible for much of the time, and the U.S. midfield, spearheaded by Zusi and

Kyle Beckerman, helped move the ball forward. Michael Bradley, who had been expected to help generate offense, seemed out of sorts. While Klinsmann expected a lot from Bradley, he knew that his team was strong as a group rather than dependent on any one individual. Klinsmann's mantra was the group over the individual. "It's not going to be a perfect game all the time. I'm not expecting perfect games from anybody. I expect him to give everything he has and then when he makes a mistake that the other guy is there to help him out," Klinsmann said.[22]

The one player, however, the Americans could rely on was Dempsey. He came up big once again, creating space and making sure he was always in a position to score. Ever the opportunist, the Seattle Sounders striker took a cross from Zusi in the 81st minute and scored his second goal of the tournament to give the United States a lead. A victory would have automatically put the Americans through to the second round. Instead, Portugal's Silvestre Varela, off a perfectly placed Ronaldo cross, scored past Howard for the tying goal in the fifth minute of stoppage time. The game ended 2–2, and the U.S. party was postponed.

"If we could have started the tournament with four points after the first two games, we would have been really happy about it. Obviously when you get a goal [against you] in the last seconds of the game when you have pretty much six points, then it's a bummer for a moment that you have to swallow. But, it was an outstanding game by all the players," said Klinsmann.[23]

The United States' final group game against Germany would be decisive. Winning would mean going through, although a draw—or even a loss—presented possibilities depending on the outcome of the Portugal–Ghana match. As for Klinsmann and whether or not he and Loew would play for a draw, the former German international said, "Our goal is to go to the next round so we will do everything in our capabilities to go into the next round. I'm not thinking about what goes on in other people's minds and situations. It's about what's important to us, so we're going to take our game to Germany and give everything we have, give them a real fight."[24]

The June 26 match in Recife was marred by heavy rain the day before. With the weather appearing to worsen just hours before kickoff, the streets surrounding the stadium and throughout the fifth-largest Brazilian city were knee-deep in water. Thousands braved the water-logged streets to get to the game. The 12-hour downpour may have flooded streets, but FIFA assured everyone that the match would go on as scheduled. The stadium's drainage system ensured that the game could go on, and an inspection of the pitch by the match officials confirmed that no delay would occur.

Rain could not keep away the thousands of loud American fans—with their "I Believe That We Will Win" chant—who had permeated stadiums in the United States' previous two games. Aside from the growing number of Americans in Brazil, the following back home had grown to levels never before seen for soccer. Bars, restaurants, and public parks had become places for people to gather. Although many may have never watched soccer before, it seemed—temporarily at least—that World Cup fever had caught on. On the field, the Americans lost 1–0 but managed to reach the Round of 16 after Portugal defeated Ghana 2–1 in the group's other game, played simultaneously in Brasilia. The lone goal came in the 55th minute from German striker Thomas Müller. Klinsmann and Loew hugged after the game, and both sides walked off the field content. "We can still improve. We have to do better . . . and we will do better," Klinsmann assured afterward.[25]

The outcome meant the United States would play Belgium (the winner of Group H) in the second round; Germany earned a date with Algeria, the second-place team from that same group. The Africans looked eager to avenge the injustice of 1982, when Germany and Austria plotted together to eliminate the Algerians in the group stage. For its part, Belgium showed plenty of heart and spunk, coming from behind to defeat Algeria 2–1 in Belo Horizonte on June 17 in its opening match, then adding a 1–0 victory (from a Divock Origi goal in the 88th minute) against Russia in Rio de Janeiro five days later to secure passage to the Round of 16. Belgium's 1–0 win on June 26 in São Paulo against South Korea put it in the same exclusive club (alongside the Netherlands, Colombia, and Argentina) of teams that had gone 3–0 in the first round. "This is truly a historic achievement for Belgium," said coach Marc Wilmots.[26]

In the battle for second, Algeria defeated South Korea 4–2 in Porto Alegre on June 22 and needed just a 1–1 draw against Russia four days later to advance to the knockout round of a World Cup for the first time in the country's history. The Russians, led by famed Italian coach Fabio Capello, fell flat—something of an embarrassment for the highest-paid manager at the tournament and for the World Cup's next host nation. Although his team failed miserably, Capello praised the level of play demonstrated at the tournament throughout the first round. "In my career, I have never seen a World Cup at this level. The quality is absolutely incredible; the pace is so intense. It's without doubt the best World Cup of all," he said.[27]

Capello was not exaggerating. The first round had produced attacking soccer, riveting finales, and some surprises. With the exception of Honduras and Ecuador, every team from North/Central and South America reached the knockout stage. Playing in South America to mostly partisan crowds had certainly helped. CONCACAF, in particular, was the big winner. Cinderella side Costa Rica had won Group D and Mexico had come close to winning Group A, losing out to Brazil only on goal differential. CONCACAF is often a difficult confederation to qualify for—something the Americans have always known—and teams from around the world had finally seen that the region could produce quality teams and players.

Furthermore, there were nearly as many goals in Brazil in 2014 after the first round (136 for an average of 2.83 per game) than in all of the 2010 World Cup (145 for an average of 2.27 per game). Costa Rica and Mexico, along with Belgium, were three of the 16 teams that advanced to the knockout stage to concede the fewest goals—just one. That statistic said a lot, especially in a tournament dominated by so many goals. Although teams would play a little more defensively in the second round, the matches were still highlighted by goals. In the end, the tournament would produce 171 goals for an impressive average of 2.67 goals per match, which equaled the record set at France '98.

## KNOCKOUT ROUND

The Round of 16 opened on June 28 when Brazil took on Chile in Belo Horizonte. While Brazil was relying on Neymar to determine the outcome of the match, Chile was hoping its defense would be strong enough to stifle that game plan. The Brazilians took the lead after 18 minutes with David Luiz. Chile equalized in the 32nd minute when Alexis Sanchez scored after the Brazilians lost the ball in their own half following a Hulk throw-in. Although Brazil dominated possession, chances were few on both sides and the game went to overtime. Chile could have won the game in the final minute of extra time, but Mauricio Pinilla's shot hit the crossbar.

The game went to a dramatic penalty shootout. With the entire nation seemingly holding its breath, the Brazilians advanced 3–2 after Chile defender Gonzalo Jara's shot hit the post. Brazil's players celebrated in the center circle as fans in the stadium and across the country rejoiced. Julio Cesar, overcome from emotion, openly wept as he spoke with reporters. "There's huge pressure in representing our country, and it was tough on a psychological and emotional level. I got very emotional four years ago, and today I am crying again, but this time out of happiness. Not many people know what I've been through, but I knew my international career wasn't over. We've got three more steps to go now and I want to see Brazil celebrating," he said.[28]

In the day's other game, played in Rio de Janeiro, Uruguay and Colombia faced off in another all–South American clash. Without Suarez in the lineup, Uruguay was unable to generate the offense seen during the first round. The Colombians, on the other hand, took the momentum of the first round and carried it with them into the knockout stage. James Rodriguez was the hero once again, scoring both goals as Colombia won, 2–0. His first goal, in the 28th minute, was one of the tournament's prettiest after he controlled the ball with his chest and unleashed a 25-yard volley that hit the underside of the crossbar and past goalkeeper Fernando Muslera. Rodriguez's second goal, in the 50th minute, came from a close-range shot just six yards out that was too strong for Muslera to stop. After the game, an ecstatic Rodriguez said, "I have always wanted to score at the Maracanã and now I have. If you want to win, every player is important. Uruguay had a lot of men behind the ball, so we needed plenty of movement up front and we got it. Now things are going to get even harder, but we can go far."[29]

On June 29, the Netherlands and Mexico took to the field under a stifling 85-degree heat in Fortaleza. Although the hot weather limited both sides from doing much in the first half, Mexico took the lead early in the second. Giovani dos Santos opened the scoring in the 48th minute on a left-footed shot. Mexico appeared well on its way to reaching the quarterfinals, a feat many would not have believed at the start of the competition. The goal opened the game up, forcing the Dutch to react. "I have to give credit to my players. I think they were in much better shape and much more focused than our opponents. They never stopped believing, right to the end. They showed belief and a lot of confidence," said Dutch coach Louis van Gaal.[30]

Despite the heat and need for FIFA-mandated water breaks, the Dutch never gave up. It drew the score level two minutes from time with Wesley Sneijder. Van Gaal had used the second-half water break to reshuffle his lineup (something coaches aren't usually able to do during soccer's nonstop action) and enact what he later called Plan B. In came substitute Klaas-Jan Huntelaar, whose fresh legs provided the Netherlands with some energy in the midfield. "We took advantage of the water break to tweak our system and created loads of chances," said van Gaal.[31]

In the fourth minute of injury time, Huntelaar converted a penalty kick for the Dutch that won them the game. The penalty came from a controversial call after Arjen Robben dropped to the ground following minimal contact from Rafa Marquez in the box. Robben was later criticized for diving—something the Mexicans were certain of. No matter. The game was over and Mexico had been eliminated. "Robben dove three times. You have to caution a player who is trying to cheat, and then if Robben did it again he would be sent off," said Herrera.[32]

Recife was the host city for the June 29 match between Costa Rica and Greece. It was Greece's first knockout game ever at a World Cup. For Costa Rica, it was the chance to repeat all it had done in the group phase. Costa Rica's 5-4-1 formation proved formidable once again versus a Greek side devoid of imagination. Midfielder Bryan Ruiz, playing on the right wing, opened the scoring in the 52nd minute. The Greeks, however, pulled off another late-game rally. Sokratis Papastathopoulos equalized in the 91st minute, pushing the match to extra time. The game went to penalties, where Costa Rica converted all five of its attempts to win 5–3. Keylor Navas's save on Theofanis Gekas proved decisive before Michael Umaña converted the winner.

The favored French took on Nigeria on June 30 in Brasilia. *Les Bleus*, riding high from its three first-round games, struggled early on. The Africans, in search of an upset, were looking to push the game to overtime. But France's Paul Pogba had other plans, netting what turned out to be the game-winner with 11 minutes left. Pogba's header got into the net after goalkeeper Vincent Enyeama failed to grab the ball off a corner kick. France put the finishing touches on its victory with a second goal in stoppage time when Nigeria's Joseph Yobo scored an own goal under pressure from Antione Griezmann.

In the second Europe–Africa contest of the day, Germany took on Algeria in Porto Alegre. The Germans remained one of the favorites to win the title and had spent the days leading up to the game training in their state-of-the-art facility in Santo Andre. The base camp, named Campo Bahia, was located along the northeast coast of Brazil and just 45 minutes away from a private airport. Not only did it make it easier to travel to games, but the base provided an oasis for both players and staff alike.

As for the game, Algeria was able to keep Germany from scoring. After the game ended 0–0 in regulation, Germany finally turned on its offense, scoring just two minutes into extra time. Half-time substitute André Schürrle scored on a backheel from a Thomas Muller cross. In the final minute of overtime, Mesut Ozil converted after Schürrle's initial attempt was blocked. In stoppage time, Algeria pulled a goal back, but it wasn't enough. Germany advanced to the quarterfinals, where it would face France. Germany also continued its streak of reaching the final eight—something it has done since the 1954 World Cup. "We were the better team after the break and in extra time," admitted Loew.[33]

The 63,000 who witnessed the Argentina–Switzerland match on July 1—many of them Argentines who had driven for days to get over the border to Brazil—saw yet another Round of 16 match that was resolved in extra time. Like the Germans, Argentina avoided a penalty shootout when striker Ángel Di María, off a Messi pass, scored in the 118th minute to put his side through to the quarterfinals. The Swiss had the chance to equalize in stoppage time, but Blerim Džemaili's header slammed against the post.

The final Round of 16 game pitted the United States against Belgium on July 1 in Salvador before a crowd of 51,227 fans, many of them Americans. Excitement for the United States had reached an all-time high. A win would equal the U.S. showing at the 2002 World Cup, while a loss would be no better than the team accomplished four years earlier in South Africa. With the hype around Klinsmann also reaching an all-time high, the pressure was on the former German international player to also get the Americans into the quarterfinals.

The United States had hoped to get Altidore back for the match, but he would end up not playing after days of speculation that he could be used as a sub. Instead, Klinsmann went with Dempsey flanked by Alejandro Bedoya and Fabian Johnson. On the other side of the field, Belgium was not lacking in offensive firepower. In the end, the Americans—known for their high-energy intensity and late comebacks—came up short. With the U.S. defense failing to stifle the Belgian attack, it was up to Tim Howard to block everything put in his path. And he did. Klinsmann's men held on for dear life as Belgium created chance after chance. Despite that, it was the Americans who could have won the game in the 90th minute when Chris Wondolowski, near the Belgian goal, blasted his shot high.

The game went to overtime tied 0–0. Three minutes into extra time, Belgium's Romelu Lukaku dribbled from midfield to the right side of the box—a ball that defender Omar Gonzalez failed to properly clear. Kevin De Bruyne retrieved the ball and fired a shot to the inside of the far left post. Howard was unable to stretch out his right leg far enough to stop the ball and Belgium was up, 1–0. In the 105th minute, Belgium seemed to put the game out of reach when Lukaku, off a De Bruyne pass, beat Howard from just six yards out. Game over? Not with the United States. With nothing to lose, Klinsmann put in Green, a fresh attacking player, in an effort to pull one back. That's exactly what he did in the 107th minute—connecting from a perfectly placed Bradley ball to volley it into the net. The goal put the Americans within one. "Even when we were down 2–0, I thought we would come back," said U.S. Soccer Federation president Sunil Gulati.[34]

However, the Belgians controlled the pace—like they had throughout much of the match—to win, 2–1. Howard was the hero of the night, recording 16 saves—the most ever in a single World Cup game in the tournament's history—but it wasn't enough to see the Americans through. "This was definitely an amazing goalkeeper performance. There is no doubt about it. He should be very proud of himself and we are proud to have him with us," said Klinsmann.

The saves served as little consolation to Howard, who was named Man of the Match. "It's heartbreaking. I don't think we could have given any more. What a great game. . . . We left it all out there. We got beat by a really good team. They took their chances well. It's heartache. It hurts," he said.[35]

Despite that heartache, the team had captured the imagination of an entire country. For the first time, it really looked as if the nation, all of it, cared about soccer and the fortunes of the U.S. team. "The country was paying attention, and I think we're building on something: Bob [Bradley] did a great job [in 2010], and Bruce [Arena] before him [in 2002]. Jurgen is building on that. We've got some new exciting players, so there's progress on the field, and it's especially progress when you

*Despite Tim Howard's amazing performance in goal, the United States was eliminated by Belgium in the Round of 16 (Credit: Action Images/FIFA.com).*

think about the number of people at home who were paying attention," said Gulati.[36]

The quarterfinals opened on July 4 with a pair of European heavyweights—Germany and France—squaring off at the storied Maracanã Stadium. Loew's team—playing in a 4-5-1 formation—continued to demonstrate its superiority, with Miroslav Klose playing as the lone striker. With the defense playing a high line and goalkeeper Manuel Neuer playing practically as a sweeper, the Germans were effective against a France team seemingly out of sorts. The game's only goal came in the 13th minute when Mats Hummels's header found the back of the net. "I was in the right place at the right time. We're playing the type of football that will give us the chance to win. We're defending well, with passion and that needs to be intensified with every coming match," said Hummels.[37]

In stoppage time, France had the chance to push overtime when Benzema's shot was saved by Neuer at point-blank range. "Compared to Germany, we are a much more inexperienced team, and they are more used to playing big international matches like this. I thought we were a little bit timid at first and they scored early. After that, we showed promise. We created chances and could have been more clinical, but Manuel Neuer had a good game. That said they could have easily

## MIROSLAV KLOSE

Miroslav Klose may be one of those players who has had a better career with his national team than at the club level. Although he has played for some of the world's biggest clubs, Klose is better known for his performances with Germany. He is the team's all-time leading scorer, with 71 goals, and has become the World Cup's top scorer, with 16 goals over a span of four tournaments in 2014.

Klose, a member of the German team that won the 2014 World Cup, played in the 2002, 2006, and 2010 tournaments as well. He scored five goals in his World Cup debut in 2002 and another five in 2006, where Germany finished third. Klose added four goals to his tally at the 2010 World Cup and two more in 2014. His goal against Brazil in the semifinals made him the tournament's all-time leading scorer with 16 goals, one ahead of Ronaldo. His goals also put him in a unique class, alongside countryman Uwe Seeler and Pelé, as the only players to have scored in four different World Cups. In another notable statistic, Germany has never lost a match in which Klose had scored.

Klose was born in Poland. His father played pro soccer there but fled the country's Communist rule in 1978 to play with French club Auxerre. As an ethnic German, Klose's father decided to move his family in 1986 to what was at the time West Germany. Although Klose was only a child and spoke very little German, he quickly learned the language, as well as his father's love for the game. The striker started his career at FC 08 Homberg, then played in the Bundesliga with famed sides such as Kaiserlautern, Werder Bremen, and Bayern Munich. Klose won two league titles with Bayern Munich before going off to Italy in 2011 to play for Serie A side Lazio. Klose, who made his Germany debut in 2001, retired from the national team following the 2014 World Cup.

## World Cup Career Statistics

Tournaments played: 4
Games: 24
Goals: 16

scored a second when we were pushing forward at the end," said France coach Didier Deschamps.[38]

That evening, Brazil took on Colombia in the day's second quarterfinal. Once again, Brazil faced a fellow South American opponent in the knockout round. The Brazilians, fearing a Rodriguez onslaught, featured striker Fred alone up top, with Neymar in a supporting role on the left flank. For Colombia, it was the first time in history that it was playing in the quarterfinals of a World Cup, and José Pékerman's men were looking to continue their Cinderalla run. With the 60,000 in attendance at Fortaleza's Castelão Stadium cheering for Brazil, Scolari's team was looking to live up to pre-tournament expectations by reaching the final.

Brazil took the lead seven minutes in when Neymar's corner kick provided the assist needed for Thiago Silva to score at close range. In the 69th minute, a long-range David Luiz free kick found the back of the net—a goal that unleashed celebrations inside the stadium and across the country. "I've been waiting all year for one like that. . . . I'm delighted it came in this game. I hit the ball well and it was lovely to watch it going in, moving like that, which made it very hard for the goalkeeper," said David Luiz.[39]

Colombia, down but not out, pulled one back in the 80th minute when Rodriguez converted a penalty kick for his sixth goal of the tournament. But the goals were not the story. Vicious fouling on both sides (the teams combined for 54 of them) marred the match. No foul was greater than when Juan Camilo Zúñiga kneed Neymar in the back. The Brazilian was taken out of the game. A subsequent medical evaluation found that Neymar had suffered a fractured vertebrae, ending his tournament. Brazil won the game 2–1 and was now in the semifinals against Germany. "We didn't have a problem with tiredness after the Chile game and the team made a full recovery, as you could see in the first half. If we'd have got the second goal then, it would have settled our nerves a bit more. The goal we conceded came about because we gave away possession and were caught off balance. [Colombia] really committed men forward with three strikers and James dropping into space. Our front men had to do a lot more running, too, but we got there in the end. We've still got two steps to go but we've got the ability to get there," Scolari said.[40]

Belgium's win over the United States ensured it a date against Argentina in the quarterfinals. With the 68,551 fans in Brasilia teeming

*Colombia's James Rodriguez won the Golden Boot after he finished as the World Cup's top scorer (Credit: Adidas/FIFA.com via Getty Images).*

with Argentine supporters and Messi in fine form, Sabella's men looked poised to advance. The teams had met two previous times at a World Cup, most recently in the semifinals of Mexico '86 when Diego Maradona led Argentina to the trophy. This time, all eyes were on Messi. Like Maradona, he could change the outcome of the game with a single pass or kick. Indeed, Messi's magic had been enough to get his side this far. In the end, Argentina did win the game, 1–0, on July 5, thanks to a Gonzalo Higuain goal after just eight minutes that put the South Americans into the semifinals. "I feel incredibly happy, and I'd like to share that happiness with my family and the whole of Argentina. Ever since the first game I've been saying that I wasn't worried, that my first goal would come, and fortunately it came at a crucial time," Higuain said.[41]

A second Higuain attempt in the second half hit the crossbar and an injury to Di María's right thigh muscle after just 33 minutes ruled him out for the remainder of the competition. Despite the victory, the sight of Di María hobbling off the field in tears made many in the Argentina camp cringe that its quest for the title would be compromised. Sabella summed the mood best, saying, "Our performance was excellent tactically, strategically, and in how a team should behave. . . . We were able to bounce back after Di María had to go off, and he was a very big loss.

We've achieved our minimum objective, which was to reach the last four, but we want more. That's what we've come for."[42]

The most riveting quarterfinal match-up came that evening in Salvador between the Netherlands and Costa Rica. The Dutch—with its experience and world-class stars—was pitted against an underdog side that had become the pride of CONCACAF and was playing in a World Cup quarterfinal for the first time. Again, the *Ticos* were able to stretch their opponents with their brand of defense and counterattacking style. The game, scoreless after 90 minutes, was headed to overtime. The frustrated Dutch had come close to scoring in the first period of overtime. First, Sneijder's free kick hit the post. Then van Persie's attempt deflected off the crossbar following Costa Rica defender Yeltsin Tejeda's save on the line. In the second half of extra time, another Sneijder shot slammed against the crossbar. In stoppage time, van Gaal proved again to be a master tactician, bringing on back-up goalie Tim Krul. In the subsequent penalty shootout, Krul saved two attempts—from Ruiz and Umaña—while the Dutch scored four goals past Navas to advance to the semifinals against Argentina.

"In terms of team spirit and togetherness, this is the best group I have ever worked with. I thought we had more quality than Costa Rica and deserved to win. . . . We have practiced [penalty shootouts]. I believe when you're used to a certain way of shooting you'll be more comfortable taking that shot. We told Tim Krul that he would be the best goalkeeper for the penalties as he's bigger; we didn't tell [Jasper] Cillessen, as we didn't want to ruin his preparation and concentration. There is no question about who will start next game, it will be Cillessen. But we felt Krul was the better choice here—and he proved that," van Gaal said in the post-match news conference.[43]

Costa Rican coach Jorge Luis Pinto added, "We're hurt but we're happy. When we came here [to Brazil] many people didn't believe in us, but during this World Cup we've done many beautiful things. Even though we have to leave the tournament, we haven't been beaten, even by the superpowers we came up against. . . . I thought we matched the Dutch and, although we can improve on certain things, we're making great progress. We've shown that we can organize ourselves, that we have good tactics and we can play football. We have left a positive and dignified impression of Costa Rican football. I am proud of the players and so is the country."[44]

## SEMIFINALS

The semifinals opened on July 8 with the much-anticipated Brazil–Germany match at Mineiro Stadium in Belo Horizonte. The Brazilians, without the injured Neymar and captain Thiago Silva through suspension, were a step away from the final. In Brazil's path stood a German team seemingly ready to take on any opponent. By the time the evening was through, Brazil had suffered its worst defeat ever at a World Cup and the most lopsided outcome ever in the semifinals. Germany's 7–1 demolition of the hosts put it through to the final and was the reward for years of hard work. For Brazil, it signaled the end of an era.

After just 11 minutes, an unmarked Müller scored from Toni Kroos's outswinging corner. The goal was enough to unhinge the backline. With the Brazilian defense in shambles, Germany scored again 12 minutes later with Miroslav Klose. The goal, his 16th at a World Cup, made Klose the tournament's all-time leading scorer, surpassing Ronaldo. Two more goals by Kroos—in the 24th and 26th minutes—and another from Sami Khedira in the 29th put the Germans ahead 5–0 at halftime. The game was over after just a half. "We took our chances well and they strained under the pressure caused by conceding," said Loew.[45]

Germany added three more goals in the second half, with Schürrle in the 69th and 79th minutes, before Oscar pulled one back for Brazil for the 7–1 final. "After losing the semifinal to Italy in 2006, we know how Brazil, the players, Scolari, and the fans feel, so we have to be modest and humble and take the next step. The emotions are great. We won, we've made it to the final. We coped with the passion of the Brazilians and we knew that if we played to our capabilities we thought we would win—but we couldn't have expected this result," said Loew.[46]

As for Brazil, the outcome was a shock—something Scolari took full responsibility for in the post-game news conference. "It's the worst moment of my soccer career and the worst day of my soccer life. But life goes on. Who is responsible for this result? I am! It's me. The blame for this catastrophic result can be shared between us all, but the person who decided the lineup, the tactics, was me. It was my choice. We tried to do what we could, we did our best, but we came up against a great German team. We couldn't react to going behind. We got disorganized and panicked after the first goal and then it all went wrong for us. Not

*Germany's rout of the host nation in the semifinals left Brazilian fans in a state of shock (Credit: FIFA).*

even the Germans can tell you how this happened, but it's because of their skills and you have to respect that. We have to learn to deal with it. My message for the Brazilian people is this: Please excuse us for this performance," he said.[47]

The other semifinal, played the following day in São Paulo between Argentina and the Netherlands, was the complete opposite of the Germany–Brazil match. Instead of a goal deluge, fans got a drought. Few chances on either side were the highlight of a game that was both tense and, at times, drab. The game ended 0–0 after regulation, and overtime was needed. Argentina had the clearest chance to score in the 115th minute when a long ball was lobbed into the path of substitute Rodrigo Palacio, but his header was too weak and Cillessen produced the easy save. The game went to penalties, where Argentina goalkeeper Sergio Romero proved decisive. His saves put Argentina on top, 4–2, in the shootout, catapulting them to the World Cup final for the first time in 24 years. His saves on Ron Vlaar's spot-kick before making a stunning save on Sneijder's kick proved decisive. Van Gaal could not muster up any magic this time around. They had been able to stop Messi, but could do little offensively to win the game. Afterward, Romero admitted that winning via a shootout had been more the product of luck than skill. "You can dive and not make it, like their goalkeeper did. I had confidence, and thank God things turned out well," he said.[48]

The final was set: Germany versus Argentina in a rematch of the 1990 final. On that occasion, West Germany had won. Now, Germany was seeking a fourth World Cup, its first as a unified nation. As for Argentina, this was Messi's big chance to come out of Maradona's shadow and lead his country to a world title. With Brazilians rooting for Germany (and against their biggest South American rivals), it looked as if the Europeans would have the edge in terms of fans. Nonetheless, Argentines continued to flood into Rio de Janeiro, despite not having tickets to the game. No matter. These fans were there to drink and dance. They wanted to soak up the enthusiasm of the World Cup and cheer on their team in the streets and in front of the large screens set up on Copacabana Beach.

Indeed, Brazilian authorities estimated that there were some 100,000 Argentina fans, many with no place to stay and opting to sleep in their cars parked along the picturesque Avenida Atlântica. In the days leading up to the final, Argentine fans gathered in large groups along Rio's streets, taunting locals with a song featuring several incendiary lyrics that had become famous during the tournament:

*Brasil, decime qué se siente tener en casa a tu papá.*
*Te juro que aunque pasen los años, nunca nos vamos a olvidar,*
*Que el Diego te gambeteó, que Cani te vacunó, que estás llorando desde*
*Italia hasta hoy,*
*A Messi lo vas a ver, la Copa nos va a traer, Maradona es más grande*
*que Pelé.*

That translates to:

*Brazil, tell me how it feels, to have your daddy in your house,*
*We'll never forget how Diego dribbled past you,*
*How Cani [Claudio Caniggia] killed you off in Italy,*
*We're going to see Messi, he's going to bring us the Cup, Maradona is*
*much better than Pele.*

Argentine fans gleefully sang on July 12 when the Netherlands added insult to Brazil's injury, taking the third-place game with a 3–0 victory against Brazil in Brasilia. The crowd showered jeers on the Brazilian players as the Dutch made it look easy. Scolari was fired within days, replaced by Dunga, the same man who had been fired after the 2010 World Cup failure. Brazil may have needed to look to the future, but it was hoping that someone from its past would help them rebuild. The World Cup's motto may have been "All in one rhythm," but the reality was that Brazil had been wildly out of sync.

## THE FINAL

With Brazil's failure one of the biggest story lines to come out of the tournament, Germany and Argentina met on July 13 at the Maracanã before 74,738 fans. The teams seemed energized from the start, with both looking to score early. The naturally frenetic start even brought with it a goal by Higuain in the 30th minute off a Lavezzi cross, but he was deemed offside by Italian referee Nicola Rizzoli. Messi looked to be a factor, but the Germans did a great job containing him. On the other side of the field, Argentina defender Javier Mascherano was doing his part to stop Müller and his teammates. The biggest moment of the first half, however, was when Germany's Christoph Kramer suffered a blow to the head after just 16 minutes. Despite the renewed focus on concussions, Kramer, visibly dazed, received medical treatment and was allowed to re-enter the match. It wasn't until the 31st minute that Loew replaced Kramer with Schürrle. The fact that Rizzoli did nothing to ensure Kramer's safety will forever be a blemish on a game that was both well played and properly officiated. In the first half of stoppage time, Germany came close when Benedikt Höwedes's header smashed the post.

With the sun setting over Rio, the second half brought with it more saves from Neuer and Romero and little from Messi and Müller. The crowd grew weary. Extra time seemed like a real possibility, and a feeling of urgency overcame both teams. The Germans dominated possession, with Ozil and Kroos linking up well in an attempt to create a scoring chance. Not to be outdone, Messi tried to score, but his attempt in the 75th minute went wide. Kroos responded with a long-range shot of his own in the 82nd minute, but that kick was also off target. With two minutes left to play, Loew made a change that would affect the outcome of the match. Out came Klose, and in his place entered striker Mario Götze.

*The legendary Maracanã Stadium in Rio de Janeiro hosted the 2014 World Cup final between Germany and Argentina (Credit: FIFA/Getty Images).*

The game ended scoreless. The final would once again go to overtime. The teams appeared relatively equal in the extra session. However, the second period of overtime was where Germany would get the victory. As the Argentines grew more frustrated, the game became increasingly tense. Bastian Schweinsteiger, the midfield workhorse who had fought for nearly every ball, took a beating from the Argentines and had to receive medical treatment for an open cut to his face. The Germans continued to maintain possession and scored in the 113th minute. The goal came together well and was executed beautifully. Götze did a fabulous job of controlling a pass from Schürrle, before controlling it with his chest and slotting a one-time shot past Romero. "I just took the shot and didn't know what was happening," Götze recalled.[49]

The goal unleashed joy from German and Brazilian supporters and tears from the many Argentines inside the stadium. "We always knew that we would need 14 players during this match and everyone in top shape, and all the players had to be ready. It was good that we had played who could come on and make an impact, and [Mario] Götze is a miracle boy, a boy wonder. I always knew he could decide the match," said Loew.[50]

With two minutes left in overtime, a Messi free kick, one last attempt by Argentina to draw level, sailed high over the crossbar. Messi was in shock, a feeling that would turn to sadness when Rizzoli blew the whistle to signal the end of the game. Germany had won a fourth World Cup title to become the first European nation to win the tournament in South America. Messi was awarded the Golden Ball as tournament MVP, little consolation as the German players celebrated on the field. "In general terms, I am very proud of my boys. They played an extraordinary World Cup. It was very exciting to see them play, and it's clear they gave everything for the Argentinean jersey. They can look themselves in the mirror and know they gave everything," said Sabella.[51]

As for the Germans, they had rebuilt their program in the mid-1990s, focusing on youth development and building the Bundesliga into one of Europe's finest domestic leagues. Once again, the Germans were the best in the world. "We started this project ten years ago and what has happened today is the result of many years' work, starting with Jurgen Klinsmann. We've made constant progress, we believed in the project, we worked a lot, and, if any group deserves it, it's this team. We've always played good soccer and I believe that over this tournament, over seven matches, we showed the best performances of any of the teams here in Brazil. The boys have also developed a team spirit which is unbelievable. They have fantastic technical capacity, and they also have the willpower that's necessary to do what is necessary," said Loew.[52]

Götze had become the unlikely hero of a World Cup that had been full of surprises. Over the course of five weeks, the tournament had featured entertaining games and thrilling goals. Despite pre-tournament fears, Brazil had avoided any major embarrassments (except for its national team's shocking collapse). In the end, Brazil 2014 would go down as one of the greatest World Cups in history.


## NOTES

1. *Marca*, "Scolari Makes a Dig at the Spanish National Side" (English edition), February 19, 2014, http://www.marca.com/2014/02/19/en/football/national_teams/1392806347.html.
2. News conference, May 24, 2014.
3. News conference, December 6, 2013.
4. Conference call, December 6, 2013.
5. News conference, June 16, 2014.

6. News conference, June 9, 2014.
7. News conference, June 12, 2014.
8. News conference, June 17, 2014.
9. News conference, June 23, 2014.
10. News conference, June 23, 2014.
11. News conference, June 13, 2014.
12. News conference, June 18, 2014.
13. News conference, June 24, 2014.
14. News conference, June 20, 2014.
15. News conference, June 20, 2014.
16. News conference, June 25, 2014.
17. News conference, June 21, 2014.
18. News conference, June 25, 2014.
19. News conference, June 16, 2014.
20. News conference, June 16, 2014.
21. News conference, June 23, 2014.
22. News conference, June 23, 2014.
23. News conference, June 23, 2014.
24. News conference, June 23, 2014.
25. News conference, June 26, 2014.
26. News conference, June 26, 2014.
27. News conference, June 26, 2014.
28. News conference, June 28, 2014.
29. News conference, June 28, 2014.
30. News conference, June 29, 2014.
31. News conference, June 29, 2014.
32. News conference, June 29, 2014.
33. News conference, July 1, 2014.
34. News conference, July 1, 2014.
35. News conference, July 1, 2014.
36. News conference, July 1, 2014.
37. News conference, July 4, 2014.
38. News conference, July 4, 2014.
39. News conference, July 4, 2014.
40. News conference, July 4, 2014.
41. News conference, July 5, 2014.
42. News conference, July 5, 2014.
43. News conference, July 5, 2014.
44. News conference, July 5, 2014.
45. News conference, July 8, 2014.
46. News conference, July 8, 2014.

47. News conference, July 8, 2014.
48. News conference, July 9, 2014.
49. News conference, July 13, 2014.
50. News conference, July 13, 2014.
51. News conference, July 13, 2014.
52. News conference, July 13, 2014.

# 11

# UNITED FRANCE

The 2018 World Cup was hosted by Russia, the first time in the tournament's long history that games would be played in an Eastern European country that also stretched across Asia. Costing an estimated $14 billion, the Russians effectively used the tournament as a propaganda tool to showcase the greatness of President Vladimir Putin and the country's rise in the post–Cold War era. More noteworthy, however, would be the quality of the soccer on display that summer.

The four years following the 2014 World Cup in Brazil had been wrought with a corruption scandal that brought down FIFA's leadership, including President Sepp Blatter, which put a spotlight on the backroom dealing that routinely took place in Zurich among nations seeking to host the World Cup, and on the role of television and marketing executives. On the eve of the World Cup in Russia, it was announced that the joint bid by the United States, Canada, and Mexico to host the 2026 World Cup was successful, beating out Morocco in a vote by all FIFA members. The choice appeared to remedy a wrong that had taken place eight years earlier when Russia and Qatar were surprisingly awarded the right to host the 2018 and 2022 tournaments, respectively.

The process of having the entire FIFA membership vote was a contrast to previous selections, when only twenty-four members cast ballots in secret. After six officials either pleaded guilty or were convicted on corruption charges by U.S. authorities, the fallout included the election of a new president, Gianni Infantino, and a series of reforms aimed at making FIFA more transparent. Whether soccer's governing body actually became less corrupt remains a matter of debate. The fallout, however, included Blatter's six-year ban from the sport. After failing to attract new sponsors as a result of the corruption allegations, FIFA decided to expand the World Cup to forty-eight teams from thirty-two in time for the 2026 tournament. It was yet another controversial decision. Some said it would water down the tournament, while others agreed that it would provide smaller countries the chance to participate in and grow the game.

In 2015 dozens of executives were arrested in Switzerland after police raided the Zurich hotel where they had been staying. The arrests were triggered by the U.S. Justice Department after uncovering bribery allegations totaling hundreds of millions of dollars. The authorities were able to make the arrests after Chuck Blazer, a former FIFA executive committee member who had been instrumental in awarding Russia the 2018 World Cup, revealed there had been wrongdoing surrounding the 2010 World Cup hosted by South Africa. Blazer, who died in July 2017 following a bout with cancer, admitted to authorities that he had abused his position to fund a lavish lifestyle that included two apartments in New York's Trump Tower—one of them for his cats. Nicknamed "Mr. Ten Percent" due to the commission he demanded as CONCACAF general secretary each time a television deal was signed, Blazer hid much of his wealth in offshore accounts. It was only after the Federal Bureau of Investigation and the Internal Revenue Service began to look into Blazer's activities on American soil—he had not filed any tax returns between 2005 and 2010—that the larger web of FIFA corruption came into focus.

Blazer had documented his travels on a personal blog, which included photos of him on a private jet with Nelson Mandela and Vladimir Putin. He was eventually charged with tax evasion, money laundering, and other charges, and given a lifetime ban from FIFA. The crooked sports-executive-turned-whistleblower had shaken the foundation of soccer's governing body to the core. As for the 2018 World Cup in Russia, FIFA found in June 2017 that the country's organizing team had done nothing corrupt—although a cloud of suspicion still hovered over the event. In a 430-page report, FIFA said Russia had done nothing illegal in obtaining the rights to host the 2018 World Cup. Nonetheless, the report did point out that the bid committee "made only a limited . . . documents available for review, which was explained by the fact that the computers used at the time by the Russia Bid Committee had been leased and then returned to their owner after the bidding process. The owner has confirmed that the computers were destroyed."[1] Those suspicious activities only cast more doubt on the process.

Making matters worse, allegations that state-sponsored doping of Russian athletes had occurred during the Winter Olympics in Sochi were later proven to be true. In December 2017, following a seventeen-month investigation, the International Olympic Committee banned Russian athletes from competing at the 2018 Olympics in PyeongChang, South Korea. Despite repeated denials from Russian officials, a report found evidence of "the systemic manipulation of the anti-doping rules and system," backing up previous allegations of government involvement in cheating in the run-up to and during the Olympics.[2] As for Russia's soccer team, they too had been accused of doping. A FIFA investigation of Russia's twenty-eight-player preliminary World Cup roster, however, cited insufficient evidence to sustain those accusations.[3]

In addition, Russian soccer had been plagued by fan violence and various racist and anti-gay incidents on the field and in the stands. Russian officials tried to downplay those concerns, saying every security measure was being undertaken—including increased use of surveillance cameras and extra police and military manpower—to ensure that fans were safe during the competition. In the end, none of those fears came to fruition. Instead, the tournament would go on to be considered one of the most successful—both on and off the field—of the modern era.

The centerpiece for the tournament was Moscow's Luzhniki Stadium. A football temple that has become as popular as the ornate Saint Basil's Cathedral in Red Square, the venue would host some of the World Cup's most memorable matches, including the July 15 final. Built in the Stalinist Empire style, the Luzhniki was completed in 1956 at the height of the Cold War. Vestiges of that era are still alive near the grounds. The façade has been restored, despite all the modern amenities located inside, and a 25-foot-high statue of Vladimir Lenin still dominates the main entrance. The venue has its roots not in soccer, but athletics. The decision by the Soviet government to construct such a stadium was in response to a brewing international phenomenon—the ability of Soviet athletes to dominate at the Summer Olympic Games. The 1952 Helsinki Games saw the Soviets capture seventy-one medals, twenty-two of them gold, for second place in the overall standings.

Those Olympics were a big success, which helped to fuel the need for the Communist regime to develop future Olympians. The move was part of larger state policy—something other Communist governments across Eastern Europe would emulate—for much of the ensuing three decades. As part of its propaganda machine, the Soviet Union embarked on the construction of a sports complex. The venue, part of a larger sports park, was to meet all modern international standards while also serving as a training base for the country's Olympic teams as well as for large domestic events.

Located in Moscow's Khamovniki District, an area known for its expensive housing, the Luzhniki is Russia's sporting jewel, despite the construction of Fisht Stadium in Sochi, which successfully hosted the 2014 Winter Olympics. The stadium was originally named the Grand Arena of the Central Lenin Stadium, a homage to the Russian revolutionary. Its current name, Luzhniki (meaning "the Meadows"), was bestowed in 1992 following the collapse of communism—inspired by the green areas near the stadium along the bend of the Moskva River.

With Central Lenin Stadium at the center of training, the country would go on to dominate at the Olympics, in an array of fields, for decades. The venue's ultimate coronation was the 1980 Summer Olympics. With an expanded capacity of 103,000 that summer, the stadium hosted both the opening and closing ceremonies. It also hosted an array of events, including track and field and football matches. The 1980 Games made history as the first time the Olympics were held in Eastern Europe. The only blemish was the boycott that enveloped the Olympics after sixty-six nations—spearheaded by the United States—opted not to participate following the Soviet invasion of Afghanistan. As a result, the Soviet Union, with no competition from American athletes, captured forty-one medals in athletics—including fifteen gold—to become the winningest country that summer. In soccer, the Soviet Union came into the 1980 Olympics among the favorites. While the sixteen-team tournament was hampered by the boycott, it did feature a few countries with rich footballing traditions, including powerhouse Czechoslovakia, winner of the 1976 European Championship, and Yugoslavia. The Soviets went on an impressive run that included a 4–0 win against Venezuela and a 3–1 victory over Zambia, with both games played before 80,000 fans at the Central Lenin Stadium. The team was managed by Konstantin Beskov, who had also coached the Soviet Union at the 1964 European Championship and would go on to guide them at the 1982 World Cup in Spain.

Although the stadium has become known for its role in Russia's sporting greatness, it is not without tragedy. On October 20, 1982, sixty-six people were killed in a stampede during a UEFA Cup second-round match featuring Spartak Moscow and Dutch HFC Haarlem. Spartak had famously defeated Arsenal 8–4 on aggregate in the first round, including a 5–2 win in the second leg at Highbury. Unusually cold and snowy conditions for October had forced stadium officials to close two of the venue's four exits. That was followed by the decision to cram all the spectators into a single section, something that would prove fatal in the end. When the 17,000 fans, including a few hundred from Holland, stormed the exit closest to the train station to beat the rush near the end of the game, the situation grew dire. What exactly caused the deaths remains a mystery. Some witnesses told investigators that a woman fell on an icy step at the bottom of a staircase after losing her shoe. Unbeknownst to the fans further back, a chain reaction of bodies pushing up against one another led to the fatal pileup. Other accounts, however, tell a different tale. Some told investigators that fans started to leave with a few minutes left in the match. The home side was ahead 1–0 following a goal from Edgar Gess after just sixteen minutes. With large numbers of fans departing, a second goal in the 89th minute by Sergei Shvetsov forced many to turn back after they had heard the roar of the crowd. It was when these two opposing groups ran into each other that tragedy ensued. The calamity remains Russia's worst sporting disaster. Although sixty-six fans—many of them children and teenagers—were officially reported killed, several subsequent investigations and eyewitness accounts put the death toll closer to 350, something that would make it the worst disaster in the history of football. The day after the game, Russian newspapers failed to mention that anyone had died or been injured at the game. President Leonid Brezhnev, who died twenty-one days later, and the Communist regime did everything in their power to suppress news and details from being made public. Four stadium officials were eventually charged and convicted for their part in the disaster. In 1992, on the tenth anniversary of the tragedy and after communism had finally collapsed, a memorial was erected near the site. On the 25th anniversary in 2007, a special match was organized at the stadium—thanks in large part to the work of former Russia manager, Guus Hiddink—between the former Spartak Moscow and Haarlem players.

In 1996, an extensive renovation project saw the construction of a roof over the stands. The venue hosted the UEFA Cup final in 1999, won by Parma 3–1 against Marseille. Parma featured a star-studded lineup that would go on to have success for Italy's national team, including goalkeeper Gianluigi Buffon and defender Fabio Cannavaro. In 2008, the Luzhniki was chosen by UEFA to host the 2008 Champions League final, won by Manchester United on penalties against Chelsea in the first all-English final. The game was incident free, much like the World Cup in the summer of 2018.

On the eve of the FIFA tournament, Alexei Sorokin, head of the 2018 World Cup Local Organizing Committee, said the Luzhniki was the perfect place to host games of such magnitude. "This is an excellent, modern stadium that has been recently revamped, fully rebuilt, preserving elements of its former looks with overhauled technologies," Sorokin told the Russian news agency, TASS. "Of course, it is unique in many respects—this is an excellent blend of memory, history and modern technologies. It is convenient and comfortable for watching football matches."[4]

## WORLD CUP QUALIFICATION

Reaching the World Cup finals proved difficult for several nations with a pedigree of winning and regularly qualifying for the finals. All 210 FIFA members were allowed to take part, with Bhutan, South Sudan, Gibraltar, and Kosovo making their World Cup qualification debuts. Myanmar—after having successfully appealed against a ban following crowd trouble during a 2014 World Cup qualifying match against Oman—was forced to play all home games outside the country. The fight for thirty-one places (after Russia automatically qualified as hosts) featured several highlights. Among these was Brazil being the first nation to qualify following a 3–0 victory against Paraguay. Peru, meanwhile, became the last team to reach the finals after defeating New Zealand 2–0 on aggregate following the playoff between South America and Oceania. Argentina, who struggled throughout qualification, needed a victory on the final day and got one thanks to a 3–1 victory against Ecuador coming via a Lionel Messi hat trick. Messi once again proved to be the deciding factor for Argentina, and the team was lucky to have had him. After losing the Copa America Centenario final

at MetLife Stadium just outside New York City, Messi had abruptly announced his retirement from the national team. It had been the ump-
teenth disaster for Argentina, and for Messi, who had achieved so much
at the club level with Barcelona, it was another example of his failure
for the national team. Argentina's football association, an organization
rife with allegations of corruption, had mishandled the national team
in recent years, and Messi's refusal to play for his country put those
problems into greater focus. Messi was eventually coaxed back to the
team as qualification heated up. Nevertheless, problems persisted, and
would come into full view at the World Cup.

Qualification, however, was more noteworthy this time around for
the teams who failed to make the finals. In South America, Chile, winners of the 2015 Copa America and 2016 Copa America Centenario, finished sixth and out of the running for the playoffs. In Africa, defending
continental champions Cameroon, along with Ivory Coast and Ghana,
also failed to qualify. In Europe, two noteworthy nations—Italy and
the Netherlands—were on the outside looking in. For Italy, the failure
to qualify marked the first time since 1958 that the Italians would not
be participating in the World Cup finals. For the Dutch, the outcome
also highlighted the decline of a program that had been competitive

*After proving to be a rising soccer power at the 2016 European Championship, Ice-
land qualified for the World Cup for the first time two years later (Credit: FIFA).*

just a few years earlier. The team had lost the 2010 World Cup final to Spain, and finished third just four years later. While those European heavyweights failed to qualify, Iceland, a nation of just 334,000 people, did. The team had reached the quarterfinals two years earlier at the 2016 European Championship after eliminating England. It would be Iceland's first trip to the World Cup finals.

In CONCACAF the United States, which had qualified for every World Cup since 1990, failed to qualify. Needing a draw in its last match against Trinidad and Tobago on October 11, 2017, the Americans still had a very good chance of advancing. After losing 2–1, a doomsday combination of a Honduras victory over Mexico and Panama's defeat versus Costa Rica dropped the U.S. team from third place to fifth in the Hexagonal. Panama qualified for the first time in history, while Honduras faced off against Australia in the intercontinental playoff (which was later won by the Aussies).

The United States had given up too many points along the way after a poor start under coach Jürgen Klinsmann. The appointment of Bruce Arena, a familiar face aimed at bringing stability to the team, proved ineffectual in the end. Despite the addition of several new players,

*Players take selfies to commemorate Panama qualifying for its first World Cup finals ever (Credit: FIFA).*

like Christian Pulisic, and a mix of veterans, such as Tim Howard and Michael Bradley, the Americans could only put together a listless first half against an opponent that had nothing but pride to play for. Down 2–0, Pulisic had pulled the score to within one in the second half, while Clint Dempsey's attempt for a draw hit the post. "We didn't qualify for the World Cup," Arena told reporters after the loss. "That was my job."[5]

The stunning defeat led to all kinds of self-questioning regarding how American players are developed and scouted. The success of the past three decades was put into doubt. As a result, U.S. Soccer president Sunil Gulati, who was up for re-election later in the year, decided not to run for the job in the end. Both he and Arena—responsible for helping build the sport in this country—had their legacies tarnished after such a poor showing.

The World Cup draw took place on December 1, 2017, in Moscow. Legends, including Pelé and Diego Maradona, were in attendance during the two-hour draw, which was hosted by former England striker Gary Lineker and Russian sports journalist Maria Komandnaya at the grandiose State Kremlin Palace. Russia headed into the draw as the lowest ranked of the thirty-two teams and having failed to advance past the group stage of any tournament since 2008. Attempting to do so at the World Cup, even with the advantages of playing on home soil, would be a difficult task. Defending champion Germany, meanwhile, would open its group on June 17 against Mexico. The Germans had already collected a trophy in Russia, winning the Confederations Cup in July 2017 and using the tournament primarily to test new players.

With President Putin looking on, Russia was placed in Group A, which would go on to be an easy group. Listed 65th by FIFA, Russia was the lowest ranked team in the entire field, and its group included the second-lowest ranked team (Saudi Arabia at 63rd) as well as Egypt, playing in its first World Cup since 1990. Unlike previous editions, all four pots were determined by each national team's October 2017 FIFA World Ranking. Pot 1 contained the highest-ranked teams, Pot 2 the next highest-ranked teams, and so on. The draw resulted in the following groups:

Group A: Russia, Saudi Arabia, Egypt, and Uruguay
Group B: Portugal, Spain, Morocco, and Iran
Group C: France, Australia, Peru, and Denmark

Group D: Argentina, Nigeria, Croatia, and Iceland
Group E: Brazil, Switzerland, Costa Rica, and Serbia
Group F: Germany, Mexico, Sweden, and South Korea
Group G: Belgium, Panama, Tunisia, and England
Group H: Poland, Senegal, Colombia, and Japan

In one of the ceremony's lightest moments, Lineker joked as Maradona pulled out his draw, saying: "He was always good with his hands"—a reference to his infamous "Hand of God" goal.[6] The draw also produced several competitive groups, spreading the teams out evenly and avoiding the creation of a dreaded "Group of Death." The toughest group, however, was Group F, with Germany, Mexico, South Korea, and Sweden, which edged the Netherlands in qualifying and knocked out Italy from the field.

## USE OF VIDEO TECHNOLOGY

As in previous editions of the World Cup, FIFA introduced some rule changes with the aim of improving the game. At the Confederations Cup in 2017, FIFA tested the Video Assistant Referee (VAR) to try to cut down on errors that could impact the outcome of matches. The use of VAR at a major tournament, which had been tested with mixed results in Serie A, Bundesliga, and in England's FA Cup, didn't go exactly as planned. In the end, the technology proved what we already knew: the video may be accurate, but humans still make mistakes. Goal Line Technology (GLT), used for the first time at the 2014 World Cup, was infallible because it was solely based on computers. GLT software would let a referee know, with the help of a microchip, whether the ball had crossed the goal line. VAR, on the other hand, needed a group of referees—the same humans who made blunders in the past by blowing calls—to review goals and determine offside using instant replay.

VAR has divided the soccer community as its inclusion in some leagues and tournaments grows. The system has been a growing source of concern after goals had been celebrated and counted, then taken away just minutes later. Offside calls, one of the most controversial decisions in the sport, have proven subjective, even with the ability to stop and slow time on the screen to get these right. Purists argue that the delay in using video review can take minutes, stalling the game and ruining some of the emotion that is part of huge moments.

There were many cases at the Confederations Cup where calls were made, with VAR help, that were either wrong or open to interpretation. As columnist Paul Gardner noted in *Soccer America*:

> To wit: in deciding whether fouls are committed, or goals are scored, soccer already operates using a skewed system. It cannot be doubted that the sport, through its rules and its referee interpretations, makes it as difficult as possible to score goals. Nor can there be any doubt that referees persistently under-call rough play—fouls are not called, penalty kicks are not given, yellow cards are issued instead of reds . . . there are three referees sitting in the VAR booth, making decisions based on video evidence, including, of course, replays. But those referees will all, to a greater or lesser extent, share the failings listed above (and I do consider them serious failings).[7]

A year later, at the World Cup, VAR would end up being successful and lauded by most as an effective tool to help referees make decisions.

*The use of VAR, featuring match officials based in Moscow, to review plays with help from the referee on the field was used at the World Cup for the first time in an effort to cut down on mistakes (Credit: FIFA).*

## OPENING ROUND

Russia opened the tournament on June 14 against Saudi Arabia at Luzhniki Stadium, before 78,011 fans. The hosts recorded the biggest opening-game win since Italy defeated the United States 7–1 in 1934, romping to a 5–0 victory with President Putin in the crowd. Going into the World Cup, the Russian prospects appeared dim. The team failed to win a game out of seven leading up to the tournament. Any fears the Russians would be humiliated were cast aside as Yury Gazinsky scored after just twelve minutes on an Aleksandr Golovin cross. Putin and Infantino smiled after the goal and shrugged as they sat with Saudi Crown Prince Mohammed bin Salman. Putin reached over to shake the prince's hand.

Ahead 2–0 at the half, the Russians scored again in the 71st minute when Artem Dzyuba, who had come into the game just 89 seconds earlier, headed the ball in off a Golovin pass. Golovin, who had two assists, tallied a goal of his own in the fourth minute of stoppage time with a superb free kick over a wall of Saudi players to make it five on the day. The win ended a sixteen-year World Cup drought for the Russians. The Saudis would end the match without a shot on target. In addition, VAR was available for the first time at a World Cup, although it wasn't used for an official review. Russia coach Stanislav Cherchesov said after the game that he was "relaxed today because I know my players. It is a pleasure to work with them. Every coach depends on the players, this is why I am relaxed. Why do I have to be stressed? I would like to underscore that we are grateful to our squad with how they fulfilled our goals, how they played in a relaxed game under the pressure stemming from this being an opening match."[8]

In the group's other game, played the following day at Ekaterinburg Arena in Yekaterinburg, Uruguay defeated Egypt 1–0. For the South Americans, the victory was the first in their opening game for the first time since 1970. While Luis Suarez looked abysmal and Edinson Cavani a lot livelier—he twice came close to scoring—Uruguay would get its goal in the 89th minute. Without Mohammed Salah after he was injured in the Champions League final won by Real Madrid against Liverpool, Egypt featured a lackluster offense. Nonetheless, it would take a Carlos Sanchez free kick, and defender Jose Gimenez rising above two defenders to head in the last-gasp winning goal. It would be the first in a long string of goals to come near the end of a match or in injury time. After the match, Uruguay coach Oscar Washington Tabarez defended Suarez, saying "I will not speculate. I've seen Messi, Pele, Maradona not having a good day, not playing to potential in matches. This is not a sin."[9]

Group A's second match day on June 19 saw Russia all but clinch a spot in the knockout round—a goal that appeared unattainable on the eve of the tournament following another resounding victory. With Salah back in the lineup for Egypt, the Africans were expecting a better performance at Saint Petersburg Stadium in Saint Petersburg. Instead, it was the upstart Russians who dominated with a 3–1 win. Up 1–0 thanks to a Ahmed Fathy own goal, the Russians put the game away in the second half by netting twice in a span of three minutes via Denis Cheryshev and Dzyuba. All Salah could do was score on a penalty kick late in the game, with his side already down by three goals. The Russians had confoundingly grim pre-tournament predictions—something not lost on the players or the coaching staff. "It's a group of solidarity and cohesion," said manager Stanislav Cherchesov, who reveled in the win by waving his arms in celebration following the final whistle. "You mention difficulties, problems. We don't like these words. We don't have this in our vocabulary. We had some issues and we dealt with it."[10]

The following day, Uruguay's 1–0 victory against Saudi Arabia—on a goal from Suarez—at Rostov Arena in the city of Rostov-on-Don officially put the South Americans through to the second round, along with the Russians. The June 25 matchup against Russia and Uruguay at Samara Arena in Samara would determine who would win the group. The Russians had momentum on their side, and home support that had reached a frenzied pitch in the days leading up to the game. The 41,970 fans in attendance made their voices heard, but it wasn't enough as Uruguay earned an easy 3–0 win against a ten-man Russian side following Igor Smolnikov's red card in the 36th minute. The attacking duo of Cavani and Suarez was paying dividends for Uruguay's veteran manager Tabarez. The two-time World Cup winners looked strong. The Russians, while failing after facing their toughest test at this tournament, remained optimistic heading into the knockout phase. "I like how my team played after we lost one player," Cherchesov told reporters. "We were rather aggressive."[11]

In Group B, the highly anticipated June 15 Iberian derby between European champion Portugal and Spain did not disappoint. Spain had come into the tournament as one of the favorites to win the title, but that confidence was shaken after Julen Lopetegui was sacked as coach on June 13, just a day after he had agreed to take over at Real Madrid after the World Cup. In a news conference at the team's training base in Krasnodar, Luis Rubiales, president of the Spanish federation, said Lopetegui's fate was sealed just two days ahead of the team's World Cup opener. In his place, the federation named the team's sporting director and former national team star Fernando Hierro as head coach. "We have been obliged to fire the national coach," Rubiales told reporters. "We wish him the best. He has done an excellent job in getting us to the tournament, but the federation cannot be left outside the negotiation of one of its employees and find out just five minutes before a public announcement."[12]

Following Iran's 1–0 win against Morocco earlier in the day to get things started in the group on June 15, Portugal and Spain played to a riveting 3–3 draw at Fisht Stadium in Sochi that evening. The match truly was one of the most exhilarating first-round matchups at a World Cup, as Spain twice recovered to cancel out Cristiano Ronaldo's goals. Spain was ahead 3–2, but a Ronaldo free kick 20 yards out, following a foul by Gerard Pique, made things even again with two minutes left in the game. "When you play against a player like Ronaldo, these things can happen," Hierro said after the match. "It's very fortunate for whatever team has Cristiano Ronaldo."[13]

On June 20, Portugal grabbed its first win of the tournament, defeating Morocco 1–0 at Luzhniki Stadium on a goal by Ronaldo after just four minutes. Ronaldo's goal marked his 85th for his country, eclipsing the total of Ferenc Puskas of Hungary to become Europe's all-time leading scorer at the senior international level. Spain also won for the first time in Russia, defeating Iran 1–0 the same day at Kazan Stadium in Kazan. A fortuitous goal from Diego Costa, after veteran Andres Iniesta was able to play the ball to him from midfield, proved to be the game winner in what had been a back-and-forth affair. A dogged effort by Iran to try and find a draw in the game's dying minutes—and with five minutes of stoppage time—and a goal ruled offside by the referee after the use of VAR brought an end to the match. "If you think of it like tennis, we had one match point today and we will have another against Portugal," said Iran's coach, Carlos Queiroz. "Everything is still open. We are still alive and still dreaming."[14]

With the group wide open going into the final match day on June 25, the inconceivable happened after Iran–Portugal and Spain–Morocco both finished in draws. Portugal's 1–0 lead couldn't hold up at Mor-

*Cristiano Ronaldo (left, with U.S. striker Carli Lloyd) helped Portugal win the 2016 European Championship, but would fall short at the World Cup after a strong opening round (Credit: Getty Images/FIFA.com).*

dovia Arena in Saransk. Despite conceding the equalizer in the third minute of stoppage time via a questionable penalty kick from Karim Ansarifard, Portugal progressed to the knockout round. Indeed, the refereeing from Enrique Caceres of Paraguay was dubious throughout the entire match. While Ronaldo's penalty kick was saved in the second half (costing the team a chance at winning the group), it was what the Portuguese star did with his elbow that infuriated Iran's bench. Queiroz said Caceres's decision to give Ronaldo a yellow card after his elbow struck Iran defender Morteza Pouraliganji in the face in the second half should have meant an automatic ejection. "Elbow is a red card in the rules," Queiroz said. "The decisions must be clear for everybody."[15]

Meanwhile at Kaliningrad Stadium in Kaliningrad, Spain won the group on goal differential after a 2–2 draw against Spain. It was a dramatic equalizer in the first minute of stoppage time by substitute Iago Aspas's back-heel off a corner kick, giving Spain the draw in what turned out to be a lively match. With Hierro doing some scoreboard watching in the second half, Spain remained unbeaten in twenty-three straight games. Nonetheless, the Spanish appeared vulnerable to defensive lapses. Despite possessing the ball for long stretches and controlling play, goals had been difficult to come by. "Until the last minute, we weren't sure who was going to finish first and second," Hierro said. "I have to say we were lucky to finish first."[16]

In Group C, France, another pre-tournament favorite, defeated Australia 2–1 on June 16 in Kazan. After a scoreless first half, a struggling France broke the deadlock thanks to a decision by referee Andres Cunha of Uruguay after he overturned his own decision and awarded a penalty. The decision came after defender Josh Risdon of Australia tackled Antoine Griezmann in the box. Cunha did not originally whistle a penalty kick. After French players complained, Cunha went to consult the video replay. It was the first time VAR was used in a World Cup game. After several tense moments, Cunha overturned his decision and whistled for a penalty kick to be taken. Griezmann converted from the spot to give France a 1–0 lead in the 58th minute. Replays showed that Risdon had made light contact with the *Les Bleus* striker.

The lead was short-lived. Four minutes later, Australia tied the score after Cunha whistled a penalty for the Socceroos following a handball in the box. The infraction was obvious and no VAR was needed. Mile Jedinak scored from the spot to level the score. The use of technology didn't end there. France took the lead nine minutes from the end when Paul Pogba saw his shot hit the crossbar and drop over the line. While the French players held off celebrating, Cunha indicated that the ball had crossed the line after GLT signaled the ball had crossed the line, lifting France to a 2–1 victory. France, despite all its attacking talent, looked lackluster in its opener.

The same day, Denmark managed a 1–0 win over Peru thanks to a counterattacking strike from Yussuf Poulsen in the 59th minute. The 40,000 Peruvians traveling to Russia over the course of the tournament to support their team outnumbered Danish supporters among the crowd of 40,502. Peru featured captain Paolo Guerrero in the lineup after the striker had initially been banned from the World Cup after testing positive for a cocaine byproduct. The thirty-four-year-old, who has denied any wrongdoing, appealed to a Swiss federal court—the final appeal in the sporting judicial system—which on May 31 agreed to lift the suspension. Guerrero had tested positive for benzoylecgonine, a metabolite of cocaine, following a World Cup qualifier in Argentina the previous year. He said it was found in his system because he drank an herbal infusion that was contaminated with coca leaf, an ingredient in cocaine widely used as a traditional remedy in South America.

Nonetheless, his appearance wasn't enough to help Peru. In goal, Kasper Schmeichel proved effective as Peru struggled to get the ball past him following six attempts. "It's good to have a good goalkeeper, let me put it that way," observed Denmark coach Age Hareide. "He is acrobatic and a very quick goalkeeper. He had a fantastic performance and we needed it. You have to acknowledge the performance of Kasper today."[17]

Five days later in Samara, Denmark and Australia played to a 1–1 draw, while France eliminated Peru 1–0 at Ekaterinburg Arena in Yekaterinburg. France's Kylian Mbappe scored the winner in the 34th minute. At just 19 years and 183 days, Mbappe became the youngest player to score for France at a World Cup, while also helping his side reach the knockout round in the process. Born just months after France won the World Cup in 1998, Mbappe said after the game: "I've always said that the World Cup is a dream for any player. It is a dream come true and I hope I will have more like this."[18] Mbappe's hopes would turn into reality by tournament's end.

The group's final match day on June 26 saw Peru eliminate Australia 2–0—rewarding the 44,000 mostly Peruvian fans at Fisht Stadium—and ending a winless run of eight World Cup games that had stretched back to the 1978 event. "Many people made the impossible trip to be here," said Peru striker Andre Carillo, who scored Peru's first goal, after the game. "I am happy to give them the victory. We are proud of them."[19] At Luzhniki Stadium, meanwhile, the 78,011 fans in attendance were treated to a dull 0–0 draw between France and Denmark. The stalemate suited both sides as French manager Didier Deschamps made several changes to his starting lineup in order to rest players ahead of the knockout stage. "We didn't have to take risks to get better," Deschamps said, "because this result was good for everyone."[20]

Group D was predicted to be one of the toughest at the tournament. Those expectations turned out to be correct as Argentina struggled for most of its first three matches, while Croatia, Iceland, and Nigeria all tried to take advantage of that sudden vulnerability. Argentina had struggled in qualifying, and friendlies leading up to the finals did nothing to quell concerns that coach Jorge Sampaoli was not up to the task. A 6–1 defeat to Spain in March sent Argentina fans reeling and Sampaoli scrambling to make excuses. "I take the blame for the goals, don't point to the players," he told reporters in the post-match news conference. "The difference [between the sides] in the game wasn't as large as the result. We have to learn from this. It cannot happen in the World Cup."[21]

Would it happen in Russia? The extra pressure on Messi to deliver a World Cup title to his country, just like Maradona had, didn't help matters. "Winning the World Cup is a huge personal challenge for me, for the group [of players Argentina have] and for the country, who have the same dreams as us. It's a nice responsibility to represent a whole country at a World Cup. I would swap a title with Barcelona for one with the national team. While I want to win things again with my club, I want to win something with the national team. I know it would be special for what it means, to be [World Cup] champions with Argentina would be different to everything, it would be something unique," Messi said in an interview.[22]

While Sampaoli had tried to wean his side off its dependence on Messi, his final twenty-three-player roster sent mixed signals. While Messi remained the fulcrum for this team, there were other players—in defense, midfield, and attack—who were also expected to have big tournaments. On the eve of the tournament, Sampaoli made it clear that his selection was based on the tactics he thought were best suited for

*Lionel Messi is all smiles after arriving in Moscow ahead of Argentina's World Cup opener against Iceland (Credit: FIFA).*

the tournament ahead of him. "We understand that these players have characteristics that will suit us," he told reporters. "With some time and the desire to play, this will be further enhanced. I have a lot of hope and, every time I see them train, the dream grows."[23]

As is the case with countries considered World Cup contenders, the names of players who don't make the cut make more news than the ones that do. The biggest omissions from Sampaoli's list included Inter Milan striker Mauro Icardi, who was coming off a great season in Serie A (where he finished as joint top scorer with twenty-nine goals). Boca Juniors forward Carlos Tevez, who last played for his country in 2015, was also not selected despite speculation that he might get a second chance to represent Argentina at a major tournament. Instead, Sampaoli went with Messi, Paulo Dybala, Sergio Agüero, and Gonzalo Higuaín. Only two of these players, Agüero and Higuaín, were pure strikers. Dybala, a playmaker, was too similar to Messi to deploy alongside the Barcelona star. Agüero deserved inclusion, but Icardi would have worked well as a trio with Agüero and Angel Di Maria (listed on the roster as a midfielder) in what certainly would have been a potent and attack-minded 3-3-1-3. Instead, Icardi's omission meant Sampaoli would be limiting his attacking options and forcing him to go with a 3-4-2-1, with Higuaín getting the start as the lone striker. A strong forward at club level for Napoli, and more recently Juventus, the burly forward had often come up short when Argentina needed him most. In both Copa America finals against Chile, in 2015 and 2016, Higuaín flubbed scoring chances early on that could have changed the course and outcome of those matches. Argentina also lost the World Cup final four years earlier after Higuaín squandered a clear chance early on.

Luck wasn't on the side of *La Albiceleste* when starting goalkeeper Sergio Romero was ruled out due to a knee injury ahead of the tournament. The Manchester United goalkeeper suffered the injury in practice and was removed from the roster as the team trained ahead of their World Cup opener on June 16 against Iceland at Moscow's Spartak Stadium. Making matters worse, the team's backup goalkeeper for the past two years, Nahuel Guzmán, was originally left off the squad. Sampaoli called in Guzmán—even after the goalkeeper's father had gone after the manager on social media after the initial exclusion. Sampaoli would give the starting job to Chelsea backup, Willy Caballero.

Argentina got the World Cup off to a positive start when Agüero put his side ahead after just nineteen minutes. The game would end in frustration for the Argentines, however, when Iceland—playing a disciplined defensive style in its first World Cup game ever—got the equalizer just four minutes later thanks to Alfred Finnbogason. Making matters worse, a Messi penalty kick attempt denied by goalkeeper Hannes Halldorsson in the second half would deal the Argentines a psychological blow early in the competition. Later that day, Croatia powered itself to a 2–0 win against Nigeria. An own goal in the 32nd minute and a penalty kick converted by Real Madrid midfielder Luka Modric in the 72nd minute put the game away. Croatia had not played a pretty game (Modric's penalty kick was Croatia's first shot on goal and only one of two clear scoring attempts), but it was enough to power the team to first place in the group. "A win is a win is a win. It doesn't matter how you score," said Croatia coach Zlatko Dalic. "What matters is that you score!"[24]

The June 21 game pitting Argentina and Croatia was already a must-win for both sides. With only the top two teams advancing from the first round, neither could afford to drop points given that the group remained wide open. The game at Nizhny Novgorod Stadium in Nizhny Novgorod would expose Argentina's vulnerabilities while further propelling Croatia's status as one of the tournament's dark horse sides. With Maradona watching from the stands, Croatia swept Argentina aside after a Caballero attempt to clear the ball following an errant back pass from defender Gabriel Mercado allowed Ante Rebic to volley the ball into the net. Caballero's massive blunder in the 53rd minute set the tone for the rest of the game. With Messi unable to get things going offensively, Croatia took advantage of Argentina's defensive lapses—now deployed with a new-look back three rather than four defenders, in an effort to play a more offensive style—put Sampaoli on the hot seat. In a desperate bid to score an equalizer, Sampaoli removed Agüero and put the scoring onus on Higuaín, Dybala, and Cristian Pavon. With Argentina exposing itself in the back and in midfield, Croatia found a second goal in the 80th minute. With Modric unmarked, the midfielder unleashed a shot from 25 yards out to beat Caballero. In stoppage time, Ivan Rakitic, a teammate of Messi's at Barcelona, beat Caballero for a third time as Croatia moved on to the knockout phase. "[Messi] is our captain. He leads the team and we simply couldn't pass to him," Sampaoli said. "We work to give Leo the ball, but our opponents also work hard to prevent him from getting the ball."[25]

Argentina, now in last place in the group, needed a victory against Nigeria in its final game—coupled with a Croatia victory against Iceland—to advance to the knockout round. Nigeria had defeated Iceland 2–0 and were very much alive in the competition. The days leading up to the game were full of drama and anxiety as tumult reigned inside the Argentina camp, with Sampaoli increasingly coming under fire and speculation that the Argentine FA could fire him at any moment. While the loss to Croatia did little to quell the "who's better" debate between Ronaldo and Messi, it did show that the Barcelona star could only succeed if his teammates helped him. They didn't once again. The pressure on Messi prior to kickoff was palpable, as Messi was caught with his eyes closed and rubbing his forehead in a moment of concentration during the playing of the national anthems. Argentina's players, with just days before the Nigeria game, were in revolt after a failed coup attempt to oust their manager. The days prior to the game were fraught with anger and frustration within the Argentine camp after the country's FA confirmed it had no plans to sack the embattled Sampaoli. The headline in *Clarin*, one of the country's largest daily newspapers, summed it up best: "Sampaoli Continues, But the Players Aren't Responding."

Tensions had risen just a day after Argentina's humiliating loss to Croatia when it was reported that a secret meeting was held, spearheaded by Messi and Javier Mascherano, that involved asking Sampaoli to step down to be replaced by technical director and 1986 World Cup star Jorge Burruchaga. In the post-match news conference, Sampaoli said, "I would beg [the fans] for their forgiveness, especially those Argentina supporters who made such a great effort to be here. And I repeat what I said, I'm responsible. I was just as dreamy-eyed as any fan before. So I'm hurt."[26] The mood was glum inside the Argentine camp, with the players no longer listening to their coach despite the team holding training sessions in the days leading up to the game. However, Claudio Tapia, the head of the Argentine FA, said the coaching staff and players had come up with a peace agreement after meeting at the team's base camp in Bronnitsy, located in suburban Moscow, and deciding to "get together and move forward."[27]

With Messi looking for his first goal at the tournament, Argentina came out aggressive against Nigeria on June 26 in Saint Petersburg. Not only did Argentina get the win it needed—and help from Croatia in the form of a 2–1 win versus Iceland—but Messi scored an exquisite goal after just fourteen minutes from a long pass from defender Ever Banega. The wild enthusiasm that followed, led by an animated Maradona in the stands, swung the momentum in Argentina's direction. While Messi, who later hit the post off a free kick, and Banega controlled the game in the first half, the rest of the team did not look up to the task. In goal, Sampaoli went with Franco Armani. The game marked the international debut of the thirty-one-year-old River Plate goalkeeper. Jitters aside, Armani performed the best he could. The Argentine defense, however, did little to instill confidence as Nigeria pushed to draw the game level.

Nigeria scored the equalizer in the 51st minute after being awarded a penalty kick following a Mascherano foul in the box. Victor Moses put the ball past Armani, a goal that would deal a blow to Argentina's hopes of qualifying for the next round. The South Americans needed a win or suffer a humiliating elimination. Once again, with the game on the line, Higuaín put an easy chance over the crossbar. With Argentina pushing forward and Sampaoli encouraging his players from the sidelines, Argentina grabbed the winner with four minutes left to play from an unlikely source when defender Marcos Rojo slotted home a volley with his right foot into the bottom corner. The goal unleashed delirium among the 64,468 in attendance, including Maradona. The former Argentine legend had to be taken to the hospital following the game after suffering chest pains. The final whistle saw Argentina go through to the knockout stage as the players huddled around Messi. Argentina had lived to see another day. "The most important thing for Leo is his human side. He cries. He suffers. He's happy when Argentina wins. I know him," Sampaoli said. "Many people say Leo does not enjoy playing for Argentina, but I do not agree. He enjoys and suffers like all the other players and that makes him even bigger."[28]

Over in Group E, another South American powerhouse, Brazil, had a much easier time advancing to the knockout stage. A 1–1 draw against Switzerland in its opener on June 17 in Rostov did little to convince, and a 2–0 win over Costa Rica five days later in St. Petersburg did little to quell concerns. It was two goals in stoppage time—Phillipe Coutino in the 91st minute and Neymar in the 97th—that lifted Brazil to victory. Neymar's playacting to get the attention of match officials had the opposite effect in the age of VAR. Furious when the referee overturned a penalty kick for Brazil, a relieved Neymar dropped to his knees after the final whistle. "The responsibility is huge when you are playing for the national team," Coutinho said after the game. "You have to be mentally strong from the beginning until the end. We fought until the end and we were rewarded."[29] Similar pressure had caused the team to implode at the World Cup four years earlier. Just four months before the tournament, Neymar had broken a bone in his right foot while playing for Paris Saint-Germain. Following an unbelievable recovery, Neymar returned to Coach Tite's lineup. Like Messi, Neymar was the key to the team's success. He had helped Brazil win its first gold medal in soccer at the Rio Olympics just two years earlier, going a long way to restore some pride in a team still reeling from the humiliation suffered at the 2014 World Cup. "We know [Neymar] had a difficult injury . . . but his joy at being on the pitch is contagious," Coutinho added.

Serbia, 1–0 winners against Costa Rica in its opener, played a pivotal game against Switzerland on June 22 in Kaliningrad. Serbia took the lead after just five minutes with Aleksandar Mitrovic's header. The Swiss stormed back, inspired by Xherdan Shaqiri, with two second-half goals. The tying goal in the 51st minute by Granit Xhaka generated controversy when he made the sign of an Albanian eagle as he celebrated the goal. The symbol was a rebuke of Serbia's role in the Yugoslavian civil war, when his Kosovan father was imprisoned during the 1980s. With emotions running high, Switzerland tied the score in the 90th minute when Shaqiri broke free from the run of play and put the ball past goalkeeper Vladimir Stojkovic. Shaqiri, who is also of Kosovan descent, made the same pro-Albanian symbol. After the match, Slavisa Kokeza, the head of Serbia's FA, said the goal celebrations "deserve to be condemned by the whole football world."[30] The politically charged actions resulted in a FIFA probe, but any chance of a suspension was set aside when the sport's governing body refused to impose those sanctions. Instead, the players were fined $12,500 apiece and cleared to play in their final Group E match against Costa Rica.

In the group's final games on June 27, Brazil clinched a berth to the second round with a 2–0 win against Serbia at Spartak Stadium in Moscow. At the same time, Switzerland, also needing a result against already-eliminated Costa Rica, had a difficult time in Nizhny Novgorod. In yet another emotion-filled match, Switzerland clawed its way to second place and a spot in the final sixteen after a 2–2 draw. Two of those goals—the 2–1 lead for Switzerland and Costa Rica's tying goal—came in the game's dying minutes. Nonetheless, advancing to the next round came with a price. Yellow cards for captain Stephan Lichtsteiner and fellow defender Fabian Schaer, their second of the competition, meant they would be suspended for the first game of the knockout round. "This is certainly not an ideal scenario," said Switzerland midfielder Blerim Dzemaili. "We don't need to look at who's not there, we need to look at who will be able to play."[31]

Group F, widely considered the toughest at the tournament, did not disappoint. The Germans, favored to repeat as champions, would go on to be one of the biggest disappointments of the first round. Germany struggled to combat Mexico's counterattacking at Luzhniki Stadium on June 17 as *El Tri* inflicted a shocking defeat on their opponents: Mexico's 1–0 victory via a Hirving Lozano strike. "We played very badly in the first half. We were not able to impose our way of playing," said Germany coach Joachim Low. "We were not effective in the spaces."[32] The following day in Nizhny Novgorod, Sweden, playing in its first World Cup in twelve years, defeated South Korea by the same scoreline in a scrappy match. The winning goal came in the 65th minute on a penalty kick by Andreas Granqvist after VAR ruled that Kim Min-woo tripped Viktor Claesson.

Mexico qualified for the knockout stage on June 23 with a 2–1 win against South Korea in Rostov-on-Don, with Javier Hernandez scoring what turned out to be the winning goal in the 66th minute. On the same day, Germany kept its World Cup dreams alive with a win against Sweden by the same scoreline as Toni Kroos scored a last-gasp goal in the fifth minute of stoppage time. It was the first time since 1974 that the Germans had to come from behind to win a World Cup game. The unusual position the Germans found themselves in, despite their depth, remained cause for concern. It was off a free kick that Kroos curled a shot into the far corner to deny Sweden's status as giant killers. "The fact Toni Kroos put it away is just incredible," said teammate Marco Reus, who tapped the ball to Kroos on the free kick. "He's shown that talent on previous occasions but really in this case it was practically the very last opportunity to win this match."[33]

June 27 marked the final match day in Group F as Mexico, Sweden, and Germany all fought for two spots. In Kazan, Germany was scrambling against South Korea during a stalemate. The South Koreans hunkered down for most of the game as Germany tried in vain to try and win. The pressure mounted in the knowledge that, at the same time in Yekaterinburg, Sweden was piling on the goals against Mexico. With Sweden topping the group after a 3–0 victory (Mexico would finish second despite the defeat), Germany would concede two stoppage-time goals. Kim Young-gwon's goal in the 93rd minute and a goal from Son Heung-min three minutes later on an empty net lifted South Korea to a 2–0 win. It marked the first time since 1938 that either Germany or West Germany had not advanced past the first round of a World Cup. "This is something for us to reckon with," Low told reporters after the game. "I am sure this will create some public uproar in Germany."[34]

Group G saw Belgium, another dark horse in the tournament, and England dominate over Tunisia and Panama. In the group opener on June 23, Belgium routed Panama 3–0 in Sochi, while England edged out Tunisia 2–1 in Volgograd. While Belgium dominated thanks to two Romelu Lukaku goals, England, as usual, struggled and was only able to grab the win via a Harry Kane strike in stoppage time. Unmarked at the far post, Kane—ever opportunistic in the penalty area and one of the world's best players for his predatory skills—redirected a header into the net. The England captain and Tottenham star had been double-teamed and fouled the entire match. After he was dragged down on two occasions, the referee refused to consult with VAR. England's energetic start and Kane's imposing game were rewarded in the end. "Maybe there was a bit of justice at the end," Kane said.[35]

Dogged by low expectations both from the news media and fans back home, English fans opted not to travel to Russia. Instead, many were expecting another poor effort despite having one of the world's best domestic leagues. Manager Gareth Southgate was pleased with his team's first game. "The pleasing thing was the movement, the pace and the interchange," Southgate told reporters. "We had good control from the back with the ball."[36] Five days later, Belgium defeated Tunisia 5–2 at Spartak Stadium in Moscow. Two goals apiece from Lukaku and Edin Hazard lifted the team to success. In Nizhny Novgorod, England romped Panama 6–1, confirming the enthusiasm in the Three Lions camp, to record its biggest margin of victory at a World Cup. A Kane hat trick and two goals from John Stones lifted England to the win. The victory allowed Belgium and England to reach the final sixteen even before the sides would meet in the final group match.

With both sides resting players ahead of the knockout stage, Belgium defeated England 1–0 on a goal from Adnan Januzaj. Although Belgium coach Roberto Martinez admitted that for the June 28 game, "the priority was not to win," the players appeared happy to have won the group. In the end, neither team really wanted to win the game or the group.[37] The defeat benefitted England as Belgium advanced to what most

considered the tougher side of the knockout-round bracket that included Brazil, Mexico, France, Argentina, Uruguay, and Portugal. England had made eight changes to its starting lineup for the game—but
the players made it clear they wanted to win every game. "We're disappointed we couldn't do that . . . I thought it was quite an even game,"
said midfielder Eric Dier. "We created some good chances. We needed
to finish one of them. That was all that was missing."[38]

The first round closed out with a wide-open Group H. While Colombia and Poland were favored to advance, no one was ruling out plucky
sides such as Japan and Senegal. That was proven in the group's opening game on June 19 when Japan shocked Colombia 2–1 in Saransk. It
marked the first time that the Japanese won a World Cup match on
European soil—thanks to a goal from Yuya Osako in the 73rd minute—
after *Los Cafeteros* were reduced to ten men after just three minutes.
Carlos Sanchez was red carded—the first of the tournament—after he
handled the ball in the box. Shinji Kagawa scored on the ensuing penalty, a lead that held for just thirty-three minutes when Juan Quintero's
free kick tied the score. Japan joined Mexico, Switzerland, and Iceland
in earning unexpected results at this tournament. The win came as a
surprise because Japan had changed coaches shortly before the tournament. "If we had actually won the World Cup, we would have had a
parade on the main street of Saransk," Japan coach Akira Nishino said.
"However, it is just one win, three points. We'll save our celebrations."[39]

On June 24, Colombia rebounded with a 3–0 win against Poland in
Kazan to keep its World Cup hopes alive. On the same day in Yekaterinburg, Japan came from behind twice to draw Senegal 2–2. The
game showcased the attacking styles of both countries, but also their
defensive lapses. Keisuke Honda's equalizer for Japan in the 78th minute put him in the history books as the first from his country to score
at three World Cups. The results meant Poland was the only team
eliminated ahead of the group's final match day. Japan left nothing to
chance. Even though the team would play Poland, Nishino would need
to impose its style—although a draw would be enough to advance—in
order to reach the final sixteen. "We need to be able to play to our full
potential rather than being reactive to the opposition's strength," he
said ahead of Japan's June 28 game against Poland.[40]

Colombia won the group with a 1–0 against Senegal, while Japan
scraped by despite a defeat by the same score. In the end, Japan finished second after finishing with a 1–1–1 record with four goals for and

four conceded—an identical record as Senegal—but advanced by virtue of having collected fewer yellow cards. The tiebreaker was controversial, but enough for Japan in the end. It also ensured that no African team reached the final sixteen at Russia 2018. Despite Nishino's promises to impose the team's style, he admitted at a news conference after the match that he "did not go for the victory" against Poland. He added: "That was slightly regrettable, but I didn't have any other plans. I am really not happy about how we played but we wanted to go through . . . and that is the only salvation that I get."[41]

## ROUND OF SIXTEEN

The knockout round opened on June 30 when France took on Argentina in Kazan. With new life breathed into Argentina, and France needing to up its game, the game did not disappoint. In fact, it exceeded expectations as the game swung back and forth while Argentina struggled to hold on. Armani got the start in goal for Argentina once again, while Sampaoli again took a tactically naïve approach with Messi as a lone striker unable to get into the game. On the other side of the field, Deschamps deployed a lineup happy to concede possession and to wait for the Argentines to tire. In an unforgettable World Cup encounter, it was a second half brace from Kylian Mbappe that sealed the place of *Les Bleus* in the quarterfinals. The teenager's blistering pace shredded the Argentine backline after the sides finished the first half 1–1. With the game tied at two halfway through the second half, Mbappe beat Armani with a shot at the near post. Four minutes later, Mbappe beat Armani again after running onto an Oliver Giroud pass.

The goals signaled a passing of the torch from Messi to Mbappe as the world's best player. "Of course, as I've already and always said, in the World Cup you have all the top-level players so it is an opportunity to show what you can do and what your abilities are," said Mbappe. "There is no better place than a World Cup."[42] Mbappe had been a constant threat with his skill and speed, helping France put together a breathtaking display. With his two goals, Mbappe became the second teenager to score multiple goals in a knockout game at a World Cup. Pelé was the other. "It is flattering to be the second one after Pelé, but let's put things in context. Pelé is in another category," Mbappe said. "It's good to be among the players to score in knockout matches."[43]

Down 4–2, Sampaoli put in Agüero in, hoping that an extra attacking player could produce more late-game heroics. He did eventually score in stoppage time, but it was too late. "It is too soon to analyze concrete mistakes we might have made," Sampaoli said after the game. "I am sure there might have been mistakes."[44] There were more than a few mistakes as Messi once again missed out on winning the World Cup. Sampaoli was fired at the end of the tournament.

On the same day, Uruguay defeated Portugal 2–1 in Sochi. The Cavani-Suarez attacking duo was once again key for the South Americans. Uruguay took the lead after just seven minutes. Cavani played a cross-field pass to Suarez on the left. He crossed the ball in to Cavani, who headed the ball home for the lead. Another header in the 55th minute by an unmarked Pepe tied the score. Ronaldo, meanwhile, was unable to score after a strong first round. Once again, Ronaldo would fail to score in a World Cup knockout game. He would end the game with a single shot on goal. "Cristiano still has a lot to give to football and I hope he will stay [on the national team] to help young players grow and develop," said Portugal coach Fernando Santos. "We have a team with many young players and we will want him there for us."[45]

Uruguay would score the winning goal in the 62nd minute when Cavani tallied a second goal of the night to win the match. Like Mbappe, Cavani stole the spotlight from one of the world's best players. In doing so, Cavani sent Ronaldo packing. "The truth is, it was really exciting," Cavani said of the victory. "There aren't words to describe this."[46] The only blemish was an injury that sent Cavani limping to the sidelines in the 70th minute, where he was replaced by Cristhian Stuani.

Two days before Russia's highly anticipated July 1 clash against Spain at Luzhniki Stadium in Moscow, Dutch coaching great Guus Hiddink, a Fox Sports analyst who had managed Russia to the European Championship semifinals ten years earlier on a run stopped by a Spanish squad at the start of their title-winning era, came by for a pep talk. "You're doing so far very well, unexpected for me, a little bit unexpected to be honest," Hiddink told the players.[47]

Spain's tiki-taka style had not worked as well as in years past. Opponents had grown wise to it. The Russians certainly had, absorbing pressure after Spain's possession game failed to penetrate the backline. Spain dominated in what turned out to be a frustrating match for them after Hierro's side completed more than 1,000 passes with 74 percent possession—but could only produce one goal. Spain led in the 12th minute after captain Sergio Ramos helped force Sergei Ignashevich to divert a crossed ball into his own goal. An error at the other end put Russia back in the game. Gerald Pique handled the ball in the box off a corner kick. Dzyuba scored on the ensuing penalty in the 41st minute to tie the score.

That's where the goals came to an end, but the heroics were just getting started. After 120 minutes, the match headed to a shootout. On penalties, goalkeeper Igor Akinfeev made two saves—on Spain's third and fifth shot—lifting the hosts to a 4–3 win. Koke saw his right-footed shot stopped by Akinfeev when the goalkeeper lunged to his right and easily blocked the ball with his hands. The decisive save came when Akinfeev used his left foot to stop Iago Aspas's left-footed shot. The save unleashed celebrations throughout Moscow that stretched across the massive country of 145 million people and 11 time zones. The unexpected win led to an outpouring of celebration and public displays of patriotism not seen since the end of World War II. As vehicular traffic leading to Red Square came to a halt and fans streamed into the street,

*Moscow's Luzhniki Stadium, with a statue of Vladimir Lenin near the main entrance, would go on to serve as the tournament's centerpiece and host a number of exciting matches, including Russia's stunning win against Spain (Credit: Courtesy of the author).*

the chants of "*Ro-si-ya! Ro-si-ya!*" filled the skies of the massive capital. "I'm not the man of the match. The man of the match is our team and our fans," Akinfeev said, referring to the cheering of the 78,011 fans inside Luzhniki Stadium.[48]

The day's second game between Croatia and Denmark in Nizhny Novgorod also produced a thriller. Like Spain, Denmark came into the game on an eighteen-game unbeaten streak, and scored early—after just fifty-seven seconds—with Mathias Jorgensen stabbing home a shot after a long throw that caught the Croatian defense flat-footed. Croatia didn't lose its nerve—tying the score just three minutes later when Mario Mandzukic took advantage of a scramble in the penalty area to fire home the ball. The sides traded shots as possession remained even. It was the goalkeeping that kept the game close.

Tied 1-1, the game went to extra time. It all became unraveled by Denmark in the 113th minute after Modric passed a ball to Ante Rebic who, after rounding Kasper Schmeichel and looking certain to score, was upended by Jorgensen. Modric's penalty kick, however, was saved by Schmeichel, the son of former Denmark goalkeeper Peter Schmeichel who was in the crowd for the game. The momentum was in Denmark's favor entering the shootout.

Schmeichel was still oozing confidence, as his two saves in the shootout showed—but those heroics were cancelled out by Croatia's Danijel Subasic. Christian Eriksen's first kick slammed against the post, while Subasic made saves on both Lasse Schone and Nicolai Jorgensen's attempts to lift his side 3-2 in a heart-stomping win. "He was a hero tonight," Dalic said. "He saved three penalties in a shootout. You don't see that every day."[49]

Mexico was trying to break its jinx of exiting in the last sixteen stage—but standing in its way was Brazil. The five-time World Cup champions raised their game on July 2 in Samara. Neymar and his constant playacting and rolling around on the ground reached new, farcical heights as Mexico played a strong first half. Neymar's overreaction to a Miquel Layun foul near the touchline earned the Brazilian striker Internet ridicule that would stick with him for the remainder of the tournament. "I'm here to win. I hope I can improve always," Neymar told reporters after the match.[50]

*El Tri*'s pressing game fell apart in the second half as Brazil got on the board. In the 51st minute, Neymar helped draw the Mexican backline out of position. In typical *Seleção* fashion, Neymar back-heeled the ball to Willian, then it went back to Neymar who put the ball into the goal. Brazil put the game away two minutes from the end when a Neymar attempt was parried by Guillermo Ochoa, but Roberto Firmino grabbed the rebound to clinch a spot in the quarterfinals. For Mexico, the defeat was disheartening. It was also record-setting for defender Rafa Marquez, who became the first player to captain a team at five different World Cups.

The day's second game in Rostov-on-Don would produce another enthralling encounter. Japan, who had sneaked into the knockout stage, were the underdogs going into this game—although no one told Belgium. The wild and chaotic game would produce a memorable second half. Japan jumped out to a 2–0 lead within a span of four minutes. Genki Haraguchi's goal gave Japan the lead. With Belgium's defense in tatters, Japan doubled the score with a play started by Shinji Kagawa's back-heel. That pass was met by Takeshi Inui, who had the space to unleash a shot from the edge of the box that beat goalkeeper Thibaut Courtois. Frustrated, Belgium's attempted comeback was thwarted by the post following an Eden Hazard shot, while a Romelu Lukaku header from close range failed to change the score.

Martinez made two key substitutions in the 65th minute, putting in Nacer Chadli and Marouane Fellaini. The move would be a stroke of coaching genius. Japan naïvely continued to play, as opposed to locking down its defense, and Belgium's experienced players took advantage of it. "It's a test of character. It's a test of the team," Martinez told reporters after the game. "You have to see how the substitutes react, how the whole team reacts."[51] The reaction paid off in the 69th minute when Japan's defense failed to clear a high ball that fell to Jan Vertonghen. The Tottenham defender took advantage of it, sending a looping header into the goal at the far post. Five minutes later, Belgium was more physically imposing following the two subs that allowed Kevin De Bruyne to play further up the field. Off a Hazard cross, Fellaini headed the ball into the goal to draw the game level. "When we were up 2–0, I really wanted to score another goal and we did have opportunities," Nishino recalled. "We were to some extent controlling the game, but Belgium upped their game when they had to."[52]

What was expected to be a mismatch became a close game. With a quarterfinal berth on the line and a meeting with Brazil on the line, the Red Devils initiated another attacking play that started with Courtois and ended ten seconds later on the other side of the field with a brilliant Chadli goal in the fourth minute of stoppage time. After Courtois grabbed a corner kick, he rolled the ball to De Bruyne, who dribbled the ball to Thomas Meunier on the right. Meunier flocked the ball across the area toward Lukaku, who let it roll by for Chadli. The sub then tapped the ball with his left foot from just seven yards to grab the improbable win. In doing so, Belgium became the first team to overturn a two-goal deficit in a World Cup knockout game since West Germany defeated England in extra time at the 1970 tournament. The game saw Belgium extend its undefeated streak to twenty-two games. The final whistle unleashed tears among the dejected Japanese players and fans, while Martinez and his players hugged one another. In the post-game news conference, Martinez was already looking ahead to Brazil, saying, "Against Brazil, I think we can enjoy it from the first minute. When you're a little boy, you dream of facing Brazil in the World Cup."[53]

On July 3, Sweden kept its fine run going with a 1–0 victory against Switzerland in St. Petersburg. Although Sweden players were not as resolute as in the recent past, a goal by Emil Forsberg, the team's main attacking threat, in the 67th minute proved to be enough against a Swiss side that came into the game never having won a World Cup knockout match. The win sent Sweden to the quarterfinals for the first time since 1994. Sweden coach Janne Andersson noted after the game that Sweden fans, a majority among the 64,000 in attendance, had been "quite extraordinary."[54]

The day's second encounter featured a tasty affair between England and Colombia in Moscow. Enthusiasm back in England had grown as fans believed that the Three Lions could win its first World Cup since 1966. It was a 1996 song called "Three Lions"—and its chorus, "It's coming home"—that could be heard in pubs across England and at games. The lyrics were actually a reference to England hosting the 1996 European Championship, its first major soccer tournament since the 1966 World Cup. Nonetheless, the words evolved to refer both to England's hopes of winning a second World Cup and to the fact that the English were also the inventors of the modern game.

As the game got underway at Spartak Stadium, England fans nestled among the 44,190 inside the venue chanted away:

*It's coming home. It's coming home. It's coming,*
*Football's coming home,*
*Everyone seems to know the score,*
*They've seen it all before,*

*They just know, they're so sure,*
*That England's gonna throw it away, gonna blow it away,*
*But know they can play, 'cause I remember*
*Three Lions on a shirt,*
*Jules Rimet still gleaming,*
*Thirty years of hurt, never stopped me dreaming.*
*So many jokes, so many sneers—but all those oh-so-nears,*
*Wear you down, through the years,*
*But I still see that tackle by Moore, and when Linekar scored,*
*Bobby belting the ball, and Nobby dancing*
*Three Lions on a shirt,*
*Jules Rimet still gleaming,*
*Thirty years of hurt, never stopped me dreaming.*

The dreaming continued against Colombia after Kane scored on a penalty kick in the 57th minute to break the scoreless deadlock. The decision to award a penalty came when Carlos Sanchez wrestled Kane down in the box. In scoring, Kane became the first player for England to tally at least one goal in six straight appearances for England since Tommy Lawton in 1939. Another stoppage time goal at this World Cup saw Colombia storm back to tie the score in the 93rd minute when an unmarked Yerry Mina scored off a play initiated from a corner kick that got past Jordan Pickford.

The contentious game was marred by fouling, with American referee Mark Geiger at risk of losing control of the proceedings after he showed Wilmar Barrios a yellow card, rather than a red, following a headbutt against Jordan Henderson. England defender John Stones called Colombia the "dirtiest team I've ever come up against," adding that his side's ability to rise above provocation was a sign of its growing maturity.[55] Colombia, without star player James Rodriguez due to a calf injury, resorted to a more defensive style and tactical fouls in an effort to break up England's possession game. But England's fine abilities from set pieces remained a threat, and Kane's penalty kick further proved that talking point.

After 120 minutes, the game went to a dreaded penalty shootout. Dreaded for England, which had never won a shootout at the World Cup in three previous editions. With Southgate calmly watching from the sidelines, England delivered a shootout victory its fans will never forget, drowning out the pro-Colombia crowd. The 4–3 win was punctuated by Eric Dier's decisive kick after Colombia's Mateus Uribe's attempt hit the crossbar and Carlos Bacca saw his kick saved by Pickford. "It was like an out-of-body experience," Dier said. "I just tried to stay in the moment."[56]

## QUARTERFINALS

France defeated Uruguay 2–0 on July 6 in Nizhny Novgorod, sending *Les Bleus* to the semifinals for the sixth time in their history. Without the injured Cavani, Uruguay was unable to generate the sufficient amount of offense needed to beat a surging French side. France's midfield looked sharp with Paul Pogba finally starting to show his potential at this tournament. Raphaël Varane gave France the lead on a header in the 40th minute. Off a free kick, Antoine Griezmann sent the ball from the right side and Varane raced across the area. He got his head to the ball and sent it into the far corner past goalkeeper Fernando Muslera. France doubled the score in the 61st minute when Griezmann's shot was deflected by Muslera into the net after failing to make what appeared to be an easy save. For Griezmann, it was his third goal of the tournament. "I was playing against a lot of friends," said Griezmann, who was teammates with Uruguay defenders Diego Godin and Jose Gimenez at Atletico Madrid, "so I think it was normal not to celebrate."[57]

France would face the winner of Brazil–Belgium, a clash of titans between two nations favored to lift the trophy. The offensive trio of De Bruyne, Lukaku, and Hazard proved tough for Brazil's defense in Kazan. Brazil maintained most of the possession, but it was Belgium that made the most of its three scoring attempts. In the end, Belgium would emerge victorious, 2–1 in a nervy affair. An own goal from Fernandinho put Belgium ahead after just thirteen minutes. De Bryune doubled the lead with Brazil's defense failing to keep up with the Red Devils' counterattacking pace. A header from Renato Augusto in the 76th minute reopened Brazil's chances, with Martinez's team locking itself in its own half in an effort to grind out the win.

Wave after wave of Brazil attacks were thwarted, with Neymar growing increasingly frustrated as the game wore on. Neymar limited his playacting versus Belgium but did get a yellow card after diving in the box. In stoppage time, a last-gasp attempt by Neymar resulted in a brilliant save from Courtois, his eighth of the game. The victory sent Belgium to the semifinals and a date with France. "Sometimes you have to accept that Brazil has this finesse, that quality, that they're going to break you down, and we just refused to accept that," Martinez said. "This is something special."[58]

England's dream of bringing the World Cup home was kept alive on July 7 as the Three Lions needed minimal effort to dispose of plucky Sweden. England upped the pace for this one and saw more set-piece success. They took the lead after thirty minutes when Harry Maguire scored on a header off an Ashley Young corner. England killed off the match in the 59th minute when a Jesse Lingard cross was met by Dele Alli's header, putting an end to an emphatic 2–0 win. "We knew set plays would be key," Maguire noted. "Also that little ball that Jesse sent in for Dele, that was great! We worked on that in practice."[59]

In reaching the semifinals for the first time since 1990, England was able to do something that David Beckham, Frank Lampard, and Steven Gerrard had failed to do in the decades since that World Cup. With chants of "football's coming home" as fans streamed out of Samara Arena, the players exited the dressing room with a confidence not seen among England players in a generation. "I know the fans here are enjoying it. The fans at home, I'm sure we'll see some videos tonight of them enjoying it," Kane said.[60]

The quarterfinal stage concluded the same day in Sochi as the Russian team, along with a nation brimming with enthusiasm, took on never-say-die Croatia. Having gone further than anyone had ever expected, Russia hoped the strategy that eliminated Spain would work again. But Dalic's side, although tired, remained energized under the leadership of Modric and his abilities at midfield. The sides traded goals in the first half—Denis Cheryshev in the 31st minute and Andrej Kramaric—to end the match 1–1 in regulation.

Extra time also produced drama as Croatia took the lead in the 101st minute on a header from Domogoj Vida. Russia, however, buoyed by the home support among the 44,287 fans at Fisht Stadium, tied the game. A header by Brazilian-born Mario Fernandes, off a free kick, sailed past Subasic and sent the crowd into a frenzy. The game ended 2–2 and would be decided by a shootout. On penalties, Akinfeev could not duplicate his previous heroics. Akinfeev made one save during the shootout, and nearly a second on Modric's attempt after the shot deflected off his hand, off the post, and into the net. In the end, Rakitic's goal helped Croatia emerge victorious, 4–3. In winning, Croatia became the second team—after Argentina in 1990—to win two penalty shootouts at a World Cup. It also marked the second time in Croatia's history that it had reached

# LUKA MODRIC

In an era in which players like Lionel Messi and Cristiano Ronaldo dominate the game, there often doesn't seem to be any room for other players to shine. The 2018 World Cup was the tournament where the spotlight finally shifted onto Luka Modric. Once a refugee, the midfielder not only helped Croatia reach the World Cup final, he proved on the international level that he deserved a place alongside Messi and Ronaldo as one of the best players of the year. FIFA named Modric the winner of the Golden Ball as the best player at the 2018 World Cup, and its player of the year two months later, breaking a ten-year lock on the prize won by either Messi or Ronaldo.

Modric had already achieved a lot at club level with Real Madrid, but the World Cup transformed itself into the perfect stage for him and his teammates to show the world that a tiny nation of just 4 million could produce top talent. A player of incredible stamina, who can be both creative offensively and pivotal in his own half, Modric revealed himself to be a superstar over the past few years.

He got his start with his local team, NK Zadar, and was later passed over by Croatian powerhouse Hajduk Split. In 2001, he signed with rivals Dinamo Zagreb at age sixteen, then was loaned out in order to gain experience. Modric's breakthrough came at the start of the 2005–2006 season when Dinamo Zagreb signed him to a ten-year contract. He helped the team win the league title that season. Modric would not finish out his contract in Zagreb after drawing interest from several English and Spanish clubs. After four years with the club, Modric had amassed thirty-one goals and twenty-nine assists in four seasons. His strongest performances in Croatia took place during the 2007–2008 season when Dinamo captured the league and domestic cup double.

In April 2008, Modric signed with Tottenham. After a slow start, Modric began to show his value in the Premier League. Modric's versatility and good attitude often meant managers would play him out of his natural position as a playmaker. That meant having to adapt to different roles and, often, not excelling. His passing abilities and accuracy rate made Modric a lethal player and one feared by many opposing defenses. Modric would go on to complete four seasons with Spurs, scoring 13 goals in 127 league matches.

Those numbers caught the attention of Real Madrid, who signed Modric to a five-year contract in August 2012. In Spain the Croatian

*(continued)*

would become a star and win lots of trophies. Playing alongside some of the world's best players, including Sergio Ramos and Cristiano Ronaldo, allowed Modric to shine. Modric's strong work ethic, composure with the ball, and ability to generate scoring chances with a pass or long-range attempt became a huge asset for Real. Modric would help the team win four Champions League titles, three FIFA Club World Cup trophies, and one league title.

Modric was born and raised in the former Yugoslavia and forced to flee as a child in 1991 as the war in the Balkans escalated. Modric's grandfather, Luka, was executed by Serb rebels in December 1991, and the family's home was burned to the ground. Modric and his family became refugees, forced to live in a hotel for the next seven years. Modric began playing soccer with other children in a nearby parking lot.

He played for Croatia at youth level, making his senior national team debut in March 2006 against Argentina. Modric was a member of the team that participated at the 2006 and 2014 World Cups as well as the 2008, 2012, and 2016 European Championships.

## World Cup Career Statistics

Tournaments played: 3
Games: 12
Goals: 2

---

the semis after a phenomenal run twenty years earlier in France. As for Russia, the team's epic run propelled the game to new heights. After the game, Russia coach Cherchesov said Putin called before and after the game to rally the players. "He congratulated us on a very good game. He said what we showed on the field was great," he said.[61]

## SEMIFINALS

For the first time in World Cup history, neither Germany, Argentina, nor Brazil were in the semifinals. Furthermore, the semifinals featured four European nations for the first time since 2006, another indication of the power and money associated with clubs that take part in domestic leagues in England, Germany, Spain, Italy, and France.

The first semifinal between France and Belgium on July 10 in St. Petersburg featured two evenly matched teams. Considering the attacking strength on both teams, many expected lots of goals. Instead, the game only produced one. There was less at stake the last time the sides played at a World Cup—a 4–2 victory for France in the third-place match in 1986. Both teams featured a galaxy of individual stars. The ability of either Deschamps or Martinez to galvanize their lineups into a cohesive unit would make the difference. Both managers had done it so far at this tournament. It was a matter of who would do it better in the semifinals. In the end, France's 4–2–3–1 formation would prove too strong for Belgium. The Red Devils, deployed in a 3–4–2–1 lineup, had gotten the best of Japan and Brazil in dramatic fashion during the knockout round—and hoped for similar heroics against France.

Instead, it was France that shone through in the end. In a match between two sides worthy of a final, Samuel Umtiti—part of France's young generation—clinched a spot in the final with a 1–0 win after scoring on a header off a corner kick in the 51st minute. Umtiti not only scored, but also played an instrumental role defensively. With France ahead, Mbappe set up Olivier Giroud with a spectacular back-heel, but Giroud's shot was thwarted by Courtois from point-blank range. Mbappe's brilliant back-heel, following a give-and-go involving Lucas Hernandez and Matuidi, was one of several plays that had Belgium's defense in a tizzy all night. France's win was even greater given that it helped thwart the highest-scoring team at the tournament and left the Red Devils' golden generation out of the final. "It's me that scored," Umtiti said, "but we all delivered a big game."[62]

France would play the winners of the second semifinal between Croatia and England on July 11. Thousands of English fans, who had previously ignored the tournament amid unfounded fears that Russia was a dangerous place to visit, flooded into Moscow for the match. Some 10,000 fans, according to Russian authorities, entered the country as ticket prices soared in the hours ahead of the game at Luzhniki Stadium. The game would not end the way the English had hoped for; football was not coming home after all, when Croatia became only the second team ever to overturn a halftime deficit in a World Cup semifinal with goals from Ivan Perisic and Mario Mandzukic to see them through to their first-ever final.

England got off to the perfect start, with yet another dead ball situation. This one, though, wasn't another well-worked corner routine but a brilliant free kick from Kieran Trippier, who curled in from the top of the box after Modric had fouled Alli. From there, the Three Lions were happy to sit back and play on the counter, with Raheem Sterling looking particularly dangerous as he outpaced Dejan Lovren and Domagoj Vida on a number of occasions. England nearly doubled their lead after a half hour, when Jesse Lingard played in Kane, whose shot was saved by Subasic, before he missed the rebound. The flag was up for offside, but a replay showed Kane was not.

Croatia, meanwhile, seriously struggled to break down England's defense. Rebic had a powerful effort saved in the 32nd minute by Pickford, but it was telling that all of his side's shots came from outside the box. They improved after the break, though, as England began to drop deeper, content to protect the lead. Perisic equalized in the 68th minute, beating Kyle Walker to knock in Sime Vrsaljko's cross. The goal rattled England, and Perisic almost got his second only three minutes later, beating Walker one-on-one before drilling a shot off the post. For the first time all tournament, Southgate's side looked out of their depth. "This is a mentally strong team," Rakitic said. "It's just unbelievable to get back in the game in this way."[63]

*England striker Harry Kane takes the time to talk with reporters. He would go on to have a wonderful World Cup, finishing with a tournament-high six goals and leading the Three Lions to an unexpected fourth-place finish (Credit: FIFA).*

England looked nervous in possession and were far too quick to lump the ball forward under pressure from Croatia, but despite a couple of half-chances for Perisic and Mandzukic, the team held on to send the match to extra time. Both sides had good chances in the first period of extra time. John Stones's header was cleared off the line by Vrsaljko, while Pickford denied Mandzukic with an excellent point-blank save in the 108th minute. Mandzukic won it shortly after the restart, capitalizing on some sloppy, tired play from England's center-backs, who failed to react when Perisic beat Trippier to a sliced clearance, sending the Juventus forward through on goal to score the winner. The victory unleashed joy back in Zagreb, where fans took to the streets to celebrate. "We are a nation of people who never give in, who are proud and who have character," said Dalic, who donned a checkered jersey to his post-game news conference. "There's no weakness in a team that is in the final."[64] England would go on to finish fourth after losing to Belgium in the third-place match 2–0 on July 14 in Saint Petersburg. Kane would be awarded the Golden Boot as the tournament's top scorer with six goals.

## FINAL

The title match on July 15 at Luzhniki Stadium was set: France, with its brash and flashy young stars, pitted against the mentally tough and hardworking Croatia. While France was a slight favorite going into the match, Croatia had to deal with the issue of fatigue. The Croatians had played a full ninety minutes more than France after contesting three consecutive thirty-minute overtimes. The final was also a rematch of the 1998 World Cup semifinals, where France won 2–1. Dalic said, "There is no weakness in a team that is in the final. [France] are a top-drawer team with fantastic players. . . . We're going to celebrate, to rest and then we will prepare for France. We're facing another daunting task, but it's going to be a fantastic match."[65]

The game was fantastic for long stretches. With 78,011 fans looking on, France started the game, preferring to play on the break. In response, Croatia dominated the ball in the opening stages with Modric and Rakitic controlling the midfield. Nonetheless, France took the lead in the 18th minute after Griezmann dived to win a free kick thirty yards

*The World Cup final between France and Croatia produced one of the tournament's most exciting matches (Credit: Courtesy of the author).*

out on the right side of the penalty area. Mandzukic flicked the ensuing delivery into his own net, the first ever own goal in a World Cup final.

Croatia responded impressively and equalized ten minutes later from another dead ball situation. After France failed to clear, the ball fell to Perisic, who took one touch past N'Golo Kanté before firing into the bottom corner. With Croatia once again beginning to take control, France retook the lead in the 38th minute, this time from the penalty spot after Perisic handled in the box. Referee Nestor Pitana had initially awarded a corner kick, but reversed his decision following a lengthy VAR consultation. The decision would impact the rest of the match. "In a World Cup final, you do not give such a penalty," Dalic said.[66]

Croatia, who came from behind to win their four previous games on the road to the final, came out quickly in the second half, but were undone by the excellent *Les Bleus* counterattack shortly before the hour mark. Pogba unleashed Mbappe with a stunning cross-field diagonal, before arriving at the top of the box to score. His first effort

*France coach Didier Deschamps (center, alongside Croatia's Luka Modric and Brazil's Marta), who won the World Cup as a player in 1998, was named FIFA's manager of the year after guiding his country to a second title (Credit: Getty Images/FIFA.com).*

was blocked, but he picked up the rebound and curled past a wrong-footed Subasic. Mbappe's goal in the 65th minute killed the match. The nineteen-year-old, the first teenager to score in a World Cup final since Pelé in 1958, controlled Lucas Hernandez's cutback before drilling past Subasic into the bottom corner.

At the other end, Hugo Lloris's awful error in the 69th minute—after the Tottenham goalkeeper tried to knock the ball past an onrushing Mandzukic, only to hit it straight at his leg, and into the net—gave some life to Croatia's attack. But as it had all tournament, the French defense held firm. There would be no Croatia comeback as France powered to a 4–2 win to capture its second World Cup in history. The six-goal game was the most in a final since England beat West Germany 4–2 in 1966. Like the 1998 team, this France roster was loaded with immigrant talent and players of African descent. Once again, the country had come together, under the leadership of Didier Deschamps, to win soccer's biggest prize. "We did not play a huge game, but we showed mental quality," Deschamps said after the game. "And we scored four goals anyway."[67]

Amid a heavy post-game downpour—mixed with gold confetti—that soaked the players, Pogba, Mbappe, and their teammates celebrated into the night. The celebration served as a wonderful ending to what many consider the best World Cup in their lifetimes.

## NOTES

1. FIFA, *Report on Issues Related to the Russian Bid Team*, n.d., https://resources.fifa.com/image/upload/rus-report-2898806.pdf?cloudid=wjbtdmp5y ghi9czewnw1.

2. International Olympic Committee, "IOC Suspends Russian NOC and Creates a Path for Clean Individual Athletes to Compete in PyeongChang 2018 Under the Olympic Flag," December 5, 2017, https://www.olympic.org/news/ioc-suspends-russian-noc-and-creates-a-path-for-clean-individual-athletes-to-compete-in-pyeongchang-2018-under-the-olympic-flag.

3. FIFA, "Update on the Investigations Following the McLaren Reports," May 22, 2018, https://www.fifa.com/worldcup/news/update-on-the-investigations-following-the-mclaren-reports.

4. TASS, "Luzhniki Is Unique Stadium Where Architecture Meets High Technologies," March 7, 2018, http://tass.com/sport/993256.

5. News conference, October 11, 2017.

6. World Cup Draw ceremony, December 1, 2017.

7. Paul Gardner, "The Gnat's Eyebrow and Other VAR Stupidity," *Soccer America*, June 26, 2017, https://www.socceramerica.com/publications/article/73920/the-gnats-eyebrow-and-other-var-stupidities.html.

8. News conference, June 14, 2018.

9. News conference, June 15, 2018.

10. News conference, June 19, 2018.

11. News conference, June 25, 2018.

12. News conference, June 13, 2018.

13. News conference, June 15, 2018.

14. News conference, June 20, 2018.

15. News conference, June 25, 2018.

16. News conference, June 25, 2018.

17. News conference, June 16, 2018.

18. News conference, June 21, 2018.

19. News conference, June 26, 2018.

20. News conference, June 26, 2018.

21. News conference, March 27, 2018.

22. Interview, *El Trece*, May 27, 2018.

23. News conference, May 21, 2018.

24. News conference, June 16, 2018.

25. News conference, June 21, 2018.

26. News conference, June 21, 2018.

27. News conference, June 23, 2018.

28. News conference, June 26, 2018.

29. News conference, June 22, 2018.

30. News conference, June 22, 2018.

31. News conference, June 27, 2018.

32. News conference, June 27, 2018.

33. News conference, June 23, 2018.

34. News conference, June 27, 2018.

35. News conference, June 23, 2018.

36. News conference, June 23, 2018.

37. News conference, June 26, 2018.

38. News conference, June 28, 2018.

39. News conference, June 19, 2018.

40. News conference, June 26, 2018.

41. News conference, June 28, 2018.

42. News conference, June 30, 2018.

43. News conference, June 30, 2018.

44. News conference, June 30, 2018.

45. News conference, June 30, 2018.

46. News conference, June 30, 2018.

47. Graham Dunbar, "Happy Hosts Russia Wait for Spain Team Under Fire at Home," Associated Press, June 29, 2018.

48. News conference, July 1, 2018.

49. News conference, July 1, 2018.

50. News conference, July 2, 2018.

51. News conference, July 2, 2018.

52. News conference, July 2, 2018.

53. News conference, July 2, 2018.

54. News conference, July 3, 2018.

55. News conference, July 3, 2018.

56. News conference, July 3, 2018.

57. News conference, July 6, 2018.

58. News conference, July 6, 2018.

59. News conference, July 7, 2018.

60. News conference, July 7, 2018.

61. News conference, July 7, 2018.

62. News conference, July 10, 2018.

63. News conference, July 11, 2018.

64. News conference, July 11, 2018.

65. News conference, July 13, 2018.

66. News conference, July 15, 2018.

67. News conference, July 15, 2018.

# APPENDIX A:
# WORLD CUP STATS

**WINNERS**

| | |
|---|---|
| 1930 | Uruguay |
| 1934 | Italy |
| 1938 | Italy |
| 1950 | Uruguay |
| 1954 | West Germany |
| 1958 | Brazil |
| 1962 | Brazil |
| 1966 | England |
| 1970 | Brazil |
| 1974 | West Germany |
| 1978 | Argentina |
| 1982 | Italy |
| 1986 | Argentina |
| 1990 | West Germany |
| 1994 | Brazil |
| 1998 | France |
| 2002 | Brazil |
| 2006 | Italy |
| 2010 | Spain |
| 2014 | Germany |
| 2018 | France |

# 1930

## Group 1

France 4, Mexico 1
Argentina 1, France 0
Chile 3, Mexico 0
Argentina 6, Mexico 3
Chile 1, France 0
Argentina 3, Chile 1

|  | Played | Win | Draw | Loss | GF | GA | Pts. |
|---|---|---|---|---|---|---|---|
| 1. Argentina | 3 | 3 | 0 | 0 | 10 | 4 | 6 |
| 2. Chile | 3 | 2 | 0 | 1 | 5 | 3 | 4 |
| 3. France | 3 | 1 | 0 | 2 | 4 | 3 | 2 |
| 4. Mexico | 3 | 0 | 0 | 3 | 4 | 13 | 0 |

## Group 2

Yugoslavia 2, Brazil 1
Yugoslavia 4, Bolivia 0
Brazil 4, Bolivia 0

|  | Played | Win | Draw | Loss | GF | GA | Pts. |
|---|---|---|---|---|---|---|---|
| 1. Yugoslavia | 2 | 2 | 0 | 0 | 6 | 1 | 4 |
| 2. Brazil | 2 | 1 | 0 | 1 | 5 | 2 | 2 |
| 3. Bolivia | 2 | 0 | 0 | 2 | 0 | 8 | 0 |

## Group 3

Romania 3, Peru 1
Uruguay 1, Peru 0
Uruguay 4, Romania 0

|  | Played | Win | Draw | Loss | GF | GA | Pts. |
|---|---|---|---|---|---|---|---|
| 1. Uruguay | 2 | 0 | 0 | 0 | 5 | 0 | 4 |
| 2. Romania | 2 | 1 | 0 | 1 | 3 | 5 | 2 |
| 3. Peru | 2 | 0 | 0 | 2 | 1 | 4 | 0 |

## Group 4

United States 3, Belgium 0
United States 3, Paraguay 0
Paraguay 1, Belgium 0

|           | Played | Win | Draw | Loss | GF | GA | Pts. |
|-----------|--------|-----|------|------|----|----|------|
| 1. USA    | 2      | 2   | 0    | 0    | 6  | 0  | 4    |
| 2. Paraguay | 2    | 1   | 0    | 1    | 1  | 3  | 2    |
| 3. Belgium | 2     | 0   | 0    | 2    | 0  | 4  | 0    |

## Semifinals

Argentina 6, United States 1
Uruguay 6, Yugoslavia 1

## Final

Uruguay 4, Argentina 2

## 1934

### First Round

Sweden 3, Argentina 2
Germany 5, Belgium 2
Spain 3, Brazil 1
Switzerland 3, Holland 2
Hungary 4, Egypt 2
Italy 7, USA 1
Czechoslovakia 2, Romania 1
Austria 3, France 2 OT

### Quarterfinals

Austria 2, Hungary 1
Italy 1, Spain 1
Italy 1, Spain 0 (replay)

Germany 2, Sweden 1
Czechoslovakia 3, Switzerland 2

## Semifinals

Italy 1, Austria 0
Czechoslovakia 3, Germany 1

## Third Place

Germany 3, Austria 2

## Final

Italy 2, Czechoslovakia 1 OT

## 1938

## Preliminary Round

Switzerland 1, Germany 1 OT
Czechoslovakia 3, Holland 0 OT
Italy 2, Norway 1 OT
France 3, Belgium 1
Hungary 6, Dutch East Indies 0
Brazil 6, Poland 5 OT
Cuba 3, Romania 3 OT

## Preliminary Round Replays

Switzerland 4, Germany 2
Cuba 2, Romania 1

## Quarterfinals

Sweden 8, Cuba 0
Brazil 1, Czechoslovakia 1 OT
Hungary 2, Switzerland 0
Italy 3, France 1

## Quarterfinal Replay

Brazil 2, Czechoslovakia 1

## Semifinals

Italy 2, Brazil 1
Hungary 5, Sweden 1

## Third Place

Brazil 4, Sweden 2

## Final

Italy 4, Hungary 2

## 1950

## Group 1

Brazil 4, Mexico 0
Yugoslavia 3, Switzerland 0
Yugoslavia 4, Mexico 1
Brazil 2, Switzerland 2
Brazil 2, Yugoslavia 0
Switzerland 2, Mexico 1

|                  | Played | Win | Draw | Loss | GF | GA | Pts. |
|------------------|--------|-----|------|------|----|----|------|
| 1. Brazil        | 3      | 2   | 1    | 0    | 8  | 2  | 5    |
| 2. Yugoslavia    | 3      | 2   | 0    | 1    | 7  | 3  | 4    |
| 3. Switzerland   | 3      | 1   | 1    | 1    | 4  | 6  | 3    |
| 4. Mexico        | 3      | 0   | 0    | 3    | 2  | 10 | 0    |

## Group 2

England 2, Chile 0
Spain 3, United States 1

Spain 2, Chile 0
United States 1, England 0
Spain 1, England 0
Chile 5, United States 2

|  | Played | Win | Draw | Loss | GF | GA | Pts. |
|---|---|---|---|---|---|---|---|
| 1. Spain | 3 | 3 | 0 | 0 | 6 | 1 | 6 |
| 2. England | 3 | 1 | 0 | 2 | 2 | 2 | 2 |
| 3. Chile | 3 | 1 | 0 | 2 | 5 | 6 | 2 |
| 4. USA | 3 | 1 | 0 | 2 | 4 | 8 | 2 |

## Group 3

Sweden 3, Italy 2
Sweden 2, Paraguay 2
Italy 2, Paraguay 0

|  | Played | Win | Draw | Loss | GF | GA | Pts. |
|---|---|---|---|---|---|---|---|
| 1. Sweden | 2 | 1 | 1 | 0 | 5 | 4 | 3 |
| 2. Italy | 2 | 1 | 0 | 1 | 4 | 3 | 2 |
| 3. Paraguay | 2 | 0 | 1 | 1 | 2 | 4 | 1 |

## Group 4

Uruguay 8, Bolivia 0

|  | Played | Win | Draw | Loss | GF | GA | Pts. |
|---|---|---|---|---|---|---|---|
| 1. Uruguay | 1 | 1 | 0 | 0 | 8 | 0 | 2 |
| 2. Bolivia | 1 | 0 | 0 | 1 | 0 | 8 | 0 |

## Final Round-Robin Group

Brazil 7, Sweden 1
Uruguay 2, Spain 2
Brazil 6, Spain 1
Uruguay 3, Sweden 2
Sweden 3, Spain 1
Uruguay 2, Brazil 1

## 1954

### Group 1

Brazil 5, Mexico 0
Yugoslavia 1, France 0
France 3, Mexico 2
Brazil 1, Yugoslavia 1 OT

|  | Played | Win | Draw | Loss | GF | GA | Pts. |
|---|---|---|---|---|---|---|---|
| 1. Brazil | 2 | 1 | 1 | 0 | 6 | 1 | 3 |
| 2. Yugoslavia | 2 | 1 | 1 | 0 | 2 | 1 | 3 |
| 3. France | 2 | 1 | 0 | 1 | 3 | 3 | 2 |
| 4. Mexico | 2 | 0 | 0 | 2 | 2 | 8 | 0 |

### Group 2

West Germany 4, Turkey 1
Hungary 9, South Korea 0
Hungary 8, Germany 3
Turkey 7, South Korea 0

### Group 2 Playoff

West Germany 7, Turkey 2

|  | Played | Win | Draw | Loss | GF | GA | Pts. |
|---|---|---|---|---|---|---|---|
| 1. Hungary | 2 | 2 | 0 | 0 | 17 | 3 | 4 |
| 2. Turkey | 2 | 1 | 0 | 1 | 8 | 4 | 2 |
| 3. W. Germany | 2 | 1 | 0 | 1 | 7 | 9 | 2 |
| 4. S. Korea | 2 | 0 | 0 | 2 | 0 | 16 | 0 |

### Group 3

Uruguay 2, Czechoslovakia 0
Austria 1, Scotland 0
Uruguay 7, Scotland 0
Austria 5, Czechoslovakia 0

|  | Played | Win | Draw | Loss | GF | GA | Pts. |
|---|---|---|---|---|---|---|---|
| 1. Uruguay | 2 | 2 | 0 | 0 | 9 | 0 | 4 |
| 2. Austria | 2 | 2 | 0 | 0 | 6 | 0 | 4 |
| 3. Czechoslovakia | 2 | 0 | 0 | 2 | 0 | 7 | 0 |
| 4. Scotland | 2 | 0 | 0 | 2 | 0 | 8 | 0 |

## Group 4

England 4, Belgium 4 OT
Switzerland 2, Italy 1
England 2, Switzerland 0
Italy 4, Belgium 1

## Group 4 Playoff

Switzerland 4, Italy 1

|  | Played | Win | Draw | Loss | GF | GA | Pts. |
|---|---|---|---|---|---|---|---|
| 1. England | 2 | 1 | 1 | 0 | 6 | 4 | 3 |
| 2. Italy | 2 | 1 | 0 | 1 | 5 | 3 | 2 |
| 3. Switzerland | 2 | 1 | 0 | 1 | 2 | 3 | 2 |
| 4. Belgium | 2 | 0 | 1 | 1 | 5 | 8 | 1 |

## Quarterfinals

Uruguay 4, England 2
Austria 7, Switzerland 5
Hungary 4, Brazil 2
West Germany 2, Yugoslavia 0

## Semifinals

West Germany 6, Austria 1
Hungary 4, Uruguay 2 OT

## Third Place

Austria 3, Uruguay 1

## Final

Germany 3, Hungary 2

## 1958

### Group 1

Northern Ireland 1, Czechoslovakia 0
West Germany 3, Argentina 1
West Germany 2, Czechoslovakia 2
Argentina 3, Northern Ireland 1
Czechoslovakia 6, Argentina 1
West Germany 2, Northern Ireland 2

### Group 1 Playoff

Northern Ireland 2, Czechoslovakia 1 OT

|  | Played | Win | Draw | Loss | GF | GA | Pts. |
|---|---|---|---|---|---|---|---|
| 1. W. Germany | 3 | 1 | 2 | 0 | 7 | 5 | 4 |
| 2. Czechoslovakia | 3 | 1 | 1 | 1 | 8 | 4 | 3 |
| 3. N. Ireland | 3 | 1 | 1 | 1 | 4 | 5 | 3 |
| 4. Argentina | 3 | 1 | 0 | 2 | 5 | 10 | 2 |

### Group 2

France 7, Paraguay 3
Yugoslavia 1, Scotland 1
Paraguay 3, Scotland 2
Yugoslavia 3, France 2
Paraguay 3, Yugoslavia 3
France 2, Scotland 1

|  | Played | Win | Draw | Loss | GF | GA | Pts. |
|---|---|---|---|---|---|---|---|
| 1. France | 3 | 2 | 0 | 1 | 11 | 7 | 4 |
| 2. Yugoslavia | 3 | 1 | 2 | 0 | 7 | 6 | 4 |
| 3. Paraguay | 3 | 1 | 1 | 1 | 9 | 12 | 3 |
| 4. Scotland | 3 | 0 | 1 | 2 | 4 | 6 | 1 |

## Group 3

Hungary 1, Wales 1
Sweden 3, Mexico 0
Mexico 1, Wales 1
Sweden 2, Hungary 1
Hungary 4, Mexico 0
Sweden 0, Wales 0

## Group 3 Playoff

Wales 2, Hungary 1

|  | Played | Win | Draw | Loss | GF | GA | Pts. |
|---|---|---|---|---|---|---|---|
| 1. Sweden | 3 | 2 | 1 | 0 | 5 | 1 | 5 |
| 2. Hungary | 3 | 1 | 1 | 1 | 6 | 3 | 3 |
| 3. Wales | 3 | 1 | 3 | 0 | 2 | 2 | 3 |
| 4. Mexico | 3 | 0 | 1 | 2 | 1 | 8 | 1 |

## Group 4

USSR 2, England 2
Brazil 3, Austria 0
USSR 2, Austria 0
Brazil 0, England 0
England 2, Austria 2
Brazil 2, USSR 0

## Group 4 Playoff

USSR 1, England 0

|  | Played | Win | Draw | Loss | GF | GA | Pts. |
|---|---|---|---|---|---|---|---|
| 1. Brazil | 3 | 2 | 1 | 0 | 5 | 0 | 5 |
| 2. England | 3 | 0 | 3 | 0 | 4 | 4 | 3 |
| 3. USSR | 3 | 1 | 1 | 1 | 4 | 4 | 3 |
| 4. Austria | 3 | 0 | 1 | 2 | 2 | 7 | 1 |

## Quarterfinals

Brazil 1, Wales 0
West Germany 1, Yugoslavia 0
France 4, Northern Ireland 0
Sweden 2,  USSR 0

## Semifinals

Sweden 3, West Germany 1
Brazil 5, France 2

## Third Place

France 6, West Germany 3

## Final

Brazil 5, Sweden 2

## 1962

## Group 1

Uruguay 2, Colombia 1
USSR 2, Yugoslavia 0
Yugoslavia 3, Uruguay 1
USSR 4, Colombia 4
USSR 2, Uruguay 1
Yugoslavia 5, Colombia 0

|  | Played | Win | Draw | Loss | GF | GA | Pts. |
|---|---|---|---|---|---|---|---|
| 1. USSR | 3 | 2 | 1 | 0 | 8 | 5 | 5 |
| 2. Yugoslavia | 3 | 2 | 0 | 1 | 8 | 3 | 4 |
| 3. Uruguay | 3 | 1 | 1 | 1 | 4 | 6 | 3 |
| 4. Colombia | 3 | 0 | 1 | 2 | 5 | 11 | 1 |

## Group 2

Chile 3, Switzerland 1
West Germany 0, Italy 0
Chile 2, Italy 0
West Germany 2, Switzerland 1
West Germany 2, Chile 0
Italy 3, Switzerland 0

|  | Played | Win | Draw | Loss | GF | GA | Pts. |
|---|---|---|---|---|---|---|---|
| 1. W. Germany | 3 | 2 | 1 | 0 | 4 | 1 | 5 |
| 2. Chile | 3 | 2 | 0 | 1 | 5 | 3 | 4 |
| 3. Italy | 3 | 1 | 1 | 1 | 3 | 2 | 3 |
| 4. Switzerland | 3 | 0 | 0 | 3 | 2 | 8 | 0 |

## Group 3

Brazil 2, Mexico 0
Czechoslovakia 1, Spain 0
Brazil 0, Czechoslovakia 0
Spain 1, Mexico 0
Brazil 2, Spain 1
Mexico 3, Czechoslovakia 1

|  | Played | Win | Draw | Loss | GF | GA | Pts. |
|---|---|---|---|---|---|---|---|
| 1. Brazil | 3 | 2 | 1 | 0 | 4 | 1 | 5 |
| 2. Czechoslovakia | 3 | 1 | 1 | 1 | 2 | 3 | 3 |
| 3. Mexico | 3 | 1 | 0 | 2 | 3 | 4 | 2 |
| 4. Spain | 3 | 1 | 0 | 2 | 2 | 3 | 2 |

## Group 4

Argentina 1, Bulgaria 0
Hungary 2, England 1
England 3, Argentina 1
Hungary 6, Bulgaria 1
Hungary 0, Argentina 0
England 0, Bulgaria 0

| | Played | Win | Draw | Loss | GF | GA | Pts. |
|---|---|---|---|---|---|---|---|
| 1. Hungary | 3 | 2 | 1 | 0 | 8 | 2 | 5 |
| 2. England | 3 | 1 | 1 | 1 | 4 | 3 | 3 |
| 3. Argentina | 3 | 1 | 1 | 1 | 2 | 3 | 3 |
| 4. Bulgaria | 3 | 0 | 1 | 2 | 1 | 7 | 1 |

## Quarterfinals

Chile 2, USSR 1
Czechoslovakia 1, Hungary 0
Yugoslavia 1, West Germany 0
Brazil 3, England 1

## Semifinals

Brazil 4, Chile 2
Czechoslovakia 3, Yugoslavia 1

## Third Place

Chile 1, Yugoslavia 0

## Final

Brazil 3, Czechoslovakia 1

## 1966

## Group 1

England 0, Uruguay 0
France 1, Mexico 1
Uruguay 2, France 1
England 2, Mexico 0
Uruguay 0, Mexico 0
England 2, France 0

|  | Played | Win | Draw | Loss | GF | GA | Pts. |
|---|---|---|---|---|---|---|---|
| 1. England | 3 | 2 | 1 | 0 | 4 | 0 | 5 |
| 2. Uruguay | 3 | 1 | 2 | 0 | 2 | 1 | 4 |
| 3. Mexico | 3 | 0 | 2 | 1 | 1 | 3 | 2 |
| 4. France | 3 | 0 | 1 | 2 | 2 | 5 | 1 |

## Group 2

West Germany 5, Switzerland 0
Argentina 2, Spain 1
Spain 2, Switzerland 1
West Germany 0, Argentina 0
Argentina 2, Switzerland 0
West Germany 2, Spain 1

|  | Played | Win | Draw | Loss | GF | GA | Pts. |
|---|---|---|---|---|---|---|---|
| 1. W. Germany | 3 | 2 | 1 | 0 | 7 | 1 | 5 |
| 2. Argentina | 3 | 2 | 1 | 0 | 4 | 1 | 5 |
| 3. Spain | 3 | 1 | 0 | 2 | 4 | 5 | 2 |
| 4. Switzerland | 3 | 0 | 0 | 3 | 1 | 9 | 0 |

## Group 3

Brazil 2, Bulgaria 0
Portugal 3, Hungary 1
Hungary 3, Brazil 1
Portugal 3, Bulgaria 0
Portugal 3, Brazil 1
Hungary 3, Bulgaria 1

|  | Played | Win | Draw | Loss | GF | GA | Pts. |
|---|---|---|---|---|---|---|---|
| 1. Portugal | 3 | 3 | 0 | 0 | 9 | 2 | 6 |
| 2. Hungary | 3 | 2 | 0 | 1 | 7 | 5 | 4 |
| 3. Brazil | 3 | 1 | 0 | 2 | 4 | 6 | 2 |
| 4. Bulgaria | 3 | 0 | 0 | 3 | 1 | 8 | 0 |

## Group 4

USSR 3, North Korea 0
Italy 2, Chile 0

North Korea 1, Chile 1
USSR 1, Italy 0
North Korea 1, Italy 0
USSR 2, Chile 1

|  | Played | Win | Draw | Loss | GF | GA | Pts. |
|---|---|---|---|---|---|---|---|
| 1. USSR | 3 | 3 | 0 | 0 | 6 | 1 | 6 |
| 2. N. Korea | 3 | 1 | 1 | 1 | 2 | 4 | 3 |
| 3. Italy | 3 | 1 | 0 | 2 | 2 | 2 | 2 |
| 4. Chile | 3 | 0 | 1 | 2 | 2 | 5 | 1 |

## Quarterfinals

Portugal 5, North Korea 3
England 1, Argentina 0
West Germany 4, Uruguay 0
USSR 2, Hungary 1

## Semifinals

West Germany 2, USSR 1
England 2, Portugal 1

## Third Place

Portugal 2, USSR 1

## Final

England 4, West Germany 2 OT

## 1970

## Group 1

Mexico 0, USSR 0
Belgium 3, El Salvador 0
USSR 4, Belgium 1

Mexico 4, El Salvador 0
USSR 2, El Salvador 0
Mexico 1, Belgium 0

|                   | Played | Win | Draw | Loss | GF | GA | Pts. |
|-------------------|--------|-----|------|------|----|----|------|
| 1. USSR           | 3      | 2   | 1    | 0    | 6  | 1  | 5    |
| 2. Mexico         | 3      | 2   | 1    | 0    | 5  | 0  | 5    |
| 3. Belgium        | 3      | 1   | 0    | 2    | 4  | 5  | 2    |
| 4. El Salvador    | 3      | 0   | 0    | 3    | 0  | 9  | 0    |

## Group 2

Uruguay 2, Israel 0
Italy 1, Sweden 0
Uruguay 0, Italy 0
Sweden 1, Israel 1
Sweden 1, Uruguay 0
Italy 0, Israel 0

|             | Played | Win | Draw | Loss | GF | GA | Pts. |
|-------------|--------|-----|------|------|----|----|------|
| 1. Italy    | 3      | 1   | 2    | 0    | 1  | 0  | 4    |
| 2. Uruguay  | 3      | 1   | 1    | 1    | 2  | 1  | 3    |
| 3. Sweden   | 3      | 1   | 1    | 1    | 2  | 2  | 3    |
| 4. Israel   | 3      | 0   | 2    | 1    | 1  | 3  | 2    |

## Group 3

England 1, Romania 0
Brazil 4, Czechoslovakia 1
Romania 2, Czechoslovakia 1
Brazil 1, England 0
Brazil 3, Romania 2
England 1, Czechoslovakia 0

|                     | Played | Win | Draw | Loss | GF | GA | Pts. |
|---------------------|--------|-----|------|------|----|----|------|
| 1. Brazil           | 3      | 3   | 0    | 0    | 8  | 3  | 6    |
| 2. England          | 3      | 2   | 0    | 1    | 2  | 1  | 4    |
| 3. Romania          | 3      | 1   | 0    | 2    | 4  | 5  | 2    |
| 4. Czechoslovakia   | 3      | 0   | 0    | 3    | 2  | 7  | 0    |

## Group 4

Peru 3, Bulgaria 2
West Germany 2, Morocco 1
Peru 3, Morocco 0
West Germany 5, Bulgaria 2
West Germany 3, Peru 1
Bulgaria 1, Morocco 1

|              | Played | Win | Draw | Loss | GF | GA | Pts. |
|--------------|--------|-----|------|------|----|----|------|
| 1. W. Germany | 3      | 3   | 0    | 0    | 10 | 4  | 6    |
| 2. Peru       | 3      | 2   | 0    | 1    | 7  | 5  | 4    |
| 3. Bulgaria   | 3      | 0   | 1    | 2    | 5  | 9  | 1    |
| 4. Morocco    | 3      | 0   | 1    | 2    | 2  | 6  | 1    |

## Quarterfinals

Brazil 4, Peru 2
West Germany 3, England 2 OT
Uruguay 1, USSR 0 OT
Italy 4, Mexico 1

## Semifinals

Brazil 3, Uruguay 1
Italy 4, West Germany 3 OT

## Third Place

West Germany 1, Uruguay 0

## Final

Brazil 4, Italy 1

## 1974

## Group 1

West Germany 1, Chile 0
East Germany 2, Australia 0

Chile 1, East Germany 1
West Germany 3, Australia 0
Australia 0, Chile 0
East Germany 1, West Germany 0

|  | Played | Win | Draw | Loss | GF | GA | Pts. |
|---|---|---|---|---|---|---|---|
| 1. E. Germany | 3 | 2 | 1 | 0 | 4 | 1 | 5 |
| 2. W. Germany | 3 | 2 | 0 | 1 | 4 | 1 | 4 |
| 3. Chile | 3 | 0 | 2 | 1 | 1 | 2 | 2 |
| 4. Australia | 3 | 0 | 1 | 2 | 0 | 5 | 1 |

## Group 2

Brazil 0, Yugoslavia 0
Scotland 2, Zaire 0
Yugoslavia 9, Zaire 0
Scotland 0, Brazil 0
Scotland 1, Yugoslavia 1
Brazil 3, Zaire 0

|  | Played | Win | Draw | Loss | GF | GA | Pts. |
|---|---|---|---|---|---|---|---|
| 1. Yugoslavia | 3 | 1 | 2 | 0 | 10 | 1 | 4 |
| 2. Brazil | 3 | 1 | 2 | 0 | 3 | 0 | 4 |
| 3. Scotland | 3 | 1 | 2 | 0 | 3 | 1 | 4 |
| 4. Zaire | 3 | 0 | 0 | 3 | 0 | 14 | 0 |

## Group 3

Sweden 0, Bulgaria 0
Holland 2, Uruguay 0
Holland 0, Sweden 0
Bulgaria 1, Uruguay 1
Holland 4, Bulgaria 1
Sweden 3, Uruguay 0

|  | Played | Win | Draw | Loss | GF | GA | Pts. |
|---|---|---|---|---|---|---|---|
| 1. Holland | 3 | 2 | 1 | 0 | 6 | 1 | 5 |
| 2. Sweden | 3 | 1 | 2 | 0 | 3 | 0 | 4 |
| 3. Bulgaria | 3 | 0 | 2 | 1 | 2 | 5 | 2 |
| 4. Uruguay | 3 | 0 | 1 | 2 | 1 | 6 | 1 |

## Group 4

Italy 3, Haiti 1
Poland 3, Argentina 2
Poland 7, Haiti 0
Argentina 1, Italy 1
Argentina 4, Haiti 1
Poland 2, Italy 1

|              | Played | Win | Draw | Loss | GF | GA | Pts. |
|--------------|--------|-----|------|------|----|----|------|
| 1. Poland    | 3      | 3   | 0    | 0    | 12 | 3  | 6    |
| 2. Argentina | 3      | 1   | 1    | 1    | 7  | 5  | 3    |
| 3. Italy     | 3      | 1   | 1    | 1    | 5  | 4  | 3    |
| 4. Haiti     | 3      | 0   | 0    | 3    | 2  | 14 | 0    |

## Final Round

*Group A*

Holland 4, Argentina 0
Brazil 1, East Germany 0
Holland 2, East Germany 0
Brazil 2, Argentina 1
Holland 2, Brazil 0
Argentina 1, East Germany 1

|               | Played | Win | Draw | Loss | GF | GA | Pts. |
|---------------|--------|-----|------|------|----|----|------|
| 1. Holland    | 3      | 3   | 0    | 0    | 8  | 0  | 6    |
| 2. Brazil     | 3      | 2   | 0    | 1    | 3  | 3  | 4    |
| 3. E. Germany | 3      | 0   | 1    | 2    | 1  | 4  | 1    |
| 4. Argentina  | 3      | 0   | 1    | 2    | 2  | 7  | 1    |

*Group B*

West Germany 2, Yugoslavia 0
Poland 1, Sweden 0
West Germany 4, Sweden 2
Poland 2, Yugoslavia 1
Sweden 2, Yugoslavia 1
West Germany 1, Poland 0

| | Played | Win | Draw | Loss | GF | GA | Pts. |
|---|---|---|---|---|---|---|---|
| 1. W. Germany | 3 | 3 | 0 | 0 | 7 | 2 | 6 |
| 2. Poland | 3 | 2 | 0 | 1 | 3 | 2 | 4 |
| 3. Sweden | 3 | 1 | 0 | 2 | 4 | 6 | 2 |
| 4. Yugoslavia | 3 | 0 | 0 | 3 | 2 | 6 | 0 |

## Third Place

Poland 1, Brazil 0

## Final

West Germany 2, Holland 1

## 1978

### Group 1

Argentina 2, Hungary 1
Italy 2, France 1
Argentina 2, France 1
Italy 3, Hungary 1
Italy 1, Argentina 0
France 3, Hungary 1

| | Played | Win | Draw | Loss | GF | GA | Pts. |
|---|---|---|---|---|---|---|---|
| 1. Italy | 3 | 3 | 0 | 0 | 6 | 2 | 6 |
| 2. Argentina | 3 | 2 | 0 | 1 | 4 | 3 | 4 |
| 3. France | 3 | 1 | 0 | 2 | 5 | 5 | 2 |
| 4. Hungary | 3 | 0 | 0 | 3 | 3 | 8 | 0 |

### Group 2

West Germany 0, Poland 0
Tunisia 3, Mexico 1
West Germany 6, Mexico 0
Poland 1, Tunisia 0

West Germany 0, Tunisia 0
Poland 3, Mexico 1

|              | Played | Win | Draw | Loss | GF | GA | Pts. |
|--------------|--------|-----|------|------|----|----|------|
| 1. Poland    | 3      | 2   | 1    | 0    | 4  | 1  | 5    |
| 2. W. Germany| 3      | 1   | 2    | 0    | 6  | 0  | 4    |
| 3. Tunisia   | 3      | 1   | 1    | 1    | 3  | 2  | 3    |
| 4. Mexico    | 3      | 0   | 0    | 3    | 2  | 12 | 0    |

## Group 3

Austria 2, Spain 1
Sweden 1, Brazil 1
Austria 1, Sweden 0
Brazil 0, Spain 0
Spain 1, Sweden 0
Brazil 1, Austria 0

|              | Played | Win | Draw | Loss | GF | GA | Pts. |
|--------------|--------|-----|------|------|----|----|------|
| 1. Austria   | 3      | 2   | 0    | 1    | 3  | 2  | 4    |
| 2. Brazil    | 3      | 1   | 2    | 0    | 2  | 1  | 4    |
| 3. Spain     | 3      | 1   | 1    | 1    | 2  | 2  | 3    |
| 4. Sweden    | 3      | 0   | 1    | 2    | 1  | 3  | 1    |

## Group 4

Peru 3, Scotland 1
Holland 3, Iran 0
Scotland 1, Iran 1
Holland 0, Peru 0
Peru 4, Iran 1
Scotland 3, Holland 2

|              | Played | Win | Draw | Loss | GF | GA | Pts. |
|--------------|--------|-----|------|------|----|----|------|
| 1. Peru      | 3      | 2   | 1    | 0    | 7  | 2  | 5    |
| 2. Holland   | 3      | 1   | 1    | 1    | 5  | 3  | 3    |
| 3. Scotland  | 3      | 1   | 1    | 1    | 5  | 6  | 3    |
| 4. Iran      | 3      | 0   | 1    | 2    | 2  | 8  | 1    |

## Final Round

*Group A*

West Germany 0, Italy 0
Holland 5, Austria 1
Italy 1, Austria 0
West Germany 2, Holland 2
Holland 2, Italy 1
Austria 3, West Germany 2

|              | Played | Win | Draw | Loss | GF | GA | Pts. |
| ------------ | ------ | --- | ---- | ---- | -- | -- | ---- |
| 1. Holland   | 3      | 2   | 1    | 0    | 9  | 4  | 5    |
| 2. Italy     | 3      | 1   | 1    | 1    | 2  | 2  | 3    |
| 3. W. Germany| 3      | 0   | 2    | 1    | 4  | 5  | 2    |
| 4. Austria   | 3      | 1   | 0    | 2    | 4  | 8  | 2    |

*Group B*

Brazil 3, Peru 0
Argentina 2, Poland 0
Poland 1, Peru 0
Argentina 0, Brazil 0
Brazil 3, Poland 1
Argentina 6, Peru 0

|              | Played | Win | Draw | Loss | GF | GA | Pts. |
| ------------ | ------ | --- | ---- | ---- | -- | -- | ---- |
| 1. Argentina | 3      | 2   | 1    | 0    | 8  | 0  | 5    |
| 2. Brazil    | 3      | 2   | 1    | 0    | 6  | 1  | 5    |
| 3. Poland    | 3      | 1   | 0    | 2    | 2  | 5  | 2    |
| 4. Peru      | 3      | 0   | 0    | 3    | 0  | 10 | 0    |

## Third Place

Brazil 2, Italy 1

## Final

Argentina 3, Holland 1 OT

## 1982

### Group 1

Italy 0, Poland 0
Peru 0, Cameroon 0
Italy 1, Peru 1
Poland 0, Cameroon 0
Poland 5, Peru 1
Italy 1, Cameroon 1

|  | Played | Win | Draw | Loss | GF | GA | Pts. |
|---|---|---|---|---|---|---|---|
| 1. Poland | 3 | 1 | 2 | 0 | 5 | 1 | 4 |
| 2. Italy | 3 | 0 | 3 | 0 | 2 | 2 | 3 |
| 3. Cameroon | 3 | 0 | 3 | 0 | 1 | 1 | 3 |
| 4. Peru | 3 | 0 | 2 | 1 | 2 | 6 | 2 |

### Group 2

Algeria 2, West Germany 1
Austria 1, Chile 0
West Germany 4, Chile 1
Austria 2, Algeria 0
Algeria 3, Chile 2
West Germany 1, Austria 0

|  | Played | Win | Draw | Loss | GF | GA | Pts. |
|---|---|---|---|---|---|---|---|
| 1. W. Germany | 3 | 2 | 0 | 1 | 6 | 3 | 4 |
| 2. Austria | 3 | 2 | 0 | 1 | 3 | 1 | 4 |
| 3. Algeria | 3 | 2 | 0 | 1 | 5 | 5 | 4 |
| 4. Chile | 3 | 0 | 0 | 3 | 3 | 8 | 0 |

### Group 3

Belgium 1, Argentina 0
Hungary 10, El Salvador 1
Argentina 4, Hungary 1
Belgium 1, El Salvador 0
Belgium 1, Hungary 1
Argentina 2, El Salvador 0

| | Played | Win | Draw | Loss | GF | GA | Pts. |
|---|---|---|---|---|---|---|---|
| 1. Belgium | 3 | 2 | 1 | 0 | 3 | 1 | 5 |
| 2. Argentina | 3 | 2 | 0 | 1 | 6 | 2 | 4 |
| 3. Hungary | 3 | 1 | 1 | 1 | 12 | 6 | 3 |
| 4. El Salvador | 3 | 0 | 0 | 3 | 1 | 13 | 0 |

## Group 4

England 3, France 1
Czechoslovakia 1, Kuwait 1
England 2, Czechoslovakia 0
France 4, Kuwait 1
France 1, Czechoslovakia 1
England 1, Kuwait 0

| | Played | Win | Draw | Loss | GF | GA | Pts. |
|---|---|---|---|---|---|---|---|
| 1. England | 3 | 3 | 0 | 0 | 6 | 1 | 6 |
| 2. France | 3 | 1 | 1 | 1 | 6 | 5 | 3 |
| 3. Czechoslovakia | 3 | 0 | 2 | 1 | 2 | 4 | 2 |
| 4. Kuwait | 3 | 0 | 1 | 2 | 2 | 6 | 1 |

## Group 5

Spain 1, Honduras 1
Yugoslavia 0, Northern Ireland 0
Spain 2, Yugoslavia 1
Honduras 1, Northern Ireland 1
Yugoslavia 1, Honduras 0
Northern Ireland 1, Spain 0

| | Played | Win | Draw | Loss | GF | GA | Pts. |
|---|---|---|---|---|---|---|---|
| 1. N. Ireland | 3 | 1 | 2 | 0 | 2 | 1 | 4 |
| 2. Spain | 3 | 1 | 1 | 1 | 3 | 3 | 3 |
| 3. Yugoslavia | 3 | 1 | 1 | 1 | 2 | 2 | 3 |
| 4. Honduras | 3 | 0 | 2 | 1 | 2 | 3 | 2 |

## Group 6

Brazil 2, USSR 1
Scotland 5, New Zealand 2

Brazil 4, Scotland 1
USSR 3, New Zealand 0
USSR 2, Scotland 2
Brazil 4, New Zealand 0

|  | Played | Win | Draw | Loss | GF | GA | Pts. |
|---|---|---|---|---|---|---|---|
| 1. Brazil | 3 | 3 | 0 | 0 | 10 | 2 | 6 |
| 2. USSR | 3 | 1 | 1 | 1 | 6 | 4 | 3 |
| 3. Scotland | 3 | 1 | 1 | 1 | 8 | 8 | 3 |
| 4. N. Zealand | 3 | 0 | 0 | 3 | 2 | 12 | 0 |

## Second Round

*Group A*

Poland 3, Belgium 0
USSR 1, Belgium 0
Poland 0, USSR 0

|  | Played | Win | Draw | Loss | GF | GA | Pts. |
|---|---|---|---|---|---|---|---|
| 1. Poland | 2 | 1 | 1 | 0 | 3 | 0 | 3 |
| 2. USSR | 2 | 1 | 1 | 0 | 1 | 0 | 3 |
| 3. Belgium | 2 | 0 | 0 | 2 | 0 | 4 | 0 |

*Group B*

West Germany 0, England 0
West Germany 2, Spain 1
Spain 0, England 0

|  | Played | Win | Draw | Loss | GF | GA | Pts. |
|---|---|---|---|---|---|---|---|
| 1. W. Germany | 2 | 1 | 1 | 0 | 2 | 1 | 3 |
| 2. England | 2 | 0 | 2 | 0 | 0 | 0 | 2 |
| 3. Spain | 2 | 0 | 1 | 1 | 1 | 2 | 1 |

*Group C*

Italy 2, Argentina 1
Brazil 3, Argentina 1
Italy 3, Brazil 2

| | Played | Win | Draw | Loss | GF | GA | Pts. |
|---|---|---|---|---|---|---|---|
| 1. Italy | 2 | 2 | 0 | 0 | 5 | 3 | 4 |
| 2. Brazil | 2 | 1 | 0 | 1 | 5 | 4 | 2 |
| 3. Argentina | 2 | 0 | 0 | 2 | 2 | 5 | 0 |

*Group D*

France 1, Austria 0
Austria 2, Northern Ireland 2
France 4, Northern Ireland 1

| | Played | Win | Draw | Loss | GF | GA | Pts. |
|---|---|---|---|---|---|---|---|
| 1. France | 2 | 2 | 0 | 0 | 5 | 1 | 4 |
| 2. Austria | 2 | 0 | 1 | 1 | 2 | 3 | 1 |
| 3. N. Ireland | 2 | 0 | 1 | 1 | 3 | 6 | 1 |

## Semifinals

Italy 2, Poland 0
West Germany 3, France 3 OT (West Germany wins 5–4 on penalties)

## Third Place

Poland 3, France 2

## Final

Italy 3, West Germany 1

## 1986

## Group A

Bulgaria 1, Italy 1
Argentina 3, South Korea 1
South Korea 1, Bulgaria 1
Italy 1, Argentina 1

Argentina 2, Bulgaria 0
Italy 3, South Korea 2

| | Played | Win | Draw | Loss | GF | GA | Pts. |
|---|---|---|---|---|---|---|---|
| 1. Argentina | 3 | 2 | 1 | 0 | 6 | 2 | 5 |
| 2. Italy | 3 | 1 | 2 | 0 | 5 | 4 | 4 |
| 3. Bulgaria | 3 | 0 | 2 | 1 | 2 | 4 | 2 |
| 4. S. Korea | 3 | 0 | 1 | 2 | 4 | 7 | 1 |

## Group B

Mexico 2, Belgium 1
Paraguay 1, Iraq 0
Mexico 1, Paraguay 1
Belgium 2, Iraq 1
Mexico 1, Iraq 0
Paraguay 2, Belgium 2

| | Played | Win | Draw | Loss | GF | GA | Pts. |
|---|---|---|---|---|---|---|---|
| 1. Mexico | 3 | 2 | 1 | 0 | 4 | 2 | 5 |
| 2. Paraguay | 3 | 1 | 2 | 0 | 4 | 3 | 4 |
| 3. Belgium | 3 | 1 | 1 | 1 | 5 | 5 | 3 |
| 4. Iraq | 3 | 0 | 0 | 3 | 1 | 4 | 0 |

## Group C

France 1, Canada 0
USSR 6, Hungary 0
France 1, USSR 1
Hungary 2, Canada 0
USSR 2, Canada 0
France 3, Hungary 0

| | Played | Win | Draw | Loss | GF | GA | Pts. |
|---|---|---|---|---|---|---|---|
| 1. USSR | 3 | 2 | 1 | 0 | 9 | 1 | 5 |
| 2. France | 3 | 2 | 1 | 0 | 5 | 1 | 5 |
| 3. Hungary | 3 | 1 | 0 | 2 | 2 | 9 | 2 |
| 4. Canada | 3 | 0 | 0 | 3 | 0 | 5 | 0 |

## Group D

Brazil 1, Spain 0
Algeria 1, Northern Ireland 1
Brazil 1, Algeria 0
Spain 2, Northern Ireland 1
Brazil 3, Northern Ireland 0
Spain 3, Algeria 0

|  | Played | Win | Draw | Loss | GF | GA | Pts. |
|---|---|---|---|---|---|---|---|
| 1. Brazil | 3 | 3 | 0 | 0 | 5 | 0 | 6 |
| 2. Spain | 3 | 2 | 0 | 1 | 5 | 2 | 4 |
| 3. N. Ireland | 3 | 0 | 1 | 2 | 2 | 6 | 1 |
| 4. Algeria | 3 | 0 | 1 | 2 | 1 | 5 | 1 |

## Group E

Denmark 1, Scotland 0
Uruguay 1, West Germany 1
Denmark 6, Uruguay 1
West Germany 2, Scotland 1
Uruguay 0, Scotland 0
Denmark 2, West Germany 0

|  | Played | Win | Draw | Loss | GF | GA | Pts. |
|---|---|---|---|---|---|---|---|
| 1. Denmark | 3 | 3 | 0 | 0 | 9 | 1 | 6 |
| 2. W. Germany | 3 | 1 | 1 | 1 | 3 | 4 | 3 |
| 3. Uruguay | 3 | 0 | 2 | 1 | 2 | 7 | 2 |
| 4. Scotland | 3 | 0 | 1 | 2 | 1 | 3 | 1 |

## Group F

Morocco 0, Poland 0
Portugal 1, England 0
England 0, Morocco 0
Poland 1, Portugal 0
Morocco 3, Portugal 1
England 3, Poland 0

|            | Played | Win | Draw | Loss | GF | GA | Pts. |
|------------|--------|-----|------|------|----|----|------|
| 1. Morocco | 3      | 1   | 2    | 0    | 3  | 1  | 4    |
| 2. England | 3      | 1   | 1    | 1    | 3  | 1  | 3    |
| 3. Poland  | 3      | 1   | 1    | 1    | 1  | 3  | 3    |
| 4. Portugal| 3      | 1   | 0    | 2    | 2  | 4  | 2    |

## Round of 16

Belgium 4, USSR 3 OT
Mexico 2, Bulgaria 0
Brazil 4, Poland 0
Argentina 1, Uruguay 0
France 2, Italy 0
West Germany 1, Morocco 0
England 3, Paraguay 0
Spain 5, Denmark 1

## Quarterfinals

France 1, Brazil 1 OT (France wins 4–3 on penalties)
West Germany 0, Mexico 0 OT  (West Germany wins 4–1 on
    penalties)
Argentina 2, England 1
Belgium 1, Spain 1 OT (Belgium wins 5–4 on penalties)

## Semifinals

West Germany 2, France 0
Argentina 2, Belgium 0

## Third Place

France 4, Belgium 2 OT

## Final

Argentina 3, West Germany 2

## 1990

### Group A

Italy 1, Austria 0
Czechoslovakia 5, United States 1
Italy 1, United States 0
Czechoslovakia 1, Austria 0
Austria 2, United States 1
Italy 2, Czechoslovakia 0

|                    | Played | Win | Draw | Loss | GF | GA | Pts. |
|--------------------|--------|-----|------|------|----|----|------|
| 1. Italy           | 3      | 3   | 0    | 0    | 4  | 0  | 6    |
| 2. Czechoslovakia  | 3      | 2   | 0    | 1    | 6  | 3  | 4    |
| 3. Austria         | 3      | 1   | 0    | 2    | 2  | 3  | 2    |
| 4. USA             | 3      | 0   | 0    | 3    | 2  | 8  | 0    |

### Group B

Cameroon 1, Argentina 0
Romania 2, USSR 0
Argentina 2, USSR 0
Cameroon 2, Romania 1
USSR 4, Cameroon 0
Argentina 1, Romania 1

|                | Played | Win | Draw | Loss | GF | GA | Pts. |
|----------------|--------|-----|------|------|----|----|------|
| 1. Cameroon    | 3      | 2   | 0    | 1    | 3  | 5  | 4    |
| 2. Romania     | 3      | 1   | 1    | 1    | 4  | 3  | 3    |
| 3. Argentina   | 3      | 1   | 1    | 1    | 3  | 2  | 3    |
| 4. USSR        | 3      | 1   | 0    | 2    | 4  | 4  | 2    |

### Group C

Brazil 2, Sweden 1
Costa Rica 1, Scotland 0
Scotland 2, Sweden 1
Brazil 1, Costa Rica 0

Costa Rica 2, Sweden 1
Brazil 1, Scotland 0

|              | Played | Win | Draw | Loss | GF | GA | Pts. |
|--------------|--------|-----|------|------|----|----|------|
| 1. Brazil    | 3      | 3   | 0    | 0    | 4  | 1  | 6    |
| 2. Costa Rica| 3      | 2   | 0    | 1    | 3  | 2  | 4    |
| 3. Scotland  | 3      | 1   | 0    | 2    | 2  | 3  | 2    |
| 4. Sweden    | 3      | 0   | 0    | 3    | 3  | 6  | 0    |

## Group D

Colombia 2, UAE 0
West Germany 4, Yugoslavia 1
Yugoslavia 1, Colombia 0
West Germany 5, UAE 1
Yugoslavia 4, UAE 1
West Germany 1, Colombia 1

|               | Played | Win | Draw | Loss | GF | GA | Pts. |
|---------------|--------|-----|------|------|----|----|------|
| 1. W. Germany | 3      | 2   | 1    | 0    | 10 | 3  | 5    |
| 2. Yugoslavia | 3      | 2   | 0    | 1    | 6  | 5  | 4    |
| 3. Colombia   | 3      | 1   | 1    | 1    | 3  | 2  | 3    |
| 4. UAE        | 3      | 0   | 0    | 3    | 2  | 11 | 0    |

## Group E

Belgium 2, South Korea 0
Uruguay 0, Spain 0
Spain 3, South Korea 1
Belgium 3, Uruguay 1
Uruguay 1, South Korea 0
Spain 2, Belgium 1

|             | Played | Win | Draw | Loss | GF | GA | Pts. |
|-------------|--------|-----|------|------|----|----|------|
| 1. Spain    | 3      | 2   | 1    | 0    | 5  | 2  | 5    |
| 2. Belgium  | 3      | 2   | 0    | 1    | 6  | 3  | 4    |
| 3. Uruguay  | 3      | 1   | 1    | 1    | 2  | 3  | 3    |
| 4. S. Korea | 3      | 0   | 0    | 3    | 1  | 6  | 0    |

## Group F

England 1, Ireland 1
Holland 1, Egypt 1
England 0, Holland 0
Ireland 0, Egypt 0
England 1, Egypt 0
Ireland 1, Holland 1

|              | Played | Win | Draw | Loss | GF | GA | Pts. |
|--------------|--------|-----|------|------|----|----|------|
| 1. England   | 3      | 1   | 2    | 0    | 2  | 1  | 4    |
| 2. Holland   | 3      | 0   | 3    | 0    | 2  | 2  | 3    |
| 3. Ireland   | 3      | 0   | 3    | 0    | 2  | 2  | 3    |
| 4. Egypt     | 3      | 0   | 2    | 1    | 1  | 2  | 2    |

## Round of 16

Czechoslovakia 4, Costa Rica 1
Cameroon 2, Colombia 1 OT
West Germany 2, Holland 1
Argentina 1, Brazil 0
Ireland 0, Romania 0 OT (Ireland wins 5–4 on penalties)
Italy 2, Uruguay 0
England 1, Belgium 0 OT
Yugoslavia 2, Spain 1

## Quarterfinals

Argentina 0, Yugoslavia 0 OT (Argentina wins 3–2 on penalties)
Italy 1, Ireland 0
West Germany 1, Czechoslovakia 0
England 3, Cameroon 2 OT

## Semifinals

Argentina 1, Italy 1 OT (Argentina wins 4–3 on penalties)
West Germany 1, England 1 OT (West Germany wins 4–3 on penalties)

## Third Place

Italy 2, England 1

## Final

West Germany 1, Argentina 0

## 1994

## Group A

United States 1, Switzerland 1
Romania 3, Colombia 1
Switzerland 4, Romania 1
United States 2, Colombia 1
Romania 1, United States 0
Colombia 2, Switzerland 0

|                  | Played | Win | Draw | Loss | GF | GA | Pts. |
|------------------|--------|-----|------|------|----|----|------|
| 1. Romania       | 3      | 2   | 0    | 1    | 5  | 5  | 6    |
| 2. Switzerland   | 3      | 1   | 1    | 1    | 5  | 4  | 4    |
| 3. USA           | 3      | 1   | 1    | 1    | 3  | 3  | 4    |
| 4. Colombia      | 3      | 1   | 0    | 2    | 4  | 5  | 3    |

## Group B

Cameroon 2, Sweden 2
Brazil 2, Russia 0
Sweden 3, Russia 1
Brazil 3, Cameroon 0
Brazil 1, Sweden 1
Russia 6, Cameroon 1

| | Played | Win | Draw | Loss | GF | GA | Pts. |
|---|---|---|---|---|---|---|---|
| 1. Brazil | 3 | 2 | 1 | 0 | 6 | 1 | 7 |
| 2. Sweden | 3 | 1 | 2 | 0 | 6 | 4 | 5 |
| 3. Russia | 3 | 1 | 0 | 2 | 7 | 6 | 3 |
| 4. Cameroon | 3 | 0 | 1 | 2 | 3 | 11 | 1 |

## Group C

Germany 1, Bolivia 0
Spain 2, South Korea 2
Germany 1, Spain 1
South Korea 0, Bolivia 0
Spain 3, Bolivia 1
Germany 3, South Korea 2

| | Played | Win | Draw | Loss | GF | GA | Pts. |
|---|---|---|---|---|---|---|---|
| 1. Germany | 3 | 2 | 1 | 0 | 5 | 3 | 7 |
| 2. Spain | 3 | 1 | 2 | 0 | 6 | 4 | 5 |
| 3. S. Korea | 3 | 0 | 2 | 1 | 4 | 5 | 2 |
| 4. Bolivia | 3 | 0 | 1 | 2 | 1 | 4 | 1 |

## Group D

Argentina 4, Greece 0
Nigeria 3, Bulgaria 0
Argentina 2, Nigeria 1
Bulgaria 4, Greece 0
Nigeria 2, Greece 0
Bulgaria 2, Argentina 0

| | Played | Win | Draw | Loss | GF | GA | Pts. |
|---|---|---|---|---|---|---|---|
| 1. Nigeria | 3 | 2 | 0 | 1 | 6 | 2 | 6 |
| 2. Argentina | 3 | 2 | 0 | 1 | 6 | 3 | 6 |
| 3. Bulgaria | 3 | 2 | 0 | 1 | 6 | 3 | 6 |
| 4. Greece | 3 | 0 | 0 | 3 | 0 | 10 | 0 |

## Group E

Ireland 1, Italy 0
Norway 1, Mexico 0
Italy 1, Norway 0
Mexico 2, Ireland 1
Rep of Ireland 0, Norway 0
Italy 1, Mexico 1

|              | Played | Win | Draw | Loss | GF | GA | Pts. |
|--------------|--------|-----|------|------|----|----|------|
| 1. Mexico    | 3      | 1   | 1    | 1    | 3  | 3  | 4    |
| 2. Ireland   | 3      | 1   | 1    | 1    | 2  | 2  | 4    |
| 3. Italy     | 3      | 1   | 1    | 1    | 2  | 2  | 4    |
| 4. Norway    | 3      | 1   | 1    | 1    | 1  | 1  | 4    |

## Group F

Belgium 1, Morocco 0
Holland 2, Saudi Arabia 1
Saudi Arabia 2, Morocco 1
Belgium 1, Holland 0
Holland 2, Morocco 1
Saudi Arabia 1, Belgium 0

|              | Played | Win | Draw | Loss | GF | GA | Pts. |
|--------------|--------|-----|------|------|----|----|------|
| 1. Holland   | 3      | 2   | 0    | 1    | 4  | 3  | 6    |
| 2. S. Arabia | 3      | 2   | 0    | 1    | 4  | 3  | 6    |
| 3. Belgium   | 3      | 2   | 0    | 1    | 2  | 1  | 6    |
| 4. Morocco   | 3      | 0   | 0    | 3    | 2  | 5  | 0    |

## Round of 16

Germany 3, Belgium 2
Spain 3, Switzerland 0
Sweden 3, Saudi Arabia 1
Romania 3, Argentina 2
Holland 2, Ireland 0

Brazil 1, United States 0
Italy 2, Nigeria 1 OT
Bulgaria 1, Mexico 1 OT
(Bulgaria wins 3–1 on penalties)

## Quarterfinals

Italy 2, Spain 1
Brazil 3, Holland 2
Bulgaria 2, Germany 1
Sweden 2, Romania 2 OT (Sweden wins 5–4 on penalties)

## Semifinals

Brazil 1, Sweden 0
Italy 2, Bulgaria 1

## Third Place

Sweden 4, Bulgaria 0

## Final

Brazil 0, Italy 0 OT (Brazil wins 3–2 on penalties)

## 1998

## Group A

Brazil 2, Scotland 1
Morocco 2, Norway 2
Scotland 1, Norway 1
Brazil 3, Morocco 0
Morocco 3, Scotland 0
Norway 2, Brazil 1

|  | Played | Win | Draw | Loss | GF | GA | Pts. |
|---|---|---|---|---|---|---|---|
| 1. Brazil | 3 | 2 | 0 | 1 | 6 | 3 | 6 |
| 2. Norway | 3 | 1 | 2 | 0 | 5 | 4 | 5 |
| 3. Morocco | 3 | 1 | 1 | 1 | 5 | 5 | 4 |
| 4. Scotland | 3 | 0 | 1 | 2 | 2 | 6 | 1 |

## Group B

Italy 2, Chile 2
Cameroon 1, Austria 1
Chile 1, Austria 1
Italy 3, Cameroon 0
Italy 2, Austria 1
Chile 1, Cameroon 1

|  | Played | Win | Draw | Loss | GF | GA | Pts. |
|---|---|---|---|---|---|---|---|
| 1. Italy | 3 | 2 | 1 | 0 | 7 | 3 | 7 |
| 2. Chile | 3 | 0 | 3 | 0 | 4 | 4 | 3 |
| 3. Austria | 3 | 0 | 2 | 1 | 3 | 4 | 2 |
| 4. Cameroon | 3 | 0 | 2 | 1 | 2 | 5 | 2 |

## Group C

Denmark 1, Saudi Arabia 0
France 3, South Africa 0
South Africa 1, Denmark 1
France 4, Saudi Arabia 0
France 2, Denmark 1
South Africa 2, Saudi Arabia 2

|  | Played | Win | Draw | Loss | GF | GA | Pts. |
|---|---|---|---|---|---|---|---|
| 1. France | 3 | 3 | 0 | 0 | 9 | 1 | 9 |
| 2. Denmark | 3 | 1 | 1 | 1 | 3 | 3 | 4 |
| 3. S. Africa | 3 | 0 | 2 | 1 | 3 | 6 | 2 |
| 4. S. Arabia | 3 | 0 | 1 | 2 | 2 | 7 | 1 |

## Group D

Paraguay 0, Bulgaria 0
Nigeria 3, Spain 2
Nigeria 1, Bulgaria 0
Spain 0, Paraguay 0
Spain 6, Bulgaria 1
Paraguay 3, Nigeria 1

|  | Played | Win | Draw | Loss | GF | GA | Pts. |
|---|---|---|---|---|---|---|---|
| 1. Nigeria | 3 | 2 | 0 | 1 | 5 | 5 | 6 |
| 2. Paraguay | 3 | 1 | 2 | 0 | 3 | 1 | 5 |
| 3. Spain | 3 | 1 | 1 | 1 | 8 | 4 | 4 |
| 4. Bulgaria | 3 | 0 | 1 | 2 | 1 | 7 | 1 |

## Group E

Mexico 3, South Korea 1
Holland 0, Belgium 0
Belgium 2, Mexico 2
Holland 5, South Korea 0
Belgium 1, South Korea 1
Holland 2, Mexico 2

|  | Played | Win | Draw | Loss | GF | GA | Pts. |
|---|---|---|---|---|---|---|---|
| 1. Holland | 3 | 1 | 2 | 0 | 7 | 2 | 5 |
| 2. Mexico | 3 | 1 | 2 | 0 | 7 | 5 | 5 |
| 3. Belgium | 3 | 0 | 3 | 0 | 3 | 3 | 3 |
| 4. S. Korea | 3 | 0 | 1 | 2 | 2 | 9 | 1 |

## Group F

Yugoslavia 1, Iran 0
Germany 2, United States 0
Germany 2, Yugoslavia 2
Iran 2, United States 1
Germany 2, Iran 0
Yugoslavia 1, United States 0

|              | Played | Win | Draw | Loss | GF | GA | Pts. |
|--------------|--------|-----|------|------|----|----|------|
| 1. Germany   | 3      | 2   | 1    | 0    | 6  | 2  | 7    |
| 2. Yugoslavia| 3      | 2   | 1    | 0    | 4  | 2  | 7    |
| 3. Iran      | 3      | 1   | 0    | 2    | 2  | 4  | 3    |
| 4. USA       | 3      | 0   | 0    | 3    | 1  | 5  | 0    |

## Group G

England 2, Tunisia 0
Romania 1, Colombia 0
Colombia 1, Tunisia 0
Romania 2, England 1
Romania 1, Tunisia 1
England 2, Colombia 0

|              | Played | Win | Draw | Loss | GF | GA | Pts. |
|--------------|--------|-----|------|------|----|----|------|
| 1. Romania   | 3      | 2   | 1    | 0    | 4  | 2  | 7    |
| 2. England   | 3      | 2   | 0    | 1    | 5  | 2  | 6    |
| 3. Colombia  | 3      | 1   | 0    | 2    | 1  | 3  | 3    |
| 4. Tunisia   | 3      | 0   | 1    | 2    | 1  | 4  | 1    |

## Group H

Argentina 1, Japan 0
Croatia 3, Jamaica 1
Croatia 1, Japan 0
Argentina 5, Jamaica 0
Jamaica 2, Japan 1
Argentina 1, Croatia 0

|              | Played | Win | Draw | Loss | GF | GA | Pts. |
|--------------|--------|-----|------|------|----|----|------|
| 1. Argentina | 3      | 3   | 0    | 0    | 7  | 0  | 9    |
| 2. Croatia   | 3      | 2   | 0    | 1    | 4  | 2  | 6    |
| 3. Jamaica   | 3      | 1   | 0    | 2    | 3  | 9  | 3    |
| 4. Japan     | 3      | 0   | 0    | 3    | 1  | 4  | 0    |

## Round of 16

Italy 1, Norway 0

Brazil 4, Chile 1
France 1, Paraguay 0 OT
Denmark 4, Nigeria 1
Germany 2, Mexico 1
Holland 2, Yugoslavia 1
Croatia 1, Romania 0
Argentina 2, England 2 OT (Argentina wins 4–3 on penalties)

## Quarterfinals

France 0, Italy 0 (France wins 4–3 on penalties)
Brazil 3, Denmark 2
Holland 2, Argentina 1
Croatia 3, Germany 0

## Semifinals

Brazil 1, Holland 1 OT (Brazil wins 4–2 on penalties)
France 2, Croatia 1

## Third Place

Croatia 2, Holland 1

## Final

France 3, Brazil 0

## 2002

## Group A

Senegal 1, France 0
Denmark 2, Uruguay 1
Denmark 1, Senegal 1
France 0, Uruguay 0

Denmark 2, France 0
Uruguay 3, Senegal 3

|    | Played | Win | Draw | Loss | GF | GA | Pts. |
|----|--------|-----|------|------|----|----|------|
| 1. Denmark | 3 | 2 | 1 | 0 | 5 | 2 | 7 |
| 2. Senegal | 3 | 1 | 2 | 0 | 5 | 4 | 5 |
| 3. Uruguay | 3 | 0 | 2 | 1 | 4 | 5 | 2 |
| 4. France | 3 | 0 | 1 | 2 | 0 | 3 | 1 |

## Group B

Paraguay 2, South Africa 2
Spain 3, Slovenia 1
Spain 3, Paraguay 1
South Africa 1, Slovenia 0
Spain 3, South Africa 2
Paraguay 3, Slovenia 1

|    | Played | Win | Draw | Loss | GF | GA | Pts. |
|----|--------|-----|------|------|----|----|------|
| 1. Spain | 3 | 3 | 0 | 0 | 9 | 4 | 9 |
| 2. Paraguay | 3 | 1 | 1 | 1 | 6 | 6 | 4 |
| 3. S. Africa | 3 | 1 | 1 | 1 | 5 | 5 | 4 |
| 4. Slovenia | 3 | 0 | 0 | 3 | 2 | 7 | 0 |

## Group C

Brazil 2, Turkey 1
Costa Rica 2, China 0
Brazil 4, China 0 ·
Costa Rica 1, Turkey 1
Brazil 5, Costa Rica 2
Turkey 3, China 0

|    | Played | Win | Draw | Loss | GF | GA | Pts. |
|----|--------|-----|------|------|----|----|------|
| 1. Brazil | 3 | 3 | 0 | 0 | 11 | 3 | 9 |
| 2. Turkey | 3 | 1 | 1 | 1 | 5 | 3 | 4 |
| 3. Costa Rica | 3 | 1 | 1 | 1 | 5 | 6 | 4 |
| 4. China | 3 | 0 | 0 | 3 | 0 | 9 | 0 |

## Group D

South Korea 2, Poland 0
United States 3, Portugal 2
United States 1, South Korea 1
Portugal 4, Poland 0
South Korea 1, Portugal 0
Poland 3, United States 1

|              | Played | Win | Draw | Loss | GF | GA | Pts. |
|--------------|--------|-----|------|------|----|----|------|
| 1. S. Korea  | 3      | 2   | 1    | 0    | 4  | 1  | 7    |
| 2. USA       | 3      | 1   | 1    | 1    | 5  | 6  | 4    |
| 3. Portugal  | 3      | 1   | 0    | 2    | 6  | 4  | 3    |
| 4. Poland    | 3      | 1   | 0    | 2    | 3  | 7  | 3    |

## Group E

Ireland 1, Cameroon 1
Germany 8, Saudi Arabia 0
Ireland 1, Germany 1
Cameroon 1, Saudi Arabia 0
Germany 2, Cameroon 0
Ireland 3, Saudi Arabia 0

|              | Played | Win | Draw | Loss | GF | GA | Pts. |
|--------------|--------|-----|------|------|----|----|------|
| 1. Germany   | 3      | 2   | 1    | 0    | 11 | 1  | 7    |
| 2. Ireland   | 3      | 1   | 2    | 0    | 5  | 2  | 5    |
| 3. Cameroon  | 3      | 1   | 1    | 1    | 2  | 3  | 4    |
| 4. S. Arabia | 3      | 0   | 0    | 3    | 0  | 12 | 0    |

## Group F

Argentina 1, Nigeria 0
England 1, Sweden 1
Sweden 2, Nigeria 1
England 1, Argentina 0
Sweden 1, Argentina 1
Nigeria 0, England 0

|            | Played | Win | Draw | Loss | GF | GA | Pts. |
|------------|--------|-----|------|------|----|----|------|
| 1. Sweden    | 3 | 1 | 2 | 0 | 4 | 3 | 5 |
| 2. England   | 3 | 1 | 2 | 0 | 2 | 1 | 5 |
| 3. Argentina | 3 | 1 | 1 | 1 | 2 | 2 | 4 |
| 4. Nigeria   | 3 | 0 | 1 | 2 | 1 | 3 | 1 |

## Group G

Mexico 1, Croatia 0
Italy 2, Ecuador 0
Croatia 2, Italy 1
Mexico 2, Ecuador 1
Italy 1, Mexico 1
Ecuador 1, Croatia 0

|            | Played | Win | Draw | Loss | GF | GA | Pts. |
|------------|--------|-----|------|------|----|----|------|
| 1. Mexico  | 3 | 2 | 1 | 0 | 4 | 2 | 7 |
| 2. Italy   | 3 | 1 | 1 | 1 | 4 | 3 | 4 |
| 3. Croatia | 3 | 1 | 0 | 2 | 2 | 3 | 3 |
| 4. Ecuador | 3 | 1 | 0 | 2 | 2 | 4 | 3 |

## Group H

Japan 2, Belgium 2
Russia 2, Tunisia 0
Japan 1, Russia 0
Belgium 1, Tunisia 1
Japan 2, Tunisia 0
Belgium 3, Russia 2

|            | Played | Win | Draw | Loss | GF | GA | Pts. |
|------------|--------|-----|------|------|----|----|------|
| 1. Japan   | 3 | 2 | 1 | 0 | 5 | 2 | 7 |
| 2. Belgium | 3 | 1 | 2 | 0 | 6 | 5 | 5 |
| 3. Russia  | 3 | 1 | 0 | 2 | 4 | 4 | 3 |
| 4. Tunisia | 3 | 0 | 1 | 2 | 1 | 5 | 1 |

## Round of 16

Germany 1, Paraguay 0
England 3, Denmark 0
Senegal 2, Sweden 1 OT
Ireland 1, Spain 1 (Spain wins 3–2 on penalties)
United States 2, Mexico 0
Brazil 2, Belgium 0
Turkey 1, Japan 0
South Korea 2, Italy 1 OT

## Quarterfinals

Brazil 2, England 1
Germany 1, United States 0
Spain 0, South Korea 0 (South Korea wins 3–2 on penalties)
Turkey 1, Senegal 0 OT

## Semifinals

Germany 1, South Korea 0
Brazil 1, Turkey 0

## Third Place

Turkey 3, South Korea 2

## Final

Brazil 2, Germany 0

## 2006

## Group A

Germany 4, Costa Rica 2
Ecuador 2, Poland 0
Germany 1, Poland 0
Ecuador 3, Costa Rica 0

Germany 3, Ecuador 0
Poland 2, Costa Rica 1

|  | Played | Win | Draw | Loss | GF | GA | Pts. |
|---|---|---|---|---|---|---|---|
| 1. Germany | 3 | 3 | 0 | 1 | 8 | 2 | 9 |
| 2. Ecuador | 3 | 2 | 0 | 1 | 5 | 3 | 6 |
| 3. Poland | 3 | 1 | 0 | 2 | 2 | 4 | 3 |
| 3. Costa Rica | 3 | 0 | 0 | 3 | 3 | 9 | 0 |

## Group B

England 1, Paraguay 0
Trinidad & Tobago 0, Sweden 0
England 2, Trinidad & Tobago 0
Sweden 1, Paraguay 0
England 2, Sweden 2
Paraguay 2, Trinidad & Tobago 0

|  | Played | Win | Draw | Loss | GF | GA | Pts. |
|---|---|---|---|---|---|---|---|
| 1. England | 3 | 2 | 1 | 0 | 5 | 2 | 7 |
| 2. Sweden | 3 | 1 | 2 | 0 | 3 | 2 | 5 |
| 3. Paraguay | 3 | 1 | 0 | 2 | 2 | 2 | 3 |
| 4. Trinidad & Tobago | 3 | 0 | 1 | 2 | 0 | 4 | 1 |

## Group C

Argentina 2, Ivory Coast 1
Holland 1, Serbia-Montenegro 0
Argentina 6, Serbia-Montenegro 0
Holland 2, Ivory Coast 1
Argentina 0, Holland 0
Ivory Coast 3, Serbia-Montenegro 2

|  | Played | Win | Draw | Loss | GF | GA | Pts. |
|---|---|---|---|---|---|---|---|
| 1. Argentina | 3 | 2 | 1 | 0 | 8 | 1 | 7 |
| 2. Holland | 3 | 2 | 1 | 0 | 3 | 1 | 7 |
| 3. Ivory Coast | 3 | 1 | 0 | 2 | 5 | 6 | 3 |
| 4. Serbia-Montenegro | 3 | 0 | 0 | 3 | 2 | 10 | 0 |

## Group D

Mexico 3, Iran 1
Portugal 1, Angola 0
Angola 0, Mexico 0
Portugal 2, Iran 0
Iran 1, Angola 1
Portugal 2, Mexico 1

|  | Played | Win | Draw | Loss | GF | GA | Pts. |
|---|---|---|---|---|---|---|---|
| 1. Portugal | 3 | 3 | 0 | 0 | 5 | 1 | 9 |
| 2. Mexico | 3 | 1 | 1 | 1 | 4 | 3 | 4 |
| 3. Angola | 3 | 0 | 2 | 1 | 1 | 2 | 2 |
| 4. Iran | 3 | 0 | 1 | 2 | 2 | 6 | 1 |

## Group E

Czech Republic 3, United States 0
Italy 2, Ghana 0
Ghana 2, Czech Republic 0
Italy 1, United States 1
Italy 2, Czech Republic 0
Ghana 2, United States 1

|  | Played | Win | Draw | Loss | GF | GA | Pts. |
|---|---|---|---|---|---|---|---|
| 1. Italy | 3 | 2 | 1 | 0 | 5 | 1 | 7 |
| 2. Ghana | 3 | 2 | 0 | 1 | 4 | 3 | 6 |
| 3. Czech Rep. | 3 | 1 | 0 | 2 | 3 | 4 | 3 |
| 4. USA | 3 | 0 | 1 | 2 | 2 | 6 | 1 |

## Group F

Australia 3, Japan 1
Brazil 1, Croatia 0
Japan 0, Croatia 0
Brazil 2, Australia 0
Brazil 4, Japan 1
Australia 2, Croatia 2

|           | Played | Win | Draw | Loss | GF | GA | Pts. |
|-----------|--------|-----|------|------|----|----|------|
| 1. Brazil | 3 | 3 | 0 | 0 | 7 | 1 | 9 |
| 2. Australia | 3 | 1 | 1 | 1 | 5 | 5 | 4 |
| 3. Croatia | 3 | 0 | 2 | 1 | 2 | 3 | 2 |
| 4. Japan | 3 | 0 | 1 | 2 | 2 | 7 | 1 |

## Group G

South Korea 2, Togo 1
France 0, Switzerland 0
France 1, South Korea 1
Switzerland 2, Togo 0
France 2, Togo 0
Switzerland 2, South Korea 0

|           | Played | Win | Draw | Loss | GF | GA | Pts. |
|-----------|--------|-----|------|------|----|----|------|
| 1. Switzerland | 3 | 2 | 1 | 0 | 4 | 0 | 7 |
| 2. France | 3 | 1 | 2 | 0 | 3 | 1 | 5 |
| 3. S. Korea | 3 | 1 | 1 | 1 | 3 | 4 | 4 |
| 4. Togo | 3 | 0 | 0 | 3 | 1 | 6 | 0 |

## Group H

Spain 4, Ukraine 0
Tunisia 2, Saudi Arabia 2
Ukraine 4, Saudi Arabia 0
Spain 3, Tunisia 1
Spain 1, Saudi Arabia 0
Ukraine 1, Tunisia 0

|           | Played | Win | Draw | Loss | GF | GA | Pts. |
|-----------|--------|-----|------|------|----|----|------|
| 1. Spain | 3 | 3 | 0 | 0 | 8 | 1 | 9 |
| 2. Ukraine | 3 | 2 | 0 | 1 | 5 | 4 | 6 |
| 3. Tunisia | 3 | 0 | 1 | 2 | 3 | 6 | 1 |
| 4. S. Arabia | 3 | 0 | 1 | 2 | 2 | 7 | 1 |

## Round of 16

Germany 2, Sweden 0
Argentina 2, Mexico 1 OT
England 1, Ecuador 0
Portugal 1, Holland 0
Italy 1, Australia 0
Ukraine 0, Switzerland 0 (Ukraine wins 3–0 on penalties)
Brazil 3, Ghana 0
France 3, Spain 1

## Quarterfinals

Germany 1, Argentina 1 (Germany wins 4–2 on penalties)
Italy 3, Ukraine 0
Portugal 0, England 0 (Portugal wins 3–1 on penalties)
France 1, Brazil 0

## Semifinals

Italy 2, Germany 0 OT
France 1, Portugal 0

## Third Place

Germany 3, Portugal 1

## Final

Italy 1, France 1 (Italy wins 5–3 on penalties)

## 2010

## Group A

South Africa 1, Mexico 1
France 0, Uruguay 0

Uruguay 3, South Africa 0
Mexico 2, France 0
Uruguay 1, Mexico 0
South Africa 2, France 1

| | Played | Win | Draw | Loss | GF | GA | Pts. |
|---|---|---|---|---|---|---|---|
| 1. Uruguay | 3 | 2 | 1 | 0 | 4 | 0 | 7 |
| 2. Mexico | 3 | 1 | 1 | 1 | 3 | 2 | 4 |
| 3. South Africa | 3 | 1 | 1 | 1 | 3 | 5 | 4 |
| 4. France | 3 | 0 | 1 | 2 | 1 | 4 | 1 |

## Group B

Argentina 1, Nigeria 0
South Korea 2, Greece 0
Greece 2, Nigeria 1
Argentina 4, South Korea 1
South Korea 2, Nigeria 2
Argentina 2, Greece 0

| | Played | Win | Draw | Loss | GF | GA | Pts. |
|---|---|---|---|---|---|---|---|
| 1. Argentina | 3 | 3 | 0 | 0 | 7 | 1 | 9 |
| 2. South Korea | 3 | 1 | 1 | 1 | 5 | 6 | 4 |
| 3. Greece | 3 | 1 | 0 | 2 | 2 | 5 | 3 |
| 4. Nigeria | 3 | 0 | 1 | 2 | 3 | 5 | 1 |

## Group C

USA 1, England 1
Slovenia 1, Algeria 0
USA 2, Slovenia 2
England 0, Algeria 0
USA 1, Algeria 0
England 1, Slovenia 0

|  | Played | Win | Draw | Loss | GF | GA | Pts. |
|---|---|---|---|---|---|---|---|
| 1. USA | 3 | 1 | 2 | 0 | 4 | 3 | 5 |
| 2. England | 3 | 1 | 2 | 0 | 2 | 1 | 5 |
| 3. Slovenia | 3 | 1 | 1 | 1 | 3 | 3 | 4 |
| 4. Algeria | 3 | 0 | 1 | 2 | 0 | 2 | 1 |

## Group D

Germany 4, Australia 0
Ghana 1, Serbia 0
Serbia 1, Germany 0
Ghana 1, Australia 1
Germany 1, Ghana 0
Australia 2, Serbia 1

|  | Played | Win | Draw | Loss | GF | GA | Pts. |
|---|---|---|---|---|---|---|---|
| 1. Germany | 3 | 2 | 0 | 1 | 5 | 1 | 6 |
| 2. Ghana | 3 | 1 | 1 | 1 | 2 | 2 | 4 |
| 3. Australia | 3 | 1 | 1 | 1 | 3 | 6 | 4 |
| 4. Serbia | 3 | 1 | 0 | 2 | 2 | 3 | 3 |

## Group E

Netherlands 2, Denmark 0
Japan 1, Cameroon 0
Netherlands 1, Japan 0
Denmark 2, Cameroon 1
Japan 3, Denmark 1
Netherlands 2, Cameroon 1

|  | Played | Win | Draw | Loss | GF | GA | Pts. |
|---|---|---|---|---|---|---|---|
| 1. Netherlands | 3 | 3 | 0 | 0 | 5 | 1 | 9 |
| 2. Japan | 3 | 2 | 0 | 1 | 4 | 2 | 6 |
| 3. Denmark | 3 | 1 | 0 | 2 | 3 | 6 | 3 |
| 4. Cameroon | 3 | 0 | 0 | 3 | 2 | 5 | 0 |

## Group F

Italy 1, Paraguay 1
Slovakia 1, New Zealand 1
Paraguay 2, Slovakia 0
Italy 1, New Zealand 1
Slovakia 3, Italy 2
Paraguay 0, New Zealand 0

|                  | Played | Win | Draw | Loss | GF | GA | Pts. |
|------------------|--------|-----|------|------|----|----|------|
| 1. Paraguay      | 3      | 1   | 2    | 0    | 3  | 1  | 5    |
| 2. Slovakia      | 3      | 1   | 1    | 1    | 4  | 5  | 4    |
| 3. New Zealand   | 3      | 0   | 3    | 0    | 2  | 2  | 3    |
| 4. Italy         | 3      | 0   | 2    | 1    | 4  | 5  | 2    |

## Group G

Portugal 0, Ivory Coast 0
Brazil 2, North Korea 1
Brazil 3, Ivory Coast 1
Portugal 7, North Korea 0
Brazil 0, Portugal 0
Ivory Coast 3, North Korea 0

|                  | Played | Win | Draw | Loss | GF | GA | Pts. |
|------------------|--------|-----|------|------|----|----|------|
| 1. Brazil        | 3      | 2   | 1    | 0    | 5  | 2  | 7    |
| 2. Portugal      | 3      | 1   | 2    | 0    | 7  | 0  | 5    |
| 3. Ivory Coast   | 3      | 1   | 1    | 1    | 4  | 3  | 4    |
| 4. North Korea   | 3      | 0   | 0    | 3    | 1  | 12 | 0    |

## Group H

Chile 1, Honduras 0
Switzerland 1, Spain 0
Chile 1, Switzerland 0
Spain 2, Honduras 0

Spain 2, Chile 1
Switzerland 0, Honduras 0

| | Played | Win | Draw | Loss | GF | GA | Pts. |
|---|---|---|---|---|---|---|---|
| 1. Spain | 3 | 2 | 0 | 1 | 4 | 2 | 6 |
| 2. Chile | 3 | 2 | 0 | 1 | 3 | 2 | 6 |
| 3. Switzerland | 3 | 1 | 1 | 1 | 1 | 1 | 4 |
| 4. Honduras | 3 | 0 | 1 | 2 | 0 | 3 | 1 |

## Round of 16

Uruguay 2, South Korea 1
Ghana 2, USA 1 OT
Germany 4, England 1
Argentina 3, Mexico 1
Netherlands 2, Slovakia 1
Brazil 3, Chile 0
Paraguay 0, Japan 0 (Paraguay wins 5–3 on penalties)
Spain 1, Portugal 0

## Quarterfinals

Netherlands 2, Brazil 1
Uruguay 1, Ghana 1 (Uruguay wins 4–2 on penalties)
Germany 4, Argentina 0
Spain 1, Paraguay 0

## Semifinals

Netherlands 3, Uruguay 2
Spain 1, Germany 0

## Third Place

Germany 3, Uruguay 2

## Final

Spain 1, Netherlands 0 OT

**2014**

## Group A

Brazil 3, Croatia 1
Mexico 1, Cameroon 0
Brazil 0, Mexico 0
Croatia 4, Cameroon 0
Brazil 4, Cameroon 1
Mexico 3, Croatia 1

|             | Played | Win | Draw | Loss | GF | GA | Pts. |
|-------------|--------|-----|------|------|----|----|------|
| 1. Brazil   | 3      | 2   | 1    | 0    | 7  | 2  | 7    |
| 2. Mexico   | 3      | 2   | 1    | 0    | 4  | 1  | 7    |
| 3. Croatia  | 3      | 1   | 0    | 2    | 6  | 6  | 3    |
| 4. Cameroon | 3      | 0   | 0    | 3    | 1  | 9  | 0    |

## Group B

Netherlands 5, Spain 1
Chile 3, Australia 1
Netherlands 3, Australia 2
Chile 2, Spain 0
Netherlands 2, Chile 0
Spain 3, Australia 0

|                | Played | Win | Draw | Loss | GF | GA | Pts. |
|----------------|--------|-----|------|------|----|----|------|
| 1. Netherlands | 3      | 3   | 0    | 0    | 10 | 3  | 9    |
| 2. Chile       | 3      | 2   | 0    | 1    | 5  | 3  | 6    |
| 3. Spain       | 3      | 1   | 0    | 2    | 4  | 7  | 3    |
| 4. Australia   | 3      | 0   | 0    | 3    | 3  | 9  | 0    |

## Group C

Colombia 3, Greece 0
Ivory Coast 2, Japan 1
Colombia 2, Ivory Coast 1
Greece 0, Japan 0

Colombia 4, Japan 1
Greece 2, Ivory Coast 1

| | Played | Win | Draw | Loss | GF | GA | Pts. |
|---|---|---|---|---|---|---|---|
| 1. Colombia | 3 | 3 | 0 | 0 | 9 | 2 | 9 |
| 2. Greece | 3 | 1 | 1 | 1 | 2 | 4 | 4 |
| 3. Ivory Coast | 3 | 1 | 0 | 2 | 4 | 5 | 3 |
| 4. Japan | 3 | 0 | 1 | 2 | 2 | 6 | 1 |

## Group D

Costa Rica 3, Uruguay 1
Italy 2, England 1
Uruguay 2, England 1
Costa Rica 1, Italy 0
Uruguay 1, Italy 0
Costa Rica 0, England 0

| | Played | Win | Draw | Loss | GF | GA | Pts. |
|---|---|---|---|---|---|---|---|
| 1. Costa Rica | 3 | 2 | 1 | 0 | 4 | 1 | 7 |
| 2. Uruguay | 3 | 2 | 0 | 1 | 4 | 4 | 6 |
| 3. Italy | 3 | 1 | 0 | 2 | 2 | 3 | 3 |
| 4. England | 3 | 0 | 1 | 2 | 2 | 4 | 1 |

## Group E

Switzerland 2, Ecuador 1
France 3, Honduras 0
France 5, Switzerland 2
Ecuador 2, Honduras 1
Switzerland 3, Honduras 0
France 0, Ecuador 0

| | Played | Win | Draw | Loss | GF | GA | Pts. |
|---|---|---|---|---|---|---|---|
| 1. France | 3 | 2 | 1 | 0 | 8 | 2 | 7 |
| 2. Switzerland | 3 | 2 | 0 | 1 | 7 | 6 | 6 |
| 3. Ecuador | 3 | 1 | 1 | 1 | 3 | 3 | 4 |
| 4. Honduras | 3 | 0 | 0 | 3 | 1 | 8 | 0 |

## Group F

Argentina 2, Bosnia-Herzegovina 1
Iran 0, Nigeria 0
Argentina 1, Iran 0
Nigeria 1, Bosnia-Herzegovina 0
Argentina 3, Nigeria 2
Bosnia-Herzegovina 3, Iran 1

|  | Played | Win | Draw | Loss | GF | GA | Pts. |
|---|---|---|---|---|---|---|---|
| 1. Argentina | 3 | 3 | 0 | 0 | 6 | 3 | 9 |
| 2. Nigeria | 3 | 1 | 1 | 1 | 3 | 3 | 4 |
| 3. Bosnia-Herzegovina | 3 | 1 | 0 | 2 | 4 | 4 | 3 |
| 4. Iran | 3 | 0 | 1 | 2 | 1 | 4 | 1 |

## Group G

Germany 4, Portugal 0
United States 2, Ghana 1
Germany 2, Ghana 2
United States 2, Portugal 2
Germany 1, United States 0
Portugal 2, Ghana 1

|  | Played | Win | Draw | Loss | GF | GA | Pts. |
|---|---|---|---|---|---|---|---|
| 1. Germany | 3 | 2 | 1 | 0 | 7 | 2 | 7 |
| 2. United States | 3 | 1 | 1 | 1 | 4 | 4 | 4 |
| 3. Portugal | 3 | 1 | 1 | 1 | 4 | 7 | 4 |
| 4. Ghana | 3 | 0 | 1 | 2 | 4 | 6 | 1 |

## Group H

Belgium 2, Algeria 1
Russia 1, South Korea 1
Belgium 1, Russia 0
Algeria 4, South Korea 2
Russia 1, Algeria 1
Belgium 1, South Korea 0

| | Played | Win | Draw | Loss | GF | GA | Pts. |
|---|---|---|---|---|---|---|---|
| 1. Belgium | 3 | 3 | 0 | 0 | 4 | 1 | 9 |
| 2. Algeria | 3 | 1 | 1 | 1 | 6 | 5 | 4 |
| 3. Russia | 3 | 0 | 2 | 1 | 2 | 3 | 2 |
| 4. South Korea | 3 | 0 | 1 | 2 | 3 | 6 | 1 |

## Round of 16

Brazil 1, Chile 1 (Brazil wins 3–2 on penalties)
Colombia 2, Uruguay 0
Netherlands 2, Mexico 1
Costa Rica 1, Greece 1 (Costa Rica wins 5–3 on penalties)
France 2, Nigeria 0
Germany 2, Algeria 1 OT
Argentina 1, Switzerland 0 OT
Belgium 2, United States 1 OT

## Quarterfinals

Germany 1, France 0
Brazil 2, Colombia 1
Argentina 1, Belgium 0
Netherlands 0, Costa Rica 0 (Netherlands wins 4–3 on penalties)

## Semifinals

Germany 7, Brazil 1
Argentina 0, Netherlands 0 (Argentina wins 4–2 on penalties)

## Third Place

Netherlands 3, Brazil 0

## Final

Germany 1, Argentina 0 OT

## 2018

### Group A

Russia 5, Saudi Arabia 0
Uruguay 1, Egypt 0
Russia 3, Egypt 1
Uruguay 1, Saudi Arabia 0
Saudi Arabia 2, Egypt 1
Uruguay 3, Russia 0

|                   | Played | Win | Draw | Loss | GF | GA | Pts. |
| ----------------- | ------ | --- | ---- | ---- | -- | -- | ---- |
| 1. Uruguay        | 3      | 3   | 0    | 0    | 5  | 0  | 9    |
| 2. Russia         | 3      | 2   | 0    | 1    | 8  | 4  | 6    |
| 3. Saudi Arabia   | 3      | 1   | 0    | 2    | 2  | 2  | 3    |
| 4. Egypt          | 3      | 0   | 0    | 3    | 2  | 6  | 0    |

### Group B

Iran 1, Morocco 0
Spain 3, Portugal 3
Portugal 1, Morocco 0
Spain 1, Iran 0
Portugal 1, Iran 1
Spain 2, Morocco 2

|              | Played | Win | Draw | Loss | GF | GA | Pts. |
| ------------ | ------ | --- | ---- | ---- | -- | -- | ---- |
| 1. Spain     | 3      | 1   | 2    | 0    | 6  | 5  | 5    |
| 2. Portugal  | 3      | 1   | 2    | 0    | 5  | 4  | 5    |
| 3. Iran      | 3      | 1   | 1    | 1    | 2  | 2  | 4    |
| 4. Morocco   | 3      | 0   | 1    | 2    | 2  | 4  | 1    |

### Group C

France 2, Australia 1
Denmark 1, Peru 0
Australia 1, Denmark 1
France 1, Peru 0

France 0, Denmark 0
Peru 2, Australia 0

|  | Played | Win | Draw | Loss | GF | GA | Pts. |
|---|---|---|---|---|---|---|---|
| 1. France | 3 | 2 | 1 | 0 | 3 | 1 | 7 |
| 2. Denmark | 3 | 1 | 2 | 0 | 2 | 1 | 5 |
| 3. Peru | 3 | 1 | 0 | 2 | 2 | 2 | 3 |
| 4. Australia | 3 | 0 | 1 | 2 | 2 | 5 | 1 |

## Group D

Argentina 1, Iceland 1
Croatia 2, Nigeria 0
Croatia 3, Argentina 0
Nigeria 2, Iceland 0
Argentina 2, Nigeria 1
Croatia 2, Iceland 1

|  | Played | Win | Draw | Loss | GF | GA | Pts. |
|---|---|---|---|---|---|---|---|
| 1. Croatia | 3 | 3 | 0 | 0 | 7 | 1 | 9 |
| 2. Argentina | 3 | 1 | 1 | 1 | 3 | 5 | 4 |
| 3. Nigeria | 3 | 1 | 0 | 2 | 3 | 4 | 3 |
| 4. Iceland | 3 | 0 | 1 | 2 | 2 | 5 | 1 |

## Group E

Serbia 1, Costa Rica 0
Brazil 1, Switzerland 1
Brazil 2, Costa Rica 0
Switzerland 2, Serbia 1
Brazil 2, Serbia 0
Switzerland 2, Costa Rica 2

|  | Played | Win | Draw | Loss | GF | GA | Pts. |
|---|---|---|---|---|---|---|---|
| 1. Brazil | 3 | 2 | 1 | 0 | 5 | 1 | 7 |
| 2. Switzerland | 3 | 1 | 2 | 0 | 5 | 4 | 5 |
| 3. Serbia | 3 | 1 | 0 | 2 | 2 | 4 | 3 |
| 4. Costa Rica | 3 | 0 | 1 | 2 | 2 | 5 | 1 |

## Group F

Mexico 1, Germany 0
Sweden 1, South Korea 0
Mexico 2, South Korea 1
Germany 2, Sweden 1
South Korea 2, Germany 0
Sweden 3, Mexico 0

|               | Played | Win | Draw | Loss | GF | GA | Pts. |
|---------------|--------|-----|------|------|----|----|------|
| 1. Sweden     | 3      | 2   | 0    | 1    | 5  | 2  | 6    |
| 2. Mexico     | 3      | 2   | 0    | 1    | 3  | 4  | 6    |
| 3. South Korea| 3      | 1   | 0    | 2    | 3  | 3  | 3    |
| 4. Germany    | 3      | 1   | 0    | 2    | 2  | 4  | 3    |

## Group G

Belgium 3, Panama 0
England 2, Tunisia 1
Belgium 5, Tunisia 2
England 6, Panama 1
Belgium 1, England 0
Tunisia 2, Panama 1

|            | Played | Win | Draw | Loss | GF | GA | Pts. |
|------------|--------|-----|------|------|----|----|------|
| 1. Belgium | 3      | 3   | 0    | 0    | 9  | 2  | 9    |
| 2. England | 3      | 2   | 0    | 1    | 8  | 3  | 6    |
| 3. Tunisia | 3      | 1   | 0    | 2    | 5  | 8  | 3    |
| 4. Panama  | 3      | 0   | 0    | 3    | 2  | 11 | 0    |

## Group H

Japan 2, Colombia 1
Senegal 2, Poland 1
Japan 2, Senegal 2
Colombia 3, Poland 0
Poland 1, Japan 0
Colombia 1, Senegal 0

|  | Played | Win | Draw | Loss | GF | GA | Pts. |
|---|---|---|---|---|---|---|---|
| 1. Colombia | 3 | 2 | 0 | 1 | 5 | 2 | 6 |
| 2. Japan | 3 | 1 | 1 | 1 | 4 | 4 | 4 |
| 3. Senegal | 3 | 1 | 1 | 1 | 4 | 4 | 4 |
| 4. Poland | 3 | 1 | 0 | 2 | 2 | 5 | 3 |

## Round of 16

France 4, Argentina 3
Uruguay 2, Portugal 1
Russia 1, Spain 1 (Russia wins 4–3 on penalties)
Croatia 1, Denmark 1 (Croatia wins 3–2 on penalties)
Brazil 2, Mexico 0
Belgium 3, Japan 2
Sweden 1, Switzerland 0
England 1, Colombia 1 (England wins 4–3 on penalties)

## Quarterfinals

France 2, Uruguay 0
Belgium 2, Brazil 1
England 2, Sweden 0
Croatia 2, Russia 2 (Croatia wins 4–3 on penalties)

## Semifinals

France 1, Belgium 0
Croatia 2, England 1 OT

## Third Place

Belgium 2, England 0

## Final

France 4, Croatia 2

# APPENDIX B:
# WORLD CUP RECORDS

**ALL TIME**

| | |
|---|---|
| Most Appearances | 21, Brazil (only country to appear in every World Cup) |
| Most Championships | 5, Brazil |
| Most Final Appearances | 8, Germany (does not include Brazil's second-place finish in 1950, which was played without an official final) |
| Most Semifinal Appearances | 13, Germany |
| Most Games Played | 109, Germany |
| Most Wins | 73, Brazil |
| Most Losses | 27, Mexico |
| Most Ties | 21, Italy |
| Most Goals Scored | 232, Brazil |
| Most Goals Conceded | 125, Germany |
| Most Red Cards | 11, Brazil |
| Most Yellow Cards | 111, Argentina |
| Most Cards (Player) | 6, Zinedine Zidane (France, 1998–2002) and Cafu (Brazil, 1994–2006) |

| | |
|---|---|
| Most Yellow Cards (Player) | 6, Cafu (Brazil 1994–2006) |
| Most Red Cards (Player) | 2, Rigobert Song (Cameroon, 1994 and 1998) and Zinedine Zidane (France, 1998 and 2006) |

## SINGLE TOURNAMENT

| | |
|---|---|
| Most Wins | 7, Brazil (2002) |
| Most Goals Scored | 27, Hungary (1954) |
| Fewest Goals Conceded | 0, Switzerland (2006) |
| Most Goals Conceded | 14, Brazil (2014) |
| Highest Average Goals Scored/ game | 5.40, Hungary (1954) |
| Most Goals Scored | 171 goals (1998 and 2014) |
| Most Goals per Game | 5.38 goals (1954) |
| Fewest Goals per Game | 2.21 goals (1990) |
| Most Red Cards | 28 in 64 games (2006) |

## INDIVIDUAL

| | |
|---|---|
| Most Titles | 3, Pelé (Brazil, 1958, 1962, and 1970) |
| Most Tournaments Played | 5, Antonio Carbajal (Mexico, 1950–1966) and Lothar Matthaeus (Germany, 1982–1998) |
| Most Games Played | 25, Lothar Matthaeus (Germany, 1982–1998) |
| Most Games Won | 16, Cafu (Brazil, 1994–2006) |
| Most Appearances in a World Cup Final | 3, Cafu (Brazil, 1994–2002) |
| Youngest Player | 17 years and 42 days, Norman Whiteside (Northern Ireland vs. Yugoslavia, 1982) |

Youngest Player in a Final       17 years and 248 days, Pelé
(Brazil vs. Sweden, 1958)

Oldest Player       43 years and 3 days, Faryd
Mondragon (Columbia vs.
Japan, 2014)

Oldest Player in a Final       40 years and 133 days, Dino Zoff
(Italy vs. West Germany, 1982)

## SCORING

Most Goals (Individual, All-Time)       16, Miroslav Klose (Germany,
2002–2014)

Most Goals (Individual, Tournament)       13, Just Fontaine (France, 1958)

Most Goals (Individual, Game)       5, Oleg Salenko (Russia vs.
Cameroon, 1994)

Most Goals (Individual, Final)       3, Geoff Hurst (England vs. West
Germany, 1966)

Fastest Goal from Kickoff       11 seconds, Hakan Sukur (Turkey
vs. South Korea, 2002)

Fastest Goal by a Substitute       16 seconds, Ebbe Sand (Denmark
vs. Nigeria, 1998)

Most Goals (Team, Game)       10, Hungary (against El Salvador,
1982)

Most Goals (Team, Final)       5, Brazil (against Sweden, 1958)

Fewest Goals (Both Teams, Final)       0, Brazil and Italy (1994)

## GOALKEEPING

Most Shutouts       10, Peter Shilton (England, 1982–
1990) and Fabien Barthez
(France, 1998–2006)

Most Consecutive Minutes without Giving Up a Goal       517 minutes, Walter Zenga (Italy,
1990)

Fewest Goals Conceded (Tournament)       0, Pascal Zuberbuhler
(Switzerland, 2006)

## COACHING

| | |
|---|---|
| Most Games | 25, Helmut Schon (West Germany, 1966–1978) |
| Most Games Won | 16, Helmut Schon (West Germany, 1966–1978) |
| Most Finals | 2, Vittorio Pozzo (Italy, 1934–1938) |
| Most Teams Coached | 5, Bora Milutinovic (Mexico, 1986; Costa Rica, 1990); USA, 1994; Nigeria, 1998; China, 2002) |
| Most Consecutive Wins | 11, Luiz Felipe Scolari (Brazil, 2002, 7; Portugal, 2006, 4) |

# BIBLIOGRAPHY

## BOOKS

Bondy, Filip. *The World Cup: The Players, Coaches, History, and Excitement* (New York: Mallard Press, 1991).

Cantor, Andres. *Goooal: A Celebration of Soccer* (New York: Simon & Schuster, 1996).

Glanville, Brian. *The Story of the World Cup* (London: Faber and Faber 1997).

Harris, Harry. *Pelé: His Life and Times* (London: Robson Books, 2000).

Morrison, Ian. *The World Cup: A Complete Record* (Derby, UK: Breedon Books Sport, 1990).

Trifari, Elio and Miers, Charles. *Soccer! The Game and the World Cup* (New York: Rizzoli International Publications, 1994).

## NEWSPAPERS AND MAGAZINES

*The Philadelphia Inquirer*
*The New York Times*
*The Washington Post*
*The Washington Times*
*World Soccer*

## WEBSITES

FIFAworldcup.com: www.fifaworldcup.yahoo.com
The BBC: www.bbc.co.uk

# INDEX

# ABOUT THE AUTHOR

**Clemente A. Lisi** has worked as a writer and editor for the past two decades. His work has appeared in the *New York Post* and ABCNews .com. Lisi is the author of *The U.S. Women's Soccer Team: An American Success Story* (2010) and *A History of the U.S. Men's National Soccer Team* (2017), both published by Rowman & Littlefield. He currently teaches journalism at The King's College in New York City.